P9-EDZ-800

The Illustrated Encyclopedia of

COUNTRY MUSIC

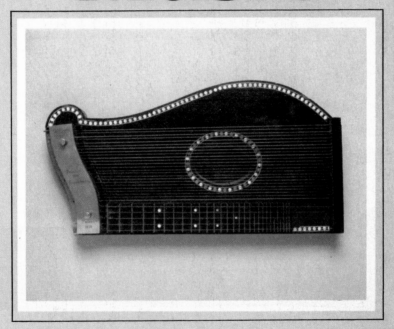

The Illustrated Encyclopedia of
COUNTRY MUSIC

a Salamander book
Published by
H·A·R·M·O·N·Y B·O·O·K·S
NEW YORK

A Salamander Book

First published 1977 in the United States by
Harmony Books, a division of Crown Publishers, Inc.
All rights reserved under the International Copyright
Union by Harmony Books. No part of this book may be
utilized or reproduced in any form or by any means,
electronic or mechanical, including photocopying,
recording, or by any information storage and retrieval
system, without permission in writing from the Publisher.

Harmony Books
A division of Crown Publishers, Inc.
One Park Avenue
New York, New York 10016

Published in Canada by General Publishing Company, Limited

Library of Congress Catalog Card Number: 77 087125

First published in the United Kingdom in 1977 by
Salamander Books Limited

Salamander Books Ltd 1977
27 Old Gloucester Street, London WC1, United Kingdom

Credits

Authors: Fred Dellar, Roy Thompson,
Douglas B. Green
Editor: Trisha Palmer
Filmset by: SX Composing Limited,
Leigh-on-Sea, Essex, England
Colour reproduction by: Metric Reproductions Ltd,
Chelmsford, Essex, England

Picture Credits

Many of the photographs in this book were provided by the
record companies mentioned in the Acknowledgements, and
we are very grateful for their help. Additionally we would
like to thank Douglas B. Green and Grease Brothers, who
supplied pictures as follows:

D. Green: pages 13, 23 (bottom), 27, 31, 33, 39, 40, 42, 50, 57,
61 (bottom), 62 (bottom), 65 (top), 72 (top), 73 (both),
74 (bottom left), 75, 87, 89, 99, 102, 114, 116, 118, 120, 127, 129,
130 (bottom), 135, 136 (bottom), 138, 139, 141, 142, 146, 149,
150, 151 (both), 152, 154, 159 (top left), 172 (bottom left), 178,
201, 208, 214, 218, 224, 225, 229 (top center), 231, 243, 247, 248.

Grease Bros: pages 16, 19, 24, 26 (both), 41, 51, 61 (top),
62 (top), 65 (bottom), 76, 98 (bottom), 112, 126, 130 (top),
159 (top right), 164, 204 (bottom right), 207 (bottom), 228, 250.

Acknowledgements

The authors acknowledge the debt they owe to such
publications as *New Musical Express*, *Music City News*,
Melody Maker, Nick Logan and Bob Woffinden's *Illustrated
Encyclopedia Of Rock*, Phil Hardy and Dave Laing's
Encyclopedia Of Rock, Irwin Stambler's *Encyclopedia Of Pop,
Rock and Soul*, Stambler and Landon's *Encyclopedia Of Folk
and Country and Western Music*, Leslie Helliwell's *Filmgoer's
Companion*, *Billboard*, *Country Music People*, *Country Music
Review*, *Old Time Music*, Joseph Murrell's *Book Of Golden
Discs*, Bill C. Malone's *Country Music U.S.A.*, Malone and
McCulloh's *Stars Of Country Music*, Christopher S. Wren's
Winners Got Scars Too, *Sing Out*, *SMG Magazine*, *Country
Song Roundup*, *Countrystyle*, Charles K. Wolfe's *Grand Ole
Opry 1925–35*. Tony Russell's *Black, Whites and Blues*,
Cashbox, Brian Chalker's *This Is Country Music*, *The Country
Music Who's Who*, Charlie Gillett and Simon Frith's *Rock File 4*,
Robert Shelton's *Country Music Story* and Joel Whitburn's
myriad chart listing compilations.

We would also like to thank the following record companies
who supplied record sleeves, illustrations and various sources
of information used in this book: A&M, Anchor, Arista, Capitol,
Capricorn, CBS, Charley, Decca, DJM, Ember, EMI, Flying
Fish, Folkways, Gusto, Island, MCA, Motown, Music For
Pleasure, Phonogram, Pickwick, Polydor, Pye, RCA, Rounder,
Shannon, Sonet, Transatlantic, United Artists, Virgin, WEA,
Westwood and Word.

Special thanks is given to Gary Wellington, Chris Diwell,
Jack Scott, Charles Webster, Debbie Bennett, David Yates,
Chas McCutcheon, John Tobler, Tom Sheehan, Leon Campadelli,
Barry Lazell, David Shrimpton, Brian Chalker, John Atkins,
Stan Britt, Dave Kunitz, Cliff Gater, Mike Craig, Geoff Thorne,
Dave Walters, Nick Kimberley, Elly Smith, Ray McCarthy,
Pete Flanagan, Murray Allen, Louis Rayner, Karen Jacobs,
Tony Byworth, Sue Baker, Carol Stein, Trisha O'Keefe
and the many, many others without whose invaluable help
this book would never have materialized.
Finally, grateful thanks and appreciation to Bruce Scott for
photographing the record covers, to Michael Stannard for
photographing the musical instruments in the introductory
spreads, Cliff Cooper for the loan of the Gibson six-string
banjo on pages 2/3 and Robert Longstaff for the Appalachian
dulcimer on pages 6/7.

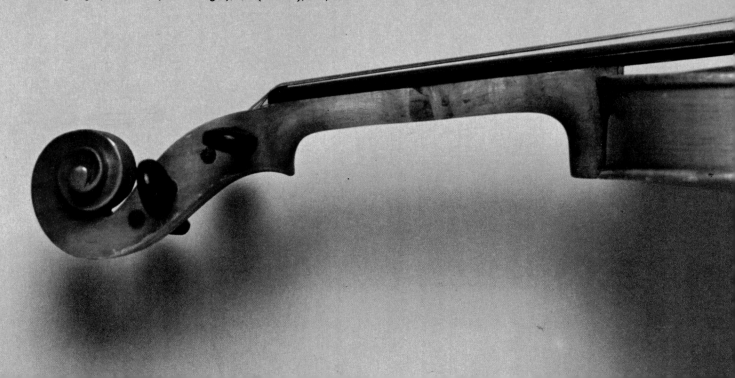

Authors

FRED DELLAR, one of the busiest journalists on the British music scene, is probably best known for his *New Musical Express* 'Information City' page. It wasn't until 1968 that he first began to write in a professional capacity, initially contributing rock and country articles to *Audio Record Review*, then writing on a wide number of subjects for *Hi Fi News*, *Disc*, *Cassettes and Cartridges*, *Album Tracking* and many other publications.

ROY THOMPSON is a country music fanatic who met Fred Dellar several years ago while working for a publishing company. Roy, who owns one of the largest collections of country records in England, has during the past few years worked with Fred on a number of musical projects. This is his first book.

DOUGLAS B. GREEN is currently editor of the *Country Music Foundation Press* and the *Journal of Country Music*, and heads the Oral History Project at the Country Music Foundation in Nashville. A former professional musician, he has contributed articles to some two score music publications including *Country Music*, *Guitar Player* and *Billboard*, and has written several liner notes for leading record companies, one of which was nominated for a Grammy award. He has contributed chapters to several books on country music and has written for both film and television. His first book, *Country Roots*, was published in 1976 by Hawthorn.

Introduction

It must have been nearly ten years ago that Roy Thompson and I first discussed the possibility of formulating a book which covered the country music phenomenon in all its many forms. Our record collections at that time included samples of western swing, bluegrass, old time and rockabilly, plus examples of a then new-fangled invention known as country-rock. And though there were certain overtly commercial performers on which neither one of us cared to spend much in the way of stylus time or writing power, it was generally agreed that an all-embracing volume, free from personal preferences, ought to be our aim. Eventually, in 1976, the opportunity to embark on our mooted project arose and we tentatively began to assemble material for this publication – at which time the problems inherent in producing such an encyclopedia became increasingly apparent.

First – who to include and who to omit?

Obviously we couldn't find space for even half the 1,352 guitar-pickers that John Sebastian claimed to inhabit Nashville. It was at this point that Roy and myself, together with Jack Scott of *New Musical Express*, drafted individual lists of artists and subjects worthy of being featured in the tome, those recurring most frequently on the three lists being the ones finally selected.

Next came the vexing question of maintaining a publishing deadline – and with this in mind we enlisted the aid of Dave Redshaw, whose writings in *Country Music People* magazine had established him as one of the most forward looking journalists on the British country scene. Then came the opportunity of assistance from Doug Green of the Country Music Foundation in Nashville, a writer with a reputation second to none in his field. It was towards Doug that we turned to fill the gaps in our collective knowledge – he checked through our already completed entries, methodically correcting any glaring errors. He also rightly observed that our coverage of the old-timey scene left much to be desired and dutifully began adding many entries of his own, thus adding a further dimension to our original concept.

Here then is final result of our collective labors, listed alphabetically in time-honored fashion, with individual artists being classified under their surnames – with such alter ego types as Ferlin Husky/Simon Crum and Pete Kirby/Bashful Brother Oswald gaining two separate headings – and groups being listed under their full title – eg the Binkley Brothers Dixie Clodhoppers will be found under 'B'.

For the discographies I take full responsibility. Complete listings were out of the question as these would have more than doubled the size of this publication – and I preferred not to indulge in the 'recommended albums' listings prevalent in books of this type, so many of these choice releases being long since unavailable to anyone wishing to learn more about particular artists. The answer – though not totally to my satisfaction – was to compile discographies listing all albums *available at the time of writing*, giving first the American label and then the British one. These discographies were compiled from catalogs supplied by the various record companies and where these were not obtainable (some companies seem strangely reluctant to show proof of their wares) the Schwann LP listing was drafted in as a secondary reference. But though many hours of work were devoted to ensuring that these discographies were as complete as possible, I fully realise that certain omissions are bound to have crept in – there are numerous minor labels, especially in the States, whose operation is mainly of a parochial nature, making their releases difficult to correlate, while even major companies sometimes manage to provide an abundance of false information regarding their own products, one leading British company working on a catalog which proved to be three years out of date! But somehow we struggled on and completed what I believe is the most comprehensive country encyclopedia currently available. Perfect it isn't – I don't believe that perfection is possible in a work such as this – so if you've got any additional information, if you wish to correct any of the facts entered here . . . or merely wish to register a complaint about your favorite country artist being totally neglected by our team, then we'd be pleased to hear from you. With your help, perfection might edge a little closer next time around.

Fred Dellar

Foreword

You know, in my many, many years in country music I have seen it grow tremendously. There are more people making a living out of country music today than ever before, and many more fans as well. Along with this there have been more and more books and magazines, and I think this a very important part of the music too.

I have seen, as the years go on – and we see it very clearly today – a great demand on the part of our public for information about Jimmie Rodgers, about the Carter Family; they want to know about the history of the Grand Ole Opry, and about Hank Williams and Patsy Cline and those that are gone. They want to learn and read about who they were and where they came from, how they came up in life and possibly what first interested them in country music or in being an entertainer.

I think that means a lot to the public. I know that people ask me all these questions and more, because of my age and because of the years I've been here at the Grand Ole Opry, and some feel I should know all this. I don't. And that's why an encyclopedia that really goes deep into the history of country music is so important.

I wish that I did know more about a lot of the older people that went ahead of me – some of them became famous, but many did not – but I'm always trying to learn. I like, and I think the majority of the public likes, to read something someone has written on country music and its history, something written with respect and with a sense of what is beautiful about someone, what is interesting about them. Not how bad they were or how good they were, but what did they accomplish, how did they accomplished it, who helped them, what influenced them to be in country music.

If somebody doesn't keep an encyclopedia and keep up with these facts and these people, one day it will all be lost to future generations. People who were, during their time, very popular and very much thought of and very much in demand will be forgotten and passed by if somebody with a love for it doesn't make the effort to get this history and record it.

I've been asked what I think about people coming from all over to study and write about our music, country music, and put it in magazines and books all over the world, and I'll tell you, I think it's wonderful. I think it reaches a lot of people that radio and television don't. You know, there are a lot of people who read for the knowledge, who want to be informed on country music. They'll pick up a book and learn more from it than they can learn about the music any other way.

I know personally, because it has happened to me so much, that there are thousands of people who would love to get to know Roy Acuff personally, who want to come up to me, to shake my hand, to ask me maybe one or two questions about my life and my career. This happens to me and to all the artists out there making their living in country music.

So I have to think how happy this encyclopedia will make thousands of people who want to know these things, and will be able to find the information right at their fingertips. Really, there will be hundreds of thousands down through the years who will turn to this book for information if it is kept in archives and taken care of. And who knows, a hundred years from today country music might be the most popular music in the whole world. It could be bigger than any of them. It makes me very proud to have played a part.

Roy Acuff

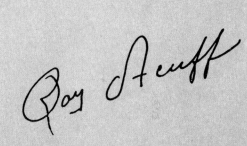

Roy Acuff

Son of a baptist minister, Roy Claxton Acuff was born September 15, 1903, in a three-room shack in Maynardsville, Tennessee. As a child, Roy, who had two brothers (Briscoe and Claude) and two sisters (Juanita and Sue) learnt jews harp and harmonica. However, it seemed that he was destined to become an athlete for, following a move to Fountain City, near Knoxville, Acuff (at that time nicknamed 'Rabbit' because he weighed only 130 pounds) gained 13 letters at high school, eventually playing minor league ball and being considered for the New York Yankees. Severe sunstroke put an end to this career, confining Acuff to bed for much of 1929 and 1930.

Following this illness Acuff, whose jobs had included that of callboy on the L&N Railroad, hung around the house, learning fiddle and listening to records by old-time players – also becoming adept with a yoyo.

In Spring, 1932, he joined a traveling medicine show, led by a Dr Haver, playing small towns in Virginia and Tennessee, by 1933 forming a group the Tennessee Crackerjacks, in which Clell Summey played dobro, thus providing the distinctive sound that came to be associated with Acuff (Pete 'Bashful Brother Oswald' (♦) Kirby providing the dobro chores in later Acuff aggregations). Soon he obtained a program on Knoxville radio station WROL, moving on to the rival KNOX for the Midday Merry-Go-Round show, starting point for Kitty Wells (♦), Bill Carlisle (♦) and many others. On being refused a raise (each musician received fifty cents per show) the band returned to WROL once more, adopting the name of the Crazy Tennesseans.

Acuff married Mildred Douglas in 1936, that same year recording two sessions for ARC (a company controlling a host of labels, later merged with Columbia), the temperature on one date being so high that the band recorded in their underwear. Tracks from these sessions included **Great Speckle Bird** and **Wabash Cannonball,** two classic items, the latter having a vocal by Dynamite Hatcher. Though Acuff's contract was with Columbia, the band's discs appeared on ARC's subsidiary labels Melotone, Conqueror and Perfect, and Columbia's subsidiary labels Okeh and Vocalion, and were not available on the main, red label until the mid-'40s. Making his first appearance on the Grand Ole Opry in 1938, Acuff soon became a regular on the show, changing the name of the band once more to the Smoky Mountain Boys, winning many friends with his sincere, mountain-boy, vocal style and his dobro-flavored band sound, eventually becoming as popular as Uncle Dave Macon (♦), who was until that time undisputed Opry main attraction.

In 1942, together with songwriter Fred Rose (♦) Acuff organised Acuff-Rose, a music publishing company destined to become one of the most important in country music. During that same period Acuff's recordings became so popular that he headed Frank Sinatra in some major music polls and caused Japanese troops to yell 'To hell with Roosevelt, to hell with Babe Ruth, to hell with Roy Acuff' as they banzai-charged at Okinawa. The war years also saw some of his biggest hits including **Wreck on the Highway** (1942), **Fireball Mail** (1942), **Night Train to Memphis** (1943), **Pins And Needles, Low And Lonely** (1943).

Nominated to run as governor of Tennessee in 1944 and 1946, Acuff failed to get past the primaries. But in 1948 he won the Republican primary, failing to win the ensuing election but nevertheless gaining tremendous support, earning a larger slice of the vote than any previous Republican candidate had ever earned in that particular political con-

Smoky Mountain Memories (DJM). A British double album.

frontation. Also in '48, Acuff opened his Dunbar Cave resort, a popular folk music park which he owned for several years.

Four years later, after being requested to change his style by Columbia, Acuff left the label, switching in turn to MGM, Decca and Capitol. And though his live performances still continued to go well and his publishing empire seemed ever-expanding, Acuff's record sales failed to maintain their previous high – **So Many Times** (1959), **Come and Knock** (1959) and **Freight Train Blues** (1965), all on his own Hickory label, being the only releases to create any real interest during the '50s and '60s.

However, his tremendous contribution to country music was recognized in November 1962, when Acuff became the first living musician to be honored as a member of the Country Music Hall Of Fame.

Severely injured in a road accident during 1965, Acuff was back and touring within a few months, at one stage making several visits to the Vietnam war front. On May 24, 1973, he entertained POW's at the White House and on March 16, 1974, was chosen to provide the President with yoyo lessons at the opening of the new Nashville Opryhouse, an incident which Acuff considers as one of the high points in his career.

Known as the 'King of Country Music', Roy Acuff has sold more than 30 million records throughout the years – his most successful disc being his Columbia version of **Wabash Cannonball,** which went gold in 1942. His film appearances include **Grand Ole Opry** (1940), **Hi Neighbor** (1942), **My Darling Clementine** (1943), **Sing, Neighbor, Sing** (1944), **Cowboy Canteen** (1944) and **Night Train To Memphis** (1946).

Albums:
Roy Acuff And His Smoky
  Mountain Boys *(Capitol/—)*
Greatest Hits *(Columbia/—)*
How Beautiful Heaven Must Be
  (Pickwick/—)
King Of Country *(Hickory/—)*

Smoky Mountain Memories
  (Hickory/DJM)
That's Country *(Hickory/—)*

*Time
(Hickory)*

*Country Music Hall Of Fame
(Hickory)*

Rex Allen

Known as the 'Arizona Cowboy', Allen was born Willcox, Arizona, December 31, 1924. A rodeo rider in his teens, he learnt to play guitar and fiddle at early age. He took an electronics course at University College of Los Angeles but opted instead for a singing career, finding his first job with radio station WTTM, Trenton, New Jersey, during the mid-forties. Like Gene Autry (♦) before him, he was a popular singer on the NBD before entering films. In 1951 he was awarded his own Hollywood radio show by CBS, subsequently getting high ratings.

He has since recorded for Decca, Mercury, Buena Vista, etc, and has made films for Fox, Republic and Universal, having the distinction of being the last of the singing cowboys on screen; but he is perhaps best known nowadays for his singing and narration chores in various Disney productions. He had a top twenty hit with **Don't Go Near The Indians,** a Mercury single, in September 1962, having previously won a gold disc for his version of **Crying In The Chapel** in 1953.

Albums:
Golden Songs Of The West
  (Vocalion/—)

Rosalie Allen

Known as The Prairie Star in her heyday, Rosalie Allen was a great cowgirl yodeler in an era of great cowgirl yodelers. Actually, she was born Julie Marlene Bedra, the daughter of a Polish-born chiropractor, in Old Forge, Pennsylvania, on June 6, 1924.

Entranced by the cowboy image and music, she gained a radio spot with longtime New York City favorite Denver Darling in the late 1930s, and through the 1940s and 1950s she was a fixture of the northeast. She signed with RCA, her biggest solo efforts being yodeling spectaculars **I Want To Be A Cowboy's Sweetheart** and **He Taught Me How To Yodel.** She was frequently paired with Elton Britt (♦) another legendary yodeler, for a number of records, the best sellers being **Quick-Silver, The Yodel Blues,** and **Beyond The Sunset.**

She turned to a career as a disc jockey over WOV in the 1950s, preferring not to travel, and gradually left her performing and recording career behind. She currently lives in rural Alabama.

Albums: none.

Amazing Rhythm Aces

Russell Smith *lead vocals, guitar*
Jeff Davis *bass*
Billy Earheart III *keyboards*
Barry 'Byrd' Burton *guitar, dobro*
Butch McDade *drums*

Memphis-based country rock band, formed during early 70s, whose **Third Rate Romance** single, penned by Smith, became top 20 hit in September 1975. Members Davis and McDade previously toured and recorded with singer-songwriter Jesse Winchester.

Albums:
Stacked Deck *(ABC/ABC)*
Too Stuffed To Jump *(ABC/ABC)*

The country rock group Amazing Rhythm Aces gained two crossover hits in 1976.

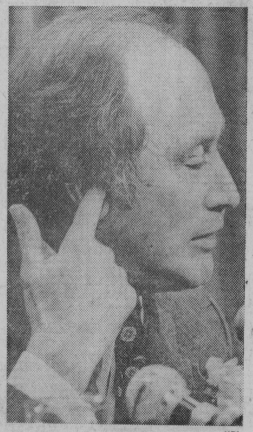

—UPI

"My wife has taught me a lot about rock," Prime Minister Pierre Trudeau told newsmen yesterday, then he stuck finger in ear.

Rev. Christenson

she is giving up all p
appearances "for the
being" because "I'm
the public."

Mrs. Trudeau said in
terview in front of the
Park West apartmen
where she is staying th
wants the press to lea
alone and "after six y
this I've had enough."

Natural

● From Page One

ronto, said there has b
medical evidence of h
contracting cancer as a
of using saccharin. He
was on the phone tall
reporters because "w
to talk about it in or
avoid a panic."

His company has r
formula on hand for
Free 7-Up, he said, b
are busy assessing. "W
we can come up with
formulation in short or
mains to be seen."

He predicted that al
mulated diet soft drin
be calorie-reduced
rather than sugar free.

In the meantime, Se
has stopped production
diet pop while it assess
sumer reaction. If t
coninued demand, pro
will resume.

Mr. Scarfe said it r

'This is your deejay, Whispering Bill Anderson, and for all those lucky folk out there in Decatur, here's a medley of my hits – it should last about a week or two.'

Stacked Deck (ABC). Well received first album from the country-rock band; financial success hadn't come easily, however, and they had undergone several lineup changes.

The American Record Company

Because of frequent references to it, the American Record Company is due a brief explanation. It controlled five labels of its own (hence the term ARC complex of labels), which were sold in 'five-and-ten' stores like Kress, W. T. Grant, and others. These labels were: Banner, Melotone, Oriole, Perfect, and Romeo. Any given song recorded for ARC might well appear on some or all of these labels.

In addition, they did recording for Sears-Roebuck, which for a time controlled its own label, Conqueror. In some cases Sears released certain materials from the ARC vaults on Conqueror, while in other cases it had its own exclusive artists – Gene Autry is the best example – on Conqueror.

As if this wasn't complicated enough, there had been a 'black label' Columbia Records in the 1920s, which folded up with the Depression. In the late 1930s a new label called Columbia was begun, an amalgamation of the Okeh, Vocalion, and ARC complex. So all rights to any of this material are currently owned by Columbia (actually now known as CBS) Records. Thus Gene Autry (♦) (after his very early recordings for a host of labels) went from Conqueror to Okeh to Columbia, although all rights are owned by Columbia. Similarly the Callahan Brothers (♦), recorded first for ARC and had their records released on Banner, Melotone, Oriole, Perfect, and Romeo, as well as a few on Conqueror. Their label, after the merger, became Vocalion, then Okeh, and finally Columbia.

Bill Anderson

Nicknamed Whispering Bill because of his lack of any real voice, Anderson was born Columbia, South Carolina, November 1, 1937. Training initially to be a journalist, he obtained a BA degree at the University of Georgia, singing and acting as a disc jockey in his spare time. Along the way, he worked as a sports writer for the weekly *DeKalb New Era* and as correspondent for the *Atlanta Journal*, opting for a full time musical career in 1958 after Ray Price (♦) heard Anderson singing his self-penned **City Lights** on a car radio and promptly covered it, thus earning a gold disc. Many other Anderson songs were then recorded by Hank Locklin (♦), Jim Reeves (♦), Porter Wagoner (♦), Faron Young (♦), Jean Shepherd (♦) etc, while his own discs (for Decca) also sold well. However, his real breakthrough as a recording artist came in 1962, with a crossover hit **Mama Sang A Song,** this being followed by **Still** and **8 x 10,** both covered in Britain by singing comedian Ken Dodd. Since that time, Anderson has waxed a stream of hits including **I Get The Fever** (1966), **For Loving You** – with Jan Howard (1967), **Wild Weekend** (1968), **Happy State Of Life** (1968), **My Life** (1969), **But You Know I Love You** (1969), **Quits** (1971), **The Corner Of My Life** and many others.

He has also appeared on many TV shows (his own Bill Anderson Show being syndicated in 126 US cities), performed in such movies as *Las Vegan Hillbillies*, *Forty Acre Farm*, *Road To Nashville*, *Country Music And Broadway* and *From Nashville With Music*, helping to make radio history by broadcasting a British concert live to station WSH Nashville via satellite.

Winner of countless awards, Anderson and his band the Po' Boys (named after **Po' Folks**, an Anderson hit) have played concerts throughout the world. He has an ultra-clean reputation – he's been called the Pat Boone of Country Music – and refused until recently to record songs having

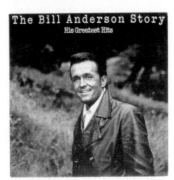

MCA Records.

MCA Records.

Bill Anderson, maker of first C&W satellite broadcast.

sexual overtones, although recent records with Mary Lou Turner (♦) like **That's What Made Me Love You** and **Sometimes** indicate that an image modification may be under way.

Albums:
The Bill Anderson Story
  (MCA/MCA)
Still *(MCA/—)*
Greatest Hits *(MCA/—)*
Greatest Hits Vol 2 *(MCA/—)*
I Love You Drops *(MCA/—)*

Gentle On My Mind
  (Pickwick/—)
Don't She Look Good? *(MCA/—)*
Country Style *(Vocalion/—)*
Bill *(MCA/—)*
Always Remember *(MCA/—)*
For Loving You *(MCA/—)*
Turn The Radio On/Talk To Me
  (MCA/—)
Whispering Bill *(MCA/—)*
Live From London *(—/MCA)*

Liz Anderson

Born Elizabeth Jane Haaby, Rosean, Minnesota, March 13, 1930, Liz married Casey Anderson, May 26, 1946 and gave birth to daughter Lynn Anderson (♦) in September '47. After business college, she worked as a secretary but became a singer-songwriter, signing a recording contract with RCA in the mid '60s. An Anderson-penned song **(My Friends Are Gonna Be) Strangers** provided Merle Haggard (♦) with a disc success in 1965, the same singer having a No 1 country hit with **The Fugitive**, another Anderson song, in December 1966. Liz herself logged over a dozen country chart-fillers while with RCA, the biggest of these being **Wife Of The Party** (1966), **The Game Of Triangles** – with Bobby Bare (♦) and Norma Jean (♦) (1966), **Mama Spank** (1967), **Tiny Tears** (1967) and **Husband Hunting** (1970). In 1971 she joined her daughter Lynn and her son-in-law Glenn Sutton at Columbia and had further hits on that company's Epic label. Nowadays she lives in virtual retirement. Her past albums include **Favorites, Cookin' Up Hits, Like A Merry Go Round** and **Liz Anderson Sings** (all on RCA).

Lynn Anderson.

Lynn Anderson

Singer Lynn Rene Anderson, daughter of Casey and Liz Anderson (♦), was born in Grand Forks, North Dakota, September 26, 1947. Later, family moved to Sacramento, where Lynn became an equestrian success, winning title of California Horse Show Queen at 1966 State Fair. Also during 1966 she joined Chart Records, recording around 100 songs for the label and producing 17 hits during the late '60s, the biggest of these being a cover version of Ben Peters' **That's A No No** (1969). After marrying producer-songwriter Glen Sutton, Lynn signed for Columbia Records, her first single for the label being **Stay There Till I Get There,** a hit written by her husband. That same year (1970), Lynn's recording of **Rose Garden** became a monster hit, winning her the CMA Female Singer Of The Year award. Other, more recent, hits include **You're My Man, How Can I Unlove You, Keep Me In Mind, Top Of The World, What A Man My Man Is** and **Sweet Talkin' Man.**

Albums:
Flower Of Love (*Pickwick/—*)
Games People Play
 (*Pickwick/—*)
How Can I Unlove You?
 (*Columbia/—*)
It Makes You Happy
 (*Pickwick/—*)

Including
Rose Garden
Snowbird
For The Good Times
Sunday Morning Coming Down
It's Only Make Believe
I Don't Want To Play House
Your Sweet Love Lifted Me
I Still Belong To You
I Wish I Was A Little Boy Again
Another Lonely Night
Nothing Between Us

Keep Me In Mind (*Columbia/—*)
No Love At All (*Columbia/—*)
Rose Garden (*Columbia/CBS*)
Smile For Me (*Columbia/—*)
Top Of The World (*Columbia/—*)
You're My Man (*Columbia/—*)
What A Man My Man Is
 (*Columbia/CBS*)

I've Never Loved Anyone More
 (*Columbia/CBS*)
Listen To A Country Song
 (*Columbia/—*)
All The King's Horses
 (*Columbia/—*)
Rose Garden/How Can I Unlove You? (*Columbia/—*)
Country Girl (*—/Embassy*)

Rose Garden (CBS). Title track was song which in 1970 brought her a giant worldwide hit and a CMA award; she has remained in the charts ever since.

Below: Lynn Anderson has spent a lot of time collecting funds for charity.

An hour-glass shaped version of the Appalachian Dulcimer is pictured here being played by Kentucky-born Jean Ritchie, who produced a book of songs from the Appalachians.

Appalachian Dulcimer

Probably originated in Northern Europe and brought to the Kentucky and North Caroline areas by immigrants, the Appalachian dulcimer is a long flat box-like instrument with a center fretboard extended over most of its length. The frets cover only the full tones of two octaves and all sharps and flats are omitted. Usually of three or four string design, the instrument is played by placing it across the knees, the left hand sliding a stick over the strings, the right hand being used for strumming. Its haunting sound was meant by its originators to imitate the sound of bagpipes with a stringed instrument.

Arkie The Arkansas Woodchopper

A longtime (1928–1970) fixture of the National Barn Dance (♦), both in its tenure on WLS (1924–1960) and WGN (1960–1970) in Chicago, Arkie was a singer, guitarist, MC, and square dance caller. Easily amused, he provided endless hours of laughter as other Barn Dance cast members attempted to make him break up in mid-song. They often succeeded.

Despite his stage name, Luther Ossenbrink was born in Missouri (on September 21, 1915), and is currently retired in that state. He did a fair bit of recording for Columbia (1928) and the ARC complex of labels, but never achieved any great success on record.

Albums: none.

Eddy Arnold

A country crooner with a smooth, very commercial voice, Arnold has probably sold more records than any other C&W artist. Born on a farm near Henderson, Tennessee, May 15, 1918, Richard Edward Arnold first became interested in music while at elementary school, his father – an old-time fiddler – teaching him guitar at the age of ten. Arnold left high school during the early 1930s to help his family run their farm. During this period he played at local barn dances, sometimes traveling to such dates on the back of a mule. He made his radio debut in Jackson, Tennessee during 1936, six years later gaining a regular spot on Jackson station WTJS. His big break came as singer/guitarist with Pee Wee King's Golden West Cowboys (♦) providing exposure on Grand Ole Opry.

As a solo act he signed for RCA in 1944, sparking off an amazing tally of hit records with **It's A Sin** and **I'll Hold You In My Heart** in 1947, the latter becoming a million-seller. This achievement was matched by later Arnold recordings: **Bouquet Of Roses, Anytime, Just A Little Lovin' Will Go A Long Long Way** (1948); **I Wanna Play House With You** (1951) and **Cattle Call** (1955), while many others sold nearly as many. Arnold's records sold to people who normally bought straight pop, so his TV appearances were not confined to just Grand Ole Opry and country shows, the singer guesting on programs hosted by Perry Como, Milton Berle, Arthur Godfrey, Dinah Shore, Bob Hope, Spike Jones and other showbiz personalities. Arnold also had own syndicated TV series, Eddy Arnold Time, plus other shows on NBC and ABC networks. Though his record sales dropped slightly by the end of the '50s, **What's He Doing In My World?, Make The World Go Away, I Want To Go With You, Somebody Like Me, Lonely Again, Turn The World Around** and **Then You Can Tell Me Goodbye**, all topped the country charts during '60s. by the beginning of the 1970's Arnold, nicknamed 'The Tennessee Plowboy' had sold well in excess of 60 million discs. A hit single 'Cowboy' marked his return to the RCA fold in 1976 after a brief period with MGM.

Albums:
Best Of Vol 1 (RCA/RCA)
Best Of Vol 2 (RCA/—)
Cattle Call (RCA/—)
Chained To A Memory (Camden/—)
One Dozen Hits (RCA/—)
Faithfully Yours (RCA/—)
Everlovin' World (RCA/—)
Love And Guitars (RCA/—)
I Love How You Love Me (Camden/—)
Misty Blue (Camden/—)
What's He Doing In My World? (RCA/—)
Portrait Of My Woman (RCA/—)
Sings Love Songs (RCA/—)

This Is Eddy Arnold (RCA/—)
Welcome To My World (RCA/—)
Then You Can Tell Me Goodbye (Camden/—)
So Many Ways/If The World Stopped Turnin' (MGM/—)
Country Gold (RCA/—)
I Wish I'd Loved You Better (MGM/MGM)
The Wonderful World Of Eddy Arnold (MGM/MGM)
World Hits (MGM/MGM)
Pure Gold (RCA/—)
Eddy (RCA/RCA
I Need You All The Time (RCA/—)
Favorites (RCA/—)

RCA Records.

RCA Records.

Area Code 615

Mac Gayden guitar, french horn
Bobby Thompson banjo, guitar
David Briggs keyboards
Ken Buttrey drums, vocals
Wayne Moss guitar
Weldon Myrick steel guitar
Norbert Putnam bass, cello
Buddy Spicher fiddle, viola, cello
Bobby Thompson banjo, guitar

Supergroup comprising Nashville and Muscle Shoals sessionmen, originally formed by Mike Nesmith (♦) who still owns unreleased tapes of Code's initial sessions. Later made two albums for Polydor then

13

split, three members forming Barefoot Jerry (♦).

Albums:
Area Code 615 *(Polydor/Polydor)*
Trip In The Country
(Polydor/Polydor)

Ernie Ashworth

Born Huntsville, Alabama, December 15, 1928. While in his teens, he played guitar and sang on local radio stations, later moving to Nashville and working for station WSIX. Carl Smith (♦) and little Jimmy Dickens (♦) were among those to record Ashworth's songs, prompting MGM to sign him to a recording contract in 1955, a number of the discs being cut for the label under the name of Billy Worth. But his luck was out and in 1957 Ashworth returned home to take a job at the Army's Redstone Arsenal. However, Wesley Rose (♦), who'd initiated the MGM contract, won Ashworth another deal, this time with Decca, his first release **Each Moment (Spent With You)** becoming a major hit in May 1960. After further successes with **You Can't Pick A Rose In September** and **Forever Gone**, came a move to Hickory Records, the hits continuing via **Everybody But Me** (1962), his first Hickory single, and **Talk Back Trembling Lips**, a No 1 in the 1963 country charts.

Wins in the Most Promising C&W Artist sections of the **Cashbox** and **Billboard** polls came in '63 and '64, Ashworth being rewarded with appearances and membership on Grand Ole Opry and other leading shows. A consistent hitmaker throughout the late '60s, **A Week In The Country, I Love To Dance With Annie, Pushed In A Corner, Because I Cared, The DJ Cried, At Ease Heart, Sad Face, A New Heart**, and **Love, I Finally Found It**, all figured among his best sellers. Ashworth, who appeared in a movie *The Farmer's Other Daughter* during 1965, has made such Hickory albums as **Talk Back Trembling Lips** and **Ernie Ashworth.**

Asleep At The Wheel

Ray Benson *vocals, guitar*
Chris O'Connell *vocals, guitar*
Tony Garnier *bass*
Danny Levin *fiddle, mandolin*
Lucky Oceans *pedal steel guitar*
Leroy Preston *vocals, guitar*
Link Davis Jr. *fiddle, saxes*
Floyd Domino *keyboards*
Bill Mabry *fiddle*

Wheel, a nine member western swing unit, began life on Ray Benson's rent-free 1,500 acre farm, near Paw Paw, West Virginia, when he, Preston and Reuben Gosfield (also known as Lucky Oceans) formed a small country band. With various personnel additions and changes the band began a series of dates alongside Poco (♦) and Commander Cody (♦), gaining further shape when female vocalist Chris O'Connell, just out of high school, became the fourth permanent member. Following a move to San Francisco, pianist Floyd Domino joined, bringing jazz influence to the band. First UA album by Wheel was near pure country in character, but subsequent albums for Epic and Capitol have seen the band employing more diverse material. Contributions by ex-Texas Playboy Johnny Gimble (♦) have, however, helped retain the Bob Wills (♦) connection. Since February 1974, Wheel have been working out of Austin, Texas, becoming an 11-piece unit in 1977.

Albums:
Comin' Right At Ya *(United Artists/—)*
Asleep At The Wheel *(Epic/—)*
Texas Gold *(Capitol/Capitol)*
Wheelin' And Dealin' *(Capitol/ Capitol)*
Wheel *(Capitol/Capitol)*

Bob Atcher

Robert Owen Atcher, born in Hardin County, Kentucky on May 11, 1914, grew up in North Dakota in a family of folk singers and championship fiddlers, and the duality of these locations gave him a broad knowledge of both traditional folk songs and cowboy songs as well, although he proved to be a very commercial country singer during his long association with Columbia Records (1937–1958).

Bob's clear tenor voice was a fixture and a cornerstone of the once-thriving country music scene in Chicago; he appeared there on WJJD and WBBM and on a host of network programs from 1931–34 and 1937–48, then joined the National Barn Dance (♦) as its top star from 1948 right through its demise in 1970.

Appearing on and off with a series of girl singers known as Bonnie Blue Eyes, Bob Atcher achieved his greatest popularity on radio, both network and local, although he recorded for Kapp and Capitol as well as Columbia Records (his biggest hit for them was a comedy version of **Thinking Tonight Of My Blue Eyes**), wrote

Hired as RCA's answer to Merle Travis, Chet Atkins has since helped to formulate the Nashville Sound.

songs, pioneered television in Chicago, and appeared as a singing cowboy in several Columbia pictures.

Although he continued to perform, Atcher's interest gradually turned to the financial and civic, and he spent nearly two decades as mayor of the Chicago suburb of Schaumburg. He has recently re-banded with his musical son and daughters, and is resuming a limited appearance schedule, still handsome, regal, and possessing that famous Atcher smile.

His past albums have included **Early American Folk Songs, Songs Of The Saddle, Dean Of The Cowboy Singers** (all Columbia); **Bob Atcher's Best** (Harmony) and **Saturday Night At The Old Barn Dance** (Kapp).

Chet Atkins

Chester Burton Atkins was born June 20, 1924, on a 50-acre farm near Luttrell, Tennessee. His elder half-brother Jim was a proficient guitarist who later went on to play with Les Paul (♦). Father James Arley Atkins was also an accomplished musician. At 18 Chet became fiddler on station WNOX in Knoxville, Tennessee, then toured with Archie Campbell (♦) and Bill Carlisle (♦), playing fiddle and guitar. He failed an audition with Roy Acuff's (♦) band in 1944 and began working for WLW, Cincinnati, a year later. After marrying Leona Johnson in 1945, Atkins joined Red Foley (♦) in 1946 then moved to Nashville in 1950, with The Carter Sisters and Mother Maybelle (♦) signing a record contract with RCA and initially cutting more vocals than instrumentals. But it was the latter that got airplay.

He became top session guitarist for RCA's Nashville sessions at end of '40s, moving up to the post of A&R assistant under Steve Sholes (♦) in 1952, first Atkins solo album, **Gallopin' Guitar** being released in 1953. After assisting Sholes on Presley's **Heartbreak Hotel** sessions in 1955, Atkins was placed in charge of the new RCA studio, becoming Nashville A&R manager in 1960 and vice-president of RCA Records just eight years later.

A guitarist able to tackle many styles, Atkins has appeared at the Newport Jazz Festival and been featured soloist with the Atlanta Symphony Orchestra. He's produced hit records for Hank Snow (♦), Waylon Jennings (♦), Perry Como, Al Hirt and many, many others, and also his own major hits in **Poor People Of Paris** (1956), **Boo Boo Stick Beat Beat** (1959), **One Mint Julep** (1960), **Teensville** (1960), **Yakety Axe** (1965) etc. Along with Floyd Cramer (♦), Hank Garland and others, he is credited with creating the highly commercial 'Nashville Sound' that brought pop acts scurrying to record in the area. For 14 consecutive years he won 'Best Instrumentalist' award in the **'Cashbox'** poll.

Albums

Best Of Vol 1 *(RCA/—)*	**Picks On The Hits** *(RCA/RCA)*
Best Of Vol 2 *(RCA/—)*	**Picks On Jerry Reed** *(RCA/—)*
Alone *(RCA/RCA)*	**Picks The Best** *(RCA/—)*
Chet, Floyd and Boots	**Goes To The Movies** *(RCA/—)*
(Camden/—)	**Chester And Lester** *(RCA/RCA)*
Country Pickin' *(Camden/—)*	**The Night Atlanta Burned**
Finger Pickin' Good	*(RCA/—)*
(Camden/—)	**Travellin' Guitar**
For The Good Times *(RCA/—)*	*(—/RCA International)*
Class Guitar/Down Home	**Me And Chet Atkins** *(RCA/RCA)*
(RCA/—)	with Jerry Reed
Me And Jerry Reed *(RCA/—)*	**Famous Country Music Makers**
Nashville Gold *(Camden/—)*	*(—/RCA)*
Now And Then *(RCA/—)*	**Atkins-Travis Travelling Show**
Superpickers *(RCA/RCA)*	*(RCA/RCA)*
This Is Chet Atkins *(RCA/—)*	

Superpickers (RCA). Originally a vocalist, but it was his guitar that won him fame. Also a prominent businessman – vice president of RCA – and successful record producer.

Austin

The capital of Texas, around the turn of the '60s Austin went from being just a pleasant university town to a byword for the new contemporary 'outlaw' country music.

Always more cosmopolitan than other Texas towns (Austin is home for whites, blacks, Mexicans, students and cowboys), '60s social and musical changes in Austin first revolved around places such as Threadgill's Bar where, around 1962, students from the university and musicians searching for an identity (such as Janis Joplin, on the run from redneck Texan mores in Port Arthur) gathered to play folk and country music. The psychedelic movement arrived and Austin evolved its own heroes in this area. Being Texans they didn't do things by halves, and bands such as Roky and the 13th Floor Elevators and the Conqueroo were larger-than-life phenomena, the Grateful Dead equivalents. By the same token, being Texans, they soon found themselves barred, busted or discriminated against, and many of the Texas rock fraternity either gave up or – like Doug Sahm (♦) – fled to California.

When the Byrds (♦) started experimenting with country rock, the stage was set for Austin's arrival as a pace-setter. By 1972, what a group of West coast hippie musicians had been experimenting with was a way of life. Through some faraway dilettante rock bands, Austin discovered its own, long forgotten Texas identity. Thus was born a new strain of honky tonk music, called, variously, 'redneck rock', 'outlaw country' and 'cosmic cowboy music'.

But the new artists carried more lyric imagination than most country stars. Kinky Friedman (♦) may have guyed country sounds and stances and Commander Cody (♦) may have presented the whole Southern music rainbow as a kind of living, honky tonk museum piece, but performers like Michael Murphey, Steve Fromholz and B. W. Stevenson came on like young, home spun idealists, using poetic imagery in their songs and playing on themes of urban alienation and changing times. The spirit of Texas revived by Peter Bogdanovich's movie 'The Last Picture Show' was being hymned for all it was worth.

In his graphic chronicle of Austin music, 'The Improbable Rise Of Redneck Rock', Jan Reid says: 'If Michael Murphey was born to play his guitar under clear skies in a meadow for retarded kids, Willie Nelson (♦) was born to assemble his band on a flat bed truck in the service ramp of a Ford dealership and play for used-car salesmen'.

Nelson had come to Austin because Texas was his home, but also because he was fleeing the commercial pressures in Nashville and needed somewhere to lay out and re-think his music. As an already established country star he gave focus to Austin music, and although Willie would continue to sing about those old country themes, beer drinking and woman troubles, he would also refine those very themes into new art forms.

As far as clubs went, the Armadillo World Headquarters (a dance hall cum beer joint whose garden had been built with the help of volunteer labor) and the Soap Creek Saloon have gained national reputations. Radio KOKE (with a decal depicting a cowboy roping an obstinate goat) set up as opposition to the established stations, peddling a mainly progressive country format.

But Texas music really made its comeback in 1972 when Willie Nelson sponsored the first Fourth of July outdoor Picnic, at Dripping Springs, Texas. Although a financial disaster the festival also featured Waylon Jennings (♦), Kris Kristofferson (♦), Charlie Rich (♦), Billy Joe Shaver (♦), Tom T. Hall (♦) and Leon Russell (who caused a great chunk of his own rock following to do a double take and followed up later by releasing a fine album of country standards called **Hank Wilson's Back, Vol 1**).

Willie balanced things up by also having Tex Ritter (♦), Roy Acuff (♦) and Bill Monroe (♦) on the bill, and the audience turned out to comprise both hard core country fans and hippies. Although the inter-cultural war was receding by 1972 the cowboys apparently felt uncomfortable (whether because of the arduous three days of heat and discomfort or because of their neighbors is uncertain) and subsequent events in this series have attracted a mainly long-haired gathering in which the atmosphere has been similar to that of the more successful rock festivals.

Austin has attracted national press attention but has not developed in the way some people predicted. Apart from Willie Nelson, none of the Austin crowd of performers is a national figure and the studios, session musicians, label offices and other things necessary to a major music town have not happened. Many Austin performers say this state of affairs suits them, and indeed it is difficult to visualize Austin increasing in importance without such commercial trappings. At present though it continues to be a pleasantly laid-back place to stay at and a vital live music center.

Autoharp

A form of miniature harp or zither that can be either laid in one's lap or cradled in the arms. A series of chord bars are fixed across the lower part of the frame, the pressing of buttons producing given chords when a pick is moved across the harp strings. An acoustic soundbox positioned behind the strings amplifies the sound. The autoharp was popularized by Mother Maybelle Carter (♦) – known as 'Queen Of The Autoharp' – her daughter June Carter, and numerous contemporary string band revivalists.

The frame of one autoharp, from the Euphrates Valley, is about 4,500 years old.

Gene Autry

Orvon Gene Autry, most successful of all singing cowboys to break into movies, was born Tioga, Texas, September 29, 1907. Taught to play guitar by mother Elnora Ozment Autry, Gene joined the Fields Brothers Marvelous Medicine Show while still at high school (at one time playing saxophone!), but after graduation in 1925 became a railroad telegrapher with the Frisco Railway at Sapulpar, Oklahoma. Encouraged by Will Rogers, following a chance meeting, Autry took a job on radio KVOO, Tulsa, in 1930, billing himself as 'Oklahoma's Singing Cowboy', and singing much in the style of Jimmie Rodgers (♦). In 1929 he had visited New York and began recording with such labels as Victor, Okeh, Columbia, Grey Gull and Gennett (often under a pseudonym), sometimes working with Jimmy Long, a singer-songwriter-guitarist, once Autry's boss on the Frisco line. On many he was assisted by Frank and Johnny Marvin (♦). Shortly after, Autry began broadcasting regularly on the WLS Barn Dance program from Chicago, his popularity gaining further momentum with the 1931 release of **Silver Haired Daddy Of Mine** (penned by Autry and Long) a recording that eventually sold over five million copies. Next came a move to Hollywood where, following a performance in Ken Maynard western 'In Old Santa Fe', he was asked to star in serial 'The Phantom Empire'. Thereafter, Autry appeared in innumerable B movies, usually with horse Champion, all but one for Republic. His list of hit records during the 1930s and '40s – he was easily the most popular country singer of the time – is awesome, including **Yellow Rose Of Texas** (1933), **The Last Roundup** (1934), **Tumbling Tumbleweeds** (1935), **Mexicali Rose** (1936), **Back In The Saddle Again** (1939), **South Of The Border** (1940), **You Are My Sunshine** (1941), **It Makes No Difference Now** (1941), **Be Honest With Me** (1941), **Tweedle-O-Twill** (1942) and **At Mail Call Today** (1945).

Autry enlisted in the Army Air Corps in July 1942 and became a pilot, flying in the Far East and North Africa with Air Transport Command. Discharged on June 17 1945, he formed a film company, continuing to star in such movies – this time for Columbia – as 'Sioux City Sue' (1947), 'Guns And Saddles' (1949) and 'Last of The Pony Riders' (1953), also appearing in the long-running 'Melody Ranch' radio program from 1939 until 1956.

His other activities included opening a chain of radio and TV stations and running a record company, a hotel chain and a music publishing firm, plus a major league baseball club, the California Angels. Since **Silver Haired Daddy**, Autry has had three other million selling discs in **Here Comes Santa Claus** (1947), **Peter Cottontail** (1949) and the over nine million seller **Rudolph The Red Nosed Reindeer** (1948). Writer of scores of hit songs, he's also starred at a series of annual rodeos held in Madison Square Garden, had an Oklahoma town named after him, and, in 1969, was elected a member of the Country Music Hall Of Fame.

Albums:
Country Music Hall Of Fame
(Columbia/—)
Christmas Time With Gene Autry *(Mistletoe/—)*
South Of The Border
(Republic/—)

All American Cowboy
(Republic/—)
Cowboy Hall of Fame
(Republic/—)
Favorites *(Republic/Ember)*
Live From Madison Square Garden *(Republic/—)*

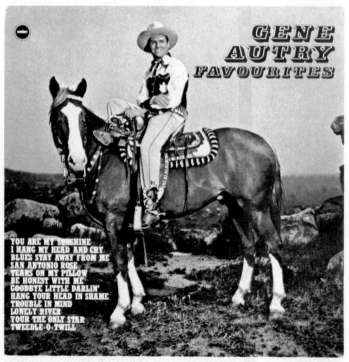

Favourites (Ember). Contains many of Autry's greatest hits from the '30s and '40s. He began as 'Oklahoma's Singing Cowboy' on radio in 1930 and became the most popular singer of the time.

Gene Autry. In 1939, he told the kids at London's Clapham Granada: 'Next time I come, I'll bring Champion'.

17

Hoyt Axton

Born in Oklahoma, son of two teachers, John Thomas Axton and his wife Mae, a lady who worked for Grand Ole Opry and wrote many fine songs – including **Heartbreak Hotel,** the Elvis Presley (♦) classic – Axton began playing guitar and singing in West Coast clubs during 1958. After a brief spell in the Navy, he cut his first record **Follow The Drinking Gourd** in Nashville, along with sessionmen Jimmy Riddle (harmonica) and Grady Martin (♦) (guitar). Axton's **Greenback Dollar** became a hit when recorded by The Kingston Trio in 1963, while **The Pusher,** another Axton song, was heard by John Kay in 1964 and subsequently became an enormous success for Kay's rock group Steppenwolf. Other Axton compositions **Joy To The World** and **Never Been To Spain** proved winners for Three Dog Night and **No No Song** scored for Ringo Starr. While Axton was once thought of primarily as a folk singer, he's now considered as one of the finest writers in country music, his songs being recorded by Waylon Jennings (♦), Tanya Tucker (♦), John Denver (♦), Glenn Yarborough, Lynn Anderson (♦), Glen Campbell (♦), Commander Cody (♦) and many others.

Albums:
Less Than The Song *(A&M/ A&M)*
Life Machine *(A&M/A&M)*
My Griffin Is Gone *(Columbia/Columbia)*
Southbound *(A&M/A&M)*
Fearless *(A&M/A&M)*
Hoyt Axton Explodes *(—/Joy)*

Snowblind Friend (MCA). Once a folk singer, Axton is a successful songwriter, having composed several rock and country hits and written for a host of country stars.

'I've always loved music – I also love women and children, rainbows, pickup trucks, wild animals, snow, clean rivers....'

The Bailes Brothers

Kyle Bailes *string bass, vocals*
Johnny Bailes *guitar, vocals*
Walter Bailes *guitar, vocals*
Homer Bailes *fiddle, vocals*

Despite the number of Bailes Brothers, the act of that name rarely consisted of all four brothers, but instead any combination of two or three was more likely. The heart of the act, however, consisted of Johnny and Walter, whose songwriting and singing made them one of the most popular groups of the 1940s.

Johnny was actually the first to work professionally, teaming up with Red Sovine (♦) early on (1937). By the time he had gone to Beckley, West Virginia, in 1939, he had not only acquired the services of Skeets Williamson, but of his sister Laverne, who became known professionally as Molly O'Day (♦). Yet another bandmember was Little Jimmy Dickens (♦). During the same period Kyle and Walter were billing themselves as the Bailes Brothers; before long it was Walter and Johnny.

In 1942 Roy Acuff (♦) heard them and arranged an audition – which was successful – for the Grand Ole Opry, a tenure which lasted through 1948, when they joined the Louisiana Hayride (♦). It was during the Opry years that they recorded many of the songs which made them famous: **Dust On The Bible, I Want To Be Loved, Remember Me, As Long As I Live,** and others, mainly for Columbia.

The act eventually broke up in 1949, Homer and Walter entering the ministry, although both Johnny and Walter, and Homer and Kyle worked as gospel duets intermittently in the 1950s. Today Kyle is in the air conditioning business, Homer is a minister, Johnny manages one of Webb Pierce's (♦) radio stations, and Walter, although still involved in church work, is the only brother actively performing on a semi-regular basis, doing gospel numbers (largely self-written) like his classic **Whiskey Is The Devil In Liquid Form.**

Albums:
The Bailes Brothers: Johnny And Homer *(Old Homestead/—)*
I've Got My One Way Ticket *(Old Homestead/—)*

DeFord Bailey

Though black musicians are a rarity in country music, it was DeFord Bailey, a black harmonica player, who opened the WSM Barn Dance programme – playing train song **Pan American Blues** –

DeFord Bailey had problems when touring, few hotels would offer him accommodation.

on the night George D. Hay (♦) reputedly named the show 'Grand Ole Opry' (♦). Born Carthage, Tennessee, in 1899, Bailey was afflicted by infantile paralysis at the age of three. Although he recovered, his growth was stunted and he suffered from a deformed back. Apart from being the first performer on the Opry, the 4ft 10in tall Bailey was also amongst the first musicians to record in Nashville, cutting several sides for Victor on September 28, 1928. He remained a member of the Opry for many years but later drifted into obscurity, in recent years operating a shoeshine stand in the Nashville area. Though he's received offers of films, records and personal appearances, all have been turned down.

19

Bakersfield

In the mid-'60s Bakersfield, California, was being touted as 'Nashville West', a center for country music that would rival Music City itself.

Bakersfield was build up mainly by Buck Owens (♦), a Texas-born singer with a hard country style who saw the opportunity to provide an alternative to the then softening music of Nashville. It was inhabited by many expatriate Oklahomans (Merle Haggard's (♦) family moved there after the 1930's Dustbowl) and Owens saw that these oil and cotton laborers would appreciate authentic, less tepid country, since many of them had grown up with it in Oklahoma and Texas.

Although Owens would not strictly carry out his promise to sing authentic modern country he did become known for just such music, and by the end of the decade he had built a reputation and the town had become such a mini-country centre that Bakersfield became known as 'Buckersfield' to many. Wynn Stewart (♦), a singer-songwriter from Alabama and a club entrepreneur, also became associated with the town.

Merle Haggard returned to his home town from prison and found it ready-made for his honest brand of country. Husky-voiced Freddy Hart (♦) too is part of the scene. Bakersfield today is a thriving center, commercially and musically.

It has not ousted Nashville as the capital (as perhaps no one quite expected it to) but is a valuable watering hole for musicians and fans in the western states, and it has played a key role in upholding the sound of basic, bar-room country music.

Larry Ballard

Up and coming self-styled honky tonk singer whose song **Young Blood And Sweet Country Music** focused attention on the increasing move among young singers towards bar room country in the early '70s – of which Ballard was part.

A native of industrial Detroit, he was born in Bay City, Michigan, November 13, 1946. Larry first played in a local rock 'n' roll band although he was generally recep-

tive to Southern music, his first favorite having been Conway Twitty (♦), but by 18 he had switched to country, a style to which he is intuitively suited.

By 1969 he was writing his own material and his gigging life took him in country bands to après-ski resorts in Colorado, to Los Angeles, Washington State and then to Nashville. When Ballard could afford to settle for good in Music City in 1973 he met Buzz Rabin, a performer and writer then working for Pete Drake (♦), and Rabin encouraged him and introduced him to Drake, the result of

which was a production deal with Drake and subsequently a contract with the progressive-minded Elektra Records. In that spring of 1974 Larry toured with Elektra stablemate Linda Hargrove (♦) but was soon big enough as an attraction to headline his own gigs.

He has a warm but hard-edged voice and his records are fairly upbeat in mood. In 1976 he was among the list of nominations for the CMA Male Singer Of The Year. His albums have included **Honky Tonk Heaven** *(Capitol)* and **Young Blood And Country Music** *(Elektra)*.

Here I Am Drunk Again (Columbia). Ex-bronco buster Bandy signed in 1976; he was previously with GRC, where he scored his first hit in 1973.

Moe Bandy

Born Meridan, Mississippi. One of six children, his mother was a pianist and his father a guitar-player, while his grandfather at one time worked the railroads with Jimmie Rogers (♦). Bandy's first band was the Mission City Playboys, organized by his father shortly after the family had moved to San Antonio, Texas. Later, after a spell as a bronco-buster, during which time he obtained several

Courtesy Columbia Records.

Left: Moe Bandy.

broken bones, Bandy formed own band The Mavericks, which he led until 1974. In 1973 he commenced recording for the then new GRC label and had an immediate hit with **I Just Started Hatin' Cheatin' Songs Today.** Following other successes via such singles as **It Was Always So Easy To Find An Unhappy Woman** and **Bandy The Rodeo Clown,** he was signed by Columbia Records in 1976 and again had an instant hit with **Hank Williams, You Wrote My Life,** a song written in the Williams style.

Albums:
It Was Easy *(GRC/—)*
I Started Hatin' Cheatin' Songs Today *(GRC/—)*
Bandy The Rodeo Clown *(GRC/—)*
Hank Williams, You Wrote My Life *(Columbia/—)*
Here I Am Drunk Again *(Columbia/—)*
I'm Sorry For You My Friend *(Columbia/CBS)*

Banjo

Ancient stringed instrument with stretched skin head. Possibly derived from the European lute-like bandore or the African banjar – though there are many other theories. Originally a four-string instrument, an American five-string version was popularized in the early nineteenth century, Joe Sweeney of Appomatox, Virginia, being credited with invention. Much used by bluegrass groups today.

Bobby Bare

The singer of million-sellers **Detroit City** and **500 Miles Away From Home,** Bare was born Ironton, Ohio, April 7, 1935. Motherless at the age of five, his sister being sent for adoption because of the father's inability to feed the whole family, Bare became a farm worker at 15, later obtaining a job in a clothing factory. He built his own guitar and learnt to play, eventually winning a job with a country band in the Springfield-Portsmouth area – for which he received no pay. He recorded his own song **All American Boy** in 1958, then joined the army, the tapes of the song being offered to various record companies and taken up by Fraternity who released the disc

Right: The multi-talented Bobby Bare.

Below: Moe Bandy has been a consistent hitmaker in 1977.

BOBBY BARE
and the family
SINGIN' IN THE KITCHEN

RCA
STEREO LSA 3196

as by 'Bill Parsons'. But though **Boy** became the nation's second biggest selling record during December 1958, Bare hardly benefited moneywise, having sold the song rights for just $50.

After service discharge, Bare began performing and writing once more, contributing three songs for Chubby Checker–Jimmy Clanton rock movie **Teenage Millionaire,** a year later having his own record hit with an RCA disc **Shame On Me.** Richard Anthony then recorded a French version of **500 Miles Away From Home** (a folk song adapted and arranged by Bare, Hedy West and Charles Williams) and obtained a gold disc, Bare also having a million-seller with **Detroit City** in 1963.

A year later, Bare appeared in an acting role in the cavalry western 'A Distant Trumpet' and also provided RCA with further hits via his versions of Hank Snow's (♦) **Miller's Cave** and Ian and Sylvia's

Four Strong Winds. After further hits, Bare left RCA to join Mercury in 1970, scoring then with **That's How I Got To Memphis, Come Sundown, Don't Tell Me How The Story Ends** and others. But he returned to RCA again, cutting classic albums **Lullabys, Legends and Lies** and **Singin' In The Kitchen** with much Shel Silverstein (♦)-penned material. In 1976, tragedy struck when Cari, Bare's 15-year-old daughter, who'd sung on **Singin' In The Kitchen,** died of heart failure.

_____

Albums:
This Is Bobby Bare *(RCA/—)*
Lullabys, Legends And Lies
  (RCA/RCA)
Memphis, Tennessee
  (Camden/—)
It's A Long Way From Home
  (Camden/—)
Hard Time Hungrys *(RCA/RCA)*
The Very Best Of Bobby Bare
  (UA/—)

Sunday AM *(RCA/—)*
I Hate Goodbyes *(RCA/—)*
For The Good Times *(—/Ember)*
Best Of Bobby Bare *(—/RCA)*
Singin' In The Kitchen
  (RCA/RCA)
Bare Country *(UA/—)*
Tunes For Two *(—/RCA)*
  with Skeeter Davis

RCA Records.

Singin' In The Kitchen (RCA). Mostly Shel Silverstein songs, performed with a little help from his family. Sadly, daughter Carrie died in 1976.

Barefoot Jerry

Jim Colvard *guitar*
Wayne Moss *guitar*
Warren Hartman *keyboards*
Russ Hicks *steel guitar*
Terry Dearmore *bass,*
  harmonica, vocals
Si Edwards *drums*

_____

Formed from the remnants of Area Code 615 (♦), only one original member – Wayne Moss, also the band's producer – still remains. Moss, born Charleston, West Virginia, began playing guitar at 12 and later worked with several rock and R&B bands before becoming a member of Brenda Lee's (♦) back-up band for two and a half years. He then became a Nashville sessionman, forming band The Escorts with drummer Kenny Buttrey and becoming owner of Cinderella recording studios. Jim Colvard is another Nashville's 400-sessions-a-year man, while Connie Smith discovery Russ Hicks has toured with Ray Price (♦), Kitty Wells (♦) and Bob Luman (♦). Terry Dearmore, a songwriter with Combine Music, has previously worked with Dennis Linde and Brewer and Shipley; Si Edwards is a studio drummer who learnt his trade from Johnny Cash sideman W. S. Holland; and newest member Warren Hartman was once a member of Stanley Steamer, a group who cut one album for MGM. A country rock unit, Jerry have recorded for Capitol, Warner Brothers and Monument.

Albums:
Watchin' TV *(Monument/—)*
You Can't Get Off With Your Shoes On *(Monument/ Monument)*
Groceries *(Monument/—)*

Barefoot Jerry (from Area Code 615), headed by Wayne Moss.

Bashful Brother Oswald

Real name Beecher 'Pete' Kirby, born Sevier County, Tennessee, this guitarist, banjoist and dobro player was one of eight brothers and two sisters, all of whom played instruments, their father being proficient on fiddle, banjo and guitar. As a young man, Kirby worked in a sawmill, a cotton mill and on a farm before becoming a guitarist in an Illinois club. Over the road at a rival establishment was a musician playing dobro and drawing large crowds – so Kirby too bought a dobro in order to compete.

During the World's Fair in Chicago he played in the local beer joints, passing his hat around, working part time in a restaurant in order to survive. Then came a move to Knoxville, Tennessee, where he joined Roy Acuff's (♦) Crazy Tennesseans on radio station WRL, becoming one of the band's stars when, as the Smoky Mountain Boys, Acuff's unit became a regular part of Grand Ole Opry at the beginning of 1939. As Bashful Brother Oswald, the bib-overall-clad Kirby sang and duetted with Acuff, utilizing the banjo for most solo work, reverting to dobro whenever Acuff's distinctive band sound was required. A member of the Smoky Mountain Boys for many years, Kirby could be found looking after Acuff's Nashville museum during the early '70s, often indulging in good-time pickin' in order to attract extra customers.

One of the stars to appear on the Nitty Gritty Dirt Band's (♦) **Will The Circle Be Unbroken?** album in 1971, Kirby cut a solo album, produced by Tut Taylor (♦), for Rounder during 1972, and has since done extensive recording with fellow Smoky Mountain Boy Charlie Collins.

Albums:
Brother Oswald *(Rounder/—)*
That's Country with Charlie Collins *(Rounder/—)*

Dr Humphrey Bate (And The Possum Hunters)

Dr Humphrey Bate *harmonica*
Burt Hutcherson *guitar*
Oscar Stone *fiddle*
Walter Leggett *banjo*
Staley Walton *guitar*
Oscar Albright *bass*
Buster Bate *guitar, tipple, harmonica, jews harp*
Alcyone Bate *vocals, ukelele, piano*

The harmonica playing leader of the most popular string band on the Grand Ole Opry, Dr Bate – a graduate of Vanderbilt Medical School who earned his living as a physician – was born in Summer County, Tennessee, in 1875. He had fronted a great many popular local string bands before he began to play on Nashville radio in 1925, joining the forerunner of the Opry late in that year. Not long after, they recorded a number of tunes and songs for Brunswick Records.

After Dr Bate's death in 1936, Oscar Stone headed the band until in 1949, when Staley Walton and Alcyone Bate took over the leadership of the Possum Hunters, whose remaining members were absorbed when the old time Opry bands amalgamated the four bands into two in the 1960s.

Bate's daughter Alcyone (now Alcyone Beasley) joined her father's band at the age of 13 as a vocalist; after a long career in radio she is still an Opry member, continuing over a half century with the show, currently playing piano for the Crook Brothers Band (♦).

Albums: none.

Dr Humphrey Bate and His Possum Hunters, the first string band to be featured on the Opry. Bate was a real *doctor.*

Molly Bee

Only ten years old when she debuted on the Rex Allen Tucson radio show, Molly Bee (real name Molly Beachwood) was born Oklahoma City, Oklahoma, August 18, 1939. When 11 she became a regular on Cliffie Stone's (♦) Los Angeles based Hometown Jamboree TV show, following this with stays on the nationally networked Pinky Lee and Tennessee Ernie Ford (♦) TV programs. A successful actress and vocalist, Mollie was booked into several Las Vegas nightspots and other major venues, breaking house records with some of her appearances. During the '60s she also began starring in West Coast productions of such stage musicals as 'The Boy Friend', 'Paint Your Wagon' and 'Finian's Rainbow', in 1967 making a well-received tour of Japan.

An MGM artist for many years, during the mid '70s she began recording for Granite, a label headed by her old mentor Cliffie Stone.

Albums:
Good Golly Miss Molly
  (Granite/Pye)

Carl Belew

Singer-songwriter and guitarist, Carl Robert Belew was born Salina, Oklahoma, April 21, 1931. For many years he played minor venues and county fairs, eventually gaining a spot on Shreveport KWKH's Louisiana Hayride (♦) and obtaining a recording contract with Decca. His first major hit for the label was **Am I That Easy To Forget?**, a self-penned song that became a top ten country hit in 1959, the success of this disc being matched by **Hello Out There**, an RCA release waxed by Belew in 1962. Other hits followed throughout the mid-'60s, namely **In The Middle Of A Memory, Crystal Chandelier, Boston Jail, Walking Shadow, Talking Memory, Girl Crazy** and **Mary's Little Lamb.** After 1968 Belew's name was absent from the charts for a long period, returning in 1971 when **All I Need Is You**, a duet recorded with Betty Jean Robinson, became a small hit.

Albums:
Carl Belew *(Vocalion/—)*
Another Lonely Night
  (Pickwick/—)
Lonely Street *(Vocalion/—)*
12 Shades *(Victor/—)*
Songs *(Vocalion/—)*

Beverly Hillbillies

An early, California-based outfit, the Hillbillies had a radio show on station KEJK (later KMPC) Beverly Hills, in 1928, the group – then comprised of Zeke and Tom Manners, Hank Skillet and Ezra Paulette – having a hit single **When The Bloom Is On The Sage/Red River Valley,** released during the following year.

Elton Britt (♦), Stuart Hamblen (♦), Wesley Tuttle (♦) and Glen Rice have all been members of the Hillbillies at some point in the group's career, Rice forming his own version of the band in later years after Zeke Manners and Elton Britt moved to New York in 1935.

The Binkley Brothers' Dixie Clodhoppers

Amos Binkley *banjo*
Gale Binkley *fiddle*
Tom Andrews *guitar*
Jack Jackson *guitar and vocals*

An early Grand Ole Opry string band, whose fine music, like most of the Opry's early acts, was severely under-recorded. Both watch repairmen by trade, the Binkley Brothers kept their band going on Nashville radio – with and without Jackson, a fine singer and yodeler – well into the mid-1930s, but only recorded during Victor's 1928 field trip to Nashville, with **Hungry Hash House** and **I'll Rise When The Rooster Crows** outstanding.

Albums: none.

Norman Blake

Leading session guitarist Blake was born Chattanooga, Tennessee, March 10, 1938. From a railroad family – one Blake home actually overlooking the Southern Railway tracks – his songs have often contained railroad themes.

After elementary school at Rising Fawn, Georgia and high school at Trenton, he joined group The Dixieland Drifters, playing radio shows in Chattanooga and Knoxville. He also played traditional Appalachian music with banjoist Bob Johnson and recorded an album of old tunes with Walter Forbes. During 1960 came a tour with June Carter (♦) and dates playing dobro and mandolin with Hylo Brown on radio station WWVA Wheeling, West Virginia.

Drafted in 1961, Blake still continued his career, though sent to Panama, recording Nashville album **12 Shades Of Bluegrass** while on leave in '62.

Discharged in 1963, Blake became a regular Johnny Cash (♦) sessionman, the same year marrying and settling down in Chattanooga but moving to Nashville in 1969 to work on Cash's ABC TV series. More sessionwork followed, including work on Bob Dylan's **Nashville Skyline.**

Since then he's toured with Kris Kristofferson (♦) and Joan Baez, worked as a solo act and formed a band with Vasser Clements (♦), Tut Taylor (♦) and John Hartford (♦). In 1977 he signed a two-year contract with Takoma Records.

Albums:
Old And New *(Flying Fish/—)*
With Tut Taylor, Vasser
  Clements etc. *(Flying Fish/ Sonet)*
Home In Sulpher Springs
  (Rounder/—)
Norman Blake And Red Rector
  (County/—)

'... Norman Blake is one of the finest guitar pickers alive ...'
  – Tut Taylor.

Jack Blanchard And Misty Morgan

The Blue Sky Boys (Camden).

Both were born in same Buffalo, New York, hospital, both in May (Jack on May 8, 1942 and Misty on May 23, 1945), both have brown hair and blue eyes, both have parents named John and Mary, plus sisters also named Mary – and both moved to Ohio while young.

Jack Blanchard spent many years as a sax player in a small combo, while Misty Morgan, who'd been involved in music since the age of nine, played piano and organ on the Cincinatti club circuit for a time before moving to Florida where she met and eventually married Blanchard. Five years passed, however, before they began working as a duo. Blanchard became a solo pianist, working with big bands as a director-arranger, later producing records in Nashville. It was at this time that he decided to cut **Big Black Bird** as a duet with his wife, thus coming up with a mild country hit. Next came **Tennessee Birdwalk,** one of 1970s biggest sellers, establishing Blanchard and Morgan as a top ranking act. Since then they've played many high rated TV shows and ob-

The Blue Sky Boys (Bluebird). The Bolick brothers split up after the war but have occasionally appeared at festivals since the mid '60s.

tained an equal number of prestige-filled dates. Their other hits for the Mega, Wayside and Epic labels include **You've Got Your Troubles, Humphrey The Camel** (1970), **There Must Be More To Life, Somewhere In Virginia In The Rain** (1970), **Just One More Song, Something On Your Mind, Down The End Of The Wine** (1974) and **I'm High On You** (1975). Their albums have included **Birds Of A Feather** *(Wayside)* and **Two Sides Of . . .** *(Mega).*

The Blue Sky Boys

Bill Bolick *vocals, mandolin*
Earl Bolick *vocals, guitar*

Both born Hickory, North Carolina, Bill on October 28, 1917, Earl on December 16, 1919, sons of Garland Bolick, who grew tobacco and worked in a textile mill. The Bolicks began playing traditional

Strictly Bluegrass (Polydor). Traditional music using string instruments, popularized by performers such as Bill Monroe and Flatt and Scruggs; one of country's most distinctive sounds.

material, working in and around the Hickory area. In 1935, Bill sang for group The East Hickory String Band – a name later changed to The Crazy Hickory Nuts after J. W. Fincher of the Crazy Water Crystal Company who had offered them a job in Nashville – and the same year, the brothers began singing duets on the local radio station. In 1936, they recorded for Victor, whose A&R man believed them to be a copy of the Monroe Brothers (♦). Their first release – on Bluebird – was **The Sunnyside Of Life**, written by Bill.

During the late 1930s and early '40s, the Bolicks mixture of old-timey and religious music became very popular but, following World War II, country fans began seeking something more commercial and RCA asked the Boys to employ an electric guitarist in their lineup – a request that they refused. In 1951, the Blue Sky Boys broke up, Bill entering college but leaving to work for the Post Office before he'd gained his degree in business, Earl working as a machinist for Lockheed. In the mid-1960s the duo began playing odd dates at folk festivals and colleges and in 1965 recorded an album for Capitol. But the Boys never returned to music on a professional basis.

Albums:
The Blue Sky Boys (Bill And Earl Bolick) *(Bluebird/—)*
Sunnyside Of Life *(Rounder/—)*
The Blue Sky Boys *(County/—)*

Bluegrass

A development of traditional string band music, usually utilizing banjo, fiddle, steel guitar, mandolin and bass, or various combinations of these instruments.

The music was formulated and popularized by Bill Monroe and His Blue Grass Boys (♦) during the late '40s and '50s. Lester Flatt and Earl Scruggs (♦), both former

25

members of the Blue Grass Boys, are among the leading musicians helping to keep bluegrass alive today. Their highspeed **Foggy Mountain Breakdown** was effectively employed as part of the score for the *Bonnie and Clyde* movie in 1967.

Bluegrass music was revitalized by the folk music boom and the development of bluegrass festivals in the middle '60s. Since then it has enjoyed explosive growth, hundreds of thousands of devotees attending hundreds of these festivals yearly, although other than **Dueling Banjos** (the theme from the film *Deliverance*) the music seems unable to generate hit records.

Dock Boggs

Possessor of a unique banjo style, Moran Lee 'Dock' Boggs was born Norton, Virginia, February 7, 1898. A miner for 41 years, Boggs played five string banjo merely as a hobby – his religious wife frowning upon any deep involvement in 'sinful' music. Acquiring his unusual playing style (employing two fingers and a thumb instead of the normal one finger and thumb claw ham-

Left: The five string banjo used in bluegrass music.

Below: Five instruments in search of a bluegrass band.

mer method) from a black musician he met in Norton, Boggs gradually developed his technique and recorded a number of sides for Brunswick in 1927, thoroughly displeasing his wife. But upon his retirement from mining, Boggs turned more of his attention to music and found himself to be an in-demand performer at various folk festivals, where his playing, his eerie, haunting songs like **Oh Death** and his nasal vocal delivery attracted much attention, encouraging Mike Seeger to record Boggs for the Folkways label. He died in the early '50s.

Albums:
Dock Boggs Vols 1 & 2
(Folkways/—)
Dock Boggs Vol 3 *(Folkways/—)*

Johnny Bond

Bond, a singing cowboy film star, was born Enville, Oklahoma, June 1, 1915. After his family moved to a farm in Marietta, Oklahoma, in the '20s, be bought a 98 cent ukelele through a Montgomery Ward catalogue and began playing it, moving on to guitar and becoming proficient on that instrument by the time he'd entered high school. In 1934, Bond made his debut on an Oklahoma City radio station; three years later, after performing at many Oklahoma venues, joining the Jimmy Wakely Trio (♦) (then known as The Bell Boys), a group heard by Gene Autry (♦) and signed for Autry's Melody Ranch CBS show in 1940.

That same year, Bond began recording for Columbia Records, for whom he recorded **Cimarron, Divorce Me C.O.D., Smoke, Smoke, Smoke, Tennessee Saturday Night, Cherokee Waltz, A Petal From A Faded Rose, 'Til The End Of The World** and many others. His strong association with Autry also led him to minor parts and sidekick roles in scores of films, while during the '50s and '60s he guested on TV shows hosted by Autry, Spade Cooley (♦) and Jimmy Wakely, becoming a co-host of Compton's Town Hall Party Show, and partner with Tex Ritter (♦) in music publishing.

A fine songwriter, Bond is responsible for such standards as **Cimarron** and **I Wonder Where You Are Tonight, Gone And Left Me Blues, Your Old Love Letters, Tomorrow Never Comes** plus around 500 other compositions. His contract with Autry's Republic Records provided that label with **Hot Rod Lincoln,** a top 30 pop hit in 1960; a 1965 recording of **Ten Little Bottles** giving another company, Starday, a top selling single.

During the 1970s, Bond – whose book *My 30 Years With Gene Autry* remains unpublished – continues to make hit records, his 1971 **Here Comes The Elephants** being a fairly recent example. His career as an author, however, has blossomed: his *Reflections: The Autobiography of Johnny Bond*, published by the John Edwards Memorial Foundation, while his *The Tex Ritter Story* was published by Chappell in 1976.

Albums:
Old Songs *(Lamb & Lion/—)*

Johnny Bond from Oklahoma – he made his name on the West Coast.

Don Bowman

Top country comedian of the '60s, Bowman was born Lubbock, Texas, August 26, 1937. While a child he sang in church, later learning to play guitar – though part of his stock in trade is that he professes to play it badly! During Bowman's school years, he became a deejay, choosing this as his profession – though he was forced to sell hub caps and pick cotton along with several other menial jobs in order to survive.

Becoming more established as a deejay at one time working with Wayton Jennings (♦), he began working more and more of his own routines into the shows, eventually opting to become a full time fun-maker, appearing at clubs in the South and South-West. In the mid '60s Chet Atkins (♦) signed Bowman to RCA, the result being a 1964 hit, **Chet Atkins Made Me A Star.** In 1966 came smaller successes with **Giddy Up Do-Nut** and **Surely Not,** which helped Bowman win the Billboard award as favorite C&W comedian of the year. His other hits include **Folsom Prison Blues No 2** (1968) and **Poor Old Ugly Gladys Jones** (1970).

Albums:
Support Your Local Prison
  (RCA/—)
All New *(Mega/—)*

Bill Boyd

Singer, guitarist, bandleader and film actor, William Boyd was born Fannin County, Texas, September 29, 1910.

A true cowboy, raised on a ranch, Boyd together with his brother Jim (born September 28, 1914) formed Alexander's Daybreakers in the late 1920s, this group metamorphizing into the Cowboy Ramblers, a Greenville, Texas, band which began recording for Bluebird in 1934, initially cutting mainly instrumental versions of traditional numbers plus cowboy songs like **Strawberry Roan** – of these, **Under The Double Eagle** (1935), a fiddle and guitar version of the popular march proving most successful, remaining in print to this day. Boyd, who cut over 300 sides for RCA over the years (his last session taking place on February 7, 1950), had his own radio show on station WRR, Dallas, Texas for innumerable years, taking time off to appear in half a dozen movies. His brother Jim has appeared in other bands at various points in his career, working with the Light Crust Doughboys (♦) in 1938–9 and the Men Of The West in 1949–51. Other Boyd hits include **New Spanish Two Step** and **Spanish Fandangs** (1939), and **Lone Star Rag** (1949).

Albums:
Bill Boyd's Cowboy Ramblers
  (Bluebird/—)

Bill Boyd's Cowboy Ramblers (Bluebird). An authentic cowboy from Texas, Boyd recorded for Bluebird for nearly 20 years; one of his 1935 instrumentals is still available.

Owen Bradley

A Nashville producer, musician, and executive who had as much, if not more, to do with the creation of the Nashville Sound and the growth of Nashville studios than any other single individual. Born on October 10, 1915 in Westmoreland, Tennessee, Bradley was a bandleading pianist who had one of the most popular dance bands in the Nashville area for some time, and served as musical director of WSM radio from 1940–1958, leading their staff orchestra as well.

In 1947 Decca's Paul Cohen asked Bradley to do some producing for him in Nashville, as Decca had already cut Ernest Tubb (♦), Red Foley (♦)

and a few others there; Bradley accepted, and by 1952 he and his younger brother Harold (now a leading Nashville session musician) had built their first studio. By 1956 they had built their legendary Quonset Hut on 16th Avenue South (which is now Columbia Studio B), which was the beginning of large scale Nashville studio activity and of the area which has come to be known as Music Row as well.

During the 1950s Bradley was instrumental in pioneering the so-called Nashville Sound, in which country music was smoothed out and given a more pop, uptown treatment, featuring lush strings and background voices. Bradley was MCA's chief staff producer, and during his time with them he produced just about every one of their artists: Loretta Lynn (♦), Conway Twitty (♦), Brenda Lee (♦), Bill Anderson (♦) and so on. He was quite open about dispensing with steel guitars, fiddles, etc., and pursuing a sophisticated recording sound which many felt was castrating country as an individual form. There is much truth in this accusation, although at the same time Bradley, with the Nashville Sound, formulated a safe, acceptable, broadly appealing sound (making much money in the process), and can justifiably be said to have brought country music in from the cold when it needed help most. Had the music not gone through this stage of its development it might well not enjoy its huge current acceptability.

In 1958 he moved up the corporate ladder to become country A&R director, a position he held for over a decade until his promotion to vice president of MCA's Nashville operation. In 1974 he was elected to the Country Music Hall of Fame and he currently continues to produce independently, having retired from MCA.

British Country Music

Though almost totally derivative, the British Country Music scene has grown steadily since the 1940s and the pioneer radio dates and music hall appearances of Big Bill Campbell. During the '70s, such acts as the Frank Jennings Syndicate, Brian Chalker, Cajun Moon, Keith Manifold, Pete Sayers, Sydney Devine and Pete Stanley and Roger Knowles all gained recording contracts with major companies, while Olivia Newton-John (♦) became the first British-born artist ever to win an American CMA award.

Fiddler Brian Golbey of Cajun Moon is one musician who has won the admiration of various American country stars, his early success coming in the mid '60s when he joined guitarist Pete Stanley to form a highly popular duo. Golbey – who became the recipient of the CMA (GB) Male Vocalist of The Year Award in 1971 – has worked with Mac Wiseman (♦) and Patsy Montana, also appearing on Ernest Tubb's (♦) Midnight Jamboree, Nashville WSM's Early Morning Show and at the CMA Internation Show, staged during Nashville's Annual Dee-Jay Convention.

Pete Sayers (vocals, dobro, guitar, autoharp and banjo), is another important figure upon the British scene. From Newmarket, Suffolk, he once worked as a night club singer and deejay in Blackley, Georgia, later moving to Nashville where he appeared on networked TV shows, performed at many concerts and became a regular on the Opry, also helping to provide the bluegrass soundtrack to 'Nashville Coyote' a Disney movie. Returning to Britain in 1971, he formed the Grand Ole Opry Roadshow, a unit which gained an enormous reputation on the club circuit but eventually split in '76, three members going on to form Telephone Bill, a band of wider horizons, while Sayers went into the studio to cut a solo album for Transatlantic.

Brian Chalker, Editor of *Country Music Review,* one of Britain's two leading C&W magazines (the other is the Tony Byworth-edited *Country Music People*) won the Top British Country Vocalist award in 1973. At various times a commercial artist, a Portsmouth (Hampshire) policeman, a detective for Pinkerton's in Canada, a stagehand and a journalist, he formed his New Frontier Band in 1970 and recorded for Chapter One, obtaining a couple of mini-hits. Possessor of a strong and character-filled voice, it seems remarkable that he hasn't yet achieved more in terms of popularity on disc.

Less impressive vocally but a fine showman is Alan Frank 'Tex' Withers, who became a country performer upon release from hospital following 18 years of treatment on a fractured spine. Another Top Male Vocal award winner, he's guested on the Tubb Midnight Jamboree, the CMA International Show and Bill Anderson's (♦) TV program and has cut an album in Nashville, using some of the finest sessionmen available. Frank Jennings, a vocalist initially influenced by Faron Young (♦), made something of a breakthrough in 1975 when he and his band, the Frank Jennings Syndicate, appeared on the Opportunity Knocks TV Show, subsequently winning an EMI recording contract, various awards from CMA (GB) and the Variety Club Of Great Britain, and a booking for the 1976 Wembley Festival Of Country Music.

Responsible for this series of Festivals is promoter Mervyn Conn, who in 1968 took a remarkable gamble and launched the first International Country Music Festival to be held outside the USA. Though Conn's initial encounter with country music promotion was hardly a financial stroke of wizardry – he promoted a tour by Johnny Cash (♦) which lost money (a later tour broke even, while a third was a resounding success) he has since seen his Festival become a major event on the C&W calender, virtually every name act in country music having played Wembley throughout the years.

And so the British scene has continued to flourish and acts such as Lorne Gibson, Ron Ryan, Kenny Johnson and Northwind, Jeannie Denver, Jon Derek, Malcolm Price, Stu Stevens, Mikki and Griff, Wildwood, Pete Nelson, Frank Yonco, Brian Maxine, plus such in-demand session steelmen as B. J. Cole and Gordon Huntley have done much to further the cause of country music, ably assisted by their Irish counterparts, Larry Cunningham, Ray Lynan and Philomena Begley.

Above: Heaven Is My Woman's Love (EMI One Up). One of Britain's most popular vocal country groups; a TV talent show led to a recording contract.

The album listing is, by necessity, a selective one.

Albums:
Brian Chalker **Songs And Ballads** (—/*Sweet Folk And Country*)
Frank Jennings Syndicate **Heaven Is My Woman's Love**
  (—/*EMI One Up*)
Jeannie Denver **Queen Of The Silver Dollar** (—/*Westwood*)
John Derek **With A Little Help From My Friends** (—/*Westwood*)
Keith Manifold **Inheritance** (—/*DJM*)
Pete Sayers **Watermelon Summer** (—/*Xtra*)
Brian Golbey **Moments** (—/*Gem*)
Pete Stanley And Roger Knowles **Picking And Singing** (—/*Xtra*)

Elton Britt

Real name James Britt Baker, born Marshall, Arkansas, June 27, 1917; the son of champion fiddle player.
  While still at school he learnt guitar on a model purchased from Sears Roebuck for $5. Britt worked in the fields as a boy, picking cotton, digging potatoes etc, but while only 14 he was discovered by talent scouts who signed him to a year's contract with station KMPC, Los Angeles, where he appeared with the Beverly Hillbillies record-

Right: Elton Britt, who won the first official gold disc for a country hit.

ing for ARC, Decca and Varsity with them and as a solo. In 1937, he signed for RCA Records, staying with the label for over 20 years during which time he recorded 672 singles and over 50 albums. Following this, he moved on to record for Decca, Ampar and ABC-Paramount. Britt, who was considered to be one of the world's greatest yodelers, obtained the first gold disc awarded to any country star when, in 1944, his version of **There's A Star Spangled Banner Waving Somewhere**, originally released in May 1942, as a B side, reached the million sales mark. Other disc successes include **Chime Bells** (1948), **Jimmie Rodgers Blues** (1968) and **Quicksilver** (1949), the latter being one of the many duets recorded with Rosalie Allen (♦).

Britt, who died June 23, 1972, appeared in several films, including *Laramie* and *The Prodigal Son*. He also made many TV appearances during the 1950s and '60s, although he was a semi-retired gentleman farmer from around 1954–1968.

Albums:
16 Great Country Performances
  (ABC/—)
Wandering Cowboy *(ABC/—)*
Yodel Songs *(RCA/—)*

Above: The Singing Hills (Fontana). A German issue of material by Elton Britt. Sadly, only three out of well over 50 albums are currently available.

Jim Ed Brown

In 1965, Bonnie and Maxine, of The Browns (♦) persuaded Chet Atkins (♦) to record Jim Ed as a solo artist, his first single **I Heard From A Memory Last Night** being a chart entry. Following this, Jim Ed began to record more frequently as a soloist, enjoying hits with **I'm Just A Country Boy, A Taste Of Heaven** (1966), **Pop A Top, Bottle, Bottle** (1967) and others – and when the Browns eventually disbanded, in 1967, Jim Ed was able to reshape his stage act and continue as a star attraction. He debuted this new act at Atlanta, Georgia, early in 1968 and was immediately signed for a lucrative engagement at a leading Lake Tahoe niterie.

Since that time his Midas touch has continued to function, virtually every one of his singles making the charts, his biggest sellers being **Morning** (1970) – a song successfully covered by singer Val Doonican in Britain – and **Southern Loving** (1973). Today, the easy-to-take vocal style of Brown is still

Below: Jim Ed Brown has had hits with his sisters and, more recently, with Helen Cornelius.

I Don't Want To Have To Marry You (RCA).

enormously popular, **I Don't Want To Have To Marry You,** a 1976 duet with Helen Cornelius, provoding him with a Country No 1. His roadshow, with his band The Gems, is still in demand, while a TV show 'Nashville On The Road', co-hosted by Brown, has also proved a moneyspinner, being carried by nearly 100 outlets.

Albums:
Evening *(RCA/—)*
Barrooms And Pop A Tops
  (RCA/—)
The Best Of Jim Ed Brown
  (RCA/—)
Hey Good Lookin' *(RCA/—)*
It's That Time Of Night
  (RCA/—)
I Don't Want To Have To Marry You with Helen Cornelius
  (RCA/RCA)

Angel's Sunday
(RCA).

Milton Brown

One of the founders of western swing, Brown was born Stephenville, Texas, September 8, 1903. In 1918 his family moved to Fort Worth, Brown attending Arlington Heights High School until graduation in 1925. After a spell in the police, with whom he broadcast as part of the Fort Worth Policeman's Quarter, Brown moved on to become a salesman – but following a meeting with Bob Wills (♦) in 1931, he began singing professionally as part of Wills' Fiddle Band, actually just a duo comprised of Wills (fiddle) and Herman Arnspiger (guitar). Then followed a number of sponsored radio shows, the band name-changing to The Aladdin Laddies, when promoting Aladdin Mantle Lamps, and The Light Crust Doughboys (♦), as pluggers of Light Crust Flour.
Following some personnel changes – which included the enrolement of Milton's brother Durwood Brown (guitar) – the band cut some sides for Victor in the guise of The Fort Worth Doughboys. But soon after, Brown formed

his own unit, The Musical Brownies, to play on radio KTAT, Fort Worth, the lineup eventually stabilizing at Milton Brown (vocals), Durwood Brown (guitar and vocals), Jesse Ashlock and Cecil Brower (fiddles), Wanna Coffman (bass) and Fred 'Papa' Calhoun (piano). This lineup – minus Ashlock – recorded a number of sides for Bluebird in April, 1934, the fiddler returning for the band's second Bluebird session in August of that year.
With the addition of jazz-playing steel guitarist Bob Dunn – the first in country music to electrify his steel – some three months later, a complete western swing sound was achieved, the band offering little allegiance to conventional country music. At the same time, Brown concluded a contract with the new Decca Record Company and with Decca the Brownies began cutting a miscellany of titles ranging from jazz items like **St Louis Blues, Memphis Blues** and **Mama Don't Allow** through to such

Western songs as **Carry Me Back To The Lone Prairie** and **The Wheel Of The Wagon Is Broken,** enjoying several best-sellers. But just when the band were moving into top gear, Brown died, following a car accident. He'd been returning home from a Crystal Springs Dance Pavilion date when his car tire burst, the vehicle overturning and finally hitting a telegraph pole, seriously injuring Brown but instantly killing his passenger, vocalist Katherine Prehoditch. Though rushed to hospital, complications set in and Brown died on April 13, 1936.
For a while the Brownies continued to fulfill contractural obligations but the band finally folded in early 1938. Brown is considered, with Wills, as a co-founder of western swing, but unfortunately did not live to fulfil his early promise, nor to reap the financial rewards the music enjoyed in the 1940s.

Albums: none.

Above: The Browns had a million seller with the Edith Piaf song Les Trois Cloches.

The Browns

The Browns – Ella Maxine Brown, born Sampti, Louisiana, April 27, 1932; her brother Jim Edward, born Sparkman, Arkansas, April 1, 1934; and younger sister Bonnie, born Sparkman, Arkansas, July 31, 1937 – began as a duo in the early '50s, when Jim and Maxine won a talent contest on Little Rock's KLRA radio station, eventually matriculating to a featured spot on KWKH's Louisiana Hayride (♦). In 1955, following an extensive concert tour, Bonnie came in to form trio, the threesome becoming a headline act on the Ozark Jubilee show. Initially signed to Abbott Records, The Browns moved to RCA after being brought to the label's attention by Jim Reeves (♦). When Jim Ed had completed his army service (his place being taken by yet

another sister, Norma, while he was away) the trio recorded a French song **The Three Bells**, which topped the charts for several weeks during 1959.

Hits such as **Scarlet Ribbons** (1959), **The Old Lamplighter, Teen-Ex, Send Me The Pillow You Dream On, Blue Christmas** (all 1960), and **Ground Hog** (1961) followed, plus a number of well received overseas tours. In 1963 The Browns became Grand Ole Opry (♦) regulars, but Bonnie and Maxine, both married, wanted to spend more and more time with their families. So, in 1967, despite success that year in the country charts with **I Hear It Now** and **Big Daddy,** the group disbanded. However, Maxine later returned to record as a solo artist for Chart, scoring with **Sugar Cane Country**

(1968), while Jim Ed Brown (♦) began a solo career on RCA Records.

Albums:
Best Of The Browns *(RCA/—)*

Ed Bruce

Recording for Phillips under the name Edwin Bruce, this singer had a brief career as a '50s rocker – but he soon returned to selling semi-shabby Chevvys at his father's used car lot in Memphis. By the mid '60s he'd moved to Nashville, there recording over a dozen singles for RCA with the aid of producer Bob Ferguson, having mild chart reaction with **Walker's**

Woods (1967), **Last Train To Clarksville** (1967) and **Painted Girls And Wine** (1968), his rich voice also being heard on an album, **If I Could Just Go Home.** In 1968, Bruce joined Monument Records cutting a fine album in **Shades Of Ed Bruce,** also having minor singles success with **Song For Jenny** and **Everybody Wants To Go Home** (1969). However, despite his strong commercial appeal, it wasn't until the '70s and an association with UA Records that Bruce finally established himself as a record seller of any consequence, his **Mamas Don't Let Your Babies Grow Up To Be Cowboys** moving high into the charts during early 1976.

Albums:
Ed Bruce *(United Artists/—)*

Above: Mainstream country singer Ed Bruce was once a Sun Records rockabilly.

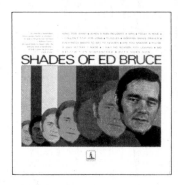

Shades of Ed Bruce (Monument)

Tom Brumley

Son of Albert E. Brumley, writer of such songs as **Turn Your Radio On** and **I'll Fly Away**, Tom Brumley was born Powell, Missouri, December 11, 1935. Being influenced by the playing of such musicians as Don Helms, Jerry Byrd(◊) and Roy Wiggins, Brumley bought his own steel guitar while still in his early teens, later becoming part of a country band with his four brothers, playing venues in Missouri and Mid-West.

After service with the armed forces in Germany, he headed for California, meeting Buck Owens (◊) at a Capitol recording session. For a while, though, he returned to Texas, taking a job in the house construction business for over a year. He eventually took up full time musical activities when asked to become a member of Owens' band The Buckeroos in December 1963, winning a CMA steel guitar award in '66. After several years with Owens, Brumley moved on to join Rick Nelson's(◊) Stone Canyon Band in February 1969, appearing on the band's four MCA albums.

Cliff Bruner

The leader of an early swing/ honky tonk band, Cliff Bruner was born April 25, 1915 in Houston, Texas, and got his start as a fiddler in Milton Brown's Musical Brownies, cutting some 48 Decca sides with Brown before his tragic death in 1936.

At that point Bruner formed his own band, the Texas Wanderers (sometimes known just as Cliff Bruner's Boys), and began a long recording association with Decca in 1937. His biggest hit on the label was the first version released of Floyd Tillman's **It Makes No Difference Now** in 1938, although one of the band's most historic milestones was cutting the first truck driving song on record: Ted Daffan's **Truck Driver's Blues** in 1939.

Bruner – who also recorded for the Ayo label in the 1940s – became increasingly inactive as the years passed, and since the early 1950s has been an insurance salesman and excutive, performing only occasionally. He currently resides in the Houston suburb of League City.

Albums: none.

Boudleaux And Felice Bryant

Boudleaux Bryant, born Shellman, Georgia, February 13, 1920, originally aimed at a career in classical music, studying to become a concert violinist and in 1938 playing a season with the Atlanta Philharmonic. Then came a switch to more popular music forms, Bryant joining a jazz group for a period. It was during this time he met his wife-to-be, Felice (born Milwaukee, Wisconsin, August 7, 1925), then an elevator attendant at Milwaukee's Shrader Hotel.

Cliff Bruner recorded one of the first truck songs – Truck Driver's Blues in 1939.

33

After marriage, the duo began writing songs together, in 1949 sending one composition, **Country Boy,** to Fred Rose (♦), who published it, thus providing Little Jimmy Dickens (♦) with material to fashion into a Top Ten hit.

In 1950, the Bryants moved to Nashville and began writing hit after hit, supplying Carl Smith (♦) with a constant source of chartbusters, one of these songs, **Hey Joe** (1953) becoming a million seller when covered by Frankie Laine. During 1955, Eddy Arnold (♦) charted with the Bryants' **I've Been Thinking** and **The Richest Man,** but it was the duo's association with the Everly Brothers (♦), commencing in 1957, that brought the song-writing team their biggest string of successes, **Bye Bye Love, Wake Up Little Susie, Problems, Bird Dog, All I Have To Do Is Dream, Poor Jenny, Take A Message To Mary,** all Bryant-penned songs, ending up on million-selling discs.

Other Bryant hits have included **Raining In My Heart** (Buddy Holly (♦) 1959), **Let's Think About Living** (Bob Luman (♦) 1960), **Mexico** (Bob Moore 1960), **Baltimore** (Sonny James (♦) 1964), **Come Live With Me** (Roy Clark (♦) 1973) and the oft-recorded **Rocky Top,** which Felice and Boudleaux wrote in just ten minutes. By 1974 *Billboard* was able to publish a list of well over 400 artists who had recorded songs by the Bryants.

Jimmy Buffett

Born Mobile, Alabama, 1947, Buffett worked for some time in the New Orleans area before moving to Nashville in 1969, there recording an album **Down To Earth,** released by Barnaby in 1970. This album failed to sell and the tapes of the follow-up were lost so Buffett, disenchanted, left for Key West in Florida, where he settled for a while, writing a whole batch of new songs. Returning to Nashville in 1972, he then cut **White Sport Coat And A Pink Crustacean,** a Don Gant produced album for Dunhill, following this with **Living And Dying In ¾ Time** and a hit single in **Come Monday** (1974). Buffett, who recorded one of the most hilariously titled tracks of '76 in **My Head Hurts, My Feet Stink And I Don't Believe In Jesus,** usually travels with his own back up unit, The Coral Reefer Band.

Albums:
White Sport Coat and A Pink Crustacean *(Dunhill/ABC)*
Living And Dying In ¾ Time *(Dunhill/ABC)*
AIA *(Dunhill/ABC)*
Havana Daydreamin' *(ABC/ABC)*

Wilma Burgess

A consistent maker of country hits during the '60s and early '70s, vocalist Wilma Burgess was born Orlando, Florida, June 11, 1939. A city girl who acquired a love of country music during high school days, it wasn't until she attended Stetson University, Florida, to major in physical education, that she began singing in public. In 1960, Wilma traveled to Nashville to demo songs for publishers, and

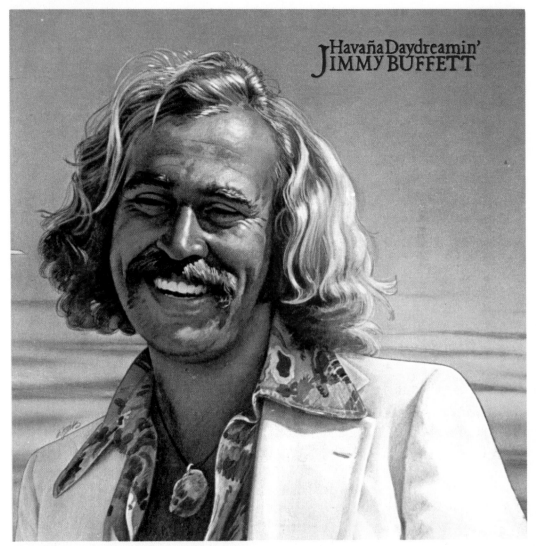

was heard by Charlie Lamb of Sound Format publications, who brought her to the attention of Decca's Owen Bradley (♦). Signed by Decca and also gaining regular appearances on various Nashville radio and TV shows, Wilma built a reputation that soared following hits with **Baby** (1965) and **Misty Blue** (1966). More recent Burgess winners have included **Parting, The Woman In Your Life, The Sun's Gotta Shine** and **Lonely For You,** while her Decca album output featured such titles as **Tear Time, Misty Blue, Don't Touch Me** and **Wilma Burgess.**

Johnny Bush

Born Houston, Texas, February 17, 1935, Bush – voted Most Promising Male Vocalist of the Year by *Record World* in 1968, an accolade duplicated by *Music City News* twelve months later – moved to San Antonio, Texas, in 1952, obtaining his first musical job at the Texas Star Inn, where he played rhythm guitar and sang. At a later stage he opted to become a drummer, eventually joining a band organized by his friend Willie Nelson (♦) during the early sixties. After a year's stay with this outfit he then moved on to become a member of Ray Price's (♦) Cherokee Cowboys, with whom he played for three years before returning to Nelson's side once more. With Nelson he became front man for the band, The Record Men, also branching out as a solo artist on Stop Records, his first release for

the label, a Nelson original titled **You Ought To Hear Me Cry** being a mild hit in 1967. His next release, **What A Way To Live,** yet another Nelson song, climbed even further up the charts.

Primarily a honky tonk singer in the Ray Price tradition, Bush moved from Stop – for whom he had major hits in **Undo The Right** (1968) and **You Gave Me A Mountain** (1969) – to RCA in 1972, enjoying his biggest ever disc success with Willie Nelson's **Whiskey River** during the Fall of that year.

Albums:
Sound Of A Heartache *(Stop/—)*
Bush Country *(Stop/Stop)*
Texas Dance Hall Girl *(Stop/—)*
Here Comes The Word Again *(RCA/RCA)*
Whiskey River *(RCA/—)*
You Gave Me A Mountain *(Stop/Stop)*

Carl And Pearl Butler

A highly popular duo during the 1960s, honky tonk vocalist Carl Roberts Butler (born Knoxville, Tennessee, June 2, 1927) and his wife Pearl (born Pearl Dee Jones, Nashville, Tennessee, September 20, 19 ?) first performed as a team in 1962. Prior to this, Carl had been a highly successful songwriter and recording artist with Capitol and Columbia, having hits for the latter label with **Honky Tonkitis** (1961) and **Don't Let Me**

Above: Havana Daydreamin' (ABC). Buffett turned to songwriting when his first recording attempts failed. Below: Johnny Bush's Whiskey River (RCA).

Cross Over (1962), the latter being released as a Carl Butler solo item but featuring Pearl on harmony vocals. When **Cross Over** became a country No 1, the Butlers realized they'd hit on a winning formula and began recording as a duo, logging a fair number of chart entries during the '60s, including **Loving Arms** (1963), **Too Late To Try Again** (1964), **I'm Hanging Up The Phone** (1964), **Just Thought I'd Let You Know** (1965), **Little Pedro** (1966) and **I Never Got Over You** (1969). Granted Opry status in 1962, the Butlers appeared in a movie, *Second Fiddle To A Steel Guitar,* during 1967.

Albums:
Greatest Hits *(Columbia/—)*

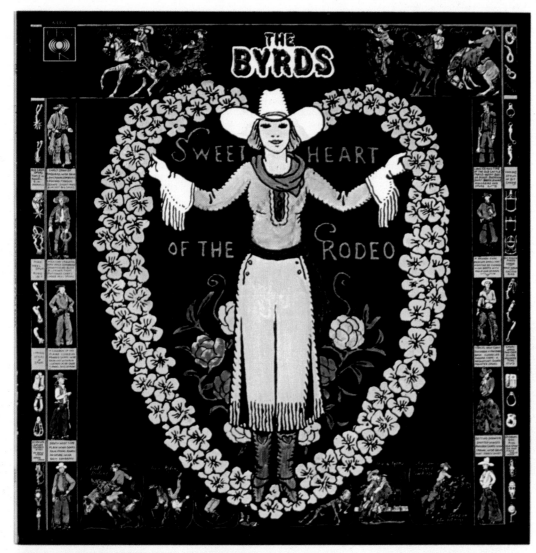

The Byrds

Initially an LA folk-rock group, formed in 1964, the Byrds produced **Sweetheart Of The Rodeo,** generally considered to be the first real country rock album in 1966. **Rodeo** contained songs penned by the Louvin Brothers (◊), Woody Guthrie (◊), Merle Haggard (◊) and others, and thereafter most Byrds albums featured some country-influenced tracks – though leader Roger McGuinn is said to have fought against the trend. The band, which folded in 1972 (McGuinn attempting a musically unsuccessful reunion album on Asylum the following year) featured, at various times, several musicians who have made some contribution to the furtherance of country music – notably Gram Parsons (◊), Chris Hillman and Clarence White (◊). A full listing of Byrds recordings is outside the scope of this publication, though **Sweetheart Of The Rodeo** (Columbia) which was recently reissued in Britain as part of a double album by CBS, is well worth investigating.

Cajun Music

A product of the Louisiana bayou country, Cajun is a mixture of jazz, blues, country and French folk music.

In original form was brought to Louisiana by French settlers deported from Nova Scotia during reign of George II. Fiddle and accordion dominated, with most vocals still in French.

The music attracted attention from major record companies way back in the '20s, the most popular of the early bands being The Hackleberry Ramblers and Miller's Merrymakers. But it was the 1946 recording of the traditional **Jole Blon,** by fiddler Harry

Below left:
Greatest Hits (Columbia).
Below:
Louisiana Cajun French Music (Rounder).

Jerry Byrd

Born in Lima, Ohio, on March 9, 1920, Jerry Byrd went on to become one of the genuine giants of the electric steel guitar. Unequalled for purity of tone and taste, he was in demand for record sessions for years, although he was never comfortable with the increasingly popular pedal steel style, preferring Hawaiian stylings. Finally growing weary of Nashville and the music business he chucked it all and caught a plane to Honolulu, where he is revered as practically a national monument for his advancement of the Hawaiian guitar,

Sweetheart Of The Rodeo (CBS). One of the first and finest country rock albums. The jacket design is from a catalog of Western clothes.

both musically and in terms of popularity.

Albums: none.

Choates, that first achieved real success for the Cajun sound. During the '50s and '60s Cajun music became more commercial, with the Bayou musicians employing steel guitar, and discs by Jimmy C. Newman (♦) and the Kershaw Brothers (♦) sold to wide audiences, Doug Kershaw's **Louisiana Man** (1961) being covered by hundreds of other artists. An offshoot of Cajun Music is Zydeco, which draws heavily on R&B influences, the principle exponent of this form being Clifton Chenier, a brilliantly inventive blues accordionist.

The Callahan Brothers

Walter T.('Joe')Callahan
guitar and vocals
Homer C. ('Bill') Callahan
guitar, mandolin, bass and vocals

Natives of Laurel, North Carolina (Walter born January 27, 1910 and Homer born March 27, 1912), the Callahan Brothers became a popular duet team of the south eastern style in the 1930s, and by 1933 were already busy on radio and were recording for the ARC complex of labels. They spent some time at WHAS in Louisville and WWVA in Wheeling before serving other stretches at WLW (1937–1939) and KVOO in Tulsa, before settling down in the North Texas area, basing their operations from either Dallas or Wichita Falls for over ten years.

It was here, for reasons best known to themselves, that they changed their names from Walter and Homer to Bill and Joe, and changed their music as well, performing more and more western and swing material, the highlight probably being their double-yodel version of **St Louis Blues**. Except for a single session with Decca (1941) and one Bill Callahan session with Cowboy Records, their 91 recorded sides were with ARC or Columbia, over a period stretching from 1934 to 1951. They became increasingly inactive in the 1950s and 1960s.

Homer/Bill died on September 10, 1971, while Walter/Joe still plays a bit of music but earns his living as a professional photographer in Dallas.

Albums:
The Callahan Brothers
(Old Homestead/—)

Archie Campbell

Honored as Comedian Of The Year in 1969 by the CMA, Campbell has been more recently involved as one of the writers and stars of the Hee Haw (♦) show.

Born Bulls Gap, Tennessee, November 17, 1914, his career really rocketed through stints on WNOX, Knoxville in 1949, an eventual TV show on WATE, Knoxville (1952–1958), coming his way. He joined the Prince Albert portion of the Grand Ole Opry in 1958, also signing a recording contract with RCA, for whom he cut a number of comedy routines including **Beeping Sleauty** and **Rindercella,** his biggest hit being with **The Men In My Little Girl's Life** (1965). With Lorene Mann he has shared a quartet of 'serious' hits, while away from show business he's known as a talented sculptor, poet and painter whose mastery of golf is almost up to professional standard.

Albums:
Archie Campbell *(Elektra/—)*

'Archie Campbell isn't only a humorist but also a humanist – in the most admirable sense'

Glen Campbell

The seventh son of a seventh son, singer-songwriter-guitarist-banjoist Glen Campbell was born Delight, Arkansas, April 22, 1936. A reasonable guitarist at the age of 6, he joined Dick Bills' (his uncle) western band while a teenager, later forming his own outfit in New Mexico, where he met Billie Nunley and married her.

Armed with his 12-string, in 1960 he opted to become one of Hollywood's busiest session musicians but found time to cut sides as a solo performer, one, **Turn Around, Look At Me,** becoming a 1961 pop hit

Depicted here with his favourite instrument, although it's not unknown for Campbell to play Amazing Grace on bagpipes.

on the local Crest label. Signed immediately to Capitol, Campbell graced the 1962 charts with Al Dexter's **Too Late To Worry, Too Blue to Cry** and Merle Travis' (♦) **Kentucky Means Paradise**, in the mid '60s supplying a couple of other minor hits while continuing his work as a sideman with the Beach Boys, Jan and Dean, Association, Rick Nelson (♦), Elvis Presley (♦) and many others. Then in 1967 he recorded John Hartford's (♦) **Gentle On My Mind**, following this monster hit with an even bigger one in **By The Time I Get To Phoenix**, a song written by Jim Webb. From then on came a succession of high selling albums and singles, the most successful of the latter being **Wichita Lineman** (1968), **Galveston, Where's The Playground, Susie?, True Grit, Try A Little Kindness** (1969), **Honey Come Back, Oh Happy Day, Everything A Man Could Ever Need, It's Only Make Believe, All I Have To Do Is Dream** – with Bobby Gentry (♦) – (1970), **Dream Baby** (1971), **Country Boy** and **Rhinestone Cowboy** (1975) and **Southern Nights** (1977).

Possessor of 11 gold records; featured artist on countless TV shows, including his own Glen Campbell Show; co-star with John Wayne in the film 'True Grit' (1969) and star of 'Norwood' (1969); Campbell is also a golf fanatic, hosting the Glen Campbell Los Angeles Open, a major event on the PGA circuit.

Albums:
Album (Pickwick/Pickwick)
By The Time I Get To Phoenix
  (Capitol/—)
Gentle On My Mind (Capitol/—)

Glen Travis Campbell
  (Capitol/Capitol)
Greatest Hits (Capitol/Capitol)
Houston (Capitol/—)
I Knew Jesus (Capitol/Capitol)

I Remember Hank Williams
  (Capitol/Capitol)
I'll Paint You A Song (Capitol/—)
The Last Time I Saw Her
  (Capitol/Capitol)
Live (Capitol/Capitol)
Oh Happy Day (Capitol/—)
Only The Lonely (Pickwick/—)
Satisfied Mind (Pickwick/—)
Try A Little Kindness
  (Capitol/Capitol)
Wichita Lineman (Capitol/—)
Anne Murray – Glen Campbell
  (Capitol/Capitol)
**Bobbie Gentry And Glen
  Campbell** (Capitol/Capitol)
Arkansas (Capitol/—)
Bloodline (Capitol/Capitol)
Reunion (Capitol/Capitol)
Rhinestone Cowboy
  (Capitol/Capitol)
Ernie Sings And Glen Picks
  (Capitol/Capitol)
Glen (—/Capitol)
Words (—/Ember)
Album (—/Capitol)
More Words (—/Ember)

Turn Around, Look At Me
  (—/Ember)
Galveston (Capitol/Ember) –
  Ember version has extra tracks
This Is Glen Campbell
  (—/Ember)
That Xmas Feeling
  (Capitol/Ember)
Two Sides Of Glen Campbell
  (—/Starline)
Wichita Lineman (—/Ember)
20 Golden Greats (—/Capitol)
The Best Of Glen Campbell
  (Capitol/—)
Capitol Country Greats Vol 1
  (—/Capitol)
Turn Around And Look At Me
  (—/Ember)
Southern Nights (—/Capitol)

Ernie Sings and Glen Picks (Capitol). On which Glen Campbell takes a backseat and picks some fine back-up guitar, while Ernie Ford handles the vocal chores.

Judy Canova

A sort of slicked up Minnie Pearl (♦) of the 1940s, Judy Canova was a country comedienne who was successful on Broadway, in some two dozen movies, and on record, as well as having a long running radio show (1943–1953) on which Eddie Dean (♦) and others were featured.

Born November 20, 1916 in Jacksonville, Florida, she and her sister Annie and brother Zeke moved to New York in 1934 to crack the big time, at which they were successful on the stage and on radio. The act broke up in the late 1930s, with Judy going solo, eventually moving to Hollywood in the early 1940s as film roles and her network radio show beckoned, a dual career which lasted into the late 1950s.

She recorded for the ARC complex of labels with her siblings, and for Okeh, Varsity, ARA, Mercury, Sterling, Sutton, Coronet, and RCA in her long career, with her theme song **Go To Sleep, Little Baby** probably her most popular, along with the haunting wartime ballad with which she closed her radio show during World War Two: **Goodnight Soldier.**

Albums: none.

Henson Cargill

From a family of political and legal background, Cargill was brought up on a ranch, where he spent considerable efforts in fighting off all intentions to turn him into a budding attorney. But though his initial aim was to become a successful rancher, he suddenly switched ambitions and headed for Nashville to cut a record session and seek a deal with a record label. There, with the aid of guitar playing producer Fred Carter Jnr he made a disc called **Skip A Rope,** which earned him a contract with Monument Records and a 1967 million seller. After other major hits with **Row, Row, Row** (1968), **None Of My Business** (1969) and **The Most Uncomplicated Goodbye** (1970), Cargill signed for the Mega label, there having minor chart entries with **Pencil Marks On The Wall** and **Naked And Crying** (both 1971). But by 1974 he was once more with a new record label in Atlantic, his first success for the company being with **Some Old California Memory.** He has a hangup about steel guitars and won't use them on his discs. By the mid '70s, Cargill was Oklahoma based, living there with his wife and three children.

Albums:
Coming On Strong
(Monument/—)
Most Uncomplicated Goodbye
(Monument/—)

Bill And Cliff Carlisle

Cliff Carlisle, born Taylorsville, Kentucky, May 6, 1904, was among the first top line dobro players. As a boy he toured as a vaudeville act, first recording for Gennett in 1930 with guitarist Wilbert Ball. An excellent yodeler, Cliff – who backed Jimmie Rodgers (♦) on some of his recordings – eventu-

Above: Cliff (left) and Bill Carlisle with Shannon Grayson on banjo. Cliff pioneered the use of Hawaiian guitar in C&W.

ally formed a duo, the Carlisle Brothers, with his younger brother, Bill (born Wakefield, Kentucky, December 19, 1908), playing dates in the Louisville-Cincinnati area. The brothers, who spiced their vocal and instrumental act with a fair degree of comedy, obtained regular radio exposure on station WLAP, Lexington, Kentucky during 1931, six years later having own show, The Carlisle Family Barn Dance, on radio station WLAP, Louisville. However, in 1947 Cliff retired (he now lives near Lexington, Kentucky) and Bill eventually formed a new group, the Carlisles. In 1954, following hits with **Rainbow At Midnight, No Help Wanted** and **Too Old To Cut The Mustard,** the Carlisles joined Grand Ole Opry, remaining cast members to this day, scoring a further hit with **What Kinda Deal Is This?** (1966). During his career, Bill Carlisle has won over 60 various country awards, his past albums including **Fresh From The Country** *(King)* and **The Best Of Bill Carlisle** *(Hickory).*

Below: Welcome To My World (Harmony). Against family expectations he decided on a career in country music, moved to Nashville and cut a million-seller.

Fiddling John Carson

An old time fiddler, he became (on June 14, 1923, in Atlanta, Georgia) the first country musician to be recorded by field recordist Ralph Peer (♦). The tracks cut, **Little Old Log Cabin In The Lane** and **That Old Hen Cackled And The Rooster's Goin' To Crow,** were initially released on 500 unlabelled discs, all immediately sold at a local old time fiddler's convention. Following a re-release on Okeh, Carson was awarded a contract with the label. Born March 23, 1868, in Fannin Country, Georgia, Carson was, at various times, a teenage jockey, a foreman in a cotton mill, a house painter and a moonshiner. Seven times fiddle champion of Georgia, he made his radio debut on September 9, 1922. Often working with a string band the Virginia Reelers (which included his daughter Rosa Lee Carson, also known as Moonshine Kate), he cut around 150 for Okeh between 1923 and 1931. Following the Depression, Carson moved to RCA, mainly re-cutting earlier successes. In later life an elevator operator, Carson died December 11, 1949.

Albums:
That Old Hen Cackled
(Rounder/—)

Martha Carson

A country gospel singer whose repertoire appealed not only to Opry fans but also the audiences at such ritzy venues as New York's Waldorf Astoria, Martha Carson was one of the most popular vocalists in her genre during the 1950s.

Born Martha Ambergay, Neon, Kentucky, March 19, 1921, her first broadcasts were relayed over station WHIS, Bluefield, West Virginia in 1939. During the '40s she toured as one half of Martha and James Carson, the other fifty per cent of the duo being her husband, the singing and mandolin-playing son of Fiddlin' Doc Roberts. They were longtime fixtures of the WSB Barn Dance in Atlanta.

Divorced in 1951, Martha began gracing the Opry with her fervent style during the following year.

The writer of well over 100 songs, including **I'm Gonna Walk And Talk With My Lord, I Can't Stand Up Alone** and **Satisfied,** Martha has recorded for such labels as RCA, Capitol, Cadence and Decca.

Albums: none.

Below: The Carters – Maybelle, A.P. and Sara. Although he is often called a pirate, many fine songs would have remained neglected but for A.P.'s efforts.

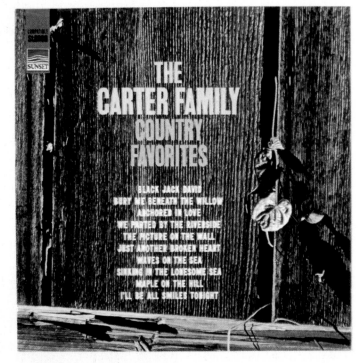

Country Favorites (Sunset). Original Family was A.P., wife Sara and sister-in-law Maybelle; A.P. and Sara were divorced in 1936 but worked together for a further seven years.

Carter Family

One of the most influential groups in country music, the original lineup was headed by Alvin Pleasant (A.P.) Delaney Carter, born Maces Spring, Virginia, April 15, 1891. One of nine children, A. P. initially sang in church quarter alongside two uncles and an elder sister. Later met Sara Dougherty (born Wise County, Virginia, July 21, 1898), a singer, guitarist, autoharp and banjo player, the two marrying on June 18, 1915. Third member of group, Maybelle Addington (born Nickelsville, Virginia, May 10, 1909) joined after marrying A.P.'s brother, Ezra Carter, in 1926. She too played guitar, autoharp and banjo.

The Carter Family were first recorded by Ralph Peer (♦) for Victor on August 1, 1927 (at the same sessions that Jimmie Rodgers (♦) cut his first sides) completing six titles, including **Single Girl, Married Girl,** at a makeshift studio in Bristol, Tennessee. After some success the family began whole series of sessions for Victor, often recording A.P.'s own songs, though **Wildwood Flower,** a traditional item cut at Camden, New Jersey, on May 9, 1928, proved to be the group's biggest seller, registering over a million sales for 78 rpm discs alone. Another important recording date occurred during June 1931, when Peer cut sides featuring collective talents of the Carters and Jimmie Rodgers.

After recording around 20 songs at one Victor session on December 11, 1934, the family moved on to ARC, waxing some 40 titles for label during period May 5–10, 1935.

Sara and A.P. obtained a divorce during the following year but continued working together in the group, next recording for Decca before moving to Texas to appear on various radio stations in the San Antonio and Del Rio areas. During this three year period, other members of Carter Family joined the group – these being Anita, June and Helen (Maybelle and Ezra's three daughters) and Janette and Joe (Sara and A.P.'s children). Sara then remarried, to Coy Bayes, and though family cut further sides for Columbia and Victor (the last sessions by the original Carter Family taking place on October 14, 1941) they disbanded in 1943, having waxed over 250 of their songs including such standards as **Wabash Cannonball, Lonesome Valley** and **I'm Thinking Tonight Of My Blue Eyes.** Maybelle then formed group with her three daughters and began a five year stint on station WRVA, Richmond, Virginia, after which came a switch to Nashville, where the quartet became regulars on Grand Ole Opry as a group and as individuals. A.P. too began his career again, working on some sides for the Acme label, during 1952–56. But this version of the Carter Family – employing Sara, Joe and Janette – made little impact. A.P. died November 7, 1960, ten years before the Carter Family's election to the Country Music Hall Of Fame.

Following A.P.'s death, Maybelle and her daughters began working as The Carter Family (previously they'd been The Carter Sisters and Mother Maybelle), June Carter eventually going solo and becoming part of the Johnny Cash (♦) road show. In 1961, Maybelle Carter (♦), plus Helen and Anita, also joined Cash, becoming regulars on his TV show in 1966. Anita's daughter Lori and Helen's son David have since appeared as part of the Carter Family road show.

Albums:
Best Of The Carter Family
(Columbia/—)
Favourite Family Songs
(Liverty/—)

Happiest Days Of All
(Camden/—)
More Golden Gems
(Camden/—)

The Carter Family
Country's First Family

KC 34266
Columbia

MOUNTAIN LADY
GOOD TIME CAKE WALK BLUES
PAPA'S SUGAR
FAR SIDE BANKS OF JORDAN
IN THE PINES (THE LONGEST TRAIN I EVER SAW)
MY SHIP WILL SAIL
MY FATHER'S FIDDLE
I'M HERE TO GET MY BABY OUT OF JAIL
NO DISTINCTION THERE
SUMMER STORMS

My Old Cottage Home
(Camden/—)
Keep On The Sunnyside
(Columbia/—)
Travellin' Minstrel Band
(Columbia/—)
Three Generations
(Columbia/—)
Green Fields Of Virginia
(RCA/—)
Famous Country Music Makers
(—/RCA)

June Carter
♦ *The Carter*
  Family
♦ *Johnny Cash*

*Right: Maybelle Carter. In 1943
she began working on WRVA's
Old Dominion Barn Dance with
her three daughters.*

*Country's First Family (Columbia). The Carter Family consisted
at this point of Mother Maybelle and daughters June, Helen and
Anita, with occasional appearances by nephews and nieces.*

Maybelle
Carter

See the Carter Family (♦).
  During '60s Maybelle became
mother figure to the New Genera-

*Mother Maybelle Carter
(Columbia).*

41

tion folkies (it was at a time when singers like Joan Baez had begun to discover and re-record Carter Family songs) and appeared on many folk bills throughout country, winning much acclaim at the Newport Folk Festival of 1963. At later Newport Festival, in 1967, she reunited with Sara Carter to record live album **An Historic Reunion,** their first recording together for 25 years. In 1971, also appeared on Nitty Gritty Dirt Band's (♦) **Will The Circle Be Unbroken** album, leading the singing on title track.

Albums:
Mother Maybelle Carter
(Columbia/—)

Wilf Carter

Born ˙Guysboro, Nova Scotia, December 18, 1904, singer-song-writer-guitarist Carter is a one time Canadian cowboy, who branched out from rodeo to radio in the early '30s when he began broadcasting on Calgary station CFCN, at the same time commencing a recording career with RCA Victor. Later, on a New York CBS radio show he adopted the guise of 'Montana Slim' under which name he became known in the United States. One of the many yodeling singers influenced by Jimmie Rodgers (♦), Carter has written over 500 songs and recorded for such labels as Bluebird, Decca and Starday.

Albums:
Montana Slim's Greatest Hits
(Camden/—)

A Living Legend (Columbia). Maybelle's popularity has increased rapidly since the '60s.

STEREO
CS 9275

STEREO
360 SOUND

||||||||||||||

CL 2475

FOR DEMONSTRATION USE ONLY NOT FOR SALE

MOTHER MAYBELLE CARTER

I Told Them What You're Fighting For
Kitty Puss
Charlie Brooks
San Antonio Rose
We All Miss You Joe
Black Mountain Rag
A Letter From Home
Tom Cat's Kitten
Let's Be Lovers Again
Give Me Your Love and I'll Give You Mine
There's a Mother Always Waiting

A LIVING LEGEND

Below: Popular Canadian-born Wilf Carter, usually known as Montana Slim.

Johnny Carver

Raised and schooled in Jackson, Mississippi, where he was born on November 24, 1940, Carver made his first public appearance at the age of five, when he, together with two aunts and an uncle, became the resident gospel group on a local radio station before moving on to play one-nighters throughout the state. At 13 he began playing guitar and within a year was leading his own band; later, after completing high school, taking a band out on the road. After a two year haul which covered some 20 States, he based himself in Milwaukee for four years, during this time meeting his wife Pat. In 1965, Carter moved to LA, becoming a regular at the Palomino Club and having his first hit record two years later when **Your Lily White Hands,** an Imperial release, charted. By this time he'd moved to Nashville where during the next few years, he provided Imperial and UA with a number of fair sized hits, before moving on to Epic and continuing his lower league success. However, an affiliation with ABC Records in 1973 took the warm voiced Carver to the top of the ladder, **Yellow Ribbon,** the title cut from his ABC debut album, moving into the coveted No 1 spot on the charts in June of that year. Since then, Carver – who won an ASCAP artist award for his **Hold Me Tight** hit in 1969 – has enjoyed continued good fortune on disc, his 1976 version of Bill Danoff's **Afternoon Delight** being among his more recent top ten items.

Albums:
Tie A Yellow Ribbon *(ABC/—)*
Don't Tell (That Sweet Old Lady Of Mine) *(ABC/—)*
Double Exposure *(ABC/—)*
Strings *(ABC/—)*
Afternoon Delight *(Dot/—)*

Afternoon Delight (Dot Records).

Above and right: Johnny Carver, one of the many country stars who performed at an early age – as part of a gospel quartet at the age of five.

Johnny Cash

Winner of six CMA awards in 1969 (best male vocalist, entertainer of the year, best single, best album, outstanding service award and even one (with June Carter (♦) for best vocal group) John R. Cash was born Kingsland, Arkansas, February 26, 1932, son of poverty stricken cotton farmer Ray Cash and his wife Carrie. In 1935 the Cash family moved to the government resettlement Dyess Colony, surviving the Mississippi river flood of 1937, an event documented in a 1959 Cash song **Five Feet High And Rising.** With the births of Joann (1938) and Tom (1940 (♦), Ray Cash's family grew to seven children, one son, Roy, putting together country band The Delta Rhythm Ramblers about this time, and broadcasting on KCLN, Blytheville. However, tragedy struck the Cashes in 1944 when son Jack died after an accident with a circular saw, an event having a lasting effect on the young John.

After high school graduation in 1950, J.R. took a job in a Detroit body plant, then worked for an Evadale margarine firm, sweeping floors and cleaning vats. But by July of that year he'd enlisted in the Air Force for a four year term. It was while serving in Germany that Cash learnt guitar and began writing his first songs.

Upon discharge in July 1954, having achieved rank of staff sergeant, Cash married Vivian Liberto and then headed for Memphis where he became an electrical appliance salesman.

In Memphis he met electric guitar player Luther Perkins and bassist Marshall Grant and began performing with them – for no pay – on station KWEM. Eventually they gained an audition with Sam Phillips of Sun Records, from which came a subsequent recording session and a single **Hey Porter/Cry, Cry, Cry,** both songs being Cash originals. Upon release, the disc – listed as by Johnny Cash And The Tennessee Two – became a hit, selling in the region of 100,000 copies. Following a success with his follow-up disc **Folsom Prison Blues** in December 1955, Cash joined KWKH's Louisiana Hayride (♦), Shreveport. He also began touring, the dates becoming even more plentiful after the release of **I Walk The Line,** a crossover hit that sold a million, and **There You Go,** another 1956 winner. In 1957, Cash joined the Opry then trekked to Hollywood to play maniacal killer in a 'B' movie titled 'Five Minutes To Live' (1958). Next came tours in Canada and Australia, grossing a quarter of a million dollars, and Cash signed for Columbia Records. Drummer W. S. Holland joined the Tennessee Two in 1960 (at which stage they became the Tennessee Three), Cash and his enlarged band playing the niteclub circuit for the first time. Much in demand, he was playing nearly 300 gigs a year, pill-popping to provide the energy.

Cash first began working with June Carter in December '61, June trying to steer him through 1962 a heavy schedule year that included a 30-hour tour of Korea and a disastrous Carnegie Hall date. At the Newport Folk Festival of 1964 he sang with Bob Dylan, that same year recording **Bitter Tears,** a classic album of songs regarding the mistreatment of the American Indian, much of the material being written by Peter LaFarge. But the pill-popping worsened and in October, 1965, Cash was arrested by the narcotics squad in El Paso, receiving a 30-day suspended sentence and a $1,000 fine. In 1966 he was jailed once more – for embarking on a 2 am flower picking spree! Also in '66 Carl Perkins (♦) became a regular

Five Feet High and Rising (Columbia).

Bitter Tears (Columbia).

part of the Cash touring show.

Though in poor health and with his weight down to 140 pounds, he produced **Carrying On,** an album with June Carter - but while his recorded work maintained a high standard, his personal life headed ever downward, Vivian Cash suing him for divorce in mid 1966. The pill addiction continued, Cash sometimes suffering complete blackouts. Under Dr Nat Winston he submitted to treatment, gradually fighting back until by the close of the '60s he was restored to complete health once more.

Since signing for Columbia in 1958 Cash had cut a tremendous quota of hit singles – the biggest of these being **All Over Again** (1958), **Don't Take Your Guns To Town** (1959), **I Got Stripes** (1959), **In The Jailhouse Now** (1962), **Ring Of Fire** (1963), **Understand Your Man** (1964), **The Ballad Of Ira Hayes** (1964), **It Ain't Me, Babe** (1964), **Orange Blossom Special** (1965), **The One On Your Right Is On Your Left** (1966), **Rosanna's Going Wild** (1967), **Folsom Prison Blues** (1968), **Daddy Sang Bass** (1968) and **A Boy Named Sue** (1969). More importantly, he'd also cut some of the most striking albums to emerge from country music – including **Ride This Train** (1960) a kind of musical hobo-ride through America; **Blood, Sweat And Tears** (1964) a tribute to the working man; the already mentioned **Bitter Tears** (1964); **Ballads Of The True West** (1965) a double album glance at western folklore; and **At Folsom Prison** (1968) an award winning affair recorded in front of perhaps the world's toughest, but most appreciative, audience.

His partnership with June Carter, whom he married in March 1968 (Merle Kilgore (♦) being best man), proved successful both on and off stage, the duo gaining a Grammy award for **Jackson,** adjudged the best country performance by a group during '67. And as the '60s rolled away, the CMA showered a whole flood of awards on the craggy faced man in black, while the film critics applauded his portrayal of an ageing gunfighter in 'The Gunfight' a 1970 release in which he pitted his acting ability against that of Kirk Douglas. During the '70s, Johnny Cash has turned increasingly towards religion, visiting Israel to make a film about life in the Holy Land and appearing on shows headed by evangelist Billy Graham. But thanks to his obvious sincerity and his crumbling rock of a voice (often placed out front over the most meager of rhythm patterns) everything he sings about, no matter how twee, always comes out sounding completely believable.

Above: Ride This Train (Columbia). A fine album that once more reflects country music's love affair with the railroad – though truckers have become the new heroes.

Left: Johnny Cash. His 1977 projects included The Rambler, a concept album involving a highway rover who meets various characters based on real people Cash has met.

Albums:
At Folsom Prison (Columbia/ CBS)
Any Old Wind That Blows (Columbia/CBS)
At San Quentin (Columbia/CBS)
Big River (Hillside/—)
Blood, Sweat And Tears (Columbia/—)
Carryin' On with June Carter (Columbia/—)
Everybody Loves A Nut (Columbia/—)
Johnny Cash And His Woman (Columbia/—)
Five Feet High And Rising (Columbia/—)
Get Rhythm (Sun/—)
Greatest Hits (Columbia/CBS)
Greatest Hits Vol 2 (Columbia/—)
Holy Land (Columbia/—)
Hymns (Columbia/—)
Hymns From The Heart (Columbia/—)
I Walk The Line (Columbia/—)
I Walk The Line (Hillside/—)
I Walk The Line/Rock Island (Pickwick/—)
Johnny Cash (Pickwick/—)
Living Legend (Sun/—)
Johnny Cash (Harmony/—)
Man In Black (Columbia/CBS)
The Man, The World And His Music (Columbia/—)
Mean As Hell (Columbia/—)
Orange Blossom Special (Columbia/—)

Original Golden Hits Vol 1/2 (Sun/—)
Original Golden Hits Vol 3 (Sun/—)
Ride This Train (Columbia/—)
Ring Of Fire (Columbia/CBS)
Rock Island Line (Hillside/—)
Roughcut King Of Country Music (Sun/—)
Showtime, with the Tennessee Two (Sun/—)
Singing Story Teller, with the Tennessee Two (Sun/—)
Story Songs Of Trains And Rivers (Sun/—)
Sunday After Church (Hillside/—)
Sunday Down South with J. L. Lewis (Sun/—)
Sings Hank Williams with J. L. Lewis (Sun/—)
Johnny Cash (Archive Of Folk/—)
John R. Cash (Columbia/CBS)
Junkie And Juicehead Minus Me (Columbia/—CBS)
One Piece At A Time (Columbia/CBS)
Sings Precious Memories (Columbia/—)
Strawberry Cake (Columbia/ CBS)
Look At Them Beans (Columbia/CBS)
Ballads Of The True West (—/Embassy)
The Gospel Road (—/CBS)
America (Columbia/CBS)
Johnny Cash (—/Embassy)

*Little Fauss and Big Halsy
(CBS) – soundtrack*

Ragged Old Flag *(Columbia/
  CBS)*
The Sound Of Johnny Cash
  (—/Embassy)
Riding The Rails *(—/CBS)*
Ballads Of The True West
  (—/Embassy)
The Great Johnny Cash
  (—/Hallmark)
Hymns By Johnny Cash
  (—/Hallmark)
The Magnificent Johnny Cash
  (—/Hallmark)
The Mighty Johnny Cash
  (—/Hallmark)
Folsom Prison Blues
  (—/Hallmark)
I Walk The Line *(—/Hallmark)*
Ballad Of A Teenage Queen
  (—/Hallmark)
The World Of Johnny Cash
  (Columbia/CBS)
**I Forgot To Remember to
  Forget** *(—/Hallmark)*
The Johnny Cash Collection
  (—/Hallmark)
Old Golden Throat *(—/Charley)*
Original Johnny Cash
  (—/Charley)
The Last Gunfighter Ballad
  (Columbia/CBS)

*Look At Them Beans
(CBS)*

Tommy Cash

Younger brother of superstar
Johnny Cash (◆), Tommy was born
in Mississippi County, Arkansas,
April 5, 1940.

He learnt guitar at age of 16 after
watching his brother play chords
and listening to other guitarists.
His first public appearance was as
a performer at Treadwell High
School in 1957; he then joined the
army at 18, becoming a disc
jockey for AFN, Frankfurt, Germany and having his own show
'Stickbuddy Jamboree'. He met his
wife Barbara during this period.

Cash began appearing with a
band at various service clubs and
eventually launched his professional career by performing alongside Hank Williams Jnr (◆) at Montreal in January, 1965. In 1969 he

*Tommy Cash. Brother of super-
star Johnny Cash, he was a one-
time disc jockey with the
American Forces Network.*

signed with Epic Records, the
same year having a *Billboard*
100 entry with **Six White
Horses,** a best selling album of
that title released in 1970. More
recently Cash, who tours with a
band called The Tomcats, has recorded for Elektra.

Albums:
Best Of Tommy Cash Vol 1
  (Epic/—)
That Certain One *(Epic/—)*
Six Horses/Lovin' Takes Leavin'
  (Epic/—)
Only A Stone *(Elektra/—)*

*Six White Horses
(Epic)*

The Cass
Country Boys

Fred Martin *accordion and lead
  vocals*
Jerry Scoggins *guitar and
  baritone vocals*
Bert Dodson *string bass and
  tenor vocals*

A smooth-singing western harmony trio who appeared in numerous films with Gene Autry (◆) as
well as appearing as his backup
band on untold personal appearances. They made a fine series of
McGregor Transcriptions, and recorded for Decca and ARA, al-

though no hit records came out of these recordings.

Albums: none.

Pete Cassell

A long-popular blind singer with a fine smooth voice which anticipated the likes of Jim Reeves (♦). Most popular in the 1940s and early 1950s, Pete recorded for Decca, Majestic and Mercury, but died all too young in 1953, a few years too early to cash in on the smooth Nashville Sound for which his voice was so well suited.

Albums: none.

Lew Childre

A native of Opp, Alabama (born November 1, 1901), 'Doctor Lew' was a Hawaiian guitar player and sophisticated rural comedian of long tenure (1945–1961) on the Grand Ole Opry. A veteran of vaudeville – as were many early country comedians – he specialized in routines involving letters to a rural physician – 'Doctor Lew' – who gave outrageous advice. He was also an adept singer and musician who featured old standards like **I'm Looking Over A Four Leaf Clover.** He and Stringbean (♦) formed a comedy team for a period (1945–1948), before each carved out a solo Opry career. He recorded little, a recently reissued album on Starday long being regarded as a collector's item.

Guy Clark

Writer of such fine contemporary songs as **Desperadoes Waiting For A Train, L. A. Freeway, Texas 1947** and **The Last Gunfighter Ballad,** Clark is a Texan (born 1941) who spent many of his early years in the town of Monahans, living with his grandmother in a run down hotel, this location providing the inspiration for many of his later songs. During the 1960s he moved to Houston, there working as an art director on a local TV station, also meeting Jerry Jeff Walker (♦) and Townes Van Zandt, whom he lists among his influences. After a stint on the coffee house circuits of Houston, Dallas and Austin (♦), he headed for LA, where he obtained a job in the Dopyera Brothers factory constructing dobros. Eventually interesting Sunbury Music in his songwriting ability, Clark became a resident of Nashville in 1971, cutting an album but scrapping it due to personal dissatisfaction. Then in 1975 came **Old No 1,** which critics hailed as the finest country debut album for many years. Possessor of a beer-stained voice, Clark writes almost poetically about losers and low-life ladies. His second album **Texas Cooking** (1976), though not quite as potent as his initial release, nevertheless provided further proof of his talent.

Albums:
Old No 1 *(RCA/RCA)*
Texas Cooking *(RCA/RCA)*

Texas Cookin' (RCA) '... we made a record of ourselves having a good time making a record – this is it.'

The rugged-looking Guy Clark has been known to wear false silver fingernails to keep his digits in full picking order.

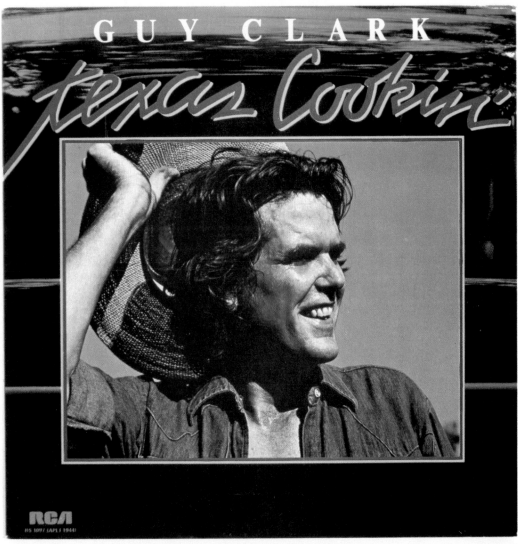

GUY CLARK

Texas Cookin'

RCA

Roy Clark

Multi talented star of the Hee Haw (♦) TV series, Roy Linwood Clark was born Meherrin, Virginia, April 15, 1933. Son of a guitar playing tobacco farmer, Clark soon picked up the rudiments of guitar technique but at an early age became even more proficient on banjo, in the late '40s, winning the National Country Music Banjo championship two years in succession. Following a move to Washington DC, Roy played as part of the Clark family group, performing at local square dances and eventually winning a solo spot on the Jimmy Dean (♦) TV Show – but getting fired due to perpetual lateness. A subsequent job found him getting fired by Marvin Rainwater (♦) – this time for earning more applause than the star himself. But better luck followed when, as a cast member of a George Hamilton IV (♦) TV series, he gained considerable recognition.

Recording initially for Four Star as Roy Clark and the Wranglers, he later moved on to Debbie, Coral and – following a tour with Wanda Jackson (♦) – Capitol, enjoying his first sizeable hit with a Capitol single **Tips Of My Fingers** in 1963. Following a contract with Dot, the hits really began to proliferate, via titles like **Yesterday When I Was Young** (1969), **I Never Picked Cotton, Thank God And Greyhound** (both 1970), **A Simple Thing Called Love, Magnificent Sanctuary Band** (both 1971), **The Lawrence Walk Counter Revolution Polka** (1972), **Come Live With Me** (1973), **Honeymoon Feeling, Somewhere Between Love And Tomorrow** (both 1974) and **If I Had To Do It All Over Again** (1976). A jovial international ambassador for country music – Clark was presented with the CMA Entertainer of the Year award in 1973.

Albums:

Lightning Fingers Of (*Capitol*/—)	**Roy Clark** (*Pickwick*/—)
Best Of Roy Clark (*Dot*/—)	**Silver Threads And Golden Needles** (*Hilltop*/—)
Country (*Dot*/—)	**Superpicker** (*Dot*/—)
Do You Believe This? (*Dot*/—)	**Take Me As I Am** (*Hilltop*/—)
The Entertainer (*Dot*/—)	**Urban, Suburban** (*Dot*/—)
Entertainer Of The Year (*Capitol*/—)	**Yesterday When I Was Young** (*Dot*/*Contour*)
Everlovin' Soul (*Dot*/—)	**Sings Gospel** (*Word*/*Word*)
Greatest! (*Capitol*/—)	**Classic Clark** (*Dot*/—)
Guitar Spectacular (*Capitol*/—)	**Family And Friends** (*Dot*/—)
He'll Have To Go (*Pickwick*/—)	**Greatest Hits Vol 1** (*Dot*/*ABC*)
Incredible (*Dot*/—)	**Heart To Heart** (*Dot*/—)
I Never Picked Cotton (*Dot*/—)	**Live With Me** (*Dot*/—)
Honky Tonk (*Pickwick*/—)	**Pair Of Fives** (*Dot*/—*ABC*)
Live! (*Dot*/—)	**Sincerely Yours** (*Paramount*/—)
Live Fast, Love Hard (*Pickwick*/—)	**So Much To Remember** (*Capitol*/—)
Magnificent Sanctuary Band (*Dot*/—)	**Introducing Roy Clark** (—/*Ember*)
The Other Side Of Roy Clark (*Dot*/—)	**Very Best Of Roy Clark** (—/*Capitol*)

Yodeling Slim Clark

Born Raymond LeRoy Clark, November 12, 1917, Springfield, Massachusetts, Yodeling Slim worked for a long period as a woodman. Winner of the World Yodeling Championship in 1947, he began recording for such labels as Continental, Remington, Wheeling and Palomino, his albums including **Yodel Songs** (*Remington* 1950), **Jimmie Rodgers Songs** (*Palomino* 1965) **and Wilf Carter Songs** (*Palomino* 1967).

Roy Clark Sings Gospel (Word). Purely religious material. Clark has recorded for several labels – Four Star, Debbie, Coral, Capital and now Dot, for whom he's scored a string of hits.

Jack Clement

Few people have mastered more phases of the music business than Jack 'The Cowboy' Clement, who currently heads up a monstrous twelve piece dance aggregation known as the Cowboy Ragtime Band.

Roy Clark. In 1973 he was judged Country Entertainer Of The Year by three of the music industry's major associations.

Clement, born in Memphis in 1932, mastered a variety of instruments as a youth, and played all kinds of music, from big band to bluegrass, on his way into the production end of the business, where he fell in with Sam Phillips at Sun Records as a session musician, engineer, and producer. He also wrote a great many songs in the era, including **Guess Things Happen That Way** and **Ballad Of A Teenage Queen** for Johnny Cash (♦)

More recently he has concentrated his energies in Nashville, where he built an extremely successful publishing firm – Jack Music – ran Jack Clement Studio, one of the most popular independent operations in town, and continued to write as well. He even found time to produce a horror film, 'Dear Dead Delilah'. Of late he says he's tired of the performers getting all the money and him getting none, and wanting a piece of the action formed the Ragtime Cowboy Band in 1976.

Other award winning Clement hits include **A Girl I Used To Know, I Know One, Miller's Cave,** and **The One On The Right Is The One On The Left.**

Albums: none.

Crossing the Catskills (Rounder).

Vassar Clements

Much respected fiddle player who worked for some time as a sessioneer in Nashville before lately finding a degree of solo fame. Born April, 1928, at Kinard, South Carolina, Vassar has been in the bands of Bill Monroe (♦), Jim and Jesse (♦), Faron Young (♦) and more recently the contemporary-slanted Earl Scruggs (♦) Revue.

He appeared on the Nitty Gritty Dirt Band's (♦) **Will The Circle Be Unbroken** and his consequent familiarity to the general public after years of being a name among recording sessions credits has meant that he has been able to get his own show together and travel the road.

Albums:
Vassar Clements *(Mercury/—)*
Superbow *(Mercury/—)*
Southern Country Waltzes
 (Rural Rhythm/—)
Hillbilly Jazz *(Flying Fish/Sonet)*

Vassar Clements. Known as Superbow because of his phenomenal fiddling, he is also adept on viola, cello, base, guitar and mandolin.

Blue Ridge Mountain Bluegrass (County).

Monroe (♦), the Stanley Brothers (♦), the New Lost City Ramblers and others during the '60s. He also enhanced his own reputation as a bluegrass musician, embarking on tours of Europe and recording a program of old time music for transmission on Radio Moscow in 1966.

By 1967, Clifton was on the move once more, he, his wife and seven children sailing for the Philippines, where he became an active member of the Peace Corps. Still in the Pacific area at the commencement of the '70s, he arrived in New Zealand, playing at a banjo players' convention and cutting an album with Hamilton County Bluegrass Band, a local outfit. Since that time Clifton has been active in both Europe and the States, Japan, Germany, Holland, Belgium, Austria and Switzerland figuring on his 1976 itinerary. But where he'll turn up next is anyone's guess!

Albums:
Blue Ridge Mountain Blues
  (County/Westwood)
Come By The Hills (County/—)
Mountain Folk Songs
  (Starday/—)
Another Happy Day – with Red
  Rector (—/Breakdown)
Goin' Back To Dixie (—/Bear
  Family)
A Bluegrass Jam Session 1952
  (—/Bear Family)
Getting Folk Out Of Country –
  with Hedy West (—/Bear Family)

A Bluegrass Jam Session 1952 (Bear Family)

Zeke Clements

'The Alabama Cowboy' was born near Empire, Alabama, on September 9, 1911, and has had one of the longest careers in country music, having appeared on radio shows in all sections of the country, as well as having the unusual distinction of having been a member of all three of the major barn dances in the course of his long career.

Zeke began on the National Barn Dance (♦) in 1928, toured for some years with Otto Gray's (♦) Oklahoma Cowboys, then joined the Grand Ole Opry in 1933 as a member of their first cowboy group, the Broncho Busters. After spending some time on the west coast on radio and in films (where he was, among many other screen parts, the voice of the yodeling dwarf Bashful in Walt Disney's *Snow White and the Seven Dwarfs*) before returning to the Opry in 1939, where he became one of the Opry's major stars throughout the 1940s. He also became known as a songwriter during this era, especially for **Blue Mexico Skies, There's Poison In Your Heart,** and as co-writer of **Smoke On The Water,** the top country record of 1945.

Clements later appeared on the Louisiana Hayride (♦) and on many other Deep South stations. He pursued a business career in Nashville in the late 1950s and 1960s, then moved to Miami, Florida, where he spent nearly a decade playing tenor banjo in a dixieland band before returning to the Nashville area in recent years.

Albums: none.

Zeke Clements, star of the Opry and Louisiana Hayride, supplied the voice of Dopey in Walt Disney's Snow White.

Bill Clifton

Perennial globetrotter Clifton was born Riderwood, Maryland, 1931. A vocalist, guitarist and autoharp player, he became interested in the music of the Carter Family (♦) during the 1940s, later forming his own group the Dixie Mountain Boys, establishing a considerable reputation among bluegrass aficionados, also cutting sides for Starday and other labels. In 1961, he recorded 22 Carter Family songs for a Starday album but some months later turned up in Britain where, using contacts made as a founder member of the Newport Folk Festival, he became instrumental in setting up tours by Bill

Patsy Cline

Patsy Cline (real name Virginia Patterson Hensley) was born Winchester, Virginia, September 8, 1932. Winner of an amateur tap dancing contest at age 4, she began learning piano at 8, and in her early teens became a singer at local clubs. In 1948, an audition won her a trip to Nashville, where she appeared in a few clubs before returning home – but her big break came in 1957 when she won an Arthur Godfrey Talent Scout show, singing **Walking After Midnight.** Her Decca single of the contest-winning song then entered the charts, both pop and country, enjoying a lengthy stay in both. In 1961, came **I Fall To Pieces,** one of Patsy's biggest hits, followed in quick succession by **Crazy, Who Who Can I Count On?, She's Got You, Strange** and **When I Get Thru With You,** most of them being massive sellers. During the same period she became a featured singer on the Opry, soon attaining the rank of top female country singer and challenging Kitty Wells (♦) as 'Queen Of Country Music'. Such hits as **Imagine That, So Wrong** and **Leavin' On Your Mind** continued to proliferate until, on March 5, 1963, Patsy died in an air disaster at Camden, Tennessee. She had been returning home from a Kansas City benefit concert with Hawkshaw Hawkins (♦) and Cowboy Copas (♦), both of whom were also killed in the crash.

But even after her death, Patsy's records continued to sell, **Sweet Dreams (Of You)** and **Faded Love** being top hits during '63, **When You Need A Laugh** and **He Called Me Baby** entering the country charts in 1964, and **Anytime** appearing in the latter as late as 1969.

In 1973 Patsy Cline was elected to the Country Music Hall Of Fame.

Albums:
Patsy Cline *(MCA/—)*
The Great Patsy Cline
  (Vocalion/—)
Greatest Hits *(MCA/—)*
Here's Patsy Cline
  (Vocalion/—)
In Care Of The Blues
  (Pickwick/—)
Portrait *(MCA/—)*
Sentimentally Yours *(MCA/—)*
Stop The World *(Pickwick/—)*
The Patsy Cline Story *(MCA/—)*
Have You Ever Been Lonely?
  (—/MCA)
Patsy Cline *(—/Hallmark)*
A Legend *(—/Ember)*
Legend Of Patsy Cline
  (Pickwick/—)
Never To Be Forgotten
  (—/Hallmark)
Patsy Cline Vol 2 *(—/Hallmark)*
Walking After Midnight
  (—/Ember)

A STRANGER IN MY ARMS
AIN'T NO WHEELS ON THIS SHIP
COME ON IN
CRY NOT FOR ME
DEAR GOD
HE'LL DO FOR YOU
HIDIN' OUT
I LOVE YOU HONEY
IN CARE OF THE BLUES
LOVESICK BLUES

Walking After Midnight
(Ember)

Patsy Cline (Hallmark). The first of three English compilations; none of her greatest hits are on this album, but the material is a fine illustration of her talents.

Bill Clifton once formed a duo, the Clifton Brothers, with guitarist Paul Clayton. Paul became Harvey Clifton, taking his name from a 1950 film that featured an invisible rabbit.

Jerry Clower

Country comedian Jerry Clower was born Liberty, Mississippi, September 28, 1926, and grew up in Amite County amid the folks he now brings to life as part of his hilarious routines. After graduation in 1944 he joined the navy, following in the path of elder brother Sonny, who did so soon after Pearl Harbor. Upon discharge came a football scholarship at Southwest Junior College, Summit, where he won a further scholarship to Mississippi State University, playing for the State football team and majoring in agriculture.

After becoming a field representative with the Mississippi Chemical Company, Clower rose to become Director of Field Services with the company, in charge of a large sales force. Sales talks became part of his stock in trade and so his **Coon Hunt Story** and other routines were introduced to make

such speeches more acceptable. A friend then suggested that Clower should record an album of his routines and, after further prompting, it was agreed that an album be cut on the Lemon label. Named **Jerry Clower From Yazoo City Talkin'** and advertised only by word of mouth, the album sold over 8000 copies in a short period, gaining Clower a contract with MCA in 1971. His album later went into the *Billboard* charts for a lengthy stay and, following the release of other high-selling LPs **From The Mouth Of Mississippi, Clower Power** and **Live In Picayune,** he became accepted as Country Music's funniest man, winning many spots on TV shows included frequent appearances on Grand Ole Opry. Father of four children, Clower, deeply religious like many country stars, is a Yazoo City Baptist deacon and an active member of the Gideon Bible Society.

Albums:
Clower Power *(MCA/—)*
Country Ham *(MCA/—)*
Live In Picayune *(MCA/—)*
Mississippi Talkin' *(MCA/—)*

The Ambassador of Goodwill (MCA).

The Heart of Hank Cochran (Monument).

Hank Cochran

Singer-songwriter Henry 'Hank' Cochran, was born Greenville, Mississippi, August 2, 1935, After completing school he moved to New Mexico, working in the oilfields during the mid '50s, eventually making his way to California, where he began entertaining in small clubs, occasionally obtaining radio and TV work. In 1954, he and the late Eddie Cochran (no relation) formed a duo, The Cochran Brothers, initially recording country material for the Ekko label but later switching to rock after watching Elvis Presley (◆) perform in Dallas.

Left: Commander Cody and his Lost Planet Airmen.

Jerry Clower from Yazoo City, Mississippi. One of country's top comedians, he also serves the Gideon cause.

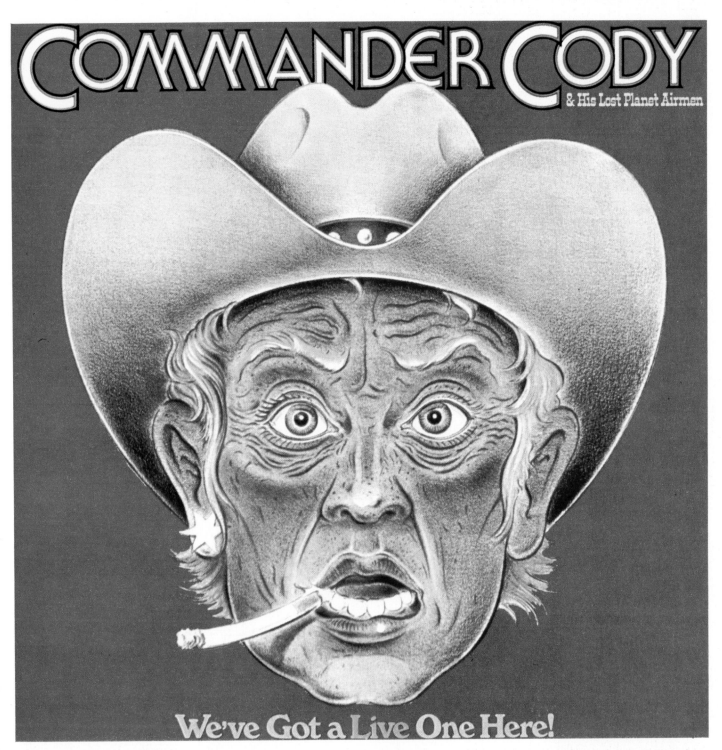

COMMANDER CODY
& His Lost Planet Airmen

We've Got a Live One Here!

After two years, the Cochrans went their separate ways, Hank going on to join the California Hayride TV show in Stockton, then in 1960 moving to Nashville in order to sell his songs. One such composition titled **I Fall To Pieces,** written with the aid of Harlan Howard (♦), became a 1961 winner for Patsy Cline (♦), after which came **Make The World Go Away** (a hit for both Ray Price (♦) and Eddy Arnold (♦)), **Willingly** (Shirley Collie and Willie Nelson (♦)); **A Little Bitty Tear** and **Funny Way Of Laughing** (Burl Ives), **I Want To Go With You** (Eddy Arnold (♦)) etc. Signed by Liberty as a recording artist in 1961, Cochran's name appeared in the charts during '62 with **Sally Was A Good Old Girl** and **I'd Fight The World,** the singer later scoring with **A Good Country Song,** on Gaylord in 1963, and **All Of Me Belongs To You,** on Monument in 1967. His albums have

included **Heart** *(Monument),* **Hank Cochran** *(RCA)* and **Going In Training** *(RCA).*

Ben Colder
♦ *Sheb Wooley*

Commander Cody And His Lost Planet Airmen

George 'Commander Cody' Frayne *keyboards, vocals*
Billy C. Farlow *vocals*
Lance Dickerson *drums, vocals*
Bruce Barlow *bass*

Bill Kirchen *guitar, trombone, vocals*
Bobby Black *pedal steel guitar*
Andy Stein *fiddle, tenor sax*
Rick Higginbotham *guitar*
Norton Buffalo *harmonica, trombone, vocals*

Zany, modern western swing outfit, named after space movie characters. Formed 1967 by leader Frayne, previously Farfisa organ player with various small time rock bands. Acquiring a sizeable reputation in California, the Airmen signed to ABC-Paramount in 1969, recording fine **Lost In The Ozone** album and subsequently gaining Top 20 hit with version of Johnny Pond's **Hot Rod Lincoln.** In 1974 they moved to Warner Bros. releasing two studio albums and a live double, **We've Got A Live One Here,** recorded during the band's 1976 British tour. Frequent lineup changes always affected Cody's unwieldy ag-

We've Got A Live One Here (Warner Bros). Recorded during their very successful British tour. Lineup changes have proved a problem but they're still going strong.

gregation and by 1976 the fate of the band was once more in doubt.

Albums:
Lost In The Ozone *(Paramount/ABC)*
Hot Licks, Cold Steel *(Paramount/ABC)*
Live – Deep In The Heart Of Texas *(Paramount/ABC)*
Country Casanova *(Paramount/ABC)*
Commander Cody And His Lost Planet Airmen *(Warner Bros/Warner Bros)*
Tales From The Ozone *(Warner Bros/Warner Bros)*
We've Got A Live One Here *(Warner Bros/Warner Bros)*

David Allan Coe

Known as the Mysterious Rhinestone Cowboy, early facts about Coe are hard to come by, though it is claimed that he entered the Starr Commonwealth Home for Boys at 9, went to boys industrial school at 14 and a further training school two years later. He's said to have spent the years between the ages of 17 and 23 at various reformatories and penitentiaries, and those between 26 and 27 at the Marion Correctional Institution.

Longhaired Redneck (Columbia)

Another claim – sometimes disputed – is that during a stay in Ohio State Penitentiary, Coe killed an inmate after being threatened with a knife, then spending three months on Death Row, only escaping the electric chair due to abolition of capital punishment.

Parole came in 1967 at which time Coe, a talented guitarist, harmonica player and singer songwriter opted for the life of a professional entertainer, in 1968 cutting an album, **Penitentiary Blues** for Shelby Singleton's (♦) SSS International label. He followed this with **Requiem For A Harlequin**, another blues-filled but poetic LP dealing with his prison experiences.

Next came a switch to country music and mild success with singles **How High's The Watergate, Martha?** and **Keep Those Big Wheels Hummin'**, the major break coming when Tanya Tucker (♦) recorded Coe's **Would You Lay With Me (In A Field Of Stone?)** and gained a hit.

Currently signed to Columbia Records, Coe won the new male vocalist (albums) award in the 1976 *Cashbox* poll.

Albums:
Penitentiary Blues *(SSS/—)*
The Mysterious Rhinestone Cowboy *(Columbia/—)*
Once Upon A Rhyme *(Columbia/CBS)*
Longhaired Redneck *(Columbia/—)*
Rides Again *(Columbia/—)*

Tommy Collins

One of the musicians who helped to put Bakersfield (♦) on the Country Music map – Buck Owens (♦) was once a member of his band – Tommy Collins – real name Leonard Raymond Sipes – was born Oklahoma City, Oklahoma, September 28, 1930. A boyhood guitarist, he began performing at local clubs while at Oklahoma

Left: David Allan Coe

The Mysterious Rhinestone Cowboy (Columbia)

State College, making appearances on such radio stations as KLPR, KOCY, KBYE and WKY. During the early '50s, he became both a resident of Bakersfield and a Capitol recording artist, his halcyon days being in 1954–55 when Collins followed **You Better**

Callin' (Starday)

Not Do That, a half-million seller, with a quartet of other Top 20 discs. In 1966 he presented Columbia with a Top Ten item in **If You Can't Bite, Don't Growl,** but his later discs, such as **Birmingham** (1967) and **I Made The Prison Band** (1968) only achieved moder-

David Allan Coe, who lived in a hearse outside the Opry on arrival in Nashville so people would know he'd hit town.

ate chart placings.

Collins' past albums include **This Is Tommy Collins** *(Capitol)*, **Dynamic** *(Columbia)*, **On Tour** *(Columbia)* and **Tommy Collins** *(Tower)*.

Jessi Colter

Writer and singer of a 1975 No 1 in **I'm Not Lisa**, Jessi Colter (real name Miriam Johnson) was born Phoenix, Arizona, the sixth of seven children born to the wife of a racing car builder. A church pianist at the age of 11, Jessi married guitarist Duane Eddy just five years later, touring England, Germany, South Africa and other countries as part of the Eddy tour-

Compton Brothers

Voted Most Promising Vocal Group of 1968–69 by *Cashbox* magazine, the Comptons, Harry and Bill, from St Louis, Missouri, won a 1965 talent contest that resulted in a Columbia recording contract. However, they later became associated with the Dot label, supplying a number of minor hits during the late '60s and early '70s, only two of these, namely **Haunted House** (1969) and **Charlie Brown** (1970), ever attaining Top 20 status. The brothers are owners of the Wepedol Publishing Co.

Ry Cooder

One time Los Angeles session man Cooder is of interest to country fans in that his music is soaked generally in southern folk styles. He first came to public notice with his tasteful and well timed mandolin excursions on bluesman Taj Mahal's first CBS album and he played with Taj's band the Rising Sons. Later, he was to impress again with his mandolin work on the Rolling Stones' **Let It Bleed** album.

He was an early student of guitar fingerpicking styles and studied guitar also by watching bluesmen such as Rev Gary Davis. Also became proficient on slide guitar and is now a rated exponent of that style. He has lately been incorporating Tex-Mex music and bolero rhythms into his live act; witness his distinctive setting of **He'll Have To Go,** the Jim Reeves (♦) classic. A real 'musician's musician', Cooder specializes in finding old folk, blues and country

Jessi (Capitol). A church pianist at 11, Jessi Colter is now married to 'outlaw' Waylon Jennings.

ing show. A singer-songwriter, she was recorded by Eddy and Lee Hazlewood for the Jamies and RCA labels, meeting Waylon Jennings (♦) during some Phoenix-based sessions.

Following a divorce from Eddy in 1968, she returned to Phoenix once more, working alongside Jennings, moving to Nashville with him in 1969 and becoming his wife during the October of that year. Jessi, who currently records for Capitol (but appears on a best selling RCA album titled **Outlaws**) has had her songs recorded by Don Gibson (♦), Anita Carter (♦) Carter Family), Patsy Sledd (♦), Marion Worth, Dottie West (♦) and several others, scoring her own hits with **I'm Not Lisa,** which she wrote in five minutes; **What Happened To Blue Eyes** (1975) and **It's Morning** (1976). She has two children, Buddy and Jennifer.

Albums:
I'm Jessie Colter (Capitol/—)
Jessi (Capitol/Capitol)
Outlaws – with Waylon Jennings, Willie Nelson and Tompall Glaser (RCA/RCA)
Diamond In the Rough (Capitol/—)

Jessi Colter's self-penned I'm Not Lisa, produced by husband Waylon Jennings and Ken Mansfield, topped the charts in '75.

One of Spade Cooley's massive lineups, with Tex Williams second from right.

tunes and restyling them almost completely.

Albums:
Ry Cooder *(Reprise/Reprise)*
The Boomer's Story
(Reprise/Reprise)
Into The Purple Valley
(Reprise/Reprise)
Paradise And Lunch
(Reprise/Reprise)
Chicken Skin Music
(Reprise/Reprise)

Spade Cooley

One time King Of Western Swing, Donell C. Cooley had literally one of the biggest bands in country music, the aggregation sometimes numbering around two dozen musicians.

Born Grand, Oklahoma, 1910, Cooley, of Scottish-Irish descent, plus a dash of Cherokee Indian, acquired the nickname of Spade from an exceptional run of spades he once held during a poker game.

Both his father and his grandfather were fine fiddle players, and Cooley, who was first taught cello, also became adept on fiddle, playing at square dances while still a boy, earning his first fee as a musician at the age of eight.

During the late-1930s he became a Hollywood extra, eventually obtaining roles in movies produced by RKO, Universal, Republic, Warner, Lippert and Columbia.

By 1942 Cooley was leading his own very successful band, in '46 leasing the Santa Monica ballroom for long term use as the band's headquarters. A radio performer during the early '40s, he was sign-

Paradise and Lunch (Reprise).

ed for a Hollywood country TV show in 1948, shortly after returning from a lengthy tour with his band. Playing a mixture of jazz, country and pure dance music, the Cooley outfit gained further fame, but the fiddle playing leader's career came to a dramatic end when he was jailed for wife-slaying. His death occurred shortly after his release from prison, Cooley suffering a heart attack in

1969 while playing at a sheriff's benefit concert in Oakland, California.

During his career, his records were released on such labels as Okeh, Columbia, RCA Victor and Decca, Cooley's biggest hit being with the self-penned **Shame On You** in 1945. During the early '50s Columbia released an album titled **Sagebrush Stomp.**

Rita Coolidge

Nashville born, on May 1, 1944, Rita Coolidge and her two sisters first began singing in a church choir (their father was a Baptist minister), Rita later working with a rock band The Moonpies, playing at fraternity parties at the University of Florida and at Florida State. In college, she also sang with a folk rock unit, then, after leaving, went to Memphis and began working for Pepper Records, cutting some sides with the label. Her sister Priscilla began working with and then married popular R&B organist-bandleader Booker T. Jones, which brought Rita into further contact with the rock scene – and engagements with such artists as Delaney and Bonnie Bramlett, Leon Russell, Eric Clapton and Joe Cocker.

Country and Western Dance-O-Rama (Decca)

Following a tour with Cocker's Mad Dogs And Englishmen in 1970, on which she was featured as a vocalist and pianist, Rita was signed to A&M as a solo artist, her first album, **Rita Coolidge**, being released in 1971. Forming a band known as The Dixie Flyers, she then began touring, playing engagements in Britain and Canada during 1971. Some time later she met Kris Kristofferson (♦), whom she married in 1973. Since that time, the duo have appeared on several tours and many TV shows, also recording two albums, **Full Moon** and **Breakaway,** together. Known as the Delta Lady (Leon Russell named the song in her honour) Rita Coolidge is considered to be one of the leading performers in country rock.

Albums:

Rita Coolidge (A&M/—)
Fall Into Spring (A&M/—)
The Lady's Not For Sale
  (A&M/A&M)
Nice Feelin' (A&M/—)
Full Moon – with Kristofferson
  (A&M/A&M)
Breakaway – with Kristofferson
  (Monument/Monument)
It's Only Love (A&M/A&M)
Anytime, Anyplace (A&M/A&M)

The Lady's Not For Sale (A&M), A 1972 album from the wife of singer-songwriter Kris Kristofersson. A fine country-rock performer, her main success has been with sophisticated M.O.R. material.

The Coon Creek Girls

Lily Mae Ledford vocals, banjo, fiddle
Daisy Lange vocals, bass
Violet Koehler vocals, guitar, mandolin
Rosie Ledford, vocals, guitar
Black Eyed Susan Ledford bass

The Coon Creek Girls were an extremely popular all girl string band of the 1930s and 1940s (although their career actually proceeded in fits and starts right up until Lily Mae Ledford's death in 1976), led by singer and multi-instrumentalist Lily Mae Ledford of Pinch-em-tight Holler, Kentucky.

Lily Mae began her career as a fiddler on the National Barn Dance (♦) in 1936, but it was John Lair (♦) who conceived of the idea of an all-girl band built around Lily Mae. It first consisted of Daisy Lange and Violet Koehler as well as younger sister Rosie Ledford, but in later years the band consisted of the three Ledford sisters only. They spent their entire career on the Renfro Valley Barn Dance (1938–1958), first over WLW and then over WHAS, and regrouped sporadically for events like the Newport Folk Festival.

Their most popular record was their theme song, **You're A Flower That Is Blooming There For Me** (Vocalion).

Albums: none.

Wilma Lee And Stoney Cooper

Born Harman, West Virginia, October 16, 1918, singer-songwriter-fiddler Dale T. 'Stoney' Cooper came from a farming family of some considerable musical ability. By the time he was 12, he'd become an accomplished musician and upon leaving school joined the Leary Family, a religious singing group, who were in need of a fiddle player. One member of the group was Wilma Lee Leary (born Valley Head, West Virginia, February 7, 1921) a singer-songwriter, guitarist and organist, whom Stoney courted and eventually married in 1939.

For several years the duo remained members of the Leary Family, appearing on radio shows and performing in churches and other venues. Then, in the mid '40s. the Coopers decided to go their own way and began playing dates on many radio stations throughout the country, in 1947 joining the WWVA Jamboree, Wheeling, West Virginia, on a regular basis.

After a ten year stay with WWVA, during which time they switched record labels from Columbia to Hickory (1955), the Coopers headed for Nashville, becoming members of the Opry in 1957. Soon after they scored hits with **Come Walk With Me, Big Midnight Special** and **There's A Big Wheel,** all three discs being top five country

Wilma Lee and Stoney Cooper. After leaving the Leary Family they formed the Blues Chasers then the Clinch Mountain Clan, recording for Rich-R-Tone in 1947.

Wilma Lee & Stoney Cooper

satisfied

Satisfied (DJM). The duo met and married while members of a religious singing group. Stoney died in 1977.

hits during 1959. Further successes followed, including **Johnny My Love** (1960), **This Old House** (1960) and **Wreck On The Highway** (1961) then, though the duo left Hickory for Decca, the hit supply seemed to dry up. However, the Coopers continued to be a tremendous onstage attraction and in the mid '70s were still rated as one of the Opry's most popular acts. Stoney Cooper's death of a heart attack on March 22, 1977 put the future of the act in doubt, although Wilma Lee and the band have been fulfilling contracted arrangements.

Albums:
Satisfied (—/DJM)
Wilma Lee and Stoney Cooper
(Rounder/—)

Wilma Lee and Stoney Cooper (Rounder).

Cowboy Copas

A victim of the 1963 plane crash that also claimed the lives of Patsy Cline (♦) and Hawkshaw Hawkins (♦), Copas' 1960 recording of

Alabam had just placed him back on top of the heap again, following his virtual disappearance from the country charts during the late '50s. Born Muskogee, Oklahoma, July 15, 1913, Lloyd 'Cowboy' Copas was brought up on a ranch, where his grandfather taught him western folklore and songs. Learning guitar at the age of 16, Copas then formed a duo with an Indian fiddler Natchee. After winning a talent contest, the twosome then played a series of dates throughout the country, Copas himself performing on 204 radio stations in North America, between 1938 and 1950. When Natchee went his own way in 1940, Copas then obtained a regular spot on a Knoxville station, eventually being featured on WLM's Boone County Jamboree and signing for King Records, for whom he made a number of hits including **Filipino Baby**, **Tragic Romance**, **Gone And Left Me Blues** and **Signed,**

Sealed And Delivered.
Becoming a featured vocalist with Pee Wee King's Golden West Cowboys (♦) on the Opry in 1946, he furthered his reputation with **Kentucky Waltz** and **Tennessee Waltz**. For a while he became a performer with an SRO reputation but after the advent of **Strange Little Girl**, a 1951 chart-climber, Copas dropped from sight. Signed to Starday in 1959, his hit recording of **Alabam** seemed set to launch him on a new career. Then came the plane disaster.

Albums: none.

Helen Cornelius

Finding fame in 1976 as Jim Ed Brown's (♦) singing partner and as a member of the Nashville On The Road TV Show, Helen Cornelius

59

has also made a considerable impression as a songwriter, her compositions being recorded by Dottsy (♦), LaCosta (♦), Liz Anderson (♦), Bonnie Guitar, Barbara Fairchild (♦) and many other artists.

Brought up on a farm in Hannibal, Missouri, she was one of an eight-strong musical family with her sisters Judy and Sharon combining with Helen to form a vocal trio, their father chauffeuring them from town to town in order to provide the threesome with opportunities to perform. As a solo act, Helen began obtaining work at various local gigs, playing some radio and TV dates, winning the Ted Mack Amateur Hour and eventually employing a backup group known as the Crossroads. At 17 she graduated from high school in Monroe City, Missouri, marrying just a year later and working for a short period as a secretary. But by 1970 she was songwriting as a profession, signing a contract with Columbia-Screen Gems and cutting some discs with Columbia Records some time later, these meeting with little response.

Signing for RCA Records in September, 1975, her first release was **We Still Love Songs In Missouri,** a well received single – but being cast as the ideal vocal foil for Jim Ed Brown proved to be the real breakthrough, the duo's version of **I Don't Want To Have To Marry You** becoming both a controversial release – many radio stations banning the disc – and a country No 1. In early 1977, **Saying Hello, Saying I Love You, Saying Goodbye** found the Cornelius-Brown partnership chart topping yet again at which point in time Helen's future in country music seemed fairly assured.

Albums:
I Don't Want To Have To Marry You – with Jim Ed Brown (RCA/RCA)

Carl Cotner

Although he spent two years with Clayton McMichen's Georgia Wildcats, Carl Cotner (born April 8, 1916 in Lake Cicott, Indiana) is best known for his more than thirty years' association with Gene Autry (♦). After two years (1935–1937) with McMichen, Cotner joined Autry as a fiddle player, soon becoming the director of his Melody Ranch band from 1939 onward. Besides fiddling, bandleading, and arranging Autry's music, he also directed many of his television shows in the early 1950s, and is still associated with Autry in his limited music business dealings.

Country Gazette

With the Flying Burrito Brothers (♦), California's most famous country rock band, now in abeyance, it was left to Country Gazette, the remains of the Burrito aggregation, to perpetuate the line. Byron Berline had originally been a

Don't Give Up Your Day Job (UA). This one came as a slight disappointment after their first album, but carries on the image of a top class non-Nashville country rock band.

championship-winning fiddle player and in-demand session man and he teamed up now with Roger Bush (string bass), Kenny Wertz (guitar, vocals) Roland White (guitar, mandolin, vocals) and Alan Munde (banjo, vocals) to bring a souped up, 1970s-style bluegrass sound to the nation.

Since bluegrass was commonplace in America their appeal there was rather limited, but in Britain and Europe they found themselves preaching to a new audience. A first British tour of clubs and colleges was hailed warmly. Gazette drew on a mixture of self-penned originals and revered standards and rounded it off with some cornpone humor in which the puckish figure of Roger Bush, with his upturned moustache, featured prominently.

They have perhaps never bettered their first album for UA, **Traitor In Our Midst,** but in spite of personnel changes they have always maintained a standard of instrumental slickness and attractive vocal harmonies and have proved to the outside world that top class country bands do not necessarily have to operate out of Nashville. On more than one occasion they have been voted Top Country Group in British award polls. Berline eventually left the band to form Sundance and was replaced for a time by Dave Ferguson. Far more popular abroad

Country Gazette 1974 Alan Munde, Byron Berline, Roger Bush and Kenny Wertz. By 1977 only Munde and newcomer Roland White were left.

than at home, the future of the band appears in doubt.

Albums:
Traitor In Our Midst *(UA/—)*
Country Gazette Live *(Antilles/Transatlantic)*
Don't Give Up Your Day Job *(UA/—)*
Sunnyside Of The Mountain *(—/Transatlantic)*
This album is known as **Out To Lunch** in the US *(Flying Fish/—)*

Country Gentlemen

One of the first progressive bluegrass groups, the Country Gentlemen played their first date on July 4, 1957.

During the group's embryonic days the personnel consisted of Charlie Waller, John Duffy, Bill Emerson and Eddy Adcock, though by the mid '70s, lead singer and flat top guitarist Waller (born Jointerville, Texas, January 19, 1935) was the only remaining member of the original lineup.

Initially from the Washington DC area, the group played two nights a week for ten years at a Georgetown niterie known as the Shamrock Club – but during the 1960s the Gentlemen gained a nationwide reputation, being featured on many networked TV shows, the group's popularity gaining ground along with the bluegrass explosion.

Eclectic in their choice of material – drawing equally from Bob Dylan, Charlie Poole (♦), Lefty Frizzell (♦) and even Hollywood film composers – the Country Gentlemen have recorded for such labels as Folkways, Rebel, Mercury, Starday and Vanguard.

Albums:
Country Songs Old And New *(Folkways/—)*
Folksongs And Bluegrass *(Folkways/—)*
On The Road *(Folkways/—)*
Going Back To The Blue Ridge Mountains *(Folkways/—)*
Bringing Mary Home *(Rebel/—)*
The Traveler *(Rebel/—)*
Play It Like It Is *(Rebel/—)*
New Look, New Sound *(Rebel/—)*
Gospel Album *(Rebel/—)*
Sound Off *(Rebel/—)*
The Award Winning Gentlemen *(Rebel/—)*
Yesterday And Today Vol 2 *(Rebel/—)*
Yesterday And Today Vol 3 *(Rebel/—)*
Live At Roanoke *(Zap/—)*
Young Fisherwoman *(Rebel/—)*
Remembrances And Forecasts *(Vanguard/—)*

Country Music Association

The CMA is a trade association formed in November, 1958 by a cadre of concerned businessmen, artists and disc jockeys to further the cause of country music. Throughout the years, the association has helped sponsor such major country music movies as *Country Music on Broadway* (1963) and *Your Cheatin' Heart* (1964), also producing its own *What's This Country Coming to?* promotional film in 1966. Other enterprises have included a series of special country albums for sale at overseas military bases, the initial establishment of the Country Music Hall of Fame (♦) in 1961 and the creation of the Country Music Foundation (♦) as a separate entity in 1964. Seminars for broadcasters, promotional TV and radio shows, promotional golfing tournaments, scholarships for country music research and the organisation of myriad exhibitions also number among the association's many achievements.

The Country Music Foundation

The Country Music Foundation is the non-profit organization which operates and administers the Country Music Hall of Fame and Museum (♦), the enormous archival holdings of the Country Music Foundation Library and Media Center located beneath the Hall of Fame, and the Country Music Foundation Press, which publishes a variety of reprints and original works on country music and the academically oriented *Journal of Country Music*.

The CMF was founded in 1964 by many of the same music business leaders who had founded the Country Music Association (♦) some years before, with the express purpose of building the Hall of Fame, the surrounding

museum, and the Library and Archives below. It sums up its goals as 'dedicated to the study and interpretation of country music's past through the display of artifacts and the collection and dissemination of data found on discs, tape, film, and in printed material'.

Country Music Hall Of Fame

The Country Music Hall of Fame is country music's major shrine, in which the greats of the past are honored for their contributions to country music. The Hall of Fame itself is actually an area located within a larger museum, housing artifacts from all eras of country music, and presenting numerous educational exhibits, slide shows, and presentations illustrating the history and development of country music.

The Country Music Hall of Fame and Museum is run by the Country Music Foundation, which houses a huge library and archive in the basement of the same building, located at 4 Music Square East, Nashville, Tennessee.

Looking suave – the Country Gentlemen, one of the first progressive bluegrass outfits.

There are currently around thirty members – one or two are elected annually – who have been so honored, both pioneer businessmen and A&R men like Art Satherley (♦), Fred Rose (♦), and George D. Hay (♦), and a long list of performers who have made country music history, including Jimmie Rodgers (♦), the Carter Family (♦), Gene Autry (♦), Bob Wills (♦), Hank Williams (♦), Bill Monroe (♦), Pee Wee King (♦), Jimmie Davis (♦), Eddy Arnold (♦), Roy Acuff (♦), Uncle Dave Macon (♦), Kitty Wells (♦), Minnie Pearl (♦), Tex Ritter (♦), and many others. There is a plaque and portrait of each of the members.

The Country Music Hall of Fame and Museum, and the parent Country Music Foundation, are non-profit organizations whose proceeds go to research and to the continued growth of the Foundation Library and Archives.

The Country Music Hall of Fame and Museum – the pilgrim's Mecca of country music.

Cousin Jody

James Clell Summey began his career as a straight musician, and was one of the fine early practitioners of the dobro. In fact, it was as a member of Roy Acuff's (♦) Smoky Mountain Boys that he recorded several of the early Acuff hits, including **Wabash Cannonball** and **The Great Speckle Bird**, and it was he as well who first joined the Opry with Acuff in 1938.

He branched out as a musician, playing electric steel (one of the first to do so on the Opry stage) with Pee Wee King's (♦) Golden West Cowboys before delving into comedy with Oral Rhodes as Odie and Jody, then joining Lonzo and Oscar (♦) for a number of years before gaining his own solo Opry spot for over a decade.

Summey was born near Sevierville, Tennessee, on December 14, 1914. Plagued by ill health in his late years, he died of cancer in 1976.

Albums: none.

A popular Opry comedian, Cousin Jody was also a very fine guitarist.

Country Rock

A trend that grew out of late '60s west coast rock – particularly around Los Angeles – and not to be confused with later, more genuine contemporary country styles.

Gram Parsons (♦) can be credited as acting as catalyst to many of the part time mandolin players and steel guitarists who were scraping a living in rock-orientated California at that time. Bob Dylan also helped encourage the trend with his **Nashville Skyline** album, giving country a further boost by recording with Johnny Cash (♦) and leaking that Hank Williams (♦) had always been one of his favorite singers.

Other country rock bands of the day included Flying Burrito Brothers (♦), Poco (♦) (whose Rusty Young has a pedal steel guitar tutor awaiting publication), the Eagles (♦), Hearts And Flowers, and Dillard and Clark.

Selected albums:
Byb Dylan **Nashville Skyline**
(Columbia/CBS)
Byrds **Sweetheart Of The Rodeo**
(Columbia/CBS)
The Flying Burrito Brothers
Gilded Palace Of Sin *(A&M/—)*
The Eagles **Desperado**
(Asylum/Asylum)
Dillard And Clark **The Fantastic Expedition of . . .** *(A&M/—)*

Earl Scruggs picks along with cowboy-hatted rocker Leon Russell.

Billy 'Crash' Craddock

Known as 'Mr Country Rock', Craddock was born in Greensboro, North Carolina. Initially part of a group called the Four Riddles along with his brother, Craddock later signed to Columbia as a solo artist, scoring heavily with a 1959 single **Don't Destroy Me.** He claims that he then quit the business because Columbia insisted on casting him in a pop role while he saw his future in C&W.

After taking many menial jobs – for a while working in a cigarette factory – he eventually signed for Ron Chancey's Chartwheel label, coming up with a whole string of rock-oriented country hits including **Ain't Nothin' Shakin', Dream Lover** and **Knock Three Times,** a revamped version of Dawn's pop hit.

Craddock is currently recording for ABC/Dot, having hits with **Easy As Pie, Walk Softly** and **You Rubbed It All Wrong** during 1976, **Broken Down In Tiny Pieces** providing a No 1 in 1977.

Albums:
Rub It In *(ABC/—)*
Two Sides Of Crash *(ABC/—)*
Great Hits Vol 1 *(ABC/—)*
Still Thinkin' 'Bout You
  (ABC/ABC)
Easy As Pie *(ABC/—)*
The Country Sound Of . . .
  (—/MFP)

The Country Sounds Of . . . (MFP). A British compilation from the country rock singer, who along with many others has suffered in the past from being forced into a pop image.

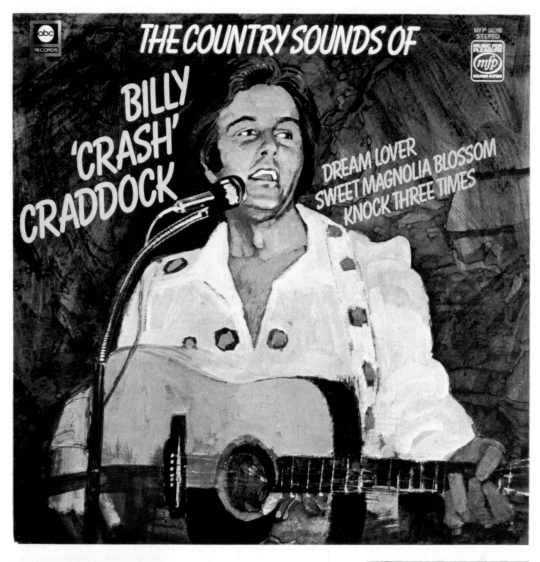

Billy 'Crash' Craddock, once formed a high school band called the Four Fiddles.

Country Piano-City Strings (RCA Victor). Nashville's most famous and distinctive pianist, who has appeared on many '50s hits, performs a selection of country music favorites.

Floyd Cramer

Pianist on a large proportion of Nashville hits during the late '50s – including Elvis Presley's (♦) **Heartbreak Hotel** – Cramer was born Shreveport, Louisiana, October 27, 1933, and grew up in Huttig, Arkansas, playing his first dates at local

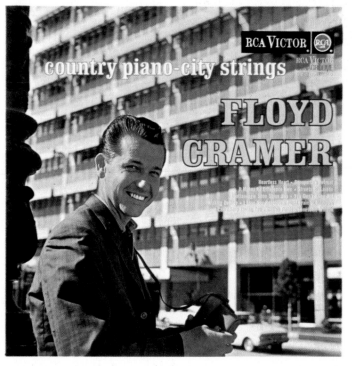

dances.

On completing high school in 1951 he returned to Shreveport where he appeared on KWKH's Louisiana Hayride (♦) show, played on sessions at the Abbott Record company and fitted in tours with Presley and other major acts.

Following various Nashville session dates, Chet Atkins (♦) advised Cramer to become a regular Music City sideman. This he did in 1955, quickly establishing himself as one of the city's most active musicians, helping to create the new Nashville Sound with his distinctive 'slipnote' piano style. He also toured and performed on many radio and TV shows including Grand Ole Opry.

Signed to RCA, his first hit record was **Flip, Flop And Bop** in 1958, following this with two self-penned million sellers, **Last Date** (1960) and **On The Rebound** (1961).

Winner of countless polls and awards, Cramer has enjoyed many other high selling discs including **San Antonio Rose** (1961), **Chattanooga Choo Choo, Hot Pepper** (1962) and **Stood Up** (1967).

In 1977 Floyd emerged with **Keyboard Kick Band,** an album on which he played no less than eight keyboard instruments including various ARP synthesizers.

Albums:
Super Hits (RCA/—)
Almost Persuaded (Camden/—)
Best Of Class Of (RCA/—)
Date (Camden/—)
Last Date (RCA/—)
Plays The Big Hits (Camden/—)
Sounds Of Sunday (RCA/—)
Country (RCA/—)
In Concert (RCA/—)
Piano Masterpieces (RCA/—)
'74 And '75 (RCA/—)
Spotlight On (Camden/—)
Young And Restless (RCA/—)
This Is Floyd (RCA/—)
Keyboard Kick Band (RCA/—)

Hugh Cross

One of country music's earliest professional entertainers was Hugh Cross, born in east Tennessee in 1904. At the age of sixteen he joined a medicine show, and by the middle 1920s was a popular singer on radio and record. A guitarist, banjoist, and songwriter **(Don't Make Me Go To Bed And I'll Be Good),** he joined the Cumberland Ridge Runners (♦) on the National Barn Dance (♦) from 1930–1933, then struck out on his own again, playing stations in the west, north west, and east, including WWVA in Wheeling.

He spent a long tenure on the WLW Boone County Jamboree, teaming there with Shug Fisher (♦) for a number of years beginning in 1938, and eventually drifted into announcing and executive capacities.

Albums: none.

Simon Crum
♦ *Ferlin Husky*

The Cumberland Ridge Runners

John Lair *leader, announcer, harmonica*
Doc Hopkins *guitar, vocals*
Linda Parker, *vocals, guitar, banjo, dulcimer*
Hugh Cross *banjo*
Slim Miller *fiddle*
Karl Davis *mandolin*
Harty Taylor *guitar*
Red Foley *bass*

The Cumberland Ridge Runners were a popular string band brought to the National Barn Dance (♦) by John Lair (♦) in 1930, and which more or less dissolved by 1935, mainly because Karl and Harty (♦), Doc Hopkins (♦), and especially Red Foley (♦) had gone on to stardom in their own right, Hugh Cross had left WLS, and Linda Parker, 'The Sunbonnet Girl', who was the real star of the act, had met an unfortunate early death.

As popular as they were for a time, their place in history is assured far more by their individual members than by the entire band itself.

Pianist Floyd Cramer, one of the original creators of the Nashville Sound.

Dick Curless

Born Fort Fairfield, Maine, March 17, 1932, Richard Curless joined a local group, Trail Blazers, soon after leaving high school. In 1948 he gained his own radio show in Ware, Massachusetts, but shortly after his marriage to wife Pauline in 1951 he was drafted into the army

Ramblin' Country (Tower Records).

and sent to Korea as a performer. There he had his own program on the Armed Forces Network and achieved great popularity using guise 'The Rice-Paddy Ranger'. Discharged in 1954, Curless returned to his home in Bangor and worked as a vocalist in a local club, but left a year later after a bout of ill health. By 1957, however, he was playing Las Vegas and Hollywood clubs, having won first place on Arthur Godfrey's TV talent show.

Then, once more, he faded from sight, first involving himself in a logging business, later playing small clubs in the Maine area. His luck changed for the better when, in 1965, he recorded **A Tombstone Every Mile** for Allagesh Records. As soon as it began chart climbing, Tower Records, a subsidiary of Capitol, bought the master and signed Curless to a contract. Following **Tombstone,** one of 1965's major country hits, Curless then proceeded to provide Tower with ten more high selling singles before moving on to the parent Capitol label in 1970, scoring once more with songs like **Hard Time Travellin' Man** and **Drag 'Em Off The Interstate Sock It To 'Em J. P. Blues.** During 1966 Curless joined Buck Owens' (♦) All-American Music Show, touring for two years, and in 1969 he recorded sountrack items for film, *Killers Three.*

Albums:
Truck Drivers' Jamboree
(Capitol/—)

Dick Curless—the Tumbleweed Kid of 1948 and Rice Paddy Ranger of Korea.

Ted Daffan

Born Beauregard County, Louisiana, September 21, 1912, singer-songwriter-guitarist Theron Eugene Daffan spent his childhood in Texas, graduating from Houston's Jeff Davis High School in 1930. During the early '30s he led the Blue Islanders, a Hawaiian band, in 1934 moving on to become steel guitarist with the Blue Ridge Playboys, a unit featuring Floyd Tillman on lead guitar. He later worked with the Bar X Cowboys, a Houston band, and after a long stay, formed a band of his own. In 1939 he wrote **Truck Drivers' Blues,** reputed to be the first ever trucking song, this being recorded for Decca by Cliff Bruner (♦), with Moon Mullican (♦) doing the vocal chores. This became such a high selling disc that Daffan and his band, The Texans, were signed to Columbia, providing that label with a 1940 hit in **Worried Mind,** which sold 350,000 copies.

The future seemed assured for Daffan but, after cutting some two dozen of his own songs for Columbia (sometimes using the songwriting nom-de-plume of Frankie Brown), World War II intervened and The Texans were forced to disband. Within two years, Daffan was recording once more, cutting **No Letter Today** and **Born To Lose,** a double sided hit that won him a gold disc for a million sale. He also formed a new band to play at the Venice Ballroom, Los Angeles, California, during the mid '40s heading back to Texas once more to organize bands in the Fort Worth and Dallas areas.

Ted Daffan, writer of the first truck-driving hit, also penned Born To Lose—virtually an anthem for the under-privileged and one of country's great songs.

Throughout the 1950s, many singers recorded Daffan's songs – including Faron Young (♦) and Hank Snow (♦), the latter becoming a partner in a Daffan music publishing enterprise in 1958.

By 1961, Daffan was once more a resident of Houston, this time as general manager of a publishing house. And that same year, yet another of his compositions ended up on a million selling disc, Joe Barry winning a gold award for his recording of Daffan's **I'm A Fool To Care,** which had been a hit nearly a decade earlier for Les Paul (♦) and Mary Ford. Other hits from the prolific Daffan pen include **Blue Steel Blues, Heading Down The Wrong Highway, I've Got Five Dollars And It's Saturday Night,** and **A Tangled Mind.**

Vernon Dalhart

A seminal figure in country music development, Vernon Dalhart (real name Marion Try Slaughter) was born Jefferson, Texas, April 6, 1883, the son of a ranch owner. While a teenager he and his mother moved to Dallas, where Dalhart obtained a job in a hardware store, later becoming a piano salesman. He also began attending Dallas Conservatory Of Music.

Next came a series of jobs in New York, during which time Dalhart sang in churches and vaudeville, auditioning for light opera. In 1912, he obtained a part in Puccini's 'Girl Of The Golden West' and later worked in other similar productions, though his first traceable recording, Edison cylinder **Can't Yo' Heah Me Callin' Caroline,** released June, 1917, featured a 'coon' song. Following this came a deluge of Dalhart recordings on various labels, the singer tackling operatic arias, popular songs, patriotic World War I ditties etc. He recorded mountain musician Henry Whitter's (♦) **The Wreck Of The Old '97** for Edison in May, 1924, then cut the same song, backed with **The Prisoner's Song,** an adaptation of a traditional folk tune, for Victor, the disc having a November 1924, release. It promptly became a massive hit, encouraging Dalhart to record more hillbilly material, though more often than not he was content to re-record his hits, **The Wreck Of The Old '97,** sung by Dalhart in various guises, appearing on more than 50 labels. Meanwhile, Victor sold over six million copies of the original version, making the disc their biggest seller of the pre-electric period.

Many of Dalhart's follow-ups, mainly written by Carson J. Robinson, (♦) dealt with the subject of disasters or news events – **The Death Of Floyd Collins, The John T. Scopes Trial** – and his records sold well until 1930. But between 1933 and 1938 Dalhart was absent from the recording studio and in 1942, following some unsuccessful 1939 sessions for Bluebird, he took a job as a night watchman with a Bridgeport, Connecticut, firm, finally becoming a night checkout clerk in a local hotel shortly before his death.

After a heart attack early in 1948, he suffered yet another and died September 14, 1948, at Bridgeport Hospital. During his lifetime Dalhart recorded under more than 100 pseudonyms, made an estimated 5,000 releases and sold around 75 million discs, most of which were country songs.

Albums:
Old-Time Songs 1925-39
(Davis Unlimited/—)

High Lonesome (Epic)

Charlie Daniels, who appeared on Dylan's Nashville Skyline and Self Portrait albums.

Charlie Daniels

Often categorized as a southern rock unit in the past, the Charlie Daniels Band has become increasingly country-oriented in recent times – which is hardly surprising in view of Daniels' history as a bluegrass player and a regular Nashville sessionman. Born Wilmington, North Carolina, 1937, the son of a lumberjack, the guitar and fiddle playing Daniels spent the years 1958–1967 (except for a short period during which he found employment in a Denver junkyard) playing with a band known as the Jaguars. He claims that the unit played every honky-tonk, dive and low-life joint from Raleigh to Texas – and it was in Texas that he met producer Bob Johnson, who headed Daniels in the direction of Nashville, where he became a sessioneer with such as Flatt and Scruggs (♦), Marty Robbins (♦), Claude King (♦) and Pete Seeger, also playing on Ringo Starr's country album and Dylan's **Nashville Skyline.** A fine songwriter – Daniels' songs have been recorded by Elvis Presley (♦), Gary Stewart (♦), Tammy Wynette (♦) etc – he began involving himself more in this area during the early '70s, and in 1971 was offered a recording contract – at which time the Charlie Daniels Band came into being.

For four years the band recorded for Kama Sutra, gaining a gold album with **Fire On The Mountain** and hit singles in **Uneasy Rider** (1973) and **The South's Gonna Do It** (1975). Then in 1976, following a year in which the CDB spent 250 days on the road, came a switch to Epic Records, the band hitting a new high with the fine **Saddle Tramp** album and the even better **High Lonesome.**

Daniels explains his work thus: 'Nashville is country but we are not Nashville. We are country – but there's a whole lot more.'

Albums:
Te John Grease And Wolfman
(Kama Sutra/Kama Sutra)
Honey In The Rock
(Kama Sutra/Kama Sutra)
Fire On The Mountain
(Epix/Kama Sutra)
Nightrider *(Epic/Kama Sutra)*
Charlie Daniels *(Capitol/—)*
Saddle Tramp *(Epic/Epic)*
High Lonesome *(Epic/Epic)*
Uneasy Rider *(Epic/—)*
The Essential Charlie Daniels
(Kuma Sutra/—)

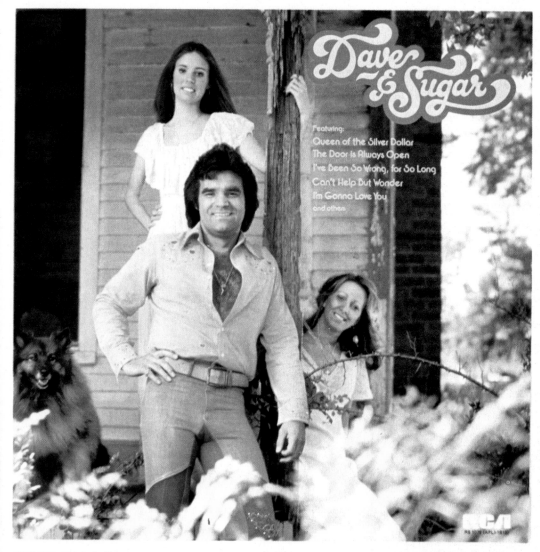

Featuring:
Queen of the Silver Dollar
The Door Is Always Open
I've Been So Wrong, for So Long
Can't Help But Wonder
I'm Gonna Love You
and others

RCA

Danny Davis

Davis, real name George Nowlan, was born Randolph, Massachusetts. He first played trumpet with high school bands during the 1930s, paying for his instrument by acting as delivery boy for a Boston fruiterer. At 17 he became a sideman with some of the best bands of the swing era, including those of Gene Krupa, Bobby Byrne, Bob Crosby, Hal McIntyre and Freddy Martin, also developing a singing style that brought him work with Vincent Lopez, Blue Barron, Sammy Kaye and others. Later he recorded under his own name, having a hit with **Trumpet Cha Cha Cha,** and in 1958 became a record producer first with Joy, then with MGM, where he helped Connie Francis on her way to six No 1 singles. During a trip to Nashville, Davis – who terms himself 'a Yankee Irishman' – met Fred Rose (♦) and Chet Atkins (♦), and became Atkins' production assistant at RCA in 1965.

He then conceived the idea of adding a brass sound to a pop-oriented country rhythm section, recording the results under the name of The Nashville Brass. The band proved a success right from the first **I Saw A Light** single, the Nashville-cum-Alpert sound of the Davis outfit appealing to such a cross section of the public that the band's first 14 albums all sold in excess of 100,000 copies, while such singles as **Wabash Cannonball** and **Columbus Stockade Blues** also made their way into the charts. By the early 1970s, Davis was living in a fabulous ranch house near Nashville, had a stake in several oil wells and a seaside

Dave And Sugar

A superior vocal group who could prove to be the Abba of the country world, Dave and Sugar is formed by Dave Rowland, a beefy, soulful singer from LA, Vicki Hackman, originally from Louisville, Kentucky, and Jackie Franc, born Sidney, Ohio.

Rowland started out as a dance band vocalist, becoming a trumpeter with the 75th Army band after being drafted, and during his tour of duty becoming the only serviceman to receive a theatrical scholarship from the Entertainment Division of the Army. Graduating from the Stamps School Of Music in Texas he became a member of the Stamps Quartet, toured with Elvis Presley (♦) and eventually became a member of the Four Guys. While still a member of the Guys he backed Charley Pride (♦) and heard that Pride required a new backup group for vocal harmony work. So Rowland held auditions and signed ex-trumpeter Jackie Frank and Vicki Hackman, who later married Pride's guitar player. Steered on course by Chardon, the company who have so astutely masterminded Pride's meteoric career, the trio obtained an immediate No 1 country single with **The Door Is Always Open** in mid 1976, following this with a second chart topper, **I'm Gonna Love You,** just a few months later. And as 1977 rolled in, a third release, **Don't Throw It All Away,** also

achieved hit status.

Albums:
Dave And Sugar (RCA/RCA)

Dave And Sugar (RCA). The first album from the vocal group who were Charley Pride's backup unit. Their first three singles all hit the charts.

Danny Davis, the self-dubbed Yankee Irishman, who lives in a huge ranch-style house and has a stake in several oil-wells.

motel and was the proud owner of a private airliner named 'Lady Barbara' after his wife. And his band had won the CMA best instrumental group award four times in a row, stopping only long enough to pick up a Grammy Award in 1970.

Albums:
You Ain't Heard Nothin' Yet
  (RCA/—)
The Best Of Danny Davis
  (RCA/—)
Caribbean Cruise *(RCA/RCA)*
Live – In Person *(RCA/—)*
Movin' On *(RCA/—)*
Travelin' *(RCA/—)*
Turn On Some Happy *(RCA/—)*
Bluegrass *(RCA/—)*
The Danny Davis Singers
  (RCA/—)
Dream Country *(RCA/—)*
Latest And Greatest *(RCA/—)*
Orange Blossom Special
  (RCA/—)
Texas *(RCA/—)*

Jimmy Davis

Elected Governor of Louisiana in both 1944 and 1960, James Houston Davis (born Quitman, Louisiana, September 11, 1902) is also an eminently successful recording artist and songwriter, his writing credits including such standards as **You Are My Sunshine, It Makes No Difference Now, Sweethearts Or Strangers** and **Nobody's Darlin' But Mine.**

Gaining a BA at Louisiana College and an MA at Louisiana State University, Davis became a professor of history at Dodd College during the late '20s. During the next decade he forwarded his musical career – recording for RCA Victor and Decca – at the same time still managing to hold down various positions of public office. A popular performer by the end of the 1930s, in 1944 he appeared in the movie *Louisiana.* When his first term of office as State Governor came to an end in 1948, Davis returned to the entertainment industry once more, concentrating much of his activity within the sphere of gospel music, winning an award as the Best Male Sacred Singer in 1957.

But politics called again in 1960 when Davis was asked to run in the primary, proving successful once more. He also won against the might of the Huey Long machine in the ensuing election, during this second stint as Governor having a hit 1962 single in **Where The Old Red River Flows.** Returning to active duty on the recording front in 1964, he immediately provided Decca with an album titled **Jimmie Davis Sings,** his other late '60s and early '70s album releases including **At The Crossing, Still I Believe, Amazing Grace** and **Christ Is Sunshine.**

In 1972, Davis was elected to the Country Music Hall Of Fame.

Albums:
Near The Cross *(MCA/—)*
Amazing Grace *(Vocalion/—)*
Christ Is Sunshine
  (Canaan/Canaan)
Greatest Hits *(MCA/—)*
Greatest Hits Vol 2 *(MCA/—)*
Highway To Heaven *(MCA/—)*
How Great Thou Art *(MCA/—)*
In My Father's House
  (Vocalion/—)

Let Me Walk With Jesus
  (MCA/—)
Memories *(MCA/—)*
No One Stands Alone
  (Vocalion/—)
Old Baptizing Creek *(MCA/—)*
Singing The Gospel *(MCA/—)*
Songs Of Consolation *(MCA/—)*
You Are My Sunshine *(MCA/—)*
Suppertime *(MCA/—)*
Sweet Hour Of Prayer *(MCA/—)*
Best Of Jimmy Davis *(MCA/—)*
Living By Faith
  (Canaan/Canaan)

Mac Davis

Born in Lubbock, Texas, Mac Davis's career has taken in rock 'n' roll, songwriting, performing and record company work.

He lived much of his early life in Atlanta, Georgia and after attending high school he worked for the Georgia State Board Of Probation. In his spare time he formed a band and toured in the south, playing mainly rock 'n' roll. Later he took up a job as a Regional Manager (in Atlanta) for Vee-Jay Records, later going to Liberty Records.

In 1968 Lou Rawls recorded one of Davis's songs, **You're Good For Me,** and Presley (♦) recorded his **In The Ghetto.** This latter was a funky departure for Presley at the time and it really brought Davis to prominence. At this time he was writing under nom-de-plumes to avoid confusion with lyricist Mack David, although he finally switched back to his own name.

He wrote some material for Elvis Presley's first television spectacular and has also written material for films. He later became a popular television performer in his own right and has made concert appearances in Las Vegas.

His hits have included crossovers in **Stop And Smell The Roses** and **Baby, Don't Get Hooked On Me,** this latter winning him a gold disc. His early pop background has given him the ability to compose commercial country material with strong melodies and this is the sort of music he currently turns out on album.

Albums:
Song Painter *(Columbia/—)*
I Believe In Music *(Columbia/—)*
Baby Don't Get Hooked On Me
  (Columbia/—)
Mac Davis *(Columbia/—)*
Stop And Smell The Roses
  (Columbia/—)
All The Love In The World
  (Columbia/CBS)
Burning Thing *(Columbia/CBS)*
Forever Lovers *(Columbia/CBS)*
Thunder In The Afternoon
  (Columbia/CBS)

Thunder In The Afternoon (Columbia)

Skeeter Davis, whose first lessons in country music came from listening to Carter Family broadcasts during her childhood.

Skeeter (RCA Victor). Her success in the pop charts during the early '60s led many to believe she had left country music behind, but she remains a member of the Opry to this day.

Skeeter Davis

Suspended by the Grand Ole Opry in December 1973 for criticizing the Nashville Police Department on a WSM broadcast – following a week in which two Opry performers had been murdered and Tom T. Hall's (♦) house burned down – it seems that Skeeter Davis' career has always been full of incident.

She began life – in Dry Ridge, Kentucky, December 30, 1931 – as Mary Frances Penick, the oldest of seven Penick children. At high school, she and her friend Betty Jack Davis (born Corbin, Kentucky, March 3, 1932) formed a harmony vocal team, the Davis Sisters, providing local performances that led to a regular program on radio station WLEX, Lexington, Kentucky. This, in turn, led to other radio shows in Detroit and Cincinnati and, eventually, to a recording contract with Fortune Records, then with RCA Victor. In 1953 their first effort, **I Forgot More Than You'll Ever Know,** became a No 1 record, claiming a chart placing for 26 weeks – and it appeared that the Davis Sisters were set for a long career. But while travelling to Cincinnati on August 2, 1953, the girls became involved in an auto accident which killed Betty Jack and critically injured Skeeter. It was some considerable time before she resumed work once more but, after a brief spell working as duo with Betty Jack's sister Georgia, Skeeter began a solo career, her first real breakthrough occurring in 1959 when her recording of **Set Him Free** established her as a chart name. A 1962 release, **The End Of The World,** proved the real clincher, the disc earning Skeeter a gold record and a worldwide reputation – and though she asked her agency not to book her into clubs where liquor was being served (Skeeter claimed that she didn't want her non-drinking fans drawn into a situation where they might be tempted to imbibe) her bookings became more and more prestigious, a date at New York's Carnegie Hall figuring among them. And her records continued to sell – **I'm Saving My Love** (1963), **Gonna Get Along Without You Now** (1964), **What Does It Take?** (1967) and **I'm A Lover – Not A Fighter** (1969) proving to be her biggest chart climbers since **World.** Along the way, she's also recorded two best selling duets with Bobby Bare (♦) – **A Dear John Letter** (1965) and **Your Husband, Your Wife** (1971) – and appeared on disc with such artists as Porter Wagoner (♦) and George Hamilton IV (♦).

Because of her pop success, plus her association with acts like Buddy Holly (♦) and the Rolling Stones, Skeeter's been often accused of betraying her country heritage. But she refuted such accusations in her sleeve notes to her **Hillybilly Singer** album, stating: 'Because of **End Of The World** and some other records getting into the pop charts, some folks thought I wasn't country anymore. But I've stayed with the Grand Ole Opry since joining in 1959 – which proves that my heart's in country!'

Albums:
Best Of Vol 2 *(RCA/RCA)*
End Of The World *(Camden/—)*
He Wakes Me With A Kiss
  (Camden/—)
Best Of Skeeter Davis *(—/RCA)*

Bring It On Home *(—/RCA)*
Love Takes A Lot Of My Time
  (—/RCA)
The Hillbilly Singer *(—/RCA)*
Tunes For Two *(—/RCA)*
Versatile Skeeter Davis *(—/RCA)*

Penny De Haven

From Winchester, Virginia (born May 17, 1948) Penny De Haven was the first female country star to entertain the armed forces in Vietnam. A frequent Opry guest, she's appeared in three films, *Valley Of Blood*, *Travelling Light* and *The Country Music Story*, and had a number of minor solo hits on the Imperial and UA labels, her highest chart placing being with **Land Mark Tavern,** a 1970 duet with Del Reeves (◆). Her albums include **Penny De Haven** *(UA).*

Eddie Dean

Born Edward Dean Glosup in Posey, Texas, July 9, 1907, Eddie began his professional career as a gospel singer with both the James D. Vaughan Quartet and with the V. O. Stamps Quartet. He and his older brother Jimmy appeared both on the WLS National Barn Dance (◆) in Chicago and on WNAX in Yankton, South Dakota, before returning to Chicago, where Jimmy appeared for a year and a half of the CBS radio soap opera 'Modern Cinderella'.

Eddie and Jimmy headed west in 1937 to try their luck in films, and both landed jobs with Gene Autry (◆), which Eddie left to join Judy Canova's (◆) radio show. He appeared in scores of films before finally landing his own series of twenty films with PRC from 1946 to 1948, in which, incidentally, Lash LaRue got his start.

Eddie's big, booming, magnificent voice somehow never seemed to find the right vehicle for a hit record, although he recorded for a great many labels, including Decca, Majestic, Mercury, Crystal, Sage and Sand, Shasta, and Capitol, his biggest records being **On The Banks Of The Sunny San Juan** *(Decca),* **No Vacancy** *(Majestic),* **One Has My Name, The Other Has My Heart** *(Crystal),* and **I Dreamed Of A Hillbilly Heaven** *(Sage and Sand)* – the last two being genuine country music classics, which he co-wrote.

Still actively performing at southern California night spots and at western film festivals, his voice is still astonishingly powerful and supple.

Albums:
Sincerely, Eddie Dean
(Shasta/—)
The Great American Singing Cowboys *(Republic/London)*

Jimmy Dean

Writer and performer of **Big Bad John,** a two million selling disc of semi-recitative nature, Jimmy Dean was born on a farm near Plainview, Texas, August 10, 1928. He began his musical career at the age of ten, first learning piano, then mastering accordion, guitar and mouth harp. While in the Air Force during the 1940s, he joined the Tennessee Haymakers, a country band comprised of service personnel, who played off-duty gigs around Washington DC, Dean continuing to play in that area after discharge in 1948.

Impresario Connie B. Gay hired

him to perform for US Forces in the Caribbean during 1952 and, following this tour, Dean and his band the Texas Wildcats began playing on radio station WARL, Arlington, Virginia, obtaining a hit record on the Four Star Label with **Bummin' Around** (1953). By '57 he had his own CES-TV network show, a program which proved popular with everyone except the sponsors, Dean gaining a CBS recording contract that same year. Initially he found hits hard to come by, but in 1961 he wrote **Big Bad John,** a somewhat dramatic tale of mineshaft heroism, and then began to supply CBS with a run of Top 20 discs that included **Dear Ivan, Cajun Queen, BT109, Little Black Book** (all 1962) and **The First Thing Every Morning,** the latter becoming a country No 1.

A star of ABC-TV during the mid

A movie still of Eddie Dean (The Golden Voice). Though now well over 70, he still turns up at film festivals.

'60s, Dean switched his record allegiance to RCA in 1966. But though this relationship began encouragingly with **Stand Beside Me,** a Top Ten item, Dean's country pop approach seemed to lose much of its appeal to record buyers as the '70s drew near – though such releases as **I'm A Swinger** (1967), **A Thing Called Love** (1968), **A Hammer And Nails** (1968) and **Slowly,** a duet with Dottie West (◆), (1971) all fared reasonably well. After this lull, he hit No 1 again in 1976 with **I.O.U.**

Albums:
Greatest Hits *(Columbia/—)*
These Hands *(RCA/—)*
I.O.U. *(GRT/—)*

Everybody's Favourite (Columbia)

Delmore Brothers

Longtime Opry favourites and writers of an enormous number of songs, including the oft-recorded **Blues Stay Away From Me,** the Delmore Brothers – Alton (born December 25, 1908) and Rabon (born December 3, 1910) – both hailed from Elkmont, Alabama. Farm raised, they were taught fiddle by their mother Aunt Mollie Delmore, in 1930 winning an old time fiddle contest in Athens, Alabama. Equally adept on guitar, the brothers soon won a contract with Columbia Records, for whom they recorded in 1931. Prior to that date, the duo had never previously faced a microphone of any kind, the Delmores' first experience of radio coming with a WSM Grand Ole Opry date during 1932. Proving extremely popular, the Delmores enjoyed a tenure of some six years on the show, leaving in 1938.

During the 1940s, came appearances on scores of radio stations, plus record dates for King, the duo's single of **Blues Stay Away From Me** becoming a top five hit in 1949 and enjoying a chart stay of no less than 23 weeks, while with King they also recorded with Grandpa Jones (♦) and Merle Travis (♦) as the Brown's Terry Four. Soon after, the Delmores became based in Houston, where Alton began drinking heavily due to the death of his daughter Sharon. And Rabon also became seriously ill with lung cancer, returning to Athens where he died on December 4, 1952.

Alton later moved to Huntsville, in which town he became a door-to-door salesman and part time guitar teacher. His death occurred on June 9, 1964, the cause being diagnosed as a hemorrhage brought about by a liver disorder.

The Delmores were posthumously honored in October, 1971, when they became elected to the Songwriters Hall Of Fame. Proficient musicians and precise harmonizers, they brought a new degree of musical professionalism to the Opry when they joined. Other hits include **Brown's Terry Blues, Freight Train Boogie, Nashville Blues, When It's Time For The Whipoorwill To Sing** and **Gonna Lay Down My Old Guitar.**

James Denny

Like Steve Sholes (♦) and J. L. Frank (♦), James R. Denny was one of the non performers whose name is now remembered by a plaque in the Country Music Hall Of Fame.

Born Buffalo Valley, Tennessee, February 28, 1911, he grew up in Nashville, where he obtained a job as a mail clerk with the National Life and Accident Company, the concern that owned WSM radio and staged the Grand Ole Opry. Gradually he climbed the ladder, working his way into the Opry organization, in 1951 gaining the post of WSM talent director. Three years later he began operating his own Cedarwood publishing company, from there breaking into the booking agency business with the Jim Denny Artist Bureau – taking with him many of the artists he had signed while with the Opry.

Although some refuse to accept John Denver as a country artist, many of his records have topped the country charts.

Eminently successful, by 1961 the Bureau was (according to *Billboard*), handling well over 3,200 personal appearances throughout the world. Winner of many showbiz honors, Denny died in Nashville on August 27, 1963 and was elected to the Country Music Hall of Fame in 1966.

John Denver

Cheerful, straw-haired product of the hippie generation, Denver is now one of the very biggest draws in showbiz.

Born John Henry Deutschendorf, in Roswell, New Mexico, December 31, 1943, he has settled in the mountain country of Aspen, Colorado, an area which he has immortalized in song, John grew up in an Air Force family and was educated in schools around the USA. His father was a pilot with three world records in military aviation and John also had flying ambitions until the music bug caught him, first via Elvis (♦) and rock 'n' roll and then through the campus folk music explosion of the '60s.

He took guitar lessons early as a boy on an old 1910 Gibson but it was during his time at Texas Tech, where he was majoring in architecture, that he felt he should try for a showbiz career, subsequently playing in west coast clubs and eventually replacing Chad Mitchell in the trio of that name. Four years later his own solo talents were sufficiently developed for RCA to sign him.

He has never been purely country although he confesses to country music having been a major influence in his career. His albums tend to contain elements of country, folk, rock and ballads. However, he has written one all-time country standard, **Country Roads,** a lyrical, uplifting song now recorded by countless artists, and he scored a pop No 1 in the US with the handclapping, bluegrass-influenced **Thank God I'm A Country Boy.** John Denver's appeal is that of clean cut, all-American boy albeit one who can appeal to two generations.

Albums:
Rhymes & Reasons (RCA/RCA)
Take Me To Tomorrow
  (RCA/RCA)
Whose Garden Was This
  (RCA/RCA)
Poems, Prayers & Promises
  (RCA/RCA)
Aerie (RCA/RCA)
Rocky Mountain High
  (RCA/RCA)
Farewell Andromeda
  (RCA/RCA)

Back Home Again (RCA/RCA)
An Evening With John Denver
  (RCA/RCA)
Windsong (RCA/RCA)
Rocky Mountain Christmas
  (RCA/RCA)
Live In London (RCA/RCA)
Spirit (RCA/RCA)
Greatest Hits (RCA/RCA)
Best Of (RCA/RCA)

Al Dexter

Leader of a country outfit known as the Texas Troopers, Dexter (real name Albert Poindexter) is best remembered for his self-penned **Pistol Packin' Mama,** a song that provided both he and Bing Crosby with million selling discs. Based on the story of Mollie Jackson (♦), whose family ran an illicit whisky still in Kentucky, the resulting disc brought Dexter a fortune in royalties and made him an overnight star – though he spent much of his later career performing at his own club in Dallas, Texas. One of the first artists to use the term

Al Dexter, who, it is claimed, went around in a shirt emblazoned with the words 'Al Dexter, Star Of Brunswick Records'.

Rocky Mountain High (RCA).
A gold album in 1972, the title track also provided a million-selling single for the ex-Chad Mitchell Trio singer and guitarist.

'honky tonk' in a song (**Honky Tonk Blues,** Dexter was born Jacksonville, Texas, on May 4, 1905. An album **Piston Packin' Mama** (*Harmony*) was released in 1962. One of country music's biggest hitmakers of the 1940s, he wrote and recorded **Too Late To Worry, Too Blue To Cry, Rosalita, Guitar Polka** and **So Long Pal,** all number one songs in that era.

DeZurich Sisters

Mary and Caroline DeZurich were a popular yodeling team on the WLS National Barn Dance (◊) for years, specializing in sky high Alpine yodels. During their long career they were also known as the Cackle Sisters. Their career lasted from the mid 1930s to the early 1950s.

Albums: none.

Little Jimmy Dickens

Provider of **May The Bird Of Paradise Fly Up Your Nose,** a monster crossover hit in 1965, the four foot, eleven inch Dickens had, at that time, already been hit-making for some 16 years.

Born Bolt, West Virginia, December 19, 1925, Dickens, the youngest of 13 children, was raised on a ranch, went to local school and later attended the University of West Virginia. At 17, he won a spot on a Beckley, West Virginia, early morning radio show, moving on to appear on WIBC Indianapolis, WLW Cincinnati, and WKNX Saginaw, Michigan, there meeting Roy Acuff (◊), who invited him to appear in a guest spot on the Grand Ole Opry. Two weeks after the date, the Opry management invited Dickens back as a regular.

Signed to Columbia Records in the late '40s, Dickens' first Top Ten disc was **Take An Old Cold Tater And Wait** (1949). This the diminutive showman followed with hits such as **Country Boy, Pennies For Papa** (1949), **A-Sleeping At The Foot Of The Bed, Hillbilly Fever** (1950), **The Violet And The Rose** (1962) and **May The Bird Of Paradise** (1965) before label hopping from Columbia to Decca, UA, Starday, Little Gem and eventually back to Columbia again, enjoying a number of minor hits along the way.

Known affectionately as 'Tater', Little Jimmy Dickens, who recently rejoined the Opry, claims to be the first country artist to circle the globe on a world tour. His TV credits are equally impressive and include dates on Hullabaloo, the Jimmy Dean Show (◊), Johnny Carson's Tonight program and Hee Haw (◊). Past albums include **Little Jimmy Dickens Sings** (*Decca*), **Little Jimmy Dickens** (*Harmony*), **Best Of Little Jimmy Dickens** (*Columbia*), **Ain't It Fun?** (*Harmony*), **Big Man In Music** (*Columbia*) and **May The Bird Of Paradise** (*Columbia*).

Little Jimmy Dickens. His recording of May The Bird Of Paradise Fly Up Your Nose was a top 20 pop hit in 1965

The yodeling DeZurich sisters brought a breath of alpine air to the country scene.

Dillards

An ethnically rated bluegrass band who score on crossover appeal to a rock audience, Rodney (born May 18, 1942) and Doug Dillard (born March 6, 1937), from Salem, Missouri, were the nucleus. They joined up with Mitch Jayne, a local radio announcer and Dean Webb (from Independence) and traveled to California where they were signed by Elektra Records – at a period before Elektra became known as a connoisseur's rock label.

The Dillards came from a strong bluegrass tradition but their novel, lighthearted approach, coupled with the fact that they themselves were a younger group, won them the plaudits of a wide public. They cut their **Back Porch Bluegrass** and **Live! Almost!** albums before meeting fiddler Byron Berline, with whom they made **Pickin' And Fiddlin',** this album being much rated and sought after by fans of old time music. Doug Dillard left to be replaced by Herb Pederson and the Dillards then pursued a more commercial, rock direction. **Wheatstraw Suite** and **Copperfields** are albums from this period and material took in Tim Hardin's **Reason To Believe** and Lennon-McCartney songs in a most pleasing manner.

Country Tracks (Elektra). A British released 'Best Of . . .' that contains no less than 24 tracks, nine of these from the band's 'Wheatstraw Suite' LP.

After recording albums for Anthem and Poppy, the Dillards began working for Flying Fish in 1977, their line up then comprising Rodney Dillard (guitar and vocals), Dean Webb (mandolin), Billy Ray Latham (banjo), Jeff Gilkinson (bass) and Paul York (drums).

Personnel changes seem to be endemic with the Dillards and more recent albums have seen a much heavier rock-influenced direction for their Anthem and Polly releases.

Albums:
Back Porch Bluegrass
 (Elektra/—)
Copperfields *(Elektra/—)*
Live! Almost! *(Elektra/—)*
Wheatstraw Suite *(Elektra/—)*
Tribute To The American Duck
 (Poppy/—)
Country Tracks – The Best Of The Dillards *(—/Elektra)*

Dirt Band
♦ *Nitty Gritty Dirt Band*

Dobro

Basically a guitar with raised strings and metal resonators designed to produce an acoustically amplified sound not dissimilar to that of the Hawaiian guitar. The name dobro, which means 'good' in Slavic, is derived from that of the DOpyera BROthers (John, Ed and Randy) of California, who originated the instrument in 1925. Principle exponents today are Josh Graves, Bashful Brother Oswald (♦), Mike Auldridge and Tut Taylor (♦).

COUNTRY TRACKS / THE BEST OF THE DILLARDS

The Dillards. Class of '73 with (left to right). Dean Webb, Rodney Dillard, Billy Ray Latham, Mitch Jaynes and Paul York.

The dobro, with which Roy Acuff achieved his notable sound, is often used by the today's country rockers.

Dottsy

A comparative newcomer to the country scene, Dottsy has been typecast as the girl you'd most like to live next to – diminutive, fresh, well scrubbed and ever smiling. She started life as Dottsy Brodt, from Seguin, Texas, her parents being of German descent. A singing prodigy, she performed at a fireman's convention while only 12 and during her teens added a long list of club appearances, conventions, talent shows and other bookings to her battle honors. By the time she was 20 she'd attracted the attention of Johnny Rodriguez's (♦) manager Happy Shahan, the result being an immediate Rodriguez-Dottsy pairing at an Austin (♦) rodeo, followed by a trip to Nashville and an RCA record deal.

Her first disc **Storms Never Last,** produced by Roy Dea – who also produced Rodriguez's initial record – was released in April, 1975, and crept into the charts, while the follow up, **I'll Be Your San Antone Rose** edged into the top 20 during January 1976, establishing Dottsy as a name to keep in mind.

Albums:
The Sweetest Thing (RCA/RCA)

Pete Drake

Session man supreme, owner of a studio and part owner of Stop Records, steel guitarist Pete Drake has played with everyone, from Jim Reeves (♦) to Bob Dylan and Ringo Starr.

Born Atlanta, Georgia, October 8, 1932, Drake didn't take up guitar until 1951, but rapidly became so proficient on the instrument that within a year he was leading his own band, The Sons Of The South. After playing on radio station WLWA, Atlanta, and WTJH, East Point, Georgia, he then worked with Wilma Lee and Stoney Cooper (♦), moving to Nashville with the duo in 1959.

Quickly becoming accepted as a sessioneer, Drake also began cutting solo discs, his 1964 **Forever** on the Smash label becoming a top 30 pop hit. Recordings bearing Drake's name have also appeared on such labels as Starday, Stop, Hillside, Cumberland and Canaan.

Albums:
Steel Away (Canaan/Canaan)

Pete Drake
Steel Away (Canaan)

Pete Drake in his studio. One of the most outstanding pedal steel men in Nashville, he is also a busy producer.

Jimmie Driftwood

Singer - guitarist - fiddler - banjoist Driftwood (real name James Morris) was born Mountain View, Arkansas, June 20, 1917, and grew up in the Ozark Mountains, where he learnt the songs and traditions of the early settlers. During high school he played at local dances, continuing his role as a part time musician and collector of folklore even after qualifying to become a teacher.

During the '50s he began performing at various festivals and concerts and in 1958 signed for RCA, producing an album titled **Newly Discovered Early American Folk Songs.** One song from the album, a revamped version of an old fiddle tune **The 8th Of January,** recorded under the title of **The Battle Of New Orleans,** became a hit single for Johnny Horton (♦) during 1959, being covered in Britain by skiffle star Lonnie Donegan. Other Driftwood songs, including **Sal's Got A Sugar Lip** and **Soldier's Joy** also came into popular use, another, **Tennessee Stud,** providing Eddie Arnold (♦) with a 20 week stay in the '59 charts. Driftwood ceased recording in 1966 but still managed to devote much of his time to the cause of folk music, helping to run the Rackensack Folklore Society and assisting with some folk festivals. His **Battle Of New Orleans** continues to be a much recorded number, Harpers Bizarre charting with the number yet again in 1968 and Buck Owens (♦) and The Nitty Gritty Dirt Band (♦) cutting versions in 1975.

Albums:
Famous Country Music Makers (—/RCA)

Above: Songs of Billy Yank and Johnny Reb (RCA). The American Civil War was a great inspiration to Jimmy Driftwood. He has also been heavily involved in American folklore since his early youth.

Roy Drusky

Born Atlanta, Georgia, June 22, 1930, Roy Frank Drusky didn't acquire an interest in country music until the late '40s, when he signed for a two year term in the Navy. While on ship, he met some C&W fans who'd organized their own band – at which point Drusky bought a guitar and taught himself to play. Upon return to civilian life, he initially tried for a degree in veterinary medicine at Emory University. Then in 1951, he formed a band, the Southern Ranch Boys, who played a daily show on a Dacatur radio station, where Drusky subsequently became a deejay. Next came a three year residency as vocalist at a local venue, during which time Drusky, a one time star athlete, made his TV debut and signed for Starday

Records.

Following a later deejay stint on KEVE, Minneapolis, he took over another residency, this time at the city's Flame Club, where he began writing more of his own songs. These he began recording for Decca, one – **Alone With You** – being covered by Faron Young (◆), providing the Shreveport singer with a hit number. However, after a move to Nashville, the Drusky hitmaking machine really went into action, first scoring with **Another** and **Anymore** in 1960, then charting five more times before switching to Mercury in 1963.

With Mercury he maintained the supply of hits right through to the early '70s, **Peel Me A Nanner** (1963), **From Now On All My Friends Are Gonna Be Strangers** (1965), **Yes, Mr Peters** (a duet with Priscilla Mitchell that went to No 1 in 1965), **The World Is Round, If The Whole World Stopped Lovin'**

(both 1966), **Where The Blue And The Lonely Go, Such A Fool** (both 1969), and **I'll Make Amends, Long, Long Texas Road** and **All The Hard Times** (all 1970) being Top Ten entries.

Drusky has appeared in two country movies – *The Golden Guitar* and *Forty Acre Feud* – enjoying a disc success with **White Lightning Express,** the title song for another.

In 1975 Drusky began having albums and singles released by Capitol, his LPs including **This Life Of Mine, Peaceful Easy** and **Country Special.** But by January 1977 not one of these was to be found in the catalog.

Albums:
New Lips *(Pickwick/—)*

Roy Drusky, one of Atlanta Tech High's star athletes, originally intended to be a veterinary surgeon.

Drusky's interest in country music started during his navy days when he and some friends formed a band.

GOOD TIMES, HARD TIMES

ROY DRUSKY

Dave Dudley

One of the several country stars who could have also made the grade in baseball, Dudley (born Spencer, Wisconsin, May 3, 1928) gained his first radio date after receiving an arm injury playing for the Gainsville Owls, Texas. While

Good Times, Hard Times (Mercury).

Dave Dudley, roadrunner and provider of trucking anthems.

recuperating, he stopped by radio station WTWT and began playing along with the deejay's choice of discs. It was then suggested that he should sing live, which he did, obtaining a positive reaction from listeners. Following stints on stations in the Idaho region during 1951–52, Dudley moved on to lead a couple of small groups, his career taking a further setback in the early '60s, when he was hit by a car while packing away his guitar after a late night gig – after which he spent several months in hospital. However, record-wise this

period proved kind to the near-rockabilly performer, hits coming on such labels as Vee, Jubilee and Golden Wing, the most important of these discs being **Six Days On The Road,** a release reputed to have commenced the whole modern truck song cycle.

In 1964 came a contract with Mercury Records and four Top Ten discs in **Last Day In The Mines** (1963), **Mad** (1964), **What We're Fighting For** and **Truck Drivin' Son-Of-A-Gun** (both 1965), Nashville local of the truckers' union providing Dudley with a

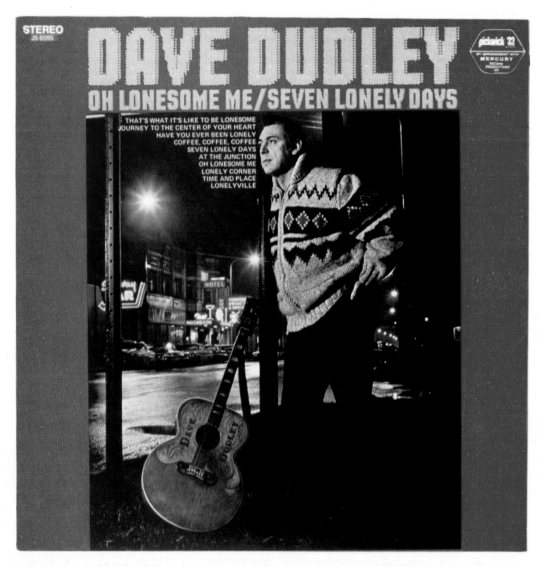

Johnny Duncan

Born on a farm near Dublin, Texas, October 5, 1938, Johnny Duncan came from a music loving family, his mother Minnie being able to both play and teach guitar. At first, Duncan thought of himself as an instrumentalist, Chet Atkins (◊), Les Paul (◊) and Merle Travis (◊) being his idols. Then during his mid teens, he realised that his singing ability was an equal asset.

After attending high school in Dublin, he went on for a stay at Texas Christian University, meeting and marrying his wife Betty during this period. Shortly after their marriage, in 1959, the Duncans moved to Clovis, New Mexico, where John joined forces with Buddy Holly (◊) producer Norman Petty, with whom he worked for the next three years. Then in 1964, following a spell as a deejay in the south west, he headed for Nashville, where he applied his talents to a number of menial jobs – including a stint at bricklaying – while waiting to break into the music industry.

After an appearance on WSM-TV Nashville, Don Law of Colombia Records signed Duncan to a contract, lining him up first with producer Frank Jones then, after 1970, with Bobby Goldsboro and Bob Montgomery. His first hit came in 1967 with the release of **Hard Luck Joe,** and since that time Duncan, who's often worked as part of the Charley Pride Roadshow (◊), has regularly slotted two or three records into the country charts every year; **Stranger,** a top five entry in July 1976, being among the most successful which he followed with the equally successful **Thinking Of A Rendezvous.**

Albums:
Sweet Country Woman
(Columbia/—)
The Best Of Johnny Duncan
(Columbia/—)

The Best of Johnny Duncan (Columbia).

Tommy Duncan

Although best known – and deservedly so – as Bob Wills' (◊) longtime lead singer, Tommy Duncan had a long and significant career of his own as well. Born January 11, 1911 in Hillsboro, Texas, he was steeped in the music of Jimmie Rodgers (◊) and loved both 'hillbilly' and the blues when he joined the Light Crust Doughboys (◊) in 1932. When their fiddler, Wills, split from the Dough-

Oh Lonesome Me/Seven Lonely Days (Pickwick). An album of Mercury recordings that capture the lonesome, between-stops side of a trucker's life.

solid gold security card in appreciation of his musical efforts on behalf of his chosen profession. With his band The Roadrunners, he's since continued on his truckstop way, accruing numerous hits – his biggest to date being **The Pool Shark,** in 1970, his most recent (and perhaps most predictable) being **Me And Old C.B.** in '76.

Albums:
Special Delivery *(UA/UA)*
Uncommonly Good *(UA/UA)*
Truck Drivin' Son Of A Gun
  (—/Philips)

Duke Of Paducah

A homespun comedian who's likely to end his routine with a rousing banjo solo, Benjamin Francis 'Whitey' Ford was born in DeSoto, Missouri, May 12, 1901.

Brought up by his grandmother in Little Rock, Arkansas, he joined the navy in 1918, learning banjo while at sea. During the '20s he toured with his own Dixieland combo, then after some time in vaudeville and a stay with Otto Gray's Oklahoma Cowboys, he became MC on Gene Autry's (◊) WLS

Chicago show, acquiring the title the Duke Of Paducah during this period. Next came an opportunity to host and script NBC's Plantation Party on WLW Cincinnati. In 1937 he, John Lair (◊) and Red (◊) and his brother Cotton Foley founded the Renfro Valley Barn Dance. In 1942 the comedian began a tour of various service installations, playing to the forces.

Following this tour, Ford gained his first date on the Grand Ole Opry, creating such an impression

that he remained a member until 1959, and has since been a constant visitor to the show. A former regular member of the Hank Williams Jnr (◊) Road Show and a performer on countless TV programs originating in Nashville, Ford – with his famous wind-up line: 'I'm goin' to the wagon, these shoes are killin' me' – still tours constantly, often providing a serious lecture – 'You Can Lead A Happy Life' – at Colleges, sales functions and various conventions.

Duke of Paducah. Although not a Paduchian, Whitey Ford has since been made honorary mayor and honorary citizen of the town.

Johnny Duncan learnt guitar from his mother. 'There'd be times when I'd come home from school and she'd stop baking to show me a chord.'

boys, Tommy Duncan joined him in the newly formed Playboys, soon known as the Texas Playboys.

Duncan's years with Wills were great for both, his mellow, bluesy, high baritone appearing on hundreds of records, **New San Antonio Rose** the biggest seller among them. He struck out on a career of his own in 1948 (taking a number of Texas Playboys with him) and although many of his Capitol re-

cordings were successful, it was nearly universal opinion that neither Wills nor Duncan were as great apart as they had been together. He spent many years touring with his new band, the Western All Stars, but it was to everyone's delight that he and Bob rejoined forces for a series of albums for Liberty in the 1960s.

Although not up to the inspired greatness of the 1930s and 1940s, these albums are tributes to the genius of two of country music's greats, and are the remaining legacy of Tommy Duncan, who died of a heart attack on July 25, 1967.

Slim Dusty

Australia's ranking country singer for some three decades has been Slim Dusty, born David Gordon Kirkpatrick in Kempsey, Australia, in June of 1927; although he prefers to call his music 'bush ballads' rather than country. A champion of the frontier ballads and music of the bush country, he has fought for their survival from the beginning of his career.

His first recording for EMI was done in 1947, and a pair of songs from his first session became the

biggest selling Australian records up to that time: **When The Rain Tumbles Down In July** and **My Faded Dream.** He rose to worldwide prominence in 1958, however, with **Pub With No Beer** and its sequel **Answer To The Pub With No Beer,** both of which were awarded with the first gold records ever presented in Australia.

Slim still tours the bush region yearly, and has become something of an elder statesman of country music in Australia and New Zealand.

Albums: none available in USA or UK.

Eagles

A West Coast country and soft rock band featuring lucid, flowing instrumental work and exquisite rough harmonies, the Eagles followed on from the Byrds (♦) and the Flying Burrito Brothers (♦) in helping bring a dash of country to acid heads and rock fans.

Founded by Randy Meisner (ex-Poco (♦) and Rick Nelson's (♦) Stone Canyon Band), Bernie Leadon (ex-Linda Ronstadt (♦), Dillard & Clark and Flying Burrito Brothers (♦)), Glenn Frey (ex-Linda Ronstadt and John David Souther) and Don Henley (ex-Shiloh), they emanated from the ethnically loose musical scene in Los Angeles but cut their first album in England under Rolling Stones' producer Glyn Johns. Later personnel changes saw guitarist and slide guitarist Don Felder boosting the lineup and, more recently, Joe Walsh joining in place of Bernie Leadon.

The Eagles scored a No 1 single in the US with the memorable **The Best Of My Love** and subsequent singles, **Lyin' Eyes** and **One Of These Nights,** notched up hit status in Britain. Their 1976 album, **Hotel California,** has also done them proud in terms of single and album sales, becoming their sixth album to achieve gold record status. The Eagles remain loosely aligned to rock but more and more country fans are 'discovering' them.

Albums:
Eagles (Asylum/Asylum)
Desperado (Asylum/Asylum)
On the Border (Asylum/Asylum)
One Of These Nights
 (Asylum/Asylum)
Hotel California
 (Asylum/Asylum)
Their Greatest Hits
 (Asylum/Asylum)

Connie Eaton

A recording artist with Chart, GRC, Stax and ABC, Connie is the daughter of Bob Eaton, a one time Opry artist best known for his 1950 hit **Second Hand Heart.** Born that same year on March 1 (in Nashville, Tennessee), Connie became hailed as 'Park concern discovery of 1964' by local paper, *The Tennessean.* Following an acting award in 1968, she met Chart Records A&R man Cliff Williamson (whom she later married) and began appearing on TV talent shows, winning $1,000 and a trophy on one major program and beating The Carpenters in the process. Stints on Arthur Godfrey, Lawrence Welk and Hee Haw (♦) shows ensued and in 1970 Connie became voted 'Most Promising Female Artist' by both *Cashbox* and *Record World* magazines, also having a fair sized record hit that year with her version of **Angel Of The Morning.** After providing several other minor hits (including two duets with Dave Peel) for Chart, Connie moved on briefly to GRC and

Stax before signing to ABC in 1974 and having her most successful release in **Lonely Men, Lonely Women,** a Top 20 single in the spring of '75. An album, **Connie Eaton,** was released later that year but has since been deleted.

The Eagles: Bernie Leadon, Don Henley, Glenn Frey, Don Felder and Randy Meisner. Leadon was later replaced by ex-James Gang guitarist Joe Walsh.

Connie Eaton, 'a traditional, conservative Lipscombe girl' – this being the Nashville college which suspended her for leaving the dorm after hours.

Rambling Jack Elliott

Born Brooklyn, New York, August 1, 1931, Rambling Jack became known as an individualistic, bohemian, folk singer; a traveling troubadour of the great outdoors and particularly the western states. Although born in New York he was widely believed to be from a rural background. He has in fact frequently wisecracked about being 'born on a 40,000 acre ranch in Brooklyn'.

At age 16 he ran away to join a rodeo, the result of a childhood fascination with western movies. He attended college in Connecticut and New York and learned to play guitar and sing cowboy songs.

He flunked out of college to live in Greenwich Village and it was there that he met Woody Guthrie (◊), a friendship that was to prove fruitful in getting him accepted as a performer. He was well received in Europe and enjoyed TV exposure and successful club bookings. In New York he also began to find popular success in Greenwich Village, particularly Gerde's Folk City – and he could be said to be a precursor of the '60s folk boom which brought Bob Dylan to fame. He played the Newport Folk Festival in 1963, and continues today to play colleges, coffee houses, and folk festivals.

Albums:
Country Style *(Prestige/—)*
Jack Elliott *(Archive Of Folk/—)*
Ramblin' *(Prestige/—)*
Talkin' Woody Guthrie
  (Delmark/Topic)
Essential Ramblin' Jack Elliott
  (Vanguard/—)
Muleskinner *(—/Topic)*

Buddy Emmons

A multi-instrumentalist of exceptional ability – he's a first class pianist, an able bass player and not a bad singer, either – Emmons is generally considered in terms of his brilliantly inventive steel guitar work.

Born Mishawaka, Indiana, January 27, 1937, he was given a six string 'lap' guitar at the age of 11 and subsequently studied at the Hawaiian Conservatory of Music, South Bend, Indiana. At 16 he appeared in Calumet City, Illinois, playing around the local clubs for most nights of the week and jamming in Chicago at weekends. By 1955 he'd moved on to Detroit where after depping for steelman Walter Haynes at a Little Jimmy Dickens (◊) gig, Emmons was awarded a permanent position with Dickens' band, which, in turn, led to dates on the Opry.

During the years that followed came lengthy stints with Ernest Tubb (◊) and Ray Price (◊), also the founding of the Sho-Bud company, he and his then partner Shot Jackson marketing the first steel guitar with push rod pedals. In 1969, Emmons left Nashville, joined Roger Miller (◊) as a bassist and became LA based, playing west coast sessions with Ray Charles, Linda Ronstadt (◊), Henry Mancini and many others between tours with Miller.

When he and the King Of The Road parted company in Decem-

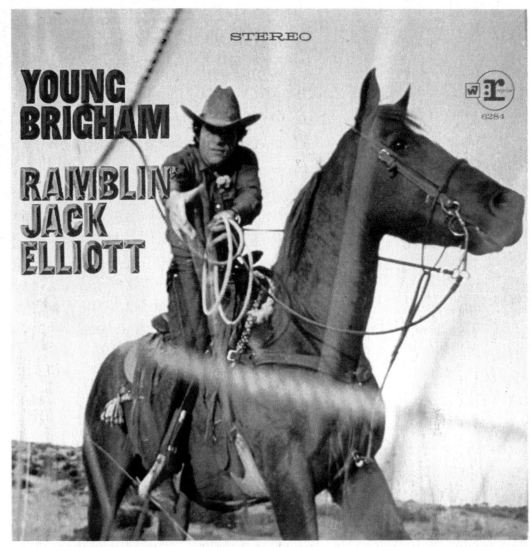

Young Brigham (Reprise). The cover shows his interest in all things Western. A cowboy singer of folky songs, his great influence was Woody Guthrie.

Buddy Emmons
Steel Guitar (Flying Fish).

ber '73, Emmons returned to Nashville once more and since that time has involved himself in an incredible amount of session work, also spending some time in promoting his own Emmons Guitar Company, his association with Sho-Bud having terminated some years ago. His **Steel Guitar** album, recorded in 1975, showcases Emmons playing in a variety of styles, paying tribute to the many 'greats' associated with that instrument.

Albums:
Sings Bob Wills *(Flying Fish/—)*

In The Sweet By And By (Word). Once dance band vocalist, Dale recorded a number of albums with husband Roy Rogers.

Steel Guitar *(Flying Fish/Sonet)*
Emmonds Guitar Inc
  (Emmons/—)
Learn To Play Pedal Steel
  Guitar *(Emmons/—)*

Dale Evans

Wife of singing cowboy superstar Roy Rogers (◊), Dale was born Frances Smith, Ulvalda, Texas, October 31, 1912.

Brought up in Texas and Arkansas, attending high school in the latter State, Dale married Thomas

The Everly Brothers during their happier days, when they toured as a team.

Fox in 1928, she and her husband parting two years later – at which time she began concentrating upon a career as a popular vocalist.

During the 1930s she became a band singer with the Anson Weeks Orchestra, then became resident vocalist on the CBS News And Rhythm Show. Following many appearances on major radio shows, including a stay on the Edgar Bergen – Charlie McCarthy Show, Dale moved into films, appearing in such productions as *Orchestra Wives* (1942), *Swing Your Partner* (1943), *Casanova In Burlesque* (1944), *Utah* (1945), *Bells Of Rosarita* (1945), *My Pal Trigger* (1946), *Apache Pass* (1947), *Slippy McGee* (1948), *Susanna Pass* (1949), *Twilight In The Sierras* (1950), *Pals*

Of The Golden West (1951) etc, many of these movies starring Roy Rogers, whom she married in 1947.

With Rogers, she's recorded a number of albums for such labels as RCA, Capitol and Word, some of these being in gospel vein, and is also the author of an armful of small books of an inspirational/religous nature.

Albums (with Roy Rogers):
Roy Rogers And Dale Evans
(Word/Word)
The Bible Tells Me So
(Capitol/—)

Everly Brothers

Mid '50s teen heart throb duo who came from a stolid country music background, made rock 'n' roll history and then returned to country.

Born Brownie, Kentucky, Don in 1937 and Phil in 1939, they were the sons of Ike and Margaret Everly, well known local country stars (and in the case of Ike, an influential guitar player). Early on the boys were joining their parents on tour and their first radio appearance with the show was on KMA, Shenendoah, Iowa.

After high school, Don and Phil branched out on their own and in 1957 they procured a record contract with Cadence. They had previously made one unsuccessful Columbia single. At Acuff-Rose music publishers they were introduced to Felice and Boudleaux Bryant (♦), the result of this liaison being their first hit, **Bye Bye Love.** The Everlys' sound was characterized by harmony singing which contrived to be velvety and whining at the same time, and which was matched with pounding, openchord guitars and songs which perfectly caught the era's mood of teenage frustration. In no time at all they were causing riots at theaters,

THE EVERLY BROS.

Pass The Chicken And Listen (RCA Victor). One of the albums which best illustrate the country music side of the Everlys.

yet they were more acceptable to adults because of their evidently modest demeanor and clean-cut looks.

Bye Bye Love was a huge international hit for them, topping pop and country charts in America and becoming the most hummed international hit that year. With rock 'n' roll losing some of its early steam the time was exactly right for this distinctive and poignant teen sound. Subsequent hits included **Wake Up Little Susie, Bird Dog, Claudette** and **All I Have To Do Is Dream,** huge sellers all of them and the last named making No 1 in the American and British pop charts.

In 1960 they left Cadence for Warner Bros, thus losing the Nashville production team (which had included Chet Atkins (♦)) and the Bryant songwriting team. However, the self-composed **Cathy's Clown** was an immediate hit for them and they followed up with **Ebony Eyes** and **Walk Right Back.** After a spell in the Marines they managed an excellent 1965 hit with **Price Of Love** but it was to be their last really big pop winner. Don had suffered from a nervous breakdown on their 1963 tour of England and gradually the brothers began to go their separate ways.

However, they now felt freer to re-explore country music, and four albums in particular – **Roots, Great Country Hits, Songs Our Daddy Taught Us** and **Pass The Chicken And Listen** – portray them in this mood. Don Everly is currently pursuing an outright solo country career.

Stories We Could Tell (—/RCA)
Don Everly solo:
Don Everly (Ode/—)
Sunset Towers (Ode/—)
Brother Jukebox (Hickory/DJM)

Phil Everly solo:
Phil's Diner (Pye/Pye)
Mystic Line (Pye/Pye)

*Golden Hits
(Warner Bros).*

*Brother Jukebox
(Hickory).*

Albums:
Greatest Hits (Barnaby/—)
Golden Hits (Warner/Warner)
Great Country Hits (Warner/—)
Very Best Of The Everly

Brothers (Warner/Warner)
Everly Brothers (—/Camden)
Everly Brothers Show
   (—/Warner)
Walk Right Back (—/Warner)

*Love's Old Song
(Columbia).*

Barbara Fairchild had two self-penned songs released on Kapp before signing for Columbia and becoming a major star.

Barbara Fairchild

A husky voiced blonde, Barbara Fairchild was born Knoble, Arkansas (population around 350) November 12, 1950. Spending her high school years in St Louis, Missouri, at 15 she'd recorded for a local station and had a regular spot on a weekly TV show. Later came the inevitable move to Nashville and a meeting with MCA staffman Jerry Crutchfield, who signed her to the company as a songwriter, Barbara's own recorded efforts appearing on Kapp.

Still working primarily as a songwriter she made some demos that came to the attention of Columbia's Billy Sherrill (♦), the result being a new recording contract and a subsequent flow of minor hits with **Love Is A Gentle Thing** (1969), **A Girl Who'll Satisfy Her Man** (1970), **(Loving You Is) Sunshine** (1971), **Love's Old Song** (1971), **Thanks For The Memories** (1972) and others, her real breakthrough coming with **Teddy Bear Song** (1973), **Kid Stuff** (1973) and **Baby Doll** (1974), all three becoming Top Five singles.

Albums:
The Fairchild Way
  (Columbia/—)
Kid Stuff *(Columbia/—)*
Love Is A Gentle Thing
  (Columbia/—)
A Sweeter Love *(Columbia/—)*
Barbara Fairchild *(Columbia/—)*
Mississippi *(Columbia/—)*
Someone Special *(Columbia/—)*
Standing In Line *(Columbia/—)*
Teddy Bear Song *(Columbia/—)*

*Love Is A Gentle Thing
(Columbia).*

*Right: On The Move
(Warner).*

Donna Fargo

Born Yvonne Vaughn, the daughter of a Mount Airey, North Carolina tobacco farmer, Donna attended High Point, North Carolina, Teacher's College and also spent some time at the University of Southern California, her musical education consisting of just four piano lessons taken at the age of ten. Nevertheless, she found herself torn between two careers, teaching, in the Corvin, California, area, and singing, which she did under a stage name, in LA clubs.

After meeting record producer Stan Silver, whom she married in 1969, Donna set out for Phoenix where she cut some sides for Ramco Records. Her initial releases flopped so Donna continued with her teaching chores, later switching her recording activities to the Challenge label, also with little success.

Taught guitar by Silver, who also encouraged her to songwrite, Donna finally won a contract with a major company in ABC-Dot, repaying their belief in her talent via a self-penned No 1 in **Happiest Girl In The Whole USA,** the CMA Single Of The Year for 1972. All possibilities of her being a one hit wonder were soon dispelled when **Funnyface,** another 1972 Fargo original, climbed the charts, to be followed by **Super Man, You Were Always There, Little Girl Gone** (all 1973), **You Can't Be A Beacon** (1974), **It Do Feel Good** (1975) and **Don't Be Angry** (1976) all Top Ten entries that benefited from the distinctive, dry-throated, Fargo vocal style. In 1977 she became part of the growing roster of Warner Bros Records country artists.

Albums:
The Happiest Girl In The Whole World *(Dot/—)*
Whatever I Say Means I Love You *(Dot/—)*
Donna Fargo *(—/MFP)*
All About A Feeling *(Dot/—)*
Miss Donna Fargo *(Dot/—)*
Best Of Donna Fargo *(Dot/ABC)*
On The Move *(Warner/Warner)*

*Above: Donna Fargo (MFP).
A British compilation.*

Charlie Feathers

An early Sun rockabilly artist, still active (in a family group) in the Memphis area. Born June 12, 1932 in Hollow Springs, Mississippi, he recorded for Flip, Sun, King, Kay, Memphis, and Holiday Inn records, and is thought of as an artistic influence who somehow never found the right rockabilly record.

Albums: none.

Narvel Felts

A native of Missouri, born 1939, Felts grew up with country, became known as a rock 'n' roller in the mid '50s and returned to country later in his career. As a boy, the first singer he remembers hearing was Ernest Tubb (♦). 'I used to wonder what his girlfriend was doing on the floor and him walking over her'.

In 1956 he won a high school talent contest by singing **Blue Suede Shoes** and in an effort to trace him and have him sing on the station, KDEX in Bernie, Missouri, put out a message for him. Narvel and his father drove the eight miles into Bernie in their pickup truck to find a telephone.

The Presley-like Narvel Felts, whose success story began with Honey Love, a rock record that sold 300,000 copies in 1959.

Performing on the station's Saturday show led to Narvel landing the bass guitar spot in Jerry Mercer's band. When Mercer left Narvel became band leader. Felts worked with both Conway Twitty (♦) (then plain Harold Jenkins) and Charlie Rich (♦) at Sun Records in 1957.

He then signed first with Mercury and then with Pink Records where **Honey Love** and **3000 Miles** made the charts. In 1970, while contracted to Hi Records, he came to Nashville hoping to find a solid country label with good distribution. Then, discussing his problems with friend and DJ Johnny Morris, they decided to evolve a new label, Cinnamon Records. In 1973, **Drift Away** (written by Mentor Williams (♦) and a pop hit for Dobie Gray) was an impressive country hit for Narvel. Later that year he scored again with **All In The Name Of Love** and in 1974 with **When Your Good Love Was Mine**.

Since joining ABC-Dot Records his three single releases have also made the country Top 20; **Reconsider Me** was a No 1 hit and was also chosen by *Billboard* as No 1 Song of the Year and *Cashbox's* No 1 Country Song of the Year for 1975. It also crossed over to the pop charts. **Funny How Time Slips Away** and **Somebody Hold Me (Until She Passes By)** have also been Top 20 country hits for Narvel. He has a strong, nasal voice, distinctive enough to handle country or rock, as his career has demonstrated.

Albums:
Reconsider Me (Dot/—)
Narvel The Marvel (Dot/—)
Doin' What I Feel (Dot/—)
Greatest Hits Vol 1 (ABC/ABC)
This Time (Hi/—)
Touch Of Felts (Dot/—)
Live (Power Pak/—)

Freddy Fender

A maverick country artist, Fender (real name Baldermar Huerta), waited 20 years for record success. Born 1937 in San Benito, a South Texas border town, Fender early in life found himself part of the migratory worker life pattern. His family worked as casual farm laborers throughout the year but made it back to the San Benito valley each Christmas. Fender remembers that music helped to make a hard life happy and that he always managed to persuade his mother to buy him a new guitar when the old one wore out.

He dropped out of high school at 16 and joined the Marines for three years but found that he preferred playing guitar in the barracks to professional soldiering. In the late '50s he was back in San Benito playing beer joints and Chicano dances. By 1958 his records, utilizing all-Spanish lyrics, were doing well in Texas and Mexico.

In 1959 he had turned to the more commercial fields of rhythm and blues and country for inspiration. To give Fender exposure, local club owner Wayne Duncan founded his own Duncan label. The nationally established Imperial

Narvel the Marvel (Dot). Yet another country singer who drifted into rock and back again; he continues to score the occasional crossover hit.

Records took an interest and Fender and Duncan leased them material. The second such release, **Wasted Days And Wasted Nights,** written by Fender and Duncan, was a big hit in 1960.

In May of 1960 Fender was busted for possession of grass, turned in by a paroled informer. Fender served three years of his five year sentence in the Angola State Penitentiary, Louisiana, cutting several titles for the Goldband and Power-pack labels while inside. The Governor of Louisiana, Jimmie Davis (♦), himself something of a country singer, helped secure Fender's release but a condition of his parole was that he should leave the entertainment business.

Fender managed to pick up his career again though, foregoing record hits but gigging steadily. He also worked as a mechanic and even went to college for two years. In 1974 though he was introduced to noted Louisiana R&B producer Huey Meaux, and Meaux set about putting Fender's distinctive voice in a country setting. In Houston, Texas, they put down many tracks, among them a re-recording of **Wasted Days And Wasted Nights.**

Fender has always leaned towards R&B and rock 'n' roll styling in his live performances but Meaux's producing talents pioneered a new country sound on record; a lispy, hurting voice with simple but tight backing arrangements and the almost claustrophobic 'presence' that was Meaux's production trademark.

Some albums were put out on Meaux's Crazy Cajun label while later albums were either leased to ABC-Dot with its acknowledged country music expertize or, as currently, released under direct contract to ABC. **Before The Next Teardrop Falls,** as a single and as an album title, was Fender's breakthrough and he now features regularly in the country charts, having the ability to give a distinctive styling to even the most mundane lyric.

Albums:
Before The Next Teardrop Falls
  (Dot/ABC)
Are You Ready For Freddy?
  (Dot/ABC)
If You're Ever In Texas
  (Dot/ABC)
Rock 'n' Country *(Dot/ABC)*
Since I Met You Baby *(GRT/—)*
Inside Louisiana State Prison
  (Power Pak/—)

Shug Fisher

Born George Clinton Fisher in Grady County, Oklahoma, on September 26, 1907, Shug got his nickname – an abbreviation of Sugar – from his mother, who 'gave it to me 'cause I was such a sweet baby'. His family moved to California in 1925, and after apprenticing as a square dance fiddler he was one of the first country musicians to adapt the string bass to the music, first with the Hollywood Hillbillies and later with the Beverly Hillbillies (♦).

Shug later teamed with Hugh Cross (♦) for several years (1935–1940) in Wheeling and Cincinnati, but came to prominence upon joining the Sons of the Pioneers (♦) as a bass player and comedian, with whom he was to spend several stints (1943–1945, 1949–1952, and 1955–1959), although in the intervening years he was to perform on his own and with Stuart Hamblen's (♦) Lucky Stars, as well as recording a host of Capitol Transcriptions and appearing in many minor film roles.

Continuing a career as an actor-comedian-musician, Shug has appeared on the Ozark Jubilee on 'Gunsmoke', and as Shorty Kellums on 19 episodes of 'The Beverly Hillbillies'. His biggest record was **Ridin' Down To Santa Fe,** on Capitol.

Albums: none.

Rock 'n' Country (Dot). As the title suggests, Fender has strong leanings towards rock music; on record, however, he has produced a new style of country.

Busted for marijuana possession in Baton Rouge during 1960, Freddy Fender spent three years working in a New Orleans bar, where his parole officer made frequent checks and kept an eye on his behavior.

Flatt & Scruggs

Flatt and Scruggs And The Foggy Mountain Boys – (left to right) Paul Warren, Earl Scruggs, Curly Secker and Lester Flatt, an 'in action' Opry shot taken during the mid '50s.

Lester Raymond Flatt, born June 19, 1914, in Overton County, Tennessee, and Earl Eugene Scruggs, born January 6, 1924, in Cleveland County, North Carolina, pioneered a particular type of bluegrass under Bill Monroe's (♦) leadership – especially Scruggs' 'three finger banjo' technique and thus helped popularize bluegrass immensely.

Both came from highly musical families. Both of Lester's parents played the banjo (in the old 'frailing' style) and Lester practiced on both guitar and banjo. He also sang in the church choir. Earl came from an area east of the Appalachians which was already using a three finger style on the five string banjo. The style was not new anyway (although the strict universal style then involved either two finger picking or simply brushing or frailing the strings). A three finger style had been used by Uncle Dave Macon (♦) and Charlie Poole (♦), and Earl himself had heard such banjoists as Snuffy Jenkins locally. But then Scruggs evolved a newer style, syncopated and rhythmic, blending in his three finger banjo eventually to make the bluegrass style sound fresh and alive, and often fast as an express train.

Lester became a textile worker but still listened to a lot of 'hillbilly' music, while also continuing to play instruments. His wife could also play guitar and sing. He was particularly a fan of Bill and Charlie Monroe (♦) who were heard a lot on Carolina radio stations in the years before World War Two. Lester was living in Covington, Virginia, and he got together with some old friends from Tennessee to play. By 1939 they had become pretty proficient and were to be heard on Radio WDBJ, Roanoke, as the Harmonizers. Then followed a period in which Lester played with the Happy-Go-Lucky Boys, one of whose members was Clyde Moody (♦) who had played and recorded with Bill Monroe. In 1943 Lester and his wife Gladys were hired by Charlie Monroe. Lester sang tenor harmony and played mandolin. He tired of the traveling and quit, trying his hand at trucking and then procuring a position with a North Carolina radio station. It was there that he received a telegram from Bill Monroe asking him to come and play with Bill on the Grand Ole Opry.

Earl had played in public with his brothers from the age of six and by 15 he was playing on a North Carolina radio station with the Carolina Wildcats. At this time (1939) he also played with the Morris Brothers (♦) on Radio WSPA, Spartanburg, South Carolina. He also became a textile worker (during the war years) but the end of the war saw him playing with 'Lost' John Miller in Knoxville. Shortly after he began to be heard widely when Miller started broadcasting on Radio WSM from Nashville. Miller then stopped touring and Earl, out of work, was hired by Bill Monroe.

At this time Monroe was known mainly around the south east but the Opry was becoming more and more popular, and Bill's show (which had featured artists and was a 'show' in the genuine sense) rapidly gained a broader appeal. Monroe switched musical duties around and Lester Flatt's high tenor voice easily adapted to singing lead when necessary. Less easy was the pace Lester was required to keep on guitar. He shortcut his guitar part sometimes by developing a characteristic run with which to catch up and finish the lines. This became known as the 'Lester Flatt G Run' since it was usually played in that chord position. Lester had also become compere and link man to the Monroe package.

Scruggs was given full rein by Monroe to develop his fluid banjo technique and helped popularize songs such as **Blue Grass Breakdown,** numbers which would remain associated with him after his departure from Monroe. Monroe even put the names of Flatt and Scruggs on some of his records. This precision and teamwork which characterized Monroe's sound was attracting many new listeners to the music and, by association, to the Opry itself.

In 1948, within weeks of each other, Earl and Lester resigned from Monroe to escape the constant traveling (Monroe has always been a dedicated touring man). Almost inevitably the two then decided to team up and do some radio work. They recruited ex Monroe men Jim Shumate, on fiddle, and Howard Watts (stage name Cedric Rainwater), on bass, and then moved to Hickory, North Carolina, where they were joined by Mac Wiseman (♦). That year, 1948, they made their first recordings for Mercury Records.

The band took its name from an old Carter Family (♦) tune, 'Foggy Mountain Top' calling themselves the Foggy Mountain Boys. Wiseman left and was replaced by mandolin player Curly Seckler. Many of the fiddle players they used had previously worked with Bill Monroe. Earl's banjo was now more to the fore and the mandolin was used less. Both Lester and Earl were prone to using guitars, Earl developing a more aggressive, Merle Travis-influenced (♦) sound on lead. The only mellower thing was Lester's vocal. In most other respects they promoted a harder, more driving music than that of Monroe.

In 1948 they moved to Bristol on the Tennessee-Virginia border and while broadcasting on radio WCYB there met the Stanley Brothers (♦) and Don Reno, both of whom developed this new sound into what we now know as 'bluegrass' and 'Scruggs-style banjo'. They broadcast for many radio stations in the south east and also booked their own out-door concerts, complete package shows that also featured local performers and at which the artists sold records and souvenirs.

In 1949 they recorded **Foggy Mountain Breakdown** and it was released the following year. It has remained one of their most consistently popular numbers, being included in the film *Bonnie And Clyde* as background to the famous car chase. In 1950 they were offered a lucrative contract by Columbia Records. However, before moving, they fulfilled some contractual obligations to Mercury by recording a series of older folk numbers and giving them the new, bluegrass treatment. Songs such as **Roll In My Sweet Baby's Arms** and **Old Salty Dog Blues** were heard in a new setting, one which many people now associate with them.

Earl also introduced the 'Scruggs peg', a device which allowed him to change easily the tuning on his banjo strings for the number **Earl's Breakdown** (1951). That year a boost was given to their career when they appeared on a show headlined by the then fashionable Ernest Tubb (♦) and Lefty Frizzell (♦). In 1953 the band began broadcasting 'Martha White Biscuit Time' on Nashville's WSM Radio, a show which not only ran for years but which saw them coming well and truly into country music prominence. 1955 consolidated their position with an equivalent syndicated TV show and at this time they also became Grand Ole Opry members. They were traveling more than they had ever done with Bill Monroe and they were also winning magazine fan polls and industry awards. The '60s folk revival also helped them, since by this time 'Scruggs picking' was already in instrument tutor terminology, Folkways released an album, compiled by Mike Seeger, titled **American Banjo Scruggs Style** and both Mercury and Columbia released similar albums with the artist himself featured.

Further recognition came in the shape of the CBS-TV series 'The Beverly Hillbillies'. The theme tune, played by Lester and Earl, **The Ballad Of Jed Clampett** was No 1 on the country charts for three months from December 1962. They became a household name and a symbol of this exciting, syncopated musical style. During the '60s they consolidated their position and sold a vast amount of records. Towards the end (mainly pushed by Earl) they began experimenting with new folk songs, with drums and with gospel style harmonies. Some of their older fans were unhappy about these changes and in 1969 they split up, Lester returning to more traditional sounds and making reunion albums with his old buddy Mac Wiseman. Lester formed the Nashville Grass, composed mainly of the Foggy Mountain Boys, but Earl went off defiantly in new directions with his Earl Scruggs Revue, utilizing his own sons and later dobro player Josh Graves into a unit which could also appeal to young, rock audiences. Earl also played a big part in getting together the old stars for the 1971 Nitty Gritty Dirt Band (♦) album **Will The Circle Be Unbroken.**

Both artists are still immensely popular in their respective fields.

Albums:
A Boy Named Sue *(Columbia/—)*
Carnegie Hall *(Columbia/—)*
Changin' Times *(Columbia/—)*
Fabulous Sounds Of
  (Columbia/—)
Foggy Mountain Breakdown
  (Hillside/—)
Greatest Hits *(Columbia/—)*
Hard Travlin' *(Columbia/—)*
Lester Flatt And Earl Scruggs
  (Archive Of Folk/—)
Blue Grass Banjos *(Hillside/—)*
Bushel Of Five String Banjos
  (Hillside/—)
Story Of Bonnie And Clyde
  (Hillside/—)
20 All Time *(Columbia/—)*
When The Saints *(Columbia/—)*
  World Of . . . *(Columbia/—)*
Flatt And Scruggs *(JS/—)*

Earl Scruggs Albums:
Nashville's Rock *(Columbia/—)*
Duelling Banjos *(Columbia/—)*
Kansas State *(Columbia/—)*

I Saw The Light *(Columbia/—)*
Earl Scruggs Revue
  (Columbia/CBS)
Scruggs Revue Vol 2
  (Columbia/—)
Rockin' Cross *(Columbia/—)*
Family Portrait *(Columbia/—)*
Live From Austin City Limits
  (Columbia/—)

Lester Flatt Albums:
Rollin' *(Power Pak/—)*
Before You Go *(RCA/—)*
Foggy Mountain Breakdown
  (RCA/RCA)
Over The Hills To The
  Poorhouse – with Mac Wiseman
  (RCA/—)
Best Of . . . *(RCA/RCA)*
Flatt Gospel *(Canaan/—)*
Lester Raymond Flatt
  (Flying Fish/—)
Live Bluegrass Festival – with
  Bill Monroe *(RCA/—)*
Living Legend *(CMH/—)*
The One And Only *(Nugget/—)*

Flatt And Scruggs With The Foggy Mountain Boys (JS). A fine album by the bluegrass pioneers who decided to work together after leaving Bill Monroe's band.

Flying Burrito Brothers

Formed in 1968 by ex Byrds Gram Parsons (♦) and Chris Hillman to bring country music to the rock fans of California. A&M Records felt that the charismatic Parsons might help generate some big sales with this new concept and they subsequently put much promotional money behind the first album, **Gilded Palace Of Sin.** Bizarre photo sessions in the desert resulted in an album sleeve depicting the Burritos in extravagant Nudie suits. The marijuana leaves embroidered on the suits emphasised a new approach. **Gilded Palace** featured some of Parsons'

Airborne (Columbia). One of the most popular country-rock bands, they were formed by Gram Parsons in 1968 and since then have gone through several lineup changes.

Far left: Dueling Banjos (Columbia).

Left: Anniversary Special (Columbia).

Red Foley – At the Opry during the early '50s. The bass player is Ernie Newton. For years, Foley closed his radio and TV shows with the words: 'Goodnight, mama, goodnight, papa'.

best-ever songs and beefed up his sensitive but none too strong voice with a rock production and Chris Hillman prominent on vocals. The line-up for this album was: Parsons (guitar, vocals), Chris Hillman (guitar, mandolin, vocals), Chris Ethridge (bass), Sneeky Pete Kleinow (pedal steel guitar) and Jon Corneal (drums). There was little country styled music being played in LA then, and this band was a real opportunity for pickers such as Sneeky Pete to make it on a national level.

In 1969 Corneal and Ethridge dropped out and Bernie Leadon (guitar, vocals) and Mike Clarke (drums) joined, Hillman switching to bass. The next two albums, **Burrito De Luxe** and **The Flying Burrito Brothers** were straighter productions but still with a good dash of country included. Parsons left between the two albums (in 1970) and in 1971 Bernie Leadon quit also, feeling that he was not being fully stretched. He formed The Eagles (♦). Sneeky Pete left also to undertake production and session work.

1971 saw a vastly expanded lineup in which Byron Berline, a top fiddle player who had recorded with The Rolling Stones, Al Perkins (pedal steel guitar), Kenny Wertz (guitar, banjo, vocals) and Roger Bush (string bass) all joined. This lineup saw the release of a good live album, **Last Of The Red Hot Burritos,** which featured much in the way of favorite material.

The addition of Alan Munde (banjo) in 1971, completed a floating aggregation which rejoiced under the title Hot Burrito Revue. The band was already perpetuating a legend on the strength of Parsons and the whole LA country rock syndrome and had built up quite a following in Holland particularly. Those bluegrass-oriented members of this loose set up who finally decided to stay became known as Country Gazette (♦). However, the Burritos were to re-form again in 1974. With a lineup of Sneeky Pete, Gib Guilbeau (a Cajun fiddle player), Gene Parsons (drums), Chris Ethridge and a new singer Joel Scott-Hill they toured American and Europe, cutting albums for CBS.

Albums:
Burrito De Luxe *(A&M/—)*
Gilded Palace Of Sin *(A&M/—)*
Last Of The Red Hot Burritos
  (A&M/—)
Flying Burrito Brothers
  (A&M/A&M)
Close Up The Honky Tonks
  (A&M/A&M)
Flying Again *(Columbia/CBS)*
Airborne *(Columbia/CBS)*
Sleepless Nights – with Gram
  Parsons *(A&M/A&M)*

Red Foley

Elected to the CMA Hall Of Fame in 1967, Clyde Julian 'Red' Foley was born Bluelick, Kentucky, June 17, 1910.

A star athlete at high school and college, at the age of 17 he won the Atwater-Kent talent contest in Louisville, in 1930 moving to Chicago to become a member of John Lair's (♦) Cumberland Ridge Runners (♦) on the WLS National Barn Dance Show (♦). Seven years later he helped to originate the Renfro Valley Show with Lair, by 1939 appearing on Avalon Time, a program in which he co-starred with Red Skelton, thus becoming the first country star to have a network radio show.

His Decca records soon proved eminently popular, Foley's versions of **Tennessee Saturday Night, Candy Kisses, Tennessee Polka,** and **Sunday Down In Tennessee** all becoming Top Ten discs during 1949. In 1950 sales escalated even further, no less than three Foley titles – **Chatternoogie Shoe Shine Boy** and the spirituals **Steal Away** and **Just A Closer Walk With Thee** – becoming million sellers. The following year, his success with religious material continued, Foley's recording of Thomas A. Dorsey's **Peace In The Valley** selling well enough to become an eventual gold disc winner. Meanwhile, his more commercial songs also accrued huge sales, **Birmingham Bounce** becoming a 1950 No 1, and **Mississippi** (1950), **Cincinatti Dancing Pig** (1950), **Hot Rod Race** (1951), **Alabama Jubilee** (1951), **Midnight** (1952), **Don't Let The Stars Get In Your Eyes** (1953), **Hot Toddy** (1953), **Shake A Hand** (1953), **Jilted** (1954), **Hearts Of Stone** (1954) and **A Satisfied Mind** – with Betty Foley (1955) all providing him with Top Ten placings.

An Opry star during the '40s, in 1954 he moved to Springfield, Missouri, where he hosted the Ozark Jubilee – one of the first successful country TV series. During the early '60s, Foley co-starred with Fess Parker on an ABC-TV series 'Mr Smith Goes To Washington' and he continued appearing on radio and TV and making many personal appearances right up to the time of his death on September 19, 1968, in Fort Wayne, Indiana.

Albums:
Beyond The Sunset *(MCA/—)*
Church In The Wildwood
  (Pickwick/—)
I Believe *(Vocalion/—)*
I'm Bound For The Kingdom
  (Vocalion/—)
Memories *(Vocalion/—)*
Red Foley *(Vocalion/—)*
Songs Of Devotion *(MCA/—)*
Red Foley Story *(MCA/—)*

Dick Foran

Although Herbert J. Yates and Nat Levine are generally given credit for creating the singing cowboy genre and casting young Gene Autry (♦) in what was to become one of the most popular film genres

of all time, it appears that Warner Brothers had come up with pretty much the same idea at the same time, for not long after the release of Autry's first major film in 1934 came a Warner Brothers western starring Dick Foran as a singing cowboy.

Possessed of a fine voice – which

The Red Foley Story (Decca). Another country performer who has had great success with religious material. This album contains many of his best-remembered songs.

sounded more at home on the Broadway stage than on the range – Foran was born June 18, 1910 in New Jersey, the son of a US Senator. Educated at Princeton, he aspired to a career on the stage and later on film, but despite his singing cowboy westerns for Warners and Universal, he aspired to, and was quite successful in, roles in high budget westerns and in numerous other non-westerns.

He is currently retired and living in southern California.

Albums: none.

Tennessee Ernie Ford

The singer who recorded **Sixteen Tons**, a mining song which sold over four million copies during the mid '50s, Ernie Jennings Ford was born Bristol, Tennessee, February 13, 1919. At school he sang in the choir and played trombone in the school band – but he also spent much time at the local radio station, WOAI, where in 1937 he began working as an announcer. Four years later, following a period of study at the Cincinnati Conservatory of Music and further announcing stints with various radio stations, Ford enlisted in the Air Force, becoming first a bombadier on heavy bombers, then an instructor. After discharge, he returned to announcing, working on C&W station KXLA, Pasadena, where he met Cliffie Stone (♦) and appeared as a singer with Stone's quartet on the 'Hometown Jamboree' show.

In 1948, Ford signed with Capitol Records, for whom his warm bass voice provided immediate hits in **Mule Train** and **Smokey Mountain Boogie** (1949), subsequently scoring with **Anticipation Blues** (1949), **I'll Never Be Free** (with Kay Starr – 1950), **The Cry Of The Wild Goose** (1950) and **Shotgun Boogie,** a Ford original that became a 1950 million seller. His own radio shows over the CBS and ABC networks gained Ford further popularity, then in 1955, following another handful of hits, he recorded **Sixteen Tons,** a superb Merle Travis (♦) song that came decked out in a fine Jack Marshall arrangement. This quickly became a massive hit, winning Ford his own NBC-TV show – a series which the singer hosted until 1961, when he took a break to spend more time with his family in California.

Since the early '60s, Ford has tended to cut down on his work, though he has appeared before capacity audiences, appeared on many TV shows and enjoyed some chart success with **Hicktown** (1965), **Honey-Eyed Girl** (1969) and **Happy Songs Of Love** (1971). During his career he has also recorded many religious albums, the biggest seller being **Hymns,** which won him a platinum plated master in November, 1963.

Albums:
Christmas Special *(Capitol/—)*
Amazing Grace *(Pickwick/—)*
Best Hymns *(Capitol/—)*
Favourite Hymns *(Capitol/—)*
Hymns *(Capitol/—)*
Hymns *(Pickwick/—)*
I Love To Tell The Story
(Capitol/—)
Jesus Loves Me *(Pickwick/—)*
Make A Joyful Noise
(Capitol/—)
Nearer The Cross *(Capitol/—)*
Need For Prayer *(Pickwick/—)*
Rock Of Ages *(Pickwick/—)*
Sweet Hour Of Prayer/Let Me
Walk With Thee *(Capitol/—)*
Tennessee Ernie Ford
(Everest/—)
America The Beautiful
(Capitol/—)
Civil War Songs Of The North
(Capitol/—)
Civil War Songs Of The South
(Capitol/—)
Country Hits Feelin' Blue
(Capitol/—)
Faith Of Our Fathers
(Capitol/—)
For The 83rd Time *(Capitol/—)*
Great Gospel Songs *(Capitol/—)*
Precious Memories *(Capitol/—)*
Sings His Great Love *(Capitol/—)*
25th Anniversary/Hymns
(Capitol/—)
Story Of Christmas *(Capitol/—)*
The Star Carol *(Capitol/—)*
The Very Best Of Tennessee
Ernie Ford *(—/Capitol)*
Ernie Sings And Glen Picks –
with Glen Campbell
(Capitol/—)

Tennessee Ernie Ford – He's had his greatest success with gospel material, many of his religious albums remaining on catalog long after his country discs have been deleted.

Wally Fowler

Cheerful, gladhanding Wally Fowler was born in February, 1917, in Bartow County, Georgia. He first achieved success as a singer and songwriter, leading an Opry band called the Georgia Clodhoppers, and writing such hits of the late 1940s as **I'm Sending You Red Roses** and **That's How Much I Love You, Baby.**

His interest turned to gospel music a little later on, and he was a member of the John Daniel Quartet before forming and leading the Oak Ridge Quartet, forerunner of the Oak Ridge Boys (♦). In later years he turned his hand to gospel promoting, sponsoring the first all night sing (in Nashville in 1948) among numerous other promotions. In his prime he recorded for both Decca and King.

Albums: none.

Curly Fox And Texas Ruby

Curly Fox, the fiddling son of a fiddler, was born Arnim LeRoy Fox in Graysville, Tennessee, on November 9, 1910. He joined a medicine show at the age of 13, and recorded as early as 1929, with the Roane County Ramblers. He also played with the Carolina Tarheels and headed his own band, the Tennessee Firecrackers, over WSB in Atlanta in 1932.

Texas Ruby was Tex Owens (♦) sister, born June 4, 1910 in Wise County, Texas, who had come to the Grand Ole Opry as early as 1934 with Zeke Clements (♦) and his Bronco Busters. She and Clements worked a bit on WHO in Des Moines, before she and Curly Fox teamed up on WSM in 1937. Not long after they became one of the most popular acts on the Opry and in country music, with their winning combination of Ruby's deep strong, sultry voice, and Curly's masterful trick fiddling. They were married in 1939.

Their biggest years were on the Grand Ole Opry in the 1940s, where they were stars of the Purina portion, and recorded for Columbia (1945–1946) and King (1947). In 1948 they journeyed to New York and then Houston, where they were to spend seven years over KPRC-TV before returning to the Grand Ole Opry. They recorded an album for Starday during this second Nashville period, just prior to Texas Ruby's death in March of 1963, when a fire raged through their house trailer. Curly went into virtual retirement afterwards, living in rural Illinois; in recent years, however, he has begun to appear at occasional bluegrass festivals and other gatherings.

Albums: none.

J. L. Frank

Elected to the Country Music Hall of Fame in October, 1967, Joe L. Frank was one of the great promoters of country music.

Born Rossal, Alabama, April 15, 1900, he moved to Chicago during the 1920s, there taking an interest in artist management and producing a country music show on radio station WLS. Later he moved his center of operations to Louisville, then, in 1939, to Nashville, which he realized was fast becoming the C&W capital.

Father in law of Pee Wee King (♦), Frank was instrumental in the success of Gene Autry (♦), Roy Acuff (♦) Ernest Tubb (♦) and many other artists. Known as the 'Flo Ziegfeld of Country Music', he died while promoting a show in Detroit on May 4, 1952.

Dallas Frazier

Respected singer-songwriter who is capable of penning country songs that 'cross over' without losing too much individuality in the process (although it must be said that one big success in this area, **Alley Oop,** molded into a novelty hit by Kim Fowley for the Hollywood Argyles, was pure gimmickry).

Born Spiro, Oklahoma, 1939, Frazier was a featured stage performer before he reached his teens and a best selling songwriter by 21. Early on, his family moved to the up and coming country center of Bakersfield (♦), California. In a talent contest sponsored by Ferlin Husky (♦) he won first prize and Husky offered him a place on his show.

He was signed by Capitol Records and moved to Nashville to pitch his songs. There, he starred on radio and TV. Ferlin Husky had one of his most famous hits with Frazier's **Timber, I'm Falling** and there were other crossovers with **There Goes My Everything** (Engelbert Humperdinck) and **Son Of Hickory Holler's Tramp** (O. C. Smith). But he could also pen a convincing dues-paying country song as he showed with **California Cotton Fields,** a title recorded by Merle Haggard (♦). Frazier has been helped in his writing career by having a stronger voice than many composers and this has enabled him to succeed as performer also. His albums have included **My Baby Packed Up My Mind And Left Me** and **Singin' My Song** (RCA).

Kinky Friedman

Leader of outlandish country rock band the Texas Jewboys, Richard Friedman was born Rio Duckworth, Texas, October 31, 1944, the son of a University of Texas professor.

Brought up on a ranch, he later attended the University in nearby Austin (♦), in which town he formed his first band, King Arthur And The Carrots. Then came some time spent in Borneo where, as a member of the Peace Corps, Friedman was employed as an agricultural extension worker, supposedly distributing seeds to many areas, though he claims that no such seeds materialized during his stay. He does claim, however, to be 'the man who brought Frisbees to Borneo'.

In 1971 he headed for LA with his band the Texas Jewboys, establishing a reputation as the Frank Zappa of country music, in 1973 cutting an album, **Sold American,**

My Baby Packed Up My Mind And Left Me (RCA Victor). Writer of several giant crossover hits, Frazier's strong voice has led to success as a performer. None of his albums are currently available.

Kinky Friedman claims that the only people who make it big in country pop are those who round off the edges, like John Denver and Mac Davis. But he likes to make the edges sharper.

LASSO FROM EL PASO

KINKY FRIEDMAN

—CHOICE MATERIAL—

Lefty Frizzell

Acquiring the nickname 'Lefty' after disposing of several opponents with his left hand during an unsuccessful attempt to become a Golden Gloves boxing champion, the Texas born (Corsicana, March 31, 1928) singer-songwriter-guitarist began life as William Orville Frizzell, the son of an itinerant oil driller. A childhood performer, at 17 he could be found playing the honky tonks and dives of Dallas and Waco molding his early, Jimmie Rodgers (♦) stylings to the requirements of his environment, thus formulating a sound that was very much his own.

In 1950, Frizzell's Columbia recording of **If You've Got The Money, I've Got The Time** became a massive hit, claiming a chart position for some 20 weeks, the ex-pugilist following this with two 1951 No 1's in **I Want To Be With You Always** and **Always Late.** Becoming an Opry star, throughout the rest of the decade he continued to supply a series of

The Legendary Lefty Frizzell (ABC).

Lasso from El Paso (Epic). All-star album from the freaky country-rock singer, who switched to Epic in 1976 after a spell with ABC.

for Vanguard. The Jewboys, who used such individual aliases as Little Jewford, Big Nig, Panama Red, Rainbow Colours and Snakebite Jacobs, signed to ABC Records during 1974 but by 1976 Friedman had switched once more to Epic, cutting **Lasso From El Paso,** an all star album featuring such dignitaries as Bob Dylan and Eric Clapton.

Albums:
Sold American
  (Vanguard/Vanguard)
Kinky Friedman *(ABC/ABC)*
Lasso From El Paso *(Epic/Epic)*

Sold American (Vanguard).

Right: Kinky Friedman.

chart high flyers, many of these in honky tonk tradition. The '60s too found Frizzell obtaining more than a dozen hits, though only **Saginaw, Michigan** – a 1964 No 1 – and **She's Gone, Gone, Gone** (1965) proved of any real consequence. As the '70s arrived, so too did one minor Frizzell success in **Watermelon Time In Georgia** – but that seemed to be his last punch. He died in 1975 after suffering a stroke – but his influence can still be heard in the work of Merle Haggard (♦) and others.

Albums:
Greatest Hits *(Columbia/—)*
Sings Songs Of Jimmie Rodgers
  (Columbia/—)
Remembering Lefty Frizzell
  (Columbia/—)
The Classic Style Of *(ABC/—)*

Lefty Frizzell Sings the Songs of Jimmie Rodgers (Columbia).

Steve Fromholz

Purveyor of what he terms 'Free form country folk science fiction gospel cum existential bluegrass-opera music', the hirsute Fromholz (born Temple, Texas, 1945) once looked likely to become the most talented has been in Austin (♦), a situation later reflected in the title of his first solo album – **A Rumor In My Own Time.**

At 18, he attended North Texas State University, meeting singer-songwriter Michael Murphey, the duo becoming part of the Dallas County Jug Band. After an abbreviated stay in the Navy, Fromholz worked with several other duos and combos, eventually befriending another singer-songwriter, Dan McCrimmon, the twosome forming Frummox and recording an album **From Here To There** for Probe (1969), the disc featuring Fromholz's ambitious **Texas Trilogy.** By 1971 the Texan had become part of Steve Stills' band moving on to form a short lived outfit known as Captain Duck and The Farmer's Co-op Boys – but he was shortly back to being a solo act once more, cutting **How Long Is The Road To Kentucky,** an LP for Mike Nesmith's (♦) Countryside label, the completed record never being released. In the wake of some live tracks cut for a small independent label, Fromholz moved to Austin (1974), there becoming an accepted part of the outlaw community, providing material and singing on Willie Nelson's (♦) **Sound In Your Mind** LP; the first *real* Fromholz solo album, **A Rumor In My Own Time,** finding a Capitol release in

Lefty Frizzell, considered by many to be the originator of laid-back country vocalism.

1976. An all star soiree featuring Red Rhodes (♦), Willie Nelson (♦), Doug Dillard (♦), John Sebastian, B. W. Stevenson and the Lost Gonzo Band, the disc fulfilled all the hopes of Fromholz's cult following, a later album, **Frolicking In The Myth,** proved him to be moving on in search of new frontiers to breach.

Albums:
A Rumor In My Own Time
  (Capitol/—)
Frolicking In The Myth
  (Capitol/Capitol)

Larry Gatlin

Born Odessa, Texas, 1949, Gatlin is a singer-songwriter whose roots are in gospel music. When only five he could be found watching the Blackwood Brothers, also at the same age appearing in an Abilene talent contest as part of The Gatlins (along with his two brothers and one of his sisters) a gospel group who toured throughout the southern states. His breakthrough occurred while he was working with The Imperials, in Vegas, as part of the Jimmy Dean Dean Show (♦).

There Gatlin met Dottie West (♦), one of Dean's guests, who offered to help him. In May 1971, he sent her eight songs – from which she selected and recorded two, **Once You Were Mine** and **You're The Other Half Of Me.** And when Dottie formed her own First Generation Music Company in 1972, Gatlin was the first writer to gain a contract. Then following further songs for Dottie West, including **My Mind's Gone To Memphis,** Gatlin sang the first verse and harmony vocals on Kristofferson's (♦) **Why Me?** hit and Johnny Cash (♦) employed several Gatlin compositions for his *Gospel Road* movie. Due to Kristofferson's insistence, Monument Records signed Gatlin in 1973, releasing singles by both he and The Gatlins that year, his first album **The Pilgrim,** appearing in 1974. More recently he's been having Top Ten hits with **Broken Lady** (1976), the winner of a Grammy award, and **Statues With-**

out Hearts (1977), and has become the newest member of the Grand Ole Opry.

Albums:
The Pilgrim *(Monument/—)*
Rain-Rainbow
  (Monument/Monument)
With Family And Friends
  (Monument/—)
Broken Lady
  (Monument/Monument)

Crystal Gayle

Loretta Lynn's younger sister (real name Brenda Gayle Webb) who has now found her own musical identity under the wing of producer Allen Reynolds.

Born Paintsville, Kentucky, 1951, at age 16 she was part of Loretta's package show. In 1970 she landed

Crystal Gayle, sister of Loretta Lynn, who made her name on the Jim Ed Brown TV show. Below: Rain Rainbow (Monument). Protege of Dottie West, Gatlin is a successful songwriter.

her first release, on Decca, **I Cried (The Blue Right Out Of My Eyes)** into the country singles charts. The following years were

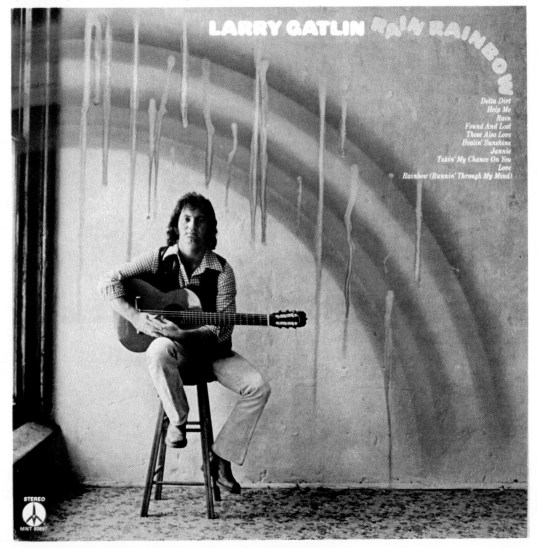

LARRY GATLIN RAIN RAINBOW

Delta Dirt
Help Me
Rain
Found And Lost
Those Also Love
Healin' Sunshine
Jannie
Takin' My Chance On You
Love
Rainbow (Runnin' Through My Mind)

STEREO
MNT 80897

not productive for chart consistency and Crystal moved to UA Records, refusing to record any material associated with Loretta and working with Allen Reynolds, the producer who had galvanised Don Williams' (◊) career. Reynolds' own composition **Wrong Road Again** brought Crystal back into the country charts. Two other singles followed the pattern, all of them from her successful first album **Crystal Gayle.**

This 1975 comeback was the start of a consistent hitmaking run and Crystal followed up with two more successful albums, **Somebody Loves You** and **Crystal.** Allen Reynolds' trademark is upon them; as with Don Williams the producer went for an uncluttered, easy going style, not too heavily country and therefore holding pop crossover possibilities. With this asset and a good vocal range Crystal Gayle is a sound bet for consistent chart success in the future.

Albums:
Crystal Gayle *(UA/—)*
Somebody Loves You *(UA/UA)*
Crystal *(UA/UA)*
I'm Not So Far Away *(UA/UA)*

Crystal
(UA).

Bobbie Gentry

In July, 1967, **Ode To Billy Joe,** a song about the suicide of a certain Billy Joe Macallister, was released. Bedecked in an imaginative, swamp flavored, Jimmy Haskell arrangement, it was one of the year's finest singles and subsequently sold a million. Thus was the public introduced to the singing and songwriting talent of Bobbie Gentry.

Of Portugese descent, she was born Roberta Streeter, Chickasaw County, Mississippi, July 27, 1944, later changing her name to Gentry after seeing *Ruby Gentry,* a movie about swampland passion involving Jennifer Jones and Charlton Heston.

A childhood singer and guitarist, Bobbie spent her early years in Greenwood, Mississippi, and then moved with her family to Califor-

nia, there attending high school in Palm Springs and later UCLA, where she majored in philosophy. Already proficient on several instruments (she plays guitar, banjo, bass, piano and vibes) Bobbie attended the LA Conservatory of Music, studying theory.

Signed to Capitol Records in 1967, she cut **Ode To Billy Joe** at one half hour session and became a star virtually overnight. Then followed a number of other crossover hits including **Okolona River Bottom Band** (1967), **Fancy** (1969), **Let It Be Me** (1969) and **All I Have To Do Is Dream** (1970), the last two being duets with Glen Campbell (◊).

Extremely popular in Britain,

Ode To Billy Joe (Warner Bros).
Soundtrack of the film of the
song that made her famous.
Despite popularity in Britain
hits have become fewer.

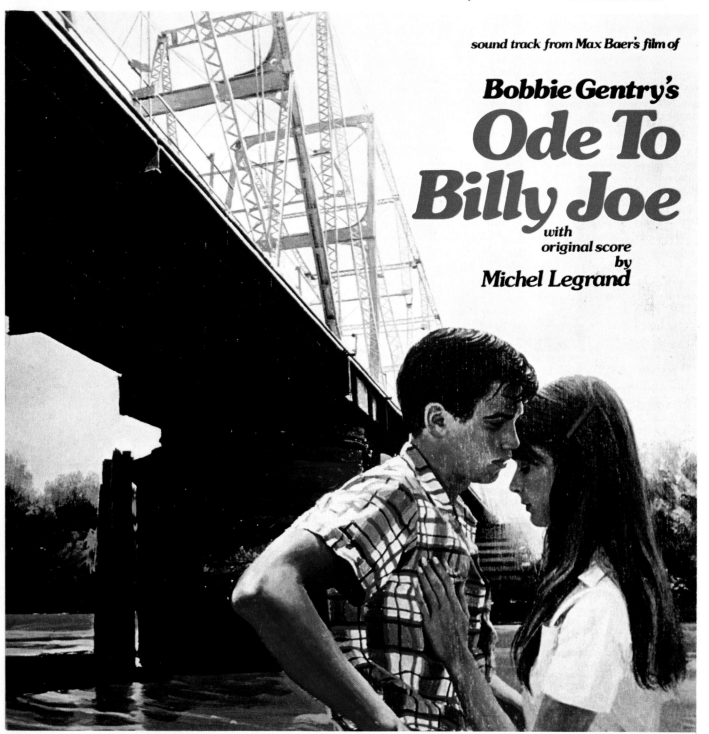

sound track from Max Baer's film of

Bobbie Gentry's

Ode To Billy Joe

with
original score
by
Michel Legrand

where she had her own BBC-TV series and gained a No 1 hit with her version of **I'll Never Fall In Love Again** (1970), Bobbie's disc sales appeared to wane as the '70s moved on. But in 1976, a film *Ode To Billie Joe*, based on the events documented in the Gentry song, reactivated some interest in her Delta ditties once more. She currently spends most of her time appearing at Las Vegas lounges and casinos.

Albums:
Ode To Billy Joe *(Capitol/—)*
Bobbie Gentry's Greatest
  (Capitol/—)
**Bobbie Gentry And Glen
  Campbell** *(Capitol/Capitol)*
Ode To Billy Joe – Soundtrack
  (Warner Bros/Warner Bros)
  title track only

*I Wrote A Song . . .
(RCA Victor).*

*Don't Stop Loving Me
(Hickory).*

Don Gibson

Rich voiced singer-songwriter Don Gibson continues to be a country music attraction while possessing the ability to appeal to pop buyers also.

Born Shelby, North Carolina, April 3, 1928, Gibson was a fairly competent guitarist before he left school. He built up a regional following via live gigs and radio broadcasts and after school moved to Knoxville where he was heard on the WNOX Tennessee Barn Dance. His first big writing success was the song **Sweet Dreams** which was a hit for Faron Young (♦).

In 1958 his best known composition **I Can't Stop Loving You** was a hit for Kitty Wells (♦), and later soul singer Ray Charles was to have an international hit with it and virtually make it his own property. Gibson himself recorded the number as the B-side of **Oh Lonesome Me,** but the latter broke through for him and gave him a name-making pop hit in the process. Total sales of **I Can't Stop Loving You** were not long in reaching the

Prolific songwriter Don Gibson's songs have been covered by scores of artists. Ray Charles won a gold disc for I Can't Stop Loving You, and Don himself gained a gold for Oh Lonesome Me.

one million mark. Later successes for Don himself were **Give Myself A Party, Blue Blue Day, Sea Of Heartbreak** and **Lonesome Number One.** The last three, and particularly **Sea Of Heartbreak,** showed that Gibson's deep voice and neatly novel songs could cross over to the pop charts sometimes. But, consistently successful in the country charts, Gibson has always kept his country image and has been critical of the inroads rock has made into country these past years. Since signing with Hickory and re-joining the Grand Ole Opry, he has proven he still has some chart muscle with songs like **One Day At A Time** and **Woman (Sensuous Woman).**

Albums:
Am I That Easy To Forget?
  (Camden/—)
Just Call Me Lonesome
  (Camden/—)
Just One Time *(Camden/—)*
Don't Stop Loving Me
  (Hickory/DJM)
The Best Of Don Gibson
  (—/RCA)
Four Sides Of Don Gibson
  (—/DJM)

During the '50s Don Gibson became a favorite in Knoxville through his many radio appearances there, and was presented with the keys to the city.

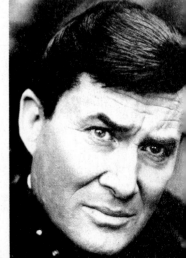

Welcome to Gilley's (Pye).

Mickey Gilley

Piano-playing cousin of Jerry Lee Lewis (♦) and a performer of similar style, Mickey Gilley was born Ferriday, Louisiana. He moved to Houston at the age of 17 to do construction work and began playing at local clubs, at this time cutting rock 'n' roll songs **Tell Me Why** and **Oo-ee-baby,** for the Houston based Minor label. This brought no success so Gilley traveled on, recording for Dot, in Memphis, Rex, in New Orleans, and Khoury, at Lake Charles, Louisiana. Later in 1960, he recorded a Warner Mack (♦) hit **Is It Wrong?** for Potomac, the disc becoming a regional best seller – but then the label folded and Gilley continued label hopping, cutting sides with Lynn, Sabra and Princess.

In 1964, he formed his own record company Astro, his second release **Lonely Wine** proving another regional hit, an album of the same title (later retitled **Down The Line With Mickey Gilley** when reissued by Paula) also being released. However, 1965 found Gilley on 20th Century Fox, from there moving to Paula, where he enjoyed a mild 1968 hit in **Now I Can Live Again** – but it wasn't until 1974, and some reaction to his Astro version of George Morgan's (♦) old **Roomful Of Roses** winner, that things slotted together for Gilley. The single was picked up for national release by Hugh Hefner's Playboy label and immediately went into the Top Five in the country charts. Since that time, Gilley's achieved huge hits with **I Overlooked An Orchid** (1974), **Window Up Above** (1975), **Bring It On Home To Me, Don't The Girls All Get Prettier At Closing Time** and **Overnight Sensation** (all 1976).

During the early '70s, the singer bought a ramshackle Houston club called Shelley's and converted it into a 1500 seater named Gilley's. He often works there, using a five piece band, his audience spanning the whole range of age groups.

Albums:
Room Full Of Roses
  (*Playboy/—*)
At His Best (*Paula/—*)
City Lights (*Playboy/—*)
Mickey's Movin' On
  (*Playboy/—*)
Overnight Sensation
  (*Playboy/—*)
Greatest Hits Vol 1 (*Playboy/—*)

Mickey Gilley owes his success to his revival of Room Full Of Roses, an old George Morgan hit, originally planned as a B side.

Welcome To Gilley's (*—/Pye*)
Smokin' (*Playboy/—*)

Johnny Gimble

Brilliant session fiddle player and writer of **Fiddlin' Around,** a number nominated for a 1974 Grammy Award, Johnny Gimble was born 1926 and grew up on a farm near Tyler, Texas.

With his brothers Gene, Jerry, Jack and Bill, the 12 year-old Johnny began playing at local gigs, Gene, Jerry and Johnny combining with James Ivie, during their high school days, to form the Rose City Swingsters, a group that played on radio station KGKB, Tyler. Leaving home in 1943, Gimble played fiddle and banjo with Bob and Joe Shelton at KWKH, Shreveport, Louisiana, also working as part of the Jimmie Davis Band (♦).

Gimble spent two or three different stints with Bob Wills (♦) and his Texas Playboys on fiddle and electric mandolin, where he was an essential part in creating the best of Bob's post war bands, although when western swing's popularity sagged he left the music business and settled down to barbering and working in a hospital.

Since 1968, however, Gimble has made a comeback and become one of the most active and in-demand session men in Nashville, recording with scores of artists and sometimes going on tour with such acts as Merle Haggard (♦), Loretta Lynn (♦) and Johnny Rodriguez (♦). But he also plays many dates as a headliner and has cut solo albums for such majors as Columbia and Capitol. He won the CMA's Instrumentalist of The Year award in 1974, and has been active as a focal point for the revival of western swing, recording with Merle Haggard, Asleep At The Wheel (♦) and others in this style.

Albums:
Fiddlin' Around (*Capitol/—*)
Texas Dance Party
  (*Columbia/—*)

Johnny Gimble, probably the most heavily employed fiddle player on the whole country scene – though Buddy Spicher might care to argue the point – he is also the best around.

Texas Dance Party (Columbia). One time Texas Playboy, Gimble's career has picked up since 1968.

Girls Of The Golden West

Dorothy Laverne (Dolly) Good
guitar and vocals
Mildred Fern (Millie) Good
guitar and vocals

Authentic westerners from Muleshoe, Texas, Dolly (born December 11, 1915) and Millie (born April 11, 1913) were one of the most popular acts in early country music history, and helped pave the way for other women singers who followed, as well as being among the earliest to exploit the cowboy image in dress and in song.

They began their career on WIL and KMOX in St Louis in 1930, then spent three years in Milford, Kansas, and on XER in Mexico, before coming to nationwide renown on the National Barn Dance (♦) from 1933–1937. They were even more popular on the Boone County Jamboree and the Midwestern Hayride (both over WLW) in Cincinnati, where they were voted the most popular act on WLW in 1945. Their appearances and performance tailed off in the 1950s, and they did not perform after about 1963. Dolly died on November 12, 1967, while Millie still lives in the Cincinnati area.

In their prime they recorded for RCA, Columbia, and Conqueror, also recording for such labels as FJC, Manco, and Bluebonnet (which put out a full six volumes of their material) late in their career. They never had any great succes on record, but were among the most popular groups of their era, and one of the most influential.

Tompall Glaser
♦ *Tompall and*
♦ *The Glaser*
Brothers

The New Opry Building, shown here, was opened in 1974 – but many rued the closure of the Ryman Auditorium, which had housed the Opry for over 30 years.

Billy Grammer

Originator of the Grammer guitar, a fine flat top instrument which by 1965 had cost around $18,000 in development and research, Billy Grammer's first guitar was installed in the Country Music Hall of Fame in March, 1969, along with the first pickup for amplifying a bass electronically, the latter designed by Everett Hull. One of 13 children fathered by an Illinois coalminer, Grammer (born Benton, Illinois, August 28, 1925) became a major star during the late '50s and early '60s. He performed on WRAL, Arlington in 1947 and by 1955 had earned a regular spot on the Washington based Jimmy Dean (♦) TV Show, moving with Dean on to a CBS network program later.

A popular bandleader, Grammer signed with Monument Records, in 1958 having his first hit – a million seller – with **Gotta Travel On,** a song adapted by The Weavers from a traditional melody. Becoming an Opry regular in 1959 and obtaining a double sided hit that year with **Bonaparte's Retreat/The Kissing Tree,** Grammer recorded for numerous labels throughout the 1960s, having minor hits on most of them via such titles as **I Wanna Go Home** (*Decca*, 1963), **The Real Thing** (*Epic*, 1966), **Mabel** (*Rice*, 1967), **Ballad Of John Dillinger** (*Mercury*, 1968) and **Jesus Is A Soul Man** (*Stop*, 1969). His past albums have included **Billy Grammer** (*Decca*, 1964), **Country Guitar** (*Decca*, 1965) and **Favourites** (*Vocalion*, 1968).

Billy Grammer at the Opry. Once lead guitarist with Clyde Moody and Jimmy Dean, Grammer obtained a gold disc for his recording of Gotta Travel On.

The Grand Old Opry

No other single show has dominated the history of country music like the Grand Ole Opry, which has been broadcast for over fifty years over WSM radio in Nashville, making it America's longest running continuous show in radio history.

It was neither the first of the radio barn dances nor was it – for at least the first fifteen years of its existence – the greatest, but through shrewd understanding of public wants and a determination to stick with country music through thick and thin, it rose to a nearly unchallengeable position of dominance, and to this day playing the Grand Ole Opry seems to be the ultimate goal of most aspiring country musicians.

The Opry was the brainchild of George D. Hay (♦), who was hired as program director of the then brand new WSM in early 1925. Having seen the success of the National Barn Dance (♦) over WLS, where he had been an announcer, Hay began a series of fitful attempts at starting a similar barn dance in Nashville. After about mid-December of 1925, however, the WSM Barn Dance was a permanent Saturday night fixture of WSM, as it is to this day. Hay, almost off-handedly, named the show the Grand Ole Opry in 1927 (see Hay's entry for a more detailed account), a name which was immediately successful with the press, the performers, and the fans.

Hay was firm about the old time type of music he wanted played on the station – 'Keep it down to earth,' and 'Keep it close to the earth, boys' were his favorite sayings, oft-repeated, and it was he who held out so long and so firmly against electric instruments and drums. Yet he was also quick to exploit the 'hillbilly' image so associated with the show, and the largely non-professional early Opry cast, who tended to show up in dignified coats and ties, were by the late 1920s (about the time an audience was admitted to the program) dressed up in outlandish hillbilly garb, and the bands given similarly outlandish names like the Gully Jumpers, the Possum Hunters, the Dixie Clodhoppers, and the Fruit Jar Drinkers.

Early Opry stars included Uncle Jimmy Thompson (♦), DeFord Bailey (♦), Theron Hale and Daughters (♦), Dr Humphrey Bate and his Possum Hunters (♦), but the major star of them all was Uncle Dave Macon (♦). However, even by the early 1930s the barn dance format was becoming a bit stale, a trend which WSM management evidently saw, although apparently – amazingly – none of the other barn dances did.

Although Hay apparently resisted the move, acts with broader appeal – like the Vagabonds (♦) and Asher and Little Jimmy Sizemore (♦) – began to appear on the show, and there seemed to be hints that the Opry was looking for a 'star' to give the show identity, particularly in relation to its rival, the National Barn Dance, which had a network show as early as 1933.

The Opry found that star in 1938, when Roy Acuff (♦) became a cast-member, delicately mixing his singing-star status with the string band sound. The same mixture was true of the singing-star-with-string-band signed the next year, Bill Monroe (♦). He was to be the last such singer with band signed, as the Opry abandoned itself to the star approach thoughout the 1940s, as Zeke Clements (♦) (1939), Minnie Pearl (♦) (1940), Paul Howard (♦) (1940), Ernest Tubb (♦) 1943), Bradley Kincaid (♦) (1944), Cowboy Copas (♦) (1946), Red Foley (♦) (1947), George Morgan (♦) (1949), Hank Williams (♦) (1949), and Hank Snow (♦) (1950) all joined within the period.

Hay was clearly unhappy with this turn of events – his role had been reduced to that of host, MC and spokesman – but it worked; within that decade the Opry became the most popular barn dance in America, leaving the National Barn Dance far behind. So quickly did its position become entrenched that when the Louisiana Hayride (♦) got rolling, developing its own Opry-type star system, instead of becoming a major barn dance it simply became a supply of talent for the Opry, providing it with its major stars of the 1950s as soon as they begun to achieve national attention, including Hank Williams, Webb Pierce (♦), the Wilburn Brothers (♦), Faron Young (♦), Jim Reeves (♦), Jimmy Newman (♦), and many, many others.

It was the only national barn dance to hang on during the rock and roll era, and with the exception of the WWVA Jamboree in Wheeling and the sporadic, fitful attempts to revive the Louisiana Hayride, it is the only radio barn dance – surely an anachronism far out of its time – still going strong.

It has survived many changes of location, first being housed in a WSM radio studio, then to a larger studio, then to the Hillboro Theater, then to the Dixie Tabernacle, then a brief period in the War Memorial Auditorium before housing itself in the Ryman Auditorium for some thirty years, beginning in 1941. It is today situated in a sparkling new Grand Ole Opry house on the grounds of a huge amusement center, Opryland USA, fifteen miles from downtown Nashville.

In a sense, the Opry has fallen from its once almighty perch, with the outlaws scorning its still-traditional approach and today's biggest stars feeling little need to appear on the show the required 26 nights a year for the exposure a lesser artist needs so badly, so the show goes on with a few too many who are obviously over the hill, and without country superstars of today.

Still, there is a magic about the name and the association with the half-century old institution which is still powerful and undeniable, and such luminaries as Tom T. Hall (♦), Ronnie Milsap (♦), and Larry Gatlin (♦) have all been eager to join its cast. Whatever its future, however, its first fifty years have been of paramount importance in the growth, development, spread, and mystique of country music.

Otto Gray and his Oklahoma Cowboys. Gray traveled in a custom-built limousine costing over $20,000.

Stars of the Grand Ole Opry 1926–74 (RCA). A wonderful double-album compilation of Opry favorites. Each copy contained a piece of the green backdrop from the old Ryman Opry House!

Claude Gray

A popular singer, guitarist and bandleader, Gray enjoyed a spate of best selling singles at the commencement of the '60s, when after recording Willie Nelson's (♦) **Family Bible,** thus gaining a Top Ten hit, he signed for Mercury and immediately scored two 1961 Top Five entries with **I'll Just Have Another Cup Of Coffee** and **My Ears Should Burn,** the latter being a Roger Miller (♦) composition.

Several minor hits later, in 1965, the 6 feet 5 inch tall Gray switched to Columbia, stopping to provide one healthy seller in **Mean Old Woman** (1966), then moved on once more to join Decca, with whom he enjoyed a lengthy stay that extended into the '70s, the relationship commencing with two best sellers, **I Never Had The One I Wanted** (1966) and **How Fast Them Trucks Can Go** (1967). Gray, who again popped into the charts during 1973 with **Woman Ease My Mind** on the Million label, was born Henderson, Texas, January 26, 1932. His albums include **Treasure Of Love** (*Hillside*).

Otto Gray

One of the most popular and influential of the very early country music professional bands was Otto Gray and his Oklahoma Cowboys, who toured in custom made limousines, helped popularize country music in the north east, and pre-presented a very slick, very rehearsed, very effective stage show.

Gray himself was from Oklahoma, but achieved his greatest success in the north east, particularly over WGY in Schenectady, New York. Not much of a musician himself, he was host and MC for the Oklahoma Cowboys, whose more prominent members included his wife 'Mommie', his son Owen, and at one time also included both Zeke Clements (♦) and Whitey Ford ('The Duke Of Paducah') (♦).

Gray had organized the Oklahoma Cowboys as early as 1924, and the band actually lasted through the mid 1940s. They recorded for Gennett, Vocalion and Okeh.

Albums: none.

Greenbriar Boys

A New York based bluegrass group formed in 1958 by Bob Yellin, John Herald and Eric Weissberg. Extremely popular at various folk festivals in the '60s, they recorded for Elektra and Vanguard, **Greenbriar Boys** (1962), **Ragged But Right** (1964) and **Better Late Than Never** (1967) being among their most well received albums for the latter label. Much changed throughout the years, the Greenbriar's personnel has included Dian Edmondson, a female lead vocalist, legendary mandolinist Frank Wakefield, fiddler Buddy Spicher, and Ralph Rinzler, one time manager of Bill Monroe (♦), organizer of numerous festivals and a leading authority on old time country music.

Albums:
Best Of The Greenbriar Boys
  (Vanguard/—)
Ragged But Right *(Vanguard/—)*
Better Late Than Never
  (Vanguard/—)

Lloyd Green

One of Nashville's top session men, Mensa member Green was born Mississippi, October 4, 1937, grew up in Mobile, Alabama, and began taking lessions on steel guitar at the age of seven, playing professionally three years later. During his high school days he played weekends at clubs and bars where 'real rough fights, shootings and stabbings were common', using material drawn mainly from the Eddy Arnold (♦) and Hank Williams (♦) songbooks. He attended the University of Southern Mississippi as a psychology major but left after two years to play in Nashville. He initially worked there with Hawkshaw Hawkins (♦) and Jean Shepard (♦), then toured with Faron Young (♦) and George Jones (♦), his first recording session in Nashville being on Jones' **Too Much Water Runs Under The Bridge** single in 1957. Though he's had hard times since – at one period being forced to take a job in a shoe shop – Green is now an in-demand steel guitar man and plays on some 500 sessions a year.

Albums:
Lloyd Green And His Steel
  Guitar *(Prize/M&M)*
Shades Of Steel *(Monument/—)*
Steel Rides
  (Monument/Monument)
Cool Steel Man *(Chart/Chart)*

Lloyd Green and his Steel Guitar (M&M).

Jack Greene

Co-host (along with Jeannie Seely (♦)) of the Wembley Country Music Festival in 1976, singer-guitarist-drummer Jack Greene was born Maryville, Tennessee, January 7, 1930.

Yet another of the long list of country entertainers who could play guitar at pre-teen stage, he first became a full time musician with the Cherokee Trio, an Atlanta GA group, moving on to become drummer with the Rhythm Ranch Boys in 1950. Then came two years of army service, followed by a sting with another Atlanta band, the Peachtree Cowboys.

Joining Ernest Tubb's (♦) Texas Troubadours in 1962, the amiable six-footer, dubbed 'Jolly Giant', soon became a favorite. And while still a member of Tubb's band, he began having solo discs released by Decca, one such release, **Ever Since My Baby Went Away**, charting in mild fashion during 1965, this being followed by two No 1's in **There Goes My Everything** (1966) and **All The Time** (1967).

During '67, Greene strolled away with four CMA awards – Best Male Vocalist, Best Album, Best Song and Single Of The Year (for **There Goes My Everything**, a Dallas Frazier (♦) composition). There-

after he continued on his hit-making way, providing Decca with five more top singles during the late '60s.

In 1969, Greene and Jeannie Seely, his co-vocalist on the Ernest Tubb TV Show, put together a roadshow, and began touring with a band called the Jolly Giants, the twosome enjoying immediate success on record with **Wish I Didn't Have To Miss You.** The first country act to play the Rooftop Lounge, King Of The Road, Nashville, in 1972, Greene and Seely received considerable acclaim for their Madison Square Garden concert in 1974. Currently they travel with a four piece band, the Renegades, attempting to cash in on the 'out-law' look and style.

Albums:
Greatest Hits *(MCA/—)*
Greene Country *(MCA/—)*
I Never Had It So Good
  (Pickwick/—)
The Best Of . . . *(—/MCA)*

With Jeannie Seely:
Two For The Show *(MCA/—)*
Jack Greene And Jeannie Seely
  (MCA/—)

Left: Lloyd Green, one of Nashville's finest pedal-steel players. His set with Johnny Gimble proved a highlight of the 1977 Country Music Festival at Wembley, England.

Ray Griff

Writer of over 500 songs, Ray Griff was born Vancouver, British Columbia, Canada, April 22, 1940, moving with his family to Calgary, Alberta, shortly before reaching his teens. A drummer in a band at the age of eight, Griff also mastered the guitar and piano, becoming a bandleader on the nightclub cir-cuit at 18. His reputation as a song-writer was enhanced when Johnny Horton (♦) recorded **Mr Moon-light,** a Griff composition, during the late '50s, Jim Reeves (♦) cutting **Where Do I Go?,** another Griff original, in 1962.

Encouraged by Reeves, he be-came Nashville based in 1964, initially involving himself in song-writing and music publishing, but later recording some sides for RCA's Groove label. An MGM re-lease, **Your Lily White Hands,** provided him with his first hit, in late '67; Griff following this with **Sugar From My Candy,** on Dot, a few months later. Label switch-ing again, he recorded Clarence Carter's **Patches** for Royal Ameri-can, gaining a 1970 success, climb-ing even higher with **The Morning**

Left: Jack Greene. In 1966 he set off on a run that saw him log eight top five singles in a row.

Below: Back In The Arms Of Love (MCA). Love songs from hit-maker Greene, now converted to the 'outlaw' movement and on the road with Jeannie Seely.

JACK GREENE
BACK IN THE ARMS OF LOVE

BACK IN THE ARMS OF LOVE
BUT YOU KNOW I LOVE YOU
I LOVE YOU BECAUSE
TO SEE AN ANGEL CRY
BIRTH OF OUR LOVE
IF NOT FOR YOU
ALL I HAVE TO OFFER YOU IS ME
LOVE ME, LOVE ME
THE KEY THAT FITS HER DOOR
I LOVE YOU MORE TODAY
THE FOOL IN ME
I CAN'T HELP IT

mca

After Baby Let Me Down in '71, and enjoying Top Ten discs with You Ring My Bell (1975) and If I Let Her Come In (1976), these two being Capitol releases.

But it's as a songwriter that the one time inveterate stutterer (for years he hardly gave an interview) has really staked a claim to fame, his compositions including Canadian Pacific (recorded by George Hamilton IV (♦)), Baby (Wilma Burgess (♦)), Better Move It On Home (Porter Wagoner (♦) and Dolly Parton (♦)), Step Aside (Faron Young (♦)), Who's Gonna Play This Old Piano (Jerry Lee Lewis (♦)), After The Laughter (Wayne Newton) and many others, the majority of these being published by Griff's own Blue Echo company.

Albums:
Ray Griff (Capitol/—)
The Last Of The Winfield Amateurs (Capitol/—)

Rex Griffin

A popular singer, guitarist, and songwriter, Rex Griffin is best known for his composition The Last Letter, although he has several other hits to his credit, including Just Call Me Lonesome. Born August 22, 1912, he became popular over WSB in Atlanta and as a host of the KRLD Texas Roundup. Probably the most fascinating aspect of his career was that he recorded Lovesick Blues for Decca, a record which went nowhere; nearly a decade later Hank Williams (♦) learned and recorded Griffin's version identically, with tremendous success. Plagued will ill health in latter years due to a lifelong drinking problem, Griffin died October 11, 1959.

Albums: none

The Gully Jumpers

Paul Warmack *mandolin and guitar*
Charlie Arrington *fiddle*
Roy Hardison *banjo*
Burt Hutcherson *guitar*

The Gully Jumpers were one of the early popular Opry string bands, and participated in that early Nashville recording session for Victor in October, 1928. Led by Paul Warmack, an auto mechanic by trade, they remained with basically the same personnel for well over two decades (they had joined the Opry about 1927), and in fact were one of the most popular and most used bands of the Opry's early years.

The group was dissolved in the middle 1960s when the four old time Opry bands were accordioned into two. Today only Burt Hutcherson survives, currently playing with the Crook Brothers Band (♦).

Albums: none.

Jack Guthrie

Born Leon Guthrie in Olive, Oklahoma in 1915, Jack moved to northern California at the age of seventeen to pursue a career in music, appearing on radio stations in Chico and Marysville. He knocked around for some years (even appearing in at least one film with Ernest Tubb (♦)) before getting a break with Capitol Records, but was soon drafted, and it was not until he was stationed on the island of Ie Shima in the South Pacific that he was informed that his recording of Oklahoma Hills (co-written with his cousin Woody (♦)), had gone to number one, and it went on to become one of the best selling records of 1945.

However, Jack was severely wounded in the South Pacific, contracting a debilitating illness as well, and although he did some touring and recording upon his return to the States he was hospitalized in mid 1947 and died January 15, 1948. His nasal, earnest voice and straightforward country material showed nothing of the social consciousness or self-consciousness of his cousin Woody. Modeled more after Jimmie Rodgers (♦) in sound and style, Jack Guthrie was a country singer pure and simple.

Albums:
Country Hits Of The '40s (Capitol/—) one track only

Below: The Gully Jumpers, one of the first string bands to play on WSM's Saturday night shows.

Woody Guthrie

Influential country folk singer and songwriter whose visual attitude and thin, fragmented vocal style have been copied by many, most notably Bob Dylan.

Born Woodrow Wilson Guthrie in Okema, Oklahoma, 1912, a hard rural upbringing amid a background of natural disasters set the tone for many of his songs. He championed the rural poor and the loser (as on Dustbowl Ballads), yet he was also capable of joyous hymns to the country itself and to the idea of man as owner of it (This Land Is Your Land).

He roamed the land extensively incorporating what he found into songs. He gave rise to what is sometimes called 'The Dustbowl Tradition', other exponents of which include Cisco Houston, Rambling Jack Elliott (♦) and Ry Cooder (♦). The slogan on his guitar read 'This machine kills fascists' and as he roamed America during the depression singing in union halls and for picket lines it was hardly surprising when the authorities, already scared by the crisis, tried to tag the 'red' label on him. In a parallel with the '60s decade, those who pointed the need for social change could find themselves ostracized or even in danger.

Guthrie's mother had died of Huntington's Chorea (a hereditary nerve disease) and Woody himself succumbed to it in 1967, having been in

Ray Griff – at the age of eight he was part of the Winfield Amateurs, an Alberta four piece with Ray on drums, his brother on banjo and a sax and piano player,

hospital since 1954 (where Bob Dylan visited him). He was a country singer in the very widest sense, a drifting son of the earth, crafting his simple songs out of experience and his own perception.

Albums:
Bound For Glory *(Folkways/—)*
Cowboy Songs – with Cisco Houston *(Stinson/—)*
Dust Bowl Ballads *(Folkways/—)*
Early Years *(Tradition/—)*
Folk Songs *(Folkways/—)*
Folk Songs Vol 1 – with Cisco Houston *(Stinson/—)*
Legendary *(Tradition/—)*
Poor Boy *(Folkways/Xtra)*
This Land Is Your Land *(Folkways/—)*
Woody Guthrie *(Archive Of Folk/Ember)*
Songs To Grow On *(Folkways/—)*
Blind Sonny Terry And Woody Guthrie *(Archive Of Folk/ Ember)*

My Love Affair With Trains (Capitol). Haggard's fascination with railroads is given full steam on this recording, one of his several concept albums.

Woody Guthrie (Ember). A true country singer, he traveled America and wrote his songs from his experiences. His life has recently been documented in the film 'Bound For Glory'.

The Hackberry Ramblers

Luderin Darbone *fiddle and leader*
Lennis Sonnier *guitar and vocals*
Edwin Duhon *mandolin*
Joe Werner *guitar*
Lonnie Rainwater *guitar*
Floyd Rainwater *bass*

An early and influential Cajun band whose records both in English and

Cajun French helped win the music a wider audience in the 1930s. In their prime – the 1930s – they recorded mainly for Bluebird. They disbanded in 1939, but in the 1960s Luderin Darbone reformed the Hackberry Ramblers for appearances at folk festivals and at weekend dances in local taverns.

Albums:
Hackberry Ramblers *(Arhoolie/—)*
Country Music: Songs Of The South And West *(New World/—)*

Merle Haggard

Country's most charismatic living legend and the proof that you don't have to forsake your musical roots to achieve fame.

The Haggard family had been driven from their farm in dustbowl East Oklahoma and were living in a converted boxcar in Bakersfield (♦), California when Merle was born, on April 6, 1937. Merle's father was a competent fiddle player although after their marriage Mrs Haggard, a strict Church of Christ member, insisted that he at least stop playing in honky tonks.

Merle was nine when his father died, and without his father's influence and music he began to run wild. His mother put him in a juvenile home for a spell to try and scare him into straightening out. He embarked on a series of petty thefts and frauds and was in and out of local prisons, and in 1957 he was charged with attempted burglary and sentenced to six months to fifteen years in San Quentin. He did some picking and some songwriting inside and was in San Quentin when Johnny Cash (♦) came to perform. A spell in solitary confinement talking with the men on death row convinced him to get himself straight, and when he left jail in 1960 he determined to try and make a go of performing, since Bakersfield was by then growing into a respectable little country music center.

He was helped initially by Bakersfield *eminence gris* Buck Owens (♦)

and by Bonnie Owens (♦), Buck's former wife whom Merle himself would eventually marry. At this time Merle ran into Fuzzy Owen, an Arkansas musician who was playing the Bakersfield clubs (the town's country music venues included a share of 'apprentice serving clubs' frequented by whooping cowbows and oil hands). Fuzzy, who is Merle's manager to this day, helped Merle get work locally and encouraged him, and when Merle returned from a stint with a band at Las Vegas in 1962 Fuzzy had him recording some sides for Tally, a label Owen had purchased from his cousin Lewis Tally.

Recording in a converted 'garage' studio, they produced a single which sold 200 copies. However, the next year saw them reach No 19 in the country charts with **Sing A Bad Song** and in 1964 **Sam Hill** reached No 45. In 1965 they put out **All My Friends Are Gonna Be Strangers**, and although it languished for some time on Tally Capitol Records later took over the Tally Catalogue and recycled the single, getting a Top Ten country hit with it.

The song was a Liz (♦) and Casey Anderson composition and in 1966 Merle had his first country No 1 with **I'm A Lonesome Fugitive,** also written by the twosome. It was the first in a long line of country hits. Merle had been trying to suppress the news of his prison record, but as the story came out the hard core country public were fascinated by this man who so obviously had lived the songs he wrote. In 1966 Merle released **The Bottle Let Me Down** (Emmylou Harris (♦) would later include the song on an album), in 1967 **Branded Man,** 1968 **Mama Tried** (which referred to his wild childhood and prison record), 1969 **Hungry Eyes** and **Workin' Man Blues** and in 1970 the well covered standard **Today I Started Loving You Again** (co-written with Bonnie Owens).

1970 also saw two other apparently innocent songs committed to record; **Okie From Muskogee** and **The Fighting Side Of Me. Okie** re-stated redneck values in the face of then current campus disturbances and Vietnam marches, yet Merle had written it as a joke, picking up a remark one of his band members had made about the conservative living habits of Oklahoma natives as the coach rolled through Muskogee one day. **Fighting Side Of Me** was another apparent putdown of those who were so bold as to disparage America's image. When Haggard premiered **Okie** for a crowd of gung-ho NCOs at the Fort Bragg, North Carolina camp they went wilder than he'd expected and from then on the song became a silent majority legend. President Nixon wrote to congratulate him on it. Haggard had been gaining a reputation as the new Woody Guthrie before **Okie,** and his hippy following was stunned yet intrigued by this new turn of events.

Haggard himself has admitted to feeling scared at the reaction the song provoked and he then backed away from further right wing involvement, refusing a proposal that had been offered him to endorse George Wallace politically. Indeed, for his next single he wanted to record a song about an inter-racial love affair **(Norma Jackson)** but Capitol advised against it.

Merle was able to settle into the straightforward country career he felt most comfortable with. He has not appeared over much on television. For one thing he lacks the easy, flip manner which TV companies seem to want from a host, and secondly he hasn't bothered to cultivate the medium. He once walked out on an Ed Sullivan show when they tried to tell him what songs to sing and how to sing them.

This is why Merle is valued so highly by country fans. In a genre where copping out into a straight showbiz format can earn one a fortune, Merle has consistently stepped back from such temptations and returned to his beloved bass fishing in the Northern California mountains.

Since **Okie,** hits have come consistently: **I Wonder What She'll Think About Me Leaving** and **It's Not Love But It's Not Bad** (written by Hank Cochran (♦) and Grady Martin) in 1972, and **If We Make It Through December** in 1975. Albums have provided an area for experimentation including one with a dixieland jazz band, **I Love The Blues (So I Recorded Live In New Orleans)** and, one of Haggard's most auspicious projects, **A Tribute To The Best Damn Fiddle Player In The World** in which he recruited original members of Bob Wills' (♦) band and teamed them with his own. Haggard had grown up with western swing, and Wills returned the compliment by inviting him to appear on Wills' own album **For The Last Time.** This was a fateful occasion since Wills suffered a stroke during these sessions from which he never recovered. Haggard has also recorded other concept albums, notably on trains (he is fascinated by the old American railroads) and religion.

Now signed to MCA, following his long association with Capitol, Merle Haggard is a classic and uncompromising country artist. His voice is hurting yet subtle with no showbiz nuances, and he gives the impression, with his sparsely instrumented band The Strangers, of being more comfortable before an ordinary working man's audience than in Las Vegas niteries. It is known that Merle wants to be remembered as a songwriter who wrote from life, like Jimmie Rodgers (♦) and Hank Williams (♦). It is certain that he will follow them into the annals of country music as one of The Godfathers.

Albums:

Same Train, A Different Time
(Capitol/—)

Okie From Muskogee
(Capitol/—)

The Fightin' Side Of Me
(Capitol/Capitol)
Tribute To The Best Damn Fiddle Player In The World
(Capitol/—)
Sing A Sad Song/High On A Hilltop *(Capitol/—)*
Hag *(Capitol/Capitol)*
The Best Of Merle Haggard
(Capitol/—)
The Best Of The Best Of . . .
(Capitol/—)
I Love Dixie Blues
(Capitol/Capitol)
Christmas Present *(Capitol/—)*
If We Make It Through December *(Capitol/—)*
His 30th Album *(Capitol/—)*
Keep Moving On
(Capitol/Capitol)
It's All In The Movies
(Capitol/Capitol)
My Love Affair With Trains
(Capitol/Capitol)
Let Me Tell You About A Song
(—/Capitol)
It's Not Love (But It's Not Bad)
(—/Capitol)

Very Best Of Merle Haggard
(—/Capitol)
A Portrait Of Merle Haggard
(—/Capitol)
The Roots Of My Raising
(Capitol/Capitol)
Merle Haggard And Bonnie Owens *(Pickwick/—)*
Songs I'll Always Sing
(Capitol/—)

Monte Hale

Just as Republic Pictures brought in young Roy Rogers (♦) to keep their recalcitrant star, Gene Autry (♦), in line, so they brought in Monte Hale when Roy became a star just in case he decided to become balky at contract time.

Same Train, A Different Time (Capitol). Like many other artists Haggard has been deeply influenced by Jimmie Rodgers, and pays tribute with a whole album of his songs.

Hale – who was born June 8, 1921 in San Angelo, Texas – went on to star in some nineteen Republic Westerns from 1945 to 1951, making him one of the last of the singing cowboys in chronological terms. Although posessed of a strong, smooth voice, his records – mainly for MGM – were not particularly successful; his singing highlights tended to come in his films, where he was backed, for the most part, by Foy Willing and the Riders of the Purple Sage (♦).

After his film making days were over (other than for a few non-singing television roles) Monte toured for a time as a singer and with rodeos before bowing out of musical and acting careers while still a young man. He currently lives in Nevada, and makes occasional appearances at Western film festivals.

Albums:
None

Theron Hale And Daughters

Theron Hale *fiddle*
Elizabeth Hale *fiddle*
Mamie Ruth Hale *piano*

Theron Hale (1883–1954) led one of the most interesting and popular of the early Opry bands from 1926 until the early 1930s. Unlike most of the raucous hoedown bands, their music was gentle and reminiscent of parlor music of the preceding century, highlighted by lovely twin fiddling. Like many other early Opry bands, they recorded only during Victor's 1928 field trip to Nashville. They were best known for popularizing **Listen To The Mocking Bird** as a trick-fiddling tune.

Bill Haley

Born William John Clifton Haley, Highland Park, Michigan, July 6, 1925. The leader of a series of good local country bands in the late 1940s and 1950s, he was undoubtedly more surprised than anyone when his creative mixture of R&B, boogie and country music took off like a rocket in 1955, with the success of **Rock Around The Clock** and later **Shake, Rattle And Roll** turning him into an international superstar overnight.

Haley had led bands which pretty much describe their musical approach – Bill Haley and The Four Aces Of Western Swing, Bill Haley and the Saddle Pals – before attempting to fuse the then all black sound of R&B with that of swing, western and country music. The result met such phenomenal reaction that it vaulted him out of the ranks of country into the ranks of rock, never to return. It is more than significant, however, that up until that turning point, his roots and approach had been firmly – if experimentally – country, a trait he shared with many of rock's originators. Though many Haley albums are available, the **Greatest Hits** and **Golden Hits** albums on US MCA and the **Rock Around The Clock** LP on British Coral tell you all you need to know about his hybrid creations.

Right: I Witness Life (Mercury).

Tom T. Hall

The Mark Twain of country music – even his band's called The Storytellers – Tom T. Hall's songs are full of colorful characters and intriguing or humorous situations. Born Olive Hill, Kentucky, 1936, the son of a preacher, he first learned to play on a broken Martin guitar, which his father, the Reverend Virgil L. Hall, restored to working order. At the age of 14, Tom T. quit school and went to

work in a clothing factory, two years later forming his first band, the Kentucky Travellers, playing local dates and appearing on radio station WMOR, Morehead, Kentucky. After the band broke up, Hall continued with WMOR, deejaying for a period of five years.

After enlistment in the army in 1957, Hall was posted to Germany, where he worked on the AFN radio network, taking the opportunity to try out a number of his own compositions – with some success. Discharged in 1961, he returned to WMOR, also working with The Technicians, another local band that enjoyed but a brief existence. More stints as a deejay followed, during which time Hall penned **DJ For A Day**, a major hit for Jimmy Newman (♦) in 1963. Next, Dave Dudley scored with **Mad** (1964), another Hall composition, and Hall promptly moved to Nashville to begin supplying songs to such acts as Roy Drusky (♦), Stonewall Jackson (♦) and Flatt and Scruggs (♦), eventually having his own hit disc with **I Washed My Face In The Morning Dew**, a Mercury release in 1967. A year

Tom T. Hall. Tremendously popular in the USA, Hall has failed to make any impression in Britain where his disc sales are dismal.

later, Jeannie C. Riley (♦) recorded **Harper Valley PTA** – a brilliant and highly commercial song about a fast-living woman and a band of small town hypocrites – and Hall became the writer of a million seller.

In recent years he's become something of a superstar – when he played Carnegie Hall in '73, the audience and the press went into raptures – while record buyers have readily snapped up such Hall releases as **A Week In A County Jail** (1969), **The Year That Clayton Delaney Died** (1971), **Old Dogs, Children And Watermelon Wine, Ravishing Ruby** (both 1973), **I Love, That Song Is Driving Me Crazy, Country Is** (all 1974) and **Fast Horses** (1976) all chart toppers from Nashville's prime yarn spinner. His albums include **Songs Of Fox Hollow** – which Hall described as 'an LP of

THE MAGNIFICENT MUSIC MACHINE
TOM T. HALL

MILOSEVICH

Director of many shows during the 1930s, Hall was still active in the music business up to the time of his death in Alabama, on April 2, 1969. Writer of such songs as **My Carolina Rose** and **My Dream Sweetheart,** he frequently guested on the WLS National Barn Dance (♦) show.

Stuart Hamblen

Born Kellyville, Texas, October 20, 1908, singer and bandleader Stuart Hamblen achieved considerable fame during the '50s as a songwriter. He attended the McMurray State Teachers College, Abilene, Texas in the 1920s but later switched to a musical career, working and broadcasting in the California area, sometimes appearing in minor roles in Western movies. In 1949, Hamblen had a Top Ten hit with a Columbia release, **But I'll Go Chasin' Women,** following this with **(Remember Me) I'm The One Who Loves You,** a few months later. An attempt to run for the Presidency of the United States, on a Prohibition Party ticket, proved a predictable failure in 1952, but in '54 he had more luck when his self-penned **This Ole House** (a song written after Hamblen had discovered a man laying dead inside a dilapidated hut many miles from the nearest habitation) became a country hit, prompting a million selling cover version by Rosemary Clooney, Billie Anthony making the British Top 20 with her recording of the same number.

Hamblen, who was responsible for many other popular songs of the '50s, followed many other artists, later turned increasingly to religious material, including the gospel standard **It Is No Secret (What God Can Do).** He currently has an album out on the gospel-oriented Word label. Other Hamblen-penned classics include **My Mary** and **Texas Plains,** both of which first became popular in the early 1930s.

Albums:
Country Church (*Word/Word*)
Men And Music (*Lamb/—*)

The Magnificent Music Machine (Mercury). Bluegrass from the son of a preacher man, whose Harper Valley PTA was a hit for Jeannie C. Riley.

songs from children of all ages' and, more recently, **The Magnificent Music Machine,** a bluegrass affair that spawned a popular single in **Fox On The Run,** Hall's highly individual version of a Tony Hazzard song that was once a 1969 pop chartbuster for Manfred Mann, and has long been a favorite of bluegrass bands.

Albums:
In Search Of Song (*Mercury/—*)
We All Got Together And . . .
 (*Mercury/—*)
The Storyteller (*Mercury/—*)
Greatest Hits (*Mercury/—*)
Songs Of Fox Hollow
 (*Mercury/—*)
**The Rhymer And Other Five
 And Dimers** (*Mercury/—*)
**For The People In The Last
 Hard Town** (*Mercury/—*)
Country Is (*Mercury/—*)
I Wrote A Song About It
 (*Mercury/—*)
Greatest Hits Vol 2 (*Mercury/—*)
Faster Horses (*Mercury/—*)
Magnificent Music Machine
 (*Mercury/—*)
**Country Classics From Tom T.
 Hall** (*—/Philips*)

A canine lover, Tom T. Hall breeds basset hounds and is apt to record such titles as The Fastest Rabbit Dog In Carter County.

Wendell Hall

Although he was by no means a true country entertainer, it was Hall's hillbilly-like recording of **It Ain't Gonna Rain No Mo',** a 1923 million seller, that encouraged Victor to embark on a search for possible country hitmakers.

Born St George, Kansas, August 23, 1896, Hall attended the University of Chicago and, after military service during World War I, began touring in vaudeville, singing and playing ukelele. Known as the Red Headed Music Maker, Hall was a friend of Carson Robinson's (♦), both going to New York to record for Victor during the early '20s.

George Hamilton IV

A pleasant voiced vocalist who has gained tremendous popularity in Canada and England as well as his native country, George Hamilton was born on July 19, 1937 and raised in Winston Salem, North Carolina. Becoming a country music fan after watching Gene Autry (♦) and Tex Ritter (♦) films at Saturday matinees, he bought his first guitar at the age of 12, earning the necessary cash on a paper round. He then began buying Hank Williams (♦) discs, frequently catching the Greyhound bus out to Nashville, where he saw Grand Ole Opry and met people like Chet Atkins (♦), Eddy Arnold (♦), Hank Snow (♦) and others.

Later he began a High School band at Reynolds High, Winston Salem, in his senior year making a demo recording of Little Jimmy Dickens' (♦) **Out Behind The Barn,** sending the results to talent scout Orville Campbell. Through Campbell, Hamilton met John D. Loudermilk (♦) and recorded his **A Rose And Baby Ruth,** which sold over a million in 1956–7. **Baby Ruth** was considered a pop hit rather than a country item and Hamilton found himself booked on the Alan Freed Show during the fall of 1956, also gaining a place on various package shows featuring Buddy Holly (♦), Gene Vincent and the Everly Brothers (♦).

Frustrated with his teenage-bopper image, Hamilton moved to Nashville in 1959, joined Grand Ole Opry and signed with RCA Records. He commenced singing primarily C&W fare, then in the early sixties, became influenced by the folk revival headed by such as Bob Dylan, Peter, Paul and Mary and Gordon Lightfoot. Becoming friendly with Lightfoot in 1965, Hamilton began recording a series of the Canadian's songs, eventually recording more Lightfoot compositions than any other artist. Through this Canuck connection, he began to work more and more with Canadian writers and later signed with RCA's Canadian division.

After a dozen years in Nashville, Hamilton moved to North Carolina once more because he felt such a move would prove beneficial to his family – by this time he'd acquired a wife, two teenage boys and a daughter.

First visiting England in 1967 en route to Nashville following a tour of US bases in Germany, he subsequently did a guest spot on the BBC's Country Meets Folk program, later becoming a regular on many British programs and being booked several times for Mervyn Conn's Country Music Festival at Wembley. In Canada, Hamilton has hosted his own TV show 'North Country' for five years, while in 1977 he became signed to Anchor, a British record label, rejoining ABC–Dot for American releases only.

George Hamilton IV. *This likeable family man has achieved star status in both Britain and Canada.*

Albums:
16 Greatest Hits *(ABC/ABC)*
Hits *(RCA/RCA)*
Bluegrass Gospel *(Lamb And Lion/Lamb And Lion)*
Canadian Pacific *(—/RCA)*
Country Music In My Soul *(—/RCA)*
Down Home In The Country *(—/RCA)*
Famous Country Music Makers *(—/RCA)*
Heritage *(—/RCA)*
International Ambassador *(—/RCA)*

Travellin' Light *(—/RCA)*
West Texas Highway *(—/RCA)*
Back Where It's At *(—/Camden)*
Trendsetter *(—/RCA)*
Back To Down East Country *(—/RCA)*
The George Hamilton Story *(—/RCA)*
This Is George Hamilton *(—/RCA)*
Best Of . . . Vol 1 *(—/RCA)*
Best Of . . . Vol 2 *(—/RCA)*
Fine Lace And Homespun Cloth *(Dot/Anchor)*

Above: Canadian Pacific *(RCA Victor). Hamilton has been influenced in the past by folk music, recording a number of Gordon Lightfoot songs, but his roots remain firmly country.*

Left: Bluegrass Gospel *(Lamb & Lion). One of the singer's few releases of religious material; his main direction lies in easy listening country songs.*

The Harden Trio: Great
Country Hits (Harmony).

Arleen Harden

One time secretary for an insurance company, Arleen Harden
(born England, Arkansas), was
part of the Harden Trio, a family
group, whose **Tippy Toeing**
charted for 21 weeks during 1966,
gaining the trio Opry membership
during 1966–68. During this time
they supplied Columbia with other
hits in **Seven Days Of Crying**
(1966), **Sneakin' Across The Border** (1967) and **Everybody Wants
To Be Somebody Else** (1968).
Arleen also became signed to the
label as a solo artist, having a first
hit with **Fairweather Lover** in
1967, and following the break up of
the Harden Trio in '68 she enjoyed
a subsequent string of minor successes, of which **Lovin' Man** (1970)
has proved the most potent to
date.

Following a stay with UA, Arleen
later signed for Capitol, cutting a
warm, easy-listening, Cam Mullins-
arranged album, **I Could Almost
Say Goodbye,** in 1975.

I Could Almost Say Goodbye
(Capitol).

Linda Hargrove

A superior singer-songwriter and
an outstanding guitarist (at least,
Pete Drake (♦) and Mike Nesmith
(♦) have said so) Linda was born in
1951 and raised in Tallahasee,
Florida, where she took piano
lessons at the age of five and
moved on to become a French
horn player in a high school band
before getting bitten by the rock
bug. Influenced by Dylan's **Nashville Skyline,** she packed her
bags and headed for Nashville in
1970, there hitting the hard times
until Sandy Posey recorded one of
her songs. Pete Drake, who sat in
on the Posey session, then offered
Linda a songwriting contract plus
some session chores as a guitarist,

Left: George Hamilton IV.

later teaching her to handle the
console at Drake's own studio.

An album featuring Linda was
cut by Mike Nesmith for his ill fated
Countryside label but never released – however, her songs met a
better fate, Leon Russell employing two on his **Hank Wilson's
Back** LP, Jan Howard (♦), Billie Jo
Spears (♦), Melba Montgomery (♦),
David Rogers (♦) and many others
also utilizing Linda's compositions
on various recordings. Since the
abortive Nesmith dates, Linda has
recorded for Elektra, cutting such
albums as **Music Is Your Mistress**
and **Blue Jean Country Queen,**
more recently becoming signed
to Capitol.

Albums:
Love You're The Teacher
(Capitol/—)
Just Like You (Capitol/—)

Linda Hargrove wanted to move into earthier and simpler music, so she went to Nashville despite
the fact that 'I used to think C&W was all cornbread and bouffants!'

Love, You're The Teacher
(Capitol).

Kelly Harrell

An early country music pioneer
who recorded as early as 1924 for
Ralph Peer (♦), then with Okeh
Records. Born Crockett Kelly
Harrell in Drapers Valley, Virginia, on September 13, 1899, he
made a number of important early
records for Victor, including
**Cuckoo, She's A Pretty Bird,
New River Train, Rovin' Gambler, I Wish I Was Single Again,
Charles Guiteau,** and **The Butcher Boy.** Often accompanied by
banjo, fiddle, and guitar, Harrell
himself played no instrument.

Despite the success of his early
records, and his songwriting
efforts in two popular early songs,
Away Out On The Mountain (as
recorded by Jimmie Rodgers (♦))
and **The Story Of The Mighty
Mississippi** (as recorded by
Ernest Stoneman), his musical
career was a brief one, and he
ended his short life working in a
rural Virginia towel factory. He
died of a heart attack on July 9, 1942.

Emmylou Harris

The First Lady of contemporary country music, Emmylou, with the help of Gram Parsons' (♦) songs, has been as responsible as anyone for making country acceptable to a wider audience. Born Birmingham, Alabama, 1949, she developed an early interest in country music and when her family moved to Washington DC she performed in the folk clubs there and in New York. An early album release on the Jubilee label in 1969 came to nothing. After this she made the ritual pilgrimage to Nashville, a fruitless journey, and also suffered a broken marriage.

Living in Virginia in the late '60s, Emmylou had become sufficiently known locally to be invited to Los Angeles by Gram Parsons to work on his first album for Warner Bros, **GP.** Warners were making a big effort to relaunch Parsons' career (by this time he was in a wasted state due to drugs and drink) and they had hired musicians from Elvis Presley's (♦) backing band to play on the album.

With Emmylou helping out and a new set of Parsons songs, it looked as if the country rock star might be on the verge of a new career. In 1973 Gram, Emmylou and the Fallen Angel Band embarked on a small tour. Tape of this tour and the evidence of those around them seemed to indicate that perhaps Gram might be finding a way back. Already, they had formulated the sound with which Emmylou would later ride to success. Gram's death occurred shortly after the recording of **Grievous Angel** in 1973 and this record is real evidence of what might have been.

Emmylou had been close to Gram and was stunned by his death. And when she picked up the threads of her own career it was to Gram's material that she turned. In 1975 she recorded **Pieces Of The Sky** for Reprise Records. It mixed country songs with some light rock 'n' roll, and although none of Gram's songs were included on this album she was using his material in her act. **Pieces Of The Sky** had not made a great dent on its release although her version of The Louvin Brothers' (♦) **If I Could Only Win Your Love** from the album did achieve No 1 status. But as Emmylou toured America and Europe her pure voice and impeccable backing band were to enchant listeners. She also has a fragile, Californian sort of beauty and those who had admired her recorded work found that her stage act was everything they had hoped for. The erstwhile Elvis Presley musicians, James Burton (guitar) and Glen D. Hardin (piano), were proving a big draw. Hardin had previously played with Buddy Holly's (♦) Crickets.

Her huge success in Europe particularly focused attention on Emmylou. Her voice had a pure, innocent, classic quality and it also lacked the nasal sound which so many non-country fans find hard to take. The second album, **Elite Hotel,** was released in 1976 and it featured three of Gram Parsons' better compositions: **Wheels, Sin City** and **Ooh Las Vegas.** As usual, it was a well balanced mix of country, ballads and rock. Emmylou's band at this time was Glen D. Hardin (piano), James Burton (guitar), Hank diVito (pedal steel guitar), Emory Gordy (bass), Rodney Crowell (rhythm guitar) and John Ware (drums). Crowell has proved himself a capable songwriter, having had a hand in three of Emmylou's best loved numbers: **Amarillo, Till I Gain Control Again** and **Boulder To Birmingham** (which last they co-wrote).

Emmylou's third album, **Luxury Liner,** was released in 1977 and follows in similar vein although James Burton has been replaced on guitar by Albert Lee, a British rock musician previously with Chris Farlowe's Thunderbirds and Heads, Hands And Feet. Emmylou now features heavily in country and pop charts and there is no doubt that she is set to be a top selling mainstream pop artist for some time.

Albums:
Emmylou Harris:
Pieces Of The Sky
(Reprise/Reprise)

Elite Hotel *(Reprise/Reprise)*
Luxury Liner *(Reprise/Reprise)*

Emmylou Harris; she has appeared on albums with Bob Dylan, Gram Parsons, Gene Clarke, Linda Ronstadt, Little Feat and many others.

Contemporary queen of the rodeo, Emmylou cut a solo album, Gliding Bird for Jubilee Records in 1969, but the label went bankrupt soon after.

Freddie Hart

Born Lochapoka, Alabama, December 21, 1933, Hart is said to have run away from home at seven, becoming – amongst other things – a cotton picker, a sawmill worker, a pipeline layer in Texas and a dishwasher in New York. By the age of 14, he'd become a marine, three years later helping to take Guam, having already been to Iwo Jima and Okinawa. A physical fitness expert and currently the possessor of a black belt in karate, he taught this form of self defense at the LA Police Academy in the '50s, eventually moving into the music business with the aid of Lefty Frizzell (♦) with whom he worked until 1953 when Hart signed a recording contract with Capitol. He subsequently recorded for Columbia (having his first hit in 1959 with **The Wall**), Monument and Kapp throughout the mid '60s, logging around a dozen chart entries, becoming a major artist after re-signing for Capitol in 1969 and having a million selling single

Easy Loving (1971), which won him the CMA Song Of The Year award in both 1971 and '72.

Since that time, Hart's enjoyed a runaway success, most of his singles claiming Top Five status, **My Hang Up Is You, Bless Your Heart, Got The All Overs For You** (all 1972), **Super Kind Of Woman, Trip To Heaven** (1973), **If You Can't Feel It, Hang On In There Girl, The Want To's** (1974), **The First Time** (1975) and **Why Lovers Turn To Strangers** (1977) being just a few of his major hits.

Now extremely wealthy, he owns many acres of plum trees, a trucking company and over 200 breeding bulls, and runs a school for handicapped children.

Easy Loving
(Capitol).

Albums:
The Best Of . . . *(MCA/—)*
Easy Loving *(Capitol/—)*
Greatest Hits *(Capitol/—)*
The First Time *(Capitol/—)*
People Put To Music *(Capitol/—)*
That Look In Her Eyes
  (Capitol/—)
Release Me *(Pickwick/—)*

John Hartford

This banjoist, fiddler, guitarist, singer-songwriter is one of the most exciting solo entertainers in country music today. Born New York, December 30, 1937, but raised in St Louis by his doctor father and painter mother, he first learnt to play on a banjo which he claims was beat up and had no head. By the time he was 13 he had also mastered fiddle and played at local square dances; next he graduated to the dobro then on to guitar. Upon leaving school, he worked as a sign painter, a commercial artist, a deckhand on a Mississippi riverboat and as a disc jockey. After marriage and the birth of a son, Hartford headed for Nashville, becoming a session musician – his work on these sessions gaining him a recording contract with RCA, for whom he cut eight albums and several singles; the first of these was **Tall Tall Grass,** a single released in 1966.

Soon many acts began recording Hartford's songs, and one, **Gentle On My Mind,** from his 1967 **Earthwords And Music** album, became a million seller when covered by Glen Campbell (♦),

Freddie Hart, a World War II teenage veterinary surgeon and black belt in karate.

John Hartford: Nobody Knows What You Do (Sonet).

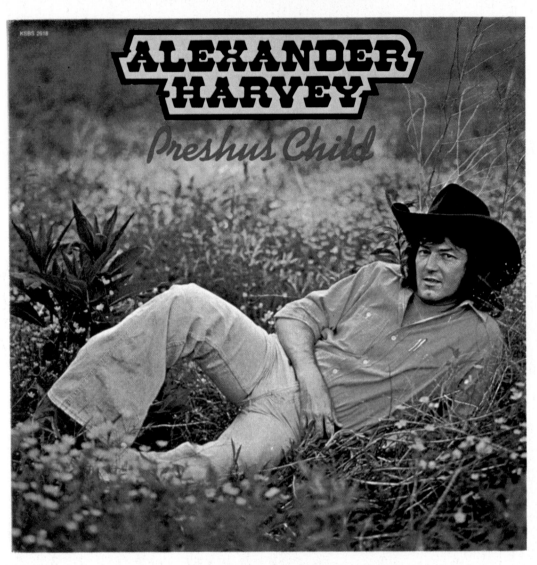

KSBS 2618

ALEXANDER HARVEY

Preshus Child

Preshus Child (Kama Sutra). Only current album by a songwriter who's provided a large number of quality hits.

Alex Harvey

Writer of **Delta Dawn, Reuben James, Tulsa Turnaround** and many other hits, Harvey was born in Brownsville, Tennessee, 1945.

Attending Murray State University, Kentucky, he obtained a degree in music and became conductor of the University Symphony Orchestra. Later he became involved in various bands and during the mid '60s moved to Nashville where he transcribed songs from tape for such aspiring writers as Kristofferson (♦), who proved unable to read or write music. Establishing himself as a quality singer-songwriter through such songs as **Molly** (a hit for Jim Glaser (♦)), **Love Of A Gentle Woman** (John Gary), **Reuben James** (Kenny Rogers (♦)) Harvey was awarded his own TV Show, Fun Farm, and also gained a Capitol recording contract.

He became a resident of Hollywood in 1970 but continued to provide an equal flow of pop and country material, Tompall and The Glaser Brothers (♦) having a hit with **Rings** in 1971, Tanya Tucker (♦) achieving a crossover success via **Delta Dawn** in '72 and Kenny Rogers recording **Ballad Of Calico,** a whole album of Harvey songs, that same year.

Harvey, who now records under the name of Alexander Harvey to save confusion with his Scottish rock singer namesake, has also made his mark in film music, contributing a score to the movie 'Fools'.

Albums:
Preshus Child *(Kama Sutra/—)*

The unpredictable John Hartford is likely to break into such zany material as Don't Leave Your Records In The Sun, sung in warped disc manner.

entering the charts in both July 1967 and September 1969, winning three Grammies in the process and becoming the most recorded song of the period. After appearances on the Smothers Brothers Comedy Hour and a regular spot on the Glen Campbell Goodtime Hour, Hartford toured with his own band for a while but eventually opted to become a solo performer. His 1976 **Mark Twang** album presents him in this role, unaccompanied by any rhythm section, Hartford providing all the percussive sounds with his mouth and feet! It went on to win a Grammy of its own, in the best ethnic/traditional category.

Albums:
Aero Plain
 (Warner Bros/Warner Bros)
Mark Twang
 (Flying Fish/Sonet)
Nobody Knows What You Do
 (Flying Fish/Sonet)

Hawkshaw Hawkins

One more victim of the plane crash that killed Patsy Cline (♦) and Cowboy Copas (♦), Harold Hawkins was born Huntingdon, West Virginia, December 22, 1921. A guitarist at the age of 15, he then won a local amateur talent show, the prize being a $15 a week spot on radio station WSAZ. By the time of Pearl Harbor, Hawkins had established himself as a radio personality – but he then enlisted and was sent for service in the Pacific area. By 1946 he was home again and singing on WWVA, Wheeling, West Virginia. Then came a recording contract with King and hit records in **I Wasted A Nickel** (1949) and **Slow Poke** (1951), plus a country classic in **Sunny Side Of The Mountain.** But despite some recordings for RCA and a 1955 contract with Grand Ole Opry, Hawkins enjoyed no further chart success until 1959, when a Columbia single **Soldier's Joy** climbed high in the country lists. Four years later – he was at this time married to Jean Shepard (♦) – his first country No 1 came with the release of **Lonesome 7-7203,** a song penned by Justin Tubb (♦). But on March 5, 1963, just two days after the disc had entered the charts, Hawkins was lying dead among the aircraft wreckage near Kansas.

His album releases included **Hawkshaw Hawkins Sings** (Camden), **All New Hawkshaw Hawkins Songs** (King), **The Great Hawkshaw Hawkins** (Harmony) and **Country Gentleman** (Camden).

The All New Hawkshaw Hawkins (London).

George D. Hay

Founder of the Grand Ole Opry, George Dewey Hay (born Attica, Indiana, November 9, 1895) was once a reporter for the *Memphis Commercial Appeal.* Shortly after World War 1, while on an assignment in the Ozarks, he attended a mountain cabin hoedown, thus conceiving an idea which later resulted in country music obtaining its most famous showcase.

When the *Appeal* moved into radio, setting up station WMC, Hay became radio editor, later, in 1924, taking up an appointment as an announcer on Chicago radio station WLS. With WLS he helped begin the National Barn Dance (♦) program, gaining high ratings, this success leading to a position of director with the newly established WSM, Nashville, in 1925. Again he instigated a similar Barndance pro-

He may be a periphary figure on the country scene, but Alex Harvey has contributed many outstanding songs to its repertoire.

gram, the first broadcast taking place on November 28, 1925, although it did not become a regularly scheduled program until December of that year. The show rapidly grew in quality and popularity. It was on December 10, 1927, that the WSM Barn Dance became officially retitled Grand Ole Opry. The show had been preceded by a program featuring the NBC Symphony Orchestra and, after an introductory number by De-Ford Bailey (♦), Hay, who announced the show, declared:

'For the past hour we have been listening to music taken from Grand Opera – but from now on we will present the Grand Ole Opry.' And so the Opry it became.

Hay, known as the Solemn Old Judge, continued to expand and develop the Opry throughout the rest of his career, extending the range of WSM's broadcasts, encouraging the best country entertainers in the country to appear in Nashville, and recruiting new talent to keep the show both vital and fresh. However, he began to show some signs of mental instability, and in 1951 he retired to live with his daughter in Virginia and

The Solemn Ol' Judge, George D. Hay, who will always be remembered as the man who named the Opry – in country's most famous speech on December 10, 1927.

died at Virginia Beach, Virginia, May 9, 1968, having been elected to the Country Music Hall of Fame in 1966.

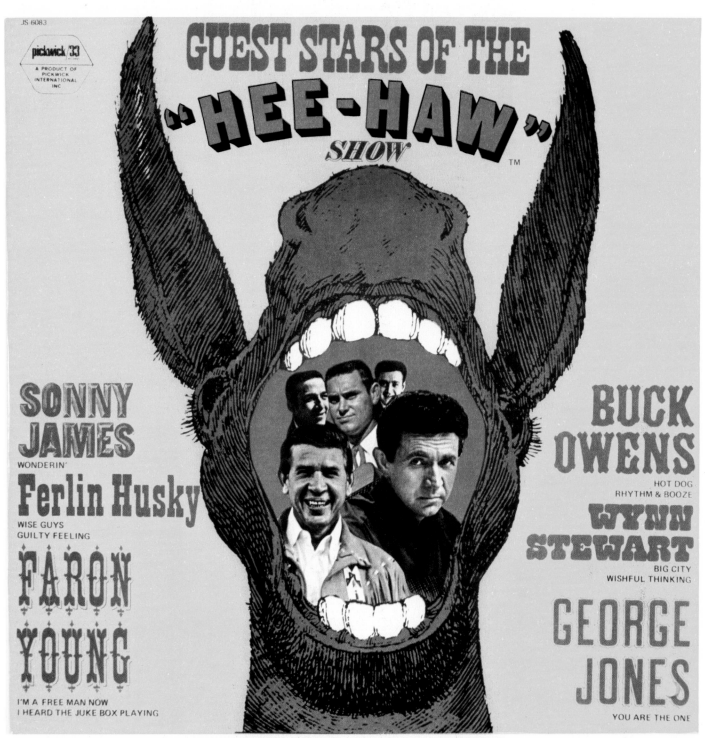

GUEST STARS OF THE "HEE-HAW" SHOW ™

JS-6083

pickwick/33
A PRODUCT OF
PICKWICK
INTERNATIONAL
INC

SONNY JAMES
WONDERIN'
Ferlin Husky
WISE GUYS
GUILTY FEELING
FARON YOUNG
I'M A FREE MAN NOW
I HEARD THE JUKE BOX PLAYING

BUCK OWENS
HOT DOG
RHYTHM & BOOZE
WYNN STEWART
BIG CITY
WISHFUL THINKING
GEORGE JONES
YOU ARE THE ONE

Guest Stars Of The Hee-Haw Show (Pickwick). A compilation from some of the most popular artists on this surprisingly young television program.

Hee Haw

Established in the summer of 1969, Hee Haw, a syndicated TV show, like the Glen Campbell (♦) and Johnny Cash (♦) Shows, brought country music to an audience who'd never previously heard of a dobro.

Full of cornporn humor, supplied by funny men like Archie Campbell (♦) (who also writes much of the script), Grandpa Jones (♦) and Junior Samples (♦), and featuring the musicianship of Buck Owens (♦), Roy Clark (♦) and many others, the show has won through despite (or perhaps because of) its lack of sophistication. Canceled by CBS-

TV in 1972, Hee Haw has continued to be marketed by Youngstreet Productions, each series reaching a huge viewing audience.

Bobby Helms

A crossover performer, Helms had a Top Ten pop hit with **Jingle Bell Rock** in 1957, the same year that he was adjudged the nation's leading country singer by *Cashbox* magazine.

Born Bloomington, Indiana, August 15, 1935, guitarist, singer-songwriter Helms appeared on radio at the age of 13, making his debut on Grand Ole Opry four years later. In 1957, he achieved a No 1 country hit with **Fraulein,** the disc remaining in the charts for a whole year, while his version of Jimmy Duncan's **My Special Angel** became both a C&W and pop hit, selling over a million copies. The impetus was maintained through-

out 1958, with **Jacqueline** (from the film *A Case Against Brooklyn*) and **Just A Little Lonesome** providing him with best sellers – but despite constant seasonal reappearances by **Jingle Bell Rock** (which took five years to become a million seller), Helms' record ca-

All New Just For You (Little Darlin').

reer faded rapidly. Between 1960–67 his name was absent from the charts, but later he achieved a series of mini hits on such labels as Little Darlin' and Cetron, as he drifted in and out of the business.

His past albums include **All New Just For You** (*Little Darlin'*), **Sorry, My Name Isn't Fred** (*Kapp*) and **Fraulein** (*Harmony*)

Albums:
My Special Angel
  (Vocalion/—)
Sings His Greatest Hits
  (Power Pak/—)

Goldie Hill

Though she went into semi-retirement shortly after her marriage to Carl Smith (♦), Goldie Hill is still remembered as one of the most popular female country singers of the 1950s, her version of **Don't Let The Stars Get In Your Eyes** be-

115

coming a Top Five hit in 1953. Born Karnes County, Texas, January 11, 1933, Goldie began her professional singing career during the early '50s, signing for Decca and appearing on Shreveport's Louisiana Hayride Show (♦) in 1952, joining the Opry the following year after the success of **Don't Let The Stars.** During the mid '50s she toured on several major shows, working on some with Carl Smith, whom she married in 1957. Though she had a best selling disc with **Yankee Go Home** in 1959, Goldie restricted her number of personal appearances during the 1960s, occasionally visiting the recording studios to cut such sides as **Loveable Fool,** a 1968 success. There are currently no Goldie Hill albums in the catalogue, though such titles as **Heartaches, According To My Heart** and **Hit Parade** graced the Decca catalogue not so very long ago.

Adolph Hofner

A native Texan of German-Slavic descent, Adolph Hofner has had a long and fascinating career playing both western swing and ethnic dance music for Texas' large German-American community. He began his career in San Antonio in the 1930s, and continues to this day, traveling five days a week within the Texas state line sponsored by Pearl Beer.

Hofner recorded for Bluebird and Okeh before World War II, and during the war hit the west coast dance circuit – where his billing was changed to Dub Hofner due to the similarity of his name to that of Germany's Fuhrer – before returning to Texas, where he recorded for Columbia, Decca, and Sarge, his biggest hits coming on Columbia: **Alamo Steel Serenade** and **Cotton Eyed Joe.**

Albums: none.

Buddy Holly

One of rock's prime movers in its early years, Buddy Holly actually began his career as a country singer, and the sound was never to leave him during his short but brilliant life; nor has the power of his songwriting seemed to diminish in recent years, as **That'll Be The Day, Every Day** and **It Doesn't Matter Any More** have all been hits in the country field in recent years.

Charles Hardin Holley (the 'e' in his last name was dropped only after he signed his first record contract) was born September 7, 1936, in Lubbock, Texas, and grew up listening to the blues and Tex-Mex music as well as to Hank Williams (♦) and Bill Monroe (♦). His first band, with longtime friend Montgomery, tells the story of their musical approach; they were called Buddy and Bob: Western and Bop.

Holly's first professional session was, in fact, a country session for Decca, produced in Nashville by Owen Bradley (♦) early in 1956, and featuring not Holly's own band but a group of Nashville sidemen. However, the combination of slick Nashville sound and raw Texas rockabilly did not mix well, and the records were not successful. It is ironic that Holly's

Buddy Holly (MCA). Although Holly is remembered mostly for his rock music and that is where his main influence lies, his first recording contract (unsuccessful) was as a country singer for Decca – produced by Owen Bradley – after he had been discovered appearing with Elvis Presley and Marty Robbins.

great success came on Coral Records, a Decca subsidiary, after the parent label had dropped him.

His career as a rock star – although many country stations continued to play his records, and many country fans continued to buy them – was brief and hectic, filled with hit records like **Oh Boy!, Peggy Sue, Rave On, Fool's Paradise** and **Raining In My Heart.** It was on one of his hectic tours that he died in a plane crash on February 3, 1959.

Still, has songs, his style, and two of his sidemen – Waylon Jennings

(♦) and Tommy Allsup – have left great marks in country music, and he was a genuine influence on it at this pivotal point in its history.

Albums:
Great Buddy Holly
  (Vocalion/—)
Rock 'n' Roll Collection
  (MCA/—)
Rave On *(—/MCA)*
Brown Eyed Handsome Man
  (—/MCA)
Greatest Hits *(—/Coral)*
Buddy Holly *(—/Coral)*
Legend *(—/Coral)*

Goldie Hill, once a contender for Kitty Wells' 'Queen of Country Music' crown.

Doyle Holly

Born June 30, 1936, Perkins, Oklahoma, Holly learnt bass guitar at an early age, forming a band with his older brothers and playing at rodeos and other venues.

A Kansas oilfield worker at 13, he remained in this occupation until 1953 when he joined the army, performing tours of duty in Okinawa and Korea.

In 1957, Holly was discharged and returned to oilfield work, this time in the Bakersfield (♦) area of California. As a part timer he played in Johnny Burnette's band along with Fuzzy Owen and Merle Haggard (♦), then, following a number of ups and downs that sometimes found him on the breadline, he joined Buck Owens (♦), becoming a regular member of the Buckaroos from August 1963, until late 1970, often being cast in the role of resident funnyman.

With his own band, The Vanishing Breed, he became signed to Barnaby Records during the early '70s and registered two fair size hits with **Queen Of The Silver Dollar** and **Lila** in 1973.

Homer And Jethro

From Knoxville, Tennessee, Henry D. Haynes (Homer), (born July 29, 1917), and Kenneth C. Burns (Jethro) (born March 10, 1923), formed a duo in 1932, the two boys winning a regular spot on station WNOX, Knoxville.

Discovering that their parodies gained more attention than their 'straight' material, they opted to become country comics, holding down a residency at the Renfro Valley, Kentucky, until war service

Gabe Ward, clarinet-playing leader of novelty band the Hoosier Hot Shots, an entertaining and zany bunch of musicians.

caused a temporary halt to their career. With Japan defeated, the duo reformed, for a decade appearing as cast members of the National Barn Dance (♦) on Chicago WLS, also guesting on the Opry and many networked radio and TV shows. Signed to RCA Records in the late '40s, they cut **Baby It's Cold Outside** with June Carter (♦) in 1948, obtaining later hits with **That Hound Dog In The Window** (1953), **Hernando's Hideaway** (1954), **The Battle Of Kookamonga** (1959) and **I Want To Hold Your Hand** (1964). The duo also recorded a number of instrumental albums (Haynes on guitar, Burns on mandolin), at one time teaming with Chet Atkins (♦) to form a recording group known as The Nashville String Band.

The 39-year-old partnership terminated on August 7, 1971, with the death of Henry Haynes.

The Hoosier Hot Shots

Gabe Ward *clarinet*
Hezzie Triesch *song whistle, washboard, drums, alto horn*
Kenny Triesch *banjo, tenor guitar, bass horn*
Frank Kettering *banjo, guitar, flute, piccolo, bass, piano*

'Are you ready, Hezzie?' always signaled the arrival of the Hoosier Hot Shots on the National Barn Dance (♦), a first rate group of comedians and musicians who had one of the most popular novelty acts in the country before Spike Jones came along.

They started out as a small dance band but their flair for comedy and unusual instruments got the best of them, and when they joined WLS in 1935 it was as a novelty group, and their success was immediate. They appeared in many films both with and without other Barn Dance castmembers, and eventually retired to California, where they still play from time to time.

Their records (for the ARC complex of labels and Vocalion) did well, but they were primarily – despite their genuinely fine musicianship – a visual comedy act that was best seen as well as heard.

Albums: none.

Doc Hopkins

Doctor Howard Hopkins – yes, that's his real name – was born January 26, 1899 in Harlan County Kentucky. He was associated for a long time (1930–1949) with station WLS and the National Barn Dance (♦), and during that period became well known as one of the best and most authentic of American folk singers. Although he spent a great deal of time on WLS and has recorded for many labels (including Paramount, Decca, and others), he has somehow never received the recognition as a country music pioneer he richly deserves. He currently lives in Chicago.

The Spectacular Johnny Horton (Columbia).

Shreveport's famed Louisiana Hayride (♦) radio show, later joining the cast as a regular member. During his teen years he completed his college education then, in the late '50s, began touring avidly, appearing also on many TV and radio shows. Signed to Epic Records in 1963, he gained an instant hit with **Mountain Of Love** which stayed in the charts for 18 weeks, winning Houston 'Most Promising Country Newcomer' plaudits from music magazines.

An accomplished yodeler and a talented guitarist-pianist, Houston went from strength to strength throughout the '60s, having No 1 hits with **Almost Persuaded** (1966) **With One Exception** (1967), **You Mean The World To Me** (1967) **My Elusive Dreams** (with Tammy Wynette – 1967), **Have A Little Faith** (1968), **Already It's Heaven** (1968) and **Baby, Baby (I Know You're A Lady)** (1969), winning two Grammy awards for **Almost Persuaded** and earning a film part in a 1967 movie, *Cottonpickin' Chickenpickers*.

During the early '70s Houston's discs continued to chart regularly, **I Do My Singing At Home** (1970), **After Closing Time** (with Barbara Mandrell (♦) – 1970), **Wonders Of The Wine** (1970), **A Woman Always Knows** (1971), **Nashville** (1971), **Home, Sweet, Home** (1971), **Soft Sweet And Warm** (1972), **Good Things** (1973) and **She's All Woman** (1973) all being Top Ten contenders. In 1976 his chart singles included **Come On Down (To Our Favourite Forget-About-Her Place) What A Night** and **The Woman On My Mind**.

Albums:
Greatest Hits *(Epic/Epic)*
Best Of Houston And Mandrell *(Epic/—)*
Day Love Walked In *(Epic/—)*
A Perfect Match – with Barbara Mandrell *(Epic/—)*
What A Night *(Epic/—)*

Twice a gold-record winner, Johnny Horton, who died in a car accident during 1960, achieved posthumous chart entries in 1961–63.

Johnny Horton

With **Battle Of New Orleans**, a Jimmy Driftwood (♦) song said to be based on an old fiddle tune known as **The 8th Of January**, Horton achieved one of the biggest selling discs of 1959, a cover version by skiffle king Lonnie Donegan becoming a Top Five record in Britain.

Born Tyler, Texas, April 3, 1929, Horton went to college in Jacksonville and Kilgore, Texas, later attending the University of Seattle, Washington. Spending some time in the fishing industry in Alaska and California, he then became a performer under the title of The Singing Fisherman, starring on Shreveport's Louisiana Hayride (♦) during the mid '50s. Completing recording stints with both Mercury

and Dot, he moved on to Columbia, his first hit being with **Honky Tonk Man** (1956) and his first country No 1 with **When It's Springtime In Alaska** (1959). Following the runaway success of the million-selling **Battle Of New Orleans**, Horton became a nationwide star, having hits with **Johnny Reb/Sal's Got A Sugar Lip** (1959) and **Sink The Bismarck** (1960), also being asked to sing Mike Phillips' **North To Alaska** in the John Wayne movie of that title, the resulting record providing the Texan with yet another million seller in 1960.

On November 5, 1960, Horton was killed in a car accident while traveling to Nashville – but still his records continued to sell, **Sleepy Eyed John** (1961), **Honky Tonk Man** (1962) and **All Grown Up** (1963) all being posthumous chart entries.

Albums:
Johnny Horton *(Columbia/—)*
Honky Tonk Man *(Columbia/—)*
Makes History *(Columbia/—)*
On Stage *(Columbia/—)*
Spectacular *(Columbia/—)*
Voice *(Columbia/—)*
World *(Columbia/—)*
Greatest Hits *(—/CBS)*

David Houston

A direct descendant of Sam Houston and Robert E. Lee, Houston was born Shreveport, Lousiana, December 9, 1938.

Brought up in Bossier City, where he was taught guitar by his aunt, Houston was aided in his career by his godfather Gene Austin (a pop singer who had 1920s million sellers with **My Blue Heaven** and **Ramona**). By the age of 12, Houston had won a guest spot on

The Best of David Houston (CBS).

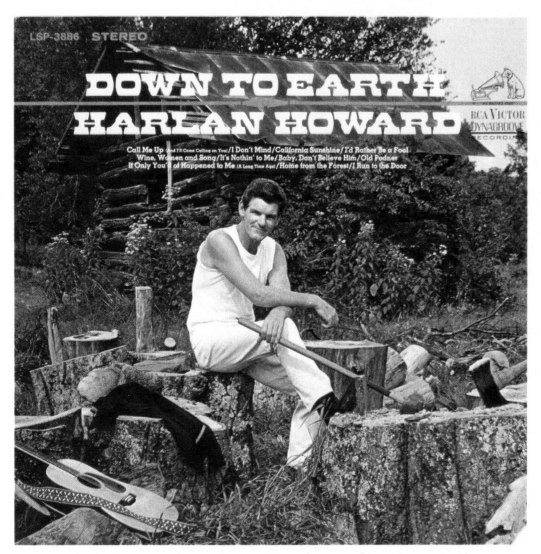

LSP-3886 STEREO

DOWN TO EARTH
HARLAN HOWARD

Call Me Up (And I'll Come Calling on You)/I Don't Mind/California Sunshine/I'd Rather Be a Fool
Wine, Women and Song/It's Nothin' to Me/Baby, Don't Believe Him/Old Podner
If Only You'd of Happened to Me (A Long Time Ago)/Home from the Forest/I Run to the Door

Down To Earth (RCA Victor). A leading country songwriter, Howard prefers to remain known as such but is also a fine singer.

Harlan Howard

An outstanding performer – as his **Down To Earth** (1968) so conclusively proves, Howard (born Lexington, Kentucky, September 8, 1929) has generally preferred to remain a songwriter, picking up numerous awards, and running his Wilderness Music Publishing Company. Raised in Detroit, he began songwriting at the age of 12. Spending four years in the paratroops following high school graduation, he became based in Fort Benning, Georgia, spending his weekend passes in Nashville whenever possible.

Later, in Los Angeles, he met Tex Ritter (♦) and Johnny Bond (♦), who began publishing his songs, hits emerging with **Pick Me Up On Your Way Down** (Charlie Walker, 1958), **Mommy For A Day** (Kitty Wells (♦), 1959) and **Heartaches By The Number** (Ray Price (♦) and Guy Mitchell (♦), 1959). In 1960, Howard along with his wife, singer Jan Howard (♦), moved to Nashville where, proving to be a veritable hit machine, he became known as the 'king' of country songwriters, a title only challenged perhaps by Dallas Frazier (♦) and Bill Anderson (♦). His many songs have included **I've Got A Tiger By The Tail, Under The Influence Of Love, A Guy Named Joe, Streets Of Baltimore, Heartbreak USA, Busted, No Charge, I Fall To Pieces** and **Three Steps To The Phone**, Howard winning no less than ten citations – a record number – for the BMI in 1961. As a recording artist he has cut albums for Monument, RCA and Nugget.

Below: David Houston (seen here with Barbara Mandrell) usually travels to gigs in a luxuriously converted bus, complete with bath.

Rock Me Back To Little Rock (MCA).

Jan Howard

The daughter of a Cherokee maid and an Irish immigrant, Jan was born at West Plains, Missouri, March 13, 1932, acquiring her present surname after marriage to songwriter Harlan Howard (♦).

An avid country music record collector in her early days, her first public performance came as a result of a meeting with Johnny and June Cash (♦), a tour with Johnny Horton (♦) and Archie Campbell (♦) ensuing. At the close of the '50s, she began recording for the Challenge label, her first release being **Yankee Go Home,** a duet with Wynn Stewart (♦). This

Jan Howard, winner of the Best Dressed Woman In Nashville award, is probably best known for her duets with Bill Anderson.

Jan followed with **The One You Slip Around With,** a 1960 hit that won her several awards in the Most Promising Newcomer category. In the wake of recordings for such labels as Capitol and Wrangle, she moved to Nashville during the mid '60s, there signing for Decca Records, also teaming with Bill Anderson (♦) as a featured part of his road and TV shows. With Anderson she cut a number of hit duets that included **I Know You're Married** (1966), **For Loving You** (a 1967 No 1), **If It's All The Same To You** (1969), **Someday We'll Be Together** (1970) and **Dissatisfied** (1971). Proving similarly successful as a solo act, a score or so of her releases attained chart status, the most prominent of these being **Evil On Your Mind** (1966), **Bad Seeds** (1966), **Count Your Blessings, Woman** (1968) and **My Son** (1968), the last named being a self penned tribute to her son Jim, who died in Viet Nam just two weeks after the song had been recorded. Following the tragic death of the second of her three sons, Jan, once contender for the Queen of Country Music crown, opted for retirement during the early '70s, although she has lately been appearing with the Carter Family on Johnny Cash's road shows. Her past MCA albums have included **Rock Me Back To Little Rock, Jan Howard** and, with Bill Anderson, **For Loving You.**

Albums:
Rock Me Back To Little Rock
  (Pickwick/—)
Sincerely (GRT/—)

120

Paul Howard

Although hot western swing on the stage of the staid Grand Ole Opry sounds a little far fetched, that was exactly Paul Howard's role in the 1940s, the height of western swing's popularity. Born July 10, 1908 in Midland, Arkansas, Howard drifted in and out of music until 1940, when he joined the Opry as a solo singer.

Always entranced by western swing, he began to build a bigger and bigger band, which grew to some nine or ten pieces, sometimes with multiple basses to make up for the lack of drums which were then still taboo on the Opry stage. His band, the Arkansas Cotton Pickers, was one of the hottest of the era, and he recorded for Columbia and King in his heyday.

Frustrated by the lack of attention western swing got in the south east, Howard left the Opry in 1949 for a circuit of radio programs and dances in Louisana, Arkansas, and Texas. He currently lives in Shreveport, where he still leads a band and plays dances.

Albums: none.

Ferlin Husky

Born Flat River, Missouri, December 3, 1927, comedian-singer-songwriter-guitarist Husky grew up on a farm. It's claimed that his first attempt to own a guitar was foiled when the hen that he swopped it for failed to lay eggs, causing neighbors to cancel the deal. He did, however, obtain a guitar at a later date and, following stints in the merchant marine and as a deejay, began performing in the Bakersfield (♦), California, area, using the name Terry Preston and eventually being discovered by Tennessee Ernie Ford (♦) manager Cliffie Stone (♦), who asked Husky to deputize for Ford during a vacation period. Around same time Husky also created a character called Simon Crum, a kind of hick philosopher who became so popular that Capitol signed the singer to cut several sides as his alter ego.

Later, recording as Terry Preston, Husky had his first hit with **A Dear John Letter,** a duet recorded with Jean Shepard (♦) in 1953, eventually obtaining a minor hit under his own name with **I Feel Better All Over,** two years on. During 1957 he appeared on a Kraft TV Theatre show playing a dramatic role, also the same year recording **Gone,** a remake of a Smokey Rogers song originally cut by Husky in his Terry Preston era, this new version becoming a million seller. By 1958 it was Crum's turn to become a chartbuster, a comedy song **Country Music Is Here To Stay** hitting the No 2 spot in the country listings. 1958 also saw Husky obtain a film role in *Country Music Holiday,* alongside Zsa Zsa Gabor and Rocky Graziano.

Since 1957 his long list of record hits have included **A Fallen Star, Wings Of A Dove** and **The Waltz You Saved For Me,** all crossover successes; and **Once** and **Just For You,** both country top ten items. Father of seven children – the youngest being named Terry Preston in memory of Husky's earlier identity – the singer has made many radio, TV and film ap-

Paul Howard and his Arkansas Cotton Pickers, one of the '40s' hottest western swing bands. Note the drum kit – banned from the Opry for many years.

pearances in recent years and recorded for ABC during the early and mid '70s. He tours with his group The Hush Puppies.

Albums:
The Best Of Ferlin Husky
  (Capitol/—)
Rambling Rose (Pickwick/—)

True True Lovin' (ABC/—)
Wings Of A Dove (Pickwick/—)
Champagne Ladies And Blue
  Ribbon Babies (ABC/—)
Sings The Foster-Rice Songbook
  (ABC/—)
Hits (Capitol/—)
Sweet Honky Tonk (ABC/—)

The Country Sounds of Ferlin Husky (ABC). Apart from the famous Simon Crum, another alias is Terry Preston, under which name he has scored a number of hits.

Aunt Mollie Jackson

An early protest singer, Aunt Mollie was born Mary Magdalene Garland, Clay County, Kentucky, 1880. Daughter of a miner, her mother died of starvation in 1886, her brother, husband and son all died in pit accidents, her father and another brother being blinded by further mining misadventures. Jailed at the age of ten for her union activities, she became a union organizer, singing at meetings and on picket lines, moving to New York in 1936 after being blacklisted throughout Kentucky because of her beliefs.

In New York, Aunt Mollie, along with her sister Sarah Ogan Gunning, continued her combined singing and union activities, and recorded a great wealth of material for the Library of Congress – though her sole commercial disc was **Kentucky Miner's Wife,** a Columbia single. She died on September 1, 1960.

Albums:
Library Of Congress Recordings
  (Rounder/—)

Carl Jackson

A fast-pickin' banjo and guitar player who's been an integral part of the Glen Campbell (♦) Show since August, 1972, Jackson was born in Louisville, Mississippi, 1953.

Ferlin Husky's alter ego Simon Crum, hick philosopher supreme, in typical pose. Fans tend to think of Crum as a star in his own right.

**Banjo Player
(Capitol).**

He learnt the banjo at the age of five and at 13 began playing with a family bluegrass outfit that included his father and uncle. During his high school days he toured as part of Jim and Jesse's (♦) band, cutting a solo album, **Bluegrass Festival,** for Prize Records during this period. He also put in some time with the Sullivan Family, a local gospel group, at one point during his career.

In 1972, he visited the Ohio State Fair, Columbus, to hear Glen Campbell (♦) and learnt that Larry McNeely, Campbell's banjoist, was leaving the group. McNeely then set up a meeting between Jackson and Campbell, the latter being so impressed by the 19 year old's

WATERLOO
I WASHED MY HANDS
IN MUDDY WATER
WILDWOOD FLOWER
DON'T BE ANGRY
"NEVER MORE"
QUOTE THE RAVEN
A WOUND TIME CAN'T ERASE
ANGRY WORDS
WHY I'M WALKING
LIFE TO GO
BLACK SHEEP
OLD SHOWBOAT

Live At The Grand Ole Opry (Columbia). Instantly successful in Nashville, Jackson is the composer of many hits and a popular performer.

Wanda Jackson

Child prodigy Wanda Jackson was born Maud, Oklahoma, October 20, 1937, the daughter of a piano playing barber. By the age of ten she could play both guitar and piano, three years later obtaining her own radio show. By 1954 she was cutting discs for Decca – charting with a Billy Grey-aided duet **You Can't Have My Love** – and began touring with Hank Thompson's (♦) band. In 1955–56, Wanda toured with Elvis Presley (♦), then became Capitol Record's leading female rocker, scoring heavily in the 1960 pop charts with **Let's Have A Party**. However, 1961 saw her return to more C&W oriented fare – and her hits such as **Right Or Wrong** and **In The Middle Of A Heartache** went into both pop and country charts.

Throughout the '60s, Wanda racked up over a score of hits – even having a major success in Japan with a rocking **Fujiyama Mama** – and though her chart-busting continued into the 1970s, in '71 she asked for her release from Capitol and switched instead to pure gospel music, cutting sides for the religious Word and Myrrh labels. Married to her manager Wendell Goodman, Wanda has two children, Gina and Greg.

Albums:
The Best Of Wanda Jackson *(Capitol/—)*
Phoenix *(Pickwick/—)*

playing that he immediately signed him as part of his touring show, six months later producing and playing on a Jackson solo album, **Banjo Player,** which was released by Capitol in 1973.

Albums:
Banjo Player *(Capitol/Capitol)*

Stonewall Jackson

His real name; he was named after the Confederate general. Born Tabor City, North Carolina, November 6, 1932, he had an impoverished childhood and obtained his first guitar at the age of ten by trading an old, tire-less bike. He figured out chords by watching other youngsters on their

guitars and would sit listening to the radio and using what he heard as the basis for constructing his own songs.

After submarine service in the navy, during which time he sometimes entertained the crews, he worked on farms and within two years, by 1956, had saved enough money to go to Nashville. Wesley Rose (♦), head of Acuff Rose publishing, heard him and signed him to a long term contract.

He had outstanding appeal as a performer and was immediately successful across the country via TV.

In 1958 he had a big country hit with **Life To Go** and 1959 saw his big crossover smash **Waterloo,** an international pop hit in which a neat country backing was combined with novelty lyrics drawing military analogies to a love affair. As a result of the hit he starred on Dick Clark's American Bandstand.

Other Jackson-composed standards were **Don't Be Angry, Mary Don't You Weep** and **I Washed My Hands In Muddy Waters.** In 1967 he came back strongly with **Stamp Out Loneliness** and also had a very successful album based around this title.

Albums:
At The Opry *(Columbia/—)*
Greatest Hits *(Columbia/—)*
Sadness In A Song *(Columbia/—)*
World *(Columbia/—)*
Greatest Hits Vol 2 *(Columbia/—)*
Greatest Hits *(GRT/—)*

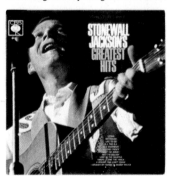

Stonewall Jackson's Greatest Hits (CBS).

Wanda Jackson, a Hank Thompson discovery, was once a full-blooded rocker whose Fujiyama Mama, Honey Bop and Let's Have A Party are prized by collectors.

Make Me Like A Child Again (Myrrh). Since 1971 Wanda has recorded exclusively gospel music.

Please Help Me I'm Falling
(Pickwick/—)
Wanda Jackson (Pickwick/—)
Now I Have Everything
(Myrrh/DJM)
Country Gospel (Word/Word)
Make Me Like A Child Again
(Myrrh/Myrrh)
**W. J. Salutes The Country
Music Hall Of Fame**
(—/Capitol)
A Portrait Of Wanda Jackson
(—/Capitol)

Sonny James

Sonny James is still thought of by many in terms of his pacesetting '50s teen hit **Young Love** (also a massive international hit for Tab Hunter) and there's no denying that his music has often been easily accessible to the MOR market, for he has a deep, rich voice with much commercial appeal.

Born Hackleburg, Alabama, May 1, 1929 (real name Jimmy Loden), part of a showbiz family, he made his stage debut at the age of four, touring with his sisters after making his radio debut. At seven he'd learned to play the violin, later becoming signed to a full time contract with a Birmingham, Alabama, radio station. Following 15 months in Korea during the early '50s – there performing before his fellow servicemen – he returned home and signed a contract with Capitol Records, obtaining his first hit with **For Rent** in 1956, that same year recording **Young Love**, an eventual million seller. After one more Top Ten entry – with the pop-slanted **First Date, First Kiss, First Love** (1957) – he saw little chart action until 1963 when he scored with **The Minute You're Gone.** That the song was successfully covered in Britain by Cliff Richard proves again just how suited James was to pop-oriented material.

During 1964, **Baltimore, Ask Marie** and **You're The Only World I Know** all charted for James, the last commencing an incredible run of Top Five singles

Right: Waylon Jennings, a favorite of the rock press, scored a massive crossover hit in 1977 with Luckenbach, Texas.

(most of them reaching the No 1 spot!) that extended well into the mid '70s. After one final hit with **That's Why I Love You Like I Do** for Capitol in mid 1972, James switched to the rival Columbia label, logging chart entries with **When The Snow Is On The Roses** and **White Silver Sands** almost immediately. More recently he's produced a hit record **Paper Roses** for Marie Osmond, recorded **200 Years Of Country Music,** one of the more interesting C&W albums of recent years, and continued his chart domination with such hits as **When Something's Wrong With My Baby, The Prisoner's Song** and **Come On In** during 1976. A remarkably consistent performer, James (known as the Southern Gentleman) has appeared in a number of minor films including *Hillbilly In A Haunted House,* a movie that also featured Lon Chaney and Basil Rathbone. An able musician on several instruments, it seems unbelievable that James has won not one CMA award at the time of writing.

Albums:
The Best Of . . . (Capitol/—)
The Biggest Hits Of . . .
(Capitol/—)
Traces (Capitol/—)
**When Snow Is On The Roses/
If She Just Helps** (Columbia/—)
Roses Are Red (Hillside/—)
Is It Wrong (Columbia/—)
South Of Saskatoon
(Columbia/—)
A Mi Esposa Con Amor
(Columbia/—)
Country Artist Of The Decade
(Columbia/—)
Guitars Of Sonny James
(Columbia/—)
200 Years Of Country Music
(Columbia/CBS)
When Something Is Wrong
(Columbia/—)

Waylon Jennings

A strong voice and strong personality have enabled this charismatic man to aspire to country music's heights. From a modestly successful career as a mainstream country and folk-country artist he is now the definitive 'outlaw' figure, a man who, with Willie Nelson (♦), spearheads the movement away from orchestral blandness in country and towards exciting, gritty, more personalized music.

Born Littlefield, Texas, 1937, Waylon could play guitar by his teens. He gained a DJ job on a Littlefield radio station at 12 and, while interested in pop in his teens, he had developed an interest in country by 21.

In 1958 he moved to Lubbock, working as a DJ there and thus meeting Buddy Holly (♦). In 1958 and '59 he toured as Holly's electric bass player. When Holly's plane crashed in 1959, killing the singer and two others, it was Waylon who, at the last moment, had given up his seat to J. P. Richardson, 'The Big Bopper' of **Chantilly Lace** pop fame.

In the early '60s, Waylon settled in Phoenix, Arizona, forming The Waylors to back him and becoming well known locally at Phoenix's famous JD's club. Chet Atkins (♦) signed him to RCA in 1965 and the following year Waylon moved to Nashville. He was featured on the Grand Ole Opry TV show, on ABC-TV's 'Anatomy Of Pop' Special and on TV generally. He also appeared in the film *Nashville Rebel.*

But Waylon was to become more than just a celluloid rebel. Nashville, and particularly its major labels such as RCA, is often tightly business-minded. Certain staff producers are insisted upon, the label's own Nashville studios are generally used and so are an elite band of like-sounding session musicians. Artists are not encouraged to record with their own bands and consequently much of the Nashville product sounds similar.

Waylon wanted to break out sufficiently to be able to have his say on material, musicians and production. He upset the RCA Nashville hierarchy by going direct to the New York bosses with his ideas about what his contract should contain. He was guaranteed an independent production package in which he would provide RCA with a number of sides per year for them to promote and sell.

The big musical change in Waylon had already become apparent on

The Southern Gentleman (Columbia).

200 Years of Country Music (CBS).

Ladies Love Outlaws where he at last succeeded in folding his own band, the Waylors, in with the session men and picking some distinctive and evocative current song material; Hoyt Axton's (♦) **Never Been To Spain** and Alex Harvey (♦)/Larry Collins' **Delta Dawn.**

But **Honky Tonk Heroes,** released the following year, in 1973, proved an even bigger watershed. Waylon extensively plundered the repertoire of one Billy Joe Shaver (♦) to come up with an album variously produced by himself, Tompall Glaser (♦), Ronnie Light and Ken Mansfield, and featuring music sounding hard and 'outlaw' as the reputation Waylon himself was already being given.

The themes, instead of lightly hymning marriage situations, love nests and the occasional bit of drinking or slipping' around, were of self-doubt, questing wanderers and good ol' boys alienated by the twentieth century – most of it couched in the imagery of the old West. The music was often sparse as the poetry but it had a sting in the tail.

Waylon was well and truly 'outlaw' country. The 1973 Nashville DJ Convention saw him ignoring the major label roster shows and setting up on a bill of his own at the Sheraton Hotel with Willie Nelson (♦), Troy Seals (♦) and Sammi Smith (♦). There were mutterings in high places about the new music but many people felt that Waylon was giving country a shot in the arm.

Waylon was still patently country (a fact he has always emphasized in interviews) but his use of a heavier instrumentation and his rock star approach has misled people. True, he played on a San Francisco bill with the Grateful Dead, but the Dead's splinter group, the New Riders Of The Purple Sage (♦) were themselves of a trucking, rock country nature and the alliance undoubtedly weaned new fans on to country.

1974 saw Waylon making the US pop charts with a double sided singles hit, **Bob Wills Is Still The King/Are You Sure Hank Done It This Way?** In 1976 he scored again with **Suspicious Minds,** an evocative duet with wife Jessi Colter (♦). 1975 had seen him (and therefore by implication, the 'outlaws') making an inroad into the CMA Awards, with the winning of Male Vocalist Of The Year. But in 1976 the **Suspicious Minds** duet involved Waylon in two awards, Duo Of The Year and Single Of The Year. That year he was also involved in Album Of The Year **(The Outlaws)** and it was evident that the new contemporary strain of country had finally gained acceptance.

Albums:

Best Of . . . *(RCA/RCA)*	Sad Songs *(RCA/—)*
Heartaches By The Number *(Camden/—)*	**The Taker/Tulsa** *(RCA/—)*
Honky Tonk Heroes *(RCA/RCA)*	**This Time** *(RCA/RCA)*
Ladies Love Outlaws	**Waylon Jennings** *(Vocalion/—)*
Good Hearted Woman *(RCA/—)*	**Are You Ready For The Country?** *(RCA/RCA)*
Lonesome, Orn'ry And Mean *(RCA/—)*	**Waylon The Ramblin Man** *(RCA/RCA)*
The Only Daddy That'll Walk The Line *(Camden/—)*	**Dreaming My Dreams** *(RCA/RCA)*
Ruby, Don't Take Your Love To Town *(Camden/—)*	**The Outlaws** – with Jessi Colter, Tompall Glaser etc *(RCA/RCA)*
	Live (1974) *(RCA/RCA)*
	Ol' Waylon *(RCA/RCA)*

The Outlaws (RCA). An award-winning release containing tracks from Jennings and other musical outlaws.

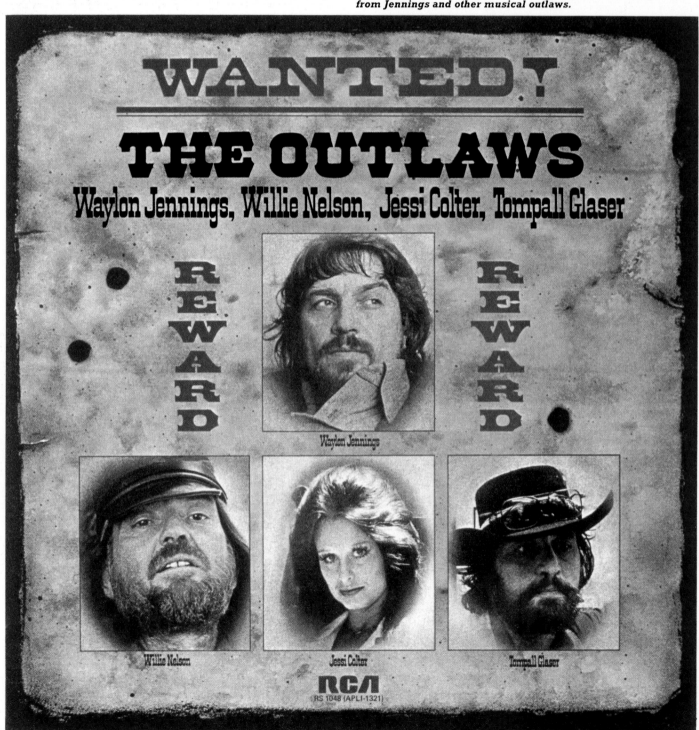

WANTED!

THE OUTLAWS
Waylon Jennings, Willie Nelson, Jessi Colter, Tompall Glaser

REWARD

REWARD

Waylon Jennings

Willie Nelson

Jessi Colter

Tompall Glaser

RCA
RS 1048 (APLI-1321)

We Like Trains/Diesel On My Trail (Epic).

Jim And Jesse

Bluegrass playing brothers Jim and Jesse McReynolds were both born in Coebrun, Virginia, Jim on February 13, 1927, Jesse on July 9, 1929. From a musical family – their grandfather was an old time fiddler who recorded with Victor – the duo began playing at local get-togethers.

With Jim on guitar and Jesse on mandolin they made their radio debut in 1947 and cut some records for the Kentucky label during the early '50s, later signing for Capitol. However, the duo's progress was terminated for a while during the Korean war when Jesse was called up for service in the armed forces, the twosome reforming once more to play on Knoxville's WNOX Tennessee Barn Dance in 1954. During the 1960s, Jim and Jesse with their band the Virginia Boys – which at that period included such musicians as Bobby Thompson and Vassar Clements (♦) – signed for Epic Records and began logging up a number of fair sized chart entries with **Cotton Mill Man** (1964), **Diesel On My Trail, Ballad Of Thunder Road** (both 1967), **The Golden Rocket** (1968) and other titles, before switching to Capitol once more for a 1971 success in **Freight Train.** Performers at both the Newport Folk Festival and the Wembley Country Music Festival, Jim and Jesse became regulars on the Opry in 1964. A fine, no-frills, bluegrass outfit specializing in smooth, haunting, sky high harmony, two of their Epic albums were re-released as a double pack in 1976.

Albums:
We Like Trains/Diesel On My Trail *(Epic/—)*
Jim And Jesse Show *(Old Dominion/DJM)*
Live In Japan *(Old Dominion/—)*
Superior Sounds Of Bluegrass *(Old Dominion/—)*
Jesus Is The Key *(Old Dominion/—)*
Paradise *(Opryland/—)*

Johnny And Jack
♦ *Johnny Wright*

Though mainly bluegrass, the McReynolds are eclectic in their choice of material and once recorded an album in tribute to Chuck Berry.

THE BEST OF GEORGE JONES

THE DOOR
THE GRAND TOUR
WE CAN MAKE IT
A PICTURE OF ME (WITHOUT YOU)
NOTHING EVER HURT ME
(HALF AS BAD AS LOSING YOU)
ONCE YOU'VE HAD THE BEST
WHAT MY WOMAN CAN'T DO
THE WEATHERMAN
LOVING YOU COULD NEVER BE BETTER
THESE DAYS (I BARELY GET BY)

The Best Of George Jones (Epic). One of the most influential and respected performers around.

George Jones the club owner: the Possum Holler, Nashville.

Saluting the Louvin Brothers (Epic).

George Jones

Known as the 'Rolls Royce of Country Singers', George Jones' vocal styling has influenced a host of country performers.

Born Saratoga, Texas, September 12, 1931, Jones grew up in a musical background. His mother played piano at the local church and his father was an amateur guitarist. He got his first guitar at age nine and was soon performing at local events. In his late teens he served with the Marines in Korea, and after discharge he worked as a house painter while also playing local evening gigs; in 1954 he had gained a sufficiently good reputation to attract the interest of industry executive H. W. 'Pappy' Daily at Starday Records in Houston.

1955 saw his first big country hit, **Why Baby Why,** and other successes before he joined his next label, Mercury, in 1958, included **You Gotta Be My Baby.** His first big hit for Mercury was **Treasure Of Love** in 1958. The following year saw him obtaining his first country No 1 with

White Lightning, an up tempo song with a novelty chorus.

In 1961 he changed labels again (Jones was by this time well enough respected to command bidding for his services among labels) and landed at UA Records where he hit what was perhaps his most fertile period, turning out songs that have become country standards but have also remained identified with Jones' name. He was particularly good at the anguished, two timing woman style of song and he delivered them as if he really meant them. 1961 saw him hit big with **Window Up Above,** 1962 with **She Thinks I Still Care** (an archetypal Jones song and one covered by countless other artists), 1963 **We Must Have Been Out Of Our Minds** (performed with his traveling co-star Melba Montgomery (♦)) and 1964 **The Race Is On.**

In 1965 he renewed acquaintance with Pappy Daily. Daily had left Starday to start his own company, Musicor, and Jones was an obvious target for him. The hits from this period, 1965 to 1967, included **Take Me, Things Have Gone To Pieces, Love Bug, I'm A People** and **You Can't Get There From Here.** Although it was a successful period music-ally Jones grew unhappy with the way he was being recorded. It should be said that Daily was a hugely respected figure in country at this time, but George felt that not enough care was being taken with the mixing of his tracks in the studio, and indeed these same tracks have since been acquired by RCA Records and remixed and engineered.

George fought to get out of his Musicor contract and eventually had to sign over his royalties to do so. At this period of time he went through a rough patch, having become divorced from his wife and beginning to drink heavily as he undertook endless overland tours. It became a case of Jones living out his own honky tonk songs. He became associated with stories of wild and destructive living, sometimes having to be helped onstage.

In 1967 he met Tammy Wynette (♦) when the two played the same package tour. Tammy was having trouble with her marriage and she and George were married before long. Thus also began the famous musical partnership between she and George. Tammy was becoming a huge star by virtue of her smooth weepie songs on Epic Records, the production work of Billy Sherrill (♦), and with George's career in something of a trough (a product of his own ill found reputation and the domi-nance of the easy-listening Nashville Sound of the '60s) it was a neat move for Sherrill to team him with Tammy.

They became known as the king and queen of country music, selling vast truckloads of albums in Middle America. As their own marriage hit problems extra piquancy was added to the partnership, Tammy riding to success on a solo basis via some old hits **D.I.V.O.R.C.E.** and **Stand By Your Man.**

In the mid '70s George's own style of music began to gain again in popularity, and he was able to tour again as a star in his own right. In 1976 the writers of the prestigious rock magazine Rolling Stone voted him their Country Singer of the Year.

Over the years, George and his popular band, the Jones Boys, have toured internationally and have appeared on many top US TV shows. Jones was an integral part of what came to be called honky-tonk music, a tough, basic, roadhouse style of country with no orchestral embellish-ments and little compromise in the lyrics. Apart from his period with Tammy and Billy Sherrill, and his gospel albums, he has largely stayed true to this style; the smooth, closed-mouth delivery with the conflicting, inherent toughness being admired enough to spawn a number by another artist called **If I Could Sing A Country Song (Exactly Like George Jones).**

We Go Together/Me And The First Lady (Epic). Jones and ex wife Tammy Wynette made a famous partnership.

Brilliant old-time banjo player Marshall Louis 'Grandpa' Jones is also a fine comedian and all-round entertainer. Still in action despite a severe heart attack.

Albums:
Best of . . . (Musicor/—)
Best Of . . . Vol 2 (RCA/—)
Close Together – with Melba Montgomery (Musicor/—)
Cup Of Loneliness (Musicor/—)
Greatest Hits (Musicor/—)
Hits (Musicor/—)
If My Heart Had Windows (Musicor/—)
I'll Share My World With You (Musicor/—)
I'm A People (Musicor/—)
In A Gospel Way (Epic/—)
Love Bug (Musicor/—)
Me And The First Lady – with Tammy Wynette (Epic/Epic)
Mr Music (Musicor/—)
My Boys (Musicor/—)
My Country (Musicor/—)
New Hits – with the Jones Boys (Musicor/—)
Nothing Ever Hurt Me (Epic/—)
Oh Lonesome Me (Hillside/—)
Old Bush Arbors (Musicraft/—)
Party Pickin' – with Melba Montgomery (Musicor/—)
The Race Is On (Camden/—)
Songs Of Dallas Frazier (Musicor/—)
Songs Of Leon Payne (Musicor/—)
George Jones Story (Musicor/—)
Walk Through This World (Musicor/—)
We Found Heaven Here (Musicor/—)

Where Grass Won't Grow (Musicor/—)
Will You Visit Me On Sunday? (Musicor/—)
With Love (Musicor/—)
You Gotta Be My Baby (RCA/RCA)
Let's Build A World Together – with Tammy Wynette (Epic/Epic)
We're Gonna Hold On – with Tammy Wynette (Epic/Epic)
Famous Country Music Makers (—/RCA)
The Best Of The Best (—/RCA)
Sings His Songs (—/RCA)
We Must Have Been Out Of Our Minds (—/RCA)
Alone Again (Epic/—)
Best Of . . . (Epic/Epic)
The Battle (Epic/Epic)
George Jones/A Picture Of Me (Epic/—)
Memories Of Us (Epic/Epic)
George And Tammy And Tina – with Tammy Wynette (Epic/Epic)
We Go Together (Epic/Epic)
Crown Prince Of Music (Power Pak/—)
Hillbilly Hit Parade with Friends (Starday/—)
Sings His Greatest Hits (Starday/—)
Golden Hits Of (Starday/—)

Grandpa Jones

A long time regular on both the Opry and Hee Haw, high-kicking, joke-cracking, story-telling, foot-stomping, vaudevillian Grandpa Jones is one of the most colorful figures on the country scene today. Born Louis Marshall Jones, in Henderson County, Kentucky, October

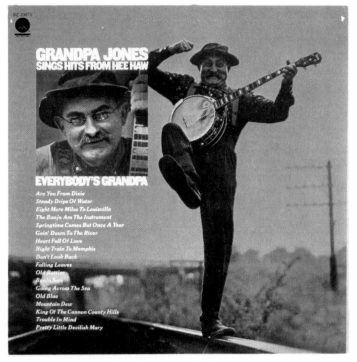

Jordanaires

A vocal group that has appeared on hundreds and hundreds of Nashville recordings, the Jordanaires were formed in Springfield, Missouri, during 1948. Initially a male barbershop quartet, performing mainly gospel material, they worked in Tennessee and nearby states, sometimes including female singers on their dates, gaining their first Opry booking in 1949.

A year later they were featured on Red Foley's (♦) million selling version of **Just A Closer Walk With Thee** and in 1956 sprang to even wider fame by commencing a long and extremely successful association with Elvis Presley (♦). Grammy award winners in 1965 (for the best religious album), the Jordanaires – who have undergone myriad personnel changes since their inception with Gordon Stoker, lead tenor, as the only constant member – have appeared on many TV and radio shows, also lending their talents to an impressive number of movie scores. Though how they find the time to indulge in their multifarious activities is beyond comprehension.

Albums:
Church In The Wildwood *(Vocalion/—)*
The Jordanaires *(Columbia/—)*

Karl And Harty

Karl Victor Davis (born December 17, 1905) and Hartford Connecticut Taylor (April 11, 1905 to October 1963), both of Mt Vernon, Kentucky, composed one of the earliest and most influential of the mandolin-guitar duets. They were brought to WLS' National Barn Dance (♦) by John Lair (♦) in 1930 as members of the Cumberland Ridge Runners (♦), and they remained on the show for some 21 years.

Their records for the ARC complex of labels (and later Capitol) were popular in their era, especially **I'm Just Here To Get My Baby Out Of Jail** (1934), **The Prisoner's Dream** (1936), and **Kentucky** (1938), all written by Karl, the mandolin player. They both left the recording and performing field in the 1950s, although Karl continues to work at WLS as a record turner to this day. Best known as a songwriter (all the above have been recorded and been hits by several groups at different times, from Mainer's Moun-

Grandpa Jones Sings Hits From Hee-Haw (Monument). Jones, who has been disguising himself as a grandpa since his twenties, is one of the Hee-Haw and Opry favorites.

'Gimme a middle C'. Nashville's most overworked vocal group, the Jordanaires, lending a helping eight hands to the studio piano tuner.

20, 1913, he began playing guitar on an instrument costing only 75 cents. At 16 he'd become so proficient a musician that he won a talent contest promoted by Wendell Hall (♦), while the year 1935 found him working with Bradley Kincaid's (♦) band, playing regularly in the north east.

Though only in his twenties, it was during this period that Jones began disguising himself as an old-timer, at the same time becoming a banjo picker in the exuberant Uncle Dave Macon (♦) style. By 1937 he was leading an outfit known as Grandpa Jones and His Grandchildren, this unit becoming regulars, first on WWVA's Wheeling Jamboree, and then Cincinnati WLW, during the late '30s and early '40s. It was here he began recording for King Records by himself, with Merle Travis (♦), and with the Delmore Brothers (♦) as the Brown's Terry Four. In 1944 Jones joined the army and was posted to Germany, where he played on AFN Radio until being discharged in '46. Almost immediately he became a member of the Opry, remaining so for many years (although he defected to pioneer television in the Washington, DC, area for several years) along the way having a brace of hit records in **All American Boy** (1959) and a version of Jimmie Rodgers' (♦) **T For Texas** (1962). Other numbers associated with Jones include **Old Rattler, Old Rattler's Pup, Mountain Dew, Tragic Romance,** and **Eight More Miles To Louisville.** He met his fiddle-playing wife Ramona while at WLW; she has been a part of his act ever since.

Albums:
Pickin' Time *(Vocalion/—)*
Hits From Hee Haw *(Monument/—)*
The Other Side Of Grandpa Jones *(King/—)*
What's For Supper? *(Monument/—)*
24 Country Hits *(King/—)*
16 Sacred Gospel Songs *(King/—)*
The Grandpa Jones Story *(CMH/—)*

taineers and the Blue Sky Boys (♦) to Linda Rondstadt (♦) and Emmylou Harris (♦)), Karl Davis was able to write a hit song as recently as the late 1960s: Hank Locklin's **Country Music Hall Of Fame.**

Albums: none.

Buell Kazee

Born Burton Fork, Kentucky, August 29, 1900, Kazee was a college educated, fully ordained minister of the church who had an avid interest in a wide range of traditional music. During 1927–29 he recorded 58 titles for Brunswick, 46 of which were released – Kazee singing and playing five string banjo on such songs as **Hobo's Last Ride** and **Rock Island Line,** also cutting some two part sketches that included **A Mountain Boy Makes His First Record** and **Election Day, Kentucky.**

Author of a book *Faith In The Victory,* Kazee performed at many folk concerts throughout his life and recorded some material for the Library of Congress. He died on August 31, 1976.

Albums:
Buell Kazee Plays And Sings
(Folkways/—)

Louisiana Man (DJM) – with Rusty Kershaw. British release from the duo, who separated in the '60s; Doug the Cajun fiddler continues to record alone.

Wayne Kemp

Born Muldrow, Oklahoma, 1941, honky tonk style vocalist Kemp, whose father was a motor mechanic, naturally enough became interested in automobile racing during his teen years, though music rapidly became his main occupation. After forming his own band and touring throughout the south west, he met Buddy Killen, who in 1963 signed him to a songwriting contract with Free Music and to a recording deal with Dial label. It was as a songwriter that he first made the grade, George Jones (♦) recording a Kemp song **Love Bug** in 1965 and enjoying a major hit. From Dial, Kemp switched to Jeb, a newly formed label, his first release, **The Image Of Me,** not gaining much public attention but proving strong enough a song to encourage a cover version by Conway Twitty (♦) – which went into the Country Top Ten. Twitty then recorded several other Kemp songs including **Next In Line, Darling You Know I Wouldn't Lie** and **That's When She Started To Stop Loving You** – all these reaching a position among the top three country sellers. This association with Twitty enabled Kemp to win a recording contract with Decca, for whom he began supplying such minor hits as **Won't You Come Home, Bar Room Habits** (1969), **Who'll Turn Out The Lights?, Award To An Angel** and **Did We Have To Come This Far?** (1971), this gradual accept-ance leading to a debut Decca album **Wayne Kemp** in '71. But since that time – despite yet another label change, this time to Dot – Kemp's name has remained virtually absent from the list of best selling discs.

Albums:
Kentucky Sunshine *(MCA/—)*

Anita Kerr

During the '50s and '60s, it seemed that the Anita Kerr Singers and the Anita Kerr Quartet were appearing on half the records that emanated from Nashville. Born Memphis, Tennessee, October 13, 1927, Anita opted for the vocal group business at an early age, having her own trio, The Grilli Sisters, even before reaching high school. A proficient pianist, she became a staff musician on a Memphis radio station at the age of 14, later moving to Nashville where, in 1949, she formed her first professional vocal group.

Quickly establishing a reputation as the best backup group in the city, the Kerr Singers began appearing on discs by Eddy Arnold (♦), Jim Reeves (♦), Chet Atkins (♦), Skeeter Davis (♦), Floyd Cramer (♦) and scores of other top artists. However, after achieving some successful Decca recordings under her own name, Anita appeared to become disenchanted with the country scene and in the mid 1960s embarked on a number of ambitious but well received re-cording ventures with singer-poet Rod McKuen. Then, during the '70s she began producing and arranging a series of easy listening vocal albums, mainly recorded in Europe. Though her records are generally excellent examples of the art of vocal group harmonies, little of Anita's recent output has been of any interest to true country music enthusiasts, one exception being a Philips album **I Sang With Jim Reeves.** However, for a time there anyway, the smooth backup sound of the Anita Kerr Singers was a major distinguishing feature of 'The Nashville Sound'.

Doug Kershaw

Cajun fiddler Douglas James Kershaw, born Tiel Ridge, Louisiana, January 24, 1936, first appeared onstage as a child, accompanying his mother, singer-guitarist-fiddler Mama Rita, at the Bucket Of Blood, Lake Arthur. In 1948, together with brothers Russell Lee 'Rusty' and Nelson 'Pee Wee' Kershaw, he formed The Continental Playboys, gaining a spot on Lake Charles KPLC-TV in 1953. Rusty and Doug then began recording as a duo for the Feature label, later obtaining a contract with Hickory and also appearing on Shreveport's Louisiana Hayride (♦) show.

With an Everly-like treatment of a Boudleaux Bryant (♦) song **Hey Sheriff,** the Kershaws made an indent on the country charts in October 1958, and even joined the Opry briefly. After Doug completed his military service the duo resumed their joint career, scoring with country classics **Louisiana Man** and **Diggy Diggy Lo,** the former being penned by Doug.

After cutting sides for Victor and Princess, the twosome parted in 1964, Doug moving on to record for Mercury, MGM and Warner Brothers, guesting with such as Johnny Cash (♦), Bob Dylan and Grand Funk Railroad, and playing in the film *Zachariah.* Meanwhile Rusty fought a struggle against alcoholism, eventually making a 'comeback' solo album for Cotillion in 1970.

Albums:
The Cajun Way *(Warner Bros/—)*
Spanish Moss *(Warner Bros/—)*
Doug Kershaw *(Warner Bros/—)*
Devil's Elbow *(Warner Bros/—)*
Douglas James Kershaw
  (Warner Bros/—)
Swamp Grass *(Warner Bros/—)*
Mama Kershaw's Boy
  (Warner Bros/—)
Flip Flop And Fly
  (Warner Bros/—)

With Rusty Kershaw:
Louisiana Man *(—/DJM)*

Merle Kilgore

Born Wyatt Merle Kilgore, Chickasha, Oklahoma, September 8, 1934, his family moved to Shreveport, Louisiana, when he was young. He learnt guitar as a boy and got a job as a DJ on Shreveport's KENT when just 16. He was already attracting attention as a performer and writer, and by the age of 18 had his first hit composition **More, More, More.** He was invited to join the Louisiana Hayride (♦) and became principal guitar accompanist on the show.

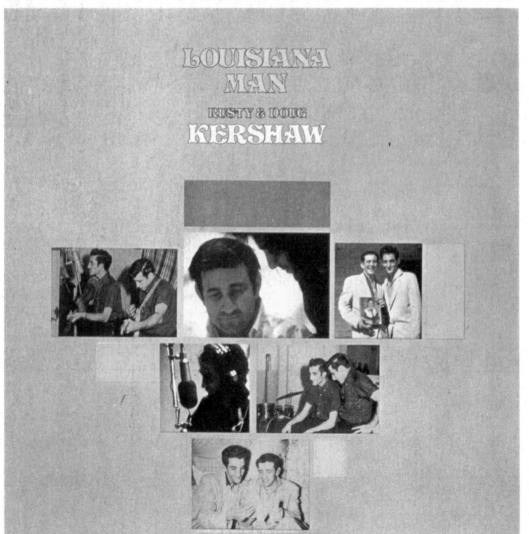

Bradley Kincaid

Bradley Kincaid. A one-off show on WLS Chicago proved so popular that he became a National Barn Dance regular.

A pioneer broadcaster of traditional Kentucky mountain music, Kincaid (born Point Leavell, Kentucky, July 13, 1895) began singing folk songs on WLS, Chicago in August, 1925, while still attending that city's George Williams College. By 1926, he'd become a regular on the WLS Chicago Barn Dance, remaining with the show (later to be known as the National Barn Dance (♦)) until 1930. Following graduation in June, 1928, Kincaid began touring, at the same time collecting folk songs from a variety of sources, publishing these in a series of songbooks. His recording career also began in '28, in which year he made a number of sides for Gennett, these discs appearing on myriad labels, sometimes under a pseudonym. Later sessions for Brunswick, in 1930, produced a similar crop of multi-labelled releases, while during the later '30s and '40s, Kincaid's name appeared on discs marketed by Decca, RCA, Majestic, Varsity, Mercury and Bullet.

A banjo picker at the age of five, Kincaid, who became known as 'The Kentucky Mountain Boy', purveyed such material as **I Gave My Love A Cherry, The Letter Edged In Black** and **Barbara Allen**, singing the latter over WLS every Saturday night for four successive years.

An ever active radio performer, he bought his own station (WWSO, Springfield, Ohio) in 1949, but sold it again in '53. His more recent recordings include albums for Bluebonnet (for whom he cut 162 titles in 1963) and McMonigle, the latter sessions stemming from 1973.

Besides appearing on nearly every major barn dance (WLW Cincinnati, WMVA Wheeling, and even the Opry from 1944–1949 as well as the National Barn Dance) Kincaid played for years in the north east, introducing folk and country music to a whole new area. Hale and hearty in his mid eighties, he still plays golf in genial retirement in Springfield.

Claude King

Wolverton Mountain – a distinctive and menacing C&W 'Jack and the Beanstalk' saga – was a 1962 million seller, written by King and Merle Kilgore (♦).

Born Shreveport, Louisiana, February 5, 1933, King attended the University of Idaho and then returned to Shreveport, to business college. He had been interested in music, having bought his first guitar from a farmer for 50 cents when he was 12. During the '50s he began writing and performing, playing clubs, radio and TV. He was signed to a record contract by Columbia in 1961, gaining country hits as follows: **Big River Big Man** (1961), **The Comancheros** (1961), **Burning Of Atlanta** (1962), **I've Got The World By The Tail** (1962), **Sheepskin Valley** (1963), **Building A Bridge** (1963), **Hey Lucille** (1963), **Sam Hill** (1963), **Tiger Woman** (1965), **All For The Love Of A Girl** (1969), **Friend, Lover, Woman, Wife** (1969), **Mary's Vineyard** (1970). **Big River, The Comancheros, Wolverton Mountain** and **Burning Of Atlanta** also crossed over into the pop charts.

The '70s have not seen King as active, and it may well be that public taste is not suited nowadays to such butch sagas of the great American outdoors. He has, however, recently signed with True Records in an effort to revitalize his career.

In 1952 he appeared on the Opry and in that same year also attended the Louisiana Tech. The following year saw him working at the American Optical Company but performing at night. He appeared on the Hayride throughout the '50s, initially recording for the Imperial and D labels. His first big hit came in 1959 with **Dear Mama,** a Starday single, Johnny Horton (♦) scoring with **Johnny Reb,** a Kilgore composition, that same year.

Another of Kilgore's Starday releases **Love Has Made You Beautiful** charted in 1960, as did **Gettin' Old Before My Time,** while in 1962 he co-wrote **Wolverton Mountain** with Claude King (♦) (a world wide pop hit for King) and **Ring Of Fire** with June Carter (♦), the latter song becoming a million seller for Johnny Cash (♦) in '63.

Though his record sales fared less successfully as the '60s wore on, the 6 foot 4 inch Kilgore became established as an impressive western actor, appearing in *Five Card Stud* (1968) and *Nevada Smith* (1966). An album, **Ring Of Fire,** was available on Hilltop Records until fairly recently.

Pee Wee King

Leader of what was claimed to be the first band to use electric guitar and drums on the Opry, King is also a noted songwriter, being writer or co-writer of such hits as **Slow Poke, Bonaparte's Retreat, You Belong To Me** and **Tennessee Waltz,** the last named being declared the state song of Tennessee in February, 1965. Born Abrams, Wisconsin, February 18, 1914, of Polish descent, Frank 'Pee Wee' King originally trained as a draftsman, though he'd learnt harmonica, accordion and fiddle while still a boy, broadcasting over stations WRIN (Racine) and WBAY (Green Bay) at the age of 14, his father having been the leader of a locally popular Polka band. After stints with WLS (Chicago) Barn Dance program during the early '30s, he joined the Gene Autry (♦) Show, taking over the band in 1934 when Autry headed for Hollywood.

Renamed the Golden West Cowboys, the band – which featured such stars as Eddy Arnold (♦), Redd Stewart (♦), Cowboy Copas (♦), Pete Pyle, Ernest Tubb (♦) and guitarist Clell Sumney at various points in its career – first graced the Opry in the mid '30s, in 1938 following Autry to Hollywood to make *Gold Mine In The Sky* for Republic Pictures, the first in a series of cowboy movies (usually with Johnny Mack Brown as the Durango Kid) featuring King and the Golden West Cowboys.

By 1941, the band could be found touring as part of the 'Camel Caravan', a show organized by the Opry to entertain at army camps and other military posts, *Billboard* later estimating that by late '42 the Caravan had played 175 shows at 68 venues, spread over a total of 19 states.

From 1947 to 1957, King hosted his own radio and TV show on Louisville WAVE, also in '47 signing a record deal with RCA Victor. In addition, he did a weekly television circuit in Cincinnati, Chicago and Cleveland.

Success also came as a composer when **Tennessee Waltz,** penned by King and Stewart, became a hit record when recorded by Cowboy Copas in 1948. Around the same time, King himself began logging a tally of hits, **Tennessee Tears** (1949), **Slow Poke** (a 1951 million seller), **Silver And Gold** (1952) and **Bimbo** (1954) all becoming Top Ten entries.

Voted top country band during 1951–55, the Golden West Cowboys were hit by the rise of rock 'n' roll during the late '50s, King adding horns in an effort to compete with the all-conquering rockers. But by 1959 the financial struggle had become uneven and King disbanded the Cowboys, forming another unit several months later when Minnie Pearl (♦) asked him to accompany her on a roadshow.

When Minnie ceased touring in 1963, King kept the unit – which included Redd Stewart (♦) and the Collins Sisters – together for a while, playing on package shows until 1968. Then he disbanded once more, relying on local musicians to support him at any of the frequent dates he currently plays.

Though King's records have failed to sell in any tremendous quantities since he terminated his contract with RCA in 1959, he remains a popular and highly respected member of the country music profession, worthily being elected to the Country Music Hall of Fame in 1974.

Albums:
The Best Of Pee Wee King And
 Redd Stewart (Starday/—)

Pee Wee King. He co-wrote such hits as Slowpoke, Tennessee Waltz, You Belong To Me and Bonaparte's Retreat, thus earning a place in the Country Music Hall of Fame.

Beecher Pete Kirby
♦ *Bashful Brother Oswald*

Eddie Kirk

A one time singer and guitarist with the Beverly Hillbillies (♦), Kirk was an amateur flyweight boxer whose yodeling ability won him the National Yodeling Championship in 1935 and '36. A singer much in the smooth style of Eddy Arnold (♦), he performed on the Gene Autry (♦) Show and on Compton's Town Hall Party shows during the late '40s, also appearing in several films. Signed to Capitol Records in 1947, he recorded **Blues Stay Away From Me** with Ernie Ford (♦) and Merle Travis (♦), obtaining two solo hits in 1949 with **Candy Kisses** and **The Gods Were Angry With Me.**

Born Greeley, Colorado, March 21, 1919, Kirk was one of the musicians who fought to have the description 'hillbilly' replaced by the more acceptable term 'country music' during the 1940s.

Pee Wee King with his Golden West Cowboys. The girl is San Antonio Rose, standing on the extreme right is Cowboy Copas and kneeling on the left is Redd Stewart.

Kris Kristofferson

Born Brownsville, Texas, June 22, 1936, son of a retired Air Force Major-General, Kristofferson's family moved to California during his high school days.

Living in San Mateo, he went to Pomona College, having success in football and taking part in the Golden Gloves boxing championship. In 1958, he won a Rhodes Scholarship to Oxford University, England, where he began writing his second novel, becoming a songwriter as a sideline, using the name of Kris Carson.

His novels rejected by publishers, he became disenchanted with a literary career and left Oxford after a year, first getting married then joining the army and becoming a helicopter pilot in Germany.

While in the army he began playing service clubs in Germany, also sending some of his songs to a Nashville publisher. Upon discharge in 1965, Kristofferson headed for Nashville, initially becoming a janitor in Columbia Records' studio, then spending some time flying men and equipment to oil rigs in the Gulf of Mexico.

Broke and with his marriage in tatters, he was about to take a construction job when Roger Miller (♦) recorded one of his songs, **Me And Bobby McGee,** the number later being covered by Janis Joplin, whose version became a million seller in 1971. During 1970, Johnny Cash (♦) waxed **Sunday Morning Coming Down,** another Kristofferson original, and the Texan cut his first solo album for Monument, Cash writing a poem documenting the singer-songwriter's lean years for use as a sleeve note.

After appearances on Cash's TV show came other triumphs including a first engagement at a name club (The Troubadour, Los Angeles, June, 1970) and another hit via Sammi Smith's (♦) version of his **Help Me Make It Through The Night,** a nationwide million selling Top Tenner in January, 1971. During the following year, the singer's **Silver Tongued Devil And I** single was declared gold, while in November, 1973, another single, **Why Me?** also qualified as a gold disc. Also in '73, two albums, **The Silver Tongued Devil And I** and **Jesus Was A Capricorn** provided Kristofferson with further gold awards.

An accomplished actor, Kristofferson played a cameo role in Dennis Hopper's film *The Last Movie* in 1971 and has since starred in such movies as *Cisco Pike, Blume In Love, Pat Garrett And Billy The Kid, Alice Doesn't Live Here Anymore, The Sailor That Fell From Grace With The Sea* and *A Star Is Born.* In 1973 he married singer Rita Coolidge (♦) and has recorded two albums with her.

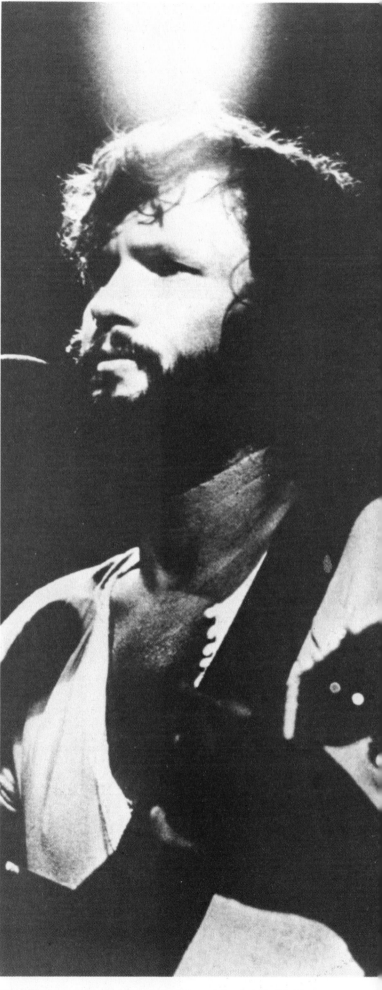

Albums:

Me And Bobby McGee
(Monument/Monument)
Border Lord
(Monument/Monument)
Jesus Was A Capricorn
(Monument/Monument)
The Silver Tongued Devil And I
(Monument/Monument)
Full Moon – with Rita Coolidge
(A&M/A&M)

Spooky Lady's Sideshow
(Monument/Monument)
Surreal Thing
(Monument/Monument)
Who's To Bless And Who's To Blame *(Monument/Monument)*
Breakaway – with Rita Coolidge
(Monument/Monument)
A Star Is Born – with Barbra Streisand *(Columbia/CBS)*

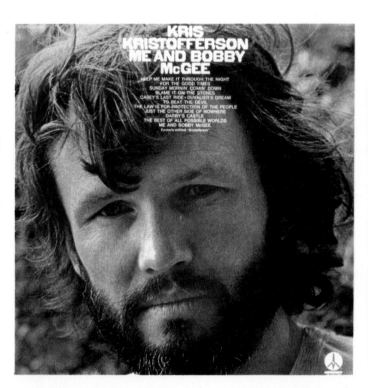

Me And Bobby McGee (Monument). Janis Joplin's version of the title track sold a million; another Kristofferson hit, Help Me Make It Through The Night, also appears.

Kristofferson, who once nearly volunteered for duty in Vietnam and during the mid '60s wrote pro-Vietnam song Vietnam Blues, utilized in flag-waving style by Dave Dudley.

KRIS KRISTOFFERSON

JESUS WAS A CAPRICORN

LaCosta

Elder sister of Tanya Tucker (♦), LaCosta entered her first talent contest at the age of four, in Snyder, Texas. During her early years, her family switched location frequently, as Beau Tucker (the girls' father and now their manager) travelled from one construction job to another. During one stay in Arizona, LaCosta and Tanya worked with a band called the Country Westerners but at that time LaCosta saw no future in a musical career and opted to become a medical records technician. Later, after marriage to Daryl Sorenson, she moved to Toltrec, Arizona, working in the local hospital. It wasn't until after Tanya's success with **Delta Dawn,** a 1972 hit, that LaCosta returned to singing once more, initially joining her sister in Las Vegas, then gaining a recording contract with Capitol Records.

Her first release **I Wanta Get To You** reached 25 in the *Billboard* country charts and since that time she's had a long string of hits, the most recent including **Get On My Love Train** and **Western Man.** LaCosta, who's appeared on several TV shows including those hosted by Bob Hope and family friend Hoyt Axton (♦), employs her own backup unit The Stone Bridge Band.

Albums:
Get On My Love Train
(Capitol/—)
With All My Love (Capitol/—)
Lovin' Somebody (Capitol/—)

John Lair

One of the grand old men of country music, and a genuine pioneer, John Lee Lair was born July 1, 1894, in Livingston, Kentucky. After a varied early career he joined WLS in Chicago as a producer of radio shows in 1927, and before long had brought to the station and to the National Barn Dance (♦) a host of his friends and acquaintances from the musically fertile area near Renfro Valley, Kentucky, including Doc Hopkins (♦), Karl and Harty (♦), Red Foley (♦), and Linda Parker. He formed a group around many of them – in which he played jug, harmonica, and generally MC'd the show – called the Cumberland Ridge Runners (♦), longtime favorites on the show from 1930 to about 1936.

Having seen the phenomenal success of barn dances in the 1930s, and having always seemed to have a longing for his central Kentucky home, he, the Duke of Paducah (♦), and Red Foley and his brother Cotton Foley bought and built the Renfro Valley Barn Dance in 1937, and it went on the air in 1938, first over WLW in Cincinnati, then over WHAS in Louisville, and finally over WCKY in Cincinnati. The show is still running, in fact, but is carried only on the local radio station WRVK.

Lair slowly acquired full ownership from the original purchasers, and kept the show traditional and local in nature from that point on. Although he sold his interest and the property in 1968, he still lives in a lovely log house overlooking the big old barn, where his dream that was forty years in the making has now been operating for an equal length of time.

Red Lane

A singer-songwriter of some consequence, Lane was born near Bogalusa, Louisiana, but spent much of his early life in Michigan.

Initially entering the music scene as a guitarist, he arrived in Nashville during the early '60s, finding some session work, then going on the road with the Justin Tubb (♦) Band. In 1967, Lane joined Dottie West's (♦) band, The Heartaches, as front man and MC, he and Dottie combining to write **Country Girl,** a West hit of 1968. By 1971 he'd become a hitmaker in his own right, two of his recordings that year, namely **The World Needs**

With All My Love (Capitol). LaCosta has had a string of country hits since returning to showbiz in 1972.

Above: LaCosta. Though she and sister Tanya Tucker once were in a band called The Westerners, she left the music biz at one time to work in a hospital.

Top left: Superstar Kristofferson was once a cleaner at a Nashville studio. And between drinks he's also been a boxer, Oxford scholar, army helicopter pilot and author.

Left: Jesus Was A Capricorn (Monument). Kristofferson appears on this 1973 album cover with singer Rita Coolidge, whom he married later that year.

A Melody and **Set The World On Fire (With Love)** becoming moderate sellers for RCA, the former title sparking off a number of cover versions. Lane, who's often collaborated with Hank Cochran (♦) on various writing projects, is also responsible for such songs as **Funky Grass Band, One Row At A Time, Charleston Cotton Mill** and **Mississippi Woman,** the last-named being a major hit for Waylon Jennings (♦) in 1971. An album, **The World Needs A Melody,** was released by RCA in September, 1971, but has since been deleted.

The World Needs A Melody (RCA Victor).

Brenda Lee

Once known as 'Little Miss Dynamite' – she's only 4ft 11in tall – Brenda is now content to put out rather characterless, easy listening albums which fall neither into country nor rock brackets.

Born Brenda Mae Tarpley, Lithonia, near Augusta, December 11, 1942, and educated in Nashville, she won a talent contest at the age of six. At a later contest in 1956, she was heard by Red Foley (♦) who asked her to appear on his Ozark Jubilee Show (March 31, 1956), her success on the show leading to further TV stints and a

Decca record contract the following May. After her initial record release – a version of Hank Williams' (♦) **Jambalaya** – she began chalking up an impressive tally of

chart entries commencing with **One Step At A Time,** which became both a country and pop hit in mid 1957. Later came a series of hard headed rockers like **Dynamite** (1957) and **Sweet Nuthin's** (1959), Brenda proving equally adept at scoring with such ballads as **I'm Sorry** (1960) and **As Usual** (1963). For a while she was undoubtedly one of the world's most popular female singers, five of her singles selling past the million mark. But after a major hit with **Coming On Strong** in 1966, her record sales tapered off considerably. In more recent years she's tended to increasingly remember her country roots. However, though she often uses Nashville sessionmen on her albums, the results are usually hybrid in nature, Brenda always keeping that wider audience in mind.

Albums:
Here's Brenda Lee
  (Vocalion/—)
Brenda Lee Now *(MCA/MCA)*
Let It Be Me *(Vocalion/—)*
New Sunrise *(MCA/MCA)*
The Brenda Lee Story
  (MCA/MCA)
10 Golden Years *(MCA/—)*
Sincerely *(MCA/MCA)*
LA Sessions *(MCA/MCA)*
Little Miss Dynamite *(—/MCA)*

Brenda Lee Now (MCA). Although started off in country music Little Miss Dynamite sticks to middle-of-the-road material on her albums.

Red Foley discovery Brenda Lee made her debut on the Ozark Jubilee Show and had her first hit with Hank Williams' Jambalaya.

Dickey Lee

Singer songwriter whose compositions have also found favor with pop audiences, his song **Never Ending Song Of Love** having become a standard in this respect with Britain's New Seekers making it into a huge pop hit.

Born in Memphis, September 21, 1941 (real name Dickey Lipscomb), Dickey was already playing professionally by the time he left high school. While still at school he and his group won a talent contest and thus secured a regular 15 minute spot on a radio station in Santa

Above: Dickey Lee's Ashes Of Love (RCA).

Bobby Lewis

Born Hodgerville, Kentucky, Bobby Lewis appeared on the Hi-Varieties TV Show at the age of 13, later working on the Old Kentucky Barn Dance radio programme, CBS' Saturday Night Country Style and the highly rated TV Show, Hayloft Hoedown.

Only 5ft 4in tall, Lewis had problems handling his heavy and bulky Gibson J-200 guitar and eventually bought a 'funny shaped small guitar' in a Kentucky music shop, the 'guitar' proving to be a lute, which he fitted with steel strings and adopted as his main instrument.

Signed to United Artists Records during the mid '60s, Lewis' first Top Ten hit came in 1964 with **How Long Has It Been,** which he followed with such other successes as **Love Me And Make It Better** (1967), **From Heaven To Heartache** (1968), **Things For You And I** (1969) and **Hello Mary Lou** (1970), **From Heaven To Heartache,** a crossover hit, earning him a Grammy nomination as Best Male Performer in 1969. In the mid '70s, after many years with United Artists, Lewis began recording for the Ace Of Hearts label, his first release being **Mr President.** His UA albums, now no longer in the catalog, include a **Best Of Bobby Lewis** and **Things For You And I.**

Below: Bobby Lewis, who is one of the few country musicians to play a lute.

Barbara, California.

He joined the Memphis Sun label in 1957, recording **Good Lovin',** and played rockabilly in Florida. His other great love was boxing and he became welterweight champion in Memphis, attending Memphis State University partly on a boxing scholarship.

His songs have achieved a remarkable record of success, some of them also providing big hits for other artists. **She Thinks I Still Care** became associated with George Jones (♦), who had a big hit with it in the '60s. Artists who have covered Dickey's material also include Glen Campbell (♦), Don Williams (♦), Anne Murray (♦) and Brenda Lee (♦).

His own pop hits have included **Patches** (written by Barry Mann and Larry Kolber) on Smash Records in 1962, **I Saw Linda Yesterday** (1962), **I Don't Wanna Think About Paula** (1963) and **The Girl From Peyton Place** (1965). Later he moved to RCA and scored country hits with **The Mahogany Pulpit** (1971), **Never Ending Song Of Love** (1971), **Rocky** (1975), **Angels, Roses And Rain** (1976) and **9,999,999 Tears** (1976).

Albums:
Rocky *(RCA/—)*
Angels, Roses And Rain
  (RCA/—)

Recent pic of Ernie Lee, one-time host Midwestern Hayride.

Ernie Lee

There are few country artists of any era more genial than Ernie Lee. Born Ernest Eli Cornelison in the musically fertile area around Berea, Kentucky, Ernie auditioned for the Renfro Valley Barn Dance in 1940 and was hired; when Red Foley (♦) left the show, it was Ernie who replaced him as host. After a stint in Detroit over WJR, Ernie came on as host of the Midwestern Hayride over WLW in Cincinnati, first on radio then pioneering it on television from 1947 through 1952.

After a brief stretch in Dayton (1953–1954) he grew weary of the strain of performing, and retired to Florida vowing simply to do a lot of fishing. However, he was soon on television there (WSUN, St Petersburg, 1954–1958), and has had an extremely popular early morning television show over WTVT in Tampa from 1958 to the present.

Although his warm personality comes across on radio and television, he was never able to hit with a big record on either RCA, MGM, or Mercury. His best effort was **Hominy Grits** on RCA in 1947.

Albums: none

Jerry Lee Lewis

Yet another example of the '50s interplay between country and rock 'n' roll, this pianist-singer with the wild stage manner was originally influenced by the pumping, honky tonk piano style of Moon Mullican (♦), incorporated the delivery of black singers into his routine and finally, after becoming a somewhat notorious rock 'n' roll household name, returned to his country music roots – he now splits his music half rock, half country, and seems to be able to satisfy the fan factions for both.

Born Ferriday, Louisiana, September, 1935, Lewis was exposed to the bayou state's wide range of music and particularly church music – his parents sang and played at the Assembly Of God church. Jerry learned piano and played his first public gig in 1948 at Ferriday's Ford car agency – to introduce a new model. He sang 'Drinkin' Wine Spo Dee O Dee'. Like many of his generation, Lewis spent time in the local black music clubs and when he cut his first sides for Sam Phillips' Memphis Sun label it was some of the wildest rock 'n' roll yet heard. Frantic rockers such as **Whole Lotta Shakin' Goin' On** and **Great Balls Of Fire** were sometimes contrasted with country sides; Lewis's first Sun release was the Ray Price (♦) hit **Crazy Arms** and it made the country charts.

His career went through a traumatic period after it was found that he had married his 13 year old second cousin. He was booed off stage in Britain and the press there crucified him. However, by the late '60s he was making a comeback, both public tolerance and rock 'n' roll being in vogue again. Jerry Lee was back and running, making more country records this time and arranging his stage act to appeal to the audience in question – in Britain he is still one of the old rocker heroes and suffers audience heckling when he tries to perform country. He scored big on US country charts of the period with out and out honky tonkers like **What Made Milwaukee Famous Has Made A Loser Out Of Me** and **Another Place, Another Time**. His best known country releases include his interpretations of **Your Cheatin' Heart, You Win Again** and **I'll Sail My Ship Alone**.

He changed his label to Smash (a Mercury subsidiary) in 1963 but much of his Sun material has been re-released in various permutations as that label has changed hands. In 1968 he featured in 'Catch My Soul', a rock musical which ran in Los Angeles. A strange personality who combines arrogance and boastfulness with an apparent respect for religion and traditional southern values, 'The Killer' was picked up by police in 1976 for waving a gun around and demanding entry to Elvis Presley's (♦) Memphis mansion. Lewis likes his public to know that he can still cut it.

Jerry Lee Lewis, who'll crack a joke and then shatter the listener with a fierce 'Are you laughing at me, boy?'

Above: Country Class (Mercury). Hellraiser Lewis looking smooth. Contains half rock, half country.

Albums:

Odd Man In (Mercury/—)	**Old Tyme Country Music** (Sun/—)
Country Class (Mercury/—)	**Old Tyme Golden Hits Vols 1-3** (Sun/—)
Taste Of Country (Sun/—)	
Sunday After Church (Hillside/—)	**Rockin' With** (—/Mercury)
Rural Route No 1 (Hillside/—)	**Southern Roots** (—/Mercury)
Roll Over Beethoven (Hillside/—)	**Whole Lotta Shakin' Goin' On** (—/Hallmark)
Drinkin' Wine Spo Dee O Dee (Pickwick/—)	**Great Balls Of Fire** (—/Hallmark)
Golden Cream Of The Country (Sun/—)	**Good Rockin' Tonight** (—/Hallmark)
High Heel Sneakers (Pickwick/—)	**The Original Jerry Lee Lewis** (—/Charly)
Jerry Lee Lewis (Pickwick/—)	**Golden Hits** (Smash/—)
Monsters (Sun/—)	**Best Of . . .** (Smash/—)
	From The Vaults Of Sun (Power Pak/—)

Above: Lewis once broke up a stand of cartridges on discovering the owner was selling pirate tapes. 'Tell 'em the killer did it!' he snarled.

Light Crust Doughboys

The Doughboys, basically a western swing outfit, first came to life when Bob Wills (♦) and Herman Arnspiger began playing at Fort Worth, Texas, venues as the Wills' Fiddle Band. With the addition of vocalist Milton Brown (♦) they became the Aladdin Laddies in 1931 and later gained a job – through Burrus Mills' executive announcer and band manager, Wilbert Lee O'Daniel (♦) – advertising Light Crust Flour on Fort Worth radio station KFJZ. At which point they became first the Fort Worth Dough-

Hank Locklin, one of the artists featured on the 1957 European tour, Concert In Country Music.

LaWanda Lindsey

Provider of many lower league hits, LaWanda was born Tampa, Florida, January 12, 1953, spending much of her early life in Savannah, Georgia, where her father Lefty Lindsey formed a group the Dixie Showboys and became manager of WEAS, the local C&W radio station. At nine she made her debut with her father's band, later becoming a regular member.

Brought to the attention of Conway Twitty (♦) after appearing on a show sponsored by one of the star's business associates, some Lindsey demo tapes were arranged by Twitty and sent to Chart Records, resulting in a 1967 contract with that label, LaWanda's first release being **Beggars Can't Be Choosers,** a Liz Anderson (♦) song.

Following an initial hit **Partly Bill** (1969), LaWanda became nominated as one of the most promising talents of 1970, in which year she had other minor hits with **We'll Sing In The Sunshine, Let's Think About Where We're Going** and **Picking Wild Mountain Berries,** the latter twosome being duets with Kenny Vernon.

Albums:
LaWanda Lindsey's Greatest Hits Vol 1 *(Chart/Chart)*

Hank Locklin

Elected mayor of his home town during the '60s, Locklin possesses a vocal style that somehow endears him to audiences of Irish extraction.

Born McLellan, Florida, February 15, 1918, Lawrence Hankins Locklin played guitar in amateur talent shows at the age of ten. During the depression years he worked on almost any job that came his way – farmwork, roadbuilding

boys, then in 1932, the Light Crust Doughboys.

The personnel of the Doughboys changed frequently during the band's career and even by 1933 – the year that the band switched to another Fort Worth station, WBAP – all of the original members had departed, O'Daniel restocking the band with new members (including his sons).

But despite the changes (the list of musicians who at one time played with the Doughboys is fairly lengthy, very impressive, and includes the names of Knocky Parker, Johnnie Lee Wills (♦), Leon Huff and Leon McAuliffe (♦)) the band continued their long association with Burrus Mills until 1942, when they became the Coffee Grinders for a while, under the sponsorship of the Duncan Coffee Co. Later, the Doughboys – who in various forms had recorded for Victor and Vocalion – reverted to their former and better known title, but never again achieving the fame that was theirs during the 1930s.

The band, in fact, reforms for special occasions to this day, under the leadership of Jack Derry.

Dennis Linde

A talented singer-songwriter, Linde (born March 18, 1943) first staked a claim to fame with a band named the Starlighters during the early '60s.

In 1968 he became a Nashville-based songwriter, cutting his first solo album, **Linde Manor,** for Intrepid in 1970, appearing as part of Kris Kristofferson's (♦) band (along with Billy Swan (♦) and Zal Yanofsky of Lovin' Spoonful fame) at the Isle of Wight that same year. After recording an album with a group called Jubal, for Elektra Records (1972) he moved on to cut two solo LPs, **Dennis Linde** (1973) and **Trapped In The Suburbs** (1974) before joining Kristofferson on the Monument label.

Though Linde has yet to enjoy any real success as a recording artist, he's certainly made it as a songwriter, his compositions being covered by everyone from the Everly Brothers (♦) and Roy Orbison (♦) through to Donny Osmond, Elvis Presley (♦) having a million-seller with his version of Linde's **Burning Love** in 1972.

Albums:
Surface Noise *(Monument/—)*

Dennis Linde (Elektra). One of two solo albums he cut for Elektra before moving to Monument; he has, however, had more success as a songwriter.

137

The Era Of Hank Locklin

ember

QUEEN OF HEARTS · MYSTERIES OF LIFE · PAPER FACE · SEND ME THE PILLOW YOU DREAM ON
I'M LONELY DARLING · COME SHARE THE SUNSHINE WITH ME · NO ONE IS SWEETER THAN YOU
A YEAR OF TIME · LET ME BE THE ONE · BORN TO RAMBLE

PLAYABLE ON MONO OR STEREOPHONIC EQUIPMENT

The Era Of Hank Locklin (Ember). A British release from the popular Locklin, who spends most of his time touring these days.

etc – gaining his first radio exposure on station WCOA, Pensacola. At the age of 20 he made his first professional appearance at a community center in Whistler, Alabama, and then embarked on a series of tours and broadcasts throughout the southern states, becoming a member of Shreveport's Louisiana Hayride (♦) during the late '40s. Record contracts with Decca and Four Star were proffered and duly signed, Locklin gaining two hits with Four Star in **The Same Sweet Girl** (1949) and **Let Me Be The One** (1953). The success of the latter, helped him to obtain Opry bookings, at the same time enabling the singer to become an RCA record artist. With RCA he began to accrue a member of best sellers – **Geisha Girl** (1957), **Send Me The Pillow You Dream On** and **It's A Little More Like Heaven** (both 1958) all being Top Ten items. But he surpassed these saleswise with the self-penned **Please Help Me I'm Falling,** a 1960 No 1 that gained its composer a golden disc – Locklin again recording the song in 1970, with Danny Davis' (♦) Nashville Brass, and once more having some chart success.

A habitual tourer, Locklin, whose many hits have included **Happy Birthday To Me** (1961), **Happy Journey** (1962) and **Country Hall Of Fame** (1967) – was among the

artists who, as part of the 'Concert In Country Music', made the first C&W tour of Europe in 1957. During the '70s Locklin based himself in Houston, appearing on KTR-TV and also on Dallas' KRID Big D Jamboree. An album, **Hank Locklin,** was released by MGM in 1975.

Albums:
Country Hall Of Fame
(Camden/—)

Send Me The Pillow You Dream On *(Camden/RCA)*
Hank Locklin *(MGM/—)*
Famous Country Music Makers *(—/RCA)*
The Era Of *(—/Ember)*
The Best Of Hank Locklin *(—/RCA)*
The First Fifteen Years *—/RCA)*
Irish Songs – Country Style *(—/RCA)*
Once Over Lightly *(—/RCA)*

Below: Hank Locklin had his first guitar before the age of ten, but failed to keep up the monthly instalments and the instrument was soon repossessed.

Lonzo And Oscar

Really the Sullivan Brothers, John (Lonzo) born Edmonton, Kentucky, July 7, 1917, and Rollin (Oscar) born Edmonton, Kentucky, January 19, 1919, Lonzo and Oscar were the top comedy act on the Opry, their 20 year stint being terminated by the death of Johnny Sullivan on June 5, 1967. Originally there was another Lonzo, a performer named Ken Marvin (real name: Lloyd George) teaming with Rollin in pre-World War II days and recording a nationwide comedy hit **I'm My Own Grandpa,** a song penned by the Sullivans. The act went into store while the brothers became part of the armed forces and shortly after their return to civilian life, Ken Marvin retired, John assuming the guise of Oscar, the duo touring with Eddy Arnold (♦) until 1947 – in which year the Sullivans became Opry regulars. Some time after the death of John, Rollin Sullivan again resurrected Lonzo and Oscar, using a new partner Dave Hooten. In its various permutations, the act has, throughout the years, recorded for such labels as RCA, Decca, Starday, Nugget, Columbia and GRC.

Albums:
Traces Of Life *(GRC/—)*

Bobby Lord

A consistent filler of lower chart places during the late '60s and early '70s, Lord, born Sandford, Florida, January 6, 1934, is a University of Tampa grad who gained something of a reputation as a cast member of Red Foley's (♦) Jubilee USA Show during the '50s. An Opry member, the singer-guitarist scored early with **Hawkeye,** and had a 1964 hit with **Life Can Have Meaning,** his most potent disc success being **You And Me Against The World,** a 1970 release. His albums, which are mainly now hard to come by, include **The Bobby Lord Show** (Hickory), **Best Of Bobby Lord** (Harmony) and **Lord's Country** (Hickory).

Bobby Lord's Country (Hickory).

John D. Loudermilk

Writer of such hits as **Talk Back Trembling Lips, Tobacco Road, Abilene, Ebony Eyes, Indian Reservation, Language Of Love, Norman, Angela Jones, Sad**

Above: Lonzo (right) and Oscar, a top Opry comedy act for many years. Their original songs included You Blacked My Blue Eyes Too Often and Take Them Cold Feet Out Of My Back.

Below: . . . Sings A Bizarre Collection. Composer of many classic songs, Loudermilk is a very popular performer but a reluctant tourer.

Movies and **A Rose And Baby Ruth,** John D. Loudermilk was once a Salvation Army bandsman.

Born Durham, North Carolina, March 31, 1934, he learned to play trumpet, saxophone, trombone and bass drum at Salvationist meetings, later learning to play a homemade ukelele, which he took to square dances. Although he made his TV debut at the age of 12 – with Tex Ritter (♦), no less – his big break came in the mid '50s, when he set a poem to music and performed on TV. George Hamilton IV (♦) heard Loudermilk's composition and recorded it, the result – **A Rose And Baby Ruth** – released in 1956, selling more than four million copies. After penning **Sittin' In The Balcony,** a 1958 smash for Eddie Cochran, Loudermilk married Gwen Cooke, a university music student and headed for Nashville, there meeting Jim Denny (♦) and Chet Atkins (♦), becoming first affiliated with Cedarwood Music, then with Acuff-Rose Publishing – also commencing a recording career with RCA.

His own recording of **Language Of Love** became a huge hit on both sides of the Atlantic during the winter of 1961–62, but all his subsequent releases have made but slight chart indentations, possibly due to Loudermilk's reluctance to perform live on any major scale. A great favorite in Britain, where he's toured with Pete Sayers, compered the Wembley Festival and appeared on several BBC shows, Loudermilk generally prefers to stay at home with his wife and two sons, enjoying the earnings afforded by his songwriting royalties.

Albums:
The Best Of . . . *(—/RCA)*
Encores *(—/RCA)*

JOHN D. LOUDERMILK SINGS A BIZARRE COLLECTION OF THE MOST UNUSUAL SONGS

RCA VICTOR DYNAGROOVE RECORDS

I'm Looking for a World/Mary's Little Boy Child/Interstate 40/Bad News/Ma Baker's Little Acre/The Lament of the Cherokee Reservation Indian/Where Have They Gone/To Hell with Love/You're Lookin'/No Playing in the Snow Today/The Little Grave/Talkin' Silver Cloud Blues

LPM-3497

Louisiana Hayride

The Hayride was an influential Saturday night show that originated on radio station KWKH, Shreveport, Louisiana. The first program (April 3, 1948) featured Johnny and Jack (♦) with Kitty Wells (♦), Bailes Brothers (♦), Four Deacons, Curley Kinsey and the Tennessee Ridge Runners, Harmie Smith and the Ozark Mountaineers, Tex Grinsey and his Texas Playboys and Pappy Covington's Band.

One of the first cast members to achieve stardom was Hank Williams (♦), a Hayride regular from August 1948 to June 1949, while others who staked a claim to fame on 'The Cradle Of The Stars', were Elvis Presley (♦), Johnny Cash (♦), Webb Pierce (♦), Slim Whitman (♦), Faron Young (♦), Jim Reeves (♦), Johnny Horton (♦) and Sonny James (♦), many of whom left the Hayride to sign for Grand Ole Opry.

An enormously successful show for a number of years, the Hayride, which gradually dropped a regular cast in favor of guest stars, petered out in the mid '60s, although several sporadic attempts have been made to revive it.

Below: Charlie Louvin, surviving member of the Louvin Brothers.

Louvin Brothers

The Louvin Brothers, Ira and Charlie, once formed one of the finest duos in country music, offering superb, close harmony vocals on songs that often showed their gospel roots.

Born Rainesville, Alabama (Ira on April 21, 1924; Charlie on July 7, 1927) the Louvins (real name Loudermilk) were raised on a farm, where they learnt to play guitar, winning their first talent show in the early '40s, some time after the family had moved to Tennessee. Drafted into the forces during the latter stages of World War II, they returned to music at the cessation of their period of active service, gaining dates on Knoxville's KNOX Mid-Day Merry-Go-Round. However, just when the brothers seemed to be making the grade (they managed to do one session for Decca), Charlie was recalled for duty during the Korean crisis.

Once more, the Louvins had to re-establish themselves and, following some appearances on a radio show in Memphis – where the brothers worked in the Post Office – came a 1951 recording contract with MGM Records, followed by a signing with Capitol Records. Their fortunes improved even further and by 1955 they'd become Opry regulars, also having a hit record with their self-penned **When I Stop Dreaming,** a disc which sparked off a run of similarly successful singles by the Louvins during the period 1955–62. Then, after one last duo hit via **Must You Throw Dirt In My Face?,** the Louvins decided to go their separate ways, Charlie proving the more popular of the two, having three 1964 chart records with **I Don't Love You Anymore, See The Big Man Cry** and **Less And Less.** Just a few months later, Ira was dead, the victim of a head on auto accident near Jefferson City, Missouri, June 20, 1965 – his wife Florence (who sang under the name of Anne Young) also dying in the accident.

Since that time, Charlie Louvin has continued as a top flight country entertainer, appearing in such films as *Music City USA* and *The Golden Guitar,* also providing Capitol with a number of chart entries – including a quartet of hit duets with Melba Montgomery (♦) – before leaving the label to join United Artists in October 1973.

Albums:
Charlie Louvin:
It Almost Felt Like Love *(UA/—)*
Somethin' To Brag About –
 with Melba Montgomery
 (Capitol/—)

Louvin Brothers:
Great Gospel Singing Of . . .
 (Capitol/—)
The Family Who Prays
 (Capitol/—)

Luke The Drifter
♦ *Hank Williams*

Above: Ten Times Charlie (Epic). Since his brother's death Charlie has had solo hits with I Don't Like You Anymore and See The Big Man Cry.

Lulu Belle
And Scotty

Husband-wife teams have long been a staple of country music performance, but one of the earliest and certainly the most popular was Lulu Belle and Scotty, staples of the National Barn Dance (♦) from 1933 through 1958.

Lulu Belle was born Myrtle Eleanor Cooper in Boone, North Carolina on December 24, 1913. Active musically as a teenager, she auditioned for the National Barn Dance in 1932 and was hired, immediately becoming one of the stars of the show. She often teamed with the young bass player for the Cumberland Ridge Runners (♦), Red Foley (♦), in duets, and they themselves were a popular team.

In 1933 another new cast member

was added to the National Barn Dance: a guitarist, banjoist, singer, and songwriter named Scott Wiseman, known professionally as Skyland Scotty. Born near Spruce Pine, North Carolina, on November 8, 1909. Scotty had appeared on radio over WRVA in Richmond as early as 1927, and appeared on WMMN in Fairmont, West Virginia, while attending Fairmont Teachers College. Although he aspired to a career as an educator (a calling he would pursue in later years), he tried his hand at music, and he too became an immediate hit upon joining the Barn Dance.

The two hit it off, of course, and became a very popular team (although some naive listeners wrote angry letters to WLS, thinking Scotty had 'stolen' Red Foley's girl), largely on the basis of their smooth duet sound and on Scotty's prolific song writing, which produced such country music standards as **Mountain Dew** (co-

written with Bascomb Lamar Lunsford), the recently revived **Remember Me,** the folk favorite **Brown Mountain Light,** and their biggest hit, **Have I Told You Lately That I Love You?**

In their years on the Barn Dance they recorded for Conqueror, Vocalion, Okeh, Columbia, Vogue, Bluebird, and after the war on Mercury, London, and Starday. They also appeared as stars of several films based around the National Barn Dance cast, including **Village Barn Dance, Hi, Neighbor, Country Fair, Sing, Neighbor, Sing,** and **National Barn Dance.** They spent a brief time away from the National Barn Dance at the Boone County Jamboree in Cincinnati (1938–1941), but were and are closely associated with Chicago, where in addition to their network and regular WLS broadcasts they had a daily television show over WNBQ from 1949–1957.

Regulars on the National Barn Dance for 25 years, Lulu Belle and Scott were during the early 40's able to ask (and get) $500 a day for public appearances.

Scotty began working toward a masters degree in education during the 1950s, and when the act bowed out of the performing limelight in 1958 they retired to their native North Carolina, where Scotty finally fulfilled his early ambition of teaching. Not one to let grass grow under her feet, Lulu Belle has now served a couple of terms in the state legislature as representative from her district.

Albums:
**Have I Told You Lately That I
  Love You** *(Old Homestead/—)*
Lulu Belle And Scotty
  (Starday/—)
Sweethearts Still *(Starday/—)*

Bob Luman Rocks (DJM). A British compilation from material recorded for Warners and Hickory during 1959–62. Includes Let's Think About Livin', his only real pop hit.

Bob Luman

Once a teenage rockabilly, Luman – who still loves to rock – became an Opry regular in August 1969.

Born Nacogdoches, Texas, April 15, 1937, Robert Glynn Luman spent much of his boyhood time listening to various country and R&B shows on the radio. Encouraged to pursue a musical career by his father, an excellent fiddler, guitarist and harmonica player, he learnt guitar but was torn between continuing as a musician or as a baseball player – Luman Jnr being a semi pro ball player of some ability. But after being offered a trial with the Pittsburgh Pirates during the mid 50s, he flunked it, from there on concentrating his energies to becoming a rock star in the Elvis Presley mold. As early as 1955 Luman had recorded tracks for a small Dallas company, then, a short time later, he won an amateur talent contest which resulted in a spot on Shreveport's Louisiana Hayride (♦), the Texan becoming a regular on the show after Johnny Cash (♦) pulled out of the cast.

Record dates with Imperial and Capitol ensued, plus Las Vegas bookings and a part in a rock movie titled *Carnival* (1957) but it wasn't until 1960 and the Warner release of a Luman single called **Let's Think About Livin'** that the real breakthrough occurred, the Boudleaux Bryant (♦) song providing the singer with a residency in both the pop and country Top Ten.

He was, however, unable to capitalize on this position. A reservist, Luman was called up for active duty, Jim Reeves (♦) taking over his band during Luman's army stay.

With the advent of the Beatles, Luman, like other former rockers, turned once more to country music, signing for Hickory and Epic and accruing over two dozen hits since 1964, the biggest of these being **The File** (1964), **Ain't Got Time To Be Unhappy** (1968), **When You Say Love, Lonely Women Make Good Lovers** (both 1972) and **Neither One Of Us** (1973) and **Still Loving You** (1974). **Alive And Well,** a 1977 album release, found Luman being produced by Johnny Cash.

Albums:
Greatest Hits *(Epic/—)*
Neither One Of Us *(Epic/—)*
When You Say Love/Lonely Women Make Good Lovers *(Epic/—)*
Satisfied Mind *(Epic/—)*
Bob Luman Rocks *(—/DJM)*
Alive And Well *(Epic/—)*

Robert Lunn

As 'The Talking Blues Boy' (or 'The Talking Blues Man' as he was later billed) Robert Lunn brought an unusual form of both comedy and blues to the Grand Ole Opry for two decades, and was long the country's foremost exponent of the talking blues, a style which was to become a staple of the folk song revival movement.

Lunn was born in Franklin, Tennessee, on November 28, 1912, He apprenticed in vaudeville before joining the Opry in 1938, and he stayed with the show, except for service in World War Two, until 1958. A left handed guitar player, he rarely sung, relying instead on his droll, dry talking blues recitations, most of which he wrote himself. His only recording was a long out of print Starday album called **The Original Talking Blues Man.** Lunn died of a heart attack on March 8, 1966.

Robert Lunn, whose forte was the talking blues, a style brought to greater prominence by the late, great Woody Guthrie.

Frank Luther

Often remembered best for his children's records, Frank Luther actually had a long career in country music, as well as some success in the pop field. Born Frank Crow in Kansas on August 5, 1905, he grew up in Bakersfield (♦), California, and his early musical experience was as singer and pianist with gospel quartets.

He moved to New York in the late 1920s, where he teamed up with a fellow Kansas, Carson J. Robinson (♦), as recording artists (frequently called on record Bud and Joe Billings), and as songwriters, collaborating on **Barnacle Bill The Sailor** and **What Good Will It Do ?** He and his wife Zora Layman also did extensive recording, some of it with Ray Whitley (♦).

He recorded a wide variety of country material in the 1920s and 1930s, for labels such as Victor, Conqueror, and Decca. He moved into the field of children's recording in the late 1930s and 1940s, recording stories, ballads, and cowboy songs, largely for Decca. In addition, he lectured on American music, and even wrote a book on the subject: *Americans And Their Songs.*

Other achievements include early country music films (*c.* 1933) shot in New York, authorship of some 500 songs, and a good bit of popular recording as well as country. In the 1950s he moved into an executive role, and lives today in retirement in the New York area.

Albums: none.

Judy Lynn

Daughter of Joe Voiten, an ex band-leader, Judy (born Boise, Idaho, April 12, 1936) was once a teenage rodeo rider, a national yodeling champion and a beauty queen, representing Idaho in the 1955 Miss America contest and emerging as a runner up. Signed to the Opry touring show after deputizing for an illness-stricken Jean Shepard (♦), in 1956 she obtained a recording contract with ABC-Paramount, her major breakthrough arriving a year later when Judy was selected to co-host, with Ernest Tubb (♦), the first national TV screening of the Grand Ole Opry show. Dressed in flamboyant western attire, Judy began touring with an eight piece band, in 1960 commencing the first of her highly popular TV shows, also switching her recording allegiance to UA and subsequently cutting **Footsteps Of A Fool,** a Top Ten hit in 1961, for that label. But though she charted twice in '63, with **My Secret** and **My Father's Voice,** her recording career seemed to peter out, despite contracts with such labels as Musicor, Columbia and Amaret, though Judy – by then Las Vegas based – did enjoy a mini-hit with **Married To A Memory** in 1971. Her albums have included **Live At Caesar's Palace,** a 1969 Columbia release, and **Parts Of Love** (Amaret).

Loretta Lynn. One of eight children, she spent her childhood in complete poverty; one Christmas her miner father had 36 cents to spend on the celebrations.

Loretta Lynn

CMA Female Vocalist Of The Year in 1967, 1972 and 1973 and, with Conway Twitty (♦), three times winner of the Association's Vocal Duo Of The Year section, Loretta, the daughter of Melvin Webb, a worker in the Van Lear coalmines, was born Butcher's Hollow, Kentucky, April 14, 1935.

Part of the musical family, she sang at local functions in her early years, marrying Oliver 'Moonshine' Lynn (known as Mooney) immediately prior to her 14th birthday. In the 1950s, the Lynns moved to Custer, Washington, where Loretta formed a band that included her brother Jay Lee Webb on guitar. Later, signed to Zero Records, the diminutive (5ft 2in) vocalist hit the charts with **Honky Tonk Girl,** a 1960 best seller, she and Mooney touring in a 1955 Ford in order to promote the disc.

The Wilburn Brothers (♦) were impressed enough to ask Loretta to come to Nashville, where Mooney took a job in a garage to support his four daughters while Loretta and the Wilburns tried to negotiate a record deal – the singer eventually signing for Decca.

With a song appropriately titled **Success,** she broke into the charts in 1962, at the same time winning the first of her numerous awards. And since then, Loretta's been the most prolific female country hitmaker of them all, virtually every one of her releases making the Top Ten, many of them, including **Don't Come Home A Drinkin'** (1966), **Fist City** (1968), **Woman Of The World** (1969), **Coal Miner's Daughter** (1970), **One's On The Way** (1971), **Here I Am Again** (1972) and **Hey, Loretta,** all reaching the premier position. Her series of duets with Conway Twitty have claimed equally impressive sales figures, **After Me The Fire Is Gone** (1971), **Lead Me On** (1971), **As Soon As I Hang Up The Phone** (1974), **Feelin's** (1975), **This Time I've Hurt Her More Than She Loves Me** and **The Letter** (both 1976) being just some of the MCA duo's successes.

A grandmother at 32, Loretta now has six children, two of which, the twins Paggey and Patsy, still live at home. Owner of a large rodeo production company and a talent agency (in partnership with Conway Twitty), Loretta also owns the whole town of Hurricane Mills, Tennessee, where she resides. In 1972, she became the first female artist to win the CMA's Entertainer Of The Year plaudit, while in 1976 her autobiography, *Coal Miner's Daughter* became a massive seller, spending nine weeks on the *New York Times'* best selling book list.

Albums:
Your Squaw Is On The Warpath
 (MCA/—)
You Ain't Woman Enough
 (MCA/—)
Write 'Em And Sings 'Em
 (MCA/—)
Woman Of The World *(MCA/—)*
Entertainer *(MCA/—)*

Who Said That God Is Dead?
 (MCA/—)
I Wanna Be Free *(MCA/—)*
Hymns *(MCA/—)*
Here I Am Again *(MCA/—)*
Greatest Hits *(MCA/—)*
Greatest Hits Vol 2 *(MCA/—)*
Fist City *(MCA/—)*

Coal Miner's Daughter (MCA). The title of her bestselling autobiography. With Conway Twitty and as a solo artist, she is the winner of countless awards.

Don't Come Home A'Dreamin'
  (MCA/—)
Coal Miner's Daughter
  (MCA/—)
Blue Kentucky Girl *(MCA/—)*
Back To Country *(MCA/—)*
Home *(MCA/—)*
**They Don't Make 'Em Like
  Daddy** *(MCA/—)*
When A Tingle Becomes A Chill
  (MCA/—)
Country Roads *(—/Coral)*
Somebody, Somewhere *(MCA/—)*
(♦ Conway Twitty for duet album
listing.)

Mac And Bob (McFarland And Gardner)

Lester McFarland
  mandolin and vocals
Robert Gardner
  guitar and vocals

Lester McFarland, born February 2, 1902 in Gray, Kentucky, and Robert Alexander Gardner, born March 16, 1897 in Oliver Springs, Tennessee, met each other at the Kentucky School for the Blind in the middle teens, and became one of the first – if not the first – of the mandolin guitar duets which became so popular in the middle 1930s.

They spent several long stints with the National Barn Dance (♦) (1931–1934, 1939–1950), as well as on WNOX in Knoxville (1925–1931), and KDKA in Pittsburgh and KMA in Shenandoah, Iowa. They began recording with Brunswick in 1926, and also recorded for the American Record Company complex of labels, Conqueror, Columbia, Dixie, Irene, and others. They were best known for **When The Roses Bloom Again,** but introduced many old time songs and ballads to the repertoire of the duet teams which followed. Although they were long favorites, their sound was rather stiff, and they were superseded by later duets like the Delmore Brothers (♦), Monroe Brothers (♦), Karl and Harty (♦), the Blue Sky Boys (♦), and others.

Bob retired in 1951, while Mac went on as a solo until 1953; a talented musician, he also played piano, trumpet, cornet, and trombone. At this writing both these fine old gentlemen are still living.

Albums: none.

Leon McAuliffe

'Take it away, Leon!' was Bob Wills' (♦) famous cry which made Leon McAuliffe's name a household word in the south west during the heyday of western swing. Although he rose to prominence with the Texas Playboys, he actually had a long career on his own as well.

Born William Leon McAuliffe on January 3, 1917 in Houston, he joined the Light Crust Doughboys (♦) in 1933 – at the age of 16 – and began his famous association with Wills in 1935. One of the first to electrify his steel, he popularized the sound for many years with Wills, ubiquitous on nearly all his Columbia Records.

Leon joined the service in 1942, and upon his return from World

War II set up his own band in 1946, the Cimarron Boys, in Tulsa. He recorded for Columbia through 1955, then Dot, ABC, Starday, Capitol, then his own label, Cimarron, and also Stoneway, before leading the newly revived Texas Playboys on Capitol. His biggest hits were **Blacksmith Blues,** and **Cozy Inn** on his own, although he wrote and performed many western swing and steel guitar classics while a Texas Playboy, including **Steel Guitar Rag, Panhandle Rag, Bluebonnet Rag** and many others.

As western swing faded in popularity in the late 1950s, Leon developed other business interests, including two Arkansas radio stations, while playing and recording only on the side. He currently leads a group of ex-Texas Playboys as western swing is once again becoming popular.

Albums:
**Bob Wills' Original Texas
  Playboys Today** *(Capitol/—)*

C. W. McCall

McCall (real name William Fries, born Audubon, Iowa, circa 1929) displayed talent as both a musician and as an artist during his boyhood days, playing clarinet in a school band and earning spare cash by painting signs on trucks and shop fronts. Becoming a fine arts major at the University of Iowa, he opted out of a musical career for many years, working his way up the advertising ladder, in 1973 winning a Cleo award for a television campaign he masterminded on behalf of the Mezt Bread Company. Creating a fictional Old Home Bread truckdriver named C. W. McCall as lead character in this series of commercials, he began using his own voice on the soundtracks. Following the popularity of the series it was suggested that he recorded a single based on the commercials. So adopting his McCall guise, Fries cut **The Old Home Filler-Up And Keep On A-Truckin' Cafe** (1974), in what he describes as his walkin', talkin', singin' style, the result being first a local hit, and then, after Fries had gained an MGM record contract, a national hit. With truckers fast becoming the national heroes of the '70s, Fries aimed further narrative-type singles at this market, scoring with such releases as **Wolf Creek Pass** (a tale about brake failure), **Classified** (which dealt with the perils of buying used vehicles), **Black Bear Road** (regarding a hectic ride through the mountains of South Colorado) and **Convoy** (which utilized the language of CB radio), the last named becoming a world-wide multi-million seller in early '76. Later that same year, Fries/McCall entered the country charts with **There Won't Be No Country Music,** a Polydor release.

Albums:
Black Bear Road *(MGM/MGM)*
Wolf Creek Pass *(MGM/—)*
Rubber Duck *(Polydor/—)*
Wilderness *(Polydor/—)*

O. B. McClinton

Born 1942, Obie Burnett McClinton

*Obie from Senatobie
(Stax).*

grew up on his father's 700 acre farm at Senotobia, Mississippi, in the company of his two brothers and four sisters, his father being the Rev G. A. McClinton. Though McClinton is black, his initial interest was in country music rather than R&B – and though he attempted to sing the latter he was singularly unsuccessful, so he turned to songwriting. After completing high school, McClinton decided that farming was not for him, so he headed for Memphis, where he'd bought his first guitar in a Beale Street shop, but got no further than working as a dishwasher. Next came a choir scholarship to Rust College, Holly Springs, Mississippi, where he graduated in 1966, moving back to Memphis once more – this time to work on radio station WDIA. Due to be drafted into the army – which he didn't want to join – McClinton volunteered for the Air Force in December '66, spending much of his

*Above: Charlie McCoy outside
a studio. His normal mouth-
harp isn't quite this big, he
just manages to make things
sound that way.*

time singing on various service talent shows.

During this period he formed a songwriting relationship with the Memphis Stax label, contributing **Keep Your Arms Around Me,** recorded by Otis Redding, **You Can't Miss What You Can't Measure,** cut by Clarence Carter, plus several other items that found their way on to disc. It was through this association that he met producer Al Bell, who heard some of McClinton's own tapes, liked them and signed the singer to Stax as an artist in January, 1971. A first album **Country** was released some months later, to be followed by **Obie From Senatobie** (1973), which contained the hilarious **Unluckiest Songwriter in Nashville,** and finally before the demise of the Stax label, a live set **At Randy's Rodeo,** featuring an unfortunate impression of Elvis (♦) singing **Heartbreak Hotel.** In 1976 McClinton became signed to Mercury Records.

Charlie McCoy

Possibly the finest harmonica player on the Nashville session scene, McCoy was born Oak Hill, West Virginia, March 28, 1941. Once a member of Stonewall Jackson's (♦) touring band, he opted for session work during the 1960s, gaining a wide audience

through his appearances on various Bob Dylan albums. He became a member of Area Code 615 (♦) in 1969, being featured on the Code's **Stone Fox Chase** track, a number later adopted as the theme to BBC TV's Old Grey Whistle Test rock show. Signed to Monument since 1963, he had a minor pop hit as long ago as May 1961 when his Cadence recording of **Cherry Berry Wine** managed to break into the *Billboard* Hot 100. A multi-instrumentalist, McCoy was adjudged CMA Instrumentalist Of The Year in both 1972 and 1973.

Albums:
Real McCoy (Monument/—)
Charlie McCoy (Monument/—)
**Fastest Harp In The South/
  Goodtime Charlie's Got The
  Blues** (Monument/—)
Nashville Hit Man
  (Monument/Monument)
Charlie My Boy (Monument/—)
Harpin' The Blues
  (Monument/—)
Christmas Album
  (Monument/—)
Stone Fox Chase
  (—/Monument)

Skeets MacDonald

A popular singer on the West Coast known best for his 1952 hit **Don't Let The Stars Get In Your Eyes.** Born October 1, 1915 in

Left: Nashville Hit Man (Monument). The harmonica-playing session man has won CMA awards two years running for his musical talents.

Below: Red River Dave with Bill Fenner and Roy Hoxton.

Greenway, Arkansas, he began his career in Michigan, where he played on a number of radio stations in Royal Oak, Flint, and Detroit before migrating to the west coast after his World War II service.

He became a longtime fixture on Town Hall Party, and recorded largely for Capitol (1952–1959) and Columbia (1959–1967). Other hits included **Call Me Mr Brown** and **You Took Her Off My Hands.** He died of a heart attack on March 31, 1968.

Albums: none.

Red River Dave McEnery

Although saga songs have long been a tradition in country music – dating back to broadside sheets – the foremost exponent of the style has been a tall, blue eyed Texan named Red River Dave McEnery. Born in San Antonio on December 15, 1914, he began a professional career in 1935, playing a host of radio stations all across the country, but finding success in New York from 1938 through 1941.

Dave returned to Texas in the early 1940s, playing the Mexican border stations, and then basing himself in San Antonio from then on, although he found time to record for Decca, Savoy, Sanora, MGM, Continental, and a whole host of smaller labels, and appeared in a film for Columbia (*Swing In The Saddle*, 1948) and a couple for Universal (*Hidden Valley Days* and *Echo Ranch*, both 1949).

He really found his niche when he wrote **Amelia Earhart's Last Flight**, however, for although he was long popular as a singer of cowboy songs, it is these modern day event songs which have become his forte. Depending on the course of current events, he has written **The Ballad Of Francis Gary Powers, The Flight Of Apollo Eleven,** and most recently **The Ballad Of Patty Hearst.**

In the early 1970s Red River Dave moved to Nashville, where he became a well known sight, with his gold boots, lariat strapped to his side, big hat and leonine white hair and goatee. At the age of sixty he was working on a comeback, and who knows, he might just make it.

Albums: none.

Sam And Kirk McGee

Members of Uncle Dave Macon's (♦) Fruit Jar Drinkers, the McGee Brothers (both born Franklin, Tennessee, Sam on May 1, 1894, Kirk on November 4, 1899) were musically influenced by their father, an old time fiddle player, and the black street musicians of Perry, Tennessee, in which town the McGees spent a portion of their boyhood. With Sam on banjo and Kirk on guitar and fiddle they became part of Uncle Dave Macon's band in 1924, joining him on the Grand Ole Opry two years later. In 1930 they worked with fiddler Arthur Smith (♦), forming a trio known as the Dixieliners (which recorded for Bluebird), Smith

Above: Warner Mack, son of a Presbyterian minister. His real name is McPherson but the label copy man at one record company took his nickname to be his surname and so the discs came out labeled that way.

leaving in the early 1940s, at which time the brothers occasionally joined a popular Opry comedy act, Sarie and Sally.

Occasional members of several of the Opry's old time bands in ensuing years, the duo eventually opted to go their own way again, becoming favorites at many folk festivals during the '60s, when a whole new generation afforded the McGees the recognition their music deserved.

Sam, who claimed to be the first musician to play electric guitar on the Opry (a claim disputed by others), was killed on his farm on August 21, 1975, his tractor falling on him.

Albums:
Sam McGee – Grand Dad Of Country Guitar Pickers *(Arhoolie/—)*
The McGee Brothers With Arthur Smith *(Folkways/—)*
God Be With You Until We Meet again – Sam McGee with Bill Lowery *(Davis Unlimited/—)*

Warner Mack

Nashville born, on April 2, 1938, singer - songwriter Warner McPherson was raised in Vicksburg, Mississippi.

While at Vicksburg's Jett High School he played guitar at various events, from there moving on to perform in local clubs. During the '50s, McPherson became a regular on KWKH's Louisiana Hayride (♦) and was also featured on Red Foley's (♦) Ozark Jamboree, his record career making progress in 1957 when his recording of **Is It Wrong?** charted in fairly spectacular manner. In the wake of this initial success, McPherson – who became Warner Mack after his nickname had inadvertently been placed on a record label – decided to return to Music City. But there was a lull in his record-selling fortunes until 1964 when, following a moderate success with **Surely,** Mack suddenly hit top gear, providing Decca with 14 successive

Top 20 hits between the years 1964 and 1970, one of which, **The Bridge Washed Out,** was the best selling country disc for a lengthy period during 1965.

A fairly prolific songwriter, Mack has written over 200 numbers, including **The Bridge Washed Out, Is It Wrong?,** and some of his other chart climbers including **Talkin' To The Wall** (1966) and **How Long Will It Take?** (1967).

Love Hungry (Decca)

Uncle
Dave Macon
THE GAYEST OLD DUDE IN TOWN

The Gayest Old Dude In Town (Bear Family). An amateur until middle age, he became an Opry favorite. Availability of several albums indicates his continuing popularity.

Uncle Dave Macon

Known variously as The Dixie Dewdrop, The King Of The Hillbillies and The King Of The Banjo Players, David Harrison Macon was the first real star of the Grand Ole Opry.

Born Smart Station, Tennessee, October 7, 1870, he grew up in a theatrical environment, his parents running a Nashville boarding house catering for traveling showbiz folk.

Following his marriage to Mathilda Richardson, Macon moved to a farm near Readyville, Tennessee, there establishing a mule and wagon transport company which operated for around 20 years. A natural entertainer and a fine five string banjoist, David Macon played at local functions for many years but remained unpaid until 1918 when, wishing to decline an offer to play at a pompous farmer's party, he asked what he thought was the exorbitant fee of 15 dollars, expecting to be turned down. But the fee was paid and Uncle Dave played, there being spotted by a Loew's talent scout who offered him a spot at a Birmingham, Alabama, theatre.

In 1923, while playing in a Nashville barber's shop, he met fiddler and guitarist Sid Harkreader, the two of them teaming to perform at the local Loew's Theatre, then moving on to tour the south as part of a vaudeville show. A year later, while playing at a furniture convention, the duo were approached by C. C. Rutherford of the Sterchi Brothers Furniture Company, who offered to finance a New York recording date with Vocalion.

Macon and Harkreader accepted, cutting 14 sides on the initial sessions, returning in 1925 to produce another 28 titles. Macon's next New York sessions (1926) found him playing alongside guitarist Sam McGee (♦), cutting such sides as **The Death Of John Henry** and **Whoop 'Em Up, Cindy** – and that same year he first appeared on the Opry, where the jovial, exuberant Macon, clad in his waistcoat, winged collar and plug hat, soon became a firm favourite.

An Opry performer – usually accompanied by his son Dorris – almost up to the time of his death, the fun loving banjoist cut many records during his lifetime, sometimes recording solo, sometimes as part of the Fruit Jar Drinkers Band (not the same as the Opry band of the same name) or, on more religious sessions, as a member of the Dixie Sacred Singers, usually employing fiddler Mazy Todd and the McGee Brothers as supporting musicians. He appeared – and virtually stole the show – in the 1940 film *Grand Ole Opry* with Roy Acuff (♦) and others.

He died, age 82, on March 22, 1952 in Readyville, just three weeks after his final appearance on Grand Ole Opry, his burial taking place in Coleman County, Murfreesboro, Tennessee.

In October, 1966, he was elected to the Country Music Hall Of Fame, his plaque reading 'The Dixie Dewdrop', from Smart Station, Tennessee, was a man whose delightful sense of humor and sterling character endeared him to millions. A professional performer on the Grand Ole

Opry for 26 years, he was a 'minstrel of the countryside' prior to that. He was a country man who loved humanity and enjoyed helping others. A proficient banjoist, he was a singer of old time ballads and was, during his time, the most popular country music artist in America.'

Albums:
Uncle Dave Macon 1926-1939
(Historical/—)
The Dixie Dewdrop (Vetco/—)
Original Masters (Folkways/—)
At Home (Davis Unlimited/—)

Gayest Old Dude In Town
(—/Bear Family)
First Row, Second Left
(—/Bear Family)
Fun In Life (—/Bear Family)

Rose Maddox

Born Boaz, Alabama, December 15, 1926, Rose Maddox began her show business career as part of a family band, an outfit justifiably known as 'the most colourful hillbilly band in the land'. With Cal on guitar and harmonica, Henry on mandolin, Fred on bass, Don providing the comedy and Rose handling the lead vocals in her full-throated emotional style, the Maddox Brothers And Rose established a reputation first in California (where the family had taken up residence during the Depres-

sion), then on the Louisiana Hayride (♦) in Shreveport.

During the 1950s, the Maddoxes produced several fine records, also putting in appearances on the Grand Ole Opry and other leading country music shows, moving their base of operations back to California as the decade came to a close. Shortly after, the group disbanded and Rose became a solo act, recording for Capitol and supplying the label with such successful records as **Gambler's Love** (1959), **Kissing My Pillow** (1961), **Sing A Little Song Of Heartache** (1962), **Lonely Teardrops** (1963), **Somebody Told Somebody** (1963) and **Bluebird, Let Me Tag Along** (1964).

During this period she also recorded a number of duets with

The Maddox Brothers and Rose, 'The most colorful hillbilly band in the land'. In 1977 Rose began recording for John Fahey's Takoma label.

Buck Owens (♦), one of which, **Loose Talk/Mental Cruelty** proved a double sided hit in 1961. Rose's albums – many of which are now hard to come by – include **Bluegrass** (Capitol – 1962) a disc made at the suggestion of Bill Monroe (♦), who played mandolin on the sessions, Don Reno and Red Smiley also taking part. After a period of semi retirement, she is once again active on the California-Nevada club circuit, and is occasionally seen at southern Californian film festivals.

J. E. Mainer

Leader of the Mountaineers, one of the first string bands to appear on records, banjoist and fiddler J. E. Mainer was born Weaversville, North Carolina, July 20, 1898. A banjo player at the age of nine, by his early teens he'd become a cotton mill hand, working alongside his father at a Glendale, South Carolina, mill. In 1913, he moved to Knoxville, Tennessee, there witnessing an accident in which a fiddler was killed by a railroad train. He then claimed the musician's broken instrument as his own, had it repaired and learnt to play it, soon becoming one of the finest fiddlers in his area. By 1922, Mainer had hoboed his way to Concord, North Carolina, there marrying Sarah Gertrude McDaniel and later forming a band with his brother Wade (♦) (banjo), Papa John Love (guitar) and Zeke Morris (mandolin/guitar). The band gained a fair degree of fame locally, though J.E. was still employed in the textile industry. But in the early 1930s came a change of fortune, when Mainer's unit, adopting the title of the Crazy Mountaineers, began a series of broadcasts from Charlottesville, sponsored by the Crazy Water Crystal Company. Record dates for RCA Bluebird followed, the Mountaineers cutting such tracks as **John Henry, Lights In The Valley, Ol' Number 9** and **Maple On The Hill.** The band's popularity continued throughout the '30s and early '40s, Mainer and the Mountaineers recording over 200 sides for RCA and broadcasting over WPTF, Raleigh, North Carolina. And by the late 1960s, J.E. was still performing and recording – one of his releases being a single featuring unaccompanied jews-harp – but the grim reaper eventually caught up with him in 1971.

Albums:
J. E. Mainer's Mountaineers
(Arhoolie/—)
J. E. Mainer's Mountaineers
(Old Timey/—)
J. E. Mainer's Mountaineers
Vol 2 *(Old Timey/—)*
The Legendary J. E. Mainer
Vols 1-20 *(Rural Rhythm/—)*
Good Ole Mountain Music
(King/—)

Wade Mainer

The banjo playing younger brother of J. E. Mainer (♦), Wade had a long and influential career of his own. Born April 21, 1907 near Weaverville, North Carolina, Wade developed an advanced two-finger banjo picking style which led to a distinctive sound on his records as well as those he made with his brother.

After splitting from Mainer's Mountaineers (they had had a big 1936 hit called **Maple On The Hill**) Wade formed his own group which at times included Clyde Moody (♦) and Zeke Morris of the Morris Brothers (♦), called Wade Mainer and the Sons of the Mountaineers.

Mainer's Mountaineers c. 1936; J. E. Mainer, Boyd Carpenter, Zeke Morris and Wade Mainer. Their daily radios shows were sponsored by the Crazy Water Hotel Company, Mineral Wells.

Possessed of a strong lead voice, his **Sparkling Blue Eyes** was a major hit in 1939, one of the last commercial successes by a string band. Wade recorded for Bluebird until 1941, and after the war spent several years with King, but without much commercial success.

After a brief retirement in North Carolina he moved to Flint, Michigan, where he has worked for Chevrolet until his retirement. Recently 'rediscovered' he has recorded again for Old Homestead, and his strong, pure country voice and unique banjo style have not much been affected by his advanced years.

Albums:
Sacred Songs Of Mother And Home *(Old Homestead/—)*
Wade Mainer And The Mainer's Mountaineers *(Old Homestead/—)*

Barbara Mandrell

Born Houston, Texas (1948) but raised in Los Angeles, Barbara could play steel guitar at the age of 11, demonstrating her instrumental and vocal skills at the Showboat Hotel, Las Vegas, that same year. Becoming a regular on LA's Town Hall Party TV show, she continued playing at Las Vegas each year – usually fitting gigs in during school holidays. Part of a family band The Mandrells – which included her father, mother and two unrelated boys – at the age of 13 she toured with Johnnie Cash (♦) and in 1966–67 visited military bases in Korea and Vietnam.

During the late '60s, Barbara recorded for the minor Mosrite label cutting titles that included **Queen For A Day** – but following

Right: Wade Mainer, taken in about 1940. At this time he had split from his brother's group, Mainer's Mountaineers, and was heading his own band, Sons Of The Mountaineers.

Above: a 1948 photo of Wade Mainer, who had a solo hit with the biggest country record of 1939, Sparkling Blue Eyes.

a family move to Tennessee, she set her sights on a Nashville contract, eventually signing for Columbia in March, 1969, and gaining her first hit later that same year with her version of Otis Redding' **I've Been Loving You Too Long.** Establishing a successful formula, Barbara recorded other R&B material including **Do Right Woman, Do Right Man, Treat Him Right** and Joe Tex's **Show Me,** enjoying some fair-sized hits as a result, also cutting some duets with David Houston, one of which, **After Closing Time** (1970), achieved Top Ten status. Her most

Midnight Angel (Dot). Once part of a family group, Barbara has been performing since the age of 11. She is, however, still in search of consistent solo hits.

popular solo effort to date has been **Standing Room Only,** a single released soon after Barbara joined Dot in early 1976. Though obviously a talented lady – she plays banjo, pedal steel, saxophone and bass – she and her band The Do Rights have sometimes proved too supperclub slick for certain mainstream country audiences.

Albums:
Midnight Oil *(Columbia/—)*
Treat Him Right *(Columbia/—)*
This Time I Almost Made It *(Columbia/CBS)*
This Is Barbara Mandrell *(Dot/ABC)*
Midnight Angel *(Dot/ABC)*

This Time I Almost Made It (Columbia).

Zeke Manners

An accordion player, singer, and songwriter, who is best known as a co-founder of the Beverly Hillbillies (◊), and for his long association with Elton Britt (◊). Manners befriended Britt when he joined the Hillbillies in 1932, and in 1935 the two of them broke away from the group and headed for New York, where they were popular – sometimes together, sometimes separately – for many years.

Aside from his Brunswick recordings with the Beverly Hillbillies, Manners recorded on his own with Variety, Bluebird, and RCA, and collaborated with Elton Britt in the late 1950s for the **Wandering Cowboy** album on ABC-Paramount.

Albums: none.

Joe And Rose Maphis

A husband and wife team whose popularity peaked during the '50s and early '60s, Otis W. 'Joe' Maphis (born Suffolk, Virginia, May 12, 1921) and Rose Lee (born Baltimore, Maryland, December 29, 1922) met on Richmond, Virginia's WRVA Old Dominion Barn Dance in 1948. Shortly after meeting they married and moved out to the West Coast, there playing on Cliffie Stone's (◊) Hometown Jamboree and Crompton's Town Hall Party for several years, also performing vocal and instrumental chores (Joe played fiddle, guitar, banjo, mandolin and bass, while Rose Lee played guitar) on various recording sessions, although he became best known at the time for his road and studio work with ricky Nelson. Starday released an album **Joe And Rose Lee Maphis** in 1964, while Joe's past solo albums have included **Golden Gospel Guitar, Guitar Goes To The Jimmy Dean Show, King Of**

The Strings (all Starday) and **Joe Maphis** (Capitol). The duo have lived in Nashville for the past five years or so.

Albums:
Joe Maphis – Gospel Guitar
(Sacred/—)

Linda Martell

From South Carolina, Linda was initially an R&B singer who regularly entertained at the USAF base in Charleston. Discovering that she received more response whenever she employed C&W material, she turned increasingly towards country music and was eventually recommended to Nashville music business man Duke Rayner, who auditioned her and then organized some Music City demo sessions. The results impressed Shelby Singleton (◊) and he signed Linda for his Plantation label, her first release, **Color Him Father,** reaching No 22 on the *Billboard* country charts in 1969. Her subsequent recordings failed to make any great impact (**A Bad Case Of The Blues** being the biggest of the lot) but Linda nevertheless made country music history by becoming the first black female singer to guest on the Grand Ole Opry.

Albums:
Colour Me Country
(Plantation/—)

Jimmy Martin

Born Sneedville, Tennessee, 1927, James Henry Martin rose to prominence as a member of Bill Monroe's (◊) Bluegrass Boys, with which outfit he was lead vocalist, guitarist and front man for much of 1949–53, his last session with the band taking place in January 1954. Next came some fine sides for Victor, which found Martin in the company of the Osborne Brothers (◊), fiddler Red Taylor (who'd played alongside Martin on Monroe's classic

Tennessee (MCA). Jimmy Martin has made a significant contribution to bluegrass.

Uncle Pen) and bassist Howard Watts, a luminary of both Monroe's band and Hank Williams' (◊) Drifting Cowboys.

Some time later, Martin formed his own regular outfit, the Sunny Mountain Boys, and began recording for Decca, sometimes employing material of novelty nature but always musicians of quality, such people as J. D. Crowe, Vic Jordan (later with Lester Flatt (◊)), Bill Emerson (with Country Gentlemen (◊)) and Allan Munde (of Country Gazette (◊)) working with the band at some point during its lifetime. Maligned for his use of drums on many of his sessions – thus horrifying some purists – Martin is perhaps one of the more

unsung heroes on the bluegrass scene, though his contribution, both vocally and instrumentally, has been of inestimable value.

Albums:
Jimmy Martin *(MCA/—)*
Big Instrumentals *(MCA/—)*
Country Music Time *(MCA/—)*
Singing All Day *(MCA/—)*
Sunnyside Of The Mountain
  (MCA/—)
This World Is Not Home
  (MCA/—)
With The Sunny Mountain Boys
  (MCA/—)

Below and right: Jimmy Martin and his Sunny Mountain Boys. The girl in the picture taken in the Golden Nugget during the early '60s is Lois Johnson.

Frankie Marvin

Following the footsteps of his elder brother Johnny (◆), Frankie Marvin (born in Butler, Oklahoma, in 1905) journeyed to New York and joined him at the peak of his popularity, doing comedy as well as playing steel guitar and ukelele. He also worked with the Duke of Paducah (◆) in a comedy team known as Ralph and Elmer, and cut numerous records for a host of companies, among the earliest country music recorded in New York.

He joined Gene Autry (◆) – whom he'd befriended in New York in 1929 – in Chicago in the early 1930s as his popularity began to grow, and went west with him to Hollywood in the mid 1930s. Frank toured, broadcast, and recorded with Autry for the next two decades, adding the distinctive steel guitar styling that was so much a part of the Autry sound. He left the Autry show in 1955, and is currently retired in the mountains near Frazier Park, California.

Albums: none.

Johnny Marvin

Born in Butler, Oklahoma, in 1898, young Johnny ran away from home at the age of twelve to pursue a career as a musician, singer, and entertainer. His quest eventually took him to New York City, where he became popular on Broadway and with a couple of hit records on Victor; **Just Another Day Wasted Away**, and **Wait For Me At The Close Of A Long, Long Day**, which was his theme song.

He also became popular in the country field as 'The Lonesome Singer Of The Air', and used his steel guitar playing brother Frankie (◆) both as a comedian and musician in his act. The two befriended young Gene Autry (◆) in 1929, and after the Depression took the wind out of Johnny's sails he went to work for Gene as a songwriter and producer on his Melody Ranch radio show. He contracted an illness while entertaining GIs in the South Seas during World War II, and died in 1945 at the age of only forty seven.

Albums: none.

Louise Massey (And The Westerners)

Louise Massey *vocals*
Curt Massey
  fiddle, trumpet, piano, vocals
Dad Massey
  vocals and various instruments
Allen Massey
  vocals and various instruments
Milt Mabie
  vocals and various instruments
Larry Wellington
  vocals and various instruments

One of the earliest, most popular and most professional Western bands in country music was first known as the Musical Massey Family, then as the Westerners, and finally as Louise Massey and the Westerners. Natives of Texas, they were among the first to dress

Frankie Marvin, an early exponent of the steel guitar. He is also an actor, songwriter and comedian; during the 1920's he partnered Whitey Ford (The Duke of Paducah) in a comedy duo.

154

in flashy cowboy outfits and exploit a Western image. They appeared for several years on WLS beginning in 1928, and also on Plantation Party and other popular radio shows.

Main vocals were by Louise Massey, whose growth in popularity is reflected in the changing band name, with many other solos by her brother Curt, who had an active and successful career in popular music both before and after his association with the Westerners, ultimately being musical director and writer of the theme songs for the Beverly Hillbillies and Petticoat Junction television shows, and actually sang the latter. Supporting vocals were done by all band members, most notably the third sibling Allen, and Louise's husband Milt Mabie.

They recorded for the ARC complex of labels, Vocalion, Okeh, and Conqueror. Their biggest hit was probably **The Honey Song,** although they are best known for Louise's composition **My Adobe Hacienda.**

Albums: none.

Ken Maynard

Ken Maynard (born July 21, 1895 in Vevay, Indiana) was a major cowboy film star in both the silent and sound era, making and losing several fortunes in his many years on the screen. His place in country music was assured by his (a) being the first cowboy to sing on film, in *The Wagon Master* in 1930; (b) being the first to use a Western song as a film title (*The Strawberry Roan,* 1933); (c) introducing Gene Autry in films, as a singer in *In Old Sante Fe* in 1934; and (d) his 1930 recording session for Columbia in which he cut eight traditional cowboy songs.

A fiddler, banjoist, guitarist, rough but appealing singer as well as a stunt man, rodeo star, and film hero of over two decades (1922–1945), Ken Maynard died in California on March 23, 1973.

Albums: none.

Jody Miller

The complete crossover singer, Jody Miller is equally at home in a pop, country or folk setting, a trait that leads to most articles on her talents commencing with the words: 'Jody Miller is difficult to classify'.

Born Phoenix, Arizona, November 29, 1941, the daughter of a country fiddle player, Jody grew up in Oklahoma, where she and school friends formed a trio known as the Melodies. Upon graduation, she decided on a solo singing career, but after heading for California, she broke her neck in an auto accident and was forced to return home to Oklahoma once more. Recuperation completed, she began establishing herself locally, joining the Tom Paxton TV Show and gaining a reputation as a folk singer. Through actor Dale Robertson she became signed to Capitol Records, in 1963 making a fairly commercial folk album in **Wednesday's Child,** later cutting a hit single in **He Walks Like A Man** (1964) and obtaining a place in the Italian San Remo Song Festival. A year later, Jody's ver-

sion of **Queen Of The House** – Mary Taylor's sequel to Roger Miller's (♦) **King Of The Road** – became a monster country and pop hit, but despite some enjoyable pop country albums that included **Jody Miller Sings The Hits Of Buck Owens** and **The Nashville Sound Of Jody Miller,** there were no further hit singles for Capitol except **Long Black Limousine,** a mild success in 1968.

Following a short retirement, during which Jody spent her time on her Oklahoma ranch raising her daughter Robin, she returned to performing once more, cutting sides for Epic, an association with producer Billy Sherrill (♦) providing her with a 1970 chart entry

titled **Look At Mine,** a Tony Hatch song. And in the '70s, she's enjoyed further Top Ten hits with **He's So Fine** (1971), **Baby I'm Yours** (1971) and **There's A Party Going On** (1972), her 1976 chart singles including **Ashes Of Love** and **Will You Still Love Me Tomorrow?** She remains a talented singer in search of that really big record.

Albums:
House Of The Rising Sun
(*Epic/—*)
Country Girl (*Epic/—*)
Will You Love Me Tomorrow?
(*Epic/—*)
Here's Jody (*Epic/—*)

Above: Two albums from Jody Miller (Epic Records). Title track of top one was a 1976 chart single.

Below: Jody Miller, a crossover singer of wide appeal.

Roger Miller

The voice and songs of Roger Miller have been heard in films ranging from *Waterhole 3*, a zany Western, to the Disney version of *Robin Hood*. He's also paid some dues as a TV actor, while his records made him one of the most successful pop country stars during the 1960s.

Born Fort Worth, Texas, January 2, 1936, Roger Dean Miller was raised by his uncle in Erick, Oklahoma, and performed his first song at the age of five, his audience being the 36 other children who attended Erick's one room schoolhouse. Influenced by the singing of Hank Williams (♦), Miller saved enough money to buy a guitar, later also acquiring a fiddle. Following a period spent as a ranch hand, Miller spent three years in the US Army in Korea, spending most of his time as a jeep driver. Upon discharge, he made his way to Nashville, booking in at the Andrew Jackson Hotel as a guest for one evening, the next morning obtaining a job as pageboy in the same establishment. In the sleeve notes to his **Trip In The Country** album, Miller describes himself at this period as being: 'a young ambitious songwriter, walking the streets of Nashville, trying to get anybody and everybody to record my songs. All in all, I wrote about 150 songs for George Jones (♦), Ray Price (♦), Ernest Tubb (♦) and others. Some were hits and some were not. In the beginning I created heavenly, earthy songs.'

Ray Price was one of the first to benefit from the Miller songwriting skill, having a 1958 hit with **Invitation To The Blues.** And signed to RCA in 1960, Miller began accruing his own country winners with **You Don't Want My Love** (1960) and **When Two Walls Collide** (1961). In 1962 he joined Faron Young's (♦) band as a drummer, also in '62 guesting on the Tennessee Ernie (♦) TV Show.

After one last hit for RCA in **Lock, Stock And Teardrops,** Miller moved to Smash, having an immediate million seller with **Dang Me,** following this with other gold disc winners in the infectious **Chug-A-Lug** (1964) and lightly swinging **King Of The Road** (1965). His endearing mixture of humor, musicianship and pure corn continued to pay dividends throughout the '60s, **Do Wacka Do** (1964), **Engine, Engine No 9, One Dyin' And A Buryin', Kansas City Star, England Swings** (all 1965), **Husbands And Wives** (1966), **Walkin' In The Sunshine** (1967) and **Little Green Apples** (1968) all being major hits.

The '70s, which have seen Roger Miller switch labels first to Mercury then to Columbia, have brought less chart success to the now Southern California-based singer-songwriter and hotel chain owner.

But he probably gets to sleep at night by merely counting his huge tally of gold singles, gold albums and numerous industry awards, including an astonishing six Grammies in a single year (1965), unequalled before or since.

Albums:
Engine No 9 *(Pickwick/—)*
Best Of *(Mercury/Mercury)*
Dear Folks Sorry I Haven't Written Lately *(Columbia/—)*
Golden Hits *(Smash/—)*
King Of The Road *(Hillside/—)*
Little Green Apples *(Hillside/—)*
Supersongs *(Columbia/CBS)*

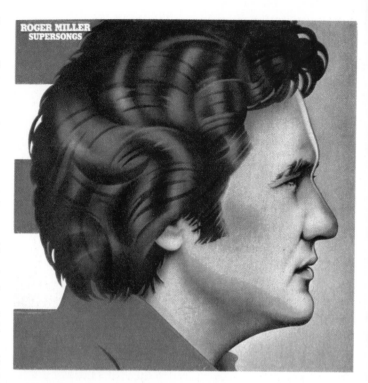

Supersongs (Columbia). Writer of many hits for other artists, Miller has had great success in pop and country charts.

Ronnie Milsap

Winner of the CMA Male Vocalist Of The Year award in 1974, Milsap is equally at home with the blues as with country ballads.

Born blind, in Robbinsville, North Carolina, he learnt the violin at the age of seven and could play piano just a year later. By 12 he'd also mastered the guitar. Attending the State School for the Blind in Raleigh, he became interested in classical music but formed a rock group The Apparitions 'because it was the thing to do'. Upon completing high school, Milsap attended Young Harris Junior College, Atlanta, studying pre-law and planning to go on to law school at Emory University where he'd been granted a scholarship. However, he quit studies to play with J. J. Cale and in 1965 formed his own band, playing blues, country and jazz, signing for Scepter Records and cutting **Never Had It So Good/ Let's Go Get Stoned,** two R&B tracks for his first single release. Attaining an essentially black sound, Milsap soon found himself playing dates alongside such artists as Bobby Bland and The Miracles. By 1969, he and his band had moved to Memphis, becoming resident group at a club known as TJ's, Milsap recording for the Chips label and coming up with a hit disc in **Loving You is A Natural Thing** (1970). After a stint with

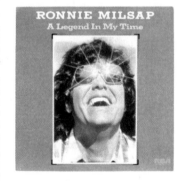

Above: A Legend In My Time (RCA).

Warner Brothers Records, the singer, who'd always featured some country material, decided to devote his career to becoming a fully fledged country entertainer and headed for Nashville, there gaining a residency at Roger Miller's (♦) King Of The Road motel and signing a management deal with Jack D. Johnson, the Svengali behind Charley Pride (♦). In April 1973 he became an RCA recording artist, his first release on the label being **I Hate You,** a Top Ten chart entry. This he followed with such titles as **The Girl Who Waits On Tables, Pure Love, Please Don't Tell Me How The Story Ends** (1974), **A Legend In My Time, Too Late To Worry, Too Late To Cry, Daydreams**

About The Night (1975), **Just In Case, What Goes On When The Sun Goes Down, (I'm A) Stand By Your Woman Man** (1976) all proving Top Five hits, many of them reaching the poll position, and **Let My Love Be Your Pillow** becoming a No 1 in early 1977.

An avid collector of old radio transcriptions, Milsap is also a radio ham.

Albums:
Where My Heart Is *(RCA/RCA)*
Pure Love *(RCA/RCA)*
20/20 Vision *(RCA/RCA)*
A Rose By Any Other *(Warner/—)*
Night Things *(RCA/RCA)*
Live *(RCA/RCA)*
A Legend In My Time *(RCA/RCA)*
Vocalist Of The Year *(Crazy Cajun/—)*
Mr Mailman *(—/DJM)*

Right: Best Of Bill Monroe and his Blue Grass Boys (MCA). The father of bluegrass music, Monroe has had lasting influence. Former members of his band such as Earl Scruggs have contributed to his definitive sound before going on to stardom of their own.

Above: Sixteen All-Time Greatest Hits (Columbia). Rock 'n' roll led to a decline in bluegrass, but the '60s saw Monroe still on top form.

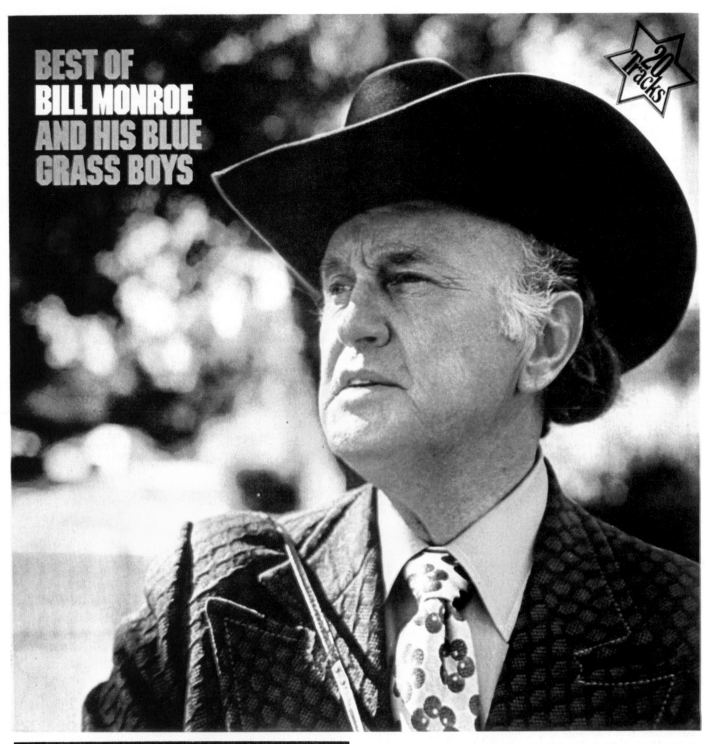

BEST OF
BILL MONROE
AND HIS BLUE
GRASS BOYS

Monroe Brothers

The virtual base upon which the whole of bluegrass music rests. William Smith (Bill) Monroe was born in Rosine, Kentucky, September 13, 1911, the youngest of eight children. Brother Charlie was next youngest having been born eight years previously, on July 4, 1903.

This gap, coupled with Bill's poor eyesight, inhibited the youngest son from many usual play activities and gave him an introverted nature which has carried through into later life, many people mistaking his shyness for standoffishness. However, this sense of isolation did allow him to develop his musical talents with great alacrity. The family farmed 655 acres and Bill, working way out in the fields where no one could hear him, developed his lung power without hindrance. Church was also a major formative influence, as with so many Southern musicians. In Bill's case he could not see to read the shape note hymnals too well and so learnt the music by ear. The shaped notes were to appear later in Bill's bluegrass music and the ear training was also important since it has obviously contributed to the man's fine sense of harmony in high vocal ranges.

The Monroe family was musical on both sides. Brother Charlie could play guitar by 11 and Birch could play fiddle. Bill's mother's side, the Vandivers, were the more musical and Uncle Pendleton Vandiver (later immortalised in Bill's perhaps most famous composition, **Uncle Pen**) would often stay overnight at the household, occasions of great musical festivity.

Uncle Pen was a rated fiddler locally and Bill was playing publically with him by 13, travelling to local square dances and backing Pen's fiddle with guitar.

Also influential on Bill then was a black musician from Rosine, Arnold Shultz. Bill would gig with him also and rated him a fine musician and with an unrivalled blues feel. At this time he also started to hear the gramophone records that were being produced featuring such performers as Charlie Poole (◊) and the North Carolina Ramblers.

Birch and Charlie left to seek work in Indiana and Bill joined them in 1929, when he was 18. Until 1934, in East Chicago, Indiana, they worked at manual jobs by day (Bill washed and loaded barrels in an oil refinery) and played dances and parties at night. For a while they went on tour with the Chicago WLS station Barn Dance, doing exhibition square dancing.

In 1934 Radio WLS, for whom the three brothers (Birch on fiddle, Charlie on guitar and Bill on mandolin) had been working on a semi pro basis, offered them full time employ. Birch decided then to give up music but Charlie and Bill reformed as a duet, the Monroe Brothers, and then followed much other radio work until in 1935 they were sponsored on Carolina radio by Texas Crystals. In that same year Bill married Caroline Brown and their children, Melissa (born 1936) and James (1941) have both performed with Bill, James eventually forming his own band, the Midnight Ramblers.

The Monroe Brothers, engaged on radio work in Greenville, South Carolina and Charlotte, North Carolina, were persuaded forcefully in 1936 by Eli Oberstein of Victor Records to do some recordings. In the Southern Radio Building at Charlotte in February of that year they cut ten sides including an early best seller, **What Would You Give (In Exchange For Your Soul).** At first they did not feel interested by the idea of recording since they were already doing well via radio and live broadcasts, but sales of the early sides were impressive enough to warrant five more such sessions in the next 12 month period. Besides featuring popular traditional material from sources such as the Skillet Lickers (♦), Carter Family (♦), Bradley Kincaid (♦) and Jimmie Rodgers (♦) (the Monroes did not write their own songs as yet) they had pioneered a distinctive style in which then-advanced mandolin and guitar techniques were coupled with a high, clear, easily recognisable vocal sound.

In 1938 they went their separate ways, partly due to differing artistic ideas, partly to personal tensions after some years together on tour. Bill formed the Kentuckians in Little Rock, Arkansas and then moved to Radio KARK in Atlanta, Georgia, where the first of his Blue Grass Boys lineups was evolved. At this time Bill began to sing lead and to take mandolin solos rather than just being part of the general sound. In 1939 he auditioned for the Grand Ole Opry and George D. Hay (♦), the 'Solemn Old Judge' and the man who first named the Opry, was impressed enough to sign him and promise that if Bill ever left it would be because he'd sacked himself. The following Saturday he played his first Opry number, the famous **Mule Skinner Blues.**

Bill Monroe's music then started to undergo subtle changes. He added accordian and banjo (played by Sally Ann Forester and Stringbean (♦) respectively) in 1945 when he joined Columbia Records and this period saw the evolution of a fuller sound with the musicians taking more solos. But in 1945 the accordian was dispensed with, never to return, and in that year the addition of Earl Scruggs (♦) with a banjo style that was more driving and syncopated than anything heard previously, put the final, distinctive seal on Monroe's bluegrass sound. Flatt and Scruggs remained with Bill until 1948.

Songs from this period include **Blue Moon Of Kentucky, I Hear A Sweet Voice Calling, I'm Going Back To Old Kentucky** and **Will You Be Loving Another Man.** Other musicians with Bill at this time were Chubby Wise (fiddle) and Howard Watts (also known as Cedric Rainwater) (bass).

Bill left Columbia in 1949 because he objected to them signing the Stanley Brothers (♦), a rival bluegrass group. With his next label, Decca, his main man was Jimmy Martin (♦), a musician with a strong, thin, highish voice, whose talents enabled Monroe to fill in more subtle vocal harmonies alongside. Compositionwise, this was Monroe's golden age. He wrote **Uncle Pen, Roanoke, Scotland** (a nod towards the source from whence so much in the way of string band jigs and reels had evolved), **My Little Georgia Rose, Walking In Jerusalem** and **I'm Working On A Building,** the last two being religious 'message' songs, always part of the Monroe tradition from the earliest days.

By the end of the decade bluegrass, although it had added a new dimension to country, was in decline due to the onset of rock 'n' roll (it is interesting to remember that when Elvis Presley (♦) released his **Blue Moon Of Kentucky** in 1954, Bill's record company rushed out a re-release of Monroe's (very different) original.

But the '60s saw a folk revival, and apart from the regional audience which had remained loyal to some extent Bill now found hordes of students eager to embrace indigenous rural white folk music. In 1963 Bill made his first college appearance at the University of Chicago; later that same year he played to 15,000 people at the Newport Folk Festival.

Bill Monroe was elected to the Country Music Hall of Fame in 1970. He has always trodden his own musical path, never bowing to commercial pressures, his contribution to country music being inestimable.

As for Charlie, he had a long and successful career – although not nearly so spectacular as Bill's – with his own band, The Kentucky Pardners, well into the early 1950s. He returned from retirement in the early 1970s to appear on the bluegrass circuit – displaying great grace and charm – –before dying of lymph cancer in 1975.

Albums:
Bill Monroe:
Bluegrass Ramble *(MCA/—)*
Bluegrass Instrumentals *(MCA/—)*
Bluegrass Special *(MCA/—)*
Bluegrass Style *(Vocalion/—)*
Bluegrass Time *(MCA/—)*
Country Music Hall Of Fame *(MCA/—)*
Greatest Hits *(MCA/—)*
High Lonesome Sound *(MCA/—)*
I Saw The Light *(MCA/—)*
Meet You In Church *(MCA/—)*
Kentucky Blue Grass *(MCA/—)*
Mr. Blue Grass *(MCA/—)*
Songs With The Blue Grass Boys *(Vocalion/—)*
Voice From On High *(MCA/—)*

Best Of Bill Monroe *(MCA/—)*
Road Of Life *(MCA/—)*
Weary Traveler *(MCA/—)*
Bean Blossom *(MCA/—)*
Best Of Bill Monroe *(—/MCA)*
Father And Son – with James Monroe *(MCA/—)*
Bill Monroe And Charlie – with Charlie Monroe *(MCA/—)*

Charlie Monroe:
Tally Ho *(Starday/—)*
Charlie Monroe On The Noonday Jamboree – 1944 *(County/County)*

Monroe Brothers:
Feast Here Tonight *(Bluebird/—)*

Melba Montgomery

Born Iron City, Tennessee on October 14, 1938, Melba was raised in Florence, Alabama, retaining her thick Alabama accent to this day. She began her singing at the local Methodist church where her father taught singing. Since he also played fiddle and guitar at home Melba grew up in a truly musical environment and polished her harmony singing early on, a facet which would stand her in good stead later when she became George Jones' (♦) singing partner. She and her brothers were part of an act in Florence which got them to the finals of an important national talent contest organised by the giant Pet Milk concern.

Melba moved to Nashville and caught the attention of Roy Acuff (♦), staying with his show for four years. In 1962 she went solo and released her first singles, **Happy You, Lonely Me** and **Just Another Fool Along The Way.**

In 1963 she teamed up with the prestigious George Jones and thus began a partnership that was to further her career greatly. With George she had the timeless hit **We Must Have Been Out Of Our Minds,** a song that was to be well covered by other artists in years to come. Melba also had solo hits at this time in **Hall Of Shame** (her chart debut) and **The Greatest One Of All.** Her voice had both strength and purity and it was becoming obvious that here was a real country find. In 1967 Melba's partnership with George ended and in 1970, on Capitol Records, she was teamed with Charlie Louvin (♦), scoring a big duet hit on **Something To Brag About.** In fact duets were a speciality of Melba's; she made a single

Above: Baby, You've Got What It Takes (Capitol).

Left: Melba Montgomery, winner of the Pet Milk Amateur contest in 1958.

and an album with Gene Pitney in 1966.

Her time at Capitol saw the start of a liaison with Pete Drake (♦), a partnership that would carry over fruitfully into her stint with the Elektra label.

Elektra were known at the turn of the '60s as the West Coast's hippest record company, having made their reputation first with folk acts and then with such rock acts as the Doors and the MC5. Melba was to represent their initial move into modern country and the result was a series of albums that were slap bang in Melba's country style, but sparkingly well produced too. Since 1973, Melba's country hit singles have included **Wrap Your Love Around Me, He'll Come Home** and **No Charge,** a sentimental 'talkover' song written by Harlan Howard (♦), with which J.J. Barrie had a No 1 pop hit in Britain during 1976. In the US it became Melba's first number one record.

Her run with Elektra also threw up some first class albums, including **Melba Montgomery, No**

Clyde Moody, ex-member of Mainer's Mountaineers and later a sideman with Bill Monroe and Roy Acuff.

Charge, Don't Let The Good Times Fool You and The Greatest Gift Of All, but by 1977 Melba had switched allegiance to the United Artists label. At the time of writing Melba lives in Nashville with her husband, industry executive and songwriter Jack Soloman.

Albums:
Melba Toast (Musicor/—)
Melba Montgomery (Elektra/—)
Miss Country Music
(Hillside/—)
Something To Brag About –
with Charlie Louvin (Capitol/—)
Don't Let The Good Times Fool
You (Elektra/—)
The Greatest Gift Of All
(Elektra/—)
No Charge (Elektra/—)
We Must Have Been Out Of
Our Minds (—/RCA)

Patsy Montana

Patsy Montana, born Rubye Blevins on October 30, 1914 in Hot Springs, Arkansas, became the first woman in country music to have a million selling record when **I Want To Be A Cowboy's Sweetheart** was released in 1935. She began her early career with silent film cowboy star Monte Montana (no relation), but was long associated with the Prairie Ramblers (♦) on the National Barn Dance (♦) (1934–1952), who backed her up on **Cowboy's Sweetheart** and most of her other hits. She recorded with them on the ARC complex of labels (1935–1942), and then on Decca (1942–1949) and RCA (1949–1951) before leaving them and Chicago for the West Coast in 1952.

She has been in and out of retirement ever since then, occasionally appearing with her daughter Judy Rose, recording in more recent years on Surf and Starday.

Albums: none.

Clyde Moody

Born in Cherokee, North Carolina, in 1915, Clyde Moody rose to prominence in the 1940s as the Hillbilly Waltz King, largely on the strength of his gold record for **Shenandoah Waltz** for King records, which sold some three million copies.

Moody apprenticed with Mainer's Mountaineers (♦), spent several successful years with Bill Monroe (♦), where he recorded the classic **Six White Horses,** and spent a bit of time with Roy Acuff (♦) before joining the Opry on his own in the mid 1940s. He achieved his greatest success on King, with other hits such as **Carolina Waltz, Next Sunday Darling Is My Birthday, I Know What It Means To Be Lonesome, I'd Stay At Home With Mother And Dad,** and many others.

He left the Opry in the late 1940s to pioneer television in the Washington DC area, then returned to his native North Carolina, where he had a long running television show and several business interests. In recent years he has returned to Nashville to resume a musical career, appearing at several bluegrass festivals yearly (those fans don't forget his years as a Blue Grass Boy), and touring over 300 days a year with Ramblin' Tommy Scott's show.

Albums:
Moody's Blue
(Old Homestead/—)

George Morgan

Writer and singer of **Candy Kisses,** the biggest country song of 1949, Morgan, for a brief period, looked capable of usurping Eddy

George Morgan, who once followed in the footsteps of Frank Sinatra and Tony Martin and recorded a duet with Dinah Shore.

Arnold's (♦) position as the undisputed king of country pop.

Born Waverly, Tennessee, June 28, 1925, he spent his teen years in Barberton, Ohio. On completing high school, Morgan worked as a part time performer but mainly earned his keep by stints as a truck driver, salesman and other occupations. Obtaining a regular singing spot on WWVA Jamboree, Wheeling, West Virginia, he there established something of a reputation and became signed to Columbia Records, his first release being **Candy Kisses,** which reached No 1 in the country charts (subsequently selling a million), while Elton Britt's (♦) cover version reached No 3. Invited to join WSM in 1948 in the dual role of deejay and vocalist, he soon became an Opry regular, scoring with more 1949 hits in **Rainbow In My Heart, Room Full Of Roses** and **Cry-Baby Heart.**

Establishing a smooth, easy style that came replete with fiddle and steel guitar, Morgan became a popular radio and concert artist but, despite major successes with **Almost** (1952), **I'm In Love Again** (1959) and **You're The Only Good Thing** (1960), his record sales remained little more than steady throughout the rest of his association with Columbia.

In 1966 he joined Starday, who provided him with elaborate orchestral trappings, a ploy which gained Morgan a quintet of mini

hits during 1967–68, but soon he was on the move again, recording with Stop, Decca, and Four Star, but only twice attaining Top 20 status, with **Lilacs And Rain,** a 1970 Stop release, and **Red Rose From The Blue Side Of Town,** a 1974 MCA item.

Morgan's death occurred in July 1975, following a heart attack sustained while on the roof of his house where he'd been fixing a TV aerial.

Albums:
Red Roses From The Blue Side
Of Town (MCA/—)
Remembering (Greatest Hits)
(Columbia/—)
Candy Mountain Melody
(MCA/—)
The Best Of . . . (Starday/—)

Sounds of Goodbye
(Saturday).

The Morris Brothers

Wiley Morris
mandolin and tenor vocals
Zeke Morris
guitar and lead vocals

Yet another of the fine duet acts which flooded country music in the mid 1930s, the Morris Brothers became well known for their smooth harmony singing and songs like **Salty Dog** and **You Give Me Your Love And I'll Give You Mine**, although they were probably best known for their version of **Tragic Romance**.

Wiley actually had a long career playing mandolin and guitar for a number of well known bands, including Wade and J. E. Mainer (♦) both together and with their separate bands, and with Charlie Monroe (♦) and his Kentucky Pardners.

The Morris Brothers' career lasted well into the 1940s, although they retired to their native western North Carolina, and have been relatively inactive musically in succeeding years, making a brief appearance on **Country Music And Bluegrass At Newport** (Vanguard) and on Earl Scruggs' (♦) ninety minute TV special 'Earl Scruggs, His Family and Friends' and the Columbia album of the same name. The reason they were included (aside from their still impressive singing); in 1940 they were the first to give a teenaged Earl Scruggs a job as a professional banjo player.

Albums: none.

Moon Mullican

Originator of a highly personal, two-finger piano style, Aubrey 'Moon' Mullican influenced many later country keyboard players including such musicians as Chet Atkins (♦) and Jerry Lee Lewis (♦). Born on his family's farm near Corrigan, Polk County, Texas, March 29, 1909, as a boy he learnt guitar from a black farmworker. His family came from religious stock and his father once bought an old pump organ in order that Mullican's sisters could practice playing church music - but Aubrey used the instrument to fashion his blues style, much to his father's dismay.

At 21 he hoboed his way to Houston aboard a freight train, upon arrival finding work in various houses of ill repute, sleeping by day and working by night, thus earning the nickname 'Moon'. During the 1930s he formed a band and began playing at clubs and on radio in the Louisiana and Texas areas, joining Leon Selph's Blue Ridge Playboys for a while in 1940 after appearing on disc with the band on a 1939 recording date. He appeared with Cliff Bruner (♦) and the Texas Wanderers during the same period.

By the mid 1940s, Mullican had become a major solo attraction, his 1947 reworking of Cajun tune **Jole Blon,** released by King as **New Jole Blon,** selling a million copies within three years of release. This he followed with **Sweeter Than The Flowers,** a 1948 high flyer, and **I'll Sail My Ship Alone,** a 1950

release that provided yet another million seller for King. In 1949 Mullican joined Grand Ole Opry for a period of six years, during which time he achieved further hits with **Mona Lisa, Goodnight Irene** (1950) and **Cherokee Boogie** (1951).

During the late 1950s and '60s he toured throughout the States and overseas, becoming part of Louisiana Governor Jimmy Davis' (♦) staff and band for four years (1960–63). During this period he gained one further hit record in **Ragged But Right** (1961) on the Starday label but he often found himself dogged by a combination of bad luck and ill health. He died from a heart attack in Beaumont, Texas, January 1, 1967. His albums included **Good Times** (Pickwick) and **Unforgettable Great Hits** (Starday).

Anne Murray

Deceptively light-voiced Canadian singer who packed enough punch on her **Snowbird** hit in the '60s to score a major international pop hit.

Born on June 20, 1946, in Spring Hill, Nova Scotia, Anne was the only girl in a family of five brothers. She obtained a bachelor's degree at the University of New Brunswick and then taught physical education, eventually finding that singing was taking more and more of her time and moving into show business entirely when offered a contract with Capitol Records.

Snowbird was one of her very first releases and its light, airy melody was soon on everyone's lips. It scored in both the pop and country charts in America and provided Anne with two potential markets which she has tightrope-walked ever since.

Anne has paid tribute to country by recording such titles as **Cotton Jenny** and **He Thinks I Still Care** (the old George Jones (♦) hit with title adapted accordingly). Her early classical music training has stood her in good stead vocally and has given her the ability to cross over into easy-listening music. On stage she often makes a point of telling an audience how she will not be tied down to one area or another. When she chooses she can also veer close to a soul sound.

Generally on album, Anne has not shown the true extremes of her talent, preferring to stay middle-of-the-road. This has made for solid commercial success but has also proved slightly tedious in sheer musical terms.

She is a major star in Canada where she has won many music awards and is a top television personality. In America she was regular guest on the CBS-TV Glen Campbell (♦) Show and she also shared top billing with Glen for four weeks at the International Hotel in Las Vegas and for a week at the Greek Theater in Los Angeles.

Albums:
Snowbird *(Capitol/Capitol)*
Anne Murray *(Capitol/—)*
Talk It Over In The Morning
  (Capitol/Capitol)
Annie *(Capitol/Capitol)*
Danny's Song *(Capitol/Capitol)*
Love Song *(Capitol/—)*
Country *(Capitol/—)*
Highly Prized Possession
  (Capitol/Capitol)

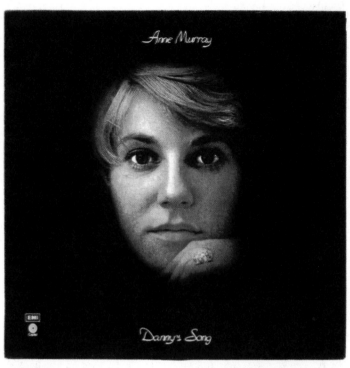

Together *(Capitol/Capitol)*
Keeping In Touch *(Capitol/—)*
Anne Murray And Glen
  Campbell *(Capitol/Capitol)*

Danny's Song (Capitol). She sticks to easy-listening songs for her album releases.

Nashville

The Tennessee capital of country music, in spite of changing styles and new regional trends. Conveniently placed inside the encircling ring of the Appalachian Mountains (the birthplace of country music), Nashville became a candidate for 'Country Capital' honors after it started to beam out the WSM 'Barn Dance', on November 28, 1925. As the music developed and record companies exploited country commercially there grew a need for a convenient recording and business center.

The radio show, sponsored by an insurance company, featured old-timey performers such as Uncle Jimmy Thompson (♦) and Sam and Kirk McGee (♦). It acquired the Grand Ole Opry (♦) tag on December 10, 1927, when the announcer, George D. Hay (♦) (known as 'The Solemn Old Judge') made a pun on the theme of grand opera – the country program followed an hour of classical music. WSM (it stood for 'We Save Millions' – the insurance company's slogan) joined the NBC network in 1941 and the Opry was soon getting to a wide audience, hungry for radio entertainment. The Opry featured music rural America could identify with, and it came to be heard all over America and in Canada. A listening habit had been established which, in the heartland of North America, endures to this day.

Initially the Opry often featured instrumental music, Uncle Dave Macon (♦) being a popular early performer, but by 1938 they could boast a genuine singing star – Roy Acuff (♦). The Opry also put on outdoor picnics and tent shows. The first one of these, in West Tennessee in 1932, attracted 8,000 people at ten cents a head.

The Opry changed with the times and was eventually able to boast such diverse stars as Eddy Arnold (♦), Ernest Tubb (♦), Hank Snow (♦), Jim Reeves (♦) and Hank Williams (♦).

Originally, the Opry was broadcast from the National Life and Accident Insurance Company's offices and as it grew in popularity an audience was invited, and then a new studio built. Two insurance officials were unable to reach their own offices one day, due to massive crowds of sightseers so, after an attempt to run the Opry without an audience, a new venue was found which would hold a small theater-full each Saturday night. This was the Hillsboro Theater, a local movie house. In 1939 they were on the move again, to the War Memorial Auditorium. Even this 2,200 seater proved too small and in 1941, the Ryman Auditorium was found, an old tabernacle with curved pews for seats. WSM bought the building, re-named it the Grand Ole Opry House and made structural alterations. But as time progressed and music became a mass entertainment form, the Opry House was found to be wanting. There was no air conditioning and the actor's union found the performers' small dressing room beneath their standards.

So 1974 saw the opening of Opryland, a modern auditorium amid an extensive amusement park, just a few miles outside the city. President Nixon opened the hall with Roy Acuff in attendance, demonstrating yo-yo techniques.

The first major artiste to record in Nashville was Eddy Arnold (♦) in 1944. Capitol was the first big label to commence a Nashville operation, in 1950, and within ten years all the major record labels had Nashville offices and studios.

The music itself was changing accordingly. Before rock 'n' roll the lines were clearly defined. Country had many strands – western swing, bluegrass, honky tonk; but it was patently recognisable as country. Rock 'n' roll brought many country careers to a standstill and many of those who could not jump on the rockabilly bandwagon were badly affected.

As the smoke cleared country redefined itself. Rock 'n' roll and the increasing urbanization of America had demonstrated that the old, homespun sounds were on the wane. Nashville saw the chance to market its produce on a pop level and to gain respectability in the process, and the result was what has become known as 'The Nashville Sound'. Country artists such as Jim Reeves (♦) found themselves increasingly being given ballads to perform. The banjos and steel guitars were phased out, and string sections, brass ensembles and vocal choruses embroidered the voices of many a former good ole boy.

In some cases the deep voices lent themselves well to this material. Johnny Cash (♦) quit his sombre, menacing, macho songs for more acceptable, pop orientated material. With **Young Love** Sonny James (♦) was launched into a financially fabulous easy-listening career. Producers looked not so much for country songs now but for melodic ballads or novelty sagas such as Jimmy Dean's (♦) **Big Bad John.**

Pianist Floyd Cramer (♦) scored a successful pop hit with his catchy **On The Rebound** and in 1960 it was estimated that Cramer was playing on 25 per cent of all Nashville's hit records. The Jordanaires (♦), Elvis Presley's (♦) harmony vocal group, were also much in demand. Many of the hits from this era, the late '50s to early '60s, were familiar to the pop-buying public, but that same public might have been surprised to know that the hits were recorded in Nashville – Jim Reeves (♦) with **He'll Have To Go,** the Willie Nelson (♦) composition **Crazy,** Skeeter Davis's (♦) **The End Of The World,** Don Gibson's (♦) **Sea Of Heartbreak,** the many hits of Bill Anderson (♦) and Roger Miller (♦).

During this period country was made acceptable to its critics. The songs were often superbly crafted (the down-home equivalents of Cole Porter or Sammy Kahn), the rural image was disappearing and, more importantly, record company bank balances were bulging. Certain record producers and certain studios had become institutions in themselves.

Inevitably this situation could not last forever and new, more authentic country stars began to find a willing public even though (as with Merle Haggard (♦) and Buck Owens (♦)) they felt obliged to operate from the wide open spaces of Bakersfield (♦), California. In the mid '60s, Charlie Pride (♦), with a voice many thought the most exciting since Hank Williams (♦), became the first black singer since DeFord Bailey (♦) to play on the Grand Ole Opry. Yet even as country began to make a come-back it was incorporated into the plans of the producers and executives – 'The Nashville Sound, Part Two'.

It manifested in smoothly produced, 'formula' country. Steels were back, even fiddles, but once the producers found a hit sound they stuck to it. There were less pop crossovers but the country market again and artists like Tammy Wynette (♦), Loretta Lynn (♦) and Lynn Anderson (♦) could become household names in parts of heartland America while remaining practically unheard of on either coast.

Chet Atkins (♦) at RCA, Ken Nelson at Capitol, Owen Bradley (♦) at MCA, Billy Sherrill (♦) and Glenn Sutton for Columbia utilized few instruments but achieved a studio sound that was both full and smooth, a perfect vehicle for offsetting a weepy country voice (like Tammy Wynette's) or a nasal one (like Tanya Tucker's (♦)).

One didn't even need to hear an artist's new album. Stylistically it was bound to sound exactly like the last one. A small but select band of studio musicians made (and make) extremely good livings doing backing duty for the Nashville Sound. They operate generally at one tenth the potential of their full musical ability, but do provide easy-to-work-with, easy-to-listen-to support for a singer.

The so-called 'Outlaw' movement shook things up yet again with the more creative and stronger-willed artists demanding more musical freedom and, in the case of Willie Nelson, breaking a sacred law and going over the heads of people in Nashville to the record company bosses in New York. The media has come to terms with 'The Outlaws'. After all, they make a lot of money and many of them still use Nashville studios even though they perhaps have independent production deals. In 1975 and 1976 the industry, through that unfailing barometer of commercial – as opposed to musical – success, the CMA Awards, started voting the Outlaws into top positions. Outlaw music had joined mainstream country.

Nashville has seen changes and will see more. Over the years, although sometimes slow, it has proved itself adaptable – certainly more adaptable than Robert Altman's movie *Nashville* depicted. There is no parallel. Philadelphia or Memphis do not hold the same sway in soul music, nor New York or Los Angeles in rock. Although the smallish area of Music Row is only one district of the city, the name Nashville means just one thing to the rest of the world – country music.

Nashville – Broadway, with Ernest Tubb's original record shop in the foreground. The famous Midnite Jamboree now takes place at his new store.

Buck And Tex Ann Nation

To Buck (born in Muskogee, Oklahoma, in 1910) and Tex Ann (born in Chanute, Kansas, in 1916) goes the credit for beginning the now popular country music parks, where Sunday afternoon crowds can picnic, relax, and listen to country music. Active in the north east, Buck and Tex Ann opened their first park in 1934, and found their greatest success in Maine, of all places.

After the duo split up, Tex Ann moved to the west coast, where she found frequent wartime employment with the bands of Merle Travis (♦), Ray Whitley (♦), and others as both a vocalist and as a fine bassist. She still resides in the Los Angeles area.

Albums: none.

The National Barn Dance

The National Barn Dance was one of the earliest, and was certainly the most influential, of the radio barn dance for some years, although the lasting success of the Grand Old Opry has tended to overshadow the dominance and importance of the National Barn Dance in the 1920s and 1930s.

Begun in 1924, early stars were Bradley Kincaid (♦), Grace Wilson, and Arkie the Woodchopper (♦), who were followed by John Lair (♦) and the Cumberland Ridge Runners (♦), Mac and Bob (♦), Karl and Harty (♦), Lulu Belle and Scotty (♦), Red Foley (♦), and others, Gene Autry (♦) among them.

The show took place in the Eighth Street Theater, and was popular for years; the 1940s saw the addition of Bob Atcher (♦) and Rex Allen (♦) to the show, but by this time they seem to have stayed with the tried and true talent too long, while the Opry was picking up all the hot new Hank Williamses (♦) and Webb Pierces (♦). WLS changed hands in 1960, and the entire station – which had first been controlled by Sears (the station letters standing for World's Largest Store) and then by the *Prairie Farmer* magazine – was converted to a rock format, and the venerable old Barn Dance was discarded.

Undaunted, the show moved to Chicago's WGN for another ten years, but neither the 50,000 watt power of WLS nor the network shows which they'd had as early as 1936 were there to help them along, and in 1970 the National Barn Dance, once the queen of them all, became history.

Jerry Naylor

Once front man with the Crickets (♦ Buddy Holly), Naylor has since moved back into country music, winning *Billboard* awards in 1973 and '74 for providing the best syndicated country radio show.

Born Stephenville, Texas, March 6, 1939, he formed his own group at the age of 14 and proved impressive enough to perform on the Louisiana Hayride (♦) show, touring with such acts as Johnny Cash (♦), Elvis Presley (♦) and Johnny Horton (♦). A deejay for a San Angelo radio station during his high school days, he later enrolled at the Elkins Electronics Institute, employing his radio knowhow for the AFRS in Germany during 1957. Following discharge from the army after a spinal injury, he returned home and recorded for Skyla Records, also befriending Glen Campbell (♦). The duo moved to Los Angeles, where Naylor worked for KRLA and KDAY. In 1961 he became a member of the Crickets, replacing bassist Joe B. Maudlin (although both musicians are depicted on the sleeve of the **Bobby Vee Meets The Crickets** album!) but, dogged by ill health, he suffered a heart attack in 1964 and left the group, taking up a solo career in country music, recording first for Tower, then for Columbia and MGM, before signing for Melodyland – for which label he provided a hit, **Is That All There Is To Honky Tonk?,** in 1974. Along the way, Naylor has also recorded material for Raystar using the pseudonym of Jackie Garrard.

Rick Nelson

Child of a showbusiness family (his parents Ozzie And Harriet had a radio and later a TV show) Nelson made the transition from teenage idol to modern country artist.

Born May 8, 1940, in Teaneck, New Jersey, he signed as Ricky Nelson first for Verve and then Imperial; his lonesome, teenthrob voice was allied to light, country-influenced backings on songs such as **Poor Little Fool, It's Late** and **Lonesome Town,** sagas of jilted love and dating frustrations, and perfectly in tune with the by then softening tone of rock 'n' roll. This was the major record companies' answer to the rawer, sharper music of Memphis. Since Nelson was also blessed with archetypal boy-next-door looks, his appeal was further propagated via concerts and TV, and riots ensued when he played.

The coming of the British Invasion swept away many of these clean cut America teen rockers, although Nelson was by then signed to MCA and had shortened his name to

Rick Nelson, whose Garden Party hit described the reaction to his country-oriented material at a Madison Square Garden rock revival gig.

Garden Party (MCA).

Rick. Although he had James Burton in his band he failed to make a real impression although two country albums, **Country Fever** and **Bright Lights And Country Music** found favor with some people.

The formation of the Stone Canyon Band in the '70s saw Nelson being accepted as a viable country rocker. This band included, at one point, Randy Meisner, also known from Poco (♦) and the Eagles (♦), and Tom Brumley (♦), Buck Owens' (♦) rated steel player for five years (Brumley, it should be noted also manufactures the famous ZB pedal steel guitars). **Garden Party,** a poignant autobiographical piece of country rock, was a gold record for Nelson although his career has since gone into decline and MCA released him from his contract.

Country Fever and **Bright Lights And Country Music** were reissued in the US only in 1973 on MCA, as a double album, **Country.**

Albums:
Country *(MCA/—)*
Garden Party *(MCA/MCA)*
In Concert *(MCA/—)*
Rudy The 5th *(MCA/—)*
Sings Rick Nelson *(MCA/—)*
Windfall *(MCA/—)*
The Very Best Of Rick Nelson *(UA/UA)*

Tracy Nelson

The big-voiced Tracy began her career in Madison, Wisconsin, as a folk singer, later joining the Fabulous Imitations, an R&B outfit. After a sting with the White Trash Blues Band she headed for San Francisco in 1967, there becoming an integral part of Mother Earth, a unit which began life as a pure blues and soul aggregation but gradually became heavily country oriented. The band split after five years, Tracy going solo and cutting **Tracy Nelson,** an Atlantic album that employed such diverse talents as Waylon Jennings (♦), Linda Ronstadt (♦), Allan Toussaint and Merry Clayton. She also recorded for Prestige, Columbia and MCA, though hit records seemed to elude her. Nashville based in the mid '70s, Tracy Nelson is held in high regard by her fellow singers, many of whom employ her on session chores.

Albums:
Deep Are The Roots
　　　　(Prestige/—)
Poor Man's Paradise
　　(Columbia/—)
Time Is On My Side *(MCA/—)*
Sweet Soul Music *(MCA/—)*
Tracy Nelson *(Atlantic/—)*

Willie Nelson

King of the Outlaw country movement in Austin (♦), Texas, Willie Nelson has run a long, hard race in country music but has, this decade, emerged as a premier stylist. Born Abbott, Texas, April 30, 1933, Nelson was raised by his grandparents after his own parents separated.

His grandparents taught him some chords and by his teens he was becoming proficient on guitar. He left Abbott in 1950 to join the Air Force. On his discharge he married a Cherokee Indian girl by whom he had a daughter, Lana. Living in Waco, Texas, Nelson took various salesman jobs, but anxious to gain a proper intro into music he talked his way into an announcing job on a local station.

Soon after, he was hosting country shows on a Fort Worth station, doubling at night as a musician in some rough local honky tonks. But he was jotting down songs whenever he could; during this period he wrote **Family Bible** and **Night Life,** songs that have become standards. When he finally made his way to Nashville and found a job in Ray Price's (♦) band as a bass player he found that he was placing his songs at last. Price, a huge name of that era, made **Night Life** his theme tune. Faron Young (♦) cut **Hello Walls,** Patsy Cline (♦) **Crazy** and Willie himself recorded **The Party's Over.** They were somber but haunting melodies, true 'white man's blues' and Willie has since incorporated them tellingly into his sparse, bluesy act. More than 70 artists have recorded **Night Life** (Willie's songs are often potential 'crossovers') but the artist himself presents them usually in a very different tone.

He poached most of Ray Price's band from him and went on the road; he saw his first marriage break up and he went off with the wife of a DJ Association president and married again, settling variously in Fort Worth, Los Angeles and Nashville.

Besides recording 18 albums in these years he also helped the career of Charley Pride (♦), featuring him on his show in the deepest South during the racially sensitive years of civil rights.

During the '60s the smooth Nashville Sound was in its ascendant and Willie found himself becoming increasingly disillusioned with big business methods, hankering as he was to make his mark as a singer rather than as a songwriter and preferably on his own terms.

A spell living in Texas while his Nashville home was being rebuilt after a fire did nothing to salve Willie's restlessness. By the early '70s he was determined to get out of his RCA contract, and with the help of one Neil Reshen (afterwards Nelson's manager) he landed a new contract from Atlantic.

Atlantic were just opening a Nashville office. Country was new to them; they had built their reputation on black music. But with Atlantic's Jerry Wexler producing in New York, Willie came up with **Shotgun Willie** and **Phases And Stages,** the second particularly a new, intense country sound displaying a deep sense of lonesome identity and making no concessions whatsoever to modern Nashville.

Nelson had by now settled in Austin with his third wife, Connie. He became a godfather there; a whiff of hardnose country authenticity amid some dedicated but basically folk-influenced young artists. Texas had always been the centre for barroom music, and now the tradition was back home again in a slightly different, but nonetheless intense, way. The glossy magazines began to home in on the phenomenon.

Atlantic's Nashville operation had folded and Willie now signed with Columbia, for whom he has made **Red Headed Stranger** and **The Sound In Your Mind.** Like **Phases And Stages, Red Headed Stranger** was a concept album, but even more personal. It threw up the national crossover hit single **Blue Eyes Cryin' In The Rain** and established Willie Nelson as a nationally known figure.

Willie is recognized as the unofficial Mayor of Austin. He has reconciled hip and redneck musical interests and helped lead a new explosion of interest in country music. Although Nashville was cagey about the Outlaws' intentions and the way they went outside the system to get what they wanted, it has recognized their contribution towards restoring massive new interest in country music generally and voted them into top positions in the annual Country Music Association awards, a sure sign of industry acceptance.

Willie also instigated the now legendary Fourth Of July Picnics, massive outdoor festivals in Texas which have featured stars such as Leon Russell and Kris Kristofferson (♦). At the tail end of '76 he joined Michael Murphey and actor Peter Fonda to make a movie, *Outlaw Blues*, filmed in Austin.

Albums:
Phases And Stages
 (*Atlantic/—*)
Shotgun Willie (*Atlantic/—*)
The Troublemaker (*Atlantic/—*)
Winners (*Camden/—*)
And His Friends
 (*Plantation/Charley*)
Best Of . . . (*UA/UA*)
Country Willie (*UA/—*)
Live (*RCA/RCA*)

Red Headed Stranger
 (*Columbia/CBS*)
What Can You Do To Me Now?
 (*RCA/—*)
Famous Country Music Makers
 (*—/RCA*)
The Sound In Your Mind
 (*Columbia/CBS*)
Wine (*RCA/—*)
Willie/Before His Time
 (*RCA/RCA*)

Below: Willie Nelson, the pickin' poet from Austin. Unlike other songwriters, he says he'd rather perform than write 'Because I'm lazy'.

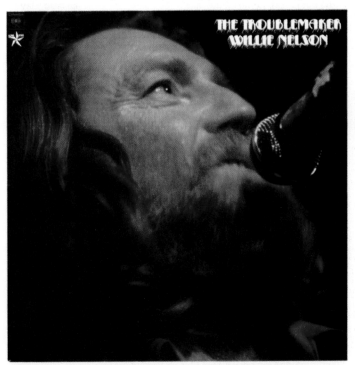

Above: The Troublemaker (Columbia). A revival meeting headed by Nelson, with Doug Sahm, Sammi Smith, Dee Moeller and Larry Gatlin. The hero of the title track is Christ.

Michael Nesmith

One of the fabulously successful Monkees, a teenybopper quartet whose main claim to artistic fame was that they were usually given good commercial song material, Nesmith left in 1969 to carve a modestly notable career as a sort of freewheeling cosmic cowboy. Although he claimed to be only nominally into country his songs have provided good country fodder, and Nesmith's records with the First and Second National Bands have their own cult audience.

Born Houston, Texas, December 30, 1942, Nesmith only learned to play guitar after his air force discharge in 1962. However, he was writing songs and his **Different Drum** was covered by Linda Ronstadt (♦).

Becoming increasingly disenchanted by the big business aura surrounding the Monkees, he had already, in 1968, produced an album of self composed instrumentals, **The Wichita Train Whistle Songs.** He put together the First National Band and was signed to RCA. The band included pedal steel player Red Rhodes (♦). In 1970 they put out the album **Magnetic South,** a Nesmith composition from this album, **Joanne,** being covered by Andy Williams among others. Another album that year was **Loose Salute.**

The First National Band split in 1971 and James Burton and Glen D. Hardin were brought in to help complete the album then being recorded, **Nevada Fighter.** Another lineup (again including Red Rhodes) recorded **Tantamount To Treason, Vol 1,** and in 1972 Nesmith and Rhodes only made **And The Hits Just Keep On Comin'.**

Nesmith founded his own label, Countryside. This was a subsidiary of Elektra and the idea was to milk some of the country music talent that was going to waste in Los Angeles. But a change of leadership at Elektra, where David Geffen replaced Jac Holzman, saw Countryside closed down.

However, Nesmith had formed another band during this time, the Countryside Band (again including Rhodes) and 1973 saw them releasing **Pretty Much Your Standard Ranch Stash.** He then moved from RCA and formed Pacific Arts, which has seen him involved in mixed media projects, notably **The Prison,** a book with a soundtrack.

It is generally agreed that Nesmith has written some very good country, or country influenced songs, one of the most famous being **Some Of Shelley's Blues.**

Albums:
And The Hits Just Keep On Comin' (—/Island)
Pretty Much Your Standard Ranch Stash (—/Island)
The Prison (Pacific Arts/Island)
The Best Of Mike Nesmith (—/RCA)

Right: Modern bluegrass outfit New Grass Revival. A previous album, no longer available, was with Merle Travis on the Takoma label.

New Grass Revival

Sam Bush
mandolin, guitar, fiddle, vocals
Courtney Johnson *banjo vocals*
Curtis Burch *guitar, vocals*
Ebo Walker and others
  electric bass

Young electric bluegrass band who evolved a distinctive hard edged picking sound during the early '70s and helped spread the appeal of bluegrass to a youth audience.

Based around the jazz-tinged fiddle talents of Sam Bush, the four man group had some success with the single **Prince Of Peace,** an evocative reworking of a Leon Russell song, this number subsequently appearing on **New Grass Revival,** an album for *Nevada Fighter (RCA Victor). 1971 album completed with Glen Hardin and James Burton after the demise of the First National Band during recording.*

Starday. Sam Bush has also played fiddle on numerous recording sessions.

Albums:
Fly Through The Country
  (Flying Fish/—)

New Riders Of The Purple Sage

Originally formed as a splinter group from San Francisco's leading acid rock band the Grateful Dead, the New Riders eventually became a name in their own right. The album **Workingman's Dead** saw the Grateful Dead moving from rock towards a more earthy, sometimes country sound, and the New Riders were the natural offshoot of this movement.

The New Riders at first played gigs with the Dead and were able to utilize Dead guitarist Jerry Garcia's latent talents on pedal steel guitar. Garcia was eventually replaced by Buddy Cage. Name West Coast rock artists who have been in NRPS include Mickey Hart and Phil Lesh (Grateful Dead), Spencer Dryden (Jefferson Airplane) and Skip Battin (Byrds). The band recently moved from Columbia to MCA and their music seems to have lost some of its freshness and vitality; witness their debut MCA album. In their day, though, a fine, trucking, country rock band.

Albums:
New Riders Of The Purple Sage
 (Columbia/CBS)
Powerglide *(Columbia/—)*
Gypsy Cowboy *(Columbia/CBS)*
The Adventures Of Panama Red *(Columbia/CBS)*
Home, Home On The Road
 (Columbia/CBS)
Brujo *(Columbia/CBS)*
Oh, What A Mighty Time
 (Columbia/CBS)
New Riders *(MCA/MCA)*
The Best Of New Riders Of The Purple Sage *(Columbia/CBS)*
New Riders *(MCA/MCA)*

New Riders of the Purple Sage (Columbia). Although considered by many to have lost direction, the Riders have drawn their members from many a fine country rock band.

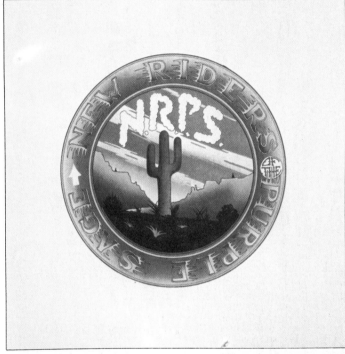

Above: Mickey Newbury, who believes in old songs and sad refrains, which he often sings to the accompaniment of falling rain.

Mickey Newbury

Called 'a poet' by Johnny Cash (♦), Newbury's often ultra sad songs have been recorded by Elvis Presley (♦), Jerry Lee Lewis (♦), Ray Charles, Lynn Anderson (♦), Andy Williams, Kenny Rogers (♦) and countless others.

Born Houston, Texas, May 19, 1940, Newbury traveled around in earlier years, eventually joining the Air Force for four years, during which time he was based in England.

'After that,' he says, 'I worked on the shrimp boats in the Gulf, diddled around, did a little writing and lots of other things. I started playing guitar when I was a kid, just enough to be able to go through three or four chords and sing something with it. But when I went into the Air Force, I ditched it all. One day I would up at a place where they served snacks and had a piano. I began playing it because I just had to get my hands on something that made music. Later I borrowed a guitar from a guy because I didn't have enough money to buy one of my own – but I didn't really start working at things and trying to write until I was 24.'

Moving to Nashville in the mid '60s, Newbury began writing songs for artists of many different styles, at one time having four songs simultaneously in the R&B Country, Easy Listening and Pop charts. As a recording artist he began cutting albums for RCA and Mercury, without making much impact, though his Mercury release **It Looks Like Rain** became a collectors' item hauling in high bids before it became repackaged as part of a double album set following Newbury's signing by Elektra in 1971. His biggest hit to date has been via **American Trilogy** (1972), a composition formed from three Civil War era songs, while his most recent album, **Rusty Tracks,** mainly produced by Bobby Bare (♦), displayed Newbury still looking back and offering soulful versions of such traditional melodies as **In The Pines, Danny Boy** and **Shanandoah.**

Mickey Newbury Sings His Own (RCA Victor).

Albums:
Frisco Mabel Joy
 (Elektra/Elektra)
Heaven Help The Child
 (Elektra/Elektra)
Live At Montezuma/It Looks Like Rain *(Elektra/Elektra)*
I Came To Hear The Music
 (Elektra/Elektra)
Lovers *(Elektra/Elektra)*
Rusty Tracks *(ABC/ABC)*

Jimmy 'C' Newman

A veteran of well over 30 hits, many of them Top Ten, Newman has remained something of an unsung country hero. Born of part-French ancestry, Big Mamou, Louisiana, August 27, 1927, he began singing in the Lake Charles area, his style employing many Cajun (♦) characteristics. During the early '50s, he became a regular on Shreveport's Louisiana Hayride (♦) and signed with the major Dot label, obtaining a Top Ten disc with **Cry, Cry, Darling** in 1954. An Opry regular by 1956, he celebrated by cutting **A Fallen Star,** his most successful record, during the following year.

Next came an MGM contract and such winners as **You're Making A Fool Out Of Me** (1958), **Grin And Bear It** (1959), and **Lovely Work Of Art** (1960) before Newman became a long term Decca artist, his run of hits continuing with the chat-filled **Bayou Talk** (1962), **DJ For A Day** (1963), **Artificial Rose** (1965), **Back Pocket Money** (1966), **Blue Lonely Winter** (1967), **Born To Love You** (1968) and others.

Proficient on virtually any type of country material, it was on such Cajun fiddle-filled releases as **Alligator Man** (1961) that Newman, with his exuberant cries of 'Aa-eee', sounded most potent.

Albums:
Alligator Man *(Pickwick/—)*

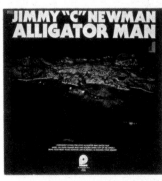

Right: Jimmy C. Newman's Alligator Man (RCA).

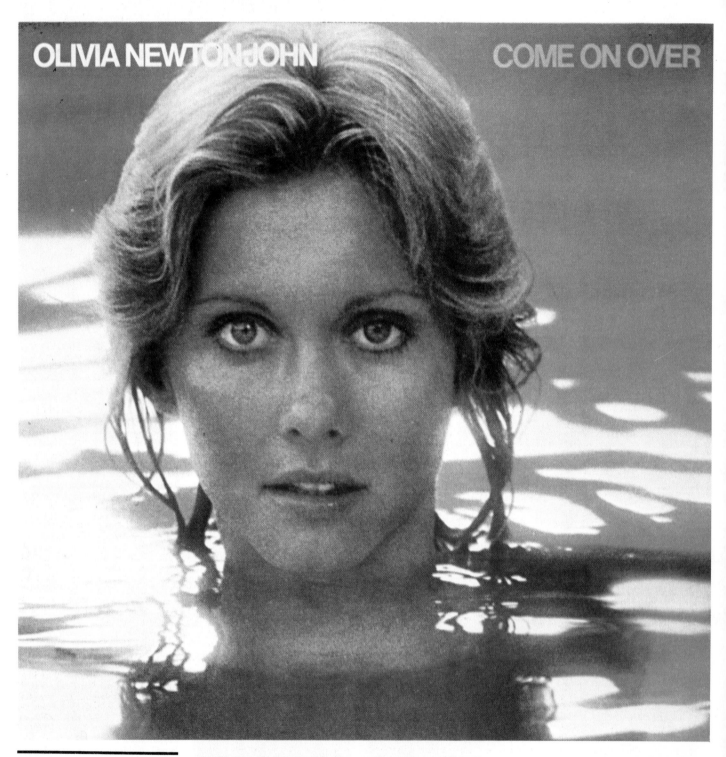

Olivia Newton-John

An extremely competent British pop vocalist who won the CMA Female Vocalist Of The Year award in 1974.

Born Cambridge, England, September 26, 1948, she grew up in Australia where her father headed a college. During the late '60s she performed as part of the Sol Four, an all girl group, eventually going solo and winning a contest that provided her with a trip to England, where she became half of Pat and Olivia, a vocal duo. In the wake of some solo and duet recordings, Olivia joined Toomorrow, a highly hyped pop group that became featured in a science fiction film of the same name. Virtually a nonstarter, Toomorrow soon split – at which time Olivia became a solo act once more, achieving a British

and US hit with **If Not For You** (1971), following this with British chart successes in **Banks Of The Ohio** (1971), **What Is Life?** (1972) and **Take Me Home Country Roads** (1973). Then came **Let Me Be There,** a countryish hit immaculately produced by John Farrar, which scored in both the US pop and country charts, thus earning Olivia no less than three Grammies and the CMA award. Since 1974 and failure in the Eurovision song contest, she's spent most of her time in the States, logging such substantial chart entries as **I Honestly Love You** (1974), **If You Love Me** (1974), **Have You Never Been Mellow?** (1975), **Please, Mr, Please** (1975), **Let It Shine** (1976), **Come On Over** (1976) and **Don't Stop Believing** (1976).

Albums:
If You Love Me, Let Me Know
  (MCA/—)
Let Me Be There *(MCA/—)*

Clearly Love *(MCA/EMI)*
Come On Over *(MCA/EMI)*
Have You Never Been Mellow?
  (MCA/EMI)
Don't Stop Believing *(—/EMI)*
First Impressions *(—/EMI)*
Long Live Love *(—/EMI)*

Nitty Gritty Dirt Band

California folk aggregation who in 1973 persuaded several revered country music figures to participate in a triple album release which would prove to give old-time music a big boost and bring country to many rock fans not yet acquainted with it.

Formed in Long Beach in 1966 by Bruce Kunkel and Jeff Hanna as the Illegitimate Jug Band (Jackson Browne was at one time a member) they engaged other like-minded local students; Jimmy Fadden,

Come On Over (EMI). One of Britain's invisible exports; she spent her early life in Australia and has now found her niche in the USA, where she has scored many hits.

Leslie Thompson, Ralph Taylor Barr and John McEuen. John's elder brother, Bill, became their manager and producer.

Their music took in blues, rock, folk, country, Cajun and jug band. In 1969 they had a hit with Mike Nesmith's (◆) **Some Of Shelley's Blues** and in 1970, Jerry Jeff Walker's (◆) **Mr Bojangles**, this last a million-seller, 1972 saw them working from the Colorado mountains but 1973 was the year in which they made their name. Good musicians all, with a liking for traditional country music, they discreetly enquired around the Nashville hierarchy as to who might be interested in collaborating on an ambitious musical pro-

ject. The result was a milestone in country history with many of country greats being heard in traditional setting on one album set.

The Dirt Band provided backings (bluegrass singer Jimmy Martin (♦) afterwards said he'd like to recruit them as his backing band, so awake were they) and the tracks featured people like Roy Acuff (♦) **(The Precious Jewel, Wreck On The Highway),** Doc Watson (♦) **(Tennessee Stud, Black Mountain Rag),** Merle Travis (♦) **(Nine Pound Hammer, I Am A Pilgrim)** and Mother Maybelle Carter (♦) of the Carter Family (♦) **(Wildwood Flower, I'm Thinking Tonight Of My Blue Eyes).** The superb music apart, this liaison provided the nation's press with a natural story, the meeting of two generations who were previously thought to have nothing in common. Imaginatively produced by Bill McEuen, the album enhanced both the reputations of the stars involved and of the Dirt Band themselves. It also sold well.

Later albums have returned to the NGDB hybrid format. They have recently shortened their name to the Dirt Band and one of the original members, Jeff Hanna, has left. Bill McEuen has formed his own label called the Aspen Recording Society, which is dedicated to a popular cause, preserving the integrity of American music.

Albums:
Will The Circle Be Unbroken
  (UA/UA)
Stars And Stripes Forever
  (UA/UA)
All The Good Times *(UA/—)*
Dream *(UA/UA)*
Dirt, Silver And Gold *(UA/—)*
Uncle Charlie And His Dog Teddy *(—/Liberty)*

Above: Nitty Gritty Dirt Band's Dream (UA).

Eddie Noack

Born Houston, Texas, April 29, 1930, Armond A. 'Eddie' Noack Jnr, graduated from the University of Houston in journalism and English. Opting for a singing career, he won an amateur talent contest at the Texas Theater, Houston, later making his first radio appearance at Bayton, Texas, in 1947.

In 1949 he signed for Gold Star Records, his first release being **Gentlemen Prefer Blondes,** but by 1951 he was to be found on Four Star, a year later appearing on the TNT label, recording **Too Hot To Handle.** The success of the song led to a contract with Starday, with whom he stayed for nearly five years.

While performing on the Hank Williams (♦) Show, he met Hank

Stars And Stripes Forever (UA). A luxuriously packaged double-album including the Dirt Band's versions of Jambalaya, Mr Bojangles plus various interviews.

Snow (♦), who expressed interest in a Noack composition titled **These Hands,** Snow eventually recording the song and taking it into the 1955 charts. More artists, including Lefty Frizzell (♦), Hawkshaw Hawkins (♦), Ernest Tubb (♦) and George Jones (♦), all covered Noack's songs but the Texan had little recording success of his own until 1958 when he joined Pappy Dailey's D Records, cutting rock discs using the name Tommy Wood but scoring with a country disc, **Have Blues Will Travel.**

When the D label was purchased by Mercury, Noack sides continued to be released but few raised much in the way of sales, and in 1960 he ceased recording for a while and moved into the publishing and songwriting scene, supplying George Jones with such songs as **Barbara Jay, Flowers For Mama, The Poor Chinee, No Blues Is Good News** and **For Better Or For Worse.**

However, Noack later returned to the recording studios once more, cutting sides for K-Ark, Ram and Wide World, making a fine

album, **Remembering Jimmie Rodgers,** for the last named.

A more recent album, **Eddie Noack,** on the Look label, contains many of his most important songs.

Norma Jean

A highly regarded performer during the '60s, Norma Jean was brought up in Oklahoma City, where she learnt guitar and performed at square dances during her teen years. By 1958 she'd become a regular on Red Foley's (♦) Ozark Jubilee TV show – and two years later, she'd not only joined the Opry but had also earned a feature spot on Porter Wagoner's (♦) Chattanooga Medicine sponsored TV program. Provided with such massive exposure Norma Jean could hardly fail – and so it was that her pure country voice soon began giving birth to such Top 20 hits as **Let's Go All The Way** (1964), **Go, Cat, Go** (1964), **I Wouldn't Buy A Used Car From**

Above: The way they were – the Dirt Band in '75.

I Guess That Comes from Being Poor (RCA Victor).

Him (1965) and **Heaven Help The Poor Working Girl** (1967). Replaced on the Wagoner show by Dolly Parton (♦) in 1967, Norma Jean's record sales dipped accordingly, though her name still cropped up on the charts well into the '70s.

Born Norma Jean Beasler, Wellston, Oklahoma, January 30, 1938, her albums have included **I Guess That Comes Of Being Poor, Norma Jean, Hank Cochran Songs, Let's Go All The Way** and **Only Way To Hold Your Man.** She currently lives as a housewife in Oklahoma, only occasionally making a stage or recording appearance.

Wayne Nutt

One of the toughest men in country music – he's survived countless barroom brawls and a car crash in which his companion was killed – Nutt was born in an Oklahoma schoolhouse on February 18, 1940. His father, a pioneer oilman, had wanted Wayne to be born in Texas but the baby arrived before the family car had got far enough along the highway.

Part Cherokee, but with Scottish ancestry, Nutt was raised on a ranch and had ridden in rodeos by the age of 14. Then in the early 1960s he moved out to work in the South Texas oilfields where he once kept going through a non stop 140 hour shift, keeping himself awake on pep pills.

Next came a lone eight month trek through the Rocky Mountains, exploring hidden valleys and fol-

The Oak Ridge Boys (Columbia). Sacred songs from the group, who now prefer to be known as The Oaks. Talents extend to country and rock.

lowing deer trails, this chapter of his life ending in September, 1969, when he married a full blooded Comanche named Judy.

With his wife, Nutt returned to the oil business, working in the Congo, Trinidad, Venezuela, Nigeria and on a North Sea oilrig. It was while based in Aberdeen, Scotland, in 1975 that he signed for CBS Records, cutting an initial album **Oil Field Man,** touring with Slim Whitman (♦) shortly after. Despite the accident of his early arrival, he still considers himself a Texan, singing of his initial misfortune in number titled **The Ballad Of Wendell Nutt.**

Albums:
Oil Field Man (—/CBS)

Oak Ridge Boys

One of the most popular gospel vocal quartets in country music, the Oaks (as they now prefer to be called) have been walking away with the Gospel Music Association's Dove Awards for many a year – in 1972, receiving Bronze Doves for Best Male Group, Best Instrumentalist (backup pianist Tony Brown), Best Album (**Light**) and even Best Album Cover and Best Liner Notes.

Formed in Oak Ridge, Tennessee, in 1957 by Smitty Gatlin, the group began working on a part time basis but became fully professional in April, 1961, commencing a recording career that has encompassed work on such labels as Cadence, Checker, Warner Brothers, Starday, Skylite, Heart-Warming and Columbia. Their appeal lies in the fact that they perform not only high quality sacred material but can equally dispense eminently palatable quantities of country, rock and soul, Boots Randolph (♦) being called in to supply his stomping sax riffs on one of the Oaks' sessions.

In 1971 they received a Grammy Award for their recording of **Talk About The Good Times,** and in 1976 did the same thing for **Where The Soul Never Dies.**

Albums:
Sky High (Columbia/—)
Oak Ridge Boys (Columbia/—)
Old Fashioned Music
  (Columbia/—)
Super Gospel Hits Vols 1 & 2
  (Columbia/—)
The Sensational . . . (Starday/—)
Oak Ridge Boys (Power Pak/—)

Above: The Oak Ridge Boys (Columbia).

Old Fashioned, Down Home, Hand Clappin', Foot Stompin', Southern Style, Gospel Quartet Music.

Lord I've Been Ready For Years
No Earthly Good
Jesus Knows Who I am
The Same Old Fashioned Way

I'm Winging My Way Back Home
Where The Soul Never Dies
It's Been Done

Doctor God
Jesus Was There
Last Train To Glory

W. Lee O'Daniel

Wilbert Lee O'Daniel, born March 11, 1890 in Malta, Ohio, became the first of many politicians to use the grass roots appeal of country music to propel him to high political office.

O'Daniel grew up in Kansas, but removed to Texas as a flour salesman, eventually rising high in the Burrus Mills company, maker of Light Crust Flour. In 1930 he formed a band around a group of struggling musicians to form the Light Crust Doughboys (♦) to advertise the product over radio – early members included Bob Wills (♦), Johnnie Lee Wills (♦), Herman Arnspiger, and Milton Brown (♦), and later Leon McAuliffe (♦).

O'Daniel himself did not play an instrument nor sing, but personally ran the band (with a heavy hand, if the rapid turnover of fine musicians is an indication), as well as serving as its announcer. In addition, he added considerably to the Doughboys' popularity by reading news, amusing stories, and his own poetry, and wrote several important songs as well, **Beautiful Texas,** and **Put Me In Your Pocket** among them.

By 1935 he severed his ties with Burrus Mills and with the Doughboys, setting up his own company and brand, Hillbilly Flour, and a new band as well; the Hillbilly Boys, led by Leon Huff and including O'Daniel's sons Pat and Mike (banjo and fiddle), and Kitty Williamson, Bundy Bratcher, Wallace Griffin, and Kermit Whalen.

However, his aspirations had begun to run higher than that of flour company executive; in 1938 he waged a grass roots campaign (taking with him the Hillbilly Boys) for Governor of Texas, winning easily, and went on to serve a term in the US Senate representing the Lone Star State as well.

Albums: none.

James O'Gwynn

Known as the Smiling Irishman, Gwynn won a modicum of fame with **My Name Is Mud,** a Mercury release of 1962.

Born in Winchester, Mississippi, but spending much of his early life in Hattisburg, O'Gwynn was part of a large musical family, his mother teaching him to play guitar. Resident in Texas during the early '50s, he played on the Houston Jamboree but later moved on to become part of Shreveport's Louisiana Hayride (♦) (1956), eventually joining the Opry in December, 1960.

On record he's cut sides for Starday, D, Mercury, Pep, UA, Hickory, Stop, Plantation, MGM, etc, his most potent period occurring during 1958–62 when he accrued six hits, O'Gwynn's popularity amazingly diminishing after the release of **My Name Is Mud,** his biggest hit. Nevertheless, he remains extremely active and gigs on a wide basis, playing dates in Britain during 1976.

Regeneration (Monument).

Roy Orbison

Born in Vernon, Texas, April 23, 1936, Orbison's roots were deep country, his first band, the Wink Westerners, being named after the town of Wink, where he was raised. He was one of the many youngsters who fell under the spell of rockabilly, and under the guidance of Sam Phillips, had his first hit on Sun Records, **Ooby Dooby,** in 1956.

However, his high, piercing, totally unique voice owes nothing to any particular genre and he moved into popular music, where after some seven million-selling singles he remains a major international star, though in the US itself he has dropped out of the limelight for many years.

A victim of tragedy since leaving Monument Records in 1965 – his career immediately plummeted, his wife Claudette was killed in a motorcycle accident and two of his children died in a fire during 1968 – Orbison resumed his rela-

Left: The Oak Ridge Boys, fast becoming rivals to the Statler Brothers with their popular gospel music.

Molly O'Day

There are more than a few people – her ex-producer Art Satherley (♦) among them – who feel that Molly O'Day is the greatest female country singer ever. Her earnest exhortative style – not unlike Roy Acuff's (♦) and Wilma Lee Coopers (♦) – is the epitome of a style and brand of old time music not found today.

She was born LaVerne Williamson in Pike County, Kentucky, on July 9, 1923, and embarked on a professional career in the summer of 1939, when she joined her fiddling brother Skeets in a band which also included Johnny Bailes (♦). Here she went by the first of her many stage names, Mountain Fern, which she changed to Dixie Lee in the fall of 1940. She married her longtime husband – and, at the time, fellow bandmember – Lynn Davis on April 5, 1941.

Molly and Lynn made the rounds of a number of south eastern radio stations for the next few years – Beckley, West Virginia; Birmingham, Alabama; Louisville (where she finally chose the name Molly O'Day), Beckley again and then Dallas and finally Knoxville, where they were heard by Fred Rose (♦), who interested Satherley in recording them. Their first Columbia session (December 16, 1946) produced many of her classics: **Tramp On The Street** (written by Hank Williamson), **Six More Miles, Black Sheep Returned To The Fold** and others. The session also marked the recording debut of Mac Wiseman (♦), who played bass on the recordings.

The records were minor hits, and they resumed the circuit of radio stations, also doing more Columbia recordings: **Poor Ellen Smith** (with Molly on the banjo), **The First Fall Of Snow, Matthew Twenty-Four** and others.

In 1950 they began recording only sacred material for Columbia (the content had already been high), and when Molly contracted tuberculosis in 1952, she and Lynn both left musical careers to become ministers in the Church of God, careers which they both follow to this day, Molly occasionally broadcasting over a Christian station based in Huntingdon, West Virginia.

There is no question that Molly O'Day quit performing and recording well before her prime; she certainly had all the talent and appeal to become country music's first really great and really popular woman singer, a role that fell to Kitty Wells (♦) just a few years later.

Albums:
Molly O'Day And The Cumberland Mountain Folks *(Old Homestead/—)*

The Heart And Soul Of Molly O'Day *(Queen City/—)*
Living Legend Of Country Music *(Starday/—)*

The Classic Roy Orbison (London). Once a rockabilly, he went on to become one of pop's most distinctive voices.
Though dogged by personal tragedy he's still making fine albums.

tionship with Monument in 1977, a subsequent album, **Regeneration,** proving to be his strongest since the early '60s.

Albums:
All Time Greatest Hits *(Monument/Monument)*
Original Sounds *(Sun/—)*
Regeneration *(Monument/Monument)*

Greatest Hits *(Monument/Monument)*
The Monumental Roy Orbison *(—/Monument)*
The Monumental Vol 2 *(—/Monument)*
The Best Of . . . *(Trip/—)*
The Exciting *(—/Hallmark)*
Focus On . . . *(—/Decca)*
The Big O *(—/Charly)*

Osborne Brothers

Among the first of the so-called progressive bluegrass outfits, the Osborne Brothers (both born at Hyden, Kentucky, Bob on December 7, 1931, Sonny on October 29, 1937) made their radio debut on station WROL, Knoxville, in the early '50s. After teaming for a time with Jimmy Martin (♦), recording for RCA, in 1956 they signed for MGM Records and became regulars on WWVA's Wheeling Jamboree show, where they specialized in precise, sky-high three part harmony with guitarist Benny Birchfield in 1959. Their gig at Antioch College that year was a milestone, sparking off a series of campus dates, while also in '59 they found themselves accepted on the Opry, later electrification enabling the group to obtain bookings at swank nightclubs and even play the White House. Constantly dismaying purists with their electric sounds and their use of steel guitar, drums and piano, the Osbornes became Decca artists in 1963, terminating their seven-year relationship with MGM. And as electric bluegrass began to prosper, the group (later featuring Ronnie Reno or Dale Sledd as the third vocalist) began accumulating a number of low-chart singles, **The King Of Woman I Got** (1966), **Rocky Top** (1968), **Tennessee Hound Dog** (1969) and **Georgie Pinewoods** (1971) proving to be among the most successful. In 1976 they cut their first album for the new CMH label, featuring accompaniment more sparse than in past years, focusing as always on Bob's awesome tenor voice and impressive harmony singing.

Albums:
Yesterday, Today (MCA/—)
Voices In Bluegrass (MCA/—)
Ru-bee (MCA/—)
Osborne Brothers (MCA/—)
Favourite Hymns (MCA/—)
Best Of . . . (MCA/—)
Pickin' Grass And Singin' Country (MCA/—)
Number One (CMH/—)

Luther Ossenbrink
♦ *Arkie The Arkansas Woodchopper*

Tommy Overstreet

Born Oklahoma, September 10, 1937, Overstreet began his career in Houston, Texas, working on a Saturday morning TV show in the guise of Tommy Dean from Abilene, a name suggested by one of his relations, the late Gene Austin, a pop singer who'd re-

Left: Bill and Sonny Osborne were among the first traditional musicians to realise that bluegrass could be a highly commercial form.

Above: Tommy Overstreet, one of whose ambitions is to record an album of songs made famous by his cousin, the late Gene Austin.

corded million selling versions of **Ramona** and **My Blue Heaven** in the late '20s.

In 1956–57 he studied radio and TV production at the University of Texas, then, following a short stint as a touring performer, came a spell of Army duty. He claims to have 'just coasted' for the next few years – at one stage recording for Dunhill but gaining little recognition – his fortunes changing in 1967 when, following a move to Nashville, he became manager of Dot Records' Nashville office, at the same time becoming a Dot recording artist.

His first tilt at the charts came with **Rocking A Melody**, a 1969 release, this being followed by one further minor hit in **If You're Looking For A Fool** (1970), before Overstreet began hitting his tally of home runs, virtually every release heading into the Top 20. These hits included **Gwen (Congratulations), I Don't Know You (Anymore)** (1971), **Ann (Don't Go Running), Heaven Is My Woman's Love** (1972), **Send Me No Roses, I'll Never Break These Chains** (1973), **Jeanne Marie (You Were A Lady), If I Miss You Again** (1974), **That's When My Woman Begins, From Woman To Woman** (1975), **Here Comes That Girl Again** (1976) and **If Love Was A Bottle Of Wine** (1977).

A regular guest on such shows as TV's Hee Haw (♦), Tonight and Midnight Special, Overstreet usually tours with a five piece band known as the Nashville Express.

Albums:
Heaven Is My Woman's Love (Dot/—)
Tommy Overstreet (Dot/—)
This Is Tommy Overstreet (Dot/—)
My Friends Call Me T.O. (Dot/—)

Woman, Your Name Is My Song (Dot/—)
I'm A Believer (Dot/—)
Greatest Hits Vol 1 (Dot/—)
Turn On To Tommy Overstreet (Dot/ABC)
Vintage 77 (Dot/—)
The Tommy Overstreet Show – Live (Dot/—)

Bonnie Owens

Wife of Merle Haggard (♦) and mother of Buddy Allan from a previous marriage to Buck Owens (♦), Bonnie Campbell Owens was born Blanchard, Oklahoma, October 1, 1932.

In her early years she sang at clubs throughout Arizona, working with Buck Owens as part of the 'Buck And Britt Show' on a Mesa radio station, later joining him in a band known as Mac's Skillet Lickers. During the '60s Bonnie – by this time sans Buck – moved to Bakersfield (♦), California, there recording with the Tally and Mar-

Turn On To Tommy Overstreet (ABC).

Just Between The Two Of Us (Capitol).

vel labels and meeting Merle Haggard, whom she married in 1965.

The twosome became signed to Capitol Records, cutting an album of duets titled **Just Between The Two Of Us,** which led to them being voted Best Vocal Group of 1966 by the Academy Of C&W Music, Bonnie also winning the top female vocalist award. Prior to this, the duo had cut a single of the same name for Tally, which had become a 1964 hit, Bonnie also achieving two solo successes with Tally via **Daddy Don't Live Here Anymore** (1963) and **Don't Take Advantage Of Me** (1964).

Following a small clutch of other minor chart entries – including **Number One Heel** (1965) and **Lead Me On** (1969), Bonnie retired from performing in 1975, devoting her time to organising Merle Haggard's various business activities.

Albums:
That Makes Two Of Us (Hilltop/—)
Merle Haggard And Bonnie Owens (Pickwick/—)

Buck Owens

Mainman behind the California Sound and the establishment of Bakersfield (♦) as a country music capital, Alvis Edgar 'Buck' Owens, the son of a sharecropper, was born Sherman, Texas, August 12, 1929.

While Buck was still young the Owens family moved to Arizona in search of a better standard of living, but they failed to find prosperity, Buck having to leave school while in his ninth grade and involve himself in farm laboring. A fine guitarist and mandolin player, he began playing with a band over radio station KTYL, Mesa, Arizona when he was barely 17. At the same age he got married – by 18 he was a father.

In 1951 he moved to Bakersfield, forming a band, the Schoolhouse Playboys, with whom he played sax and trumpet. He also established himself as a first class sessionman on guitar, backing such Capitol recording stars as Wanda Jackson (♦), Sonny James (♦) and Faron Young (♦). And following a stint as a lead guitarist with Tommy Collins' (♦) band he became signed as a Capitol recording artist on March 1, 1957. His first chart entry was with **Second Fiddle** (1959), then followed a long sojourn in the Top Five via such releases as **Under Your Spell Again** (1959), **Above And Beyond, Excuse Me, I Think I've Got A Heartache** (1960), **Fooling Around** and **Under The Influence Of Love** (1961) – by

Best of Buck Owens Vol. 3

Left: Best of Buck Owens Vol 3 (Capitol). One of the great hitmakers, Owens was instrumental in making Bakersfield a center for recording artists in the mid '60s.

which time Owens had become one of the biggest stars in country music.

With his band the Buckaroos – an outfit that has featured such fine musicians as Don Rich (♦), Doyle Holly (♦), and Tom Brumley (♦) – Owens began playing to sellout crowds at such prestigious venues as New York's Madison Square Garden and Los Angeles' Olympic Auditorium, his record sales becoming increasingly phenomenal, Owens registering no less than 17 No 1 hits between 1963–69, these recordings including such titles as **Act Naturally** (1963), **My Heart Skips A Beat** (1964), **I've Got A Tiger By The Tail** (1965), **Buckaroo** (1965), **Waitin' In The Welfare Line** (1966), **Sam's Place** (1967), **How Long Will My Baby Be Gone?** (1968) and **Tall Dark Stranger** (1969), many of these being written or part written by Owens himself.

During the early '60s, the bandleader had recorded a series of extremely successful duets with Rose Maddox (♦), and at the onset of the '70s Owens revived this practice, employing Susan Raye (♦) as a partner and logging up hits with **We're Gonna Get Together, Togetherness** and **The Great White Horse**. And though some had begun to suggest that Owens had become **Too Old To Cut The Mustard** – the title of a 1971 chart single featuring Owens and his son Buddy Allan – the Baron of Bakersfield continued to supply Capitol with such major discs as **The Kansas City Song, I Wouldn't Live In New York City** (1970), **Bridge Over Trouble Water, Ruby (Are You Mad?), Rollin' In My Sweet Baby's Arms** (1971), **I'll Still Be Waiting For You, Made In Japan** (1972) and **It's A Monster's Holiday** (1974). However, in 1976 he terminated his long association with the label, signing instead with Warner Brothers and releasing an album entitled, characteristically, **Buck 'Em!**

Albums:
The Best Of (Capitol/—)
(It's A) Monster's Holiday (Capitol/—)
A Merry Hee Haw Christmas (Capitol/—)
Best Of Vol 4 (Capitol/—)
County Singer's Prayer (Capitol/—)
Buck Owens (Pickwick/—)

If You Ain't Lovin' (Pickwick/—)
Ain't It Amazing, Gracie (—/Capitol)
The Buck Owens Show (Pickwick/—)
You're For Me (Pickwick/—)
Buck 'Em (Warner Bros/—)
Best Of Vol 2 (—/Capitol)
Sweethearts In Heaven (Starday/—)

Tex Owens

Born in the Lone Star State in 1892, Tex Owens was a popular star and co-host of the KMBC Brush Creek Follies as well as the WLW Boone County Jamboree and several other radio shows. But he is best known and remembered for writing and singing his 1935 hit **Cattle Call** on Decca. He died at his home in Baden, Texas, in 1962. From a musical family, his daughter, Laura Lee, had a long career as Bob Wills' (♦) first girl singer and later with husband Dickie McBride; in addition, his sister was Texas Ruby (♦), longtime Opry star.

Albums: none.

Left: Early '30s Tex Ownes.

Vernon Oxford

Highly regarded in Europe, Oxford was born June 8, 1941, in Benton County, Arkansas, one of seven children of one of the area's leading fiddle players. In his early childhood, Oxford would join the whole family in evening singing, later – after a move from the Ozarks to Wichita, Kansas – becoming a member of the local church choir. Like his father, he became a fiddler, entering the well known Cowtown contest and also the Kansas State championship.

After forming his own band and touring throughout the mid west, Oxford then moved on to Nashville, where he was turned down by several record companies as being 'too country'. Eventually, in 1965 he became signed to RCA, who released seven singles and an album before dropping him. He also signed for Stop, with continued lack of real recognition.

In 1971, fans in Britain and Sweden organized a petition urging RCA to release Oxford's discs once more – and, two years later, British RCA duly obliged with a double album in their **Famous Country Music Makers** series, a release which accrued impressive sales figures.

This encouraged RCA Nashville to re-sign Oxford in 1974, the singer immediately responding by providing, first, a minor hit in **Shadows Of My Mind** (1975), then a major one with **Redneck** (1976).

Albums:
Famous Country Music Makers (—/RCA)
By Public Demand (—/RCA)
I Just Want To Be A Country Singer (RCA/RCA)

By Public Demand (RCA).

Vernon Oxford, who gave his first public appearance at the age of four in church, but had to wait till 1975 to gain real recognition.

Ozark Mountain Daredevils

A country rock band from Springfield, Missouri, who acquired a strong local reputation although none of them had much prior experience in top line groupdom.

Their first album in 1973 was well received and they scored a pop hit single in 1974 with a self penned composition, **If You Want To Get To Heaven.** Their second album, in 1974, **It'll Shine When It Shines,** was even better received and is generally considered to be their best. The third, **The Car Over The Lake Album,** came out in 1976 and was recorded in Nashville. The Ozarks believe in an eclectic approach since album one was recorded at Randle Chowning's ranch in Missouri and the first in London with top British producer Glyn Johns.

Much of the Ozarks' stage act consists of rock 'n' roll but their country picking is slick, and they display vocal harmonies that are sometimes reminiscent of the Eagles.

Albums:
Ozark Mountain Daredevils
(A&M/A&M)
It'll Shine When It Shines
(A&M/A&M)
The Car Over The Lake Album
(A&M/A&M)

Andy Parker (And The Plainsmen)

Born near Mangum, Oklahoma, on March 17, 1913, Andy Parker began his radio career at the age of 16 on KGMP in Elk City, Oklahoma, a career which eventually took him to San Francisco where he assumed the role of the singing cowboy on NBC's 'Death Valley Days' from 1937 to 1941. After working a bit in defense plants he moved to Los Angeles in 1944, and by 1946 had formed a western harmony group known as Andy Parker and the Plainsmen, with KNX in Hollywood as their home base.

Andy and the Plainsmen appeared in some eight PRC films with Eddie Dean (♦) and signed with Capitol Records in December of 1947. However, they were never able to establish a firm identity apart from the host of western harmony groups abounding at the time, despite Parker's fine lead voice, excellent harmony, and the strong lineup of Charlie Morgan (of the Morgan Family) on lead guitar, Clem Smith on bass, George Bamby, who had worked with Spade Cooley (♦) before and would work with the Sons of the Pioneers (♦) afterward as arranger and accordionist, and the legendary jazz steel guitarist Joaquin Murphy.

Andy Parker and the Plainsmen had no particularly big selling records, on either Capitol or Coast Records, although they did cut a fine series of Capitol Transcriptions. In later years a heart condition kept Parker from performing and touring, and he is retired in the San Francisco area today.

Albums: none.

THE CAR OVER THE LAKE ALBUM

The Car Over The Lake Album (A&M). Even with a relatively inexperienced lineup they are regarded as one of the best bands of the '70s.

Above: Grievous Angel (Warner Bros).

Above: Sleepless Nights (A&M).

Gram Parsons

Seminal figure in the country rock movement of the late '60s. Born Cecil Connor in Winterhaven, Florida, November 5, 1946, his father, 'Coon Dog' Connor, owned a packing plant in Waycross, Georgia. Coon Dog shot himself when Gram was 13 and Gram's mother married again, to Robert Parsons, a rich New Orleans businessman. Parsons formally adopted Cecil and changed the boy's name to Gram Parsons.

With much drinking in both real and adoptive families and a hitherto uprooted life, Gram ran away at age 14 and at 16 he was in New York's Greenwich Village following the folk boom and singing protest songs. At one time he formed a folk band with Jim Stafford and a later band, Shiloh, specialized in a commercial and regionally successful brand of folk.

Studying theology at Harvard in 1965, Gram formed the International Submarine Band. After he dropped out of university the band reformed in New York and an album on Lee Hazlewood's label showed them following a fairly purist country path. This album is now a very rare collector's item.

By the time the album came out Gram had joined The Byrds (♦). Meeting Chris Hillman of that band in Los Angeles in 1968 he convinced Hillman that the hitherto rock-orientated Byrds should experiment with country. The result was **Sweetheart Of The Rodeo,** the first real country rock album. Although much of Gram's contribution was mixed out, the album set a new style among rock groups and reminded many a Southern-bred rocker just where his roots lay. The Byrds appeared on the Grand Ole Opry and sang Gram's own composition, **Hickory Wind.**

Gram's fantasy about marrying country with rock charisma was nurtured by his association with the Rolling Stones. He quit the Byrds on the eve of a South African tour, causing a welter of ill feeling. However, he reunited with Chris Hillman again in 1969 when his country aspirations were more fully realised in the Flying Burrito Brothers (♦). **The Gilded Palace Of Sin,** in which the band posed for publicity shots in Nudie suits, has been hailed as a country rock classic and it showcased Parsons compositions that have since become standards via the talents of Emmylou Harris (♦).

But Parsons was getting into the West Coast drug lifestyle and by the recording of the second album, **Burrito DeLuxe,** he seemed more interested in hanging out with Jagger and Richard in Europe. With his trust fund providing him extensive monies to indulge his lifestyle, and a fantasy about getting on to rock superstar level, Gram's preoccupations were tending more towards drugs and drink than productive musical output. However, Warner Reprise came up with a contract and, better still, there was a possibility of Merle Haggard (♦) producing his next album. Parsons went to visit Haggard in Bakersfield (♦), but Merle appeared to have a change of heart at the last moment. However, a session finally went ahead using Haggard's engineer Hugh Davis. Also booked were Glen D. Hardin, James Burton and a new girl singer from Baltimore, Emmylou Harris. Gram was evidently drunk to the point of falling down for the first sessions. Even so, the album showed that his writing ability was still there. **GP** was not a big commercial success on its release in 1972, and it was followed by **Grievous Angel** which featured a similar lineup and more classic Parsons songs. Both albums have since been re-released. A tour around this time with Emmylou Harris and the Fallen Angel Band gave hints of what might have been for Gram had he lived. It has been left to Emmylou to perpetuate the songs and the legend.

Parsons probably did not expect to live long and on September 19, 1973, at Joshua Tree in the California desert, he died of a heart attack. The causes were apparently a heavy mix of drink and drugs followed by (according to Byrd Roger McGuinn) a lovemaking bout with his wife. But at the Los Angeles International Airport the body was snatched and instead of ending up at New Orleans for a family funeral, was driven to the desert at Joshua Tree and unofficially cremated – before he died, Gram had made a pact with his friend and manager Phil Kaufman that whoever died first would be taken to the desert and cremated. As a result of this bizarre incident no autopsy was possible and no official cause of death established. Parsons has since become a cult figure, following one of his country idols, Hank Williams (♦), to an early and mysterious death. But unlike Williams, Parsons had to wait until after his demise for recognition.

Albums:

Sleepless Nights – with the Flying Burrito Brothers *(A&M/A&M)*	**GP** *(Reprise/Reprise)* **Grievous Angel** *(Reprise/Reprise)*

Dolly Parton

Born on a farm in Locust Ridge, Sevier County, Tennessee, January 19, 1946, Dolly Rebecca Parton was the fourth of 12 children born to a mountain family. At the age of ten she was already an accomplished performer, her first regular radio and TV dates being on the shows of Cas Walker, in Knoxville. At 13 she was cutting sides for a small Louisiana record company, the same year making an appearance on Grand Ole Opry.

Graduating from Sevier County High School in June, 1964, she immediately left for Nashville, where she at first scraped by as part of a songwriting team (with her uncle, Bill Owens), her first success coming in 1967, with two hit records on Monument (**Dumb Blonde** and **Something Fishy**) and a contract to join the Porter Wagoner (♦) television and road show. Also that year, Dolly began recording for RCA, her duet with Wagoner on Tom Paxton's **Last Thing On My Mind** entering the charts in December '67 and rapidly climbing to become a Top Ten item.

For the next six years, the Parton-Wagoner partnership continued to flourish, over a dozen of their duets becoming RCA best sellers. However, it seemed that Dolly was gradually becoming the major attraction on disc, obtaining a No 1 with her recording of **Joshua** in 1970. By 1974, she'd branched out as a true solo act, though continuing to record duets with Wagoner and utilize his talents on some of her sessions. The result was a move away from mainstream country in an attempt to gain a wider audience. And the bid proved profitable, Dolly's recording of **Jolene** (1974) becoming a world-wide hit and such further releases as **I Will Always Love You, Love Is Like A Butterfly** (1974), **The Bargain Store, The Seeker, We Used To** (1975) and **All I Can Do** (1976), all gaining positions in the top five.

Winner of numerous accolades – CMA Female Singer Of The Year 1975 and 1976 – Dolly Parton is undoubtedly one of the most important singers in country music today, her songwriting ability also becoming increasingly more potent throughout the years, with lyrics that are often more ambitious than those found in standard country pop fare.

Albums:

As Long As I Love/Hello, I'm Dolly (The World Of Dolly Parton) *(Monument/Monument)*	**All I Can Do** *(RCA/RCA)* **This Is Dolly Parton** *(—/RCA)* **Best Of ... Vol 2** *(—/RCA)*
The Best Of ... *(RCA/RCA)*	**New Harvest – New Gathering** *(RCA/RCA)*
Bubbling *(RCA/—)*	
Coat Of Many Colours *(RCA/—)*	
Fairest Of Them All *(RCA/—)*	**With Porter Wagoner:**
Jolene *(RCA/RCA)*	**The Best Of Porter Wagoner And Dolly Parton** *(RCA/RCA)*
Just The Way I Am *(Camden/—)*	**Say Forever You'll Be Mine** *(RCA/RCA)*
Mine *(Camden/—)*	**Porter 'N' Dolly** *(RCA/—)*
My Tennessee Mountain Home *(RCA/RCA)*	**Love And Music** *(RCA/—)*
Love Is Like A Butterfly *(RCA/RCA)*	**We Found It** *(—/RCA)*
Bargain Store *(RCA/RCA)*	**Two Of A Kind** *(—/RCA)*
Dolly *(RCA/RCA)*	**Just The Two Of Us** *(—/RCA)*

Above: Jolene (RCA) and Right: All I Can Do (RCA).

Left: Dolly Parton. On one of her tracks she used Roy Acuff, Kitty Wells, Chet Atkins, Minnie Pearl, Ernest Tubb, Carl and Pearl Butler, Grandpa Jones and her parents as backup singers!

Les Paul

One of the most influential guitarists – country or otherwise – in popular music history was born Lester William Polfus in Waukesha, Wisconsin, on June 9, 1915. He began his career as a country musician (guitar and harmonica) and comedian, Hot Rod Red, before changing that to Rhubarb Red. He toured for some time with a popular Chicago group, Rube Tronson and his Texas Cowboys, as well, but his growing interest in jazz led him to play with big bands and small combos for a time. In fact from 1934 to 1935 he had a country show as Rhubarb Red over WJJD (Chicago) in the morning, and an afternoon jazz show as Les Paul on WIND.

In 1936 he, vocalist and rhythm guitarist Jim Atkins (Chet Atkins (♦) old half brother) and bassist Ernie Newton (a longtime Opry and Nashville session bassist in the 1940s and 1950s) auditioned in New York as the Les Paul Trio, and spent the next five years with Fred Waring.

Les moved to Los Angeles late in 1941, where he spent much of his time in the studios as well as a stint in the services. In 1947 he teamed with a girl singer, an ex-Gene Autry (♦) bandmember named Colleen Summers, whom he later married, who was such a fine guitarist she had played lead guitar in Jimmy Wakelys (♦) band and sung harmony with him on his hit **One Has My Name, The Other Has My Heart.**

Colleen became Mary Ford, and the combination of her singing, his extraordinary playing, and his then unique use of multiple track record-ing for guitar and voice made the team immensely popular in the late 1940s and early 1950s, and produced eleven number one records for Capitol, including **Nola, Lover, Caravan, Just One More Chance, How High The Moon, Vaya Con Dios, Confessin', I'm A Fool To Care,** and **The World Is Waiting For The Sunrise.**

Les had experimented with electric guitars as early as the late 1930s – in fact, he had never stopped being fascinated by electronics since he got his first crystal radio set in 1927 – and in 1952 Gibson began putting out their fabulously successful series of Les Paul guitars, designed by Les himself. Long the favorite of rock players, these solid body electrics are now becoming increasingly commonplace in country as well.

After he and Mary Ford divorced in 1962 Les retired from performing, turning to inventing in his New Jersey home. The boom in interest in the Les Paul guitar, however, had made his name a household word among musicians, and in 1973 he began performing again on a limited scale. Still deeply interested in electronics – his personal Les Paul guitar, which he calls the Les Pulverizer, is light years ahead of the standard Gibson production model – he is also still a superb musician. In fact, his duet album with Chet Atkins, **Chester And Lester,** won a Grammy as the Best Country Instrumental Performance of 1976.

Albums:

Chester And Lester – with Chet Atkins *(RCA/RCA)*

The World Is Still Waiting For The Sunrise – with Mary Ford *(Capitol/—)*

The Very Best Of Les Paul And Mary Ford *(—/Capitol)*

Now *(London/Decca)*

RCA
RS 1068 (APL1-1665)

175

Johnny Paycheck

Though in 1976 Paycheck temporarily adopted the stance of a Nashville renegade, calling himself John 'Austin' Paycheck in honour of the Music City's major rival (♦), the Ohio-born (May 31, 1941, real name Don Lytle), singer-songwriter began his career as a Music City sideman, enjoying a brief stay as bass guitarist with Porter Wagoner's (♦) Wagonmasters, then becoming a member of Faron Young's (♦) Deputies before moving on to play with both George Jones (♦) and Ray Price (♦). During this period he switched to steel guitar, rejoining Jones'

band as a guitarist during 1959–60. As a rockabilly he cut some sides for Decca, using the pseudonym of Donny Young – then came sessions for Mercury and Hilltop, Paycheck scoring two fair sized hits on the latter label with **A-11** (1965) and **Heartbreak, Tennessee** (1966). He then helped to form Little Darlin' Records, providing the label with several good sellers during the '60s, the biggest of these being **The Lovin' Machine,** a Top Ten entry during 1966. It was at this time that Paycheck also made the grade as a writer, his **Apartment No 9** affording Tammy Wynette (♦) her first hit; **Touch My Heart,** another of his compositions, being a Top Ten item via a version cut by Ray Price.

Little Darlin' folded at the end of the '60s, a period during which

Paycheck virtually hit rock bottom, becoming a self-confessed alcoholic.

Paycheck, however, proved not to be a quitter. He took the cure and fought back with considerable determination, teaming up with producer Billy Sherrill (♦) to cut some sides for Epic, his first release on the label being **She's All I Got,** which reached the top of the country charts in 1971. Since then, Paycheck's name has hardly been out of the Top Ten, such releases as **Someone To Give My Love To** (1972), **Mr Lovemaker** (1973), **Song And Dance Man** (1974) and **For A Minute There** (1975) establishing him as an artist of considerable ability.

Albums:
11 Months And 29 Days *(Epic/—)*

Greatest Hits *(Epic/—)*
Loving You Beats All *(Epic/—)*
Song And Dance Man *(Epic/—)*
She's All I Got *(Epic/—)*
Someone To Give My Love To *(Epic/—)*

Heartbreak, Tenn. (Hilltop).

Loving You Beats All I've Ever Seen (Epic).

Below: Ex-rockabilly Johnny Paycheck cut sides for Decca under the name Donny Young.

Jimmy Payne

A fine songwriter, Payne was born in Arkansas, 1939, moving to Gideon, Missouri in the mid '40s. While in the army, during the late '50s he met Chuck Glaser of the Glaser Brothers (♦), and played lead guitar with Glaser's band. However, it was as a songwriter that he first moved to Nashville, in 1962, where, encouraged by the Glasers, he cut a single **Ladder In The Sky** for the K-Ark label, gaining no reaction. He then left Nashville, taking up a job as a paint sprayer in St Louis, but later returned to the Music City where in 1963 he cut a version of John Hartford's (♦) **Every Little Pretty Girl** for Vee-Jay.

Signed to the Glasers' publishing company, Payne co-wrote **Woman, Woman,** which the Union Gap turned into a 1967 pop million seller, and since that time he's continued to provide hits for others. However, as a solo record artist he's made little impact, having achieved only two minor chart entries with **L. A. Angels** (on Epic, 1969) and **Rambling Man** (on Cinnamon, 1973), the latter being a country version of an Allman Brothers number.

Leon Payne

Smooth-voiced singer and multi-instrumentalist Payne was blind from childhood. Born Alba, Texas, June 15, 1917, he attended the Texas School For The Blind between 1924-35, learning to play guitar, piano, organ, drums, trombone and other instruments. During the mid '30s he began playing with various Texas bands, occasionally joining Bob Wills and his Texas Playboys. During the late 1940s, he became a member of Jack Rhodes' Rhythm Boys, in 1949 forming his own outfit, The Lone Star Buddies, and playing on Grand Ole Opry.

A prolific songwriter, Payne penned a great number of much covered songs including **Lost Highway, Blue Side Of Lonesome, They'll Never Take Her Love From Me** and **I Love You Because,** the latter providing him with his own hit record in late 1949.

Payne, who recorded with such labels as MGM, Bullet, Decca, Capitol and Starday, suffered a heart attack in 1965 and during his last few years had to curtail many of his performing activities. He died September 11, 1969.

Albums:
Country Hits Of The 1940s
(one track only) *(Capitol/Capitol)*

Minnie Pearl

With her flower-bedecked straw hat and old time summer dress, Minnie Pearl is the most instantly recognizable lady in country entertainment today.

Born Sarah Ophelia Colley, in Centreville, Tennessee, October 25, 1912, she majored in stage technique at Nashville's Ward-Belmont College during the 1920s, then taught dancing for a while before joining an Atlanta production company as a dramatic coach in 1934. By 1940, Sarah had become Minnie Pearl from Grinder's Switch (Grinder's Switch being a railroad switching station just outside of Centreville) and made her debut on Grand Ole Opry in this guise. She became an instant Opry favorite and has since appeared on numerous tours, radio and TV shows, also appearing on the first country music show ever to play New York's Carnegie Hall (1947). Much honored by the music industry, Minnie, Nashville's Woman Of The Year – 1965, was elected to the Country Music Hall Of Fame in 1975. She has recorded for such labels as Everest, Starday and RCA, though few of her albums appear to be currently available, her act appealing as much to the eye as to the ear.

Albums:
Grand Ole Opry Stars – with Grandpa Jones *(Camden/—)*
Stars Of The Grand Ole Opry *(RCA/RCA)* one track only

Ralph Peer

The most notable talent scout of the 1920s and discoverer of such artists as Jimmie Rodgers (♦) and the Carter Family (♦), Ralph Sylvester Peer was born Kansas City, Missouri, May 22, 1892. Appointed recording director of Okeh Records in 1920, he first recorded many leading blues artists including Mamie Smith. Then, following the success of Wendell Hall's (♦) **It Ain't Gonna Rain No More** quasi-hillybilly hit for the rival Victor company, Peer was authorized to organize various field recording centers throughout the south, his 1923 sessions with

Fiddlin' John Carson (♦) proving to be a landmark in country music recording. In August, 1927, Peer, then working with Victor, recorded the first sessions of both Jimmie Rodgers and the Carter Family, thus assuring himself of a place in country music history.

In 1928 he formed the Southern Music Publishing Company – a concern heavily involved in the publication of country songs – becoming sole owner in 1932. Its BMI branch is known as Peer International, the entire concern today called the Peer-Southern Organization.

During the remainder of his life, Peer became active in many fields – even receiving a gold medal for his work in horticulture – and died in Hollywood, California, on January 19, 1960. His wife Monique and son Ralph Junior today are the controllers of this multi million dollar firm.

Hank Penny

One of the few easterners who tried to bring a western swing sound to country music of the 1940s was Hank Penny, who was born August 18, 1918 in Birmingham, Alabama. He began his career as early as 1933, but rose to prominence over WWL in New Orleans and spent a good bit of time on the Midwestern Hayride over WLW in Cincinnati, before departing for the West Coast in the mid 1940s. In later years he turned his talents from vocals to that of comedy, and is still active in the southern California area as a comedian. In his heyday he recorded for Columbia, RCA, King, and Decca, his biggest hit probably **Bloodshot Eyes** for King.

Albums: none.

Carl Perkins

Although Perkins is known as one of the seminal figures of Memphis rock 'n' roll he came from a solid country background and his albums are dotted with country numbers.

Born April 9, 1932, in Lake City, Tennessee, in a poor farming community, he started his career performing at local country dances and honky tonks with brothers Jay and Clayton. They called themselves the Perkins Brothers. Independently of Elvis (♦), Carl realized that country was moving in new directions and when he first approached Sam Phillips at Sun studios in Memphis, Phillips insisted that he cut country music, since Elvis had the other scene tied up. The result was three country singles; **Turn Around, Let The Juke Box Keep On Playing** and **Gone, Gone, Gone.** But Perkins persuaded Phillips to let him do some faster material and the result of that was **Blue Suede Shoes,** which, in 1956, topped the pop, country and R&B charts simultaneously. Perkins looked set to be the next superstar from the Sun stable but later that year he was on his way to do the Perry Como and Ed Sullivan shows in New York when, in his own words; 'the Chesapeake Bay Ferry was the last thing I remembered for three days'. The car crash left Perkins with multiple injuries and a broken career. His brother Jay

later died as a result of the crash.
However, Elvis had recorded **Blue Suede Shoes** and Perkins was at least assured of a place in the rock 'n' roll honors list.

Carl's solo career seemed to be at a standstill. Elvis had overtaken him as a rock 'n' roll star (Perkins says that there were times in the early days of package tours when Elvis would die a death trying to follow him. He was drinking heavily but a tour of Britain in 1964 and then as headliner in 1965 convinced him that he was at least a star in some countries. Also, the Beatles had recorded **Honey Don't** and **Everybody's Trying To Be My Baby.** After this, Perkins was approached by Johnny Cash (♦) to be in his road show and was for years a part of the package. Nowadays he has more chance to do country material and played the big British Country Festival at Wembley in 1976 and 1977.

Lately he has formed his own band with his sons on drums and bass, his show consisting of re-creations of the amazing number of hits he's written, which in addition to the above include **Match Box Blues, Boppin' The Blues,** and **Daddy Sang Bass.**

Albums:
Original Golden Hits *(Sun/—)*
Blue Suede Shoes *(Sun/—)*
Greatest Hits *(—/Embassy)*
The Original Carl Perkins
  (—/Charley)
Long Tall Sally *(—/Embassy)*

Bill Phillips

An integral part of the Kitty Wells (♦) – Johnny Wright (♦) Roadshow for many years, William Clarence Phillips was born Canton, North Carolina, January 28, 1936. A guitarist during his high school years, Phillips originally became an upholsterer by trade, his musical career really blossoming in 1955 when he joined the cast of the Old Southern Jamboree on WMIL, Miami, Florida – in which city he gained a residency at the Granada

club.
In 1957 he moved to Nashville, there signing as a songwriter with Cedarwood Publishing, supplying Webb Pierce (♦) with **Falling Back To You,** a 1958 Top Ten hit that resulted in its composer obtaining a recording contract from Columbia.

Phillips began cutting such titles as **Sawmill, Georgiatown Blues** and **You Are The Reason,** prompting few sales but creating enough interest to obtain dates on the Opry during the late '50s.

However, after becoming a Decca act in 1963 he began accumulating a desirable number of chart entries, the first being **I Can Stand It (As Long As She Can),** the most successful proving to be **Put It Off Until Tomorrow,** **The Company You Keep** (1966) and **Little Boy Sad** (1969), these three all gaining Top Ten status. A Phillips composition, **We'll Stick Together,** was the first song that Kitty Wells and Johnny Wright recorded as a duet. His past albums have included **Bill Phillips** (1966) and **Action** (1968), both of these being Decca releases.

Webb Pierce

Born West Monroe, Louisiana, August 8, 1926, Webb Pierce became a distinctive stylist in the heavily electric modern country of the '50s decade.

Early in his youth he learned to play good guitar and was soon gaining notice playing at local events. After a regular stint on Radio KMLB in Monroe, Pierce moved to Shreveport, home of the Louisiana Hayride (♦), to try and gain attention. He was noticed by no less than Horace Logan, program director of KWKH, sponsoring station of the Hayride, and was

Right: Webb Pierce, once voted Top Folk Singer by Ranch and Farm Magazine. Also an 'in' name with rockabilly fans, his old discs being prized artifacts.

Carl Perkins (CBS). Beaten to the post by Presley in the race to become a rock 'n' roll superstar, Perkins now concentrates on country music.

quickly to become a popular radio performer.

He joined the Hayride. During this period, the early '50s, his band included many who were themselves to find fame; Faron Young (◊), Jimmy Day, Floyd Cramer (◊). Early 1950s hits with Decca included **That Heart Belongs To Me** and **Wandering Back Street Affair** and he co-wrote the hit **Last Waltz.** In 1953 he was successful enough as a hit artist to gain a No 1 Singer award by the American Juke Box Operators.

By 1955 he had moved to Nashville and joined the Grand Ole Opry and in that year he had three No 1 country hits; **In The Jailhouse Now, Love Love Love** and **I Don't Care.** 1956 saw him scoring duet hits with Red Sovine (◊); **Why Baby Why** and **Little Rosa.** Getting in also with the burgeoning spirit of the times, he recorded **Teenage Boogie,** an item now much sought after by rockabilly collectors. He followed up with Top Ten country hits on **Bye Bye Love** (the Bondleaux and Felice Bryant (◊) composition made famous by the Everly Brothers (◊)), **Honky Tonk Song** and **Tupelo County Jail.** Pierce epitomized '50s country music. His voice had the authentic, nasal, modern country ring and his songs had a bar room edge, uncluttered by the excess orchestration later to dominate Nashville recording. But this very authenticity seems itself to have become dated and Pierce, although a revered name, is now something of a museum piece.

He has become extensively involved in the business side of things – a publishing company, Cedarwood, which was responsible for putting Charley Pride (◊) on to Pride's future manager, Jack Johnson; radio stations, and a failed record label. He is one star who does actually own that Nashville cliche, the guitar shaped swimming pool. However, although Webb changed labels in 1975 and had a minor country hit on Shelby Singleton's (◊) Plantation label with **The Good Lord Giveth And Uncle Sam Taketh Away,** an odd effort with honking R&B saxes, he is no longer a trendsetting force.

Albums:
Greatest Hits *(MCA/—)*
Country Favourites *(MCA/—)*
I'm Gonna Be A Swinger *(MCA/—)*
Songs *(Vocalion/—)*
Best Of . . . *(MCA/—)*

Webb's Choice (Decca).

Right: An early days pic of country-rock Poco, during their Deliverin' era.

Ray Pillow

Voted Most Promising Male C&W Artist of The Year by *Billboard* and *Cashbox* in 1966, singer-guitarist Pillow was born Lynchburg, Virginia, July 4, 1937. Following four years in the forces during the late '50s, he completed a stay at college, obtaining his degree, then opted for a signing career,

working on the local club circuit.

Later signed to Capitol Records, he gained his first sizeable hit with **Take Your Hands Off My Heart** in 1965, the same year seeing the release of **Thank You Ma'am,** a Top 20 entry. During 1966 came four more chart fillers, including **I'll Take The Dog,** a duet with Jean Shepard (◊) that was destined to become Pillow's most successful record. Also that year – on April 30 – he became a member of WSM's Grand Ole Opry, thus fulfilling one of his great ambitions.

Throughout the '60s, Pillow continued to rack up minor hits, first with Capitol, then with ABC and Plantation – but since **Reconsider Me** (1969), his name has been absent from the best sellers.

Albums:
People Music *(Plantation/—)*
Countryfied *(Dot/—)*
Slippin' Around *(Mega/—)*

Poco

A country-slanted rock band, Poco formed in 1969 when ex-Buffalo Springfield cohorts Richie Furay (guitar and vocals) and Jim Messina (guitar and vocals), linked with Rusty Young (pedal steel, banjo, guitar, vocals), Randy Meisner (bass) and George Grantham (drums).

Three desertions took place during the band's nine-album stay with the Epic label – Messina moving out to join Kenny Loggins as half of a hit-making duo; Meisner becoming part of Rick Nelson's (◊) Stone Canyon Band before joining the Eagles (◊); and Furay

Left: Ray Pillow. Though he missed out on winning the important National Pet Milk contest, he managed to climb the ladder and become an Opry member in 1966.

Live (Epic).

eventually helping to form the Souther-Hillman-Furay Band. In the wake of some commercially unsuccessful but musically interesting attempts to create an 'orchestral country' style – as exemplified by the title track of their **Crazy Eyes** album (1973) where Bob Ezrin's full-blooded string orchestrations are permeated by some pure mountain banjo pickin' – Poco completed their obligations to Epic and, after dickering with the possibility of becoming stablemates to the Eagles on Asylum, signed a deal with ABC Records, the immediate result being **Head Over Heels** (1975), one of their best-received albums. And though it had been rumored that the band would fold in 1973, by 1977 Poco were still intact and offering up their high-flying vocal harmonies on **Indian Summer,** the band's line-up then

being Paul Cotton (guitar, vocals), and Timothy B. Schmit (bass, vocals) with founder members Young and Grantham, this personnel having been established for some four years.

Cotton was born February 26, 1943; Young was born at Long Beach, California, February 23, 1946; Grantham hails from Oklahoma, born on November 20, 1947, and Schmit is another Californian, born Sacramento, October 30, 1947.

Albums:
Poco (Epic/CBS)
Pickin Up The Pieces
    (Epic/Epic)
Deliverin' (Epic/Epic)
From The Inside (Epic/Epic)
A Good Feelin' To Know
    (Epic/Epic)
Crazy Eyes (Epic/Epic)
Seven (Epic/Epic)
Catamos (Epic/Epic)
Live (Epic/Epic)
The Very Best Of . . .
    (Epic/Epic)
Head Over Heels (ABC/ABC)
Rose Of Cimmaron (ABC/ABC)
Indian Summer (ABC/ABC)

Below: Poco (CBS). As strong as ever today despite several lineup changes, which made it likely that they would split. For a long time the band were bored stiff with rock journalists' obsession with Furay and Messina and their early days with the now defunct Buffalo Springfield.

Charlie Poole

Leader of the North Carolina Ramblers, one of the most popular bands to emerge from that area during the 1920s, five string banjo player, singer, and hard drinker Charlie Poole was born Alamance Country, North Carolina, March 22, 1892. A textile worker for much of his life, in 1917 he met Posey Rorer, a crippled miner who played fiddle, the duo teaming up and playing together in the West Virginia-North Carolina area, eventually adding guitarist Norman Woodlieff and recording for Columbia on July 27, 1925. Among their first sides was **Don't Let Your Deal Go Down,** one of the band's most requested numbers.

Personnel changes followed throughout the ensuing years, Roy Harvey replacing Woodlieff on the band's Columbia sessions of September, 1926, and Posey Rorer leaving in 1928, to be succeeded first by Lonnie Austin, later by Odell Smith.

Invited to provide background music for a Hollywood movie in 1931, Poole readied himself for a move to California. But that same year, on May 21, he suffered a heart attack and died at the age of 39.

Albums:
Charlie Poole And The North Carolina Ramblers Vols 1-3 (County/—)
Charlie Poole (Historical/—)

Seven (Epic).

Poplin Family

The Poplins, of Sumter, South Carolina, represent a family tradition more than a commercial musical group. Their father, Henry Washington Poplin, arrived in Sumter in 1870 and passed on vocal, guitar and banjo tutorage to his children Edna and China, besides teaching them many traditional songs.

In 1941 China began playing on WIS Radio, Columbia South Carolina, having already brushed up his fiddle talents by gigging at square dances. He was in two groups for his radio work, the Musical Millers and the Royal Crown Rangers. With World War Two rationing limiting his touring activities he moved to Charleston where he took up construction work and lost part of a finger, an

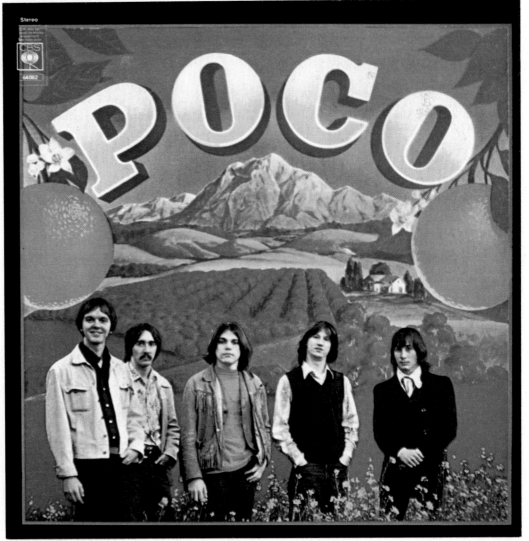

Gwine Back To Sumter (Melodeon). Mentioned on both their available albums, Sumter was the town settled by the Poplins' father in 1870.

incident which later caused him to adopt a revised banjo chording.

In 1943 Edna managed to reinterest him in playing and they provided music for local dances.

They also entered fiddle conventions and have won prizes at Galax, Virginia and Union Grove, North Carolina. Their first commercial recording was released on the Folkways label in 1964 and was titled **The Poplin Family Of Sumter, South Carolina.** A second album, on Melodeon, **Gwine Back To Sumter,** sees them with Edna's daughter Laura, and with Margie Reece from Knoxville, Tennessee. Many of the songs on this album are traditional; **Columbus Stockade Blues, Maggie, My Pretty Quadroon,** and the sound is delightfully old-timer with some innocently touching harmony singing and China playing a splendidly hard and percussive style of banjo.

Albums:
The Poplin Family Of Sumter, South Carolina (Folkways/—)
Gwine Back To Sumter (Melodeon/—)

The Prairie Ramblers

Chick Hurt *mandolin, tenor banjo*
Jack Taylor *string bass*
Tex Atchison *fiddle*
Salty Holmes *guitar, harmonica, jug*
Willie Thawl *clarinet*
Alan Crockett *fiddle*
Patsy Montana *guitar, vocals*
Ken Houchens *guitar*
Bob Long *guitar*
Rusty Gill *guitar*
George Barnes *guitar*
Wade Ray *fiddle*
Wally Moore *fiddle*

The Prairie Ramblers, long associated with WLS and the National Barn Dance, were one of the most influential of the early string bands, although their style progressed through the years from south eastern string band to western swing in their Barn Dance tenure from 1932–1956.

As the above list indicates there were numerous band changes, but the nucleus of the band was formed by Chick Hurt and three of his neighbors, Taylor, Atchison, and Holmes, in western Kentucky. Originally called the Kentucky Ramblers, they began on radio on WOC in Davenport, Iowa, but within a few months were members of the National Barn Dance, where they teamed for many years with Patsy Montana (♦), backing her on many of her records and in person.

Their early style was excellent string band, and they introduced many important songs like **Feast Here Tonight, Shady Grove,**

Below: Golden Hits Vol 2 (RCA). Presley's move from Sun Records to RCA signalled the start of the 'respectable' hitmaking era.

Rolling On; as time went on, however, their style became increasingly swingy. An interesting aside: they also recorded a number of risqué (for the times, anyway) songs under the name Sweet Violet Boys.

Atchison left the band in 1937, heading to California where he appeared in many films and with the bands of Jimmy Wakely (♦), Ray Whitley (♦), Merle Travis (♦) and others. Holmes left and returned, then went on to a career that took him to the Opry for a time with his wife Maddie (Martha Carson's (♦) sister) as Salty and Maddie. Atchison was replaced by Crockett, who shot himself in 1947, and he was replaced in turn by Wade Ray, later to lead his own swing band and record for RCA. Wally Moore was his replacement, and when the band finally ground to a halt in 1956, Hurt, Taylor (the original members) and Moore were playing with a polka band, Stan Wallowick and his Polka Chips, which they continued to do for nearly another decade.

They recorded for the ARC complex of labels, Conqueror, Vocalion, Okeh, Mercury, and both Victor and Bluebird.

Elvis Presley

When Elvis Presley took country music into undreamed-of realms in 1955 many thought that he had killed it for all time. For there was no doubt that Presley was a country singer up till then and that, until the term rock 'n' roll was coined, the new music was believed to be just country with an extra hard backbeat and some wild gimmicks.

Elvis Aaron Presley was born on January 8, 1935, in Tupelo, East Mississippi and brought up in a religious family atmosphere. He sang with his parents at revival meetings, at concerts and in church, soon learning to play some guitar also. The family moved to Memphis when he was 13 and he began to sing for local dances. After graduation from high school he was employed as a truck driver, playing with local groups at night. That year he cut his first record, a private recording of **My Happiness,** to give to his mother as a birthday present. The people at Sam Phillips' Memphis studio became interested in this country boy with the strange inflections in his voice and later that year they set up some experiments in the studio with Presley, Scotty Moore and Bill Black to try and find a sound that suited Presley.

Country songs were found to be not quite suitable but when Elvis started a wild version of blues singer Arthur Crudup's **That's All Right Mama** they knew it was the missing piece of the puzzle. The backing to this is fast, almost breathless, country, but Presley's vocals are wild and uninhibited. However, he was to keep his country connections, backing each 45 rpm record he released with a country title. Charlie Feathers (♦) has described Presley's **Blue Moon Of Kentucky** as classic rockabilly – bluegrass, speeded up and with a colored feel. Presley particularly was influenced by the blues and by black musicians generally. He tended to dress in the extravagently colored suits of the black street hipsters – it was an upfront pose that sometimes courted trouble when he began touring in the hard core redneck South.

That's All Right Mama was doing well locally where DJ Dewey Phillips had plugged it. A local country agent, Bob Neal, Presley's manager for a while, got him some bookings on local country shows.

But it was his next manager, 'Colonel' Tom Parker, a hustling wheeler dealer who, in earlier days, would undoubtedly have been running a successful medicine show, who procured him vital exposure on the prestigious Louisiana Hayride (♦) on March 3, 1955. The Hayride was the next most important radio broadcast to the Saturday night Grand Ole Opry from Nashville and indeed Presley was to play on the Opry himself.

He toured on country bills with people like Hank Snow (♦) and Johnny Cash (♦) and the receptions got wilder, girls trying to get at him and tear his clothes. Parker eventually negotiated a deal for him to join the major RCA label and Presley's days as a country styled rock 'n' roller were over as RCA smoothed him gradually into an 'acceptable' young singer. Sam Phillips got $35,000 for Presleys' contract and the Sun masters went with the deal.

Presley would never again reach those primitive but exciting heights as he settled into a career of Las Vegas concerts and second rate films. He had taken country to the limit, using black influences to pep up the music, and in so doing badly bruised the country market for some years. Even honky tonk country seemed tame by comparison now. However, it is as well conversely to remember country's contribution to rock 'n' roll. When archivists came to rediscover the roots of rock years later they were led to a whole wealth of half forgotten '50s music and were able to bring it from the shadow of the then prevailing smooth Nashville Sound. Presley may have utilized black music to launch rock 'n' roll but country enthusiasts might also argue that he sounded not unlike the fashionable bar room wailers of the day, taken to their wild, bopping conclusion. His albums are too numerous to list and few contain tracks of any real interest to country music enthusiasts; however, **World Wide 50 Gold Award Hits Vol 1,** a four album, boxed set, released by RCA, contains most of Presley's hit singles.

On August 16, 1977, Presley died at the age of 42 of 'acute respiratory distress', mourned by millions around the world.

Kenny Price

Known at RCA as the Round Mound Of Sound, Price, a chunky singer-multi instrumentalist and Hee Haw (♦) regular, was born Florence, Kentucky, May 27, 1931.

Reared on a Boone County, Kentucky, farm, he learnt to play a guitar bought from Sears Roebuck, and began playing country music at local functions.

Stationed in Korea throughout much of his service career, he successfully auditioned for the Horace Heidt USO Show and upon discharge decided to pursue a serious career in music. After enrolling at the Cincinnati Conservatory of Music, he joined Cincinnati's WLW in 1954, becoming a regular on the station's Midwestern Hayride for several years – initially as lead singer with the Hometowners, later spending two years as compere – before moving on to Nashville, where he lately has joined Hee Haw TV Show.

While with the Hayride he met Bobby Bobo, another cast member, who founded his own company, Boone Records. Signed to Boone, Price registered an immediate hit with **Walking On New Grass** (1966), the same year obtaining a second Top Ten item with **Happy Tracks,** both songs being Ray Pennington compositions. Further hits for Boone flowed, the biggest of these being **My Goal For Today** (1967). But in 1969, Price took his happy sound to RCA – two of his 1970 releases, **Biloxi** and **The Sherriff Of Boone County,** becoming Top Ten entries.

Albums:
Turn On Your Love Light
(RCA/—)

Top: Kenny Price.
Above: Supersideman (RCA).

Ray Price

Born on a farm in Perrybille, East Texas, January 12, 1926, Ray Noble Price, the 'Cherokee Cowboy', was brought up in the city of Dallas. After high school, he spent several years in the forces, returning to civilian life in 1946 and attending college with the avowed intention of becoming a veterinary surgeon. However, an able singer-songwriter-guitarist, he began performing at college events and local clubs, eventually making his radio debut as an entertainer in 1948 on station KRBC, Abilene. Later came further exposure on Big D Jamboree, a Dallas radio show that received some network coverage.

Price began recording for Bullet during the early '50s, his first release being a song called **Jealous Lies.** Then, in 1951, came a contract with Columbia, many of his early records for the label reflecting the influence of Hank Williams (♦); Price's band, the Cherokee Cowboys, was formed from the remnants of Williams' outfit, the Drifting Cowboys.

By the end of 1952 Price was an Opry regular with two hit singles to his credit – **Talk To Your Heart** and **Don't Let The Stars Get In Your Eyes** both charting during the year. And though his name was absent from the charts for the next 14 months, in February, 1954, he began a non stop run of hits that has lasted almost up to the present time, the most prominent of these being: **Crazy Arms** (a 1956 million seller), **I've Got A New Heartache** (1956), **My Shoes Keep Walking Back To You** (1957), **City Lights** (another million seller, 1958), **Heartaches By The Number** (1959), **The Same Old Me** (1959), **One More Time** (1960), **Soft Rain** (1961), **Make The World Go Away** (1963), **Burning Memories** (1964), **The Other Woman** (1965), **Touch My Heart** (1966), **For The Good Times** (1970), **I Won't Mention It Again** (1970), **I'd Rather Be Sorry** (1971), **Lonesomest Lonesome** (1972), **She's Got To Be A Saint** (1973), **You're The Best Thing** (1973) and **Roses And Love Songs** (1975). An astute judge of the country music market, Price has always been able to switch styles (from honky tonk to sheer pop balladry) at what appears to be exactly the right moment. And throughout his career, he has always employed a top flight band, past versions of the Cherokee Cowboys including Buddy Emmons (♦), Johnny Bush (♦), Willie Nelson (♦), Roger Miller (♦) and Jimmy Day. In 1971, Price's Columbia release (he currently records for ABC/Dot) **I Won't Mention It Again** was adjudged CMA Album Of The Year.

Albums:
All Time Hits (Columbia/—)
Danny Boy (Columbia/—)
Greatest Hits (Columbia/—)
Greatest Hits Vol 2
   (Columbia/—)
Burning Memories (Columbia/—)
I Won't Mention It Again
   (Columbia/—)
The Other Woman
   (Columbia/—)
She's Got To Be A Saint
   (Columbia/—)
Take Me As I Am (Columbia/—)
Touch My Heart (Columbia/—)
Welcome To My World
   (Columbia/—)
Western Strings (Columbia/—)

World (Columbia/—)
You're The Best (Columbia/—)
For The Best Times
   (Columbia/CBS)
Lonesomest Lonesome
   (Columbia/—)
Make The World Go Away
   (Harmony/—)
This Time, Lord (Myrrh/Myrrh)
Christmas Album (Columbia/—)
If You Change Your Mind
Rainbows And Tears (Dot/—)
Say I Do (Dot/—)
Hank 'N' Me (Dot/—)
Reunion – With The Cherokee Cowboys (Dot/—)

Below: I Won't Mention It Again (Columbia).

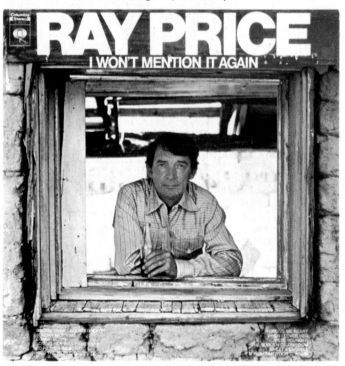

Charley Pride

Easily the most successful black entertainer to emerge from the country music scene, Charley Pride was born on a Delta cotton farm in Sledge, Mississippi, March 18, 1938.

One of 11 children, Pride picked cotton alongside his parents during his boyhood days, eventually saving enough cash to purchase a $10 Silvertone guitar from Sears Roebuck. Despite being born in blues territory, Pride preferred playing country music – but it was to baseball, not show business, that he turned initially – playing for the Memphis Red Sox as a pitcher and outfield player in 1954. Two years later, he was drafted into the forces, during this period marrying Rozene, a girl he met in Memphis. Returning to civilian life in 1959, he quit baseball following a wage disagreement, becoming a construction worker for a while. Several jobs later he settled down in Helena, Montana, working at a zinc smelting plant, also playing semi-pro ball in the Pioneer League. And though he continued efforts to break into major league ball, he found himself turned down by the California Angels in 1961 and by the New York Mets, a year later.

However, his secondary career reaped some reward when in 1963 Pride sang a song on a local show headed by Red Sovine (♦) and Red Foley (♦), earning praise from Sovine, who urged him to try his luck in Nashville. Taking this advice, Pride made the move, Chet Atkins (♦) eventually hearing some of his demo tapes and signing him to RCA.

Pride's first RCA single, **Snakes Crawl At Night,** was released with little in the way of accompanying publicity in December, 1965, few of the deejays playing the disc realising that the singer was anything

Right: Charley Pride. When his first single was released his management deliberately refrained from publicising the fact that Charley was black.

Below: Ray Price. Backed by his Cherokee Cowboys Price has had consistent hits since 1954, despite having most of his band poached by former member Willie Nelson.

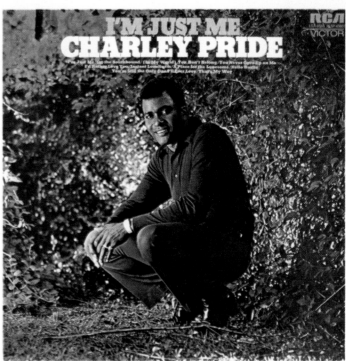

Country Feelin' (RCA). Ex-cottonpicker Pride was born in blues land but found his career in country music after failing to make it as a professional baseball player.

I'm Just Me (RCA). Helped greatly by Willie Nelson, who took him on his roadshow in the racially sensitive South, Pride is country's most successful black singer.

but pure Aryan. But by the following Spring, the Mississippian had lined up a huge hit with **Just Between You And Me,** his performance gaining him a Grammy nomination. A couple of hits later, in January, 1967, and he was on the Opry, his introduction, by Ernest Tubb (♦), receiving a warm reception.

As the '70s rolled in, Pride reached superstar status. Having logged five No 1's in a row with **All I Have To Offer Is Me, I'm So Afraid Of Losing You** (1969), **Is Anybody Goin' To San Antone?, Wonder Could I Live There Anymore** and **I Can't Believe That You've Stopped Loving Me,** he has adjudged Performer Of The Year 1971 by the CMA, also winning the association's Male Vocalist of the Year award, a title he retained in 1972.

Since then he's continued to make all the right moves and kept his generally love-saturated hits flowing with almost production-line regularity, **I'd Rather Love You, I'm Just Me, Kiss An Angel Good Morning** (1971), **All His Children, It's Gonna Take A Little Longer, She's Too Good To Be True** (1972), **A Shoulder To Cry On, Don't Fight The Feelings, Amazing Love** (1973), **We Could, Mississippi Cotton Pickin' Delta Town** (1974), **I Ain't All Bad, I Hope You're Feeling Me** (1975), **The Happiness Of Having You, My Eyes Can Only See As Far As You, A Whole Lotta Things To Sing About** (1976) and **She's Just An Old Love Turned Memory** (1977) being among the numerous best sellers that Pride has accumulated.

Possessing a warm baritone voice, Charley Pride sounds as pure country as Hank Williams (♦) – sometimes even more so. And paradoxically he has become RCA's biggest seller since Elvis Presley (♦) – a country boy who tried his hardest to sound black.

Albums:
(Country) Charley Pride
 (RCA/RCA)
Amazing Love *(RCA/RCA)*
Best Of . . . *(RCA/RCA)*
Best Of . . . Vol 2 *(RCA/RCA)*
Did You Think To Pray
 (RCA/RCA)
Country Feelin' *(RCA/RCA)*
From Me To You *(RCA/—)*
Sings Heart Songs *(RCA/RCA)*
I'm Just Me *(RCA/RCA)*
In Person *(RCA/RCA)*
Incomparable *(Camden/—)*
Pride Of America *(RCA/RCA)*
Songs Of Love *(RCA/RCA)*
A Sunshiny Day *(RCA/RCA)*
Sweet Country *(RCA/RCA)*
Tenth Album *(RCA/RCA)*
 (titled **Charley Pride Special**

in Britain)
Country Way *(RCA/RCA)*
Christmas In My Home Town
 (RCA/RCA)
Best Of . . . Vol 3 *(RCA/RCA)*
Charley *(RCA/RCA)*
The Happiness Of Having You
 (RCA/RCA)
Just Plain Charley *(—/RCA)*
Make Mine Country *(—/RCA)*
Pride Of Country Music
 (—/RCA)
Sample Charler Pride *(—/RCA)*
Sensational Charley Pride
 (—/RCA)
Songs Of Pride – Charley That Is
 (—/RCA)
Sunday Morning With *(—/RCA)*
From Me To You *(—/RCA)*

John Prine

Original and witty songwriter-singer, Prine was discovered by Kristofferson (♦) in a Chicago club and has since gained a sound reputation among contemporary

folk and country critics while not yet enjoying wide commercial success.

Born October 10, 1946, in Maywood, Illinois, Prine took up guitar at age 14 and then served his time in the US Army and the US Post Office. He was able to pursue his musical talents from 1969 whence

Above: John Prine (Atlantic). First album from the Kristofferson discovery.

he gained a cult following in local and Chicago folk clubs.

His first album showed what seemed to be an orthodox nasal country voice, but with backings lighter and frothier than average. Also, Prine's lyrics ranged engagingly over dope, war casualties and long drawn out love situations. On that first album, **John Prine,** the track **Your Flag Decal Won't Get You Into Heaven Anymore** was a direct challenge to unthinking patriotic hysteria.

Yet Prine was an easygoing person, something of a good ol' boy, and he was able to slip the material over to such audiences as Kentucky miners (he played miner's benefits and sang in **Paradise** of how open-cast mining had raped the land).

Subsequent albums have found Prine with sparser folk or heavier rock backings. Although all his songs are interesting he has never quite equalled the overall strength of the first one. His song **Paradise** has been recorded by many artists and it looks like passing into country legend already.

Albums:
John Prine *(Atlantic/Atlantic)*
Diamonds In The Rough
 (Atlantic/Atlantic)
Sweet Revenge *(Atlantic/Atlantic)*
Common Sense *(Atlantic/Atlantic)*

Ronnie Prophet (RCA).

Ronnie Prophet

Described by Chet Atkins (♦) as 'the greatest one-man show I've seen', singer-guitarist Prophet grew up on a farm at Calumet, Quebec, Canada, and began playing at square dances in his early teens. During his teens he moved to Montreal and later began playing club dates in Fort Lauderdale, his first Nashville appearance occurring in 1969.

He obtained a residency at Nashville's Carousel Club, his drawing power proving so potent that the venue became renamed Ronnie Prophet's Carousel Club. Signed to Chardon (the company that managed Charley Pride (♦), Dave And Sugar (♦), Gary Stewart (♦) etc) in July, 1976, Prophet's first US album release occured shortly after, the LP containing such tracks as **Shine On, Sanctuary** and **It's Enough,** all hit singles in Canada. An all round entertainer – he provides impressions and spices his country repertoire with instrumental work-outs on such unlikely material as **Malaguena** and **The Third Man Theme** – Prophet employs a considerable amount of electrical gimmickry on his live performances.

Albums:
Ronnie Prophet *(RCA/RCA)*

Above: Self-taught musician Ronnie Prophet has a chromium-plated nightclub act that has brought him dates at the Sands, *Las Vegas, Harrah's in Reno, the Blue Max in Chicago and the Palomino in Hollywood.*

Welcome To The Sunshine (MCA). Jeanne's first big hit came in 1973 with Satin Sheets, but even before this she was a guest on the Opry.

Jeanne Pruett

Jeanne, a singer-songwriter from Pell City, Alabama, was one of ten children who spent a fair portion of their childhood indulging in harmony vocals or joining their mother and father in listening to the Opry on an old battery radio.

Now a mother herself – with a 21 year old son and a 19 year old

Below: Jeanne Pruett, who worked as a songwriter for Marty Robbins Enterprises for seven years.

daughter – Jeanne first came to Nashville in 1956, along with her husband Jack, a guitarist who played lead with Marty Robbins (♦) for almost 14 years.

It was Robbins who was responsible for her being signed to RCA Records in 1963, at which time she cut six titles. And though there was little reaction, the following year found her making her debut as a guest on Grand Ole Opry.

Despite spending much of her time raising her children, Jeanne continued writing and performing, eventually securing a new record contract with Decca in 1969 and enjoying a minor hit in

'71 with **Hold On To My Unchanging Love.**

But the real breakthrough came in 1973 when her recording of **Satin Sheets** became a phenomenal seller, crossing over to enter the pop charts. Since then, she has been a consistent hitmaker through such releases as **I'm Your Woman** (1973), **You Don't Need To Move A Mountain** (1974) and **Just Like Your Daddy** (1975), also becoming an Opry regular in July, 1974.

One of Nashville's finest cooks – many of her interviews seem to come laced with recipes – Jeanne's avowed ambition is to own a restaurant that serves up first class country cooking.

Albums:
Love Me *(MCA/—)*
Jeanne Pruett *(MCA/—)*
Honey On His Hands *(MCA/—)*
Introducing Jeanne Pruett *(—/MCA)*

Riley Puckett

One of the pioneers of recorded old time country music, George Riley Puckett was born Alpharetta, Georgia, May 7, 1894. When only three months old he suffered an eye infection – and following incorrect treatment of the ailment lost his sight. Educated at a school for the blind in Macon, Georgia, he learnt to play five string banjo, later moving on to guitar. During the early '20s Puckett worked with a band led by fiddle player Clayton McMichen, then joined Gid Tanner's Skillet Lickers (♦) in 1924, remaining featured vocalist with the outfit until its disbandment some ten years later. Puckett's many solo recordings include **Rock All Our Babies To Sleep,** reputed to be one of the first discs to feature a country yodeler, cut three years prior to Jimmie Rodgers' (♦) initial sessions. From 1934 to 1941 Puckett recorded for RCA Victor – also cutting a few sides for Decca in 1937 – and

worked on radio stations in Georgia, West Virginia, Kentucky and Tennessee up to his death in East Point, Georgia, on July 13, 1946.

At the time of his death – caused by blood poisoning from an infected boil on the neck – Puckett was working with a band called the Stone Mountain Boys, on radio station WACA, Atlanta.

His exuberant – sometimes even wild – bass-run guitar style was very influential on country guitarists of his day, the forerunner of the pulsing style which characterizes bluegrass.

Albums:
The Skillet Lickers Vol 1-2 *(Country/—)*
Riley Puckett *(GHP/—)*

Pure Prairie League

George Ed Powell *guitar, vocals*
Mike Reilly *bass, vocals*
John David Call *pedal steel guitar, dobro, banjo, vocals*
Larry Goshorn *guitar, vocals*
Michael O'Connor *keyboards*
Billy Hinds *drums*

Formed Cincinnati, 1971, this country rock band took its name from a Womens' Temperance Society that once appeared in an Errol Flynn movie.

League signed for RCA in '71, the line up then being: Craig Fuller (guitars, vocals), George Ed Powell (guitars, vocals), Jim Lanham (bass, vocals), Jim Caughlan (drums) and John David Call (steel guitar), By the time their second album **Bustin' Out** appeared, only Fuller and Powell remained from the original band.

Pure Prairie League: John David Call, Mike Reilly, William Frank Hinds, Larry Goshorn, George Ed Powell and Michael Connor.

Pure Prairie League (RCA). Their first album, containing Country Song, a high-grade piece of pickin'.

In 1973, after further personnel problems, PPL ceased recording and the record company thought the band had broken up. But the group continued playing live dates, such response being caused by these appearances that RCA was forced to reissue **Bustin' Out,** plus **Amie,** a single taken from the album, the latter going into the national charts in 1975. PPL, which was then comprised of Powell and Call from the '71 band plus new members Mike Reilly and Michael O'Connor, from the Lee Riders, also guitarist Larry Goshorn, re-signed with RCA once more and have since achieved considerable success via albums and concerts. All PPL's album sleeve designs are based around an 'oldtimer' originally created by *Saturday Evening Post* artist Norman Rockwell.

Albums:
Pure Prairie League *(RCA/RCA)*
Bustin' Out *(RCA/RCA)*
Two Lane Highway *(RCA/RCA)*
If The Shoe Fits *(RCA/RCA)*
Dance *(RCA/RCA)*

Eddie Rabbitt

Considered by many pundits to be pure MOR, vocalist Eddie Rabbitt (real name Edward Thomas, born Brooklyn, New York, November 27, 1941) would, nevertheless, appear to have numerous friends among country music record buyers, such Rabbitt releases as as **Forgive And Forget** (1975), **I Should Have Married You** (1975), **Rocky Mountain Music** (1976), **Drinkin' My Baby (Off My Mind)** (1976) and **Two Dollars In The Jukebox** (1977) all becoming major hits.

A one time truck driver, soda jerk, boat helper and fruit picker, Rabbitt recorded for 20th Century Fox and Columbia during the '60s before achieving chart status with his Elektra releases.

Albums:
Eddie Rabbitt *(Elektra/—)*
Rocky Mountain Music
  (Elektra/—)

Marvin Rainwater

Of Indian ancestry, Rainwater – a singer and prolific songwriter who also plays guitar and piano – became a star during the 1950s, when several of his records sold well over a million copies each.

Born Wichita, Kansas, July 2, 1925, his real name was Marvin Percy, Rainwater being his mother's maiden name, which he later adopted for his stage work. Although he was always interested in music as a child and began composing songs at the age of eight, he actually began his career by training as a veterinary surgeon, becoming a pharmacist's mate in the Navy during World War II. Upon discharge he then opted for a career in the music business, his first major breakthrough coming in 1946, when he debuted on Red Foley's (♦) Ozark Jubilee Radio Show, the station receiving so

many enquiries about 'that singer with the Indian name' that Rainwater was signed to a regular spot on the program.

During the early '50s he began touring and cutting records for Four Star and Coral, another high point in his career occurring when he entered the Arthur Godfrey CBS Talent Scout TV Show in 1955 was brought back for four consecutive weeks, at the same time gaining a position on Godfrey's morning radio show.

In January 1956 he signed with MGM Records and with his second release, the self-penned **Gonna Find Me A Bluebird,** won his first gold disc. Promoted by MGM as a full blooded Cherokee brave, Rainwater then usually appeared bedecked in Indian head dress and similar paraphernalia. And maybe the idea worked for him because in 1958 his rocking **Whole**

Lotta Woman became a worldwide hit, reaching the No 1 position in the British charts and ensuring Rainwater of a season at the London Palladium.

However, in the USA reaction to the disc was mixed and some radio stations banned the song as being 'too suggestive'.

Soon after – following another million seller with his version of

Gonna Fine Me A Bluebird (MGM). Rainwater won his first gold disc with the title track in 1956; at this time he used to perform on stage dressed as a Red Indian.

VICTOR STEREO   **RCA SF 8320**

Woman—Tears—Country Song—It's All on Me—Harmony Song—You're Between Me—Take It Before You Go—Doc's Tune

Above: Especially For You (Westwood).

189

John D. Loudermilk's **Half-Breed** (1959) – Rainwater and MGM parted company, the singer moving on to record for such labels as Warner Brothers, UA, Warwick and his own Brave Records, with little real success. Then in the mid '60s came a serious throat ailment that resulted in an operation, after which Rainwater was not to record for nearly four years.

In 1971 he again visited Britain, recording an album with British band Country Fever. Since then he has visited the country several times, like George Hamilton IV (♦) and (until recently) Vernon Oxford (♦) enjoying a higher reputation in Britain than in his homeland.

Albums:
New Country Sounds (—/Gem)
Especially For You
(—/Westwood)

Boots Randolph

A premier Nashville sessionman for many years, Randolph began playing saxophone in bands throughout the middle west, eventually being spotted by Homer and Jethro (♦), who saw him at a Decatur, Illinois, club and promptly relayed their enthusiasm to Chet Atkins (♦). Later Atkins was to hear a tape of Randolph playing **Chicken Reel** in his good-timey, slap-tongued style, and was similarly impressed. He invited Randolph to Nashville and enthused about the sax-man's talents to his

friends. Within a few days Owen Bradley (♦) hired him for a Brenda Lee (♦) session and from then on he became a much-sought-after sessioneer and an established part of the Nashville Sound, recording as a solo artist for both RCA and Monument. In 1963 he obtained a major hit with **Yakety Sax**, following this with such other pop successes as **Hey, Mr Sax Man** (1964), **The Shadow Of Your Smile** (1966), **Temptation** (1967). But perhaps the most interesting Randolph disc, at least to C&W fans, is **Country Boots**, a 1974 album made in the company of Maybelle Carter (♦), Chet Atkins, Uncle Josh Graves and a host of other stellar pickers. The majority of his other album releases fall outside the scope of this book.

Eddy Raven

Eddy Raven was born and raised in the bayou country of Southern Louisiana, one of nine children whose father traveled all over the South as a musician and trucker. At seven Eddy had his first guitar and at 13 his first band. Although his father advised him towards country music Eddy followed the prevailing rock 'n' roll path even though he admitted he was more concerned about lyrics than rhythm.

He lived in Georgia and had his own radio slot on WHAB and a local hit on the Cosmo label. But his father moved the family back to Lafayette, Louisiana. There he

This Is Eddy Raven (Dot).

met Lake Charles record entrepreneur Bobby Charles and wrote him a country/blues hit which sold 60,000 on Charles' label.

After an experimental period in the '60s when Eddy performed all around the Gulf Coast (and at one time played with two young albino brothers called Edgar and Johnny Winter) he tired of the traveling life and, in 1970, went to Nashville where fellow cajun Jimmy C. Newman (♦) put him on to Acuff-Rose publishing.

Eddy's first big writing success was **Country Green** which provided a good hit for Don Gibson (♦). He did likewise for Jeannie C. Riley (♦) (**Good Morning Country Rain**) and Don Gibson again (**Touch The Morning**). Roy Acuff (♦), Roy Clark (♦) and Roy Orbison (♦) have covered Raven's material and Eddy himself has his own re-

Love Sure Feels Good In My Heart (EMI).

cording contract with ABC Records.

Albums:
Cajun (Louisianne/—)
This Is Eddy Raven (Dot/—)

Susan Raye

A regular on the Buck Owens (♦) Show and a star of Hee Haw (♦) since the show's inception, Susan Raye was born Eugene, Oregon, 1944. Initially showing no interest in country music, she became a member of a rock group during her high school days. However, she won an audition held by a local radio station, who were looking for a country singer, and for the next year worked on a late morning C&W show, filling in the afternoons with a deejay spot.

Next came nightclub stints and regular appearances on the Hoedown TV show – at which time she was seen by Jack McFadden, Buck Owens' manager, and invited to Bakersfield (♦) to meet Owens. Joining Owens as a full member of his show in 1968, Susan also signed for Capitol Records, her first single being **Maybe If I Closed My Eyes**, a Buck Owens original, released in September, 1969.

Just a few months later, in January 1970, her version of Jackie DeShannon's **Put A Little Love In Your Heart** pop hit went into the best selling lists, to be followed by **We're Gonna Get Together**, **Togetherness** and **The Great White Horse**, all 1970 duets with Buck Owens. Solowise, Susan's biggest successes have been with **Willy Jones** (1970), **LA International Airport, Pitty Pitter Patter** and **(I've Got A) Happy Heart** (all 1971).

Albums:
Best Of Susan Raye
(Capitol/—)
Honey Toast And Sunshine
(Capitol/—)
Watcha Gonna Do With A Dog Like That (Capitol/—)

Jerry Reed

One of Nashville's most remarkable 'pickers', Reed was born Jerry Hubbard in Atlanta, Georgia, March 20, 1937. A cotton mill worker in his early days, he began playing at local Atlanta clubs,

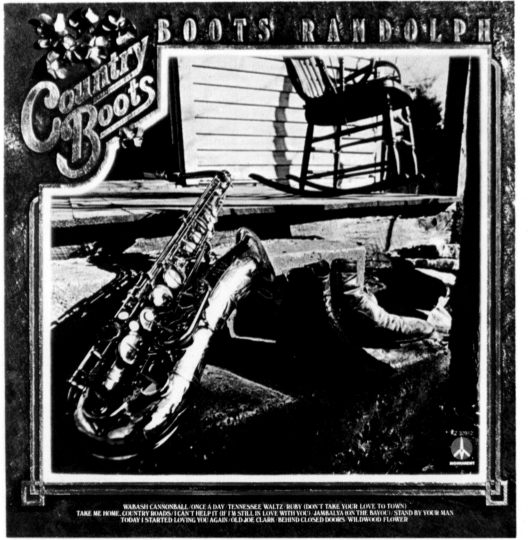

Left: Country Boots (Monument). Probably Randolph's most country-oriented album, on which he's assisted by Maybelle Carter, Chet Atkins et al.

Above: Susan Raye, longtime regular on the Buck Owens show, a singer of 'heart songs and happy songs'.

obtaining a record contract with Capitol in 1955 and cutting some rockabilly tracks. These made little impact, however, Reed's first claim to fame arising through his songwriting ability, predominantly with **Crazy Legs,** which Gene Vincent waxed in 1956.

Following a two year stint in the forces, Reed then settled in Nashville, there providing Columbia with two minor 1962 hits in **Goodnight Irene** and **Hully Gully Guitars.**

Establishing himself as a superior session man, Reed was signed to RCA as a solo act in 1965, his first hit for the label being the rocking **Guitar Man** (1967), which Elvis Presley (♦) covered in '68, thus thus gaining a pop chart success. That same year, Presley also scored with **US Male,** another

Reed composition.

The Georgian's own records continued to sell, **Tupelo Mississippi Flash** (1967), **Remembering** (1968), **Are You From Dixie?** (1969), **Talk About The Good Times** (1970), **Georgia Sunshine** (1970), all reaching high chart positions. Then, late in 1970, came **Amos Moses,** one of Reed's swaprock specials; the song was a Top Ten pop hit and resulted in Reed being nominated CMA's Instrumentalist Of The Year. He also won a Grammy for the Best Country Male Vocal Performance of 1970.

In recent years Reed has concontinued on his winning way, his recording of **When You're Hot You're Hot** becoming a country No 1 in 1971, and **Lord Mr Ford** reaching the same position in '73. A maker of somewhat erratic

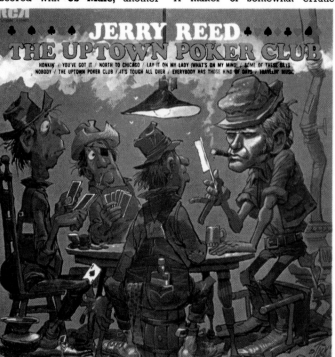

The Uptown Poker Club (RCA). Title track is revival of Darktown Poker Club, a hit for the fast-talking Phil Harris during the late 1940s. Released in 1974, the album is already deleted in the USA.

Ko-Ko Joe (RCA). Apart from performing Reed is a fine songwriter and actor.

albums – he tends to mix hardheaded rockers with sunshiny singalongs – his series of guitar duets with Chet Atkins (♦) have resulted in some fine music. In films, Reed has won critical acclaim as an actor, his performance as the corrupt Bama McCall in *Gator* being highly lauded. Formerly he appeared in *W.W. And The Dixie Dance Kings,* in which Burt Reynolds starred.

Albums:
Best Of . . . *(RCA/—)*
Oh What A Woman *(Camden/—)*
Tupelo Mississippi Flash *(Camden/—)*
When You're Hot You're Hot *(RCA/—)*
Red Hot *(RCA/—)*
Mind Your Love *(RCA/—)*
Both Barrels *(RCA/—)*
Me And Jerry Reed – with Chet Atkins *(RCA/—)*
Me And Chet – with Chet Atkins *(—/RCA)*
Uptown Poker Club *(—/RCA)*

Del Reeves

Singer-songwriter, multi-instrumentalist, Franklin Delano Reeves was born Sparta, North Carolina, July 14, 1934. At the age of 12 he had his own radio show in North Carolina then, after attending Appalachian State College and spending four years in the Air Force, he became a regular on the Chester Smith TV Show in California. By the late '50s Reeves had his own TV show, which he fronted for four years before moving to Nashville, signing for Frank Sinatra's Reprise label in 1958 (the first country artist to do so) and writing songs with his wife Ellen Schiell Reeves. These were recorded by such acts as Carl Smith (♦), Sheb Wooley (♦) and Roy Drusky (♦). Reeves' own initial hit disc came with **Be Quiet Mind,** a Decca release of 1961.

The Del Reeves Album (UA).

Above: Del Reeves.

But despite label changes and a couple of minor chart entries on Reprise and Columbia, it wasn't until 1965 and a contract with UA that he obtained his first No 1 with a song titled **Girl On The Billboard.** In October, 1966, just four hits later, Reeves became a member of Grand Ole Opry, since which time he's continued to supply a continual stream of chart fillers, among the most successful of these being **A Dime At A Time** (1967), **Looking At The World Through A Windshield, Good-Time Charlies** (both 1968), **Be Glad** (1969) and **The Philadelphia Fillies** (1971). More recently he's been cutting a series of duets with Billie Jo Spears (♦), one of these – **On The Rebound** – reaching the Top 20 during 1976.

Star of his own weekly TV show for a time, Del Reeves Country Carnival, the talented Carolinian has also appeared in such movies as *Second Fiddle To A Steel Guitar, Sam Whiskey, Cottonpickin' Chickenpickers* and *Forty Acre Feud.* Named 'The Dean Martin of Country Music' by some members of the media because of his easy style, Reeves currently lives on the outskirts of Nashville with his wife and three daughters.

Albums:
Live At The Palamino *(UA/—)*
Strings And Things *(UA/—)*
10th Anniversary *(UA/—)*
By Request – with Billie Jo Spears *(UA/—)*

Goebel Reeves

An early century Woody Guthrie (♦) figure, Reeves, known as the Texas Drifter, specialized in songs of hobos and hard times, writing from his own experience on the road.

Born Sherman, Texas, October 9, 1899, he came from a solid middle class background but chose to live a rough traveling life. After a stint in the army, during which time he saw front line action in World War I, he traveled the states gathering experience for his hobo and cowboy songs and recording some of them for the Okeh and Brunswick labels. He played in vaudeville, the main outlet for music at that time, also did some radio work, and claims to have taught Jimmie Rodgers his yodeling style. His songs include **Hobo's Lullaby, Hobo And The Cop, Railroad Boomer, Bright Sherman Valley** and **Cowboy's Prayer.** For a while he was in the Industrial Workers Of The World organization. He died in 1959 in California.

Jim Reeves

Originally a stone country singer, smooth-toned Jim Reeves from Texas reached amazing heights as a pop ballad singer and since his death in an air crash his fame has burgeoned into cult proportions.

James Travis Reeves was born on August 20, 1923, at Galloway, Panola County, Texas. His father died when he was young and his mother supported a large family by working in the fields. Early on in life he heard the sound of Jimmie Rodgers (♦) on the phonograph and thus was born his interest in music. He acquired a guitar at the age of five; it had strings missing but an oil construction worker fitted it up for him and taught him some basic chords. At nine he made his first radio broadcast, a 15-minute program on a Shreveport, Louisiana station.

By high school, in Carthage, Texas, he was just as interested in sport as in music and he soon became a star of the school baseball team, although he was still playing at local dances and high school events. He entered the University of Texas at Austin (♦) and his baseball prowess as a pitcher soon attracted the attention of the St Louis Cardinals scouts who signed him up. But an unlucky slip on a wet pitch gave him an ankle injury that was to halt his career.

In 1947 he met and married a school teacher named Mary White who encouraged his musical interest. Jim had majored from university in phonetics and pronunciation and he now sought a job in radio, becoming a DJ and news reader for station KGRI in Henderson, Texas. He aspired to the position of Assistant Manager (and later bought the station).

Jim then made a momentous journey. He and Mary, having decided to make a determined effort to further Jim's career, drove out in their car and, at the crossroads of High 80 in Texas, they tossed a coin to determine whether to proceed to Dallas or Shreveport. Shreveport won and Jim ended up with a job as announcer of KWKH, the station that owned Louisiana Hayride (♦).

It was one of Jim's jobs to announce the Saturday night Hayride show and he was even allowed to sing occasionally. One night in 1952 Hank Williams (♦) failed to arrive, and Jim was asked to fill in. In the audience was Fabor Robison, owner of the Abbott Record Company and Jim was straight away signed to contract. He had already made four obscure singles for the Macy label (belonging to a Houston chain store) and these records only came to light in 1966. However, his Abbott deal soon began bearing fruit. With **Mexican Joe,** his second Abbott release in 1953, he gained No 1 position in the pop charts and became a featured star on the Hayride.

In 1956 he recorded **Bimbo** which, beside earning him a second gold disc, also earned him a nickname, 'Bimbo Boy'. He recorded 36 discs for Abbott, all of them in an earthy country style.

By now he was attracting attention from major record labels and in 1955 he signed for RCA amid some competition. That same year he joined the Grand Ole Opry in Nashville at the recommendation of Ernest Tubb (♦) and Hank Snow (♦). A string of country hits followed; **Yonder Comes A Sucker** (his own composition), **According To My Heart, My Lips**

Jim Reeves On Stage (RCA Victor). One of nearly 50 albums still available. Like many other artists who died tragically, his following today is as loyal as ever.

Are Sealed and Am I Losing You? (another self-composition). In 1957 he undertook a major European tour in the company of The Browns (♦), Del Wood (♦) and Hank Locklin (♦). The February 1957 release of Four Walls was a major turning point. Jim was still in Europe when the song hit in both pop and country fields, gaining him his third gold disc. Unaware of his good fortune he returned to find radio and TV offers in abundance, including NBC-TV's prestigious Bandstand show. That year he also gained his own daily show on ABC-TV.

Jim had become firmly established in the broad pop market and from that time his music started to soften. However, there were three more minor hits in Anna Marie, Blue Boy and Billy Bayou before Jim recorded his all-time greatest hit in 1959, He'll Have To Go. The theme was familiar enough. Ten years earlier it might have been called a honky tonk song. But the treatment, with Reeves' dark, intimate, velvet tones gliding over a muted backing, was something different again. Another gold disc and this time truly international stardom. Over the next few years Jim traveled to every state in America and to most parts of the world. His 1962 tour of South Africa with Chet Atkins (♦) and Floyd Cramer (♦) broke every known attendance record in the entertainment field.

In 1963 he returned to South Africa to star in his only film, Kimberley Jim, the story of a con man in South Africa's diamond strike days. He had not toured British venues in these years because of Musician's Union restrictions, but in 1964 he was in Britain for TV shows, to promote his new single I Love You Because. Other hits of the '60s included You're The Only Good Thing (1960), Am I Losing You? (1961), Adios Amigo (1962), Guilty, Welcome To My World (1963), I Love You Because, I Won't Forget You (1964).

On a flight back to Nashville from Arkansas on July 31, 1964, following the negotiation of a property deal, Jim and his manager Dean Manuel reported that their single engine plane had run into heavy rain while crossing remote hills a few miles from Nashville's Beery Field airport. The plane was making its approach to land at 5 pm when it disappeared from the airport radar screen.

A search was instigated involving 12 planes, two helicopters and a ground party of 400 (which included some prominent industry people). Two days later the wreckage and the bodies were discovered amid thick foliage.

On August 2, 1964, services were held for Jim and Dean and most of the country music fraternity was present. Jim's body was flown back to Carthage where hundreds filed past the coffin. Honorary pall bearers included Chet Atkins (♦) and Steve Sholes (♦), the man who had signed Jim to RCA.

But the legend lived on and Jim's records continued to hit the charts, perhaps with greater emphasis. His British fan club was not formed until 1966. Pop hits for Jim Reeves after his death included There's A Heartache Following Me, Distant Drums, This World Is Not My Home, Is It Really Over?, I Won't Come In While He's There and When Two Worlds Collide.

Jim Reeves was voted into the Country Music Hall Of Fame in 1967.

Albums:
Jim Reeves (Camden/—)
Am I That Easy To Forget? (RCA/—)
Best Of . . . (RCA/RCA)
Best Of . . . Vol 2 (RCA/—)
Best Of . . . Vol 3 (RCA/—)
Best Of Sacred Songs (RCA/—)
12 Songs Of Christmas (RCA/RCA)
Distant Drums (RCA/RCA)
God Be With You (RCA/Camden)
Good 'n' Country (Camden/Camden)
Great Moments (RCA/—)
Have I Told You Lately That I Love You? (Camden/Camden)
I'd Fight The World (RCA/RCA)
Moonlight And Roses (RCA/RCA)
Touch Of Velvet (RCA/RCA)
We Thank Thee (RCA/Camden)
Young And Country (Camden/RCA)
I Love You Because (RCA/RCA)
Kimberly Jim (Camden/—)
Legendary Performer (RCA/—)
Songs Of Love (RCA/RCA)
According To My Heart (—/RCA)
50 All-Time Worldwide Favourites (—/RCA)

25 All-Time Worldwide Favourites Vol 1 (—/RCA)
25 All-Time Worldwide Favourites Vol 2 (—/RCA)
Gentleman Jim (—/RCA)
He'll Have To Go (—/RCA)
International Jim Reeves (—/RCA)
Intimate Jim Reeves (—/RCA)
And Some Friends (—/RCA)
On Stage (—/RCA)
Jim Reeves Way (—/RCA)
Writes You A Record (—/RCA)
Missing You (—/RCA)
My Cathedral (—/RCA)
My Friend (—/RCA)
Something Special (—/RCA)
Talkin' To Your Heart (—/RCA)
Touch Of Sadness (—/RCA)
Welcome To My World (—/RCA)
Yours Sincerely (—/RCA)
Country Side Of Jim Reeves (—/Camden)
Songs To Warm The Heart (—/Camden)
Sings With Some Friends (—/Camden)
The Best Of . . . (—/Camden)
Welcome To My World (—/Camden)
Bimbo (—/Camden)

Jim Reeves' records continue to sell in enormous quantities, his version of It's Nothin' To Me becoming a top 20 country hit in 1977. His widow, Mary, still promotes his discs.

Velvet Hammer In A Cowboy Band (Countryside).

Red Rhodes

Born Orville J. Rhodes, East Alston, Illinois, December 30, 1930, he began playing dobro at the age of five, his mother teaching him A major tuning. Within a short space of time, he'd become proficient on the instrument but at 15 switched to lap steel guitar, which he fixed to a stand, playing his first paid gig at the Bill Jones Bar in Illinois along with his step-father who played rhythm guitar and sang.

Moving to LA in 1960, he became a sessionman, playing on such Byrds (♦) hits as **You Ain't Goin' Nowhere** and **Wasn't Born To Follow,** also Fraternity Of Man's **Don't Bogart The Joint** and many others, leading his own band at the Palomino C&W club (he recorded an album **Live At The Palomino** for Happy Tiger) and gaining several awards. His work on various sessions with the Monkees led him to become steel guitarist with Mike Nesmith's (♦) First National Band in 1969, remaining as part of the Second National Band and Nesmith's Countryside outfit.

A fine solo album **Velvet Hammer In A Cowboy Band** was produced by Nesmith for his ill fated Countryside label in 1973, but since that time Rhodes has been content to revert to session work, appearing on albums by Bert Jansch and others. He also runs his own guitar workshop, in which establishment he is depicted on the sleeve of **Velvet Hammer.**

Bobby G. Rice

Rice started in rock 'n' roll, and although he later switched to country his records often retained a strong commercial feel.

Born in Boscobel, Wisconsin, July 11, 1944, he grew up on a farm with four sisters and a brother, all musically minded. They ran a successful dance hall called the Circle D and by the mid '50s had their own show on Radio WRCO, Richmond, a gig that lasted for seven years.

The family group broke up in 1964 when two sisters married, and Rice then formed a duo with his sister Lorraine, adapting to a more country style and doing local TV. When his sister quit he formed the Bobby Rice Band and was signed by Royal American Records. 1970 saw country chart hits in **Sugar Shack,** Bruce Chanel's **Hey Baby, A Hundred Pounds Of Clay** and **Lover Please.** Royal American was purchased by Metromedia and other hits followed; **You Lay So Easy On My Mind** (1972) and **You Give Me You** (1973). Another new label, GRT, saw **Write Me A Letter** hit the charts in 1975 and **Pick Me Up On Your Way Down** in 1976.

Albums:
She Sure Laid The Lonelies On Me *(GRT/—)*
Instant Rice *(GRT/—)*
Write Me A Letter *(GRT/—)*
With Love *(GRT/—)*

Below: Bobby G. Rice, guitarist and banjo player.

Charlie Rich

Originally a cult favorite in the field of rockabilly, Rich has now become one of the best selling artists in modern country. Born in Colt, Arkansas, December 14, 1934, Rich's high school and University of Arkansas days saw him heavily influenced by jazz and blues. He studied music formally at college and when the USAF posted him to Oklahoma in the early fifties one of his first groups, the Velvetones, secured a slot on local TV. The Velvetones played jazz and blues and Rich's wife Margaret handled vocals.

Upon his discharge Rich moved to West Memphis, Arkansas, to work on his father's cotton farm. After sitting in one night in Bill Justis's band (Justis had a Sun Records hit in 1958 with the instrumental, **Raunchy**) Rich was invited to Sam Phillips' studio in Memphis to lay down some trial tracks. He was told that he was too jazzy, handed a pile of Jerry Lee Lewis (♦) records and told to come back when he could get that bad!

After playing sessions with Warren Smith, Ray Smith and Billy Lee Riley, Rich landed his own rockabilly hit in 1959, **Lonely Weekends.** The demise of Sun saw Rich without a record label and Bill Justis, now an employee of RCA, persuaded him to sign for Groove, an RCA subsidiary, in 1963. The foot-stomping hit single **Big Boss Man** came from this period. In 1965 Rich moved to Smash where Shelby Singleton (♦) encouraged Rich to utilize both rock and country influences. That year he scored another hit single in the national charts with **Mohair Sam.**

After an unproductive stint with the Memphis label Hi (he recorded overtly sentimental country weepers and standards there) Epic signed him in 1968, making him part of their modern country push under producer Billy Sherrill (♦). Although Sherrill was becoming the doyen of the 'Nashville Sound' he had trouble stimulating more than average sales with Rich, although local critical acclaim was heard for such titles as **Raggedy Ann** and **I Almost Lost My Mind.**

But in 1972 the smoothly soulful country coupling **I Take It On Home** backed with **Peace On You** was a country and pop hit and was nominated for a Grammy award. The album **The Best Of Charlie Rich** swept up many of the earlier Epic titles, re-presenting them to the public, and suddenly Rich was a big country name. But success really came with the next album, **Behind Closed Doors.** By this time Sherrill and Rich had hit a winning combination and the new, urbane country sound (immediately dubbed 'countrypolitan') was the talk of the 1973 CMA Awards. Not only had Rich topped the country charts, he was being bought by pop fans who might previously have bought Frank Sinatra albums. A flood of Rich 'countrypolitan' albums have followed with RCA re-releasing much of their product on Rich. Although Rich looks set to continue recording in this vein his stage shows are more of a musical mixture, showcasing his rock and blues roots. An Epic release **The Silver Fox** also acknowledged this eclecticism.

Behind Closed Doors (Epic). The album which made Rich a real country name – the sound was 'countrypolitan' and appealed to a new middle of the road audience.

Albums:

Behind Closed Doors (Epic/—)	**There Won't Be Anymore** (RCA/RCA)
Best Of (Epic/—)	**She Called Me Baby** (RCA/RCA)
Early Years (Sun/—)	**Time For Tears** (Sun/—)
Entertainer Of The Year (Pickwick/—)	**Tomorrow Night** (RCA/RCA)
Golden Treasures (Sun/—)	**Very Special Love Songs** (Epic/Epic)
Lonely Weekends (Sun/—)	**Every Time You Touch Me** (Epic/—)
Lonely Weekends (Pickwick/—)	**Greatest Hits** (Epic/—)
Memphis Sound (Sun/—)	**Favorites** (—/RCA)
She Loved Everyone But Me (Camden/—)	**Great Hits** (RCA/—)
Silver Fox (Epic/Epic)	**Silver Linings** (Epic/—)
Sings Hank Williams (Hi/—)	**World Of** (RCA/—)
Songs For Beautiful Girls (Pickwick/—)	**Take Me** (Epic/—)
Sun's Best (Sun/—)	**Original Charlie Rich** (—/Charley)

Don Rich

Born Olympia, Washington, August 15, 1941, Rich learnt to play guitar at a very early age, performing on radio while only five. Soon mastered the fiddle and at 11 won a talent contest and a trip to Hollywood.

In 1958 came his first meeting with Buck Owens (♦). And though the duo found themselves to be musically compatible, Rich then decided to enter college, where he qualified as a music teacher. However, by 1960 he was back with Owens on a full time basis, becoming a prominent part of the Owens sound as lead guitarist, fiddler, and tenor singer with the Buckaroos.

As a composer, Rich wrote many fine songs, including **Waiting In Your Welfare Line,** a No 1 for Owens in 1966. And his work as a musician has been aptly captured on the many albums recorded by the Buckaroos, his fiddle playing

being featured on such numbers as **Faded Love, Turnwater Breakdown** and the perennial **Orange Blossom Special.** Never much of a hitmaker with the Buckaroos – their recordings of **Anywhere USA, Nobody But You** (both 1969) and **The Night They Drove Old Dixie Down** (1970) only grazing the charts – Rich did enjoy one fairly substantial hit when he recorded **Cowboy Convention** with Owens' son Buddy Alan in 1970. On July 17, 1974, Rich died tragically while riding his motor cycle near Morro Bay, California. That same year, the CMA honored him the Top Instrumentalist Of The Year award.

Jeannie C. Riley

An international star on the strength of just one record – a multi-million selling version of

Tom T. Hall's (♦) **Harper Valley PTA** (1968) – the booted, mini skirted Jeannie (born Anson, Texas, October 19, 1945) had only minimal experience in the entertainment industry prior to her arrival in Nashville. In Music City she worked as a secretary for some time, cutting a few demo discs but generally having little success until Shelby Singleton (♦) signed her to launch his new Plantation label with **Harper Valley PTA,** a brilliant song dealing with small town hypocrisy. An immediate hit which sold four million copies in the US alone, the single sparked off an album of the same title, which also qualified for a gold disc, while Jeannie C. was awarded a Grammy as the Best Female Country Vocalist of '68.

The Girl Most Likely (1968), **There Never Was A Time** (1969), **Country Girl** (1970), **Oh Singer** (1971) and **Good Enough To Be Your Wife** (1971), were other Plantation releases that achieved Top Ten status, but following a label switch to MGM in 1971 Jeannie's disc sales began to taper off and its been quite a time now since her name last appeared on the charts.

Albums:
Country Girl (Plantation/—)
Generation Gap (Plantation/—)
The Girl Most Likely (Plantation/—)
Greatest Hits (Plantation/—)
Harper Valley PTA (Plantation/—)
Jeannie (Plantation/—)
Things Go Better With Love (Plantation/—)
World Of Country (Pickwick/—)
Yearbooks And Yesterdays (Plantation/—)

Tex Ritter

Born near Murvaul in Panola County, Texas, on January 12, 1905, Woodward Maurice Ritter aspired to a career in law at the University of Texas and at Northwestern before abandoning it for a career on the Broadway stage, where he appeared in five plays in the early 1930s, including 'Green Grow The Lilacs' in 1930. During his New York years he also appeared as a dramatic actor on radio's popular 'Cowboy Tom's Round-Up' and co-hosted the WHN Barn Dance with Ray Whitley (♦), and he made his first records for ARC in 1934.

One of the first to follow Gene Autry (♦) into films as a singing cowboy, Tex moved to Hollywood in 1936, where he was to star in some sixty films for Grand National, Monogram, Columbia, Universal, and PRC up until 1945. After several unsuccessful years with Decca (1935–1939) he was the first country singer to sign with the new Capitol label in 1942, and responded with a long string of hits for them. He was one of country music's biggest sellers of the 1940s.

When his film career declined he turned to touring, and had few rivals in the number of miles travelled year in and year out. In addition, he and Johnny Bond (♦) co-hosted 'Town Hall Party' from 1953 to 1960, and his rendition of the theme song for the film *High Noon* won an Academy Award in 1953.

Ritter moved to Nashville in 1965, where he joined the Grand Ole Opry and took over a late night radio program on WSM. He acted on a longstanding desire to run for political office when he ran – unsuccessfully – for the US Senate in 1970, incurring debts that were to haunt him for the rest of his life.

A lifelong student of western history, he was instrumental in setting up the Country Music Foundation (♦) and the Country Music Hall Of Fame (♦),

Fall Away (Capitol). A now deleted album from one of the first singing cowboys, who scored many hits and turned to live performances after making dozens of films.

to which he was elected in 1964. Rated purely as a singer, he did not have a great voice, but his unusual accent, odd slurs and phrasing, and a strong feeling of genuine honesty – sometimes plaintive, sometimes gruff – made his voice one of the most appealing in country music's history, and his long string of hits includes **Jingle, Jangle, Jingle** (1942), **Jealous Heart** (1944), **There's A New Moon Over My Shoulder** (1944), **I'm Wasting My Tears On You** (1945), **You Two Timed Me One Time Too Often** (1945), **Rye Whiskey** (1945), **Green Grow The Lilacs** (1945), **High Noon** (1952), **The Wayward Wind** (1956), and **I Dreamed Of A Hillbilly Heaven** (1961). He died on January 2, 1973 after a heart attack at the Metro Jail, Nashville, where he was arranging bail for one of his band members; he was pronounced dead on arrival at Baptist Hospital.

Albums:

An American Legend
  (Capitol/—)
Hillbilly Heaven *(Capitol/—)*
The Very Best Of . . .
  (Capitol/—)
Comin' After Jimmy
  (Capitol/—)

Deck Of Cards *(—/MFP)*
Tex *(Pickwick/—)*
Love You Big As Texas
  (Pickwick/—)
High Noon *(Pickwick/—)*

Marty Robbins

In a music where 'western' has often been considered a misnomer, Marty Robbins has emphasized the western of country and western through a series of memorable cowboy/Mexican style ballads, many of them crossing over to the pop fields.

Born Glendale, Arizona, September 26, 1925, he grew up in a desert area, his earliest musical recollections involving his harmonica-playing father and the songs and stories of his grandfather, Texas Bob Heckle, a traveling medicine man. Many of Robbins' own songs, such as **Big Iron,** owe much to his grandfather's tales.

Influenced by the films of Gene Autry (♦), Robbins developed an ambition to become a singing cowboy and, following a three year term of service in the Navy, he began playing at clubs in the Phoenix area, also appearing on radio station KPHO. Soon he gained his own TV show, Western Caravan, at one time having Little Jimmy Dickens (♦) as guest, Dickens being so impressed by Robbins' performance that he contacted Columbia Records who immediately signed him, releasing his first disc **Love Me Or Leave Me Alone,** in 1952.

With his third Columbia release, **I'll Go On Alone,** Robbins hit the country music Top Ten, that same year (1953) making a return visit with **I Couldn't Keep From Crying.** He'd already guested on Grand Ole Opry and in '53 became a regular on the show, celebrating his signing with two 1954 hits in **Pretty Words** and **That's All Right,** the latter being the same Arthur Crudup up tempo blues with which Elvis Presley (♦) made his name. Robbins thus established a rock 'n' roll connection which haunts him today and followed up by recording the hummable **Singing The Blues** (1956), **Knee Deep In The Blues, The Story Of My Life, White Sport Coat** and **Teenage Dream** (1957) some of these becoming huge international hits and spawning equally successful cover versions in Britain. Robbins is a convincing rock 'n' roller, a fact not lost on the British Teddy Boy fraternity, one of whom,

Originally known as 'Mr Teardrop' because of his penchant for cry-in-your-beer balladry, Marty Robbins later moved on to tackle rock, pop, and various areas of country music.

at the 1976 Wembley Country Festival shouted 'You gotta rock, Marty' when it became apparent that the singer was bent on doing an exclusively country set.

The crossover hits continued, at least in America, where Robbins had success in 1958 with **She Was Only Seventeen** and **Stairway Of Love.** And in 1959 came his biggest ever, **El Paso,** the lyrics of which would have made a convincing Western film and the rhythm of which slipped insistently along, tinged with Mexican nuances. This was the archetypcal Robbins, purveying a mixture of macho Western feel and melodic sentiment in a dramatically powerful but held-back voice. Following **Don't Worry,** a 1961 country No 1, **Devil Woman** struck the same response as **El Paso** among pop fans and they again brought Robbins into the pop charts on both sides of the Atlantic.

Since that time Robbins' records have rarely been absent from the country Top 20 – one statistician recently estimating that Marty's discs have occupied *Billboard* chart positions for 73 per cent of the time since 1959, among them being listed such substantial sellers as **Ruby Ann** (1962), **Begging To You** (1963), **Ribbon Of Darkness** (1965), **Tonight Carmen** (1967), **I Walk Alone** (1968), **My Woman, My Woman, My Wife** (1970) and **El Paso City** (1976). An actor of some substance – Robbins has appeared in such films as *The Gun And The Gavel, The Badge Of Marshal Brennan* and *Buffalo Gun* – he is also a successful album artist and has maintained a very prolific output in this area, showing an ability in latter years to appeal to the middle of the road market with his releases. He has appeared on most major American TV shows and tours heavily, displaying a varied, entertaining style in which his own mickey-taking chit-chat features predominately. An Opry favorite for 24 years, the one time desert rat has the distinction of being the last person to perform at the Ryman Auditorium.

When he returned to the Opry after major heart surgery in 1970, he was forced to remain on stage for 45 minutes by his appreciative fans.

STEREO 360 SOUND

"devil woman"
MARTY ROBBINS

DEVIL WOMAN ■ AIN'T LIFE A CRYING SHAME ■ TIME CAN'T MAKE ME FORGET
IN THE ASHES OF AN OLD LOVE AFFAIR ■ THE HANDS YOU'RE HOLDING NOW ■ WORRIED
LITTLE RICH GIRL ■ PROGRESSIVE LOVE ■ I'M BEGINNING TO FORGET
LOVE IS A HURTING THING ■ KINDA HALFWAY FIXED ■ THE WINE FLOWED FREELY

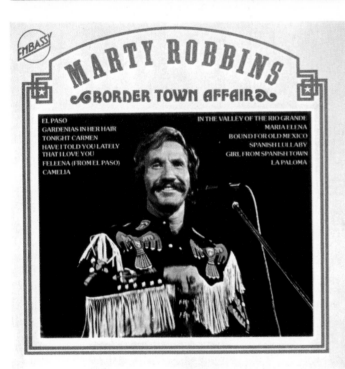

MARTY ROBBINS
BORDER TOWN AFFAIR

EL PASO
GARDENIAS IN HER HAIR
TONIGHT CARMEN
HAVE I TOLD YOU LATELY
THAT I LOVE YOU
FELEENA (FROM EL PASO)
CAMELIA

IN THE VALLEY OF THE RIO GRANDE
MARIA ELENA
BOUND FOR OLD MEXICO
SPANISH LULLABY
GIRL FROM SPANISH TOWN
LA PALOMA

Above: Devil Woman (Columbia). The title track was a pop hit that kept alive Robbins' image as a rock 'n' roller.

A first rate songwriter, his musical versatility is astonishing. In addition to the straight country, cowboy, and '50s rock mentioned above, he has recorded songs or albums of Hawaiian, Caribbean, and religious music.

Albums:
All Time Greatest Hits
  (Columbia/—)
Marty's Country (Columbia/—)
Devil Woman
  (Columbia/Embassy)
The Drifter (Columbia/CBS)
More Greatest Hits
  (Columbia/CBS)
Greatest Hits Vol 3
  (Columbia/CBS)
**Gunfighter Ballads And Trail
  Songs** (Columbia/—)
I Walk Alone (Columbia/—)
More Gunfighter Ballads
  (Columbia/CBS)
Return Of The Gunfighter
  (Columbia/—)
**Have I Told You Lately That I
  Love You?** (—/CBS)

Tonight Carmen (Columbia/—)
Portrait Of Marty (—/CBS)
Double-Barrelled (—/CBS)
  (a double package of
  Gunfighter Ballads and
  More Gunfighter Ballads
What God Has Done
  (Columbia/—)
The World Of . . . (Columbia/—)
No Signs Of Loneliness Here
  (Columbia/—)
Marty Robbins (MCA/—)
El Paso City (Columbia/CBS)
Adios Amigo (Columbia/CBS)
El Paso (—/Hallmark)
The Marty Robbins Collection
  (—/Hallmark)
Border Town Affair (—/Embassy)
Two Gun Daddy (—/MCA)
Good 'N' Country (—/MCA)

Left. Border Town Affair (Embassy). Contains his biggest ever crossover hit, El Paso, and concentrates throughout on songs with the Robbins-favored Mexican tinge.

Below: Marty Robbins. He began cutting his hit El Paso City album while under contract to MCA, but when he switched back to Columbia was allowed to take the master recordings with him.

Kenny Roberts

A super-yodeler known best in the north and north east, although he was actually born in Lenoir City, Tennessee, on October 14, 1927. He has recorded for Decca, Coral, Dot, King, and Starday, with his biggest hits being the yodeling extravaganzas **Chime Bells** and **She Taught Me How To Yodel.**

Albums:
Yodelin' Country Songs
(Vocalion/—)

Eck Robertson

Born Delaney, Madison County, Arkansas, November 20, 1887, old time fiddler Alexander 'Eck' Campbell Robertson grew up in Texas, and was probably the first country musician to make records. Following a Confederate Reunion, held in Virginia during 1922, he and fiddler Henry C. Gilliland, dressed as Western plainsmen, traveled to New York, where they persuaded Victor to let them record. On June 30 and July 1, 1922, they cut six titles, the first of these – including Robertson's version of **Sally Goodin** – being released in April, 1923. A month earlier, in March, 1923, Robertson had played **Sally Goodin** and **Arkansas Traveller** – the latter also being among the recorded tracks – over radio station WBAP, thus becoming the first country performer to promote his own discs over the air.

Carson J. Robison

Composer of such songs as **Barn-acle Bill The Sailor, Open Up Them Pearly Gates, Carry Me Back To The Lone Prairie, Little Green Valley, Blue Ridge Mountain Home, Left My Gal In The Mountains,** and the hit monolog **Life Gets Teejus Don't It,** Robison's formula of vaudeville, news songs and pure hillbilly made him one of the most popular country songwriters of his era.

Born Oswego, Kansas, August 4, 1890, he first sang at local functions in the Oswego area, moving to Kansas City in 1920, where he became one of the first country singers to ever appear on a radio show. In New York during 1924 he recorded as a whistler for Victor, teaming (as guitarist and co-vocalist) with ex-opera singer Vernon Dalhart (◆) to form a formidable hitmaking partnership that lasted for four years. After the termination of this association, Robison formed another duo – with Frank Luther (◆) (Francis Luther Crowe), whose voice resembled Dalhart's – also moving on to lead such bands as the Pioneers, the Buckaroos, the Carson Robison Trio and the Pleasant Valley Boys throughout the years.

Based in Pleasant Valley, New York, during the 1940s and '50s, Robison remained an active performer and writer right up to the time of his death on March 24, 1957.

Rockabilly

A fusion of rhythm and blues, western swing and pure honky tonk, rockabilly was the link between country and rock. Carl

Below: Jimmie Rodgers' My Time Ain't Long (RCA). Perhaps a preview of his early death – he had suffered ill health since childhood and died of tuberculosis in 1933.

Perkins (♦) often demonstrates the link between the rhythms of Hank Williams' (♦) **Kaw-Liga** and early rock as part of his act while chunks of pure rockabilly occur on the Ernie Ford (♦) boogies of the early '50s. The heyday of the style occurred between 1954 and 1958, the catalyst being Memphis, where an ex-radio announcer named Sam Phillips set up Sun Records, releasing Elvis Presley's (♦) initial **That's All Right** in 1954 and Carl Perkins' **Blue Suede Shoes** (the first million selling rockabilly disc) in 1956. Other Sun rockers included Charlie Feathers (♦), Johnny Carroll, Charlie Rich (♦), Jerry Lee Lewis (♦), Sonny Burgess and Roy Orbison (♦) while even such now generally accepted 'pure' country stylists as George Jones (♦), Ed Bruce (♦) and Dickey Lee (♦) appeared on Phillips' rockabilly sessions.

Eventually virtually every record company had its share of rockabillies, though today it is LA's Rollin' Rock label that spearheads the attack, providing regular releases by such performers as Jackie Lee Cochran, Ray Campi and Mac Curtis. The two volumes of **Rare Rockabilly** released by British MCA are also highly recommended.

Johnny Rodriguez

Young Chicano country star Juan Raul Davis Rodriguez was born Sabinal, Texas, December 10, 1952, the second youngest of nine children born to Andre and Isabel Rodriguez. Given a guitar by his brother Andres at the age of seven, during his high school days he became vocalist and lead guitarist with a rock outfit, though his main interest lay in country music. At 17 he recorded a demo disc in San Antonio but a possible record deal fell through. Then, following a couple of minor offenses (including the barbecuing of a goat he and some friends had stolen) Rodriguez was taken by a friendly Texas Ranger to see the owner of the Alamo Village resort in Bracketville – the belief being that if he obtained a regular job in music he would be more likely to

stay out of trouble. Employed by Happy Shahan (now Rodriguez's co-manager), he spent the summers of 1970 and '71 at the Village, driving a stagecoach, riding horses and singing for the tourists. It was during '71 that Tom T. Hall (♦) and Bobby Bare (♦) heard Rodriguez in Bracketville and urged him to come to Nashville.

This he did a few months later when, following the deaths of both his father and his brother Andres, he headed for the Music City to become guitarist with Tom T. Hall's band, The Storytellers. Hall, signed to Mercury Records, obtained the Chicano an audition with the label, Rodriguez proving impressive on the session and gaining an immediate contract.

His first release, **Pass Me By,** became a Top Ten hit before the end of '72, the follow up, **You Can Always Come Back,** being even more popular and heading some charts. Aided by his striking good looks and obvious sex appeal,

Rodriguez has since established himself as a performer of some substance, averaging three hits a year throughout 1973–76, all of his albums selling at gold level. His annual earnings are currently reputed to be in excess of half a million dollars, his possessions including a 27½ acre farm near Nashville.

Albums:
Introducing (Mercury/—)
All I Ever Meant To Do Was Sing (Mercury/—)
Just Get Up And Close The Door (Mercury/—)
Love Put A Song In My Heart (Mercury/—)
The Greatest Hits Of . . . (Mercury/—)
Reflecting (Mercury/—)

Johnny Rodriguez, goat thief, was arrested by a kindly Texas Ranger who believed in him and set him on the road to stardom; his story reads like a Hollywood script.

Above: Johnny Rodriguez' Reflecting (Mercury). Latest album from the successful Chicano singer.

Jimmie Rodgers

Known as The Father Of Country Music, James Charles Rodgers was born Meridian, Mississippi, September 8, 1897, the son of a section foreman on the Mobile and Ohio Railroad. Always in ill health as a child (his mother died of TB when Rodgers was four), he left school in 1911, becoming a water carrier on the M&O.

Working among the black railroad laborers, he picked up elements of their music, learning to play basic chords on both guitar and banjo.

He later moved on to perform other tasks on the railroad, holding down a job as a brakeman until ill health caught up with him once more and he was forced to seek a less strenuous occupation. An amateur entertainer for many years, he became a serious performer in 1925, initially becoming a black-face artist with a traveling medicine show then, in 1926, appearing in Johnson City, Tennessee, as a yodeler, assisted by guitarist Ernest Helton. Also in '26, Rodgers and his wife Carrie – whom he married in 1920 – moved to Asheville, North Carolina, there organizing the Jimmie Rodgers Entertainers, a hillbilly band comprised of Jack Pierce (guitar), Jack Grant (mandolin/banjo), Claude Grant (banjo) and Rodgers himself on banjo. Together they broadcast on station WWNC, Ashville, in 1927 for a period of six weeks, then set out to play a series of dates throughout the south east. Upon hearing that Ralph Peer (♦) of Victor Records was setting up a portable recording studio in Bristol, on the Virginia-Tennessee border, the Entertainers headed in that direction. But due to a dispute within their ranks (♦ The Tenneva Ramblers) Rodgers eventually recorded as a solo artist, selecting a sentimental ballad, **The Soldier's Sweetheart,** and a lullaby, **Sleep, Baby, Sleep** as his first offerings, these tracks being released in October, 1927, alongside the first release by the Carter Family (♦). The record met with instant acclaim, achieving encouraging sales, thus causing Victor to record further Rodgers sides throughout '27, these including **Ben Dewberry's Run, Mother Was A Lady** and **T For Texas,** the latter originally issued as **Blue Yodel** and becoming a million seller. By the middle of 1928, two more Blue Yodels (the series was eventually to include 13 such titles) were in the catalog and Rodgers had become America's

'Blue Yodeler', his amalgam of blues, country, folk music and down-to-earth songs, having worldwide appeal, thus making him the first true country superstar. Victor began to provide the ex-brakeman with various backing groups, jazzmen accompanying him on some tracks, Hawaiian musicians being drafted in to assist on others, even a whistler named Bob McGimsey being signed to accompany Rodgers on **Tuck Away My Lonesome Blues.** Rodgers' popularity grew daily, **Brakeman's Blues** becoming his third million-selling disc. He toured throughout the south and south west, appeared on radio and even made a short movie *The Singing Brakeman* (1929). And even though the Depression had hit America, his fans still bought his records by the tens of thousands. But Rodgers was gradually wasting away, the illness that he sang about in such songs as **TB Blues,** often forcing him to cancel performances. In 1931, he joined humorist Will Rogers in a series of concerts in aid of the drought sufferers in the south eastern regions, while in 1932 he began a twice-weekly radio show from station KMAC, San Antonio, Texas, but quit when he became hospitalized in early '33. However, later that year, though critically ill, he returned to Victor's New York recording studios on 24th Street, there cutting 12 sides over a period of eight days, a special cot being erected in which Rodgers rested between takes. The final song **Fifteen Years Ago Today** was completed on May 24, but during the following day Rodgers began to hemorrhage and then lapsed into a coma from which he never regained consciousness. He died on May 26, 1933.

Rodgers never appeared on any major radio show or even played Grand Ole Opry during his lifetime. But he, Fred Rose (♦) and Hank Williams (♦) were the first persons to be elected to the Country Music Hall Of Fame in 1961, which is indicative of his importance in the history of country music.

Albums:
Best Of The Legendary (RCA/—)
This Is Jimmie Rodgers (RCA/—)
My Rough And Rowdy Ways (RCA/—)

Famous Country Music Makers Vol 1 (—/RCA)
Famous Country Music Makers Vol 2 (—/RCA)

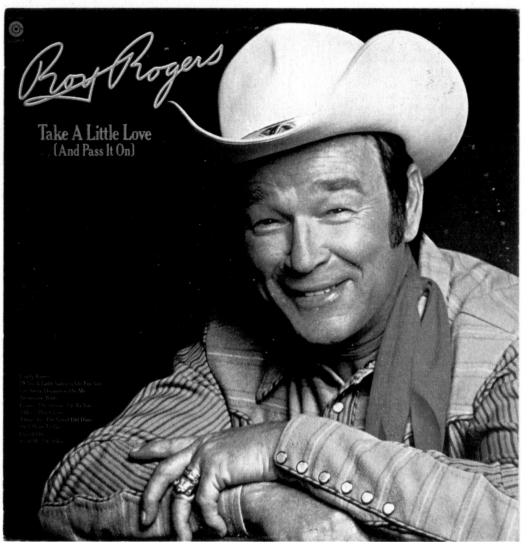

Take A Little Love (Capitol). *One of the most successful Western double acts (with horse Trigger), Rogers has also been recording for many years.*

David Rogers

David Rogers grew up in a country music environment, listening to Grand Ole Opry every Saturday night of his boyhood. Born Atlanta, Georgia, March 27, 1936, Rogers set his sights on becoming an entertainer at an early stage – but though in 1956 he was auditioned by Roger Miller (♦), then part of the Third Army Special Services Division, he failed to become a forces entertainer, merely being drafted in the normal manner. Upon his return to civilian life in 1958, he then began working at various venues in the Atlanta, Georgia, area, in 1962 signing for the city's Egyptian Ballroom, where he continued to work for nearly six years.

In October, 1967, he became a full member of Wheeling WWVA's Jamboree show, his first strong selling disc coming in 1968 via **I'd Be Your Fool Again,** a Columbia release. After further success that year with **I'm In Love With My Wife,** Rogers decided on a move to Nashville and began appearing on various package shows, also receiving bookings for top flight clubs and several syndicated TV programs.

Following a run of money-spinning discs, including **A World Called You** (1969), **I Wake Up In Heaven** (1970), **She Don't Make Me Cry, Ruby, You're Warm** (both 1971) and **Need You** (1972), Rogers signed for Atlantic, becoming the label's first country

act. Immediately he provided a top 20 hit in **Just Thank Me** (1973), following this with **Loving You Has Changed My Life,** a Top Ten hit during 1974. After a hit album in **Farewell To The Ryman,** Rogers then switched to the Republic label, having a modicum of chart success with a single, **Whispers And Grins,** during 1976.

Kenny Rogers

Born Houston, Texas, circa 1941, Rogers signed his first recording contract during his high school days. Later, after attending the University of Houston where he studied music and commercial art he began working with various groups including the Bobby Doyle Trio, the Kirby Stone Four and the New Christy Minstrels. Together with other ex-Minstrels he formed The First Edition in 1967, the group signing for Reprise Records and having a Top Five pop hit in 1968 with their version of Mickey Newbury's (♦) **Just Dropped In (To See What Condition My Condition Was In).** Other monster-selling discs followed, including **But You Know I Love You** (1969), **Ruby Don't Take Your Love To Town,** a fine Mel Tillis (♦) song about a disabled war veteran (1969), **Reuben James** (1969), **Something's Burning** (1970), **Tell It All, Brother** (1970) and **Heed The Call** (1970), the group's popularity gradually tapering off somewhat following the release of **Someone Who**

Cares, a 1971 high seller. Later becoming a solo artist – it had always been his grainy voice that helped to sell the Edition's brand of folk/country/pop – Rogers gained a recording contract with UA, having some success on the country scene with **Love Lifted Me,** a chart single in early 1976, but making even more impact with **Lucille,** a pure country saga regarding a faithless wife, which reached No 1 in the country charts during April, 1977, and made a surprising impact on popular charts as well.

Albums:
The First Edition's Greatest Hits *(Reprise/—)*
Kenny Rogers *(UA/UA)*
Love Lifted Me *(UA/—)*

Above Kenny Rogers (UA). His first solo album after leaving the First Edition, and the only one currently available in the UK.

Roy Rogers

A major Western movie star between 1938 and 1953 and known as the King Of The Cowboys, Rogers started out as Leonard Slye, born Cincinnati, Ohio, November 5, 1911, his biggest early musical influence being his father, who played mandolin and guitar. He grew up on a farm in Portsmouth, Ohio, area, and following High School became employed in a Cincinnati shoe factory for a while. During the 1920s he began playing and singing at local functions and in 1930 hitched a ride to California, initially becoming a peach picker then a truck driver. After stints with such groups as the Rocky Mountaineers and the Hollywood Hillbillies, he formed his own band The International Cowboys, later – with the aid of Tim Spencer and Bob Nolan – forming the Sons Of The Pioneers (♦). Though this outfit established a considerable reputation, Slye set his sights higher and began playing bit parts in films, first under the name of Dick Weston and then assuming his guise as Roy Rogers, eventually winning a starring role in *Under Western Skies*, a 1938 production. With his horse Trigger and frequent female co-star Dale Evans (♦) (whom he married in 1947) and occasional help from such people as the Sons Of The Pioneers and Spade Cooley (♦), Rogers became Gene Autry's (♦) only real rival, starring in over 100 movies and heading his own TV show in 1952–54. His films include *Carson City Kid* (1940), *Robin Hood Of The Pecos* (1942), *The Man From Music Mountain* (1944), *Along The Navajo Trail* (1946), *Night Time In Nevada* (1946) and *Son Of Paleface* (1952). A recording artist with RCA-Victor for many years, Rogers has recently cut albums for Word and 20th Century.

Albums:
Best Of Roy Rogers
(Camden/—)
Roy Rogers And Dale Evans
(Word/Word)
The Bible Tells Me So
(Capitol/—)
Happy Trails To You
(20th Century/—)

Linda Ronstadt

Excellent West Coast ballad singer who at one time sang plenty of country, but whose liaison with producer Peter Asher has made her into a top class singer of most rock styles.

Born July 15, 1946, in Tucson, Arizona, she arrived in Los Angeles in 1964 and formed the Stone Poneys. They signed to Capitol and 1967 saw the release of two albums, **Stone Poneys** and **Evergreen,** featuring a middle of the road approach and vocal harmonies. **Stone Poneys** yielded a hit single, Mike Nesmith's (♦) composition **Different Drum.** Linda next went out as a solo name and made two more albums, **Hand Sown, Home Grown** and **Silk**

Purse, the latter made with Nashville musicians.

Linda moved more towards her latter day direction in 1971 with the formation of a backing band consisting of future Eagles (♦) Glenn Frey, Don Henley and Randy Meisner, and the release of **Linda Ronstadt.**

A move to Asylum Records brought her Peter Asher as producer and **Don't Cry Now,** an album which made the US pop charts in 1973. 1974 saw the last of her Capitol albums (and many say her best to date) released. **Heart Like A Wheel** was an album she 'owed' Capitol, the last one of her contract with them and it broke her as a major artist containing as it did three gold singles. The pattern was set for an orgy of lushly enjoyable soft rock with **Prisoner In Disguise** and **Hasten Down The Wind** providing further riches. Linda is sometimes thought to be lacking in interpretive subtlety, but there is no doubt her voice is one of modern music's most distinctive and winning sounds.

The production on her records is immaculate, the backing work

deceptively loose. The heartfelt ballad is her forte but she has a penchant for material by Hank Williams (♦), the Everly Brothers (♦) and Buddy Holly (♦).

Albums:
Stoney End – with the Stone
  Poneys *(Pickwick/—)*
Silk Purse *(Capitol/—)*
Linda Ronstadt *(Capitol/—)*
Heart Like A Wheel *(Capitol/—)*
Different Drum *(Capitol/—)*
Don't Cry Now *(Asylum/—)*
Hand Sown, Home Grown
  (Capitol/—)
Beginnings – with the Stone
  Poneys *(Capitol/—)*
Prisoner In Disguise
  (Asylum/—)
Hasten Down The Wind
  (Asylum/—)
Greatest Hits *(Asylum/—)*
A Retrospective *(Capitol/—)*

Fred Rose

A founder of the Acuff-Rose Music Publishing Co, Rose was also an outstanding songwriter, his credits including **Be Honest With Me, Blue Eyes Crying In The Rain,**

Tears On My Pillow, Kaw-Liga, I'll Never Get Out Of This World Alive, Crazy Heart, Take These Chains From My Heart, Texarkana Baby, Settin' The Woods On Fire and a host of other country hits, many of which he wrote in partnership with such people as Gene Autry (♦), Hy Heath, Ray Whitley (♦) and Hank Williams (♦), Rose himself often writing under such assumed names as Floyd Jenkins and Bart Dawson.

Born Evansville, Indiana, August 24, 1897, Rose began his career as a honky tonk pianist in Chicago. He recorded for Brunswick, also for QRS, he and Fats Waller cutting piano rolls for the latter company. A pianist with Paul Whiteman's Orchestra during the King Of Jazz's heyday, Rose later formed a duo with singer-whistler Elmo Tanner, then moved into radio, gaining a CBS network show in Chicago during the early '30s. Already established as a songwriter, having penned such numbers as **Red Hot Mama** and **Deed I Do** for Sophie Tucker, Rose's travels took him to New York, Nashville and Hollywood, where he wrote a large quantity of songs

Fred Rose, empire builder, in kindly gangster pose.

for film usage, 16 of these for Gene Autry.

Returning to Nashville once more, he set up Acuff-Rose Publishing with Roy Acuff (♦) in 1942 – and though a member of ASCAP (American Society Of Composers, Authors And Publishers), he swung his weight behind the then less powerful fledgling BMI (Broadcast Music Incorporated) licensing organization, thus helping to break the hold that New York had on the songwriting industry. He also encouraged many songwriters and artists, in 1945 handing over the driving seat at Acuff-Rose to his son Wesley (♦) while he himself helped to establish the career of the up-and-coming Hank Williams (♦).

Rose died in Nashville, December 1, 1954, but his vast contribution to the cause of country music as a songwriter, publisher, producer, and executive was remembered in 1961, when he along with Jimmie Rodgers (♦) and Hank Williams became the first members of the Country Music Hall Of Fame.

Right: Mendocino (Oval). Doug Sahm and his band scored a hit with the title track in Mexican style, but are going on to the 'outlaw' vein.

Wesley Rose

Brought in to operate Acuff-Rose in December, 1945 (see Fred Rose (♦)), Wesley, who'd obtained a BS degree in accounting at Chicago's Walton School of Commerce, had formerly been employed in the accounting department of Standard Oil. Following his move to Nashville, he began expanding the whole horizon of Acuff-Rose's business, turning the first publishing company in Music City into one of the most successful in the world.

Following his father's death in 1954 Rose moved increasingly into the field of record production, initially fashioning material for such majors as RCA, Mercury, MGM and Columbia but later forming his own Hickory label and signing artists that included Sue Thompson (♦), Doug and Rusty Kershaw (♦), Don Gibson (♦), the Newbeats, Carl Smith (♦), Donovan and, of course, Roy Acuff (♦) himself. He was also instrumental in guiding the career of the Everly Brothers (♦).

A music industry leader, Wesley Rose was one of the founder members of the Country Music Association. He was born Chicago, Illinois, February 11, 1918.

Doug Sahm

Although Doug Sahm became known originally through his teeny-bop hit **She's About A Mover** (1965) and moved on to utilize blues, Mexican music, rock and country in his recordings; he has recently looked set to move more firmly into the country vein via the so-called Outlaw community of Austin (♦), Texas, where he now resides.

Born 1941 and raised in San Antonio, he was subject to the varied root musical influences of that area, but nevertheless found himself part of the mid '60s garage band movement in which many young American groups emulated the English bands of the day, with long hair and trendy clothes playing at least as important a part as the music. **She's About A Mover** featured a pumping 4/4 beat, Sahm's strange whining vocal and the amateurish sounding organ dabs of Augie Meyer. It is a sound that has since become Sahm's

trademark, with various refinements. The Sir Douglas Quintet, as his band was known, then moved to the burgeoning San Francisco and scored another, similar hit with the catchy **Mendocino.**

But Sahm was still a native Texan (a sentiment he has expressed in the song **Lawd, I'm Just A Coun-**try Boy In This Great Big Freaky City**) and the '70s have seen him in more ethnic mood, pursuing his love of blues, Mexican conjunto and good-time country. In 1973, he cut the impressive **Doug Sahm And Band** for Atlantic Records, his guests on that occasion including Bob Dylan, Dr John and David Bromberg.

Sir Douglas Quintet
Mendocino
SMASH

STEREO SRS 67115
PLAYABLE ON MODERN MONAURAL EQUIPMENT

Albums:
Mendocino (—/Oval)
Texas Rock For The Country Rollers (ABC/ABC)

Below: Doug Sahm with his Texas Tornadoes. 'You just can't live in Texas if you don't have a lot of soul' – the book of Sahm, 1969 Mendocino edition.

Above: Sir Douglas Quintet (Philips) from Doug Sahm, now resident in Austin.

Buffy Sainte-Marie

Hardly a pure country singer – she began as a folk singer and has since headed every which way – Buffy has nevertheless made several recordings of interest to C&W enthusiasts, her musical pleas on behalf of the Indian nation also being worthy of investigation by those professing an interest in western culture. Her birthplace is clouded in mystery though Sebago Lake, Maine (February 20, 1941) is the location most generally accepted. Born to Cree Indian parents, she was adopted at an early age and raised mainly in Massachusetts, never knowing her real family. She broke into the folk scene via appearances at New York's Gaslight Cafe, in Greenwich Village, during the early '60s, learning to play Indian mouth-bow from singer-songwriter and fellow Cree Patrick Sky. A codeine addict at one point in her career, she wrote a classic song, **Cod'ine,** about her experiences, though it proved to be Donovan's version of her **Universal Soldier** that brought her songwriting into perspective. Achieving considerable kudos through her appearances at the Newport Folk Festivals during the '60s, Buffy became signed to Vanguard Records, cutting her first album, **It's My Way** (containing both **Cod'ine** and **Universal Soldier**) for the label in 1964. By 1968, Buffy's intense vibrato was to be heard in a Nashville studio where she cut a pure country album **I'm Gonna Be A Country Girl Again,** achieving a mild pop hit with the title track, but having even more success with **Soldier Blue** (1971) the theme song from a somewhat horrific movie dealing with the massacre of the Indians during the last century.

Leaving Vanguard in 1973, she signed for MCA but after only two albums moved on to ABC, making a strong album **Sweet America** in 1976.

One Sainte-Marie composition, **Until It's Time For You To Go,** recorded by Buffy in 1965, later became a 1972 million seller for Elvis Presley (♦). Much of Buffy's recorded work lies outside the scope of this book but **I'm Gonna Be A Country Girl** and **A Native North-American Child** (both on Vanguard) the latter album being a plea on behalf of the North-American Indian, should be heard.

Above: Buffy Sainte-Marie. Hard to tie to any particular totem pole, you'll also find her name in rock and folk books.

Above: I'm Gonna Be A Country Girl Again (Pye)

Right: Moonshining (Chart)

Junior Samples

From Cumming, Georgia, he weighs nearly 300 lbs and is proud of being dubbed 'the world's biggest liar'. A sawmill worker for most of his life, during the early '60s Samples could be usually found spending his time with his wife and six children or merely fishing, drinking and relating his hilarious tales.

One such story told to a game warden eventually came to the ears of a Macon, Georgia, deejay, who interviewed Samples for his radio program. When the tape was played on the air it caused such a reaction that Chart Records purchased the recording and released a single **The World's Biggest Whopper,** which became a mild hit in mid 1967. This was followed by an album, **The World Of Junior Samples,** and a second ad lib LP, **Bull Session At Bull's Gap,** with Archie Campbell (♦). As a result of this success on record, Samples has become one of the mainstays on the Hee-Haw (♦) CBS-TV Show.

Art Satherley

Born Bristol, England, October 19, 1889, Arthur Edward Satherley, the son of a clergyman, worked on a Somerset farm during his boyhood days. Later, after being provided with a public school education, he joined the army, upon discharge becoming employed by the Triumph Motorcycle Company.

Fascinated by tales of the American West, in 1913 he traveled to Wisconsin, there obtaining a job grading timber for the Wisconsin Chair Company, makers of cabinets for Thomas Edison's phonographs. He became involved in the fast-growing record industry, helping to publicize Paramount Records as a 'race' label, selling blues discs by such as Blind Lemon Jefferson and Ma Rainey, and helping to break the stranglehold on the market achieved by Columbia, Okeh and Victor. But Paramount lagged behind after the development of the new electric recording process in 1925 and in 1928 Satherley left Paramount – where he'd become recording manager – to work for QRS Records. By 1930 he was working for ARC (♦), a firm which controlled a number of labels including Perfect, Oriole, Banner, and Melotone. Already established as a first rate blues talent scout, Satherley began to build up the company's country music catalog, signing Gene Autry (♦) in 1931 and gradually helping ARC to become the top country company in the land.

When ARC became Columbia in 1938, Satherley was retained by the company, continuing in an A&R role until his retirement in 1952, having added such acts as Lefty Frizzell (♦), Marty Robbins (♦), Little Jimmy Dickens (♦), Bill Monroe (♦) and Carl Smith (♦) to Columbia's roster. Satherley, who was also instrumental in aiding the careers of Roy Acuff (♦), Bob Wills (♦), Al Dexter (♦), Red Foley (♦), Tex Ritter (♦) and many others, was elected to the Country Music Hall Of Fame in 1971 for his work as a record pioneer.

Earl Scruggs
♦ Flatt And Scruggs

Below: Pioneer five-string banjoist Earl Scruggs.

Now Presenting Troy Seals (Atlantic). He has not been too successful on disc but is the composer of much-covered hits for other people, many of them on this album.

Troy Seals

Singer-songwriter Seals (born Big Hill, Kentucky, November 16, 1938) became a guitar player in his pre-teen years, later forming a band that played both rock and country material. While touring he met and married pop singer Jo Ann Campbell, forming a duo that recorded for Atlantic, but getting little reaction. Disenchanted, they left the music business, Seals working for a construction firm in Indianapolis. A year later he arrived in Nashville and began writing songs with such partners as Will Jennings, Don Goodman and Donnie Fritts, also striking up a friendship with sessionman David Briggs, who obtained Seals many bookings as a guitarist on record dates – the Kentuckian appearing on sessions with Ray Stevens (♦), Waylon Jennings (♦), Dobie Gray, Brenda Lee (♦) and others.

After cutting demos for Monument under the direction of Ray Pennington, some sides were mooted for Polydor but plans proved abortive and Seals eventually became one of Atlantic's initial country signings. However, within a year the company decided on a change of policy and Seals found himself label-less and forced to move on once more – this time to Columbia.

Despite his lackluster career on disc, Seals has fared well as a songwriter, providing **There's A Honky Tonk Angel** (a No 1 for Conway Twitty (♦) in 1974), **You Almost Slipped My Mind** (Kenny Price (♦)), **Girl In New Orleans** (Sammi Smith (♦)), **Country Red** (Gary Stewart (♦)) and the much-covered **We Had It All**.

Albums:
Troy Seals (Columbia/—)

Jeannie Seely

An Opry member since 1966, Jeannie was born in Pennsylvania, July 6, 1940 and grew up in the Titusville area. She began singing on local radio in Meadville, Pennsylvania at the age of 11 and during her high school era appeared on the prestigious Midwest Hayride show. Although she studied banking and associated subjects at the American Institute of Banking, Jeannie preferred the trappings of showbiz and moved to LA, signing for Four Star Music as a writer, and cutting a couple of unsuccessful discs for Challenge Records. With encouragement from Hank Cochran (♦), who later became her husband, she upped and headed for Nashville in 1965, becoming a writer for Tree International Music, a regular on the Porter Wagoner (♦) Show (replacing Norma Jean (♦)), also signing for Monument Records and having an instant hit with Cochran's **Don't Touch Me** (1966), a release which won her a Grammy award for the

Once a sawmill worker, Billy Joe Shaver lost two fingers in an accident. A controversial writer and personality, he has been married three times to the same woman!

Best Female C&W Vocal Performance.

In the wake of eight chart singles for Monument – these including **It's Only Love** (1966), **A Wanderin' Man** (1966) and **I'll Love You More** (1967) – Jeannie became a part of the Jack Green Show in 1969. Joining Green on the Decca label, the duo favorably impressed record buyers via **I Wish I Didn't Have To Miss You,** a Top Five disc in 1969, Jeannie's biggest solo hits arriving with **Can I Sleep In Your Arms?** in 1973, and **Lucky Ladies** (1974).

Albums:
Greatest Hits (Monument/—)

Billy Joe Shaver

A new wave singer-songwriter who rose to prominence while in his mid '30s, Shaver was a part time poet who set his sights on Nashville after hearing Waylon Jennings (♦) sing.

Born Corsicana, Texas, he moved to Waco at the age of 12, spending his early life employed at a sawmill, punching cattle, doing carpentry or performing various menial tasks as a farmhand. His ambitions as a songwriter later led him to Nashville where he found his wares rejected by every publisher. Shaver, on the brink of starvation, was forced to return to Texas. However, on a later trip to the Music City he sold a song to Bobby Bare (♦) that became the B side of a hit and he became signed as a writer to Bare's own Return Music Publishing Company, achieving something of a breakthrough when Kristofferson (♦) recorded his **Good Christian Soldier** (1971). Next, Tom T. Hall latched on to Shaver's songs, likewise Dottie West (♦), Jan Howard (♦), Jerry Reed (♦), Tex Ritter (♦) and Jim Ed Brown (♦), his reputation as one of the most potent new writers in Nashville being established when Waylon Jennings cut **Honky Tonk Heroes** (1973) an album of songs, all but one of which had been penned by Shaver. An often controversial writer – one of his songs **Black Rose** deals with the subject of interracial marriage – he became a fully fledged recording artist when Kris Kristofferson produced **Old Five And Dimers Like Me,** Shaver's first album, for the Monument label. He is perhaps best known for his tribute to Willie Nelson (♦), a theme song of the Austin (♦) movement called **Willie The Wandering Gypsy And Me.**

Albums:
When I Get My Wings (Capricorn/—)

Dorothy Shay

Known as the Park Avenue Hillbilly, Dorothy's gimmick was to attire herself in exquisite gowns then perform such incongruous, novelty hillbilly numbers as **Another Notch On Father's Shotgun** and **Makin' Love, Mountain Style.** Very popular during the 1940s, she recorded for Columbia her biggest hit **Feudin' And Fightin'** (1947), a song originally from the score of a Broadway show. Born 1923, she appeared in an Abbott and Costello movie *Comin' Round The Mountain* in 1951.

JEAN SHEPARD, "I'm A Believer"

Jean Shepard

A leading supporter of ACE, an association devoted to keeping country music free from pop contamination, Jean Shepard will certainly consider many areas of this book as being outside the pale. 'John Denver (♦), Glen Campbell (♦) and Mac Davis (♦) are not country,' she proclaimed at the Wembley Festival in April, 1977. Accordingly her own work is pure '50s type country, full of hard-sob ballads and full throttle honky tonk, all of which she sings with almost unbelievable conviction.

Born Pauls Valley, Oklahoma, November 21, 1933, Jean originally sang and played bass with an all-girl western swing outfit known as the Melody Ranch Girls. After impressing Hank Thompson (♦) via a Melody Ranch Girls – Brazos Valley Boys joint gig, Jean became signed to Capitol Records in 1953,

that same year gaining her first No 1 with **Dear John Letter,** a duet recorded with Ferlin Husky (♦). Next came a sequel, **Forgive Me, John** (1953) then a brace of 1955 solo winners with **Satisfied Mind** and **Beautiful Lies.** Jean became a regular on the Red Foley (♦) Show over KWTO, two years later moving to Nashville and attaining Opry status. But her hits remained infrequent until 1964 (shortly after the death of husband Hawkshaw Hawkins (♦)) when her recording of **Second Fiddle (To An Old Guitar** sparked off a long flow of successes that has included **Happy Hangovers To You** (1966), **If Teardrops Were Silver** (1966), **Your Forevers (Don't Last Very Long)** (1967), **Then He Touched Me** (1970), **Another Lonely Night** (1970), **Slippin' Away** (1973) and **At The Time** (1974). Jean, who also cut a trio of hit singles with Ray Pillow (♦) during 1966–67, was still sing-

Above: I'm A Believer (UA). Jean's favorite cause is the purity of country music.

Right: Jean Shepard, whose introduction to country music was listening to Jimmie Rodgers on a wind-up Victrola.

ing with as much authority as ever during the mid '70s, being one of the best-received female vocalists on that '77 Wembley gig.

Albums:
Slippin' Away *(UA/—)*
I'm A Believer *(UA/UA)*
For The Good Times
  (Capitol/—)
Mercy Ain't Love Good
  (UA/UA)
Poor Sweet Baby *(UA/UA)*
The Good Shepard *(—/UA)*
The Best Of Jean Shepard
  (—/Capitol)
Best Of . . . *(Power Pak/—)*

T. G. Sheppard

Backing musician, rock singer, record promotion man and country singer, T. G. Sheppard got his break in 1976 when his single **Devil In The Bottle** topped the country charts. His own description of his style: 'an earthy country sound with pop overtones' does ring true (besides showing the born promotion man's ability to make simultaneous pitches and still appear credible).

Originally influenced by country and gospel music in his birthplace of Humboldt, Tennessee, T. G. (real name Bill Browder) later settled in Memphis and became guitarist and backup singer in Travis Whymark's band. Securing a contract with Atlantic Records and using the name Brian Stacy, he had a number of pop-styled singles released in the early '60s, including **High School Days** which was a small pop hit. In 1965 he got married and took a hard look at his modest singing career, but as he still wanted to stay in records he became a promotion man. After a stint as the RCA Memphis promotion man he formed his independent production and promotion company, Umbrella Pro-

ductions. He picked up **Devil In The Bottle** from writer Bobby David and, in desperation, after several companies turned it down, demoed it himself, eventually finding an unlikely outlet in Tamla Motown who were just getting into country.

Since the name Bill Browder would coincide with his promotional activities he called himself T. G. Sheppard, after spotting a bunch of German shepherd dogs through an office window.

Another single, **Solitary Man,** also entered the country charts in 1975, and the latest Sheppard hit is the Sterling Whipple song **Show Me A Man.** The record label Melodyland has now become Hitsville after a Los Angeles church named Melodyland claimed the name.

Right: Solitary Man (Hitsville). Title track was a country hit.

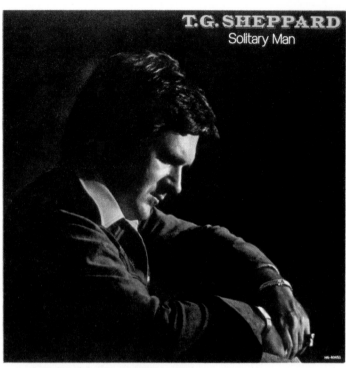

T.G. SHEPPARD
Solitary Man

Albums:
T. G. Sheppard *(Melodyland/—)*
Motels And Memories *(Melodyland/—)*
Solitary Man *(Hitsville/—)* – a slightly different version of this album is available on British Hitsville under the title **Nashville Hitmaker.**

Below: T. G. Sheppard. His early singing career was in pop; he scored a few small hits but went into promotion before returning as a country singer.

Billy Sherrill

Ex R & B producer who developed a smooth line in modern country production during the '60s, Sherrill sparked off success for Tammy Wynette (♦), and later for Tanya Tucker (♦), and in the early '70s he helped revitalize the career of ex rock 'n' roller Charlie Rich, the seductive, soporific, late-night sound being dubbed 'Country-politan' by the critics.

Working for Columbia and Epic, Sherrill evolved a masterly way of balancing steel guitars and orthodox country instruments against orchestras. Such was the success of this fine balance, with all the rough edges knocked off, that records made by Sherrill sold in spectacular quantities and helped identify the 'Nashville Sound' as mainstream country to most people when in fact it was just part of a larger whole.

Steve Sholes

Chiefly known for his activities as A&R Manager for RCA's Country Music and R&B Division, Stephen Sholes was born Washington DC, February 12, 1911. In 1929 he commenced working for RCA, only breaking this long relationship while attending college and performing Army service during World War II. In 1945 Sholes returned to RCA once more, receiving an appointment to his A&R position later that year. He became instrumental in the label, accumulating one of the most impressive country music rosters in the world; he signed such acts as Jim Reeves (♦), Hank Snow (♦), The Browns (♦), Elvis Presley (♦) and Chet Atkins (♦), whom he originally visualized as RCA's answer to Capitol's Merle Travis (♦), but later appointed as his A&R assistant.

Above: R&B piano and sax player Billy Sherrill, now producing country for Epic.

During the late '50s and early '60s, the dynamic Sholes gained promotion after promotion within the framework of RCA – though he never lost touch with Nashville, and helped to conduct a fund-raising campaign aimed at building the Country Music Hall of Fame and Museum.

Elected to the Hall of Fame himself in 1967, Sholes died on April 22, 1968, while en route to the airport from RCA's Nashville studios.

Shel Silverstein

Cartoonist with *Playboy* magazine for over 20 years, Silverstein is a bald-pated, sometimes anarchistic singer-songwriter whose early albums include **Hairy Jazz** (1961), cut with the Red Onion Jazz Band. Though as a performer he has hardly been country-oriented, he has nevertheless provided numerous songs for country artists (predominantly Bobby Bare (♦)), the most notable of these being **A Boy Named Sue,** a Grammy award winner for Johnny Cash (♦)

Above: Freakin' at the Freakers' Ball (CBS)

in 1969. Prime provider of material for Dr Hook, an outrageous rock band with some country pretensions, Silverstein's more recent albums have included **A Boy Named Sue** (RCA), **Freaking At The Freakers' Ball** (Columbia) and **Inside** (Atlantic). He also wrote a film score for **Who Is Harry Kellerman And Why Is He Saying Those Terrible Things About Me?**

Although as a songwriter he specializes in the catchy and clever, occasionally he proves himself capable of the sincerity and sensitivity inherent in country songwriting, as with his **Here I Am Again** (recorded by Loretta Lynn (♦).

Below: Shel Silverstein illustrating the benefits of being employed by Playboy magazine. How does he find time to write songs and make albums?

Shelby Singleton

One of the shrewdest businessmen on the country music scene, producer-publisher-record company owner Singleton (born Waskom, Texas, December 16, 1931) first moved into the music business as a promotion man in the Shreveport, Louisiana, area, there meeting his wife Margie – a singer who later had hits on Starday, Mercury and Ashley. With Mercury Records he worked in New York and Nashville, first as a product manager, then as a producer, fashioning such hits as Brook Benton's **Boll Weevil Song** (1960) and Bruce Channel's **Hey, Baby** (1962). Placed in charge of Mercury's Smash subsidary, he rose to become vice-president of the parent company, along the way signing Jerry Lee Lewis (♦), Charlie Rich (♦) and other major artists. But in 1966, following a nine year stay with Mercury, Singleton resigned and set up his own production company, having his biggest success when in 1968 he produced a session by a then unknown singer named Jeannie C. Riley (♦) for his own Plantation label, the result being **Harper Valley PTA**, a single that sold several million copies.

Owner of Sun Records, which he purchased in 1969, thus acquiring a supply on invaluable masters by Johnny Cash (♦), Jerry Lee Lewis and others, Singleton has also been instrumental in setting up several other labels, including SSS and Silver Fox, and also runs a publishing company, Shelby Singleton Music, which employs well over 30 writers.

Asher And Little Jimmy Sizemore

One of the early professional bands on the Grand Ole Opry consisted of Asher Sizemore (born June 6, 1906, in Manchester, Kentucky) and his young son Jimmy (born January 29, 1928), who specialized in sentimental hearth and home type ballads and songs, and were one of the first Opry acts to put out a very successful songbook. Asher had little Jimmy on the radio as early as the age of three, and the Opry's Harry Stone, having heard them on WHAS in Louisville, brought them to the Opry where they stayed for some ten years (1932–1942), recording for Bluebird Records as well, although no big hits emerged.

After the war they appeared on KXEL, Waterloo, Iowa, SMOX, St Louis, WHO in Des Moines, and WSB in Atlanta, often with Asher's younger son Buddy Boy, who was killed in Korea late in 1950. Jimmy Sizemore is currently a radio executive in Arkansas, while Asher died some years ago.

Asher and Little Jimmy in a photo taken from the front of the 1936 edition of Fireside Treasures, a folio of old songs.

The Skillet Lickers

Gid Tanner *fiddle*
Clayton McMichen *fiddle*
Riley Puckett *guitar*
Lowe Stokes *fiddle*
Bert Layne *fiddle*
Fate Norris *banjo, harmonica*
Ted Hawkins *mandolin, fiddle*
Arthur Tanner *banjo, guitar*
Mike Whitten *guitar*
Hoke Rice *guitar*
Gordon Tanner *fiddle*

An extremely popular and influential Atlanta-based string band of the 1920s and 1930s. Led by Gid Tanner, the band included two other country music figures of great importance in their own right: Clayton McMichen and Riley Puckett.

Tanner (1885–1960), like all the bandmembers through the years a Georgian, first recorded with Puckett (1894–1945), the b-ind guitarist, for Columbia in 1924, and continued to record with various permutations of the Skillet Lickers for Columbia and Victor for the next decade, although the band name did not actually exist until McMichen (1900–1970) joined Tanner, Puckett, and Norris in 1926.

Their material, for the most part, was composed of fiddle breakdowns, minstrel songs, and a bizarre and hilarious series of eighteen spoken comedy records called **A Corn Likker Still In Georgia,** although the fiddle breakdown **Down Yonder** is probably most closely associated with them.

Their sound together was rough and wild, typically featuring the fine twin fiddling of McMichen and Layne, falsetto shouts and snatches of verses by Tanner, and often Puckett's bluesy singing. All three mainstays went their separate ways after 1934, Tanner dying on May 13, 1960, but the legacy of The Skillet Lickers is one of humorous, extremely good natured old time music played in the most spirited of styles. They were unique, but their sound was in many ways the sound of an old time substyle of country music already on the way out as they were recording it.

Albums:
The Skillet Lickers *(County/—)*
The Skillet Lickers, Vol 2 *(County/—)*
Gid Tanner And His Skillet Lickers *(Rounder/—)*
A Corn Likker Still In Georgia *(Voyager/—)*
Riley Puckett *(GHP/—)*

Jimmie Skinner

A songwriter of some skill, Skinner never really climbed past the half way stage on the ladder of success as a performer and at one time was probably better known as the owner of a mail order record store, the Jimmie Skinner Music Center, in Cincinnati, though he has since given up this business and moved to the Nashville area.

Born near Berea, Kentucky, Skinner's first success came as a songwriter, one of his compositions, **Doin' My Time,** proving a minor hit in 1941. A deejay during the '40s, he had his own show on WNOX, Knoxville, Tennessee, also appearing on other stations. He signed as a performer with Mercury Records during the mid '50s and had Top Ten hits with **I Found My Girl In The USA** (1957) and **Dark Hollow** (1957), also gaining further chart entries and cutting a much sought after album of Jimmie Rodgers (♦) songs. Since that time he's recorded for such labels as Decca, Starday, King and, more recently, Vetco. Many of his songs have become standards in bluegrass repertoire, including (in addition to the above) **You Don't Know My Mind,** and **Will You Be Satisfied That Way.**

Albums:
Requestfully Yours *(Vetco/—)*
Sings The Blues *(Vetco/—)*
Sings Bluegrass *(Vetco/—)*
Original Greatest Hits *(Power Pak/—)*

Patsy Sledd

A popular performer, Patsy has worked on the George Jones (♦) and Tammy Wynette (♦) Show, often making backup appearances on Wynette recordings. Her TV dates have included spots on Hee-Haw (♦) and Midwestern Hayride, while she has also sung on shows headed by Del Reeves (♦), Billy Walker (♦) and the Wilburn Brothers (♦).

Born Falcon, Missouri, January 29, 1944, Patsy initially sang with her sisters in a group known as the Randolph Sisters, performing in churches and at other Falcon venues. In 1965, she moved to Nashville with her then-husband Dale Sledd, longtime guitarist with the Osborne Brothers (♦), there impressing Roy Acuff, who invited her to work on his Caribbean tour in 1967. Patsy later joined the Acuff Show for Stateside tours and a trip to Vietnam. Signed to United Artists Records in 1968, she had three singles released and sunk without trace. But better luck came with a Mega contract in 1972, with her first release, **Nothing Can Stop My Love** becoming a sizeable hit.

Albums:
Chip, Chip *(Mega/—)*

Arthur 'Guitar Boogie' Smith

Leader of an outfit known as the Crackerjacks, guitarist-banjoist-mandolin player Arthur Smith was born April 1, 1921, in Clinton, South Carolina. One of the State's most popular performers, he played on radio station WBT, Charlotte for over 20 years, achieving national fame when his recording of **Guitar Boogie,** originally issued by the Superdisc label, was subsequently released on MGM, providing Smith with a 1947 million-seller. After several years of hits for MGM, many of which were of the eight-to-a-bar genre, Smith moved on to other labels. He became signed to Starday and Dot during the '60s, more recently cutting material for Monument and CMH. His **Feuding Banjos** (frequently called **Dueling Banjos**) became internationally well known as a result of its prominent part in the film *Deliverance.*

Albums:
Mister Guitar *(Starday/—)*
Battling Banjos *(Monument/—)*

Below: Arthur 'Guitar Boogie' Smith and his Crackerjacks. A gold record winner for MGM during the 1940s, he was still banjoing for Monument in the '70s.

Fiddlin' Arthur Smith

Born Dixon County, Tennessee, Smith was a railroad worker who during the early '30s joined Sam and Kirk McGee (♦) in a trio known as the Dixieliners. Becoming an Opry favorite, Smith toured under the auspices of WSM for several years, sometimes playing with the McGees, at other times working with his own trio; the latter group acquired something of a national reputation with their recording of **There's More Pretty Girls Than One** in 1936.

Later, Smith moved on to play with the Delmore Brothers (♦) and throughout the '40s and '50s worked variously as a sideman or with units of his own, much of it on the West Coast, where he appeared in many western movies with Jimmy Wakely (♦) and others. The 1960s brought him a new lease of life, thanks to the advent of the folk festivals and the rediscovery of many folk heroes by a new and youthful audience – this period of fresh acceptance was marked by **Fiddlin' Arthur Smith,** an album for Starday in 1963, and a Mike Seeger-masterminded Smith-McGee Brothers set for Folkways.

Albums:
The McGee Brothers With Arthur Smith (Folkways/—)

Below: Cal Smith.

Cal Smith

Born Calvin Grant Shofner on April 7, 1932, Gans, Oklahoma, Smith was raised in Oakland, California. After the usual round of talent contests and local engagements, he became a regular on the California Hayride TV show, gaining his first regular club job in San Jose, California, during the early 1950s. Later, after engagements that included a spell as a deejay, Smith became MC and vocalist with Ernest Tubb's (♦) Texas Troubadours, remaining for the band for a period of five and a half years. Through Tubb, Smith became signed to Kapp Records, initially charting with **The Only Thing I Want,** in 1967, then continuing to keep the label supplied with a number of lower-level hits (**Drinking Champagne, It Takes All Night Long, Heaven Is Just A Touch Away** etc) through to 1971, when his discs began appearing on Decca. Around the same time, his chart placings began to rise; **I've Found Someone Of My Own** became a Top Five hit in 1972, a year during which Smith spent 202 days on the road, playing in such places as Alaska and Hawaii. In 1973, he earned yet another top placing with **The Lord Knows I'm Drinking,** capping even this success with that of **Country Bumpkin,** a massive seller during mid 1974 and a release that won him his first CMA award – for Single Of The Year. Ernest Tubb once predicted that it would take Cal Smith a long time to get to the top but that he would certainly get there someday. It seems he knew what he was talking about.

Albums:
Best Of Cal Smith (MCA/—)

Country Bumpkin (MCA/—)
I've Found Someone Of My Own (MCA/—)
Jason's Farm (MCA/—)
My Kind Of Country (MCA/—)
Time To Pay The Fiddler (MCA/—)
Introducing Cal Smith (—/MCA)

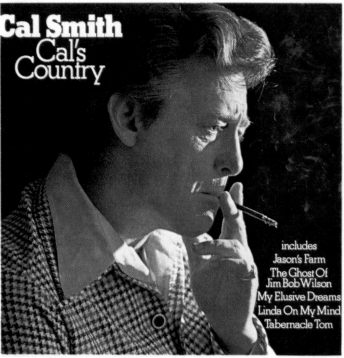

Above: Cal's Country (MCA) from the ex-Texas Troubador.

Above: Carl Smith Sings
Bluegrass (Columbia).
A break from his normal
ballad style.

Right: A Way With Words
(DJM). A British release
containing twelve tracks
recorded for Hickory and
produced by Wesley Rose.

CARL SMITH
A Way With Words

Carl Smith

Born Maynardsville, Tennessee, March 15, 1927, Carl Smith sold flower seeds to pay for his first guitar, then cut grass to pay for lessons. His first break in show business came a few years later, with radio station WROL, Knoxville, Tennessee. Then in 1950, Jack Stapp, at that time program director of WSM, asked Smith to come to Nashville and work on the WSM morning show. Soon after, he won a place on the Opry, signed a contract with Columbia Records and, with his second release, **Let's Live A Little,** had a smash hit. That same year (1951), he was voted No 1 country singer by several polls and accrued three further chartbusters via **If Teardrops Were Pennies, Mr Moon** and **Let Old Mother Nature Have Her Way.** During the '50s and '60s he was rarely out of the charts, averaging around three hits per year, the biggest of these being **Don't Just Stand There, Are You Teasing Me?** (1952); **Trademark, Hey, Joe** (1953); **Loose Talk, Back Up, Buddy Boy, Go, Boy, Go** (1954); **Kisses Don't Lie, There She Goes** (1955) and **Ten Thousand Drums** (1959), all Top Five items. Following his success on radio Smith moved on to TV, working for such shows as Four Star Jubilee (ABC/TV) and Carl Smith's Country Music Hall, a weekly networked show in Canada, syndicated to several US stations. He's also guested on many other shows and been featured in two movies – *The Badge Of Marshall Brennan* and *Buffalo Guns.*

In 1957, Smith married country singer Goldie Hill (♦) (his second wife; the first having been June Carter) and moved to a ranch near Franklin, Tennessee, to bring up his four children, Carlene, Lorri Lynn, Carl Jnr and Larry Dean. Today he owns a 500 acre ranch with a ranch-styled home, a two storey colonial house converted into an office, another house used for storage, plus some 50 horses and 200 head of cattle. Early in 1974, the singer left Columbia Records after a 24 year stay with the label (during which time he sold around 15 million discs) and moved on to Hickory Records, for whom he's since had some minor success.

Albums:
Bluegrass (Columbia/—)
Country On My Mind
  (Columbia/—)
Don't Say You're Mine
  (Columbia/—)
Greatest Hits (Columbia/—)

Greatest Hits Vol 2
  (Columbia/—)
A Tribute To Roy Acuff
  (Columbia/—)
The Way I Lose My Mind
  (Hickory/—)
A Way With Words (—/DJM)

Born in the same town as Roy Acuff, Carl Smith has had a long and consistently successful career, mainly with Columbia. Today he spends most of his time on his ranch near Franklin, Tennessee.

211

Connie Smith

In 1963, Connie Smith was just another pretty Ohio housewife, but in winning an amateur talent contest she was heard by Bill Anderson (♦) – the result being an offer to sing with Anderson and an opportunity to embark on a recording career which has, at the present time, allowed her to accrue a tally of nearly 30 Top Ten hits.

Born Elkhart, Indiana, August 14, 1941, one of a family of 16, Connie learned to play guitar while hospitalized with a serious leg injury. A performer at local events, she later married and settled down to a normal life of household chores. But following her discovery by Anderson she became signed to RCA Records, creating a tremendous impact with her initial release **Once A Day,** an Anderson-penned song that became a country No 1 in 1964. An overnight success, Connie was signed to make her TV debut on the Jimmy Dean Show (♦), won the plaudit Most Promising Singer of 1964 from *Billboard* and – in the wake of three early '65 hits with **Then And Only Then, Tiny Blue Transistor Radio,** and **I Can't Remember** – Connie became an Opry star on June 13, 1965.

Since that time, Connie has appeared on scores of TV and radio shows, and has featured in such country-oriented movies as *Las Vegas Hillbillies, Road To Nashville* and *Second Fiddle To A Steel Guitar*. Also, recording mainly Bill Anderson and Dallas Frazier (♦) numbers, she's had hits with **Ain't Had No Lovin', The Hurtin's All Over** (both 1966), **Cincinnati, Ohio, Burning A Hole In My Mind** (both 1967), **I Never Once Stopped Loving You** (1970), **Just One Time** (1971), **If It Ain't Love, Just For What I Am** (both 1972), **Love Is What You're Looking For** (1973), **Til (I Kissed You)** and **I Don't Wanna Talk About It Anymore** (1976).

One of the many country artists with deep religious convictions, the diminutive Connie, who

Above: Connie Smith. 'Five days on the road each month is what I allow myself,' she once said. 'The rest of the time is for Christianity and my family.' She never works clubs where alcohol is served.

spends a great deal of her time doing social work, toured Australia, New Zealand and Japan during 1972, raising funds for the children of Bangladesh.

Albums:
God Is Abundant *(Columbia/—)*
If It Ain't Love *(RCA/—)*
That's The Way Love Goes
  (Columbia/—)
I Never Knew *(Columbia/—)*
I've Got A Lot Of Hurtin' Done Today/I've Got My Baby Back On My Mind *(Columbia/—)*
Sings Hank Williams Gospel
  (Columbia/—)
The Song We Fell In Love To
  (Columbia/CBS)
I Don't Wanna Talk
  (Columbia/—)
Even The Bad Times Are Good
  – with Nat Stuckey *(Camden/—)*
Back In Baby's Arms *(—/RCA)*
Best Of Connie Smith *(—/RCA)*
Greatest Hits – Vol 1 *(—/RCA)*

Connie Smith Sings Hank Williams Gospel (Columbia).

If It Ain't Love (RCA Victor).

As Long As There's A Sunday (Elektra).

Sammi Smith

Now considered as a country rebel – to be mentioned alongside Jennings (♦), Nelson (♦) and Co, Sammi originally made her mark as a crossover artist of some potential, her version of Kristofferson's (♦) **Help Me Make It Through** (CMA Single Of The Year, 1971) selling over two million copies.

Born Orange, California, August 5, 1943, she grew up in Oklahoma, playing clubs in that area at the age of 12. Encouraged in her career by Oklahoma City songwriter/recording studio owner Gene Sullivan, she was heard by Tennessee Three bassist Marshall Grant, who persuaded her to make the inevitable trip to Nashville where she became a Columbia recording act. Some moderate hits followed – including **So Long, Charlie Brown** (1968) and **Brownsville Lumberyard** (1969) – after which Sammi moved on to the Mega label in 1970, recording Mega's first album, **He's Everywhere,** the title track becoming a chart single. A second track from the same album was then selected as a follow up, the amazingly successful **Help Me Make It Through The Night,** the sales of which prompted Mega to retitle the parent album in line with the single and to embark on a re-promotion campaign.

However, since that initial monster single, little else has gone Sammi's way on disc. **Then You Walk In,** released a few months later, did manage to sneak into the Top Ten during 1971 – but, despite a change of record companies, she's had no further major chart entries credited to her name.

Albums:
The Very Best Of . . . *(UA/—)*
As Long As There's A Sunday *(Elektra/—)*

I've Got To Have You (Pye).

Left: Connie Smith, performer at PTA meetings and other local functions in her home town.

Hank Snow

The most revered of all Canadian country performers, Clarence Eugene Snow was born Liverpool, Nova Scotia, May 9, 1914. Leaving home at 12, he became a cabin boy on a freighter for four years but in his teens began singing in Nova Scotia clubs, obtaining his first radio show in 1934, on CHNS, Halifax, Nova Scotia. Known initially as the 'Yodeling Ranger' and later as the 'Singing Ranger', he became signed to RCA-Victor in 1934, his first sides for the company being **Lonesome Blue Yodel** and **Prisoned Cowboy.**

Despite a move to the US during the mid '40s and appearances on such shows as the WWVA Jamboree, Snow remained virtually unknown south of the Canadian border until 1949 when, following a disappointing Opry performance on January 7, his recording of **Marriage Vows** became a Top

Ten hit. In 1950 he became an Opry regular, that same year seeing the release of **I'm Moving On,** a self-penned hit that became a US No 1, remaining in the country charts for well over 40 weeks. Throughout the '50s and early '60s Snow continued to provide RCA with a huge number of Top Ten singles – several of them being train songs, revealing his debt to Jimmie Rodgers (♦), a singer he had idolized as a boy. His immaculately annunciated ballads also attracted the attention of myriad record buyers. Too numerous to list, Snow's hits include **Golden Rocket** (1950), **Rhumba Boogie** (1951), **I Don't Hurt Anymore** (1954) and the tongue-twisting **I've Been Everywhere** (1962), all country No 1's, **I'm Moving On** and **I Don't Hurt Anymore** both becoming million sellers.

Snow, who has consistently fought against what he believes to be over-commercialization of country music, has proved to be one of C&W's most traveled ambassa-

dors, appearing in his somewhat stagey cowboy attire at venues all over the world, including some that were uncomfortably close to the Vietnamese war front.

His eldest son, Jimmie Rodgers Snow, is both a country performer and a traveling evangalist.

Albums:
Best Of Hank Snow (RCA/RCA)
Best Of Vol 2 (RCA/RCA)
Grand Ole Opry Favorites (RCA/RCA)
Hello Love (RCA/—)
Lonesome Whistle (Camden/—)
Snowbird (Camden/—)
When My Blue Moon Turns To Gold (Camden/—)
Wreck Of The Ol' '97 (Camden/—)
I'm Movin' On (Camden/—)
That's You And Me (RCA/RCA)
You're Easy To Love (RCA/RCA)
Tracks And Trains (—/RCA)
Live From Evangel Temple (RCA/—) – with Jimmie Rodgers Snow
Hits Covered By Snow (—/RCA)

Above: Sons of the Pioneers (l to r) Karl Farr, Bob Nolan, Tim Spencer, Hugh Farr and Len Slye (Roy Rogers).

Songs of Tragedy (RCA Victor).

Famous Country Music Makers (—/RCA)
Famous Country Music Makers Vol 2 (—/RCA)
Award Winners (—/RCA)

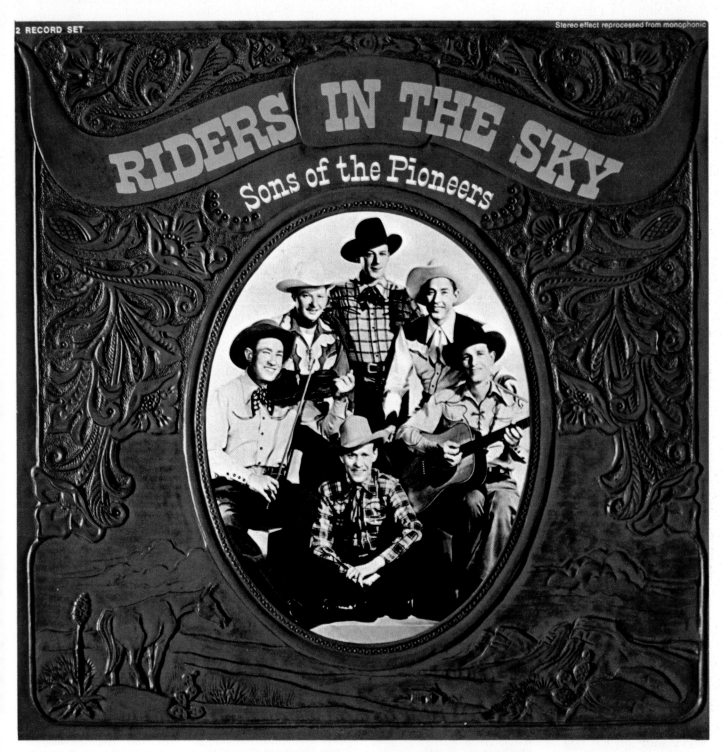

2 RECORD SET

Stereo effect reprocessed from monophonic

RIDERS IN THE SKY
Sons of the Pioneers

Sons Of The Pioneers

Originally a guitars/vocals trio when formed by Roy Rogers (♦) Bob Nolan and Tim Spencer in 1934 as the Pioneer Trio, the name changed to the Sons Of The Pioneers in deference to the American Indian heritage of new members Karl and Hugh Farr. They did much radio work during the '30s and recorded variously for Decca, Columbia and RCA. Movies also figured large for them and they appeared in many of those featuring Rogers after he had left the band to pursue his film career. A few of the films in which the Sons were involved included *Rhythm On The Range* (1936), *Hollywood Canteen* (1944), *Gay Rancheros* (1944) and *Melody*

Time (1948). Other members of the group have included Lloyd Perryman, Ken Carson, Ken Curtis, Pat Brady, Doye O'Dell, Dale Warren, Duece Spriggins, Tommy Doss, Shug Fisher (♦) and Rusty Richards. Bob Nolan composed the group's biggest hits **Tumbling Tumbleweeds** and **Cool Water,** and Spencer, who left in 1950 but managed the Sons until 1955, composed **Cigareetes, Whiskey And Wild Wild Women, Careless Kisses** and **Roomful Of Roses.** Spencer died in the early '70s aged 65, in California; however, the Sons were still going strong in 1977, led by Perryman, who'd originally joined the group 41 years earlier.

A word should be said about Bob Nolan, whose songwriting may be the finest ever to appear in country music. A brilliant poet with an inventive ear for melody and harmony, he virtually invented

the sound and style of western harmony singing single-handedly, and he supplied the once thriving field with the great majority of its classic songs, which, in addition to the above, include **Trail Herding Cowboy, A Cowboy Has To Sing, One More Ride, Way Out There,** and **Song Of The Bandit.**

Albums:
Best Of . . . *(RCA/—)*
Riders In The Sky *(Camden/—)*
San Antonio Rose *(Camden/—)*
Tumbleweed Trails
  (Vocalion/—)
Cool Water *(RCA/—)*
Western Country *(Granite/—)*

Red Sovine

King of truck driving songs and narrations, Woodrow Wilson Sovine was born Charleston, West Virginia, July 17, 1918.

Above: Riders In The Sky (Camden) from Sons of the Pioneers, one of country music's most influential and durable groups.

Like many other country entertainers he learnt guitar at an early age and tuned in to C&W radio stations, obtaining his own first radio job with Jim Pike's Carolina Tar Heels on WCHS, Charleston, West Virginia, in 1935. Later the unit moved on to play the WWVA Jamboree, Wheeling, West Virginia.

During the late 1940s Sovine formed his own band, The Echo Valley Boys, he and the group gaining their own show on WCHS. Then on June 3, 1949, Hank Williams (♦) left the Louisiana Hayride (♦) to become an Opry regular and Sovine's band was drafted in as a replacement, the Echo Valley Boys also taking over Williams' daily

15 minute Johnny Fair Syrup Show stint. From 1949 until 1954 Sovine remained a star attraction on the Hayride, during that period striking up a friendship with Webb Pierce (♦). The twosome performed duets on the show, combining to write songs and, in turn, both becoming Opry regulars. On disc they joined up for **Why, Baby,**

Why?, a country No 1 in 1956, following this with **Little Rosa,** a Top Ten hit that same year. Though Sovine remained a top rated performer throughout the late '50s and early '60s his name disappeared from the charts until 1964, when a Starday release, **Dream House For Sale,** climbed into the listings to be followed a few months later

by **Giddyup Go,** which provided the singer with yet another No 1.

From that time on, Sovine continued adding to his list of chart honors, making a major impression in 1967 with **Phantom 309,** his classic tale of a truck-driving ghost. Then in the mid '70s, following a flood of recordings based on tales of CB radio, Sovine came into his own, achieving one of his biggest-ever successes with **Teddy Bear,** a highly sentimental tale regarding a crippled boy, his CB radio and a number of friendly truckers. He had, at the age of 58, finally earned a million-selling record.

Albums:
Phantom 309 (Starday/—)
Sunday With Sovine (Starday/—)
Classic Narrations (Starday/—)
The Best Of Red Sovine
  (Starday/—)
Teddy Bear (Starday/RCA)
The Greatest Grand Ole Opry
  (Chart/Chart)
Little Rosa (—/Hit)
Woodrow Wilson Sovine
  (Starday/—)

Billy Jo Spears

Though she's got a voice that's hardly in Opry tradition – take away the country backings and you're left with a bluesy sound befitting an uppercrust torch singer – Billie Jo was country raised (born Beaumont, Texas) and appeared on the Louisiana Hayride (♦) in her early teens, performing **Too Old For Toys, Too Young For Boys,** a ditty which she recorded on the reverse of a Mel Blanc Bugs Bunny type disc at the age of 13. Graduating from high school, she worked

Billie Joe Spears: she couldn't sing at her first public appearance because of nerves.

in a variety of jobs, becoming a carhop at a Beaumont drive in for a period of four years. In 1964, country songwriter Jack Rhodes heard her sing and talked her into a trip to Nashville where she became signed to UA Records. However, her first country hit came with **He's Got More Love In His Little Finger,** a Capitol release of 1968, Billie Jo reaching the Top Five during the following year with **Mr Walker It's All Over.** Apart from an elongated chart stay with **Marty Gray** (1970), her other Capitol sides, though fair sellers (five other titles reaching the charts) failed to emulate the success of **Mr Walker.** A change of fortune occurred following a switch to UA Records in 1974, **Blanket On The Ground** (1975), a Roger Boling song dealing with the delights of alfresco lovemaking, establishing Billie Jo with an international reputation. Since then she's scored with **Silver Wings And Golden Rings, Misty Blue, On The Rebound** (with Del Reeves (♦) and **What I've Got In Mind** and seems set to extend her run of winners for some time to come, her appeal being much wider than that of a 'straight' country singer.

Albums:
Help Me Make It Through The
  Night (Hillside/—)
Billie Jo (UA/—)
Blanket On The Ground
  (UA/UA)
What I've Got In Mind (UA/UA)
If You Want Me (UA/UA)

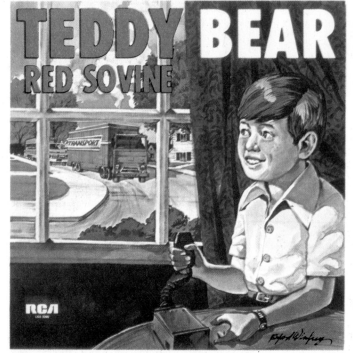

Above: Teddy Bear (RCA). The title track of this album was Red Sovine's first million seller – at the age of 58.

Carl T. Sprague

Known as the Original Singing Cowboy, Sprague was born near Houston, Texas, in 1895. A cowboy music enthusiast in his college days, he led a band while at Texas A&M, playing on the campus radio station. In August, 1925, inspired by Vernon Dalhart's hit record **The Prisoner's Song,** he recorded ten songs for Victor, his initial release – **When The Work's All Done This Fall** – selling nine hundred thousand copies. Further sessions (in 1926, '27 and '29) ensued, at which Sprague recorded mainly traditional cowboy material from the late nineteenth century. A man of many occupations – including insurance salesman, army officer, coach, garage operator etc – Sprague, who settled in Bryan, Texas, performed at various folk festivals during the 1960s, recording for the German Folk Variety label as recently as 1972.

Albums:
Carl T. Sprague
 (—|Bear Family)

Joe Stampley

Raised in Springhill, Louisiana, Stampley was influenced by both country entertainers and rock 'n' rollers like Jerry Lee Lewis (♦) and the Everly Brothers (♦). Becoming a member of the Uniques, a pop outfit that had late '60s hits with **Not Too Long Ago** and **All These Things** on the Paula label, Stampley supplied the group with many of their songs, signing a writing contract with Gallico Music. While still with the Uniques he began recording for Dot as a country artist, failing to achieve much in the way of sales with his initial output. However, his **Takes Time To Know Her** broke mildly into the charts during early 1971, since which time Stampley has achieved an impressive tally of major hits via such releases as **If You Touch Me** (1972), **Soul Song, Bring It On Home** (1973), **I'm Still Lovin' You, Take Me Home To Somewhere** (1974), **Penny, Roll On Big Mama** (1975), **All These Things, Whiskey Talking, The Night Time And My Baby, Everything I Own** (1976) and **There She Goes Again** (1977). Signed to Epic in 1975, Stampley has often found his newer recordings competing with belatedly released Dot material – often both old and new making the grade chartwise.

Albums:
Soul Song *(Dot|—)*
I'm Still Loving You *(Dot|—)*
Take Me Home To Somewhere
 (Dot|—)
Joe Stampley's Greatest Hits
 Vol 1 *(Dot|—)*
All These Things *(Dot|—)*
Billy Get Me A Woman *(Epic|—)*
Golden Hits (with the Uniques)
 (Paula|—)
Joe Stampley *(Epic|—)*
Sheik Of Chicago *(Epic|—)*
Ten Songs About Her *(Epic|—)*

Right: Joe Stampley; like so many others, once a pop artist but finding his niche in country music.

The First Popular Singing Cowboy (Folk Variety).

Above: Two albums by Joe Stampley – The Sheik of

Chicago (Epic) and Soul Song (Ember).

Stanley Brothers

Responsible for some of the most beautiful harmony vocals to ever emerge from the bluegrass scene, guitarist and lead vocalist Carter Glen Stanley (born McClure, Virginia, August 27, 1925) and his brother, banjoist and vocalist Ralph Edmond Stanley (born Stratton, Virginia, February 25, 1927), formed an old time band, the Stanley Brothers and The Clinch Mountain Boys, in 1946, and began broadcasting on radio station WCYB, Bristol, Virginia. Recording for the small Rich-R-Tone label, in 1948 they cut **Molly And Tenbrooks,** the band switching direction and playing in the bluegrass style of Bill Monroe (◆), Ralph Stanley utilizing the three-finger method of banjo playing popularized by Monroe sideman Earl Scruggs (◆ Flatt and Scruggs).

In March, 1949, the Stanleys signed for Columbia Records and began cutting a series of classic bluegrass sides (all vocals), retaining mandolin player and vocalist Pee Wee Lambert from their previous band and adding various fiddle and bass players at different sessions, George Shuffler replacing Lambert and becoming part of the Stanley Brothers' sound just prior to the band's last Columbia session in April, 1952. Throughout the '50s and '60s, the Stanleys recorded for such labels as Mercury, Starday and King, often cutting purely religious material. They also engaged on many tours, playing a prestigious date at London's Albert Hall as part of their European tour in March, 1966. But it was to be the Stanley Brothers' only British appearance;

Carter Stanley died in a Bristol, Virginia, hospital on December 1 that same year. Since the death of his brother, Ralph Stanley has kept the tradition of the Clinch Mountain Boys alive – though his music has become increasingly traditional in character.

Albums:
That Little Old County Church House (County/—)
Long Journey Home (County/—)
Recorded Live Vol 1 (Rebel/—)
Recorded Live Vol 2 (Rebel/—)
Folk Concert (Starday/—)
Hymns Of The Cross (King/—)
Good Old Camp Meeting Songs (Starday/—)
The Best Of . . . (Starday/—)
For The Good People (King/—)
First Album (Melodeon/—)
Together For The Last Time (Rebel/—)
The Stanley Brothers On The Air (Wango/—)

Banjo In The Hills (Starday/—)
Sing The Songs I Like Best (King/—)
In Person (Power Pak/—)

Ralph Stanley:
Hills Of Home (Starday/—)
Old Home Place (Rebel/—)
The Stanley Sound Around The World (King Bluegrass/—)
Plays Requests (Rebel/—)
With The Clinch Mountain Boys (Rebel/—)
Ralph Stanley, A Man And His Music (Rebel/—)
I Want To Preach The Gospel (Rebel/—)
A Cry From The Cross (Rebel/—)
Let Me Rest On Peaceful Mountain (Rebel/—)
Old County Church (Rebel/—)

Below: Bluegrass harmony vocal duo, the Stanley Brothers; Carter (left) and Ralph.

Above: The fresh-faced and innocent Kenny Starr.

Kenny Starr

Loretta Lynn (♦) protege Kenny Starr was born Topeka, Kansas, September 21, 1953, his family later moving to Burlingame, Kansas, where Starr grew up.

At an early age he began visiting the local Veterans Of Foreign Wars hall, where he would unplug the jukebox and sing for nickles and dimes. By the age of nine he was leading his first band, The Rockin' Rebels, this being quickly superseded by another group Kenny And The Imperials which toured the area, earning Starr between $10 and $15 a night.

At 16 he became a country entertainer, initially leading a band called The Country Showman, later winning a talent contest held in Wichita after singing his version of Ray Price's (♦) **I Won't Mention It Again.** Local promoter Hap Peebles saw Starr's performance on the show and asked if he would appear on a forthcoming Loretta Lynn and Conway Twitty (♦) concert, which Starr did, winning a standing ovation. After the concert Loretta suggested that he should move to Nashville and offered him a job in her own road show. Soon after, she also helped him obtain a recording contract with MCA. A singer-songwriter-guitarist, Starr had a No 1 country hit with his own **The Blind Man In The Bleachers** in January, 1976, following this up with a minor success in **Tonight I Face The Man.**

Albums:
The Blind Man In The Bleachers (MCA/—)

Statler Brothers

Vocal Group:
Lew De Witt – born Roanoke County, Virginia, March 8, 1938.
Philip Balsley – born Augusta County, Virginia, August 8, 1939.
Harold Reid – born Augusta County, Virginia, August 21, 1939.
Don Reid – born Staunton, Virginia, June 5, 1945.

Voted CMA Vocal Group of the Year every year since 1972, the Statlers – then Harold (bass), Lew (tenor), and Phil (baritone) began singing together in 1955 at Lyndhurst Methodist Church in Staunton, Virginia. In 1960, Harold's younger brother Don joined the

group – then known as the Kingsmen – and became front man, the quartet passing an audition to become part of the Johnny Cash Show (♦) some three years later . . . at which point they changed their name to the Statler Brothers after espying the name Statler on a box of tissues in a hotel room.

In 1965 they went further up the ladder after recording **Flowers On The Wall,** a song penned by De Witt, this Columbia release becoming a Top Five pop hit, also gaining a high place on the country charts. The group won two Grammy awards (Best New Country Group and Best Contemporary Performance By A Country Group) as a consequence.

Further hits followed – **Ruthless** and the delightfully titled **You Can't Have Your Kate And Edith Too** (both 1967) proving among the most popular – but it wasn't until 1970 and a new recording contract with Mercury that the Statlers moved into top gear, immediately gaining a second crossover hit with **Bed Of Roses.** Since that time they've become undisputed kings of country vocal groups, though the Oak Ridge Boys (♦), now more secular than in their early history, could make a strong challenge in time to come. But meanwhile the Statlers, like the product from which they took their name, continue to clean up!

Albums:
Bed Of Roses (Mercury/—)
Pictures Of Moments To Remember (Mercury/—)
Innerview (Mercury/—)

Above: Oh Happy Day (Columbia).

Country Music Then And Now (Mercury/—)
Sing Country Symphonies In E Major (Mercury/—)
Alive At The Johnny Mack Brown High School (Mercury/—)
Sons Of The Motherland (Mercury/—)
Best Of . . . (Mercury/—)
Holy Bible – Old Testament (Mercury/—)
Holy Bible – New Testament (Mercury/—)
Harold, Don, Phil and Lew (Mercury/—)
The Country America Loves (Mercury/—)

Below: Carry Me Back (Mercury).

Below: Statler Brothers.

Red Steagall

Writer of the brilliant **Texas Red**, an allegory concerning the life of Christ, Russell 'Red' Steagall (born Gainsville, Texas) learned his music in an atmosphere pervaded by the sounds of Bob Wills (♦). Polio struck when he was 15, leaving Steagall without the use of his left hand and arm – but he used the months of therapy and recuperation to master the guitar and mandolin, and later began playing in coffee houses during his stay at West Texas State University, where he studied animal husbandry – just in case he didn't make it in show biz.

However, his first job found him working for an oil company as a soil chemistry expert, with performing remaining a sideline until 1967 when **Here We Go Again,** a Steagall original penned with the aid of co-writer Don Lanier, provided Ray Charles with a chart record. Other Steagall songs subsequently found their way on to disc and the Texan became involved on the song publishing side of the industry, eventually signing a recording contract with Dot in 1969. Since that time he has cut several hit singles for Capitol (**Party Dolls And Wine, Somewhere My Love, Someone Cares For You, Fiddle Man, I Gave Up Good Morning, Darling** and **If You've Got The Time I've Got The Song**) and rejoined Dot once more, obtaining a 1976 best seller with **Lone Star Beer And Bob Wills Music,** the title track from a fine album.

Albums:
Party Dolls And Wine
  (Capitol/—)
If You've Got The Time, I've Got The Song (Capitol/—)
Lone Star Beer And Bob Wills Music (Dot/—)
Texas Red (Dot/—)

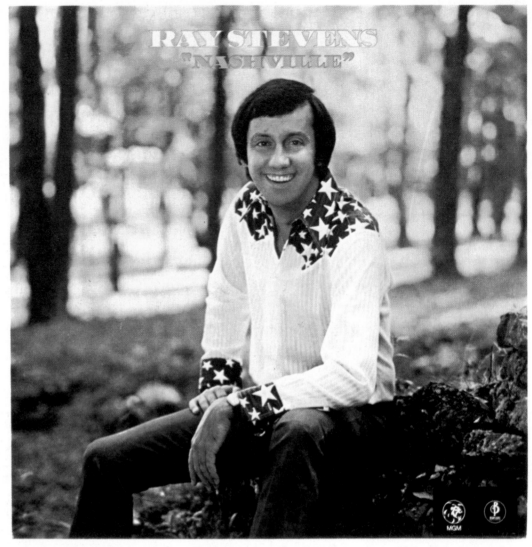

Nashville (Barnaby). An album that spotlights Stevens' multi-instrumental ability and produced by himself.

Above: If You've Got The Time, I've Got The Song (Capitol). A heavy early influence was Bob Wills. Red Steagall didn't get his first recording contract until 1969 – for Dot – having studied animal husbandry in case he didn't make it.

Ray Stevens

A talented singer-songwriter, arranger, producer and multi-instrumentalist, Stevens (born Ray Ragsdale in Clarkdale, Georgia, 1939) studied music at Georgia State University, then moved to Nashville, where he began recording such novelty hits as **Sergeant Preston Of The Yukon** (a 1959 success that had to be withdrawn after objections from a company that held the rights to the television show of that name); **Ahab The Arab** (1962); **Gitarzan** (1969) and **Along Came Jones** (1969), not forgetting **Jeremiah Peabody's Polyunsaturated, Quick Dissolving, Fast Acting, Pleasant Tasting, Green And Purple Pills** (1961). Since the end of the '60s Stevens, who has recorded for such labels as Judd, Mercury, Monument, Barnaby, Janus and Warner, has turned increasingly to country music, scoring with such discs as **Turn Your Radio On** (1971), **Nashville** (1973) and a semi-bluegrass version of **Misty** (1975), also appearing on Jerry Kennedy's **And Friends** album (1974) playing keyboards on a fine version of his **Everything Is Beautiful** in the company of several Nashville stars. But from time to time he still produces pieces of sheer lunacy, like **The Streak,** just to prove that he's not to be categorized. Perhaps **Nashville** (Barnaby) is the Stevens album of most interest to country fans.

Gary Stewart

A new wave singer-songwriter whose vibrato-filled voice places him in a love or hate category, Stewart was born and raised in Kentucky, moving to Florida with his family when he was 12.

His recording career began in 1964 with **I Loved You Truly,** a single for Cory which did little. Stewart then went on the road, playing bass with the Amps, a rock outfit, eventually returning home to work for an aircraft firm. In 1967 he met policeman Bill Eldridge, an ex-rocker who had contacts in Nashville. Together they began writing songs, one becoming a minor hit for Stonewall Jackson (♦), commencing a deluge that included **Sweet Thang And Cisco,** a 1969 hit for Nat Stuckey (♦); **When A Man Loves A Woman** and **She**

Out of Hand (RCA).

Above: The ubiquitous Stevens.

Right: Gary Stewart. Although his first recordings never got beyond the demo stage they won him an RCA contract.

Goes Walking Through My Mind, both 1970 Top Five discs for Billy Walker (◆), and other material for such artists as Kenny Price (◆), Jack Greene (◆), Johnny Paycheck (◆), Cal Smith (◆), Hank Snow (◆) and Warner Mack (◆).

But with his own recording contract with Kapp petering out, Stewart returned to Fort Pierce, Florida, leaving behind some demo sessions he had made of Motown material, cut while he was working in various capacities at Bradley's Barn studio.

These demos were later heard by Roy Dea, a Mercury producer who subsequently was signed to RCA by Jerry Bradley. He immediately signed Stewart for his new label, his belief in the singer paying off when Stewart's **Drinkin' Thing,** a second-time-round release, became a Top Ten hit in 1974. Since that time, Stewart's had other major chart discs with **Out Of Hand** (1975), **She's Actin' Single (I'm Drinkin' Doubles)** (1975) and **In Some Room Above The Street** (1976), all of which have helped establish the one-time Charley Pride (◆) sideman as a solo performer of considerable potential.

Albums:
You're Not The Woman You Used To Be *(MCA/—)*
Steppin' Out *(RCA/RCA)*
Out Of Mind *(RCA/RCA)*
Your Place Or Mine *(RCA/RCA)*

John Stewart

One time member of the Kingston Trio and writer of the Monkees' hit **Daydream Believer,** this Californian folk-country artist with the tremulous, macho singing voice and poetic grasp of imagery has had limited commercial success as a performer so far but commands a strong critical following and fanatically devoted pockets of fans, particularly in Britain where a magazine, *Omaha Rainbow*, is named after a line in one of his songs.

Born in San Diego, California, in September 1939, his father trained race and show horses. Stewart's early influences were rock 'n' roll and folk and he played in several garage bands in his youth. His folk interest then had him pitching songs to the Kingston Trio (then huge) – he simply turned up to one of their gigs with a banjo and played the songs. A result of the Trio recording Stewart's songs was an invitation from Roulette Records to form a folk group, the Cumberland Three.

He later replaced Dave Guard in the Kingston Trio but left in 1967, disillusioned with the slickness of the music. After a short songwriting stint with John Denver (♦) (during one session they demoed **Leaving On A Jet Plane** and **Daydream Believer!**) he hitched up with singer Buffy Ford and experimented with mixed-media, using themes and images from Andrew Wyeth, the painter. Wyeth's subjects of an older, simpler, rural America were to permeate Stewart's work. His first such album, **Signals Through The Glass,** is now a very rare collector's item. In the late '60s he worked on the Robert Kennedy election campaign and utilized some of his experiences into the song **Omaha Rainbow.**

Stewart's greatest recording successes have been with producer Nik Venet, and although some of the albums were recorded in Nashville only a limited number of tracks could truly be called country. Even so, Stewart's music is constructed in such a way that the heroic sagas of old, rural America and the characters portrayed appeal to many a country buff. His musical style is simple, his delivery direct. A live album, **The Phoenix Concerts,** is an excellent representation of his style, recorded in a district where he has a large American following. Phoenix, Arizona, land of deserts and canyons is perhaps the right place for Stewart to find his most avid disciples. To date he has not attracted mass acceptance, however, having been discarded by more than one record company.

Albums:
California Bloodlines
  (Capitol/—)
Willard *(Capitol/—)*
Signals Through The Glass –
  with Buffy Ford *(Capitol/—)*
Cannons In The Rain
  (RCA/RCA)
Phoenix Concerts *(RCA/RCA)*
Wingless Angels *(RCA/RCA)*

John Stewart, the lonesome picker, who initially climbed the ladder as a member of the Kingston Trio, a popular folk act. Records now with RSO.

Redd Stewart

Henry Redd Stewart, born Ashland City, Tennessee, May 27, 1921, began his career by writing a song for a car dealer's commercial at the age of 14. He then formed and played in bands around the Louisville, Kentucky area until 1937, when Pee Wee King (♦) came to Louisville to play on radio station WHAS and signed Stewart as a musician, Eddy Arnold (♦) being the band's vocalist at the time although Redd was Eddy's replacement as vocalist when Arnold went off on his own. Then came Pearl Harbor – and Stewart was drafted for army service in the South Pacific, during which period he wrote **A Soldier's Last Letter,** a major hit for Ernest Tubb (♦). After the war he rejoined King and began taking a serious interest in songwriting, teaming with King to write **Tennessee Waltz** (a hit for both King and Cowboy Copas (♦) but a 1950 six million seller for pop singer Patti Page), following this with **Slow Poke** (a 1951 gold disc for King), and **You Belong To Me** (which in the Jo Stafford version topped the US charts for five weeks during 1952), and the reworked old fiddle tune, **Bonaparte's Retreat.**

Stewart's own career on disc has been less successful – despite stints with such labels as RCA, Starday, King and Hickory – and it seems that he'll generally be remembered for his songwriting and his 30 year association with Pee Wee King.

Albums:
The Best Of Pee Wee King And Redd Stewart *(Starday/—)*

Redd Stewart, composer of Tennessee Waltz, a hit for the Fontaine Sisters, Les Paul and Mary Ford, Anita O'Day, Patti Page, Pee Wee King, Jo Stafford, Spike Jones, Guy Lombardo . . .

Wynn Stewart

Singer-songwriter, born Morrisville, Missouri, June 7, 1934. Stewart received early singing experience in church, and at 13 appeared on KWTO, Springfield, Missouri. Later his family moved to California where he made his first recording at the age of 15.

During the mid '50s Stewart became signed to Capitol Records, later that decade switching to Jackpot Records, a subsidiary of Challenge. His song **Above And Beyond** provided a big hit for Buck Owens (◆) in 1960, while some of Stewart's own Jackpot sides featured the voice of Jan Howard (◆). For Challenge itself Stewart provided such hits as **Wishful Thinking** (1959), **Big Big Day** (1961) and **Another Day, Another Dollar** (1962) around that period opening up his own club in Las Vegas, and appearing on his own TV show.

Some two and a half years later he sold the club and moved to California, signing once more for Capitol and promoting his discs by tours with a new band The Tourists. Purveying his California style of honky tonk and beer-stained ballads, Stewart made friends and influenced record buyers, the result being a flow of country chart entries that has included **It's Such A Pretty World Today** (a No 1 in 1967), **'Cause I Have You** (1967), **Love's Gonna Happen To Me** (1967), **Something Pretty** (1968), **In Love** (1968), **World Wide Travelin' Man** (1969) and **It's A Beautiful Day** (1970), Stewart extending his run of winners in 1976 with **After The Storm,** a Top Ten release on Playboy. His Capitol albums – now all deleted – included **You Don't Care What Happens To Me, It's A Beautiful Day, Songs Of Wynn Stewart** and **Baby It's Yours.**

Below: You Don't Care What Happens To Me (Capitol). Honky tonk and ballad singer Stewart's albums are all now deleted.

Above: Wynn Stewart. At the age of five he was singing solo in church in his home town; by 13 he was appearing regularly on radio.

Cliffie Stone

Born Clifford Gilpin Snyder in Burbank, California, on March 1, 1917, Cliffie grew up in a rich country music tradition: his father was the well known area banjo player-comedian professionally known as Herman the Hermit. Despite this background, Cliffie began his musical career as bassist for big bands such as Anson Weeks and Freddie Slack. He soon got into country radio, however, and served as a disc jockey, MC and performer on several Los Angeles area stations, and was bandleader and featured comedian on the Hollywood Barn Dance.

Cliffie moved into the executive end of the music business in 1946 with the newly formed Capitol Records, with whom he stayed for over two decades, recording a half dozen albums of his own as well as guiding the careers of Tennessee Ernie Ford (◆) and many others. He stayed busy as a performer, however, leading the Hometown Jamboree, a pioneering Los Angeles television show, and co-writing such hits as **No Vacancy, Divorce Me C.O.D., New Steel Guitar Rag, So Round So Firm So Fully Packed,** and **Sweet Temptation.**

In the middle 1960s he turned his attention to several music business enterprises, including his publishing company Central Songs, which he sold to Capitol in 1969. Lately he has entered the record field once again, heading up the new Granite label.

Albums:
Square Dance USA *(Capitol/—)*
Cliffie Stone Sing-Along *(Capitol/—)*
Party's On Me *(Capitol/—)*

Stoneman Family

One of the most famous family groups in Country Music, the

David 'Stringbean' Akeman (left) and his sometime partner, Bijou. Stringbean got his nickname when a radio announcer forgot his real one.

June 14, 1968.

Although the Stonemans were – and still are – considered one of the finest semi-bluegrass bands, Pop's early record output – with his Dixie Mountaineers – featured sentimental ballads of the nineteenth century, British traditional melodies, dance tunes, much religious material and even a number of humorous sketches. He is reputed to be the first musician to record with an autoharp.

Albums:
In The Family *(MGM/—)*
The Stoneman Family
  (Folkways/—)
The Stonemans *(MGM/—)*
Stoneman's Country *(MGM/—)*
Tribute To Pop Stoneman
  (MGM/—)
Great *(MGM/—)*
Ernest V. Stoneman And The
  Dixie Mountaineers 1927-28
  (Historical/—)
Mountain Music Played On An
  Autoharp *(Folkways/—)* –
  with Kilby Snow etc

Stringbean

Born Annville, Kentucky, June 17, 1915, real name David Akeman. Son of a fine banjo player, Stringbean made his own first banjo at the age of 12 and began playing professionally six years later in the Lexington area, eventually working with Cy Rogers' Lonesome Pine Fiddlers on radio station WLAP. It was during this period that the 6 ft 2 in performer became dubbed Stringbean and adopted a more comic direction with his act. During the late '30s he worked with Charlie Monroe (Monroe Brothers ♦), then joined Bill Monroe (♦) on the Grand Ole Opry in July, 1942, staying with Monroe for three years. Also known as 'The Kentucky Wonder', Stringbean, an outstanding banjo player in the style of Uncle Dave Macon (♦), was a longtime member of the Opry but perhaps won even more fame through his appearances on the Hee-Haw (♦) TV series. He died on November 10, 1973, he and his wife Estelle being brutally murdered after returning home from the Opry.

Albums:
Salute To Uncle Dave Macon
  (Starday/—)
Me And My Old Crow
  (Nugget/—)

Ernest V. Stoneman and the Blue Ridge Corn Shuckers (Rounder).

Stonemans revolved around Ernest V. 'Pop' Stoneman (born Monorat, Carroll County, Virginia, May 25, 1893), a carpenter who in 1924 wrote to Okeh and Columbia seeking an audition. A jews' harp and harmonica player by the age of ten and a banjoist and autoharp player in his teens, Pop was eventually heard by Okeh's Ralph Peer (♦) who recorded some test sides in September, 1924, cutting a number of finally accepted sides the following January, these including **The Sinking Of The Titanic,** one of the biggest selling records of the '20s. Between 1925–29 Pop, sometimes with his wife or other members of his family, cut well over 200 titles for Okeh, Gennett, Paramount, Victor and other companies, also playing on

dates with such acts as Riley Puckett (♦) and Uncle Dave Macon (♦). High spenders, having spent their royalties on cars and other luxuries, the Depression of 1929 hit the Stonemans hard, only one recording date, featuring Pop and his son Eddie, emanating from this period, Pop had to resume his former occupation as a carpenter in a Washington DC naval gun factory. Meanwhile, his wife Hattie struggled to bring up her family – which eventually numbered 13 children.

Several of the children became musicians and Pop formed a family band during the late '40s, playing in the Washington area and recording an album for Folkways in 1957 that helped spark off a whole new career.

Proving popular on the major folk festivals and on college dates, the Stonemans became an in-demand outfit, making their debut on Grand Ole Opry in 1962 and recording for Starday that same year. During the mid '60s the family moved to Nashville, appeared on the Jimmy Dean (♦) ABC-TV show, and were signed to appear in their own TV show Those Stonemans in 1966. A year later, they won the CMA award for the Best Vocal Group, the band then consisting of Pop (guitar, autoharp), Scotty (fiddle), Jim (bass), Van (guitar), Donna (mandolin) and Roni (banjo).

However, a stomach ailment began to affect Pop and he died in Nashville on June 14, 1968, his last recording session taking place on

Nat Stuckey

Perhaps an underrated performer – though he has been a consistent supplier of medium sized hits – Nat Stuckey was born Cass County, Texas, December 17, 1937. Employed for some considerable time as a radio announcer – he studied at Arlington State College, Dallas, in order to enhance his radio career – Stuckey also worked with a jazz group in 1957–58, becoming leader of a country band, the Corn Huskers, in 1958–59.

In 1966, Buck Owens (♦) recorded his fellow Texan's **Waitin' In The Welfare Line** – the most programmed country record of the year – at which stage Stuckey, who'd been working with the Louisiana Hayriders (♦) and recording for the Sims label, switched to Paula Records, scoring his own Top Ten hit with **Sweet Thang.**

Below: Nat Stuckey.

Seven chart records later, in 1968, he label-hopped once more, this time signing for RCA and immediately scoring five major disc successes with **Plastic Saddle** (1968), **Joe And Mabel's 12th Street Bar And Grill, Cut Across Shorty, Sweet Thang And Cisco** and **Young Love** (all 1969), the last named being a duet with Connie Smith (♦).

Since that time, Stuckey has never really enjoyed the quota of potent singles expected of him, only **She Wakes Me Every Morning With A Kiss** (1970) and **Take Time To Love Her** (1973) establishing his name in the upper regions of the charts. But Stuckey, who became an MCA artist in the mid '70s, still promises much, his **What I've Got In Mind,** a Top 20 single in 1976, being accompanied by **Independence,** one of the year's most rewarding albums.

Albums:
Favorites *(Paula/—)*
The Best Of . . . *(RCA/—)*
Independence *(MCA/MCA)*

Above: New Country Roads (RCA Victor). Although never a scorer of massive hits Stuckey has been a consistent chart performer. Has lately moved to MCA.

James Clell Summey
♦ *Cousin Jody*

Billy Swan

A comparative unknown when his **I Can Help** single hit the charts in 1974, Swan turned out to have a long pedigree in Southern music generally. Born in Cape Girardeau, Missouri, he had written **Lover Please** at age 16. The song was recorded by his band of that time, Mirt Mirley and the Rhythm Steppers, but Clyde McPhatter made it a huge R&B hit.

Swan tried his luck in Nashville eventually, taking odd jobs. He followed Kris Kristofferson (♦) as janitor at Columbia's Nashville studios. While working for Columbia Music Swan became involved with Tony Joe White and produced that artist's first three, and most important, albums. He also backed

Above: Four (Columbia). Swan has followed Kristofferson from janitor to recording star.

Kristofferson at the 1970 Isle of Wight Festival and was later to join Kinky Friedman's (♦) band for a while.

The 1974 album release of **I Can Help** revealed an artist with a liking for country, rock 'n' roll and rhythm and blues. He made an impressive version of Presley's (♦) **Don't Be Cruel** and in 1975 he had another pop single hit with

Above: Billy Swan. Didn't have his first hit until 1974 but he'd been around for a long time before that.

Everything's The Same. He has since toured with such rated Nashville musicians as Kenny Buttrey and Charlie McCoy (♦) as backing musicians and Elvis Presley paid him the honor of recording **I Can Help,** besides giving Swan a pair of his socks as a gift.

Albums:
I Can Help
(Monument/Monument)
Rock 'n' Roll Moon
(Monument/Monument)
Billy Swan
(Monument/Monument)
Four *(Monument/Monument)*

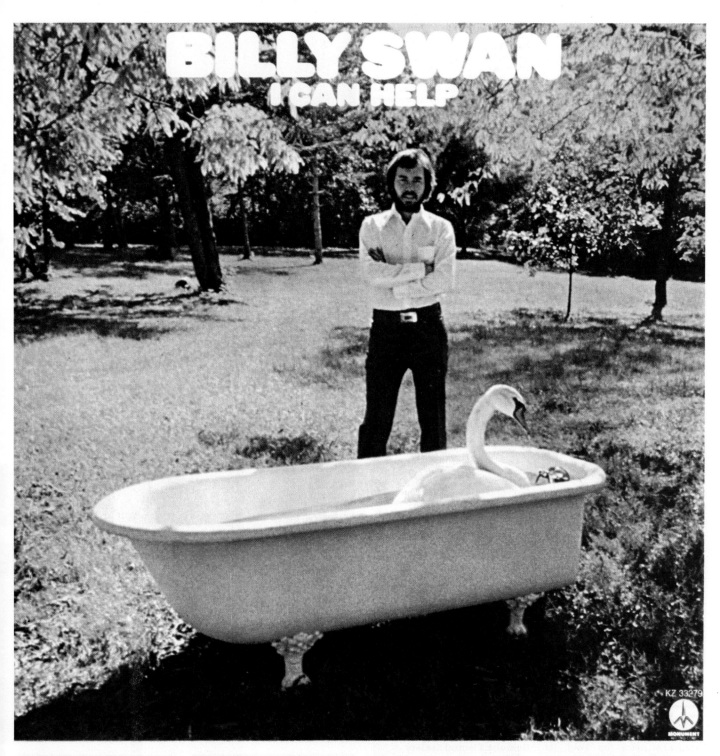

BILLY SWAN
I CAN HELP

KZ 33279

James Talley

Purveyor of music he calls 'contemporary American', Talley was born Tulsa, Oklahoma but spent much of his early life among the trailer camps of Washington state during the late '40s, his family eventually settling down in Albuquerque, New Mexico, when Talley reached the age of eight. His first musical instrument was a beat-up trumpet which he played in a high school band – but this he later traded in for a guitar. Employed as a welfare worker among the Chicanos, he wrote a collection of songs and ballads that formed an extended work (yet to be recorded) known as **The Road To Torreon**, composing his first song **Ramon Esteban** (about a ditch-digging highway worker that Talley once befriended) following a meeting (and subsequent advice) from

Pete Seeger.

After stints in graduate school, at UCLA and at the University of New Mexico, there majoring in American Studies and art forms of the '30s, he moved to Nashville, working for several years in the cause of public health programs. His community work took him into the black ghetto areas where he became exposed to the music of B. B. King, Muddy Waters and other bluesmen. He also became increasingly interested in country music – his father had been a western swing fanatic – and met Johnny Gimble (♦) and Josh Graves (♦), both of whom later played on Talley's albums. Opting to become a professional performer, he worked some club and college dates during the early '70s but often had to take construction jobs in order to provide for his wife and two sons. A deal in which Talley offered to help build a recording

studio in exchange for studio time led to his first album **Got No Bread, No Milk, No Honey, But We Sure Got Love** in 1974, the singer pressing 1,000 copies of the disc which he mailed to various country radio stations. Impressed by the reaction, Capitol Records signed Talley, gave his self-produced LP a nationwide release and then financed him for further albums **Trying Like The Devil** (1976) and **Blackjack Choir** (1977). Though his music finds its roots in Rodgers (♦) and Guthrie (♦), other influences, predominantly those of R&B, are allowed to infiltrate.

Albums:
Got No Bread, No Milk, No Honey, But We Sure Got Love
(Capitol/—)
Trying Like The Devil
(Capitol/—)
Blackjack Choir
(Capitol/Capitol)

Above: I Can Help (Monument). Contains Presley's Don't Be Cruel. 'Billy Swan sure does Don't Be Cruel kinda slow . . . by the time he'd got to the next line I'd had a shower.'
– Billy Sherrill.

Jimmie Tarlton

Though his name is now almost forgotten, it was John James Timbert Tarlton (born Chesterfield County, South Carolina, 1892) who first recorded the old folk song **Birmingham Jail,** an oft-recorded country favorite. The son of a sharecropper, Tarlton became proficient on banjo, guitar and harmonica while still a boy, his repertoire being drawn not only from the traditional material learnt from his mother but also from the blues songs of the black workers. During his twenties he began hoboing his way around the country, his route taking him to New York, Chicago and Texas, where he became an oil field worker. After a spell in the cotton mills of Carolina and a trek through the mid-west with a medicine show, he opted for a full time career in music, a 1926 partnership with Georgian guitarist Tom Darby proving eminently successful and resulting in a recording session for Columbia. In November, 1927, Darby and Tarlton recorded **Birmingham Jail** and **Columbus Stockade Blues,** the ensuing disc attaining impressive sales figures. For the next three years the duo continued to provide Columbia with discs, their contract finally terminating in 1930. And though no recordings were made in 1931, Tarlton taking up temporary work in a South Carolina cotton mill, dates with Victor (1932) and ARC (1933) followed, the partnership dissolving in '33 when Darby returned to a farming career. Tarlton, however, remained an active musician for many years, at one time working with Hank Williams (♦) in a medicine show. He was rediscovered by a new generation during the 1960s and began playing club dates and festivals, even cutting an album, **Steel Guitar Rag.** But this proved to be his swansong; he died in 1973.

Albums:
Darby And Tarlton
(Old Timey/—)
Darby And Tarlton
(—/Bear Family)

Darby and Tarlton
(Bear Family).

Chip Taylor

Brother of actor Jon Voigt (of *Midnight Cowboy* fame) and son of a golf pro, Taylor was born James Wesley Voigt, Westchester County, New York, 1940. A singer-songwriter, he has penned several hit numbers on the pop side, writing **Wild Thing** (Troggs), **Angel Of The Morning** (Merrilee Rush) and **Anyway That You Want Me** (American Breed), while in country he has contributed **Sweet Dream Woman** (Waylon Jennings (♦)), **Just A Little Bit Lower On Down The Line** (Bobby Bare (♦)), **If You Were Mine, Mary** (Eddy Arnold (♦), Jim Ed Brown (♦)) and **The Long Walk Home** (Floyd Cramer (♦)).

A rockabilly singer with King during the '50s, Taylor later went into record production then joined singer-songwriter Al Gorgoni to form a duo, the group expanding to a trio with the arrival of Trade Martin. After cutting two albums for Buddah they split, Chip continuing on Buddah for one solo

album, **Gasoline** (1972) which included his version of **Angel Of The Morning,** before moving on to Warner Brothers and making the critically acclaimed **Chip Taylor's Last Chance** (1973). Taylor is that unusual animal, a New York country artist who until recently has recorded outside of Nashville – but so far he has not thoroughly capitalized on the reputation he made with **Last Chance.**

Albums:
Last Chance
(Warner Bros/Warner Bros)
This Side Of The Big River
(Warner Bros/Warner Bros)
Somebody Shoot Out The Jukebox *(Columbia/—)*

Tut Taylor

Noted for his unusual flat picking dobro style, Robert 'Tut' Taylor hails from Milledgeville, Georgia, where he was born November 20, 1923. A mandolin player since the age of 12, he also plays fiddle, guitar, dulcimer, autoharp and banjo and is renowned as a collector, builder and dealer in string instruments, operating Tut Taylor's General Store on Nashville's Arlington Avenue.

During the mid '60s he cut a series of albums for the World Pacific label – some as part of the Folkswingers (a pickup unit that sometimes included Glen Campbell (♦) on 12-string) and one as featured player with the Dixie Gentleman (along with Vassar Clements (♦)), the latter **Blues And Bluegrass,** later being re-released on Old Homestead Records. Featured on Porter Wagoner's (♦) **Bluegrass Story** (1965), Taylor also appeared on John Hartford's (♦) **Aeroplane** album in 1971 and has since worked closely with Hartford and Norman Blake (♦) on various projects, one Taylor-Blake brainchild being a band of pickers known as the Dobrolic Plectral Society. He was also among the all-star musical lineup which helped Leon Russell make his **Hank Wilson's Back** album.

An interesting point is that some of Taylor's Folkswinger releases were pressed on pink vinyl, these pressings now being highly sought after by collectors.

Albums:
Friar Tut *(Rounder/—)*
Dobrolic Plectral Society
(Takoma/—)
Walnut Valley Spring Thing
(Takoma/—) - with John Hartford and others
Blues And Bluegrass
(Old Homestead/—)
The Old Post Office
(Flying Fish/—)

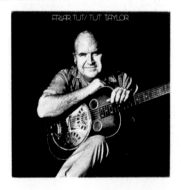

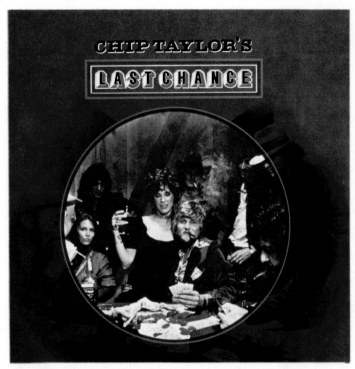

Chip Taylor's Last Chance (Warner Bros). A successful songwriter and a rockabilly singer in the '50s, he received wide praise for this first album on WB.

Below: Tut Taylor. A collector and dealer in old string instruments, he included a list of Martin guitar serial numbers on the sleeve of his Friar Tut album.

The Tenneva Ramblers

Claud Grant *vocals and guitar*
Jack Grant *mandolin*
Jack Pierce *fiddle*
Claude Slagle *banjo*

A relatively popular band of the late 1920s and early 1930s, best known because of their association with Jimmie Rodgers (♦). Originally known as the Jimmie Rodgers Entertainers, they were set to record for Ralph Peer (♦) in that historic weekend in August of 1927. At the last moment they all defected from Rodgers, and made up the new band name, which reflected the location of the session: Bristol, a city divided in half by the state line between Tennessee and

Virginia. They were moderately successful in their recording efforts, but going it alone seemed not to have hurt Jimmie Rodgers a bit.

Albums: none.

Al Terry

Born Allison Joseph Theriot on January 14, 1922, Al Terry was a Cajun who hit it big when rockabilly came along, with his **Good Deal Lucille.** Other than this nationwide hit, Terry has been pretty much a regional favorite, playing Louisiana and east Texas. He recorded for Hickory from 1954–1962, and also Dot, Index, and Rice, but another **Good Deal Lucille** never came his way.

Left: Tut Taylor's Friar Tut (Rounder).

Above: A guitar called Hank Thompson with a man of the the same name.

Movin' On (Ember).

Above: Hank Thompson. Though some of his early tracks are prized by rock fans he's really a swing era artist who cuts songs brought to fame by Nat King Cole et al.

Hank Thompson

For 13 consecutive years (from 1953–1965) Thompson's Brazos Valley Boys won just about every western band poll, and even today Thompson's influence pervades the '70s country-rock scene, influencing such neo-swing bands as Asleep At The Wheel (♦) and Commander Cody's Lost Planet Airmen (♦).

Born Henry William Thompson, Waco, Texas, September 3, 1925 he initially became a harmonica ace, winning many talent contests by his playing. Later he graduated to guitar, learning to play on a second-hand instrument costing only $4, bought for him as a Christmas present by his parents. During the early 1940s he began broadcasting from a local radio station and found a sponsor in a flour company, who presented him in a show titled 'Hank The Hired Hand'. A few months later, in 1943, Thompson joined the navy for a period of three years, upon discharge returning to country music and winning himself a spot on Waco radio station KWTX. He also formed a western swing band, The Brazos Valley Boys, and began recording for Globe Records in August, 1946, the results of session providing single **Whoa Sailor/Swing Wide Your Gate Of Love** that became a regional hit. This reached the ears of Tex Ritter (♦), who then suggested to Capitol Records that they sign the Waco singer.

In 1948 Thompson commenced a career with the label that was to last 18 years, scoring immediately with national hits in **Humpty, Dumpty Heart** and **Today,** following these with 1948 successes **Green Light** and a remake of **Whoa Sailor.** From then on came a perpetual stream of hits, the biggest being Thompson's version of a Carter-Warren song **The Wild Side Of Life,** which became a million seller in 1952. Though his last appearance in the pop charts was with **She's A Whole Lot Like You,** back in July, 1960, Thompson has provided a non stop flow of country chart winners, including **Oklahoma Hills, Hangover Tavern, On Tap, In The Can Or In The Bottle, Next Time I Fall In Love (I Won't)** and **I've Come Awful Close,** while he and the Brazos Valley Boys continue to play many dates world-wide. In 1966 Thompson moved from Capitol to Warner Brothers, then on to Dot in 1968. Though for a time it seemed that he might be rejecting the western swing style that first brought him to prominence, a 1977 album release **Back In The Swing Of Things** proved Thompson to be playing his strongest suit once more.

Albums:
The Best Of . . . (Capitol/—)
The Best Of . . . Vol 2 (Capitol/—)
Simple Simon (Pickwick/—)
On Tap, In The Can Or In The Bottle (Dot/—)
Sings The Hits Of Nat King Cole (Dot/—)
Back In The Swing Of Things (Dot/ABC)
Movin' On (—/Ember)
Country Sounds Of Hank Thompson (—/MFP)

Back In The Swing Of Things (ABC). After a brief departure, this album signalled Thompson's return to the western swing that made him famous.

Above: The Sue Thompson Story (DJM).

Sue Thompson

Known as the lady with the itty-bitty voice, even today Sue Thompson still sounds like a teenybopper. Born Nevada, Missouri, Eva Sue McKee (her real name) grew up on her parent's farm, spending her spare time listening to country music or viewing Western films – her hero was Gene Autry (♦). At seven she received her first guitar and began playing in church and at social events. During her high school days, she won a San Jose talent contest, the reward being a two week engagement at a local vaudeville theatre; Sue's first real break came on Dude Martin's San Francisco KGO-TV show Hometown Hayride, where she became a regular cast member and cut two sides with Martin's Round-Up Gang, one side **If You Want Some Loving** encouraging Mercury to sign her as a solo act. She was married to Martin for a time, and later spent some years as the wife of another entertainer, Hank Penny (♦).

Moving to Los Angeles she appeared in cabaret alongside many major artists, and in the late '50s made a number of appearances on Red Foley's (♦) portion of the Grand Ole Opry. Following record dates for Columbia and Decca, Sue signed for Hickory Records in December, 1960, having an initial hit with **Sad Movies,** a gold disc winner. Others followed, including **Norman** (another million-seller), **James (Hold The Ladder Steady), Paper Tiger, Have A Good Time** and **Angel, Angel,** most of her songs being in pure pop vein. Becoming increasingly country-oriented during the late '60s, she made a lengthy tour of the Vietnam war zone. Today she's still going strong, her version of **Big Mabel Murphy,** a Dallas Frazier (♦) song, becoming a 1975 best-seller.

Albums:
The Sue Thompson Story
   (—/DJM)

Uncle Jimmy Thompson

The first featured performer on the Saturday night barn dance show which was to develop into the Grand Ole Opry was Uncle Jimmy Thompson, born in Smith County, Tennessee, in 1848. While he primarily farmed for a living for over half a century in both Tennessee and Texas, he was an avid participant and frequent winner of nationwide fiddle contests.

Excited by the then-new medium of radio, he applied – at the age of 78! – for a spot on WSM, and in 1925 his Saturday night show, the forerunner of the Opry, first came on the air. He stayed with the Opry (then still known as the WSM Barn Dance) until 1928, then toured a bit and recorded for both Columbia (1926) and Vocalion (1930) before passing away, probably of pneumonia, on February 17, 1931, at the ripe old age of 83.

Mel Tillis

Though Tillis has always had problems with his speech – having a life-long stutter – he's had little trouble putting words (and music) down on paper, his songwriting efforts including **Detroit City, Honky Tonk Song, Ruby Don't Take Your Love To Town, I'm Tired, One More Time, Crazy Wild Desire, A Thousand Miles Ago** and many other Top Ten entries.

Born Tampa, Florida, August 8,

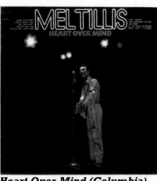

Heart Over Mind (Columbia).

1932, Tillis grew up in Pahokee, Florida, there graduating from High School. A drummer in the school band, he later studied violin but opted out to become a footballer of some distinction. However, next came a spell in the US Air Force followed by a stint on the railroad. During this time Tillis developed his writing and performing ability and in 1957 headed for Nashville with three of his songs

– all of which became hits for other singers. Tillis' own first hit disc came late in '58 with **The Violet And The Rose,** a Columbia release; this was followed by **Finally** (1959), **Sawmill** (1959) and **Georgia Town Blues,** a duet with Bill Phillips (♦) (1960). Following a switch to the Ric label and a first time Top 20 item in **Wine** (1965), he became signed to Kapp, his career flourished from this point; he obtained Top Ten hits with **Who's Julie?** (1968). **These Lonely Hands Of Mine** (1969), **She'll Be Hanging 'Round Somewhere, Heart Over Mind** (both 1970) then moved on to MGM to continue his personal hit parade via **Commercial Affection, Heaven Everyday** (1970), **The Arms Of A Fool, Brand New Mister Me** (1971), **I Ain't Never** (1972), **Neon Rose, Sawmill** (1973), **Midnight, Me And The Blues, Stomp Them**

M-M-M-Mel Tillis! An inveterate stutterer, he turned his impediment to good use and made it part of his act.

Old Faithful (Kapp).

Grapes, Memory Maker (1974) **Best Way I Know How** and **Woman In The Back Of My Mind** (1975), many others only just missing the upper bracket. To this list can be added two hit duets with Sherry Bryce and **How Come Your Dog Don't Bite Nobody But Me,** a diverting duet with Webb Pierce (♦) that hit the middle region of the charts in 1963.

One of the most prolific and versa-tile songwriters in country music – his material ranges from pure un-diluted goo through to raunchy honky tonk – he's equally diverse as a performer, being able to handle almost any type of song in convincing manner. Which is why he deservedly won the CMA Entertainer Of The Year Award in 1976.

Albums:
Big 'n' Country *(Vocalion/—)*
Detroit City *(Pickwick/—)*
Greatest Hits *(MCA/—)*
Heart Over Mind *(Columbia/—)*
In Person *(MCA/—)*
Night Train To Memphis
  (Pickwick/—)
Best Of *(MCA/—)*
Love Revival *(MCA/—)*
M-M-Mel *(MGM/—)*
Welcome To Country *(MGM/—)*
Best Way *(MGM/—)*

Below: Floyd Tillman. A Western Union messenger at the age of 13, he heard some Jimmie Rodgers records while delivering a message and was immediately hooked on country music.

Floyd Tillman

One of country music's most suc-cessful songwriters, Floyd Till-man was born Ryan, Oklahoma, December 8, 1914. A Western Union messenger at the age of 13, he became singer, guitarist, man-dolin and banjo player with the Mark Clark Orchestra and the Blue Ridge Playboys during the '30s, signing for Decca Records in 1939 and cutting the self-written **It Makes No Difference Now,** a C&W classic.

During the late '40s Tillman, who became a Columbia recording artist in 1946, wrote such composi-tions as **I Love You So Much It Hurts** (1948), **Slipping Around** (1949) and **I'll Never Slip Around Again** (1949), his records of these songs all becoming hits. But they became even bigger hits when recorded by Jimmy Wakely (♦), big band vocalist Margaret Whit-ing duetting with Wakely on the two 1949 successes.

Though his name remained absent from the record charts during the '50s, in 1960 Tillman scored again with **It Just Tore Me Up,** a Liberty release. Other Till-man songs include **Each Night At Nine, I'll Keep On Lovin' You,** and **Daisy Mae.** An LP, **The Best Of Floyd Tillman,** was re-leased on the Harmony label in July, 1964, while a **Greatest Hits** album has also appeared on Pick-wick.

Above: Floyd Tillman – His Greatest Hits of Loving (Fontana).

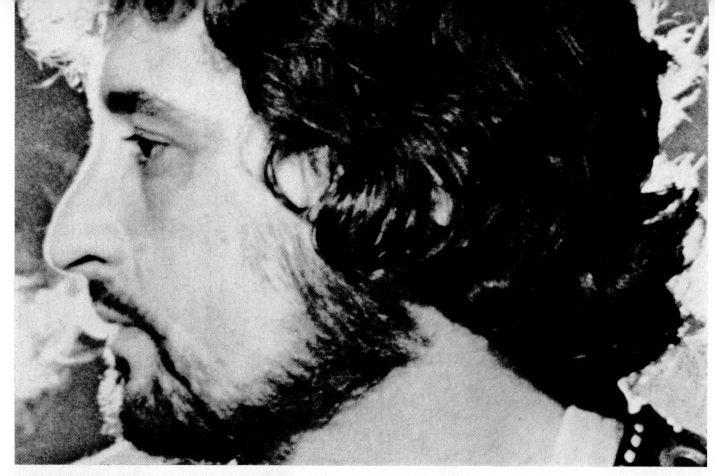

Tompall And The Glaser Brothers

Listenable, harmony vocal group who won many awards and have since split to follow solo careers, Tompall having become a top ranker in the 'outlaw' movement.

Born on a ranch in Spalking, Nebraska, early interest in music was generated by the boys' parents, who were both country devotees.

During the early '50s they formed a band and played local clubs and dance halls. As their reputation spread they gained a 13-week series on KHAS, Hastings, Nebraska. Following their winning top place on the Arthur Godfrey Talent Show and consequent national attention, they traveled to Nashville in 1958 and were soon seen on tour with Marty Robbins (◆). Signed by Decca Records, they recorded folk music (while performing country on stage) and were not entirely happy with it. Their first album for Decca, **This Land,** was pure folk.

But in 1962 they became members of the Grand Ole Opry and followed

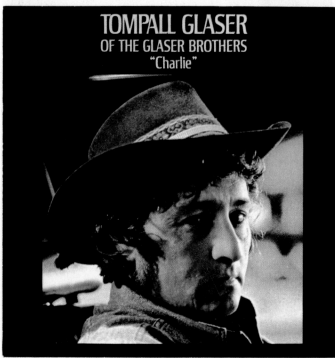

Above: Tompall Glaser; with his Outlaw Band he has become part of the country 'outlaw' movement.

a country direction from then on. Also in that year they toured with Johnny Cash (◆) and the dates this package played at Las Vegas and Carnegie Hall brought them an even wider audience.

In 1966 they signed with MGM Records and began a noteworthy recording career. Their delightful harmony voices and acoustic guitar work (although they employed full country backing also) were particularly suited to the more melodic country material, and they kept abreast of the latest songwriting trends too, using material from many sources.

Record World magazine, in 1974, voted them Vocal Group Of The Decade and in England too they won awards, becoming very popular visitors at the annual Easter Wembley Country Festival.

In 1973, after 15 years, the group split up. They already had a successful recording studio and publishing company to their name but Nashville was undergoing the trauma of the new movement, sparked off by the likes of Kris Kristofferson (◆), and Tompall particularly had ideas about the songs he wanted to write. He has now become simply Tompall (and his Outlaw Band) and his first solo album **Charlie** in 1973 indicated a change of direction, particularly in terms of lyrics, where Tompall began to delve into more personal, introspective themes. The song **Charlie** spoke of a man's past and future lives and seemed prophetic. Both single and album were well received, critically and saleswise.

Later albums have seen Tompall in the same mood, exploring themes and music that would not have been possible with the more melodic Glaser Brothers. A noteworthy single from his second album, **Take The Singer With The Song,** was the evocative **Lay Down Beside Me.** Tompall tours with Waylon Jennings (◆) and Willie Nelson (◆) as part of the 'Outlaws' package and he was a part of their 1976 **Wanted, The Outlaws** album on RCA. He has a gruff, dark brown voice with a catch in it and his sound often becomes a mite too dark and introspective. This led to an unsatisfactory level of sales as far as MGM were concerned, and in 1977 he changed labels to ABC-Dot. His first album for them was **Tompall And His Outlaw Band,** a set which featured a further move towards heavier, funkier backings. Tompall also enjoys a reputation as something of a high liver.

Brother Chuck runs Nashville's premier 'outlaw' booking agency, Nova, handling Waylon Jennings, David Allan Coe (◆) and others. He has immersed himself more in the business and record production side of things and has had a hand in some important productions, among them Kinky Friedman's (◆) excellent first album, **Sold American.** Chuck had a bad stroke shortly after the Glaser Brothers split up but recovered well, although he still suffers from some paralysis.

Jim Glaser is currently pursuing a less spectacular but mainstream country career.

Albums:

Tompall Glaser:	Tompall Glaser And His
The Great Tompall And His	**Outlaw Band** (ABC/ABC)
Outlaw Band (MGM(MGM)	**The Outlaws** (RCA/RCA) –
Tompall (MGM/—)	some tracks only

Left: Charlie (MGM). His first solo album after the Glasers had split up. They performed melodic, popular country; Tompall is deeper and more introspective.

Diana Trask

One of an extremely rare breed – an Aussie who's made it to the top in country-pop, Diana Trask was born in Melbourne, Australia, June 23, 1940. Winner of her country's top talent award at 16, she toured with a small group for a while then in 1959 headed for the States.

On the poverty line at first, her breakthrough came via a week with Don McNeill on ABC-TV's Breakfast Club. Diana, then purely a pop vocalist, became signed to Columbia Records, obtaining a guest spot on the Jack Benny Show, then being signed as a regular on Mitch Miller's Sing Along With Mitch TV show and even being offered a film contract by 20th Century Fox. However, her showbiz plans got momentarily sidetracked when Diana got married, returned to Australia and began raising a family. But during a trip to the CMA convention during the late '60s she became bitten by the country bug and stayed on in Nashville, having her first country hit with **Lock, Stock And Teardrops** (1968) before joining Dot Records and cutting an album, **Miss Country Soul,** which sparked off a number of chart entries that have included **I Fall To Pieces** (1969), **Beneath Still Waters** (1970), and **The Chokin' Kind** (1971).

Albums:
Diana's Country *(Dot/—)*
Sings About Loving *(Dot/—)*
Lean It All On Me *(Dot/—)*
The Mood I'm In *(Dot/—)*
Believe Me Now Or Believe Me Later *(ABC/—)*

Merle Travis

Easily one of the most, if not the most, multi-talented men ever to enter the music business was Merle Travis, born in Rosewood, Muhlenberg County, Kentucky on November 29, 1917. A singer and songwriter of major proportions and a guitar stylist of monumental influence, he also proved adept as an actor, author and even cartoonist.

Merle learned the basics of his celebrated guitar style from Mose Rager (also Ike Everly's teacher) who in turn learned it from a black railroad hand, fiddler, and guitarist named Arnold Shultz. Merle sophisticated the finger style to a degree of complexity unknown in that era (it was to prove extremely influential to Chet Atkins (♦) and many others), and his renown won him a job first with a group called the Tennessee Tomcats, before joining Clayton McMichen's Georgia Wildcats on WLW's Boone County Jamboree. There he also became a part of the Brown's Ferry Four and the Drifting Pioneers and appeared on NBC's 'Plantation Party'.

After a wartime stint in the Marines, Travis relocated on the west coast, perfecting his songwriting, appearing in minor roles in a host of westerns, playing in bands with Cliffie Stone (♦), Ray Whitley (♦), Jimmy Wakely (♦), Wesley Tuttle (♦), Tex Ritter (♦), and others. He also signed with Capitol Records and had several of the biggest hits of the era: **Divorce Me C.O.D.** (1946) and **So**

Round, So Firm, So Fully Packed (1947), and several others which ranked on the charts, **Dark As A Dungeon** (1947) and **Sixteen Tons** (1947), a 1955 hit for Tennessee Ernie Ford (♦).

A writer or co-writer of all his hits, he also co-wrote **No Vacancy** with Cliffie Stone and **Smoke! Smoke! Smoke!** with Tex Williams (♦). He was also adept at reworking folk tunes, and **John Henry, I Am A Pilgrim,** and **Nine Pound Hammer** were all adapted by and integrated into the Travis style.

In the 1950s Merle became a southern California fixture, appearing regularly on the Hometown Jamboree, Town Hall Party, and made a striking appearance as a guitar playing sailor in *From Here To Eternity*. He still lives in southern California (although he moved to Nashville for a time in the 1960s), and is still busy touring. A shoo-in for induction into the Country Music Hall of Fame, he would have achieved great fame as a singer only, more yet as a songwriter, and even more as one of the handful of most influential guitarists in country music history: Merle Travis possessed all these talents, and more.

Albums:
The Merle Travis Guitar *(Capitol/—)*
The Best Of . . . *(Capitol/—)*
The Atkins-Travis Traveling Show *(RCA/RCA)*

Above: Miss Country Soul (Dot). Originally a pop vocalist, this is Diana Trask's first country album.

Below: The Atkins-Travis Traveling Show (RCA).

Ernest Tubb

The sixth member to be elected to the Country Music Hall Of Fame; headliner on the first country music show ever to be presented at Carnegie Hall; a regular member of the Opry since 1943 – these are just a few of the achievements credited to Ernest Dale Tubb, the son of a

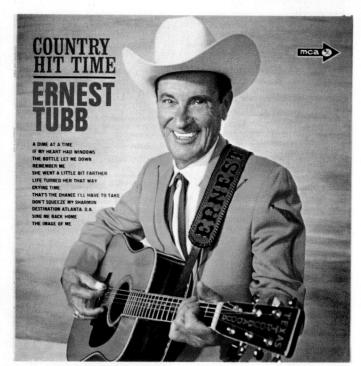

Ernest Tubb Record Shop (Decca). One of country music's most famous radio shows, the Midnight Jamboree, comes from Tubb's record shop in Nashville and has done since 1947.

Country Hit Time (MCA). A now deleted offering from the non-smoking teetotaller, who is constantly on tour and just as busy today as when he started in the early '30s.

Texas cotton farm overseer. Born Crisp, Texas, February 9, 1914, Tubb's boyhood hero was the great Jimmie Rodgers (♦). But though he had dreams of emulating Rodgers and sang at various local get-togethers during his early teens, Tubb was almost 20 before he owned his first guitar.

The year 1934 proved important for him, Tubb then obtaining his initial radio dates on San Antonio KONO – during this period marrying Lois Elaine Cook.

But 1935 also brought its incidents, Tubb's eldest son Justin (♦) being born in the August of that year – and a meeting with Carrie Rodgers (Jimmie's widow) taking place. She and Ernest Tubb became good friends, Mrs Rodgers loaning him her husband's original guitar (still in his posession) and also arranging an RCA record session at which Tubb cut two sides; **The Passing Of Jimmie Rodgers** and **Jimmie Rodgers' Last Thoughts**.

However, Tubb's luck wasn't always that good. His second son, Rodger Dale, was born July, 1938 but died after just a few weeks. Things began to look brighter after the birth of a daughter, Violet Elaine, on December 3, 1939, then Decca offered him a new record contract and he obtained a job on Fort Worth's KGKO, which later led to Tubb being sponsored by Universal Mills, makers of Gold Chain Flour.

It was at this stage that he became the Gold Chain Troubador, earning $75 a week promoting Universal's wares. It was a nickname which preceded his famous Texas Troubador image. By 1941 he'd also moved into movies, appearing in *Fightin' Buckaroos*, a Columbia release. Then came his recording of **Walking The Floor Over You**, a self-penned composition. Released in the fall of '42, it became a million-seller, helping Tubb gain his first appearance on the Opry in December, 1942, regular membership coming during the following year.

He continued logging up successful discs and film appearances in such productions as *Ridin' West* (1942), *Jamboree* (1943) and *Hollywood Barn Dance* (1947), also in '47 opening his now famous record shop near Nashville's Ryman Auditorium and commencing his Midnight Jamboree program over WSM, advertising the shop and showcasing the talents of up-and-coming country artists.

Tubb married again in 1949, his new wife being Olene Adams, mother of Erlene, Olene, Ernest Jnr, Larry and Karen Tubb. That year he appeared on hit records with the Andrews Sisters and Red Foley (♦), also managing to achieve Top Ten placings with no less than five of his solo efforts, the biggest of these being **Slippin' Around** and **Blue Christmas**. And until 1969 he became the charts' Mr Consistency, thanks to such discs as **Goodnight Irene** (with Red Foley 1950), **I Love You Because** (1950), **Missing In Action** (1952), **Two Glasses Joe** (1954), **Half A Mind** (1958), **Thanks A Lot** (1963), **Mr And Mrs Used-To-Be** (with Loretta Lynn (♦) 1964), and **Another Story, Another Time, Another Place** (1966), his only real absence from the hit listing being between 1952 and 1954 when, following an exhausting Far East tour, Tubb suffered from an illness that kept him off the Opry from some considerable while.

Nowadays he doesn't smoke, doesn't drink, and keeps himself fit for his constant touring by myriad rounds of golf. And although 63 he's never happier than when on the road with his Texas Troubadors – a band which has spawned such talents as Jack Greene (♦) and Cal Smith (♦).

And still the radio shows from his record store continue – though they currently emanate from Tubb's new shop on Nashville's Demonbreun Street.

Albums:
Golden Favourites *(MCA/—)*
Great Country *(Vocalion/—)*
Greatest Hits *(MCA/—)*
Greatest Hits Vol 2 *(MCA/—)*
Just Call Me Lonesome *(MCA/—)*
My Hillbilly Baby *(Hillside/—)*
Stand By Me *(Vocalion/—)*
Ernest Tubb Story *(MCA/—)*
Texas Troubadors *(Vocalion/—)*
Ernest Tubb *(MCA/—)*

Justin Tubb

Eldest son of Ernest Tubb (♦), singer-songwriter-guitarist Justin was born San Antonio, Texas, August 20, 1935. One of the many country singers who began entertaining during their high school days, he claims that his career received a real fillip when his father recorded one of his songs in 1952. That year, he and two of his cousins formed a group and began playing clubs in and around the Austin area, where Tubb was attending the University of Texas. But after just a year of college came the inevitable move to Nashville and a deejaying job on radio station WHIN in nearby Gallatin, Tennessee, where Tubb not only spun discs but also entertained his listeners with his own songs.

In 1953 he signed with Decca, the following year having two hits with **Looking Back To See** and **Sure Fire Kisses**, both duets with Goldie Hill (♦). Although Tubb became an Opry regular in '55, his records only sold moderately well and he began to label hop, leaving Decca in 1959 and cutting sides for Challenge and Starday. Then, after a Top Ten Groove release in **Take A Letter, Miss Gray** (1963) came a long association with RCA and a trio of moderate chart visits via **Hurry, Mr Peters** (1965), **We've Gone Too Far Again** (1966) – both duets with Lorene Mann – and **But Wait There's More,** a solo item from 1967.

Once an inveterate tourer, Tubb has played in all but two states, and has also appeared in Canada, Bermuda, Spain, Britain, West Germany and Panama. And during 1967 he took a show to the Far East, entertaining servicemen in Vietnam and other areas. Nowadays he rarely makes personal appearances, but manages a publishing company and is also in charge of the Ernest Tubb Midnight Jamboree, a live show broadcast from the Ernest Tubb Record Shop on Demonbreun Street in Nashville, immediately after the Grand Ole Opry program. He has also enjoyed considerable success as a songwriter, his most notable composition being a number called **Lonesome 7-7203**.

Tanya Tucker

When she was nine years old, people at both MGM and RCA Records wanted to sign her. At 14 she'd gained a Top Ten hit and a year later her face bedecked the cover of The Rolling Stone. Shortly after, she'd come up with the biggest country single in the land, also acquiring a reputation as a musical Lolita for employing songs with provocative lyrics.

Born Seminole, Texas, October 10, 1958, Tanya Denise Tucker, the daughter of a construction worker, spent her early years in Wilcox, Arizona, moving to Phoenix in 1967. There, Tanya and her father began attending as many country concerts as possible, visiting local fairs to hear Mel Tillis (♦), Leroy Van Dyke (♦), Ernest Tubb (♦) and others, Tanya often joining the stars onstage for an impromptu song.

Following a cameo role in the movie *Jeremiah Johnson*, Tanya, then 13, cut a demo tape that included her renditions of **For The Good Times, Put Your Hand In The Hand** and other songs, the results eventually impressing Columbia executive Billy Sherrill (♦), who signed Tanya to the label

Above: Ernest Tubb. In October 1947 he headed the first ever country date at Carnegie Hall – a Grand Ole Opry team.

Columbia KC 32272

TANYA TUCKER WHAT'S YOUR MAMA'S NAME *FEATURING* **BLOOD RED AND GOIN' DOWN**

Teddy Bear Song
Horseshoe Bend
California Cotton Fields
Rainy Girl
Pass Me By
The Missing Piece Of Puzzle
Song Man
The Chokin' Kind
Teach Me The Words To Your Song
What's Your Mama's Name

and promptly produced her recording of Alex Harvey's **Delta Dawn.** The result was a 1972 Top Ten item, after which the Tucker-Sherrill partnership moved into further action to provide further chartbusters with **Love's The Answer, What's Your Mama's**

Here's Some Love (MCA).
Tanya changed labels in 1975.

Name?, Blood Red And Going Down (1973), **Would You Lay With Me (In A Field Of Stone)** and **The Man That Turned My Mama On** (1974), **Would You Lay With Me** becoming a hit of international proportions.

In 1975, following a million-dollar deal, Tanya signed for MCA, thus terminating her association with Sherrill and creating some doubts as to her ability to survive without the guiding hand of the Columbia Svengali. But the doubts were quickly dispelled when **Lizzie And The Rainman, San Antonio Stroll** (1975), **You've Got Me To Hold On To, Don't Believe My Heart Can Stand Another You, Here's Some Love** (1976) and **Riding Rainbows** (1977) all rocketed up the charts. Tanya's older sister, LaCosta (◆), is also a country star of some considerable merit.

Albums:
Delta Dawn *(Columbia/—)*

What's Your Mama's Name (Columbia). Following an early interest in country music, Tanya Tucker was signed by Columbia and had an incredible run of success.

What's Your Mama's Name?
(Columbia/—)
Greatest Hits *(Columbia/CBS)*
Here's Some Love *(MCA/MCA)*
Tanya Tucker *(MCA/MCA)*
Lovin' And Learnin'
(MCA/MCA)
Ridin' Rainbows *(MCA/MCA)*

Wesley Tuttle

Tuttle, born in Lamar, Colorado, became west coast based, after various radio stints that included a

stay on WLW, Cincinnati, appearing in films and as a regular on Compton's Town Party along with Tex Williams (◆), Cliffie Stone (◆), Tex Ritter (◆) etc. Tuttle became signed to Capitol Records in 1945, one of his most successful sides for the label being his version of **Crying In The Chapel** (1953). He also recorded several duets with his wife Marilyn, the duo making some albums for RCA in the late '50s but later fading from the mainstream country scene when Tuttle began working as an evangelist, recording only religious material.

Conway Twitty

Real name Harold Lloyd Jenkins, born Friars Point, Mississippi, September 1, 1933, Twitty learnt guitar on board a riverboat piloted by his

236

country music-loving father. Almost signed by the Philadelphia baseball team (he nowadays runs his own softball squad known as the Twitty-birds), Twitty was drafted before the contract could be concluded and spent two years in the army instead.

During the mid '50s he became a rock and roll singer, playing on many radio stations and scoring with a Mercury single **I Need Your Lovin'** (1957). Shortly after, he joined MGM Records and won a gold disc for **It's Only Make Believe,** one of 1958s biggest sellers. Hardly out of the pop charts between September 1958 and April 1961, he also appeared in three teen-angled films during this period – *Sex Kittens Go To College*, *Platinum High School* and *College Confidential*. It was at this time that Twitty began writing country songs, his **Walk Me To The Door** being recorded by Ray Price (♦) in 1960. By June 1965, he himself was cutting country sides under Decca's Owen Bradley (♦), at the same time settling down in Oklahoma City playing with a band known as the Lonely Blue Boys and (in June, 1966) commencing a syndicated TV program, The Conway Twitty Show.

During the late '60s, Twitty moved to Nashville and began amassing an incredible number of massive selling discs – his list of country hits (which began in 1966 with **Guess My Eyes Were Bigger Than My Heart**) being swelled by **Next In Line, I Love You More Today, To See My Angel Cry, Hello Darlin', 15 Years Ago, How Much More Can She Stand?, You've Never Been This Far Before, She Needs Someone To Hold Her, The Games That Daddies Play, Play Guitar Play** and many others, the majority of his releases attaining the pole position in the charts. A series of duets with Loretta Lynn (♦) quickly established the twosome as the most popular country couple of the '70s, Twitty and Lynn winning the CMA Vocal Duo Of The Year award in 1972, '73, '74 and '75.

Originally named after a famous silent film comedian, he took his stage name from the towns of Conway (in Arkansas) and Twitty (in Texas). Made honorary chief of the Choctaw nation in the early '70s, he was also awarded an Indian title Hatako-Chtokchito-A-Yakni-Toloa – which translates into 'Great Man Of Country Music'.

Albums:
Greatest Hits *(MGM/—)*
Greatest Hits Vol 1 *(MCA/—)*
Hello Darlin' *(MCA/—)*
Honky Tonk Angels *(MCA/—)*
I'm Not Through Loving You *(MCA/—)*
To See My Angel Cry *(MCA/—)*
Shake It Up *(Pickwick/—)*
You've Never Been This Way/ Baby's Gone *(MCA/—)*
Greatest Hits Vol 2 *(MCA/—)*
High Priest Of Country *(MCA/—)*
Linda On My Mind *(MCA/MCA)*
Now And Then *(MCA/MCA)*

Twitty *(MCA/—)*
Best Of Conway Twitty *(—/MCA)*
Play Guitar Play *(MCA/MCA)*

With Loretta Lynn:
Louisiana Woman, Mississippi Man *(MCA/—)*
We Only Make Believe *(MCA/—)*
Country Partners *(MCA/MCA)*
Feelin's *(MCA/MCA)*
United Talent *(MCA/MCA)*
Never Ending Song Of Love *(—/Coral)*

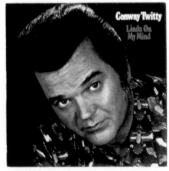

Above: Two from Twitty, Linda On My Mind and To See An Angel Cry (MCA)

T. Texas Tyler

Tyler, real name David Luke Myrick, was born June 20, 1916, near Mena, Arkansas. Educated in Philadelphia, he began his career at the age of 14, heading east and appearing on the Major Bowes Amateur Hour in New York during the '30s. He became widely known as 'The Man With A Million Friends'.

Later came a further move to West Virginia, while in 1942 Tyler was in Louisiana, becoming a member of Shreveport KWKH's Hayride (♦) show.

A period in the armed forces followed, Tyler settling down in the Hollywood area upon discharge and forming the T. Texas Western Dance Band, a popular unit whose lifespan lasted some 12 years. It

was during this period that Tyler wrote and recorded **Deck Of Cards,** a hit for the Four Star label in 1948. A somewhat sentimental but ingenious monolog regarding a soldier who employs a deck of cards as his Bible, prayer book and almanack, the number became a million-seller when recorded by Wink Martindale, also becoming a hit for Tex Ritter (♦) and British comedian Max Bygraves. Following this record, which won the *Cashbox* award for the best country disc of 1948, Tyler produced several more winners, the most potent of these being **Dad Gave The Dog Away** (1948), **Bumming Around** (1953), **Courting In The Rain** (1954) and his theme song, **Remember Me.**

During 1949 the Arkansas traveller appeared in *Horseman Of The Sierras*, a Columbia movie, and

won a fair amount of acclaim for Range Round-Up, his Los Angeles TV show. In the '50s and '60s, he continued performing both live and on TV, but despite some worthwhile Starday releases Tyler failed to place his name on the record charts during the later stages of his career. He died from natural causes on January 28, 1972 in Springfield, Missouri.

T. Texas Tyler – His Great Hits (Hilltop). Includes his theme song, Remember Me.

Uncle Henry's Original Kentucky Mountaineers

A fine and popular old time string band which, by making certain concessions to modernity, remained active well into the 1940s. 'Uncle Henry' Warren was born in Taylor County, Kentucky, in 1903, and possessed a deep love for old time music. Although he did not play an instrument, he was the leader of the band as MC and comedian.

The band began as early as 1928, over KFLV in Rockford, Illinois, but rose to prominence in Louisville where they spent four years over WHAS, hosting the WHAS Morning Jamboree. They also spent time at WNOX in Knoxville, WLAP in Lexington, and WHIS in Bluefield, West Virginia. In 1940 they moved to the WJJD Suppertime Frolic in Chicago, where they spent the war years and well into the late 1940s, cutting an extensive series of transcriptions for Capitol during this period.

Band members included Paul South, singer and writer of much of their original material; Sally and Coon Hunter, a duet team; Dell Remick, steel guitarist; and Jimmy Dale Warren, Uncle Henry's son, who eventually moved to the west coast and has spent the past 24 years as the lead singer for the Sons of the Pioneers (♦).

Albums: none.

The Vagabonds

Herald Goodman *vocals*
Curt Poulton *vocals and guitar*
Dean Upson *vocals*

A smooth singing harmony trio who were with the Grand Ole Opry from 1931–1938. They were unique on the Opry at the time, for they were non-Southerners (all were from the midwest), they had acquired and used formal musical

training, they were primarily a vocal band using only Poulton's guitar for backup, and they were the first real professional band the Opry ever had, depending on music for their full time living.

Upson had formed the Vagabonds at WLS in 1925; Poulton joined in 1928 and Goodman completed the trio at KMOX in St Louis in 1930. They were best known for their extremely popular **When It's Lamp Lighting Time In The Valley,** and recorded a host of similar sentimental tunes for Bluebird and other smaller labels. The Vagabonds broke up in 1938 when Goodman left to head the Saddle Mountain Roundup over KV00 in Tulsa. Poulton turned to MC and occasional guitar work, while Upson eventually became a WSM executive.

Albums: none.

Leroy Van Dyke

Co-writer (with Buddy Black) and singer of **The Auctioneer,** a 1956 gold disc winner that incorporated a genuine high-speed auctioneering routine, Van Dyke (born Spring Fork, Missouri, October 4, 1929) originally decided on a career in agriculture, obtaining a BS degree in that subject at the University of Missouri. After serving with army intelligence during the Korean War he became a livestock auctioneer and agricultural correspondent, utilizing his writing skills to pen songs. He sang **The Auctioneer** on a talent show and subsequently won a contract with Dot Records, his song providing his first release – a 2½ million seller. A regular on the Red Foley (♦) TV Show, he later became signed to Mercury, providing that label with **Walk On By,** yet another million seller, in 1961, following this with other major hits like **If A Woman Answers** and **Black Cloud** during the following year. Since that period, however, his releases have rarely charted impressively, only **Louisville** (1968) making any real impression.

Van Dyke, who made his film debut in *What Am I Bid* (1967) has recorded for Warner, Kapp and Decca since leaving Mercury in 1965.

Albums:
Golden Hits *(Sun/—)*
Greatest Hits *(MCA/—)*

Porter Wagoner

Once a grocery store clerk, Wagoner (born West Plains, Missouri, August 12, 1930) whiled away slow trading periods by picking guitar and singing, his performances being so impressive that he was engaged to promote the business over an early morning radio show. His popularity on radio eventually led to a weekly series on KWTO, Springfield in 1951, Wagoner later moving on to TV when KWTO became the home of Red Foley's (♦) Ozark Jubilee show. In 1955 he became signed to RCA, supplying his first Top Five that same year with **Satisfied Mind.** Following two similarly successful singles in **Eat, Drink And Be Merry** (1955) and **What Would You Do (If Jesus**

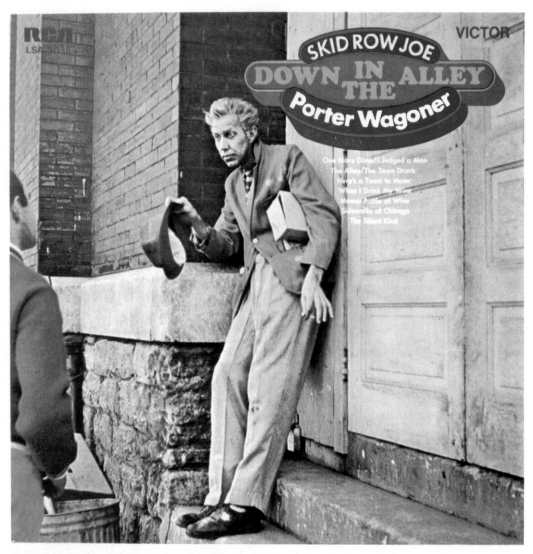

pop vocalist Margaret Whiting, the disc soon became a million-seller for Capitol Records. Other hits with Margaret Whiting followed (including **I'll Never Slip Around Again**), the duo logging no less than seven Top Ten discs within two years. Meanwhile, Wakely also did well in a solo capacity, such records as **I Love You So Much It Hurts** (1949), **I Wish I Had A Nickel** (1949), **My Heart Cries For You** (1950) and **Beautiful Brown Eyes** (1951), charting impressively. His 1948 hit **One Has My Name, The Other Has My Heart,** in fact, started a whole cycle of 'Cheatin' songs' which **Slippin' Around** accelerated.

But during the mid '50s, the Wakely career seemed to run out of steam, and though he had a CBS networked radio show until 1958 and co-hosted a TV series with Tex Ritter (♦) in 1961, his record sales diminished, Wakely forming his own label, Shasta. By the middle of the '70s Wakely was still in showbiz, mainly playing to clubs in LA and Las Vegas, using an act that featured his children Johnny and Linda Lee.

Albums:
Big Country Songs (Vocalion/—)
In Person, Jimmy Wakely, The Singing Cowboy (Shasta/—)
Reflections (Shasta/—)
Country Hits Of The '40s
 (Capitol/—) – two tracks only
The Great American Singing Cowboys (Republic/—)

Billy Walker

Once billed as 'The Traveling Texan – The Masked Singer Of Country Songs', William Marvin Walker was born Ralls, Texas, January 14, 1929.

In 1944, at the age of 15, while Walker was attending Whiteface High School, New Mexico, he won an amateur talent show, the prizes being a chocolate cake and three dollars. But the contest also gained him his own 15-minute Saturday radio show on KICA, Clovis, New Mexico, Walker hitchhiking 80 miles to play on the program, then hitching his way home again. Joining the Big D Jamboree in Dallas during 1949 he adopted his masked singer guise; the ploy worked, gaining the Texan a considerable following and a subsequent record contract from Columbia.

Other shows followed, Walker appearing on the Louisiana Hayride (♦) in the early '50s, the Ozark Jubilee between 1955–60 and joining the Opry in 1960. His first hit disc came in 1954 with **Thank You For Calling,** but it wasn't until 1962 and the release of **Charlie's Shoes,** a nationwide No 1, that Walker began to dominate the charts. The majority of his discs became Top 20 entries during the following decade, providing Columbia with such hits as **Willie The Weeper** (1962), **Circumstances** (1964), **Cross The Brazos At Waco** (1964), and **Matmoros** (1965) before signing with Monument and scoring with **A Million And One** (1966), **Bear With Me A Little Longer** (1966), **Anything Your Heart Desires** (1967), **Ramona** (1968) and **Thinking About You, Baby** (1969). By 1970 Walker had joined MGM, gaining

---

Down In The Alley (RCA Victor). A popular and oft-repeated theme of Wagoner's – the life and times of a derelict, in startling contrast to his love duets with Dolly Parton. An earlier singing partner on his TV show was Norma Jean.

Came To Your House) (1956), the Missourian joined the Opry (1957), in 1960 moving on to formulate his own TV show with singer Norma Jean (♦) (later replaced by Dolly Parton (♦)) and his band The Wagonmasters. Filmed in Nashville and initially syndicated to 18 stations, by the late '60s the program was being screened to over 100 outlets throughout the USA and Canada, establishing Wagoner's touring show as one of the most popular on the country circuit. Predominantly straight country in his own musical approach, although sometimes seemingly a catalyst for more startling innovations (Buck Trent first began playing electric banjo on the Wagoner program while Porter has also been involved in some of Dolly Parton's more contemporary moves) he's managed to gain a consistent foothold in the upper reaches of the charts throughout the years, having Top Ten solo hits with **Your Old Love Letters** (1961), **Misery Loves Company** (1962), **Cold Dark Waters** (1962), **I've Enjoyed As Much Of This As I Can Stand** (1962), **Sorrow On The Rocks** (1964), **Green, Green Grass Of Home** (1965), **Skid Row Joe** (1965), **The Cold, Hard Facts**

Of Life (1967), **Carroll County Incident** (1968) and **Big Wind** (1969), also sharing an impressive number of hit duets with Dolly Parton, the more recent of these including **Burning The Midnight Oil** (1971), **Please Don't Stop Loving Me** (1974) and **Is Forever Longer Than Always?** (1976). Wagoner's albums have included 'live' recordings made in 1964 and 1966; a bluegrass offering, cut in '65; some 'downer' sessions, typified by such releases as **The Cold Hard Facts Of Life** and **Confessions Of A Broken Man,** both releases dealing with the seamier side of humanity, and a number of duet LPs with Skeeter Davis (♦) and Dolly Parton.

Albums:
Best Of . . . (RCA/RCA)
Carroll County Incident (RCA/—)
The Farmer (RCA/—)
Silent Kind (Camden/—)
Tore Down (RCA/—)
Highway Heading South (RCA/RCA)
Sing Some Love Songs, Porter Wagoner (RCA/RCA)

With Dolly Parton:
Best Of Porter Wagoner And Dolly Parton (RCA/RCA)
Love And Music (RCA/—)
Porter And Dolly (RCA/—)
Say Forever You'll Be Mine (RCA/RCA)
Two Of A Kind (—/RCA)
We Found It (—/RCA)
Just The Two Of Us (—/RCA)

Jimmy Wakely

One of country music's major stars during the '40s and early '50s, James Clarence Wakely was born in a log cabin at Mineola, Arkansas, February 16, 1914. Raised and schooled in Oklahoma, where he took such jobs as a sharecropper, journalist and filling station manager, he became a professional musician during the mid '30s, forming the Jimmy Wakely Trio with Johnny Bond (♦) and Scotty Harrell in 1937, the group appearing daily on Oklahoma City's WKY radio station. In 1940, Gene Autry (♦) guested on the show, liked the trio and signed them for his Hollywood-based Melody Ranch CBS radio program.

On Melody Ranch, Wakely quickly established himself as a star in his own right – eventually securing parts in over 50 Hollywood movies (in 1948 he was nominated as the fourth most popular Western film actor – only Roy Rogers (♦), Gene Autry and Charles Starrett being rated higher). And after two years on the Autry show he left to form his own band, employing such musicians as Cliffie Stone (♦), Spade Cooley (♦), Merle Travis (♦) and Wesley Tuttle (♦). By 1949 he'd become so popular that he beat both Frank Sinatra and Bing Crosby in the *Billboard* pop vocalist poll, enjoying a huge hit with his version of Floyd Tillman's (♦) **Slippin' Around.** Recorded as a duet with

The Hand Of Love (MGM). A deleted album from The Masked Singer of Country Songs, who has been a chart regular and Opry member since the early '60s.

high chart placings with **When A Man Loves A Woman** (1970), **I'm Gonna Keep On Loving You** (1971) and **Sing A Love Song To Baby** (1972) but by 1975 had switched to RCA, obtaining minor chart positions with **Don't Stop The World, (Here I Am) Alone Again** and **Love You All To Pieces** in 1976.

Walker has also made some movie appearances, two of which were in *Second Fiddle To A Steel Guitar* and *Red River Round-Up*.

Albums:
Portrait/Darling Days
  (Monument/—)
Lovin' And Losin' *(RCA/—)*
Alone Again *(RCA/—)*

Charlie Walker

Born Collins County, Texas, November 2, 1926, Walker was a precocious singing and writing talent, becoming a good musician in his teens and joining Bill Boyd's Cowboy Ramblers in 1943. Later he was successful on radio, his announcing style being much sought after and getting him rated in *Billboard*'s Top Ten Country Music Disc Jockey listing. He signed with Columbia Records in the mid '50s and in 1958 had his first big hit with **Pick Me Up On Your Way Down**. During the '60s and early '70s, he recorded for Columbia and Epic, having hits with several songs, among them being **Who'll Buy The Wine?** (1960), **Wild As A Wild Cat** (1965) and **Don't Squeeze My Sharmon** (1967), also cutting a series of honky tonk titles that has included **Close All The Honky Tonks** (1964), **Honky Tonk Season** (1969) and **Honky Tonk Women** (1970). His announcing capabilities helped him gain many cabaret residencies, most notably at the Las Vegas Golden Nugget. A capable golfer, Walker has won respect as a knowledgeable golf-

ing broadcaster. In 1972 he became an RCA recording artist, his albums for that label including **Charlie Walker, Break Out The Bottle** and **I Don't Mind Going Under.**

I Don't Mind Goin' Under (RCA).

Jerry Jeff Walker

Originally a folkie operating out of New York, Jerry Jeff (born Oeneota, New York, March 16, 1942) has more recently become associated with the new wave country movement emanating from Austin (♦), Texas.

During the mid '60s he formed a rock group, Circus Maximus, with Austin songwriter Bob Runo, the band recording for Vanguard. However, Walker opted to become a solo act in 1968 and cut the self-penned **Mr Bojangles**, a memorable song regarding a street dancer he once met in a New Orleans jail, also providing Acto with an album of the same title. But though **Mr Bojangles** became

a much covered song and provided the Dirt Band (♦) with a Top Ten hit in 1970, Walker's career seemed to remain fairly stationary for a considerable period. Signed to MCA in the early '70s, he began recording a series of increasingly interesting country-oriented albums, often employing material of good-timey or barroom nature. Also he began employing a backup unit known as the Lost Gonzo Band, who have since become a recording band in their own right.

Albums:
Drifting Way Of Life
  (Vanguard/—)
Jerry Jeff Walker *(MCA/—)*
Viva Terlingua *(MCA/—)*
Collectibles *(MCA/—)*
Ridin' High *(MCA/—)*
It's A Good Night For Singin'
  (MCA/MCA)

Jerry Wallace

Billed as 'Mr Smooth' – though he's been known to rock – Wallace is a one time pop vocalist who swung into country music during the mid '60s and has since amassed over a score of hits.

Born Kansas City, December 15, 1933, singer-songwriter-guitarist Wallace was raised and educated

It's A Good Night For Singin' *(MCA)*. Once a folk singer and now based in Austin, this album is typical of Walker's poker-playing and drinking songs.

Shutters and Boards (Mercury).

in California. Following a brief term of service in the Navy, he made his first chart impact in 1958 when his recording of **How The Time Flies,** on Challenge, reached 11th place in the pop charts. The following year brought even more success when Wallace's version of **Primrose Lane,** a number later used as a theme for Henry Fonda's 'Smith Family' TV series, became a million-seller.

After providing Challenge with 11 hit discs, Wallace signed for Mercury and cut more country-oriented material, **Life's Gone And Slipped Away** (1965) gaining him his first country chart entry. Since that time, he has cut sides for such labels as Liberty, Decca, MCA and MGM, his major C&W hits including **The Morning After** (1971), **To Get To You** (1972), **Do You Know What It's Like To Be Lonesome?** (a No 1 in 1973), **Sound Of Goodbye** (1973), **Don't Give Up On Me** (1973), **Guess Who?** (1974) and **Coming Home To You** (1975). A performer on many top TV programs, Wallace's voice has been heard on myriad commercials and even on such unlikely TV series as 'Hec Ramsey' and Rod Serling's 'Night Gallery'.

Albums:
Wives And Lovers *(MCA/—)*
Do You Know What It's Like To Be Lonesome? *(MCA/—)*
Superpak *(UA/—)*
Primrose Lane *(MCA/—)*
I Wonder Whose Baby (You Are Now) *(MCA/—)*
Jerry Wallace *(MGM/—)*
Greatest Hits *(MGM/—)*

Doc Watson

Folk legend and heir to an old time country tradition, guitarist, banjoist, singer, Arthel (Doc) Watson was rediscovered in the boom folk years of the '60s and again in the '70s when the Nitty Gritty Dirt Band (♦) brought his music to the newly-enthusiastic country rock public.

Born Deep Gap, North Carolina, March 2, 1923, Doc was son of a farmer who was prominent in the singing activities of the local Bap-

tist church. Doc's grandparents lived with his immediate family and they taught the boy many traditional folk songs. He also listened to records of the Carter Family (♦) and Gid Tanner's Skillet Lickers (♦). His first appearance was at the Boone, North Carolina, Fiddler's Convention. He achieved fame locally but with country music 'smartening up' and with rock 'n' roll finally hitting the scene, the mountain tradition was not foremost in the mind of national America.

In 1960 some east coast recording executives came to cut Clarence Ashley's String Band and Ashley then appeared on a New York 'Friends Of Old Time Music' bill

Two Days In November (Poppy) - with Merle Watson. After the arrival of country rock in the early '70s Doc's career revived strongly, as it had done in the folk-laden '60s.

Doc & Merle Watson
"Two Days In November"

POPPY

in 1961. Doc was invited along on the bill. As a consequence he scored a solo gig at Gerde's Folk City in Greenwich Village, being rapturously received. The hunger of young people for an antidote to a pop business then backsliding into blandness was fed by ethnic artists such as Doc. In 1963 he consolidated his reputation considerably with an appearance on the Newport Folk Festival.

Doc relies heavily on traditional material. His voice, his guitar and banjo playing have a simplicity and intense profundity, and songs like **Tom Dooley** and **Shady Grove** he has almost made his own.

During the '60s he recorded for Folkways. He has variously been heard on record with his mother, Mrs G. D. Watson, Jean Ritchie, his brother Arnold, Arnold's father-in-law Gaither Carlton and, recently and most fruitfully, with son Merle.

In 1964 he signed with Vanguard Records. In the early '70s his career was to undergo another revival. The Nitty Gritty Dirt Band (♦) championed the cause of traditional acoustic country by recording a three-album set for UA with guests from the cream of country and folk music circles. With their rock following, the Dirt Band and **Will The Circle Be Unbroken** certainly did no harm to Doc's career. He is now a revered figure among old and young alike, drawing wild receptions quite out of keeping with his down-home musical style.

Albums:
Doc Watson *(Vanguard/—)*
And Son *(Vanguard/—)*
Elementary *(Vanguard/—)*
Essential *(Vanguard/—)*
Old Time Music At Clarence Ashley's Vol 1 *(Folkways/—)*
Old Time Music At Clarence Ashley's Vol 2 *(Folkways/—)*
Jean Ritchie And Doc Watson At Folk City *(Folkways/—)*
And Family *(Folkways/—)*
Home Again *(Vanguard/—)*
In Nashville *(Vanguard/—)*
On Stage *(Vanguard/—)*
Southbound *(Vanguard/—)*
Then And Now – with Merle Watson *(Poppy/—)*
Two Days In November – with Merle Watson *(Poppy/—)*
And The Boys *(UA/—)*
Memories *(UA/—)*

Gene Watson

A singer with an easy-flowing style and a penchant for tearstained ballads, Watson is a Texan who initially worked out of Houston. After gigging with the Wilburn Brothers (♦) he became the resi-

Because You Believed in Me (Capitol).

dent singer at the Dynasty Club in Houston and began cutting sides for various independent record labels. Obtaining a regional hit with **Love In The Hot Afternoon** he became signed to Capitol Records, who made the disc into a Top Five country chart success in mid 1975, following this with such other impressive chart entries as **Where Love Begins** (1975), **You Could Know As Much About A Stranger** (1976), **Because You Believed In Me** (1976) and **Paper Rosie** (1977).

Albums:
Love In The Hot Afternoon *(Capitol/—)*
Because You Believed In Me *(Capitol/—)*
Paper Rosie *(Capitol/Capitol)*

Above: Paper Rosie (EMI), Gene Watson's third album.

Dennis Weaver

A character actor best known for his TV roles in Gunsmoke (as the limping, slow drawling Chester – 1958–64), Kentucky Jones (1965) and McCloud (1970 onwards), the easy-going Weaver has acquired both a western image and a reasonable reputation as a country singer. Born 1924, he hails from Joplin, Missouri. A Western movie addict as a child, he later became a top grade athlete in track events, just failing to qualify for the Olympic Games in 1948.

Following graduation from Oklahoma University, he became part of the New York Artists Studio, making his Broadway debut in 'Come Back Little Sheba' with Shirley Booth (1951). By the following year he'd moved into films, appearing in *The Raiders*, later making *War Arrow* (1954), *Dragnet* (1954), *Seven Angry Men* (1955), *A Touch Of Evil* (1958), *The Gallant Hours* (1960), *Duel At Diablo* (1966) and many others. Recording his first country album, **Dennis Weaver,** for the Impress label in 1972, he subsequently signed for Ovation, for whom he made **One More Road.** And by 1976, he'd gone the whole hog, spending some time in Nashville with producer Ray Pennington and emerging with a second album titled **Dennis Weaver,** adjudged his strongest bet to date.

Albums:
One More Road *(Ovation/DJM)*
British title **McCloud Country**
Dennis Weaver *(—/DJM)*

Freddy Weller

Born September 9, 1947, Atlanta, Georgia, before becoming a coun-

Above: Gene Watson, another 'overnight sensation' who's been on the scene for a number of years. His version of Paper Rosie was a top five hit.

try artist and obtaining a contract with Columbia Records Weller achieved a fair degree of fame in the field of pop, both as a member of hit-parading rock group Paul Revere And The Raiders, with whom he debuted on the Ed Sullivan Show during April, 1967, and also as co-writer of many songs with Tommy Roe, including the million-sellers **Dizzy** (1968) and **Jam Up, Jelly Tight** (1969).

Once a bassist and guitarist with Joe South, Weller has also worked as a studio musician in Atlanta and toured as part of Billy Joe Royal's backup group.

After achieving a Top Ten country hit with **Games People Play** in 1969, Weller enjoyed a successful patch through to 1971, **These Are Not My People, Promised Land, Indian Lake** and **Another Night Of Love** all charting impressively during this period. In late '74 Weller signed for Dot and cut one album for the label, resigning for Columbia after just a year.

Albums:
Too Much Monkey Business *(Columbia/—)*
Sexy Lady *(Columbia/—)*
Roadmaster *(Columbia/—)*
Freddy Weller *(Dot/—)*
Another Night Of Love *(Columbia/—)*
Greatest Hits *(Columbia/—)*
Liquor, Love and Life *(Columbia/—)*

Freddy Weller (Columbia)

Kitty Wells

The acknowledged Queen Of Country Music, Kitty Wells (real name Muriel Deason) was born Nashville, Tennessee, August 30, 1918. As a child she sang gospel music at the neighborhood church, at 14 learning to play guitar. Within a year she was playing at local dances, sometime later obtaining her first radio dates. While appearing on station WXIX's 'Dixie Early Birds' show, she met Johnny Wright (Johnny And Jack (♦)), whom she married two years later (1938). By this time she had become a featured artist on the Johnny and Jack touring show, adopting the name Kitty Wells from a folk song called 'Sweet Kitty Wells'.

With their backup unit The Tennessee Mountain Boys, Johnny and Jack and Kitty Wells toured widely during the late '30s and the war years of the '40s, their biggest breaks on radio coming in 1940 on WBIG, Greensboro, North Carolina, then later on WNOX Knoxville's 'Mid-Day Merry-Go-Round'. In 1947 came Johnny, Jack and Kitty's membership on Grand Ole Opry, after which they moved to Shreveport to become the stars of KWKH's new Louisiana Hayride (♦). Five years later came an offer of a regular spot on the Opry, plus a record contract from Decca (she'd previously recorded with RCA-Victor), the same year seeing the release of **It Wasn't God Who Made Honky Tonk Angels,** an answer disc to Hank Thompson's (♦) **Wild Side Of Life,** that enabled Kitty to become the first female to have a No 1 country hit – although Patsy Montana's I Wanna Be A Cowboy's Sweetheart would have reached No 1 if charts had existed in 1935.

Since that time Kitty Wells has amassed an amazing number of chart entries, including duets with Roy Drusky (♦), Red Foley (♦), Roy Acuff (♦), Johnny Wright (♦) and Webb Pierce (♦), the biggest of her solo successes being with **Paying For That Back Street Affair** (1953), **Making Believe** (1955), **Searching** (1956), **Jealousy** (1958), **Mommy For A Day** (1959), **Amigo's Guitar** (1959), **Left To Right** (1960), **Heartbreak U.S.A.** (1961), **Unloved, Unwanted** (1962), **Password** (1964) and **You Don't Hear** (1965). Her awards are equally numerous and include *Billboard*'s No 1 Country Music Female Artist Of The Year 1954–65, a 1974 Woman of the Year award from the Nashville Association of Business and Professional Women, plus a Most Outstanding Tennessee Citizen citation presented by the late Governor of Tennessee, Frank G. Clement, in 1954.

Kitty, who has three children – Ruby, Carol Sue and Bobby (Bobby Wright (♦)) – eventually terminated her long association with Decca during the mid '70s, signing for the Macon-based Capricorn label and cutting an album, aptly named **Forever Young.** And in 1976 she received the supreme accolade – being elected to the Country Music Hall Of Fame.

Albums:
The Kitty Wells Story
  (MCA/MCA) British and
  American versions differ
Open Up Your Heart
  (Pickwick/—)
Kitty Wells (Vocalion/—)

Heart (Vocalion/—)
Greatest Hits (MCA/—)
Dust On The Bible (MCA/—)
Golden Favourites – with Red
  Foley (MCA/—)
Forever Young (Capricorn/—)

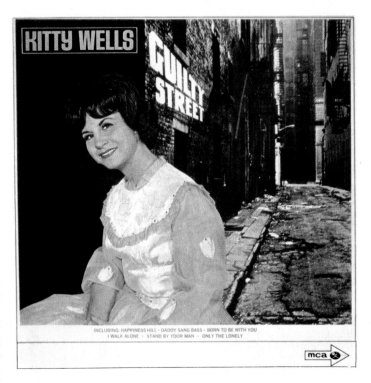

Above: Guilty Street (MCA). One of country music's most successful female singers, she has been in the business for over 40 years after starting as a church singer.

Above: A Bouquet of Country Hits (MCA). She has had a string of chart records as a solo artist and in duets, but here she covers a selection of other people's hits.

Dottie West

Known as the 'Country Sunshine' girl after writing and recording a song of that title for a Coke commercial, she was born McMinnville, Tennessee, October 11, 1932, one of ten children. Farm raised, Dorothy Marie still had time to gain a college degree while helping to work the cotton and sugar cane fields.

She later incorporated these experiences into her songs, but one of Dottie's strengths has also been her ability to adapt pop stylings – she has, in recent years, trodden a line between country sentiments and commercial productions with

If It's All Right With You (RCA)

considerable success.

In the early 1950s, she studied music at Tennessee Tech and there met Bill West, her future husband. Bill was studying engineering but he played steel guitar and accompanied Dottie at college concerts. Both eventually majored in their respective subjects and then moved to Ohio where they appeared as a duo on local TV in the Cleveland area. While visiting relatives in Nashville during the early 1960s they met some executives from Starday Records and were given a record contract; this resulted in some live appearances but little else, Dottie later switching to the Atlantic label, again with virtually no result. Success eluded her until 1963 when Dottie, by this time signed to RCA, recorded **Let Me Off At The Corner,** a Top 30 disc. A year later came the big one – **Here Comes My Baby** – a West original that became covered by Perry Como, providing him with a pop hit but also earning Dottie a Grammy award. From that moment on it became freewheeling for Dottie – she became an Opry regular (1964), arranged and worked with the Memphis and Kansas City Symphony Orchestra, provided RCA with such major solo hits as **Would You Hold It Against Me?** (1966), **Paper Mansions** (1967), **Country Girl** (1968), **Forever Yours** (1970), **Country**

Sunshine (1973), **Last Time I Saw Him** (1974) and **When It's Just You And Me** (1977) and also recorded hit duets with Jim Reeves (♦) (**Love Is No Excuse** – 1964) and Don Gibson (♦) (**Rings Of Gold** and **There's A Story Goin' Round** – both 1969).

Between collecting numerous awards, making a few movies, writing some 400 songs and commercials, and fitting in recording dates and several tours, she has also found time to raise four children and marry again – her second husband being drummer Bryon Metcalf.

Albums:
Best Of . . . (RCA/RCA)
Carolina Cousins (RCA/RCA)
Country Sunshine (RCA/RCA)
House Of Love (RCA/RCA)
Would You Hold It Against Me ?
  (Camden/—)
Careless Hands (—/RCA)
I'm Only A Woman (—/RCA)

Billy Edd Wheeler

Despite critical acclaim following the release of his **Nashville Zodiac** album in 1969, Wheeler, now in his forties, still hasn't attained all that was expected of him.

Born Whitesville, West Virginia, December 9, 1932, Billy Edd is that none too usual animal, the college-educated country artist. He has a BA degree from Berea College, Kentucky, attended Yale Drama School and has been, variously, an editor, a music business executive, a Navy pilot, and an instructor at Berea College. The Kingston Trio had a Top Ten pop hit with his **Reverend Mr Black** in 1963 and Wheeler himself enjoyed a rare hit single with **The Little Brown Shack Out Back,** which nearly (but not quite) topped the country charts in '64, helping him earn an ASCAP writer's award. But despite various changes of record company (he has been with such labels as Monitor, Kapp, UA and RCA) his only *real* influence upon the charts during recent years has been through the medium of his songwriting, Johnny Cash (◆) and June Carter (◆) adding to Wheeler's royalty check by recording his **Jackson,** a crossover hit in 1967.

A collector of folk material – and author of a folk play – Billy Edd Wheeler was responsible for creating a special music room in the Mountain Hall Of Fame, Richwood, West Virginia.

Clarence White

A rock musician with a bluegrass background, guitarist Clarence White was born Lewiston, Maine, June 7, 1944. Raised in California, he played with the Country Boys at the age of ten, the group's other members being his brothers Roland (16) and Eric (12). A bluegrass unit, working at various barn dances and local functions in the Burbank area, the Country Boys materialized into the Kentucky Colonels in 1962, the lineup then being Clarence (guitar), Roland (mandolin), Roger Bush (bass), Billy Ray Latham (banjo) and Leroy Mack (dobro). Two albums were recorded, one for World Pacific and the other for Briar, before Clarence left in 1965 to become a sessionman, appearing on discs with Ricky Nelson (◆), the Everlys (◆), the Byrds (◆), Gene Clark, Flying Burritos (◆), Wynn Stewart (◆) and many others.

After cutting a never-released solo album for the Bakersfield International label and working sporadically with Cajun Gib and Gene (Gib Guilbeau and Gene Parsons), White formed Nashville West, a short lived country rock unit that featured both Guilbeau and Parsons plus bassist Wayne Moore. But in September, 1968, he moved on to become a regular member of the Byrds, remaining with the group until its final demise. Returning to session work once more, White began fashioning a new solo album, also putting in some gigs with the re-formed Kentucky Colonels. However, the solo album was never completed; White was knocked down and killed by a drunken woman driver while loading equipment on to a van following a gig on July 14, 1973.

Albums:
Kentucky Colonels (—/UA)
Livin' In The Past *(Takoma/—)*

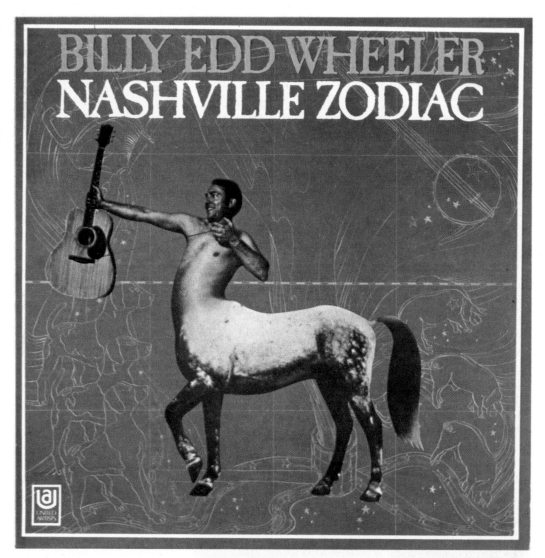

Above: Nashville Zodiac (UA). This album was widely praised on its release, but Billy Edd Wheeler hasn't achieved much since then.

Ray Whitley

Despite a late start, Ray Whitley became a quite successful jack of all trades in the era of the singing cowboy. Born in 1901 near Atlanta, Georgia, Whitley spent some time in the Navy and as an electrician and steelworker in Philadelphia and New York, where he pursued music as a hobby. He auditioned for radio in New York City, and rapidly rose to co-host (with Tex Ritter (◆)) of the WHN Barn Dance in the middle 1930s. Here he also recorded for the American Record Company complex, and also for Decca, his biggest hits being his theme song, **Blue Yodel Blues,** and **The Last Flight Of Wiley Post.**

He was one of the earliest singing cowboys to invade Hollywood, appearing in films as early as 1936. He spent 1938–1942 at RKO, where he made 18 musical shorts of his own and was the singing sidekick to George O'Brien and Tim Holt before spending some more time in similar roles at Universal. Film work trailed off in the late 1940s,

Right: Ray Whitley, one of Hollywood's earliest singing cowboys. His last film was Giant in 1956.

and his last role was as Watts, James Dean's manager in *Giant*.

He was active musically during his film period, both as a cowboy singer and fronting a western swing dance band for several years during the war. He continued to record for Decca, and later Okeh, Conqueror, Cowboy, and Apollo. An active songwriter, he wrote or co-wrote as Fred Rose (♦) many of Gene Autry's (♦) big hits, including **Back In The Saddle Again, Lonely River, I Hang My Head And Cry,** and **Ages And Ages Ago.**

In addition, Whitley also managed both the Sons of the Pioneers (♦) and Jimmy Wakely (♦) for a time, and helped Gibson design and build their first J-200 guitar, which quickly became popular among country and cowboy singers.

Long retired from active performing, Whitley has of late been a fixture at western film festivals, still singing and doing tricks with his bullwhip.

Albums: none.

Slim Whitman

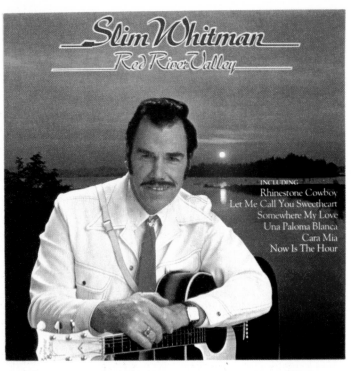

Red River Valley (UA). A best selling album in Britain in '77; he is better known here, where he has been scoring hits since the early '50s, than in his home country.

Born Otis Dewey Whitman Jnr, Tampa, Florida, January 20, 1924, Whitman's early interest was in sport rather than music. He became a star pitcher with his Tampa high school team and hoped to make a career in the game. However, on leaving school he took a job in a meat-packing plant, where he met his wife-to-be. Just prior to Pearl Harbor Whitman became a shipyard fitter in Tampa, enlisting in the Navy during 1943 and serving on the USS Chilton until discharged in 1945. While in the Navy he learned guitar and entertained at shipboard events, upon return to civilian life splitting his time between baseball and entertaining when not working in the shipyard.

In 1946 he gained a contract with the Plant City Berries of the Orange Belt League – but his musical career also prospered via radio spots on Tampa WDAE and many local club bookings. It was at this point that Whitman opted for music as a full time occupation and began establishing his reputation beyond the bounds of Tampa, in 1949 winning a record contract with RCA. After gaining some attention with a release titled **Casting My Lasso To The Sky,** he moved to Shreveport, becoming a regular on the Louisiana Hayride (♦). Later, in 1952, he signed for Imperial Records and staked an immediate claim to stardom with his semi-yodeled version of **Indian Love Call,** a former operetta favorite penned by Harbach, Hammerstein and Friml. A massive seller – in Britain it topped the pop charts for five straight weeks during 1955 – it provided Whitman with a gold disc and an audience ready to snap up such other offerings as **Keep It A Secret** (1952), **North Wind** (1953), **Secret Love, Rose Marie** (both 1954), **Cattle Call** (1955), **More Than Yesterday** (1965), **Guess Who?** (1970) and **Something Beautiful** (1971), all of which have entered the Top Ten in the country listings.

Whitman's reliance on mainly sweet, romantic ballads, purveyed in a rich voice that switches easily to falsetto, has made him a worldwide favorite. But nowhere is he more popular than in Britain where he became the first country vocalist to perform at the London Palladium. His British tours are usually in the SRO bracket while such albums as **The Very Best Of Slim Whitman** and **Red River Valley** topped the UK charts in 1976 and '77 respectively.

Albums:
Best Of Vol 2 (*UA/—*)
15th Anniversary
  (*Imperial/Liberty*)
I'll See You When (*UA/UA*)
Irish Songs (*Imperial/Liberty*)
Love Song Of The Waterfall
  (*Imperial/Sunset*)
Song Of The Old Waterwheel
  (*Imperial/—*)
Everything Leads Back To You
  (*UA/—*)
Yodelling (*—/Liberty*)
Country Songs – *City Hits*
  (*—/Liberty*)
A Travellin' Man (*—/Liberty*)
A Time For Love (*—/Liberty*)
Great Performances (*—/Liberty*)
Country Memories (*—/Liberty*)
Cool Water (*—/Liberty*)
In Love The Whitman Way
  (*—/Liberty*)
Happy Street (*—/Liberty*)
Straight From The Heart
  (*—/Liberty*) ✦
Tomorrow Never Comes
  (*—/Liberty*)
God's Hand In Mine (*—/Sunset*)
Christmas Album (*—/Sunset*)
Reminiscing (*—/Sunset*)
I'll Walk With God (*—/Sunset*)
Slim Whitman Collection
  (*—/UA*)
Snowbird (*—/UA*)
It's A Sin To Tell A Lie (*—/UA*)
25th Anniversary Concert
  (*—/UA*)
Golden Songbook (*—/UA*)
Happy Anniversary (*—/UA*)
Very Best Of . . . (*—/UA*)
Red River Valley (*—/UA*)

Henry Whitter

One of the earliest country musicians to be recorded – it's claimed that his earliest recordings were pre-dated only by those of Eck Robertson (♦) – William Henry Whitter was born near Fries, Virginia, April 6, 1892. Working in a cotton mill to earn a living, he learnt guitar, fiddle, piano, harmonica and organ, and began performing around the Fries area. In March, 1923, he visited New York, gaining an audition with the General Phonograph Company and recording two numbers – which were promptly shelved. However, in the wake of Fiddlin' John Carson's (♦) success with his Okeh sides, Whitter was recalled to New York in December, 1923, there waxing nine numbers for Okeh release, the first of these, **The Wreck On The Southern Old '97,** backed with **Lonesome Road Blues,** being issued in January, 1924. Later that year, **Old '97** was to be recorded in a slightly different version by Vernon Dalhart (♦), which became a multi-million-selling record.

Whitter continued to record as a soloist, an accompanist (with Roba Stanley – one of the first female country singers to record) and as a bandleader, with Whitter's Virginia Breakdowners. He also form-

ed a successful musical alliance with blind fiddler George Banman Grayson, recording with him several times between 1927 and 1929. This partnership terminated when Grayson died in a road accident during the mid '30s, and though Whitter continued in a solo role until the commencement of the 1940s his health gradually deteriorated. He died from diabetes in Morganton, North Carolina, on November 10, 1941.

Wilburn Brothers

Once part of a family act that included their father, mother, elder brothers and a sister, Doyle (born Thayer, Missouri, July 7, 1930) and Teddy Wilburn (born Thayer, November 30, 1931) began as hometown street corner singers, the Wilburn Family eventually touring the South and establishing a reputation that led ultimately to an Opry signing in 1941. In the wake of the Korean War, Teddy and Doyle began working as a duo, touring with Webb Pierce (♦) and Faron Young (♦). Obtaining a record contract with Decca, they scored a Top Ten disc in 1956 with **Go Away With Me,** this being the first of an impressive tally of hits that extended into the early '70s. With a repertoire that extended into virtually every area of country music, the Wilburns appealed to a wide audience, a fact reflected in their record sales of 1959 when three of their releases, **Which One Is To Blame?, Somebody Back In Town** and **A Woman's Intuition,** all became major hits.

Founders of the Wil-Helm Talent Agency in conjunction with Smiley Wilson, the Wilburns found themselves representing many of Nashville's leading talents – including Loretta Lynn (♦), whom they featured on their own highly popular TV show and for whom they ob-

tained her recording contract with Decca. Also founders of Sure-Fire Music, a music publishing company, the Wilburns were responsible for such Top Ten discs as **Trouble's Back In Town** (1962), **Tell Her So** (1963), **It's Another World** (1965), **Someone Before Me** (1966) and **Hurt Her Once For Me** (1966).

Albums:
I Walk The Line (*Vocalion/—*)
Portrait (*MCA/—*)
Take Up Thy Cross (*MCA/—*)
That Country Feeling (*Coral/—*)

Curly Williams

Curly Williams led a popular band on the Grand Ole Opry throughout the 1940s called the Georgia Peach Pickers, and is best known for having written **Half As Much** which, because it was popularized by Hank Williams (♦) and because the writer's credit is usually listed as 'Williams', is frequently thought of as Hank's song.

Curly returned to Georgia in the late 1940s and gradually drifted out of performing. He was with Columbia from 1945 through 1951, and his biggest hits for the label were **Southern Belle (From Nashville Tennessee)** and **Georgia Steel Guitar.**

Albums: none.

Doc Williams

Although he's never had a hit record, one of the most popular regional acts in country music has been Doc Williams and his wife Chickie, and their band the Border Riders. They still play hundreds of dates a year, filling houses in the north east and in the Canadian Maritimes, largely on the strength of their longtime association with WWVA and the Wheeling Jamboree.

Above: Don Williams'
Harmony (ABC).

also gained several disc hits with **Come Early Morning, Amanda, Till The Rivers Run Dry, I Wouldn't Want To Live, The Ties That Bind, Say It Again, Turn Out The Light, You're My Best Friend** and others.

Albums:
Don Williams Vol 1 *(Dot/ABC)*
Don Williams Vol 2 *(Dot/ABC)*
Don Williams Vol 3 *(Dot/ABC)*
Greatest Hits *(Dot/ABC)*
You're My Best Friend
 (Dot/ABC)
Harmony *(Dot/ABC)*
Pozo Secon Singers
 (Power Pak/—)

Above: A Portrait (MCA).
Proficient in every aspect
of country music, the
Wilburn Brothers have
kept up a stream of
hits since 1956.

Born Andrew J. Smik, of Bohemian descent, on June 26, 1914, he grew up in the musically rich area of eastern Pennsylvania. And except for brief stays at WREC in Memphis (1939) and WFMD in Frederick, Maryland (1945), he has remained in that area: Cleveland from 1934–1936, then Pittsburgh, and finally Wheeling, from 1937 until the present day.

In 1948 he married Jessie Wanda Crupe, who became known as Chickie, and they have had many regionally popular records on their own label, Wheeling: **Beyond The Sunset, Mary Of The Wild Moor, Silver Bells,** and Doc's own composition **Willie Roy, The Crippled Boy.**

A staunch traditionalist and a longtime spokesman for Wheeling, WWVA, and the Wheeling Jamboree, Doc Williams never achieved national success or huge record sales, but has been a great influence in the north east and in Canada.

Albums:
From Out Of The Beautiful
 Hills Of West Virginia
 (Wheeling/—)
Doc 'n' Chickie Together
 (Wheeling/—)
Wheeling Back To Wheeling
 (Wheeling/—)

Don Williams

One of the major new names in country music, Williams was born near Plainview, Texas, and grew up around the Corpus Christi area. He first came to prominence with the pop-folk group, the Pozo-Secon singers, in 1965; the group (comprised of Williams, Susan Taylor and Lofton Cline) having a major hit the following year with **Time.** Between 1966–67 the Pozos also had best sellers with **I'll Be Gone, I Can Make It With You, Look What You've Done, I Believed It All** and **Louisiana Man,** but gradually their popularity waned in 1971 Williams returned to Texas to join his father-in-law in his furniture business.

A solo recording venture by former Pozo Susan Taylor had him return to Nashville in a writing capacity but he soon began singing once more, a solo album **Don Williams Vol 1** being released on Jack Clements independent JMI label during 1973.

His debut solo single had been **Don't You Believe** (June, 1972) but it was his second, **The Shelter Of Your Eyes,** that gave him his first major bite at the country charts. Williams, who tries to keep his public appearances down to a minimal number and spends most of his time writing songs, recording or tending his farm near Ashland City, Tennessee, has appeared in a Burt Reynolds movie *W.W. The Dixie Dancekings* and

Right: The Legend of Hank
Williams (MGM).

Hank Williams Snr

One of the most charismatic figures in country music – his Opry performance of June 11, 1949, when his audience required him to reprise **Lovesick Blues** several times is still considered as the Ryman's greatest moment – he was born Hiram King Williams, Georgiana, Alabama, September 17, 1923.

A member of the church choir at six, he was given a $3.50 guitar by his mother a year later, receiving some tuition from Tee-Tot (Rufe Payne) an elderly black street musician. When barely a teenager he won $15 singing **WPA Blues** at a Montgomery amateur contest, then formed a band The Drifting Cowboys which played on station WSFA, Montgomery, for over a decade. In 1946 Williams signed with Sterling Records, switching to the newly formed MGM label in '47. Though virtually an alcoholic, he was booked as a regular on KWKH's Louisiana Hayride (♦), and in 1949, having scored with his recording of **Lovesick Blues,** came a contract with Grand Ole Opry. An early recording, **Move It Over,** has already been a minor hit for Williams but after the runaway success of **Lovesick Blues** (a song waxed by yodeler Emmett Miller in 1925), he began cutting Top Ten singles with almost monotonous regularity. With Fred Rose (♦) masterminding every Williams recording session, arranging, playing, producing and often participating in the songwriting, such hits as **Wedding Bells, Mind Your Own Business, You're Gonna Change** and **My Buckets Got A Hole In It** all charted during 1949, the following year providing **I Just Don't Like This Kind Of Livin', Long Gone Lonesome Blues, Why Don't You Love Me?, Why Should We Try Anymore?** and **Moaning The Blues.** These were followed by **Cold Cold Heart, Howlin' At The Moon, Hey Good Lookin', Crazy Love, Baby We're Really In Love** (1951), **Honky Tonk Blues, Half As Much, Jambalaya, Settin' The Woods On Fire** and **I'll Never Get Out Of This World Alive** (1952), the latter ironically released just before his death (from a heart attack brought on by excessive drinking) on New Year's Day, 1953. He and his Drifting Cowboys had been booked to play a show in Canton, Ohio, and Williams hired a driver to chauffeur him through a snowstorm to the gig. He fell asleep along the way – but when the driver tried to rouse him at Oak Hill, Virginia, he was found to be dead. After his

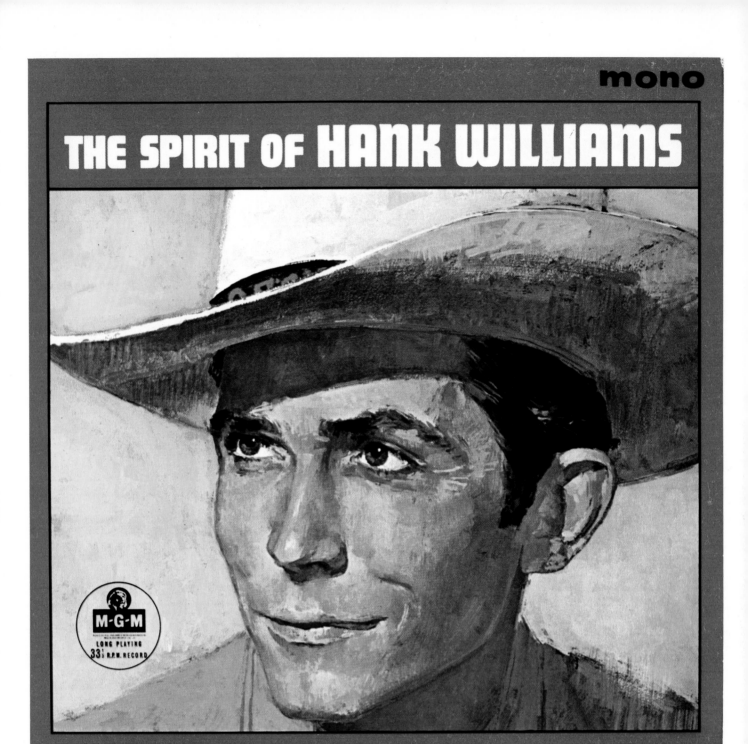

THE SPIRIT OF HANK WILLIAMS

mono

The Spirit of Hank Williams (MGM). Sadly, his drinking had led to many problems with his career and finally caused his fatal heart attack in the '50s.

death, his records continued to sell in massive quantities, **Your Cheatin' Heart, Take These Chains From My Heart, I Won't Be Home No More** and **Weary Blues From Waitin'** all charting during the year that followed. The last months of Williams' life – though financially rewarding – were ultra-tragic. A drug user in order to combat a spinal ailment caused by being thrown from a horse at the age of 17, he was fired from Grand Ole Opry in August '52, because of perpetual drunkenness and was also divorced by his wife Audrey Sheperd – though he re-married, to Billie Jean Jones, daughter of a Louisiana police chief, soon after.

Though a difficult man to work with, being moody and uncommunica-tive, he was much respected and well loved by the country music fraternity, over 20,000 people attending his funeral in Montgomery, at which Roy Acuff (♦), Carl Smith (♦), Red Foley (♦) and Ernest Tubb (♦) paid tribute in song.

His songs were well accepted in pop music as well – his compositions providing million-selling discs for Joni James (**Your Cheatin' Heart** – 1953), Tony Bennett (**Cold, Cold Heart** – 1951), Jo Stafford (**Jambalaya** – 1952) etc – Williams' material has been recorded by rock bands, folk singers and black music acts.

Elected to the Country Music Hall of Fame in 1961 his plaque reads: 'The simple, beautiful melodies and straightforward plaintive stories in his lyrics of life as he knew it will never die'.

His son, Hank Williams Jnr (♦), still carries on the Williams tradition today and in 1964 provided the music to *Your Cheatin' Heart*, a Holly-wood scripted film biography, in which George Hamilton portrayed Hank Snr.

Albums:
Greatest Hits *(MGM/MGM)*
Greatest Hits Vol 2 *(MGM/MGM)*
On Stage Vol 1 *(—/MGM)*
On Stage Vol 2 *(—/MGM)*
Essential Hank Williams
  (—/MGM)
Collectors Hank Williams Vol 1
  (—/MGM)
Live At The Grand Ole Opry
  (MGM/MGM)
Memorial Album *(—/MGM)*
Greatest Hits Vol 3 *(MGM/—)*
Home In Heaven *(MGM/—)*
I Saw The Light *(MGM/—)*
Life To Legend *(MGM/—)*
Luke The Drifter *(MGM/—)*
24 Great Hits *(MGM/—)*
Very Best Of . . . *(MGM/—)*
Very Best Vol 2 *(MGM/—)*

Above: Live At The Grand Ole Opry (MGM). Hank Williams Sr was a much-loved member of the Opry for many years.

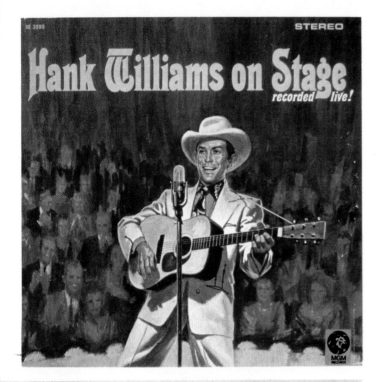

SE 3099 STEREO

Hank Williams on Stage
recorded live!

Hank Williams On Stage (MGM). An extremely popular Opry and live performer for years, Williams was one of country music's leading and best loved artists.

Hank Williams Jnr

Son of the late Hank Williams (♦) and his wife Audrey, Hank Jnr was born Shreveport, Louisiana, May 26, 1949 – though he was taken to Nashville when only three months old and grew up in the country capital.

During his high school days he exceled in swimming, football, boxing and other sports, becoming a health fanatic. When barely a teenager he toured with his mother's 'Caravan Of Stars' show, at the age of 15 having national hits via MGM releases **Long Gone Lonesome Blues** and **Endless Sleep,** following these with other such high-selling discs as **Standing In The Shadows, It's All Over But The Crying, Cajun Baby, Custody** (as Luke The Drifter Jnr), **I'd Rather Be Gone, All For The Love Of Sunshine, Raining In My Heart, I've Got A Right To Cry** and **Ain't That A Shame.**

His films include *My Cheatin' Heart,* a highly glossy, Hollywood version of his father's life that became one of the most money-spinning country movies ever made – grossing ten times its original investment of $1.2 million – while his appearance with Johnny Cash (♦) at Detroit's Cobo Hall, in 1969, broke all then existing country records with a take of $93,000.

Hank Jnr, who plays guitar, piano and fiddle and who tours in a private Greyhound Scenicruiser called The Cheatin' Heart Special, suffered severe injuries to his head when he fell down a rock face during a hunting trip in 1975, and has recently returned to record-ing and performing, albeit with an Allman Brothers-sounding southern rock sound.

Albums:
14 Greatest Hits *(MGM/—)*
Hank And Friends *(MGM/MGM)*
Eleven Roses *(—/MGM)*
Greatest Hits Vol 2 *(—/MGM)*

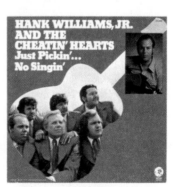

Above: Just Pickin' . . . No Singin' (MGM).

Left: The son of a country legend, Hank Williams Jr lived on his father's memory for a number of years – cutting albums like Songs My Father Left Me. But recently he's headed his own way.

Leona Williams

A member of the Merle Haggard (♦) Roadshow during the mid '70s, Leona was one of the first women to emulate Johnny Cash (♦) and record a live album in a penitentiary. Born Leona Helton, Vienna, Missouri, January 7, 1943, she became part of the Helton family band at an early age – her father, mother, four brothers and seven sisters all being instrumentalists of one kind or another. Obtaining her own radio show Leona Sings on KWOS, Jefferson City, Missouri, at 15, she married bassist Ron Williams a year later, the duo becoming members of Loretta Lynn's (♦) backup unit, Leona playing bass and singing and her husband moving in behind the resident drum kit.

Following a guest appearance on the Grand Ole Opry, a demo recording was arranged by Lonzo and Oscar (♦), the result being a contract with Hickory Records in January, 1968. This association lasted until 1974 when Leona became an MCA acquisition for spell.

A straight down-the-line country singer, Leona's more successful singles have included **Once More** (1969) and **Country Girl With Hot Pants On** (1971) while her songwriting efforts have been recorded by such as Tammy Wynette (♦) and Loretta Lynn.

Albums:
San Quentin's First Lady
(MCA/—)
A Woman Walked Away
(—/DJM)

A Woman Walked Away (DJM)

Tex Williams

Writer (with Merle Travis (♦)) and performer of **Smoke, Smoke, Smoke (That Cigarette),** a 1947 hit that sold around two and a half million copies, Williams was, during his heyday, a predominantly West Coast-based bandleader, who appeared in many films during the 1940s.

Born Sol Williams in Ramsey, Fayette County, Illinois, August 23, 1917, he had his own one man band and vocal show on radio WJBL, Decatur, Illinois, at the age of 13, later touring throughout the States, Canada and Mexico with various western and hillbilly aggregations. During the late 1930s he became Hollywood based, there befriending Tex Ritter (♦) and working in films. After a long stay as lead vocalist and bass player with Spade Cooley (♦), he formed his own band, The Western Caravan, in 1946, signing to the up and coming Capitol label. Following the success of **Smoke, Smoke, Smoke,** the band's third release, Williams became a star of international proportions, working on scores of network TV and radio shows, his band playing to capacity audiences at choice venues. And though his run of record success seemed to peter out following the release of **Bluebird On Your Windowsill** (1949), he continued recording for such labels as Decca and Liberty, cutting a live album **Texas Williams At The Mint,** for the latter in 1963. However, a record deal with a Kentucky company, Boone, renewed Williams' acquaintance with the charts once more – albeit on a lower level – the singer accruing goodly sales with **Too Many Tigers** (1965), **Bottom Of A Mountain** (1966), **Smoke, Smoke, Smoke '68** (1968) and several other titles. By 1970 he'd signed for Monument, obtaining a Top 30 disc with **The Night Miss Nancy Ann's Hotel For Single Girls Burned Down** in 1971.

Albums:
Those Lazy Hazy Days
(Granite/Pye)

*Those Lazy Hazy Days
(Pye)*

Foy Willing

Born Foy Willingham in Bosque County, Texas, in 1915, Foy aspired to a musical career while still in high school, appearing on radio as a solo singer and with a gospel quartet. He eventually found his way to New York City, where he appeared on radio for Crazy Water Crystals from 1933 to 1935, when he returned to Texas to work in radio as an executive and announcer.

Willing moved to California in 1940 and founded the Riders of the Purple Sage, originally composed of himself, Al Sloey, and Jimmy Dean (♦), although later members included Scotty Harrell, fiddler Johnny Paul, accordionist/arranger Billy Leibert, accordionist Paul Sells, guitarist Jerry Vaughn, clarinetist Neely Plumb, and steel guitarist Freddy Traveres. The group was formed in 1943 as cast members of the Hollywood Barn Dance, and through the rest of the 1940s they appeared on many radio shows including All Star Western Theater, the Andrews Sisters Show, the Roy Rogers (♦) Quaker Oats Show, and appeared in many Republic films as well with Monte Hale (♦) and Roy Rogers (♦).

They recorded for Decca, Capitol, Columbia, and Majestic Records, their biggest hits being **No One To Cry To** and **Cool Water** on Majestic, and **Texas Blues** and **Ghost Riders In The Sky** on Capitol. The Riders of the Purple Sage disbanded in 1952 when Willing left active performing, although there was an occasional regrouping for special appearances, a couple of quick albums on Roulette and Jubilee, and a 1959 tour with Gene Autry (♦). Foy Willing has, however, lately been recording, writing songs, and appearing at Western film festivals.

Willis Brothers

The Willis Brothers (Guy, born Alex, Arkansas, July 15, 1915; Skeeter, born Coalton, Oklahoma, December 20, 1917; and Vic, born Schulter, Oklahoma, May 31, 1922), were originally known as the Oklahoma Wranglers, their radio career commencing on KGEF, Shawnee, Oklahoma; in 1940 the trio moved on to become featured artists on the Brush Creek Follies Show on KMBC, Kansas City, Missouri.

*Above: Goin' To Town
(London).*

With Guy as front man and guitarist, Vic on accordion and piano, and Skeeter appearing in his role

Above: Foy Willing and the Riders of the Purple Sage, following in the hoofmarks of Sons of the Pioneers.

as the 'smilin' fiddler', the brothers appeared to be on the way to establishing a healthy reputation, but then World War II intervened and the Willis Brothers joined the forces for four years. They regrouped in 1946 and became Opry members until 1949, striking up an association with Eddy Arnold (♦), on whose show they appeared for some eight years. Also during this period they became the first group to back Hank Williams (♦) on Sterling Records, and in a sense were the original Drifting Cowboys, although they did not tour with him.

Rejoining the Opry in 1960, the group enjoyed some hit Starday singles throughout the '60s via such titles as **Give Me Forty Acres** (1964), **A Six Foot Two By Four** (1965), **Bob** (1967) and

Somebody Loves My Dog (1967). Often employed as session musicians, the Willis Brothers have recorded for several labels including RCA, Mercury, Sterling, Coral, Starday and MGM. They also bear the distinction of being the first country act to play a concert at Washington DC's Constitution Hall, formerly a venue for classical concerts only. Despite Skeeter's death of lymph cancer in 1976, the Willis Brothers were still active at the time of writing.

Albums:
Best Of . . . *(Starday/—)*
The Singing Cowboy Rides Again – with Johnny Bond *(CMH/—)*
The Return Of The Singing Cowboy – with Johnny Bond *(CMH/—)*

Vic and Guy Willis; a third brother, Skeeter, died in 1976.

Remembering . . . (Columbia). Although Bob Wills is dead, the Playboys were re-formed in 1976; western swing is also being revived by a whole new range of artists.

Bob Wills

Leader of the finest western swing band ever to grace country music, and in fact the originator of the style, the late Bob Wills is currently undergoing an upswing in popularity, his influence being acknowledged by countless new-wave artists.

Born near Kosse, Limestone County, Texas, March 6, 1905, James Robert Wills was the first of ten children of a fiddle-playing father. In 1913 the Wills family moved to Memphis, Texas, where Jim Rob began playing fiddle at square dances, his initial instrument having been mandolin.

Living on a West Texas family farm until 1929, that year he arrived in Fort Worth, becoming 'Bob' Wills after working in a medicine show that possessed one too many Jims. Forming a duo, the Wills Fiddle Band, with guitarist Herman Arnspiger during the summer of '29, the fiddler began playing for dances in the Fort Worth area. And during 1930 he added vocalist Milton Brown (♦), the unit later metamorphosizing

Hall of Fame (with Tommy Duncan) (UA). Duncan left the Light Crust Doughboys with Bob and Johnnie Willis in 1933; the resulting Texas Playboys had lasting influence.

into the Light Crust Doughboys (♦), a band whose broadcasts over radio station KFJZ proved extremely popular.

The Doughboys recorded for Victor in February, 1932, Brown leaving soon after, to be replaced by Tommy Duncan (♦), a vocalist selected from over 70 other applicants.

Fired from the Doughboys in August 1933 – due to excessive drinking and his inability to get along with Doughboys' leader W. Lee O'Daniel (♦) – Wills took Duncan and his banjo playing brother Johnnie Lee Wills (♦) with him, forming his own outfit, Bob Wills and his Playboys, gaining a regular spot on WACO in Waco. And though beset by legal problems, activated by Wills' ex-sponsors, the Burrus Mill and Elevator Company (the makers of Light Crust flour), the band struggled on, eventually making a base in Tulsa, where they became an institution on station KVOO with Bob and Johnnie Lee heading programs on the station for the next 24 years.

Now known as Bob Wills And His Texas Playboys, the band began recording for Brunswick, cutting some sides in Dallas during September, 1935. Their record success, their KVOO programs, and their regular dances at Carn's Academy, as well as the power and inventiveness of the bandmembers, made their Tulsa years their most memorable.

A swing band with country overtones – The Playboys comprised 13 musicians by the mid '30s and grew into an 18-piece during the 1940s – Wills' outfit played a miscellany of country ballads, blues and riffy jazz items with horns and fiddles vying for the front line positions. This sound proved tremendously popular and when in April, 1940, Wills re-recorded his self-penned **San Antonio Rose** (the band had already cut the number as an instrumental in 1938) as a vehicle for Tommy Duncan's vocal artistry, the resulting disc became a million-seller. Another version of the same song – by Bing Crosby – also sold past the million mark, though it appears that Wills earned little in the way of royalties.

Many more hits followed – but with the advent of Pearl Harbor, the band began to break up as its various members enlisted in the forces, Wills himself joining the army in late '42. Physically unfit for service life, he was discharged the following July, at which time he headed for California where he appeared on radio shows and made several movies. During the post-war period, with big bands generally fading, Wills was forced to use a smaller band, and began featuring fiddles and string instruments more prominently than he had with his earlier Tulsa unit, using the instrument much in the manner of jazz horn soloists. Again, the public loved the sound but Wills was unsure where he was heading, both musically and home-wise, his wife and children having to move 14 times in 20 years.

His health also began to fail and during 1962 Wills suffered his first heart attack. Still he continued to tour with the Playboys, but in 1964 came another heart attack and he was forced to call a halt to his band-leading days.

Nevertheless, he still made a more limited number of appearances as a solo artist and continued making records – his efforts on behalf of country music receiving due recognition in October, 1968, when Wills' name was added to those already honored in the Country Music Hall Of Fame.

Also honored by the State of Texas on May 30, 1969, Wills was paralyzed by a stroke the very next day. But though bedridden for many months, with even his power of speech impaired, he fought back and by 1972 began to appear at various functions, albeit in a wheelchair.

In December, 1973, he attended his last record date, many of the original Texas Playboys, plus Merle Haggard (♦), taking part. In two days, 27 titles were cut for UA – but Wills was only present for a portion of the time, suffering a severe stroke after the first day. He never re-gained consciousness, although his actual death did not occur until some 17 months later on May 13, 1975.

However, though Wills had gone his music lives on, the Playboys reforming in late '76 under the leadership of vocalist-guitarist Leon McAuliffe and cutting a new album for Capitol.

Albums:

Anthology (Columbia/—)	**The Texas Playboys** (MCA/—)
Hall Of Fame – with Tommy Duncan (UA/—)	**Time Changes Everything** (MCA/—)
Greatest String Band Hits (MCA/—)	**The Last Time** (UA/—)
King Of Western Swing (MCA/—)	**In Concert** (Capitol/—
A Living Legend (MCA/—)	**Best Of . . .** (MVA/—)
Remembering (Columbia/—)	**Best Of . . . Vol 2** (MCA/—)
Sings And Plays (Liberty/—)	**Fathers And Sons** – with Asleep At The Whrel (Epic/—)
Western Swing Along (Vocalion/—)	**The Tiffany Transcriptions** '45-'48 (Tishomingo/—)
	24 Great Hits By . . . (MGM/—)

Johnnie Lee Wills

Although often cast deep in the shadow of his elder brother Bob (♦), Johnnie Lee Wills actually carved out quite a long and successful career of his own. Born in east Texas in 1912, Johnnie Lee got his start playing tenor banjo with Bob as a member of the Light Crust Doughboys (♦), and left the band with him when Bob formed

the Playboys, soon to become the Texas Playboys.

Business got so good for Bob around 1940 that he formed a second band around Johnnie Lee, which grew to as many as 14 or 15 pieces. Called Johnnie Lee Wills and his Boys, they became extremely popular in the Tulsa area, and at one time or another contained many of the finest western swing musicians of the era, including Leon Huff, Joe Holley, and Jesse Ashlock.

They signed with Bullet Records in the mid to late 1940s, and had the

two biggest country hits that label was to produce: **Rag Mop,** and **Peter Cottontail.** They also recorded for Decca, Sims, RCA and a few smaller labels.

When western swing slumped in popularity in the 1950s, Johnnie Lee continued to run his famous Tulsa Stampede, and opened a still-thriving western wear shop. He still appears at various western swing reunions.

Albums: none.

Mac Wiseman

One of the revered figures of old time music, Mac Wiseman has recently undergone an upsurge in popularity.

Malcolm B. Wiseman was born near Waynesboro, Virginia, on May 23, 1925, and raised in an area which he says is 'just like The Waltons on TV'. Country music in this area of the Shenendoah Valley was very much a folk art and Mac learned his music from the people around him. Mac has become known as a bluegrass artist although his music also encompasses old-time, modern, and even pop styles as well. Mac has floated in and out of the accepted Monroe/Earl Scruggs (♦) bluegrass style in his time and has indeed specialized in more traditional, sentimental material such as **Jimmy Brown The Newsboy** and **Letter Edged In Black.**

He attended the Shenendoah Conservatory of Music in Dayton, Virginia and then joined the announcing staff of radio station WSVA in Harrisburg, Virginia, as newscaster and disc jockey. At this time he also wrote copy for station advertisements and worked nights with local country bands. He possesses a warm, clear, tenor voice and this 'classicism' has been eagerly utilized by some of the top names in bluegrass, notably Bill Monroe and Elatt and Scruggs, both acts having included Mac live and on record early in his career. He in fact began his career with another country music legend, Molly O'Day (♦).

He has starred on Shreveport's Louisiana Hayride, Atlanta's WSB Barn Dance and the Knoxville Tennessee Barn Dance, and his guested on the Opry. He began recording on then-new Dot Records in 1951 and his hits with them included **Tis Sweet To be Remembered, Jimmy Brown, The Newsboy, Ballad Of Davy Crockett** and **Love Letters In The Sand,** (**Jimmy Brown The Newsboy** topped the country charts for 33 weeks). Mac became Dot's Country A&R director and also ran that company's country music division for a few years. In 1962 he moved labels to Capitol. He moved back to Dot again where he experimented with, among other things, a string-backed album, and then left for RCA. He currently records for CMH.

Lately, apart from the increasing number of bluegrass festivals he plays, Mac has been featured at Carnegie Hall and the Hollywood Bowl. He has a very strong student following and has also been active

Left: Mac Wiseman, an outstanding bluegrass guitarist who helped to popularize his boyhood songs from the Shenandoah Valley.

Right: On The South Bound (RCA Victor). Wiseman works mainly with bluegrass artists but his range extends to old time and sentimental material.

behind the scenes in the industry.

Until quite recently a rotund figure (he was known to consume two dishes per course to other people's one) in 1974 he underwent an operation and has trimmed down considerably, having lost in excess of 100 pounds.

Albums:
Old Time Country Favorites
(Rural Rhythm/—)
The Mac Wiseman Story
(CMH/—)
Country Music Memories
(CMH/—)
Concert *(RCA/—)*
Johnny's Cash And Charley's Pride *(—/RCA)*
16 Great Performances *(ABC/—)*

Del Wood

Probably the second (after Maybelle Carter) female country instrumentalist to achieve any real degree of fame, pianist Del Wood recorded a corny, ragtime version of a fiddle tune called **Down Yonder** (previously a 1934 hit for Gid Tanner (♦ Skillet Lickers)) on the Tennessee label in 1951 and came up with a million-seller. Nashville born (on February 22, 1920), Del became an Opry member in 1951 and has remained on the show ever since, even playing on the Japanese version of the Opry during her Far East tour of 1968. Perpetuator of several other best-selling discs in heavy handed ragtime/honky tonk style, Del has recorded for RCA, Mercury, Class, Decca, Lamb & Lion, etc.

Albums:
Ragtime Glory Special
(Lamb & Lion/Lamb & Lion)
Tavern In The Town
(Vocalion/—)

Above: Adelaide Hazelwood, honky-tonk piano player.

Sheb Wooley

A highly versatile performer, Wooley was voted CMA Comedian

Of The Year in 1968 for his alter ego character Ben Colder, while in '64 he won a *Cashbox* magazine award for 'his outstanding contributions to country and popular music as a writer, recording artist and entertainer'.

In the role of Pete Nolan, he co-starred in the TV series Rawhide and as Ben Colder he's scored with such recorded comedy hits as **Don't Go Near The Eskimos** (1962), **Almost Persuaded No 2** (1966), **Harper Valley PTA (Later That Same Day)** (1968) and **15 Beers Ago** (1971).

Born Erick, Oklahoma, April 10, 1921, Wooley spent his early years on his father's farm, becoming a competent horseman at the age of four and a rodeo rider during his teens. He formed his own band while still at school, later having his own network radio show for three years. In 1948, he was awarded his first major recording contract by MGM.

It was at this stage that Wooley, who'd studied at the Jack Koslyn School of Acting, moved to California and began working on *Rocky Mountain*, a Warner Brothers' movie starring Errol Flynn. He's since been featured in more than 30 films, among these being *Little Big Horn*, *Boy From Oklahoma*, *Giant*, *Distant Drums*, *Man Without A Star* and *High Noon*, in which Wooley received considerable acclaim for his performance as the whiskey drinking killer, Ben Miller.

Co-star in 105 episodes of Rawhide, Wooley has appeared on countless TV shows. And as a recording star under his own name (as opposed to releases using his Colder identity) he has enjoyed a six-week stay at the top of the pop charts with his 1959 **Purple People**

Above: Sheb Wooley, rodeo rider and musician.

Eater, three years later topping the country charts with **That's My Pa.**

Above: Bobby Wright, talented son of Kitty Wells and Johnny Wright. Ernest Borgnine and Owen Bradley are among those who have helped his career.

Bobby Wright

The son of Johnny Wright (♦) and Kitty Wells (♦), Bobby Wright (born Charleston, West Virginia, March 30, 1942) was brought up in a show business atmosphere, appearing on Shreveport's Louisiana Hayride (♦) at the age of eight and becoming a Decca recording artist at 11. Completing his education at Middle Tennessee State University, he auditioned for and gained the part of Willie in the TV series 'McHale's Navy', remaining with the show for a four year run. A frequent performer on various syndicated TV shows and a member of his parent's family show, Wright's first hit record came in 1967 with the Decca release **Lay Some Happiness On Me** – his most successful disc to date being **Here I Go Again**, a Top 20 entry in 1971.

Johnny Wright

Wright (born Mt Juliet, Tennessee, May 13, 1914) came from a musical family, his grandfather being a champion old time fiddler and his father a five string banjo player. In 1933 he moved to nearby Nashville, then in its infancy as a country music center, there meeting and marrying Kitty Wells (♦), also working with singer-guitarist Jack Anglin (born Columbia, Tennessee, May 13, 1916) on radio station WSIX, Nashville and forming a duo, Johnny and Jack, with Anglin in 1938. During the early '40s, Johnny and Jack toured with their band, The Tennessee Mountain Boys, playing on WBIG, Greensboro, North Carolina, WNOX, Knoxville and many other radio stations. By 1948, they, together with Kitty Wells (still only a featured singer, not yet a star), joined the Grand Ole Opry, then left to become stars of Shreveport's Louisiana Hayride (♦), their popularity on the show leading to an opportunity to rejoin Opry members in 1952, the threesome becoming regulars for a period of 15 years.

Signed initially to Appollo, an R&B label (there cutting such sides as **Jolie Blon** and **Paper Boy**), Johnny and Jack switched to the more country-oriented RCA in the late '40s, scoring Top 20 hits with

Poison Love (1951), **Crying Heart Blues** (1951), **Oh Baby Mine (I Get So Lonely)** (1954), **Beware Of It** (1954), **Goodnight, Sweetheart, Goodnight** (1954), **Stop The World** (1958), **Lonely Island Pearl** (1958) and **Sailor Man** (1959). Other hits included **Ashes Of Love** and **I Can't Tell My Heart That.** But shortly after one last success with **Slow Poison**, a 1962 Decca release, Jack Anglin

was killed (on March 8, 1963) in a car crash en route to a funeral service for Patsy Cline (♦) – at which point Wright formed a new roadshow and became a solo recording act, notching a chart No 1 in 1965 with **Hello Vietnam.**

His son Bobby (♦) proving a success chartwise during the late '60s Wright formed the Kitty Wells-Johnny Wright Family Show in 1969, doing extensive touring, he

Above: Johnny Wright. With Jack Anglin he formed the successful duo Johnny and Jack.

and Bobby recording an album of Johnny And Jack material for Starday during 1977.

Albums:
Here's Johnny And Jack
(Vocalion/—)

252

Tammy Wynette

One of the most successful female country singers of all time, Tammy Wynette was adjudged CMA Female Vocalist Of The Year for three consecutive years (1968–70), while her recording of **Stand By Your Man,** a No 1 in the US during 1968 and a major British hit in 1975, was the biggest selling single by a woman in the entire history of country music.

Tammy began life as Wynette Pugh, born near Tupelo, Mississippi, May 5, 1942. Her father died when she was but a few months old and her mother moved to Birmingham, Alabama, to engage in war work, leaving her in the care of grandparents until the end of World War II. Brought up on a farm, Tammy learnt to play the collection of instruments once owned by her father, taking a lengthy series of music lessons with a view to a career in singing.

But, getting married at 17, she had little time for music during the next three years. Instead she became the mother of three children, her marriage breaking up before the third child was born. The baby, a girl, developed spinal menigitis, and Tammy had to supplement her earnings as a Birmingham beautician in order to pay off various bills incurred as a result of the child's ill health. She turned to music once more, becoming featured vocalist on station WBRC-TV's Country Boy Eddy Show during the mid '60s, following this with some appearances on Porter Wagoner's (♦) syndicated TV program.

Soon she began making the rounds of the Nashville-based record companies, in the meantime working as a club singer and a song-plugger in order to support her children. Following auditions for UA, Hickory and Kapp, Tammy was signed by Epic's Billy Sherrill (♦) and recorded **Apartment No 9,** a song written by Johnny Paycheck (♦) and Bobby Austin. Released in 1966, the disc proved a great success. And the next release – **Your Good Girl's Gonna Go Bad** (1967) – proved to be even stronger, becoming a top five item. From then on it was plain

Tammy Wynette's Stand By Your Man, claimed to be the biggest selling single by a female country singer, was released five times in Britain before scoring.

sailing throughout the '60s as **I Don't Wanna Play House** (1967), **My Elusive Dreams** (with David Houston (♦), 1967), **Take Me To Your World, D-I-V-O-R-C-E, Stand By Your Man** (all 1968), **Singing My Song** and **The Ways To Love A Man** (both 1969) qualified as chart-toppers.

Married to George Jones (♦) in 1968, Tammy and he recorded a series of fine, Sherrill-produced albums together. But their home life was ever-stormy, resulting in a 1975 divorce.

However, on disc Tammy continues to do little wrong – **He Loves Me All The Way, Run, Woman, Run** (both 1970), **Good Lovin'** (1971), **Bedtime Story** (1972), **Till I Get It Right** (1973), **Another Lonely Song** (1974) and **'Til I Can Make It On My Own** (1976) being just a few of the major hits her crying voice has endowed during the 1970s, while her **Greatest Hits** album (which remained in the charts for over 60 weeks) has earned well in excess of one million dollars.

It seems that Tammy Wynette is forever destined to chronicle her life through Billy Sherrill's choice of song – her hits forming a kind of musical diary. Equally, it appears that there's an enormous public just waiting to hear the next chapter.

Albums:
Your Good Girl's Gonna Go Bad *(Epic/—)*
World Of . . . *(Epic/—)*
Stand By Your Man *(Epic/Epic)*
Kids Say The Darndest Things *(Epic/—)*
Inspiration *(Epic/—)*
Greatest Hits *(Epic/—)*
First Songs *(Epic/—)*

Divorce *(Epic/—)*
Another Lonely Song *(Epic/Epic)*
Greatest Hits Vol 3 *(Epic/—)*
I Still Believe In Fairy Tales *(Epic/Epic)*
Bedtime Story *(Epic/—)* re-released with **Stand By Your Man** as a double-pack in the US
Woman To Woman *(Epic/Epic)*

You And Me (Epic). Tammy Wynette and George Jones were a successful singing duo during their marriage, but Tammy continued as a popular solo artist at the same time.

'Til I Can Make It On My Own
  (Epic/Epic)
You And Me *(Epic/Epic)*
Christmas With Tammy Wynette *(—/Epic)*
Superb Country Sounds
  (—/Embassy)
We Sure Can Love Each Other
  (—/Epic)
The Best Of Tammy Wynette
  (—/CBS)
No Charge *(—/Embassy)*

With George Jones:
Let's Build A World Together
  (Epic/Epic)
We're Gonna Hold On
  (Epic/Epic)
George And Tammy And Tina
  (Epic/Epic)
We Go Together/Me And The First Lady *(Epic/Epic)*
  available only as separate albums in Britain

Skeets Yaney

One of country music's great regional stars, who has been unfairly overlooked because of lack of big record sellers. A spectacular yodeler, Skeets – born Clyde A. Yaney in Mitchell, Indiana – was a longtime star on KMOX in St. Louis, one of the main members of the KMOX Barn Dance in the 1930s and 1940s. He still lives in the St Louis area.

Albums: none.

Faron Young

Affectionately known as 'The Sheriff', Faron has been a stalwart

of the country music industry for some three decades.

Born Shreveport, Louisiana, February 25, 1932, he was raised on a farm outside the town and spent his boyhood days picking up guitar chords while minding the family's cows. He formed his first band at school becoming proficient enough to play local fairs and hoedowns. After college he found that he'd gained something of a reputation in Louisiana and was invited to join KWKH and subsequently the Louisiana Hayride (♦) itself. It was then that Webb Pierce (♦) employed him as a featured vocalist. In 1951 he was signed by Capitol Records and had coun-

try hits with **Tattle Tale Eyes** and **Have I Waited Too Long?** Joining the Opry in 1952, Young then spent from 1952–54 in the US Army, touring widely to entertain the troops. His first major success came with the Ted Daffan (♦) song **I've Got Five Dollars And It's Saturday Night**, and with his bid for the teenage market in **Going Steady.**

The '50s saw him gaining many hits and massive popularity, obtaining a No 1 disc with **Sweet Dreams** and later with **Country Girl** (1959), following this in 1961 with another chart-topper in **Hello Walls.** Throughout the '60s, the hits continued to flow, **Backtrack**

(1961), **Three Days, The Comeback, Down By The River** (1962), **The Yellow Bandana, You'll Drive Me Back (Into Her Arms Again)** (1963), **Walk Tall** (1965), **Unmitigated Gall** (1966), **I Just Came To Get My Baby** (1968), **Wine Me Up, You Time's Comin'** (1969) and **Keeping Up With The Joneses,** a 1964 duet with Margie Singleton, figuring among his Top Ten successes for the Mercury label, to which Young became contracted in 1961.

A versatile entertainer who presents an alive and amusing show with his own witty comments much to the fore, Young has retained his popularity over an extensive period, as such major '70s hits as **It's Four In The Morning** (a Top Five pop hit in Britain during 1972), **This Little Girl Of Mine** and **Just What I Had In Mind** clearly demonstrate.

He has appeared in a number of low-budget film productions including *Daniel Boone, Hidden Guns, Country Music Holiday* and *Raiders Of Old California* while his out of showbiz interests include a booking agency, a music publishing firm, and magazine publishing – Young being the current owner of the monthly publication *Music City News*. He even has contributed to Nashville's rising skyline, owning the Faron Young Executive Building near Music Row.

Albums:
The Best Of . . . *(Mercury/—)*
I'd Just Be Fool Enough
  (Mercury/—)
Best Of Vol 2
  (Mercury/Mercury)
Hello Walls *(Capitol/—)*

Faron Young, a prosperous businessman as well as a popular entertainer – owner of the Jailhouse nightclub.

INDEX

This index does not set out to be comprehensive, but concentrates on those personalities whose names recur throughout. It also provides an alphabetical guide to any acts and artists of stature not given their own entry in the book, and supplements the cross-reference system (denoted by ♦ or ◊) used throughout. The main A-Z entries are not all included so please check with the main listing first. References to main entries are indicated here by **bold** type.

M

Milt Mabie 154, 155
Mac and Bob 145, 162
Leon McAuliffe 137, **145**, 169, 249
C. W. McCall **145**
O. B. McClinton **145**
Charlie McCoy 145-6, 226
Skeets MacDonald 146-7
Red River Dave McEnery 146-7
Bill McEuen 166
John McEuen 166
Lester McFarland **145**
Sam and Kirk McGee 147, 148, 160, 210
Roger McGuinn 35
Warner Mack 96, **147**, 221
Clayton McMichen 60, 209
Uncle Dave Macon 9, 61, 87, 99, 127, 147, 148-9, 160, 225
Jim and Jesse McReynolds 125
Maddox Brothers 149
Rose Maddox 149, 172
Mainer's Mountaineers 127-8, 150, 159
J. E. Mainer **150**, 160
Wade Mainer 150-1, 160
Barbara Mandrell 118, 119, **151**
Keith Manifold 28, 29
Tom Manners 24
Zeke Manners 24, **152**
Ken Mansfield 56, 124
Joe and Rose Maphis 152
Linda Martell **152**
Fred Martin 46, 67
Jimmy Martin 152-3, 158, 167, 171
Frankie Marvin 16, **154**
Johnny Marvin 16, **154**
Louise Massey 154-5
Brian Maxine 28
Ken Maynard 16, **155**
Randy Meisner 80, 162
Melody Ranch Band 60
Melody Ranch Girls 205
Men of the West 28
Mikki and Griff 28
Midnight Ramblers 157
Miller's Merrymakers 35
Jody Miller **155**
Roger Miller 81, 99, 131, 155, **156**, 161, 184, 200
Ronnie Milsap 99, 156
The Miracles 156
Bill Monroe 16, 25, 49, 50, 61, 87, 99, 100, 116, 145, 149, 152, **157-8**, 159, 204, 218, 225, 250
Birch Monroe 157
Charlie Monroe 87, 145, **157-8**, 160, 225
Patsy Montana 28, **159**, 182
Melba Montgomery 109, 140, **158-9**
Clyde Moody 98, 150, **159**
Moonpies 57
Charlie Morgan 173
George Morgan 97, 99, **159**
Misty Morgan 25
Wiley Morris 87, 150, **160**
Zeke Morris 87, 150, **160**
Wayne Moss 13, 22, 23
Moon Mullican 65, 136, **160**
Alan Munde 60, 152
Michael Murphey 16, 93, 163
Joaquin Murphy 173
Anne Murray 135, **160**
Music Shoals 13
Musical Brownies 31, 33
Musical Millers 181

N

Nashville Brass 67, 138
Nashville Express 171
Nashville String Band 117
Buck Nation 162
Tex Ann Nation **162**
Jerry Naylor **162**
Pete Nelson 28
Rick Nelson 33, 38, 80, **162**, 180, 243
Tracy Nelson **162**
Willie Nelson 16, 34, 53, 93, 94, 99, 123, 124, 161, **163**, 184, 204, 213, 232
Michael Nesmith 13, 93, 109, **164**, 166, 194, 200
New Frontier Band 28
New Grass Revival **164**
New Lost City Ramblers 50
New Riders of the Purple Sage 124, **165**
New Seekers 134
Newbeats 202
Mickey Newbury **165**, 209
Jimmy C. Newman 36, 99, 105, **165**, 190
Olivia Newton-John 28, **166**
Nitty Gritty Dirt Band 23, 42, 75, 88, **166-7**, 239, 240, 241
Eddie Noack **167**
Norma Jean 12, **167**, 204, 238
Fate Norris 209
North Carolina Ramblers 157, 181
Northwind 28
Wayne Nutt 167-8

O

Oak Ridge Boys 91, **168**, 219
Mike O'Daniel 169
Pat O'Daniel 169

Wilbert Lee O'Daniel 136, **169**, 249
Molly O'Day 19, **169**, 250
James O'Gwynn **169**
Oklahoma Cowboys 50, 78, **99**
Roy Orbison 137, **169**, 190, 199
Original Kentucky Mountaineers 237
Osborne Brothers 152, **170-1**, 209
Donny Osmond 137
Marie Osmond 123
Luther Ossenbrink *see* Arkie
Tommy Overstreet **171**
Bonnie Owens 103, **171**
Buck Owens 20, 33, 55, 65, 75, 103, 115, 116, 161, **171-2**, 190, 195, 224, 226
Tex Owens 91, **172**
Vernon Oxford **172**, 190
Ozark Mountain Daredevils **173**
Ozark Mountaineers 140

P

Pappy Covington's Band 140
Andy Parker **173**
Linda Parker 64, 133
Gene Parsons 89, 243
Gram Parsons 35, 62, 88, 89, 110, **173-4**
Dolly Parton 102, 167, **174**, 238
Paul Revere and the Raiders 241
Les Paul 15, 65, 78, **175**, 223
Ezra Paulette 24
Johnny Paycheck **176-7**, 221, 253
Jimmy Payne **177**
Leon Payne **177**
Minnie Pearl 39, 61, 99, 130, 174, **177**
Herb Pederson 73
Ralph Peer 40, 109, **177-8**, 199, 225, 228
Hank Penny **178**, 230
Carl Perkins 45, **178**, 199
Bill Phillips **178**, 230
Sam Phillips 49, 178, 183, 195, 199
Webb Pierce 19, 99, 140, 162, **178-9**, 180, 216, 242, 244, 254
Ray Pillow **180**, 205
The Plainsmen **173**
Pleasant Valley Boys 198
Poco 14, 62, 80, 162, **180**
Charlie Poole 61, 87, 157, **181**
Poplin Family 181
Possum Hunters **23**
Prairie Ramblers 159, **182**
Elvis Presley 18, 38, 52, 63, 66, 67, 68, 71, 110, 122, 127, 136, 137, 140, 142, 145, 158, 161, 162, 165, 178, **183**, 186, 191, 196, 199, 203, 207, 226
Terry Preston 120, 121; *see also* Ferlin Husky
Kenny Price **183**, 221
Malcolm Price 28
Ray Price 11, 23, 34, 53, 81, 119, 136, 156, 163, 176, 184, 219, 237
Charley Pride 67, 78, 156, 161, 163, 180, **184-5**, 186
John Prine **186**
Ronnie Prophet **186-7**
Jeanne Pruett **188**
Riley Puckett **188**, 209, 225
Pure Prairie League **188**

R

Eddie Rabbitt **189**
Marvin Rainwater 48, **189**
Ralph and Elmer 154
Randolph Sisters 209
Boots Randolph 168, **190**
Eddy Raven **190**
Susan Raye 172, **190-1**
Red Onion Jazz Band 207
Margie Reece 182
Jerry Reed **190-1**, 204
Del Reeves 70, **191**, 209
Goebel Reeves **191**
Jim Reeves 11, 31, 47, 75, 99, 101, 128, 140, 142, 160, 161, **192-3**, 207, 242
Renegades 101
Jack Rhodes' Rhythm Boys 177, 216
Red Rhodes 94, 164, **194**
Rhythm Steppers 226
Bobby G. Rice **194**
Charlie Rich 16, 85, **195**, 199, 207, 208
Don Rich 172, **195**
Cliff Richard 123
Riders of the Purple Sage 105, 248
Jeannie C. Riley 105, 190, **195**, 208
Rising Sons 56
Jean Ritchie 13
Tex Ritter 16, 27, 61, 107, 119, 139, **195-6**, 204, 229, 233, 236, 237, 238, 243, 247
Roane County Ramblers 91
Marty Robbins 66, 188, **196-7**, 204, 232
Kenny Roberts 198
Eck Robertson **198**, 244
Carson J. Robison 66, 106, 143, **198**
Rockin' Rebels 219
Jimmie Rodgers 20, 39, 40, 42, 61, 78, 92, 93, 102, 104, 109, 127, 158, 177, 178, 188, 192, **198-9**, 201, 209, 214, 227, 228, 234

Johnny Rodriguez 75, 97, **199**
David Rogers 109, **200**
Kenny Rogers 112, 165, **200**
Roy Rogers 81, 104, **200**, 215, 238, 248
Roky 16
Rolling Stones 56, 68, 80, 89, 173
Linda Ronstadt 80, 81, 110, 128, 162, 164, **200-1**
Rose City Swingsters 97
Fred Rose 9, 34, 61, 67, 169, 199, **201-2**, 244, 245
Wesley Rose 14, 122, 201, **202**
Dave Rowland 67
Royal Crown Rangers 181
Leon Russell 16, 57, 58, 62, 163, 164
Ron Ryan 28

S

Saddle Pals 105
Doug Sahm 16, 163, **202**
Buffy Sainte-Marie **203**
Sarie and Sally 147
Art Satherley 61, 169, **204**
Pete Sayers 28, 29, 139
Schoolhouse Playboys 171
Jerry Scoggins **46**
Joel Scott-Hill 89
Scotty (Scott Wiseman) **141**, 162
Earl Scruggs 25, 49, 62, 66, **87-8**, 105, 158, 160, 204, 218, 250
Troy Seals 124, **204**
Mike Seeger 27, 210
Jeannie Seely 100, 101, **204**
Billy Joe Shaver 16, 124, **204**
Dorothy Shay **204**
Jean Shepard 11, 100, 113, 120, 143, 180, **205**
T. G. Sheppard **206**
Billy Sherrill 84, 126, 155, 161, 176, 195, **207**, 227, 234, 253
Steve Sholes 15, 71, 193, **207**
Shel Silverstein 22, **207**
Shelby Singleton 55, 152, 180, 195, **208**
Asher and Little Jimmy Sizemore 99, **208**
Skillet Lickers 158, 171, 188, **209**, 240, 251
Hank Skillet 24
Jimmie Skinner **209**
Dale Sledd 171, **209**
Patsy Sledd 56, **209**
Arthur 'Guitar Boogie' Smith **209**
Fiddlin' Arthur Smith 147, **210**
Cal Smith **210**, 221, 234
Carl Smith 14, 34, 115, 119, 191, 202, 204, **211**, 246
Connie Smith 23, **212-3**, 226
Sammi Smith 124, 131, 163, **213**
Smoky Mountain Boys 9, 23, 62
Hank Snow 15, 22, 65, 99, 107, 160, 167, 183, 192, 207, **214**, 221
Sol Four 166
Sons of the Mountaineers 150
Sons of the Pioneers 86, 173, 200, **214-15**, 237, 244, 248
Sons of the South 75
John David Souther 80
Southern Ranch Boys 75
Red Sovine 19, 180, 184, **215-16**
Billy Jo Spears 109, **216**
Buddy Spicher 13, 97, 100
Carl T. Sprague **217**
Jo Stafford 223, 246
Joe Stampley **217**
Stanley Brothers 50, 88, 158, **218**
Stanley Steamer 23
Pete Stanley 28, 29
Kenny Starr **219**
Ringo Starr 18, 66, 75
Statler Brothers **219**
Red Steagall **220**
Steppenwolf 18
Ray Stevens 204, **220**
Stu Stevens 28
Gary Stewart 66, 186, **220-1**
John Stewart **222**
Redd Stewart 130, **223**
Wynn Stewart 20, 119, **224**, 243
Stone Bridge Band 133
Stone Canyon Band 33, 80, 180
Stone Mountain Boys 188
Cliffie Stone 24, 90, 120, 152, **224**, 233, 236, 238
Stoneman Family **224-5**
Storytellers 105
Stringbean 47, 158, **225**
Nat Stuckey 220, **226**
Colleen Summers *see* Mary Ford
Clell Summey *see* Cousin Jody
Sunny Mountain Boys 152
Glenn Sutton 12, 161
Billy Swan 137, **226-7**
Sweet Violet Boys 183

T

James Talley **227**
Gid Tanner 209
Gordon Tanner 209
Jimmie Tarlton **227-8**
Chip Taylor **228**
Harty Taylor 64, 127
Tut Taylor 23, 24, 74, **228**
Telephone Bill 28
Tennessee Crackerjacks 9
Tennessee Firecrackers 91
Tennessee Haymakers 70
Tennessee Mountain Boys 242
Tennessee Ridge Runners 140
Tennessee Tomcats 233

Tennessee Two 45
Tenneva Ramblers 199, **228**
Al Terry **228**
The Texans 65
Texas Playboys 79, 140, 177, 249
Texas Ruby **91**, 172
Texas Troopers 72
Texas Troubadours 100, 210
Texas Wanderers 33, 160
Texas Wildcats 70
13th Floor Elevators 16
Bobby Thompson 13, 125
Hank Thompson 205, **229**, 242
Sue Thompson 202, **230**
Uncle Jimmy Thompson 99, 160, **230**
Thunderbirds and Heads 110
Mel Tillis **230-1**, 234
Floyd Tillman 65, 231, 238
Tompall *see* Glaser
Toomorrow 166
Trail Blazers 64
Diana Trask **233**
Merle Travis 14, 38, 71, 78, 87, 90, 127, 130, 162, 167, 183, 207, **233**, 238, 247
Ernest Tubb 28, 81, 85, 88, 91, 99, 100, 101, 102, 130, 143, 156, 160, 161, 167, 174, 186, 192, 210, **233-4**, 235, 246
Justin Tubb 113, 133, **234**
Beau Tucker 133
Tanya Tucker 18, 55, 112, 133, 161, 207, **234**, 236
Wesley Tuttle 24, 233, **236**, 238
Conway Twitty 20, 28, 85, 128, 137, 144, 145, 219, **236-7**
T. Texas Tyler **237**

U

Uncle Henry's Original Kentucky Mountaineers **237**

V

The Vagabonds 99, **237**
Leroy Van Dyke 234, **237**
Vanishing Breed 116
Virginia Boys 125
Virginia Breakdowners 244
Virginia Reelers 40

W

Porter Wagoner 11, 68, 102, 167, 174, 176, 204, 228, **237-8**, 253
Wagonmasters 238
Frank Wakefield 100
Jimmy Wakely 27, 175, 183, 210, 231, 233, **238**, 244
Billy Walker 209, 221, **238-9**
Charlie Walker **239**
Jerry Jeff Walker 47, **239**
Jerry Wallace **239-40**
Charlie Waller 61
Stan Wallowick and his Polka Chips 183
Joe Walsh 80
Doc Watson 167, **240-1**
Gene Watson **241**
The Waylors 123, 124
Dennis Weaver **241**
The Weavers 98
Dean Webb 73
Freddy Weller **241**
Larry Wellington 154
Kitty Wells 9, 23, 61, 96, 116, 119, 140, 169, 174, 178, **242**, 252
Kenny Wertz 60, 89
Dotty West 56, 70, 94, 133, 204, **242**
Western All Stars 79
The Westerners 133, **154-5**
Billy Edd Wheeler **242-3**
White Trash Blues Band 162
Clarence White 35, **243**
Ray Whitley 143, 162, 183, 195, 201, 233, **243-4**
Slim Whitman 140, 168, **244**
Henry Whitter 66, **244**
Wilburn Brothers 99, 144, 209, 241, **244-5**
Wildwood 28
Andy Williams 164, 165
Curly Williams 244
Doc Williams **244-5**
Don Williams 95, 135, **245**
Hank Williams 61, 62, 99, 100, 102, 104, 107, 116, 134, 140, 152, 156, 160, 161, 162, 167, 169, 174, 184, 186, 192, 199, 201, 215, 228, 244, **245-6**, 247, 248
Hank Williams Junior 46, 78, 246, **247**
Leona Williams **247**
Tex Williams 57, 233, 236, **247-8**
Skeets Williamson 19, 169
Foy Willing 105, **248**
Willis Brothers **248**
Bob Wills 31, 97, 104, 136, 145, 169, 172, 177, 204, 220, **249**
Johnnie Lee Wills 137, 169, **249-50**
Wink Westerners 169
Mac Wiseman 28, 87, 88, 169, **250-1**
Tex Withers 28
Del Wood 193, **251**
Sheb Wooley 191, **251**
The Wranglers 48
Bobby Wright 242, **252**

Johnny Wright 125, 178, 242, **252**
Tammy Wynette 66, 118, 126, 161, 176, 207, 209, 247, **253-4**

Y

Skeets Yaney **254**
Frank Yonco 28
Anne Young 140
Faron Young 11, 28, 49, 65, 96, 99, 100, 102, 140, 156, 163, 171, 176, 180, 244, **254**

proost Turnhout (Belgium)